# The Christian
# Bed & Breakfast
## Directory

**1996-1997 Edition**

# The Christian
# Bed & Breakfast
## Directory

### 1996-1997 Edition

Edited by
*Rebecca Germany*

A Barbour Book

ISBN 1-55748-794-4

Published by Barbour and Company, Inc.
P.O. Box 719
Uhrichsville, Ohio 44683

**Front and back cover:**   The Ashley Inn Bed and Breakfast,
Charleston, South Carolina.

# Table of Contents

# How To Use This Book

Have you ever dreamed of spending a few days in a rustic cabin in Alaska? Would you like to stay in an urban town house while taking care of some business in the city? Would your family like to spend a weekend on a midwestern farm feeding the pigs and gathering eggs? Maybe a romantic Victorian mansion in San Francisco or an antebellum plantation in Mississippi is what you've been looking for. No matter what your needs may be, whether you are traveling for business or pleasure, you will find a variety of choices in the 1996-1997 edition of *The Christian Bed & Breakfast Directory*.

In the pages of this guide you will find over 1,300 bed and breakfasts, small inns, and homestays. All of the information has been updated from last year's edition, and many entries are listed for the first time. Although not every establishment is owned or operated by Christians, each host has expressed a desire to welcome Christian travelers.

The directory is designed for easy reference. At a glance, you can determine the number of rooms available at each establishment and how many rooms have private (PB) and shared (SB) baths. You will find the name of the host or hosts, the price range for two people sharing one room, the kind of breakfast that is served, and what credit cards are accepted. There is a "Notes" section to let you know important information that may not be included in the description. These notes correspond to the list at the bottom of each page. The descriptions have been written by the hosts. The publisher has not visited these bed and breakfasts and is not responsible for inaccuracies.

It is recommended that you make reservations in advance. Many bed and breakfasts have small staffs or are run single-handedly and cannot easily accommodate surprises. Also, ask about taxes, as city and state taxes vary. Remember to ask for directions, and if your special dietary needs can be met, and confirm check-in and check-out times.

Whether you're planning a honeymoon (first or second!), family vacation, or business trip, *The Christian Bed & Breakfast Directory* will make any outing out of the ordinary.

REBECCA GERMANY, EDITOR

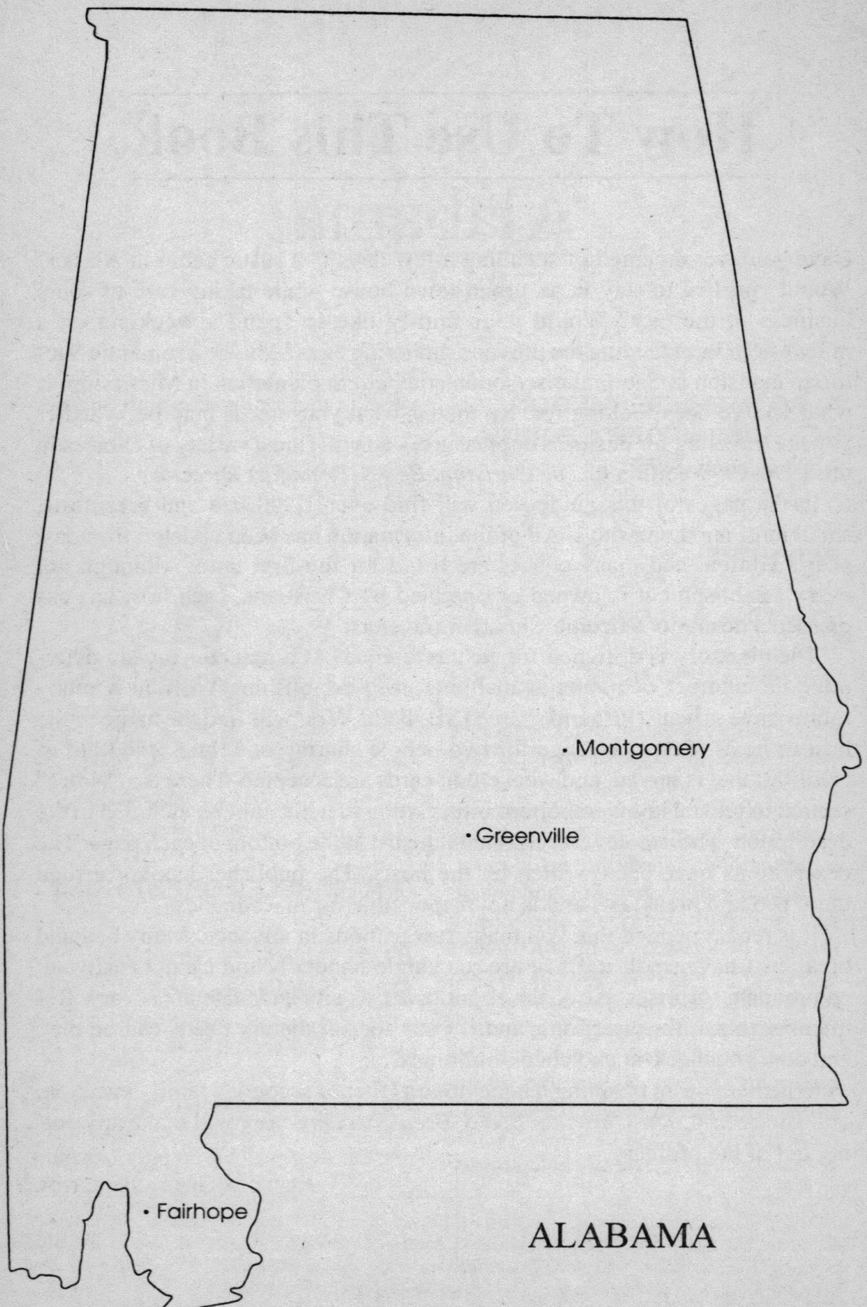

• Montgomery

•Greenville

• Fairhope

**ALABAMA**

# Alabama

**ALSO SEE RESERVATION
SERVICES UNDER GEORGIA
AND MISSISSIPPI**

## FAIRHOPE

### The Green House
23360 Main Street, 36559
(334) 928-4567; (800) 763-5672

Conveniently located along scenic 98
which traces the Eastern Shore of Mobile Bay, The Green House features two
beautifully appointed upstairs bedrooms
with vaulted ceilings and fans. Each has
a private bath, telephone, refrigerator,
coffee bar, cable television, and queen-
size bed. Both bedrooms open onto a
gracious living room, from which guests
may step to a private balcony perfect
for sunbathing. Available on the ground
floor is a luxurious, complete apartment
with a private entrance and fully-
equipped kitchen. A spacious living
room with queen-size sofa bed will
comfortably sleep four guests. Cable
TV, and private phone and bath are pro-

vided in this easily accessible suite.

Hosts: Candy and Bob Bousson
Rooms: 3 (PB) $85-95
Full Breakfast
Credit Cards: A, B, C
Notes: 5, 7, 8, 9, 10, 12

The Green House

## GREENVILLE/FOREST HOME

### Pine Flat Plantation
### Bed and Breakfast
c/o 1555 Dauphin St., Mobile 36604
(334) 471-8024 or (334) 346-2739

Pine Flat Plantation Bed and Breakfast
was built in 1825 by an ancestor of the
present owner. This country, comfort-

---

NOTES: Credit cards accepted: A Master Card; B Visa; C American Express; D Discover;
E Diners Club; F Other; 2 Personal checks accepted; 3 Lunch available; 4 Dinner available;
5 Open all year; 6 Pets welcome; 7 Children welcome; 8 Tennis nearby; 9 Swimming nearby;
10 Golf nearby; 11 Skiing nearby; 12 May be booked through travel agent.

able home has recently been lovingly restored and warmly decorated with cheerful fabrics and interesting antiques. Located just minutes off I-65 between Greenville and Pine Apple, Alabama, this plantation home provides a relaxed, romantic country setting for weary travelers, hunters who want more than just a hunt, or city folks looking for a peaceful place to unwind.

Hosts: Jane and George Inge
Rooms: 4 (PB) $70-90
Full Country Breakfast
Credit Cards: A, B
Notes: 2, 4, 5, 7, 10, 12

Pine Flat Plantation Bed and Breakfast

Red Bluff Cottage

## MONTGOMERY

### Red Bluff Cottage

551 Clay St., P.O. Box 1026, 36101
(334)264-0056; FAX (334) 262-1872

This raised cottage, furnished with family antiques, is high above the Alabama River in Montgomery's Cottage Hill district near the state capitol, Dextor Avenue, King Memorial Baptist Church, the first White House of the Confederacy, the Civil Rights Memorial, and Old Alabama Town. It is convenient to the Alabama Shakespeare Festival Theater, the Museum of Fine Arts, and the expanded zoo. 3 Crown ABBA rated

Hosts: Mark and Anne Waldo
Rooms: 4 (PB) $65
Full Breakfast
Credit Cards: A, B, C, D
Notes: 2, 5, 7, 10, 12

---

NOTES: Credit cards accepted: A Master Card; B Visa; C American Express; D Discover; E Diners Club; F Other; 2 Personal checks accepted; 3 Lunch available; 4 Dinner available;

# Alaska

## ANCHORAGE

### Artic Loon B&B

P.O. Box 110333, 99511
(907) 345-4935 (voice and FAX)

Elegant accommodations await guests in this 6,500 square-foot Scandinavian home in the hillside area of South Anchorage. Breathtaking, spectacular views of Mount McKinley, the Alaskan Range, and the Anchorage Bowl are presented from every room. An eight-person jacuzzi hot tub, sauna, rosewood grand piano, and pool table provide relaxation after a full, gourmet breakfast served on English bone china. Fully licensed, quiet mountain setting near golf course, Chugack State Park, hiking trails, and zoo.

Hosts: Jamie and Lee Johnson
Rooms: 3 (1PB; 2SB) $85-105
Full Breakfast
Credit Cards: A, B
Notes: 2, 5, 7, 8, 9, 10, 11, 12

### Crossroads Inn

1406 West 13th Ave., 99501
(907) 258-7002; FAX (907) 258-7007

Ours is a split-level family home, downtown near Coastal Trail. Two rooms have cable TV, and all three rooms have access to business machines. Business travelers welcome. Healthy foods. Owners are Mary, a musician/teacher, and Dick, a management consultant/facilitator. Quiet neighborhood. Your comfort is important to us, and you'll enjoy Alaskan hospitality.

Hosts: Mary and Dick LaFever
Rooms: 3 (SB) $70-80 (plus $15 for child)
Continental Plus Breakfast
Credit Cards: A, B, C, E (only for 3 or more night stay)
Notes: 2, 5, 7, 8, 10, 11

### Hospitality Plus

7722 Anne Circle, 99504-4601
(907) 333-8504; FAX (907) 337-1718

A comfortable home, delightful and thematically decorated rooms, caring and knowledgeable hosts, sumptuous breakfast elegantly served, a mountain range within reach, a profusion of wildflowers and moose in the yard. Add to that years of various Alaskan adventures, a Hungarian refugee's escape story, exceptional tour and guiding experience, an avid fisherman, storytelling experts and artistic achievements, and then sum

---

5 Open all year; 6 Pets welcome; 7 Children welcome; 8 Tennis nearby; 9 Swimming nearby; 10 Golf nearby; 11 Skiing nearby; 12 May be booked through travel agent.

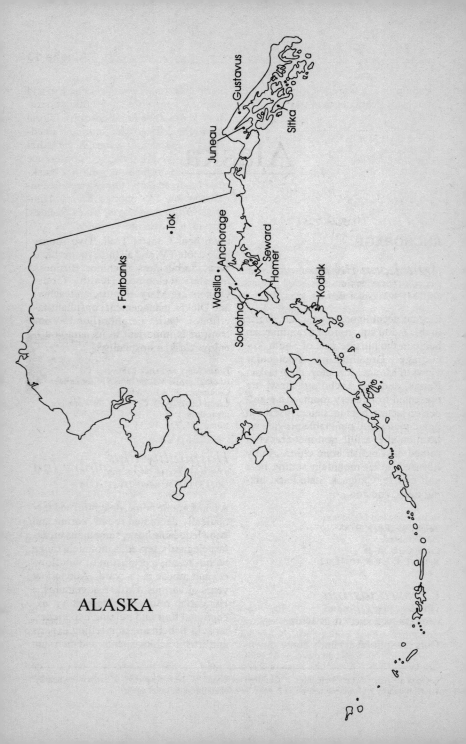

ALASKA

it all up in one word: HOSPITALITY. It doesn't get better than this!

Hosts: Charlie and Joan Budai
Rooms: 3 (1PB; 2SB) $50-75
Full Breakfast
Credit Cards: None
Notes: 2, 5, 7, 8, 9, 10, 11, 12

## Poppy Seed Bed and Breakfast

616 East 72nd Ave., 99518
(907) 344-2286; (907) 349-2286 (message)

Our large comfortable home has guest accommodations on one level. Guests share living and dining area, kitchen with laundry, guests' only bath, phone, and freezer. We offer warm hospitality, comfy beds, and scrumptious breakfasts. Shopping, restaurants, Taku Lake Park, Campbell Creek, Greenbelt, bike trails, beaver lodges, fishing, skiing, bus to Alyeska Resort, city bus, airport, and downtown are just minutes away. Your hosts are 20-year Alaska residents. Referrals to other B&B's statewide.

Hosts: Tony and Gael Petrone
Rooms: 3 (PB) $50-60
Continental Breakfast
Credit Cards: none
Notes: 2, 5, 6, 7, 9, 10, 11

## FAIRBANKS

## 7 Gables Inn

PO Box 80488, 99708
(907) 479-0751; (907) 479-2229(FAX)

Historically, Alaska's 7 Gables was a fraternity house. It is within walking distance of the University of Alaska, Fairbanks campus, yet near the river and airport. The spacious 10,000 square-foot Tudor-style home features a floral solarium, a foyer with antique stained-glass and an indoor waterfall, cathedral ceilings, wedding chapel, conference room, and dormers. A gourmet breakfast is served daily. Other amenities include cable TV, phones, library, laundry facilities, jacuzzis, bikes, canoes, and skis. Suites are available.

Hosts: Paul and Leicha Welton
Rooms: 11 (9PB; 2SB) $50-120
Gourmet Breakfast
Credit Cards: A,B,C,D,E
Notes: 2, 5, 7, 9, 10, 11, 12

Glacier Bay Country Inn

## GUSTAVUS

## Glacier Bay Country Inn

P.O. Box 5, 99826
(907) 697-2288; FAX (907) 697-2289
Winter: P.O. Box 2557, St. George, UT 84771
(801) 673-8480; FAX (801) 673-8481

Set in a clearing by lush, green rainforest and a majestic mountain backdrop, the Glacier Bay Country Inn will capture your heart at first sight. Its unique architecture includes multi-angled roofs, dormer windows, log-beamed ceilings, and large porches. Meals feature freshly baked breads and

NOTES: Credit cards accepted: A Master Card; B Visa; C American Express; D Discover; E Diners Club; F Other; 2 Personal checks accepted; 3 Lunch available; 4 Dinner available; 5 Open all year; 6 Pets welcome; 7 Children welcome; 8 Tennis nearby; 9 Swimming nearby; 10 Golf nearby; 11 Skiing nearby; 12 May be booked through travel agent.

desserts, garden fresh produce, and local seafood—crab, halibut, and salmon. Some of the best whalewatching in the world (humpbacks and ocras), kayaking, hiking—and time to just relax!

Hosts: Ken (Ponch) and Sandi Marchbanks
Rooms: 9 (8PB; 1SB) $238 AP (includes 3 meals, transfers, and bikes)
Full Breakfast
Open May through September
Credit Cards: none
Notes: 2, 3, 4, 7, 12

## HOMER

### Beeson B&B

1393 Bay Ave., 99603
(907) 235-3757 (voice and FAX)

Enjoy all the beauty and wonder of Homer, the halibut capital of the world. Stay with us in a beautiful yet cozy room with a private bath, cable TV, and a magnificent view of Kathemak Bay, the snow-capped mountians, and the famous Homer Spit. We can accomodate large groups. Your hostess promises that "you'll never feel this much at home anywhere else—unless of course you are at home!" Jacuzzi included.

Hostess: Doni Beeson
Rooms: 8 (PB) + 1 cottage; $75-105
Continental Breakfast
Credit Cards: none
Notes: 2, 5, 10, 12

### Brass Ring B&B

P.O. Box 2090, 99603
(907) 235-5450

In the midst of towering spruce trees, the Brass Ring Bed and Breakfast is a country log home located on a quiet cul-de-sac within walking distance of area shops and restaurants. Our five guest bedrooms are individually decorated and, for your enjoyment, we have Alaskan videos, cable TV, coin laundry, a FAX machine, and limited freezer space. We serve a gourmet, Alaskan, full breakfast and, for early risers, we prepare our famous picnic breakfast. Also, the small town of Homer offers many different activities for you to enjoy during your stay.

Hosts: Dave and Vicki VanLiere
Rooms: 6 (1PB; 5SB) call for rates
Full Breakfast
Credit Cards: A, B
Notes: 2, 7 (over 5), 12

## JUNEAU

### Alaska Wolf House

P.O. Box 21321, 1900 Wickersham, 99802
(907) 586-2422 (voice and FAX)

Alaska Wolf House is a 4,000 square foot western, red cedar log home located one mile from downtown Juneau. Built on the side of Mt. Juneau, it features a southern exposure enabling the viewing of sunrises and sunsets over busy Gastineau Channel and the moon rising over the statuesque mountains of Douglas Island. Hosts Philip and Clovis Dennis serve an excellent breakfast in The Glassroom overlooking the channel and mountains. Within a short walk is the Glacier hiking-jogging-biking trail and public transportation. Smoke-

NOTES: Credit cards accepted: A Master Card; B Visa; C American Express; D Discover; E Diners Club; F Other; 2 Personal checks accepted; 3 Lunch available; 4 Dinner available;

free rooms are available with private or shared bathrooms. Suites have kitchens. Plan to enjoy all the amenities of home while experiencing "Our Great Land of Foreverness."

Hosts: Philip and Clovis Dennis
Rooms: 5 (2PB; 3SB) $75-105
Full Breakfast
Credit Cards: A, B
Notes: 2, 3, 4, 5, 7, 9, 10, 11, 12

Pearson's Pond Luxury Inn

## Pearson's Pond Luxury Inn

4541 Sawa Circle-CD, 99801-8723
(907) 789-3772; FAX (907) 789-6722

Private studio/suites on scenic pond. Hot tub under the stars, rowboat, bicycles, BBQ, guest kitchenette. Complimentary cappuccino, fresh breads, gourmet coffee, and popcorn. Near glacier, fishing, rafting, skiing, ferry, airport, and Glacier Bay departures. Smoke-free. Quiet, scenic, and lots of privacy in fully equipped studio with private entrance and deck. In-room dining and TV, VCR, and stereotapes provided. Hosts will make all travel, tours,

excursion arrangements. Guests say it's a definite "10" . . . where expectations are quietly met. Winner of AAA and ABBA excellence awards.

Hosts: Steve and Diane Pearson
Rooms: 3 (1PB; 2SB) $69-169
Continental Breakfast
Credit Cards: A, B, C, E
Notes: 2, 5, 8, 9, 10, 11, 12

## KODIAK

## Country Bed and Breakfast

1415 Zentner Ave., 99615
(907) 486-5762; (voice and FAX)

Our bed and breakfast radiates a homey atmosphere with its homemade bread, granola, yeast rolls, abelskievers (a Danish donut), and "made-from-scratch" buttermilk pancakes and berry syrup. Thirteen skylights brighten the living room, kitchen, hall, bathroom and one of the bedrooms of our cedar-sided home located in a quiet neighborhood. All remodeling was done by my husband who retired five years ago from the Coast Guard base here in Kodiak after 38 years of federal employment, while I have majored in being a homemaker, wife, and mother which has prepared me well for a bed and breakfast hostess.

Hosts: Sally and Ken Van Dyke
Rooms: 4 (SB) $70-80 + tax
Full Breakfast
Credit Cards: none
Notes: 2, 5, 6, 7, 8, 9, 10, 11, 12

5 Open all year; 6 Pets welcome; 7 Children welcome; 8 Tennis nearby; 9 Swimming nearby; 10 Golf nearby; 11 Skiing nearby; 12 May be booked through travel agent.

## SEWARD

### The White House B&B

PO Box 1157, 99664
(907) 224-3614; FAX (907) 224-7499

This 5,000 square-foot home is surrounded by a panoramic mountain view. One-half of the home is for guest use. Country charm abounds with quilts and hand crafts. Guest TV room and fully equipped kitchen is in common area. Breakfast is self-serve buffet in guest dining area. The Historical Iditarod Trail close by. Also the famed Kenai Fjords National Park is accessed by road or boat.

Hosts: Tom and Annette Reese
Rooms: 5 (3PB; 2SB) $50-65(winter) $65-85 (summer)
Expanded Continental Breakfast
Credit Cards: A, B
Notes: 2, 5, 7, 11, 12

The White House Bed and Breakfast

## SITKA

### Alaska Ocean View Bed and Breakfast

1101 Edgecombe Dr., 99835
(907) 747-8310 (voice and FAX); (800) 520-6870

You will enjoy casual elegance and affordable rates at this superior quality B&B where guests experience a high degree of personal comfort, privacy, and friendly knowledgeable hosts. Open your day with the tantalizing aroma of baking bread and a wonderful generous breakfast. Close your day with a refreshing soak in the bubbling patio jacuzzi and complimentary snack. In room 45-channel CATV/VCR and private phone. Video/book Alaskana library. Business center. Central location. Smoke-free. On airport and ferry shuttle-bus route. Awarded AAA three-diamond rating. Business travelers and vacationers rate this lodging superior in every way. "Absolutely the best!"

Hosts: Bill and Carole Denkinger
Rooms: 3 (PB) $79-115 (suite); cash discount
Full Breakfast
Credit Cards: A, B, C
Notes: 2, 5, 6 (outdoors only!), 7, 8, 9, 12

## SOLDOTNA

### Scout Lake Bed and Breakfast

Box 3705, 99669
(907) 262-5575

Stay in a clean and beautiful log home on the lake. Eat sourdough pancakes served by a lifelong Alaskan. You have your own entrance and have available TV/VCR and freezer space. Located eight miles east of Soldotna close to World class fishing on the Kenai and Moose Rivers, Swanson River, canoe trails, golf course, great hiking, excep-

---

NOTES: Credit cards accepted: A Master Card; B Visa; C American Express; D Discover; E Diners Club; F Other; 2 Personal checks accepted; 3 Lunch available; 4 Dinner available;

tional clamming, and big game hunting.

Hostess: D.J. McCaslin
Rooms: 2 (SB) $80-85
Full Breakfast
Credit Cards: none
Notes: 2, 5, 7, 9, 10, 11 (cross-country)

## TOK

## *Cleft of the Rock Bed and Breakfast*

Sundog Trail, Box 122, 99780
(907) 883-4219; (voice and FAX; call first)

Cleft of the Rock Bed and Breakfast offers you sparkling, well-mannered accommodations and warm, friendly, Christian hospitality. Nestled in black spruce just three miles west of Tok. You can find an inviting, homelike atmosphere in one of our guest rooms, or cabins. A hot hearty Alaskan breakfast. Children 12 and under stay free.

Hosts: John and Jill Rusyniak
Rooms: 5 (3PB; 2SB) $65-105
Full Breakfast
Credit Cards: A, B
Notes: 2, 5, 6 (with approval), 7, 9, 11, 12

Yukon Don's

## WASILLA

## *Yukon Don's Bed and Breakfast*

1830 E. Parks Hwy., Suite 386, 99654
(907) 376-7472; (800) 478-7472;
FAX (907) 376-6515

When you're traveling in Alaska, you don't want to miss staying at Yukon Don's Bed and Breakfast, "Alaska's most acclaimed B&B Inn." Each spacious, comfortable guest room is decorated with authentic Alaskana; stay in Iditarod, Fishing, Denali, Hunting rooms or select the Matanuska or Yukon executive suites. Our guests are pampered by relaxing in the Alaska room, complete with Alaskan historic library, video library, pool table, cable TV, and gift bar. The all-glass-view room on the second floor offers the grandest view in the Matanuska Valley, complete with fireplace, sitting chairs and observation deck. We also offer phones in each room, Yukon Don's own expanded continental breakfast bar, a sauna, exercise room, and, according to Commissioner Glenn Olds (world traveler) "the grandest view he has ever seen from a home." Judge William Hungate, St. Louis, MO said, "It's like seeing Alaska without leaving the house."

Hosts: "Yukon" Don and Kristan Tanner
Rooms: 7 (3PB; 4SB) $75-115
Expanded Continental Breakfast
Credit Cards: A, B, C
Notes: 2, 5, 7, 8, 10, 11, 12

---

5 Open all year; 6 Pets welcome; 7 Children welcome; 8 Tennis nearby; 9 Swimming nearby; 10 Golf nearby; 11 Skiing nearby; 12 May be booked through travel agent.

# ARIZONA

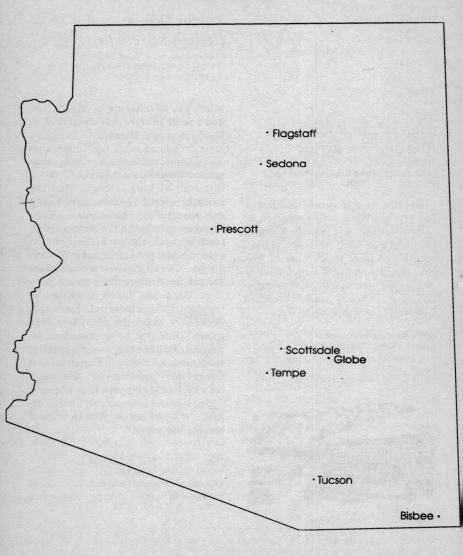

Flagstaff

Sedona

Prescott

Scottsdale
Globe
Tempe

Tucson

Bisbee

# Arizona

## Mi Casa Su Casa Bed and Breakfast Reservation Service

P.O. Box 950, **Tempe**, AZ 85280-0950
(602) 990-0682; (800) 456-0682 (reservations);
FAX (602) 990-3390

Our reservation service has over 160 inspected and approved homestays, guest cottages, ranches, and inns in Arizona, Utah, New Mexico, and Nevada. In **Arizona**, listings include Ajo, Apache Junction, Bisbee, Cave Creek, Clarkdale, Dragoon, Flagstaff, Mesa, Page, Patagonia, Payson, Pinetop, Phoenix, Prescott, Scottsdale, Sedona, Sierra Vista, Tempe, Tombstone, Tuscon, Yuma, and other cities. In **New Mexico**, we list Albuquerque, Algodones, Chimayo, Los Cruces, Silver City, Sante Fe, and Taos. In **Utah**, listings include Moab, Monroe, Salt Lake City, Springdale, St. George, and Tropic. In **Nevada**, we list Las Vegas. Rooms with private and shared baths range from $40-175. Full or continental breakfast. Ruth Young, coordinator.

## Old Pueblo Homestays Reservation Service

P.O. Box 13603, 85732
(520) 790-0030; (800) 333-9776 (reservations);
FAX (520) 790-2399

A B&B reservation service featuring accommodations in individual homes in Arizona, ranging from very modest to luxurious, including continental to gourmet breakfast. Brochure $2 with SASE. William A. Janssen, coordinator. Master Card and Visa accepted.

## BISBEE

### The Greenway House

401 Cole Avenue, 85603
(520) 432-7170; (800) 253-3325;
FAX (520) 432-7917

The Greenway House, built in 1906, is one of the country's finest historic Craftsman-style mansions. The inn, with the ambiance of yesteryear combined with the comforts of today, is ideally suited for romantics, tourists, and business travelers. Eight guest suites

---

NOTES: Credit cards accepted: A Master Card; B Visa; C American Express; D Discover; E Diners Club; F Other; 2 Personal checks accepted; 3 Lunch available; 4 Dinner available; 5 Open all year; 6 Pets welcome; 7 Children welcome; 8 Tennis nearby; 9 Swimming nearby; 10 Golf nearby; 11 Skiing nearby; 12 May be booked through travel agent.

are furnished with beautiful antiques. Guests are greeted with complimentary fruit baskets, fresh flowers, and candy. Kitchens are supplied with continental breakfast. Homemade blueberry muffins are delivered each morning. Private baths have clawfoot tubs with showers. Amenities include luxury soaps, bubble bath, robes, and hair dryers. Billiard room. Patios. Private entrances. Off-street parking. Air-conditioned. AAA approved, three-diamond award, and quality rated by Mobile.

Hostess: Joy O'Clock
Rooms: 8 (PB) $90-130
Credit Cards: A, B
Contintental Breakfast
Notes: 2, 5, 6 and 7 (limited), 8, 10, 12

## FLAGSTAFF

### Comfi Cottages
1612 N. Aztec St., 86001
(520) 774-0731

Near the Grand Canyon, great for families. Five individual cottages with antiques and English country motif. Three cottages are two bedroom, one bath; one is a one-bedroom honeymoon cottage and another is a large three bedroom, two baths. Fully equipped with linens, towels, and blankets. Kitchens have dishes, pots, pans, coffeepot, etc. Ready-to-prepare breakfast foods in fridge. Color cable TV and telephone. Bicycles on premises, washer/dryer, picnic tables, and barbecue grills at each cottage.

Hosts: Ed and Pat Wiebe
Rooms: 7 (PB) $65-195 (for entire cottage)
Guest Prepared Full Breakfast
Credit Cards: A, B
Notes: 2, 5, 7, 8, 9, 10, 11, 12

### The Inn at 410 Bed and Breakfast
410 N. Leroux St., 86001
(520) 774-0088; (800) 774-2008

The Inn at 410 offers guests four seasons of hospitality in a charming 1907 Craftsman home. Eight spacious guest rooms, some with fireplace or whirlpool, are uniquely decorated; one room wheelchair accessible. The innkeepers pamper each guest with a personal touch that includes oven-fresh cookies and scrumptious, healthy breakfasts. An easy jaunt to the Grand Canyon, Sedona, hiking, biking, or skiing in the San Francisco Peaks.

Hosts: Howard and Sally Krueger
Rooms: 8 (PB) $100-150
Full Breakfast
Credit Cards: A, B, C
Notes: 2, 5, 7, 10, 11, 12

## GLOBE

### Cedar Hill Bed and Breakfast
175 East Cedar, 85501
(520) 425-7530

Cedar Hill B&B was built in 1903 by the Trojonavich family. Who were owners of Glober Lumber Company, which accounts for the wainscoting walls in the kitchen and rear porch. The property has many fruit trees and flower beds, including a grape arbor for the enjoyment of our guests. Guests may enjoy both a front porch with porch swings and our back patio with shade trees. The back yard is fenced for the protection of children and pets you may

NOTES: Credit cards accepted: A Master Card; B Visa; C American Express; D Discover; E Diners Club; F Other; 2 Personal checks accepted; 3 Lunch available; 4 Dinner available;

wish to bring! Cable TV and VCR are available in the living room. Within driving distance of both Tuscon and Phoenix. Discounts for senior citizens and for stays longer than overnight.

Hostess: Helen Gross
Rooms: 2 (SB) $40-50
Full Breakfast
Credit Cards: none
Notes: 2, 5, 6, 7, 9

## PRESCOTT

### *Hassayampa Inn*
122 E. Gurley St., 86301
(520) 778-9434 (voice and FAX)
(800) 322-1927

Times have changed, but the Inn, now listed on the National Register of Historic places, still retains the charm of yesteryear with the amenities of today. The classic overnight rooms, lace curtains, oak period furniture, and modern bathrooms, along with exceptional service provided by a caring staff, will enhance your visit. Discriminating travelers will find the Inn the ideal destination; just steps from the center of town, Courthouse square, antique shops, museums, and stately Victorian homes. For the finest in cuisine visit the acclaimed Peacock Room; for a light snack and beverage, relax in the quaint Bar and Grill, or just sit back and enjoy the beauty of the magnificent lobby at the Hassayampa Inn.

Hosts: William M. Teich and Georgia L. Teich
Rooms: 68 (PB) $89-175
Full Breakfast
Credit Cards: A, B, C, D, E
Notes: 2, 3, 4, 5, 7, 8, 9, 10, 12

Hassayampa Inn

## SCOTTSDALE

### *Valley O' The Sun Bed and Breakfast*
P.O. Box 2214, 85252
(602) 941-1281 (voice and FAX); (800) 689-1281

"Cead Mile Faite" are the words in Gaelic on the doormat of the Valley O' The Sun Bed and Breakfast. It means "100,000 welcomes." This B&B is more than just a place to stay. Kathleen wants to make your visit to the great Southwest a memorable one. Ideally located in the college area of Tempe, but still close enough to Scottsdale to enjoy the glamour of its shops, restaurants, and theaters. Two guestrooms can comfortably accommodate four people. One bedroom has a full-size bed and the other has twin beds. Each room has its own TV. Within minutes of golf, horseback riding, picnic area and swimming, bicycling, shopping, and tennis, and walking distance from Arizona State University.

Hostess: Kathleen Kennedy Curtis
Rooms: 2 (1SB,) $35
Continental Breakfast
Credit Cards: none
Notes: 2 (restricted), 5, 7 (over 10), 8, 9, 10, 11, 12

---

5 Open all year; 6 Pets welcome; 7 Children welcome; 8 Tennis nearby; 9 Swimming nearby; 10 Golf nearby; 11 Skiing nearby; 12 May be booked through travel agent.

## SEDONA

### Briar Patch Inn

HC 30, Box 1002, 86336
(520) 282-2342; FAX (520) 282-2399

Eight acres of beautiful grounds along
Oak Creek and spectacular Oak Creek
Canyon. Rooms and cottages are all
delightfully furnished with southwestern charm. A haven for those who appreciate nature amid the wonders of
Sedona's mystical beauty. Suitable for
small workshops.

Hosts: Joann and "Ike" Olson
Rooms: 16 (PB) (includes 12 cottages)
$135-195
Full Breakfast
Credit Cards: A,B
Notes: 2, 5, 7, 8, 9, 10, 11, 12

### The Graham B&B

150 Canyon Circle Dr., 86351
(520) 284-1425; (800) 228-1425;
FAX (520) 284-0767

The Graham Inn is an impressive contemporary Southwest inn with huge
windows allowing great views of
Sedona's red rock formations. Each
guest room has a private bath, balcony,
and TV/VCR and some rooms have a
jacuzzi and fireplace. All rooms have
many individual features which make
each unique and delightful. Pool and
spa invite guests outdoors. Mobile Four
Star Award and AAA Four Diamond
Award. Sedona's Finest.

Hosts: Carol and Roger Redenbaugh
Rooms: 6 (PB) $99-209
Full Breakfast
Credit Cards: A, B, D
Notes: 2, 5, 7, 8, 9, 10, 11, 12 (no fee)

The Graham Bed and Breakfast

### Territorial House, An Old West B&B

65 Piki Dr., 86336
(520) 204-2737; (800) 801-2737;
FAX (520) 204-2230

Our large stone and cedar house has
been tastefully decorated to depict
Arizona's territorial era. Each room is
decorated to recall different stages of
Sedona's early history. Some rooms
have private balcony, jacuzzi tub, or
fireplace. An enormous stone fireplace
graces the living room and a covered
veranda welcomes guests at the end of
a day of sightseeing around Sedona.
Relax in our outdoor hot tub. A full
hearty breakfast is served at the harvest
table each morning. All of this is served
with Western hospitality.

Hosts: John and Linda Steele
Rooms: 4 (PB) $90-130
Full Breakfast
Credit Cards: A, B
Notes: 2, 5, 7, 8, 9, 10, 11, 12

NOTES: Credit cards accepted: A Master Card; B Visa; C American Express; D Discover;
E Diners Club; F Other; 2 Personal checks accepted; 3 Lunch available; 4 Dinner available;

## TUSCON

### Bonnie's B&B

5902 E. 9th, 85711
(602) 747-8943

This beautiful ranch-style home is located near the Tuscon International Airport, University of Arizona, library, and shopping. It is a home where families are welcome and couples will find it quiet and relaxing. Bonnie and Lee have an extensive Christian tape, video, and book library available. You will be served fresh citrus picked from our backyard with your choice of breakfast. Offering a three room suite or a fully furnished guest cottage. Visit Old Tuscon movie location and the Desert Museum. Call for additional rates.

Hosts: Bonnie and Lee Myers
Rooms: cottage + 3-room suite (PB) $55-75
Full Breakfast
Credit Cards: none
Notes: 2 (and travelers'), 6 and 7 (cottage only), 8, 9, 10, 11, 12

Bonnie's Bed and Breakfast

### Casa Alegre Bed and Breakfast

316 E. Speedway Blvd., 85705
(520) 628-1800; (800) 628-5654;
FAX (520) 792-1880

Casa Alegre Bed and Breakfast is a Craftsman-style home located only a few minutes from the University of Arizona and downtown Tuscon. Each guest room is a well-appointed reflection of Tuscon's past. The Inn's serene gardens feature a swimming pool and hot tub for your relaxation and enjoyment. A full scrumptious breakfast is served either in the formal dining room or on the patio.

Hostess: Phyllis Florek
Rooms: 5 (PB) $80-95
Full Breakfast
Credit Cards: A, B, D
Notes: 2, 5, 8, 9, 10, 11, 12

Casa Alegre

### El Presidio Bed and Breakfast Inn

297 N. Main Ave., 85701
(520) 623-6151; (800) 349-6151

Experience Southwestern charm in a desert oasis with the romance of a country inn. Garden courtyards with Old Mexico ambiance of lush, floral displays, fountains, and cobblestone surround richly appointed guest house and suites. Enjoy antique decors, robes, complimentary beverages, fruit, snacks, TVs, and telephones. The 1880s Victorian adobe mansion has been featured in many magazines and the book *The*

---

5 Open all year; 6 Pets welcome; 7 Children welcome; 8 Tennis nearby; 9 Swimming nearby;
10 Golf nearby; 11 Skiing nearby; 12 May be booked through travel agent.

*Desert Southwest.* Located in a historic district; walk to fine restaurants, museums, shops, and the Arts District. Close to downtown. Mobile and AAA three-star rated.

Hostess: Patti Toci
Rooms: 3 suites (PB) $85-110
Full Breakfast
Credit Cards: none
Notes: 2, 5, 8, 9, 10, 12

## Elizabeth's Bed and Breakfast

1931 W. Calle Campana de Plata, 85745
(602) 884-8874

This modest, attractively decorated home is within walking distance of a bus stop, regional park, and golf courses. This comfortable home is in a quiet neighborhood three miles west of the University of Arizona. The hostess is a world traveler who enjoys meeting new people. She takes pride in her home and will make you very welcome. The guest bedroom has a queen-size bed, large closet, dresser space, TV, radio, and telephone.

Hostess: Elizabeth
Rooms: 1 (PB) $45-55
Continental Breakfast
Credit Cards: None
Notes: 2, 3, 5, 8, 9, 10, 12

## Jeremiah Inn

10921 E. Snyder Rd., 85749
(520) 749-3072

For centuries travelers have paused at quiet inns to refresh themselves before continuing life's journey. The Jeremiah Inn is one such place (Jeremiah 9:2a). Santa Fe style with spacious contemporary comforts are offered in this 1995 constructed inn, a 3.3 acre desert retreat in the shadows of the Catalina Mountains. Birding, star-gazing, hiking, swimming, queen beds, afternoon cookies, and smoke-free premises are offered.

Hosts: Robert and Beth Miner
Rooms: 3 (PB) $70-100
Full Breakfast
Credit Cards: A, B
Notes: 2, 5, 7, 8, 9, 10, 11

## June's Bed and Breakfast

3212 W. Holladay, 85746
(602) 578-0857

Mountainside home with pool. Majestic towering mountains. Hiking in the desert. Sparkling city lights. Beautiful rear yard and patio. Suitable for receptions.

Hostess: June Henderson
Rooms: 3 (1PB; 1SB) $45
Continental Breakfast
Credit Cards: none
Notes: 2, 5, 8, 9, 10, 11

---

NOTES: Credit cards accepted: A Master Card; B Visa; C American Express; D Discover; E Diners Club; F Other; 2 Personal checks accepted; 3 Lunch available; 4 Dinner available;

# Arkansas

Bonnybrooke Farm Atop Misty Mountain

## EUREKA SPRINGS

### Bonnybrooke Farm Atop Misty Mountain

Rt. 2, Box 335A, 72632
(501) 253-6903

If your heart's in the country . . . or longs to be . . . we invite you to share in the sweet quiet and serenity that awaits you in your place to come home to. . . . Five cottages, distinctly different in their pleasure to tempt you: fireplace and jacuzzi for two, full glass fronts and mountaintop views, shower under the stars in your glass shower, wicker porch swing in front of the fireplace and a wonderful jacuzzi . . . you're gonna love it! In order to preserve privacy our lo-cation is not made public and is given to registered guests only.

Hosts: Bonny and Josh Pierson
Rooms: 5 cottages (PB) $85-125
Basket Breakfast
Credit Cards: none
Notes: 2, 5, 9, 12

The Brownstone Inn

### The Brownstone Inn

75 Hillside Ave., 72632
(501) 253-7505

A present part of Eureka's past in this historical limestone building, located on trolley route to historic downtown and an easy short drive to the Great Passion Play. Victorian accommodations, private outside entrances, private baths, and gourmet breakfasts with coffee, tea, or juice at your doorstep before break-

---

5 Open all year; 6 Pets welcome; 7 Children welcome; 8 Tennis nearby; 9 Swimming nearby; 10 Golf nearby; 11 Skiing nearby; 12 May be booked through travel agent.

# ARKANSAS

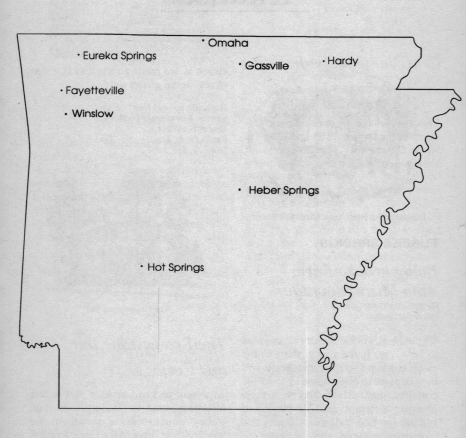

fast. Featured in *Best Places to Stay in the South*.

Hosts: Marvin and Donna Shepard
Rooms: 4 (PB) $85-95
Full Breakfast
Closed January and February
Credit Cards: A, B
Notes: 2, 5, 10, 12

## Crescent Cottage Inn

211 Spring, 72632
(501) 253-6022; (800) 223-3246 (res.only)
FAX (501) 253-6234

Crescent Cottage Inn is a landmark Victorian home built in 1881 and is on the National Register. There are four guest areas all having private baths, queen beds, cable TV, and telephones—two have private, double jacuzzi spas and refrigerators. All rooms and two (of three) porches overlook forested mountains. A great full breakfast. Antiques throughout and recently redecorated. Walk to town, trolley stop, and 1886 church. Rare AAA rating.

Hosts: Ralph and Phyllis Becker
Rooms: 3 + 1 two-room suite (PB) $75-115
Full Hearty Breakfast
Credit Cards: A, B, D
Notes: 2, 5, 7, 8, 9, 10, 12

Crescent Cottage Inn

Gardeners Cottage

## Gardeners Cottage

11 Singleton, 72632
(501) 253-9111; (800) 833-3394

Tucked away in a private, wooded, historic district location, this delightful cottage is decorated in charming country decor with romantic touches, cathedral ceilings, skylight, full kitchen, and a jacuzzi for two. The spacious porch with its swing and hammock is for leisurely lounging. Great for honeymooners or a long peaceful stay.

Hostess: Barbara Gavron
Rooms: 1 cottage (PB) $95-115
No Breakfasts
Credit Cards: A, B, C, D
Notes: 2, 9, 10, 12

## The Heartstone Inn and Cottages

35 Kings Hwy., 72632
(501) 253-8916; (800) 494-4921;
FAX (501) 253-6821

An award-winning inn with all private baths, private entrances, and cable TV. King and queen beds. Antiques galore. Renowned gourmet breakfasts. In-

---

NOTES: Credit cards accepted: A Master Card; B Visa; C American Express; D Discover; E Diners Club; F Other; 2 Personal checks accepted; 3 Lunch available; 4 Dinner available; 5 Open all year; 6 Pets welcome; 7 Children welcome; 8 Tennis nearby; 9 Swimming nearby; 10 Golf nearby; 11 Skiing nearby; 12 May be booked through travel agent.

privileges. Large decks and gazebo under the trees; great for bird-watching. Recommended by: *New York Times, Country Home Magazine, America's Wonderful Little Hotels and Inns, Recommended Inns of the South*, and many more.

Hosts: Bill and Iris Simantel
Rooms: 10 + 2 cottages (PB) $63-118
Full Breakfast
Closed Christmas through January
Credit Cards: A, B, C, D
Notes: 2, 9, 10, 12

## Piedmont House B&B

165 Spring St., 72632
(501) 253-9258; (800) 253-9258

Built as travelers' lodging in 1880, Piedmont House is located in the heart of the Victorian, historic district. Each room has private baths, air-conditioning, ceiling fans, and private entrance from the wraparound porches. Best mountain views and just a short walk to historic downtown shopping and great restaurants. A home away from home with the warmest hospitality you could ever find.

Hosts: Sheri and Ron Morrill
Rooms: 8 (PB) $69-129
Full Breakfast
Credit Cards: A, B, C, D, E
Notes: 2, 5, 7 (over 12), 10

## Ridgeway House B&B

28 Ridgeway, 72632
(501) 253-6618; (800) 477-6618

Prepare to be pampered! Sumptuous breakfasts elegantly served, luxurious rooms, antiques, flowers, desserts, quiet street within walking distance of eight churches, five-minute walk to historic downtown, trolley one block. Porches, decks, private jacuzzi suite for anniversaries/honeymoons. All our guests are VIPs!! Open all year.

Hosts: Becky and "Sony" Taylor
Rooms: 5 (3PB; 2SB) $79-129
Full Breakfast
Credit Cards: A, B
Notes: 2, 5, 7, 12

## Singleton House B&B

11 Singleton, 72632
(501) 253-9111; (800) 833-3394

This old-fashioned Victorian house with a touch of magic is whimsically decorated and has an eclectic collection of treasures and antiques. Breakfast is served on the balcony overlooking a wildflower garden and fish pond. Walk one block to the historic district, shops, and cafés. Passion Play and Holy Land tour reservations can be arranged. A guest cottage with jacuzzi is also available at a separate location. Hands-on apprenticeship program available! Featured in over 15 Bed and Breakfast Guidebooks. Celebrating our 12th year!

Hostess: Barbara Gavron
Rooms: 5 (PB) $60-95
Cottage: 1 (PB) $95 (no breakfast)
Full Breakfast
Credit Cards: A, B, C, D
Notes: 2, 5, 7, 9, 10, 12

## Sunnyside Inn

5 Ridgeway, 72632
(501) 253-6638; (800) 554-9499

Lovingly restored, circa 1880 Victorian home in the Historic District. Beauti-

---

NOTES: Credit cards accepted: A Master Card; B Visa; C American Express; D Discover; E Diners Club; F Other; 2 Personal checks accepted; 3 Lunch available; 4 Dinner available;

fully appointed. Quiet, restful surroundings are smoke and alcohol free. Full country breakfasts, private baths, honeymoon suite with jacuzzi, walking distance to downtown. Breakfast is served on a tree top deck overlooking a wilderness area.

Hostess: Gladys Rose Foris
Rooms: 6 (PB) $80-95
Full Breakfast
Credit Cards: None
Notes: 2, 5, 7, 12

The Tweedy House

## The Tweedy House
16 Washington St., 73632
(501) 253-5435; (800) 346-1735

Built in 1883, Tweedy House is an elegant Victorian home located on the Historic Loop. Inside Tweedy House you will find three stories of antiques, family heirlooms, and quality furnishings. The third floor features a romantic honeymoon hideaway. The second floor features two large guest rooms with private baths, and one two-room suite. Amenities include: jacuzzi, TV/VCRs, guest sunroom, decks/porches, hot tub, refreshments, full breakfast,

evening dessert, and friendly service!

Hosts: Ed and Kathy Greiner
Rooms: 4 (2 are suites) (PB) $79-129
Full Breakfast plus evening dessert
Credit Cards: A, B, D
Notes: 2, 5, 7, 8, 9, 10, 12

## FAYETTEVILLE

### Hill Avenue Bed and Breakfast
131 S. Hill, 72701
(501) 444-0865

This century-old home is located in a residential neighborhood near the University of Arkansas, downtown square, Walton Art Center, and Bud Walton Arena. Comfortable common areas and a large porch and deck are available to guests. Breakfast is served on the deck or in the formal dining room. Both a hearty country breakfast and a low-fat breakfast are offered.

Hosts: Cecelia and Dave Thompson
Rooms: 2 (SB) $40-50
Full Breakfast
Credit Cards: none
Notes: none

## GASSVILLE

### Lithia Springs Lodge
R 1, Box 77A, Hwy. 126 N., 72635
(501) 435-6100

A lovingly restored, early Ozark health lodge, six miles southwest of Mountain Home in north central Arkansas. Fishing, boating, and canoeing in famous lakes and rivers. Scenic hills, valleys,

5 Open all year; 6 Pets welcome; 7 Children welcome; 8 Tennis nearby; 9 Swimming nearby; 10 Golf nearby; 11 Skiing nearby; 12 May be booked through travel agent.

and caverns. Silver Dollar City, Branson, and Eureka Springs are within driving distance. Enjoy walking in the meadow and woods and browse through the adjoining Country Treasures Gift Shop.

Hosts: Paul and Reita Johnson
Rooms: 5 (3PB; 2SB) $50-70
Full Breakfast
Credit Cards: A, B
Notes: 2, 5, 8, 9, 10, 11 (water), 12

Olde Stonehouse Bed and Breakfast Inn

## HARDY

### Olde Stonehouse Bed and Breakfast Inn

511 Main St., 72542
(501) 856-2983; (800) 514-2983;
FAX (501) 856-4036

Historic, native Arkansas stone house with large porches lined with jumbo rocking chairs provides the perfect place to relax and watch the world go by. Each room is individually and comfortably furnished with antiques. Central heat and air, ceiling fans, queen beds, private baths, and luxurious two-room suites. In-town location, a block from Spring River and the unique shops of Old Hardy Town. Three country music theaters, golf courses, horseback riding, canoeing, and fishing nearby. Attractions: Mammoth Springs State Park, Grand Gulf State Park, Evening Shade, AR, Arkansas Traveler Theater. Breakfast is a treat, like Grandma used to make, gourmet but hearty! Evening snacks. Special occasion packages available. Murder mystery dinner parties and packages. Gift certificates. Approved by AAA and ABBA.

Hosts: David and Peggy Johnson
Rooms: 7 + 2 suites (PB) $55-95
Full Breakfast
Credit Cards: A, B, C, D
Notes: 2, 3, 4, 5, 8, 9, 10, 12

## HEBER SPRINGS

### The Anderson House Inn

201 E. Main St., 72543
(501) 326-5266; (800) 264-5279;
FAX (501) 362-2326

A country inn in the bed and breakfast tradition. Enjoy a wonderful lodging alternative in a beautiful Ozark foothills setting. The Anderson House Inn is convenient to Greens Ferry Lake and Little Red River fishing and water sports. Trophy trout fishing is available. We feature handmade quilts, antiques, and a southern flavor. Our Great

NOTES: Credit cards accepted: A Master Card; B Visa; C American Express; D Discover; E Diners Club; F Other; 2 Personal checks accepted; 3 Lunch available; 4 Dinner available;

room has a large screen TV for guests to enjoy.

Hosts: Jim and Susan Hildebrand
Rooms: 16 (PB) $58-75
Full Breakfast
Credit Cards: A, B, C, D
Notes: 2, 5, 8, 9, 10, 12

## HOT SPRINGS

### Vintage Comfort B&B

303 Quapaw, 71901
(501) 623-3258 (voice and FAX)

Situated on a tree-lined street, a short walk from Hot Springs' historic Bath House Row, art galleries, restaurants, and shopping. Guests enjoy a comfortably restored Queen Anne house built in 1907. Four spacious rooms are available upstairs, each with private bath, ceiling fan, and period furnishings. A delicious full breakfast is served each morning in the inn's dining room. Vintage Comfort B&B is known for its comfort and gracious Southern hospitality.

Hostess: Helen R. Bartlett
Rooms: 4 (PB) $65-85
Full Breakfast
Credit Cards: A, B, C
Notes: 2, 5, 7 (over 5 years), 8, 9, 10, 12

## OMAHA

### Aunt Shirley's Sleeping Loft B&B Inn

Route 1, Box 84-D, 72662
(501) 426-5408

*Quiet *Romantic *Relaxed atmosphere *Rustic country setting with the conveniences of home *A/C *Private bath *Clean *Beautiful view and walkways *Patio *Gas grill *Campfires available for cookouts *Swings under the trees *Big country breakfast *Lots of Southern hospitality *Children welcome *Ten miles north of Harrison *Spend a memorable vacation at an affordable price *Member of Harrison Chamber of Commerce *Listed in *Arkansas off the Beaten Path* *Near Branson and Eurika Springs.

Hosts: Buddy and Shirley LeBleu
Rooms: 2 (SB) 1cabin w/loft; $50-60
Full Breakfast
Credit Cards: A, B
Notes: 2, 5, 6, 7, 9, 10, 12

## WINSLOW

### Sky-Vue Lodge

22822 N. Hwy. 71, 72959
(501) 634-2003; (800) 782-2003

Located on Scenic 71 near Fayetteville, Sky-Vue Lodge offers a 25 mile view of the Ozarks. Enjoy the spectacular view from the porch of your charming cabin, which has heating and air conditioning for year-round comfort. Hike our 83 acres, or enjoy activities at two nearby state parks. We are family oriented and alcohol free. Facilities are ideal for retreats, conferences, reunions, and weddings. Full breakfast included, other meals available.

Hosts: Glenn and Janice Jorgenson
Rooms: 7 cottages (PB) $45-55
Full Breakfast
Credit Cards: A, B
Notes: 2, 4, 5, 7, 8, 9

---

5 Open all year; 6 Pets welcome; 7 Children welcome; 8 Tennis nearby; 9 Swimming nearby; 10 Golf nearby; 11 Skiing nearby; 12 May be booked through travel agent.

# CALIFORNIA

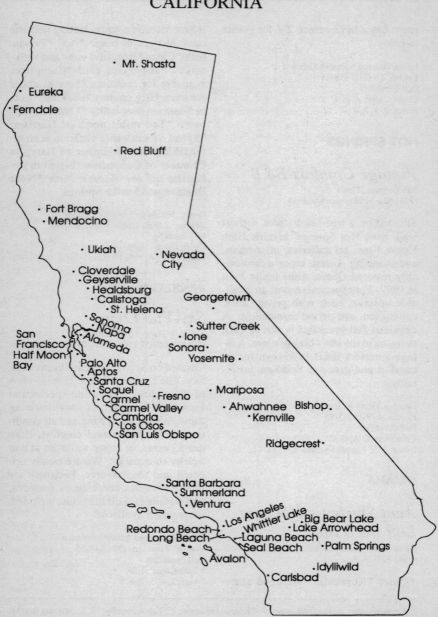

Mt. Shasta

Eureka
Ferndale

Red Bluff

Fort Bragg
Mendocino

Ukiah

Nevada
City

Cloverdale
Geyserville
Healdsburg
Calistoga
St. Helena

Georgetown

Sonoma
Napa
Alameda

Sutter Creek
Ione
Sonora
Yosemite

San
Francisco
Half Moon
Bay

Palo Alto
Aptos
Santa Cruz
Soquel
Carmel
Carmel Valley
Cambria
Los Osos
San Luis Obispo

Fresno

Mariposa

Ahwahnee   Bishop
Kernville

Ridgecrest

Santa Barbara
Summerland
Ventura

Los Angeles
Whittier Lake
Redondo Beach
Long Beach
Laguna Beach
Seal Beach
Avalon

Big Bear Lake
Lake Arrowhead

Palm Springs

Idyliwild
Carlsbad

# California

## Bed and Breakfast of California—A State-Wide Reservation Service

3924 E 14th Street, Long Beach 90804
(310) 498-0522

Bed and Breakfast of California helps travelers make reservations anywhere in California. Our accommodations include private home-stays in San Diego, Los Angeles, Santa Barbara, Malibu, Cambria, San Francisco and dozens of others throughout the state. We also work with historic inns, guest houses, and ranches. Rates range from $45-95 per night, including a full breakfast.

Our **"Kids Welcome"** program is geared toward family travel state-wide. These homes emphasize comfort, hospitality, and affordability. Please call for information or to order a directory.

## AHWAHNEE

### Silver Spur B&B

44625 Silver Spur Tr., 93601
(209) 683-2896

Silver Spur Bed and Breakfast is nestled in the Sierra Nevadas of California, just off historic Highway 49, key to the California Gold Country, near the South and West gates of famed Yosemite National Park, and minutes from many outdoor sports. We feature beautiful clean rooms with private baths and entrances, tastefully decorated in American Southwest. Outdoor rest and dining areas boast outstanding Sierra views. A continental breakfast is served daily. Come enjoy Yosemite and be treated to old-fashioned hospitality and great value!

Hosts: Patty and Bryan Hays
Rooms: 2 (PB) $45-60
Expanded Continental Breakfast
Credit Cards: A, B, D
Notes: 2, 5, 6 (sometimes), 7, 9, 10, 11, 12

## ALAMEDA

### Garratt Mansion

900 Union, 94501
(510) 521-4779; FAX (510) 521-6796

This 1893 Victorian halts time on the tranquil island of Alameda. Only fifteen miles to Berkeley or downtown San Francisco. We'll help maximize your vacation plans or leave you alone to regroup. Our rooms are large and comfortable, and our breakfasts are nutri-

---

NOTES: Credit cards accepted: A Master Card; B Visa; C American Express; D Discover; E Diners Club; F Other; 2 Personal checks accepted; 3 Lunch available; 4 Dinner available; 5 Open all year; 6 Pets welcome; 7 Children welcome; 8 Tennis nearby; 9 Swimming nearby; 10 Golf nearby; 11 Skiing nearby; 12 May be booked through travel agent.

tious and filling.

Hosts: Royce and Betty Gladden
Rooms: 7 (5PB; 2SB) $80-130
Full Breakfast
Credit Cards: A, B, C, E
Notes: 2, 5, 7, 8, 9, 10, 12

Bayview Hotel

## APTOS

## *Bayview Hotel, A Country Inn*

8041 Soquel Dr., 95003
(408) 688-8654; (800) 4-BAYVIEW;
FAX (408) 688-5128

The Bayview Hotel is proud to be the oldest operating inn on the Monterey Bay. This elegant Victorian-Italianate structure was built in 1878 by Joseph Arano who imported fine furniture for his "grand hotel." All rooms have private baths, some have fireplaces and extra-large soaking tubs. Some of the original furniture is still at the Inn and many photographs tell of times past. One of the Bayview's contemporary amenities is the Veranda, a four-star restaurant serving the finest regional American cuisine.

Hostess: Gwen Burkard
Rooms: 11(PB) $90-150
Full Breakfast
Credit Cards: A, B, C, D
Notes: 2, 3, 4, 5, 7, 8, 9, 10, 12

## AVALON

## *Gull House*

344 Whittley Ave., P.O. Box 1381, 90704
(310) 510-2547; FAX (310) 510-9569

Two deluxe suites on the lower level of our contemporary home, each with a separate entrance, large living room with gas-log fireplace, a morning room with refrigerator and table, bedroom, and bath. Also, two large guest rooms overlooking patio, pool, and spa with baths. Breakfast is served on the patio by the pool, spa, and gas barbecue. Within walking distance of all island activities—beaches, golf, tennis, boating, fishing, biking, horseback riding, and picnic facilities. Full payment 10 days prior to arrival.

Hosts: Bob and Hattie Michalis
Rooms: 2 suites (PB) $145-185
Continental Plus Breakfast
Credit Cards: none
Notes: 2 (in advance), 7, 8, 9, 10, 11, 12

## BIG BEAR LAKE

## *Truffles—A Special Place Bed and Breakfast*

P.O. Box 130649, (Bow Canyon Rd.), 92315
(909) 585-2772

Gracious hospitality in peaceful surroundings describe this elegant, country, manor inn nestled on ¾ acre at a 7,000 foot high mountain resort. Skiing, golf, hiking, and lake close by. Five guest rooms are individually appointed with private baths and feathertop beds. Full breakfasts, afternoon appetizers, and evening desserts topped off with

NOTES: Credit cards accepted: A Master Card; B Visa; C American Express; D Discover; E Diners Club; F Other; 2 Personal checks accepted; 3 Lunch available; 4 Dinner available;

truffles on bedtime pillows make for a memorable stay. This spacious establishment includes comfortable traditional and antique furnishings with lots of attention to detail. No smoking.

Hostesses: Marilyn Kane and Carol Bracey
Rooms: 5 (PB) $110-135
Full Breakfast
Credit Cards: A, B
Notes: 10, 11

## BISHOP

### The Chalfant House B&B

213 Academy, 93514
(619) 872-1790

This 1900 semi-Victorian, two-story house includes country antique furnishings and handmade quilts. There are five rooms and two suites. Tea is served in the afternoon; ice-cream sundaes are served in the evenings. Enjoy TV/VCR, library, and a fireplace in the parlor. Central air and ceiling fans. No smoking.

Hosts: Fred and Sally Manecke
Rooms: 7 (PB) $60-90
Full Breakfast
Credit Cards: A, B, C
Notes: 2, 5, 7, 8, 9, 10, 11

## CALISTOGA

### Calistoga Wayside Inn

1523 Foothill Blvd., 94515
(707) 942-0645; (800) 845-3632;
FAX (707) 942-4169

A warm, inviting Mediterranean-style home, built in the 1920's and situated in a secluded garden setting. Rooms have king or queen beds and private baths. Enjoy the garden and patio, or curl up by the fireplace. Savor a Calistoga country breakfast, afternoon refreshments, and herb tea in the evening. Restaurants, shops, wineries, and spas nearby. Gift certificates.

Hosts: Pat and Carmine
Rooms: 3 (PB) $100-135
Full Breakfast
Credit Cards: A, B, C
Notes: 2, 5, 7, 8, 9, 10, 12

### Foothill House

3037 Foothill Blvd., 94515
(707) 942-6933; (800) 942-6933;
FAX (707) 942-5695

"The romantic inn of the Napa Valley," according to the *Chicago Tribune* travel editor. In a country setting, located in the western foothills just north of Calistoga, the Foothill House offers spacious suites individually decorated with antiques. All suites have private baths and entrances, fireplaces, small refrigerators, and air-conditioning. Some have jacuzzis. A luxurious cottage is also available. A gourmet breakfast is served each morning and appetizers and refreshments each evening.

Hosts: Gus and Doris Beckert
Rooms: 3 (PB) $135-250
Full Breakfast
Credit Cards: A, B, C
Notes: 2, 5, 8, 9, 10, 12

### Hillcrest B&B

3225 Lake Co. Hwy., 94515
(707) 942-6334

Hilltop, rambling country home filled

---

5 Open all year; 6 Pets welcome; 7 Children welcome; 8 Tennis nearby; 9 Swimming nearby;
10 Golf nearby; 11 Skiing nearby; 12 May be booked through travel agent.

with antique silver, china, artwork, and furniture. Rooms have balconies with breathtaking views of lush Napa Valley. Swimming, hiking, and fishing on 40 acres of family owned property since 1870. Guests have use of spa, pool, balcony barbecue area, fireplace in guest parlor, and grand piano.

Hostess: Debbie O'Gorman
Rooms: 6 (4PB; 2SB) $45-90
Continental Breakfast
Credit Cards: none
Notes: 2, 5, 6, 8, 9, 10, 11, 12

## CAMBRIA

## The Pickford House Bed and Breakfast

2555 MacLeod Way, 93428
(805) 927-8619

Eight large rooms done in antiques. All private baths with clawfoot tubs and showers. The front three rooms have fireplaces and a view of the mountains and valley. All rooms have a TV and king- or queen-size bed. Wine and fruitbreads served at 5 PM. Located near beaches and wineries and only seven miles from the Hearst Castle. Third person only $20. Full breakfast served from 8-9 AM in our antique dining room with cozy fireplace. Gift certificates available. Abundance of parking space. Check in after 3 PM, check out at 11 AM.

Hostess: Anna Larsen
Rooms: 8 (PB) $85-130
Full Breakfast
Credit Cards: A, B
Notes: 2, 5, 7

## CARLSBAD

## Pelican Cove Inn

320 Walnut Ave., 92008
(619) 434-5995; FAX (619) 434-6015

This romantic inn is located 200 yards from the beach and features eight rooms all with private baths (some spas), feather beds, down comforters, fireplaces, and TVs. A full breakfast that can be enjoyed in your room, the gazebo, or the sun deck is included. Excellent restaurants and shopping are within walking distance.

Hosts: Kris and Nancy Nayudu
Rooms: 8 (PB) $85-175
Full Breakfast
Credit Cards: A, B, C
Notes: 2, 5, 8, 9, 10, 12

The Stonehouse Inn

## CARMEL

## The Stonehouse Inn

P.O. Box 2517, 93921
(408) 624-4569; (800) 748-6618

The Stonehouse Inn is an impressively built stone structure with windows allowing inspirational ocean views which are some of California's finest. The inn was built in 1906, the year of the tragic

---

NOTES: Credit cards accepted: A Master Card; B Visa; C American Express; D Discover; E Diners Club; F Other; 2 Personal checks accepted; 3 Lunch available; 4 Dinner available;

San Francisco earthquake. All of its rooms are decorated to have many individual features which make each unique and delightful. The Inn is in a quiet neighborhood setting, yet its location is close enough to walk to many area attractions. Exploring Carmel Beach, Point Lobos State Park, or even the areas world renowned shops are just a few of the ways you can spend your time. Also, an evening can be spent dining at one of Monterey Peninsula's excellent restaurants. Come to the Stonehouse Inn to relax and experience the wonderful accommodations here by the beautiful Carmel Bay.

Host: Ad Navaille
Rooms: 6 (SB) $90-135
Full Breakfast
Credit Cards: A, B, C
Notes: 5, 7 (over 12), 8, 9, 10, 12

## CARMEL-BY-THE-SEA

## Sunset House

P.O. Box 1925, 93921
(408) 624-4884 (voice and FAX)

Sunset House, a romantic Inn, located on a quiet residential street, captures the essence of Carmel. Experience the sound of the surf, being close to the beach and yet only two blocks from quaint shops, galleries, and restaurants that make Carmel famous. Two rooms have ocean views and all rooms have brick, wood-burning fireplaces, and charming sitting areas, and all rooms are furnished with lovely antiques.

Hosts: Camille and Dennis Fike
Rooms: 4 (PB) $140-180
Expeanded Continental Breakfast
Credit Cards: A, B, C
Notes: 2, 5, 8, 9, 10

## CARMEL VALLEY

## The Valley Lodge

Carmel Valley Rd. at Ford Rd., P.O. Box 93, 93924
(408) 659-2261; (800) 641-4646;
FAX (408) 659-4558

A warm Carmel Valley welcome awaits the two of you, a few of you, or a small conference. Relax in a garden patio room or a cozy one or two bedroom cottage with fireplace and kitchen. Enjoy a sumptuous continental breakfast, our heated pool, sauna, hot spa, and fitness center. Tennis and golf are nearby. Walk to fine restaurants and quaint shops of Carmel Valley village, or just listen to your beard grow.

Hosts: Peter and Sherry Coakley
Rooms: 31 (PB) $95-135; $155 one bedroom
Expanded Continental Breakfast
Credit Cards: A, B, C
Notes: 2, 5, 6 (extra fee), 7, 8, 9 (on-site), 10, 12

## CLOVERDALE

## Ye Olde' Shelford House

29955 River Rd., 95425
(707) 894-5621; (800) 833-6479

This 1885 country Victorian is located in the heart of wine country, with 6 beautifully decorated rooms with family antiques, fresh flowers, homemade quilts and porcelain dolls by Ina. A gourmet breakfast is served in our delightful dining room. We will make reservations for you at one of the many good restaurants nearby. Before you retire, you can enjoy the many games in the recreation room, then get into the

---

5 Open all year; 6 Pets welcome; 7 Children welcome; 8 Tennis nearby; 9 Swimming nearby; 10 Golf nearby; 11 Skiing nearby; 12 May be booked through travel agent.

hot tub to relax after a busy day. Pool and tandem 10-speed bicycles available. Air-conditioned.

Hosts: Sheila Haverson and Al Sauder
Rooms: 6 (PB) $85-110; Closed January
Full Breakfast
Credit Cards: A, B, D
Notes: 2, 5, 7, 8, 9, 10, 12

## COLOMA

### Coloma Country Inn
345 High St., P.O. Box 502, 95613
(916) 622-6919

Built in 1852, this country Victorian farmhouse is surrounded by five acres of private gardens in the middle of a 300-acre state park. Main house has five guest rooms and the carriage house has two suites. All rooms feature country decor, including quilts, stenciling, American antiques, and fresh flowers. Hot-air balloon with your host from the backyard meadow or white-water raft from the South Fork American River one block from the inn.

Hosts: Alan and Cindi Erhgott
Rooms: 7 (5PB; 2SB) $89-120
Full Breakfast
Credit Cards: none
Notes: 2, 5, 7, 9, 10, 12

Fallon Hotel

## COLUMBIA

### Fallon Hotel
11175 Washington St., 95310
(209) 532-1470; FAX (209) 532-7027

Since 1857 the Fallon Hotel in the historic Colombia State Park has provided hospitality and comfort to travelers from all over the world. It has been authentically restored to its Victorian grandeur, and many of the antiques and furnishings are original to the hotel. We welcome you to come visit our Fallon Hotel, Fallon Theater, and old-fashioned ice cream parlor for a taste of the Old West.

Host: Tom Bender
Rooms: 14 (13PB; 1SB) $50-90
Continental Breakfast
Credit Cards: A, B, C, D
Notes: 2, 4, 5 (weekends only Jan-March), 7, 8, 9, 10, 11, 12

## EUREKA

### "An Elegant Victorian Mansion" B&B Experience
1406 "C" St., 95501
(707) 444-3144 or (707) 443-6512

An award-winning 1888 NATIONAL HISTORIC LANDMARK featuring spectacular gingerbread exteriors, opulent Victorian interiors, antique furnishings, and an acclaimed French-Gourmet breakfast. Eureka's most prestigious and luxurious bed and breakfast experience - EXCLUSIVELY for the non-smoker. Breath-takingly authentic, with all the nostalgic trimmings of a century ago, this meticulously restored Victorian masterpiece offers both HISTORY and HOSPITALITY, combined with ROMANCE and PAMPERING. Enjoy the regal splendor of this spectacular STATE HISTORIC SITE, and indulge in four-star luxury. Eureka's only AAA OFFICIALLY APPOINTED bed and breakfast has been rated by inn-goers state-wide as the "Best Bed and Breakfast in California." *World Traveler* magazine calls it "The best lodging value in California."

Hosts: Doug and Lily Vieyra
Rooms: 4 (2PB; 2SB) $65-135
Full French Gourmet Breakfast
Credit Cards: A, B
Notes: 2, 3, 5, 8, 9, 10, 11, 12

## Carter House Victorians

301 "L" Street, 95501
(707) 444-8062; (800) 404-1390;
FAX (707) 444-8067

Carter Victorians encompassed three lovely Victorians: the Carter House Inn, an exact replica of a circa 1884 San Francisco house that was destroyed in the 1906 earthquake; the classic 25-room Hotel Carter, and the newest addition, the three-room, single-level Bell Cottage. Each offers a distinctly clean and artful blend of classic Victorian architecture with stylish, contemporary interior settings, all in a warm, hospitable environment. A great variety of luxurious rooms, each appointed with original local art, fine antiques, and generous amenities such as fireplaces,

whirlpools, bay views, skylights, double-head showers, soaking tubs with marina views, king-size beds, telephones, VCRs and a video tape library, honor bars, and minifridges. "The best of the best," according to *California Living Magazine.*

Hosts: Mark and Christi Carter
Rooms: 32 (PB) $115-225
Full Breakfast
Credit Cards: A, B, C, D, E
Notes: 2, 4, 5, 7, 8, 9, 10, 12

Carter House Country Inn

## Shannon House

2154 Spring St., 95501
(707) 443-8130

The Shannon House is an 1891 Victorian that has been lovingly restored by the owners. It features period wallpaper and antiques throughout. The inn is situated on a quiet residential street in Eureka, a town of about 25,000. The town offers a walk through history with its various museums featuring Indian history, logging, working with steam engines, and maritime history. Within short distance there are miles of trails running through old growth redwood

5 Open all year; 6 Pets welcome; 7 Children welcome; 8 Tennis nearby; 9 Swimming nearby; 10 Golf nearby; 11 Skiing nearby; 12 May be booked through travel agent.

forests along secluded beaches.

Hosts: David and Barbara Shannon
Rooms: 3 (1PB; 2SB) $65-85 + tax
Full Breakfast
Credit Cards: C, D
Notes: 2, 5, 7, 8, 9, 10, 12

## A Weaver's Inn

1440 B St., 95501
(707) 443-8119

A Weaver's Inn is the home and studio of a fiber artist and her husband. The home is a stately Queen Anne Colonial Revival house built in 1883 and remodeled in 1907. Placed in a spacious fenced garden, airy and light, cozy and warm even when veiled by wisps of fog. Arriving early you might visit the studio, try the spinning wheel before the fire, or weave on the antique loom, before having refreshments. The Victorian parlor offers a piano and elegant relaxing.

Hosts: Bob and Dorothy Swendeman
Rooms: 4 (2PB; 2SB) $65-110
Full Breakfast
Credit Cards: A, B, C, D
Notes: 2, 5, 6, 7, 8, 10, 12

## FERNDALE

## The Gingerbread Mansion Inn

400 Berding St., P.O. Box 40, 95536
(707) 786-4000; (800) 952-4136;
FAX (707) 786-4381

Nestled between the giant redwoods and the rugged Pacific Coast, is one of California's best-kept secrets: the Victorian village of Ferndale. A State His-

toric landmark and listed on the National Historic Register, Ferndale is a community frozen in time with Victorian homes and shops relatively unchanged since their construction in the mid-to-late 1800s. One of Ferndale's most well-known homes is the Gingerbread Mansion Inn. Decorated with antiques, the eleven, romantic guest rooms offer private baths, some with old-fashioned clawfoot tubs, and fireplaces. Also included is a full breakfast, high tea, five parlors, and formal English gardens. Rated 4 Diamonds by AAA.

Hosts: Ken and Sandie Torbert
Rooms: 9 (PB) $125-195
Full Breakfast
Credit Cards: A, B, C
Notes: 2, 5, 10, 12

The Gingerbread Mansion Inn

## FORT BRAGG

## Glass Beach Bed and Breakfast Inn

726 N. Main St., 95437
(707) 964-6774

We are a gracious guest house offering

elegance, relaxation, and the comforts of home. Built in the early 1920s and renovated in 1980. Each room is furnished in its own distinct style. All rooms have private baths with tub/shower combination. We offer our guests one of the best breakfasts in town. Mention this add October 1st through June 30, Monday through Thursday and stay two nights for the price of one!

Hostess: Nancy Cardenas
Rooms: 9 (PB) $80-125
Full (Prepared to Order) Breakfast
Credit Cards: A, B, D
Notes: 2, 5, 7, 8, 9, 10, 12

## Grey Whale Inn

615 N. Main St., 95437
(707) 964-0640; (800) 382-7244;
FAX (707) 964-4408

Handsome four-story Mendocino Coast Landmark since 1915. Cozy rooms to expansive suites, all have private baths. Ocean, garden, hill, or town views. Some rooms have fireplaces or TV, one has a jacuzzi tub, and all have phones. Recreation area: pool table/library, fireside lounge, and TV theater. Sixteen-person conference room. Full buffet breakfast features blue-ribbon breads. Friendly, helpful staff. Relaxed seaside charm, situated six blocks to beach. Celebrate your special occasion on the fabled Mendocino Coast!

Hosts: John and Colette Bailey
Rooms: 14 (PB) $85-180
Full Breakfast
Credit Cards: A, B, C, D
Notes: 2, 5, 7, 8, 9, 10, 12

## Pudding Creek Inn

700 N. Main St., 95437
(707) 964-9529; (800) 227-9529;
FAX (707) 961-0282

Two lovely 1884 Victorian homes, adjoined by a lush garden court, offer comfortable and romantic rooms all with private baths. Your stay includes buffet breakfast with fresh fruit, juice, main dish, and tantalizing homemade coffee cakes served hot. Antiques, fireplaces, personalized sightseeing assistance. Near scenic Skunk Train excursion, beaches, dining, shops, galleries, hiking, tennis, and golf. Mention this book for a 15% discount off room rate.

Hosts: Garry and Carole Anloff
Rooms: 10 (PB) $65-125
Full Breakfast
Credit Cards: A, B, C, D
Notes: 2 (prior arrangement), 5, 7, 8, 9, 10, 12 (10%)

## FRESNO

## Mary Lou's B&B

5502 W. Escalon Ave., 93722
(209) 277-2650

Mary Lou's B&B in Fresno, CA is just three miles east of Hwy. 99 off the Herndon ramp. Stop on your way to Yosemite or Sequoia National Parks. Twin beds, private bath, guest sitting room, and air-conditioning await your arrival.

Hosts: Mary Lou and Merle Robinson
Rooms: 1 (PB) $50-60
Full Breakfast
Credit Cards: none
Notes: 2, 5, 7, 10

---

5 Open all year; 6 Pets welcome; 7 Children welcome; 8 Tennis nearby; 9 Swimming nearby; 10 Golf nearby; 11 Skiing nearby; 12 May be booked through travel agent.

## GEORGETOWN—GOLD COUNTRY

### Historic American River Inn

P.O. Box 43, Main at Orleans St., 95634
(916) 333-4499; (800) 245-6566;
FAX (916) 333-9253

Innkeepers Will and Maria Collin carry on the century old tradition of graciousness in a setting far removed from the fast pace of modern living. You are invited to cool off in a beautiful mountain pool or relax in the spa. Some may choose a day of bicycling amid the colorful breathtaking daffodils, iris and the brilliant yellow-gold scotch broom. The bicycles are provided. Their historic Queen Anne Inn can provide the ideal setting for your corporate off-site meeting or retreat. All meeting necessities and food catering services are available. The inn can accommodate up to 17/60 participants. Please call for detailed information for your group.

Hosts: Will and Maria Collin
Rooms: 18 (12PB; 6SB) $85-115
Full Gourmet Breakfast
Credit Cards: A, B, C, D, E, F
Notes: 2, 3, 5, 7, 8, 9, 10, 11, 12

## GEYSERVILLE

### Campbell Ranch Inn

1475 Canyon Rd., 95441
(707) 857-3476; (800) 959-3878

A 35-acre country setting in the heart of the Sonoma wine country offers a spectacular view, beautiful gardens, tennis court, swimming pool, hot tub, and bicycles. We have five spacious rooms with private baths, fresh flowers, fruits, king beds, and balconies. Full breakfast is served on the terrace, and we offer an evening dessert of homemade pie or cake. A wine country destination resort.

Host: Mary Jane and Jerry Campbell
Rooms: 5 (PB) $100-165
Full Breakfast
Credit Cards: A, B, C
Notes: 2, 5, 10, 12

Old Thyme Inn

## HALF MOON BAY

### Old Thyme Inn

779 Main St., 94019
(415) 726-1616

The Inn has seven guest rooms, all with private baths. The Inn is a restored 1889 Queen Anne Victorian, located on historic Main Street in the downtown area. Some rooms have fireplaces and double size whirlpool tubs. The theme is our English-style herb garden; all rooms are named after herbs. Atmosphere is friendly and informal. We serve beverages in the evening and a hearty breakfast each morning. Nearby activities include golf, whale-watching, tidepools,

---

NOTES: Credit cards accepted: A Master Card; B Visa; C American Express; D Discover; E Diners Club; F Other; 2 Personal checks accepted; 3 Lunch available; 4 Dinner available;

and shopping. Many fine restaurants are closeby, many within walking distance.

Hosts: George and Marcia Dempsey
Rooms: 7 (PB) $75-210
Full Breakfast
Credit Cards: A, B
Notes: 2, 5, 7, 8, 9, 10, 12

## HEALDSBURG

### Healdsburg Inn on the Plaza

110 Matheson St., 95448
(707) 433-6991; (800) 431-8663

A quiet place in the center of town where history and hospitality meet. This historic 1900 brick Victorian, once a Wells Fargo Express building, now houses our ten room bed and breakfast. Rooms done in sunrise/sunset colors feature fireplaces, queen beds, private bathrooms, fluffy towels, and a rubber ducky. Breakfast is served in our sun-filled solarium. Enjoy browsing through our art gallery, and antique and gift shops on the first floor.

Hosts: Genny Jenkins and LeRoy Steck
Rooms: 10 (PB) $145-195 (midweek rates discounted)
Full Breakfast
Credit Cards: A, B
Notes: 2, 5, 8, 9, 10

### The Honor Mansion

14891 Grove St., 95448
(707) 433-4277

A beautifully restored 112-year-old "Italiante" Victorian in the heart of the Sonoma County Wine Country. Enjoy the comfort of immaculate guest rooms, a dip in the pool, or a peaceful rest beside the Koi pond waterfall. Wonderful food; warm hospitality. Your best vacation ever!

Hostess: Cathi Fowler
Rooms: 5 (PB) $115-135
Full Breakfast
Credit Cards: A, B, D
Notes: 5, 10, 12

The Honor Mansion

## IDYLLIWILD

### The Pine Cove Inn

Box 2181, 23481 Hwy. 243; 92549
(909) 659-5033; FAX (909) 659-5034

Enjoy clean air with great views of Mount San Jacinto and Mount Tahquitz. Our units are spacious and tastefully appointed in a variety of styles. Relax, read a book, or hike on 75 miles of marked trails in the San Jacinto wilderness area. Get acquainted with paradise.

Hosts: Bob Bollman and Michelle Johanson
Rooms: 9 (PB); $70-90
Full Breakfast
Credit Cards: A, B
Notes: 2, 5, 7, 10, 11, 12

---

5 Open all year; 6 Pets welcome; 7 Children welcome; 8 Tennis nearby; 9 Swimming nearby; 10 Golf nearby; 11 Skiing nearby; 12 May be booked through travel agent.

Wilkum Inn

## Wilkum Inn B&B

P.O. Box 1115, 92549
(909) 659-4087; (800) 659-4086

Come home to warm hospitality and personal service in a friendly mountain ambiance. The two-story, shingle-sided inn is nestled among pines, oaks, and cedars. Warm knotty pine interiors and a cozy river rock fireplace are enhanced by the innkeepers' antiques and collectibles. Expanded continental breakfast of fruits and breads, such as crepes, Belgian Waffles or abelskivers, fortify guests for a day of hiking or visiting unique shops and art galleries.

Hostesses: Annamae Chambers and Barbara Jones
Rooms: 5 (3PB; 2SB) $65-95
Expanded Continental Breakfast
Credit Cards: none
Notes: 2, 5, 12

## IONE

## The Heirloom

214 Shakeley Ln., P.O. Box 322; 95640
(209) 274-4468

Travel down a country lane to a spacious, romantic English garden and a petite Colonial mansion built circa 1863. The house features balconies, fireplaces, and heirloom antiques, along with gourmet breakfast and gracious hospitality. Located in the historic gold country, close to all major northern California cities. The area abounds with antiques, wineries, and historic sites. Within walking distance to a golf course.

Hostesses: Melisande Hubbs and Patricia Cross
Rooms: 6 (4 PB; 2 SB); $60-92
Full Breakfast
Credit Cards: A, B, C
Closed Thanksgiving and Christmas
Notes: 2, 5, 8, 9, 10

## JULIAN

## Butterfield Bed and Breakfast

2284 Sunset Drive, 92036
(619) 765-2179; (800) 379-4262;
FAX (619) 765-1229

Butterfield Bed and Breakfast captures the gold mining and apple growing heritage of the historic mountain hamlet of Julian. The inn's five guest rooms, each with private bath, offer guests day's end luxury in the French Bedroom Suite, Country Rose, Feathernest Room, Apple "Sweet," or the Rosebud Cottage. Each morning guests are treated to a gourmet breakfast. Butterfield offers holidays specials, carriage rides, and candlelight dinner or just a quiet place to relax. From the lilac and apple blossoms of spring, the wild flowers of summer, and the glorious hues of fall to the white frosting of winter, Butterfield Bed and Breakfast delivers a mother lode of

NOTES: Credit cards accepted: A Master Card; B Visa; C American Express; D Discover; E Diners Club; F Other; 2 Personal checks accepted; 3 Lunch available; 4 Dinner available;

hospitality all year long.

Hosts: Ray and Mary Trimmins
Rooms: 5 (PB) $79-119
Full Breakfast
Credit Cards: A, B
Notes: 2, 4, 5, 7, 8, 10, 12

## Julian Gold Rush Hotel

P.O. Box 1856, 2032 Main St., 92036
(619) 765-0201

Built in 1897 by a freed slave, Albert
Robinson, and his wife, Margaret, the
Hotel fit beautifully into the emerging
Victorian society of the 1890's. The
Hotel was often called the "Queen of
the Back Country" and was a frequent
stopping place of Lady Bronston, Ad-
miral Nimitz, the Scripps, and the
Whitneys. The hotel register even
boasts the presence of many a senator
and congressman. Popular also with the
townfolk, the Hotel served as a Julian
social center after the monthly townhall
dances when Margaret Robinson hosted
and prepared much anticipated midnight
feasts.

Hosts: Steve and Gig Ballinger
Rooms: 17 (5PB; 12SB) $72-160
Full Breakfast
Credit Cards: A, B, C
Notes: 2, 5, 7, 8, 9, 10, 12

Julian Gold Rush Hotel

Julian White House

## Julian White House

P.O. Box 824, 92036
(619) 765-1764; (800) 948-4687

Secluded on a mountaintop, this petite
Colonial mansion has four guest rooms
all with private baths and queen beds.
The Honeymoon Suite offers a mountain view from bed. Rates range from
$90-135/night which includes a full
breakfast and evening dessert. Featured
on Home Garden TV, and recommended by K-ABC's Elmer Dills.

Hosts: Alan and Mary Marvin
Rooms: 4 (PB) $90-135
Full Breakfast
Credit Cards: A, B
Notes: 2

## Pinecroft Manor

P.O. Box 665, 92036
(619) 765-1611

Contemporary English Tudor-style
home. Five level manor in wooded area
with English Garden, flagstone grotto,
and sitting areas. Interior has Alpine
Flair with exposed beams, cathedral
ceilings, and is furnished in antiques.
Guest rooms located on three levels,
hosting a parlor, fireplace, library, game

5 Open all year; 6 Pets welcome; 7 Children welcome; 8 Tennis nearby; 9 Swimming nearby;
10 Golf nearby; 11 Skiing nearby; 12 May be booked through travel agent.

and TV/VCR room. Each guest room has queen-size bed, private ½ bath with shared shower/tub. "English Ivy" or "Garden Room" themes. Full breakfast in dining room, evening hospitality, and bed-time tea/cocoa.

Hosts: Diane and Fred Boyer
Rooms: 2 (SB) $90-95 (3 separate cabins available with PB)
Full Breakfast
Credit Cards: A, B
Notes: 2, 5, 7, 9, 12

## KERNVILLE

### Kern River Inn Bed and Breakfast

P.O. Box 1725, 119 Kern River Drive, 93238
(619) 376-6750; (800) 986-4382

A charming, classic country riverfront B&B located on the wild and scenic Kern River in the quaint little town of Kernville within the Sequoia National Forest in the southern Sierra Mountains. We specialize in romantic getaways. All bedrooms have private baths and feature river views; some with whirlpool tubs and fireplaces. Full breakfast. Walk to restaurants, shops, parks, and museum. A short drive to giant redwood trees. An all-year vacation area with fishing, skiing, hiking, biking, whitewater rafting, and Lake Isabella.

Hosts: Jack and Carita Prestwich
Rooms: 6 (PB) $79-99
Full Breakfast
Credit Cards: A, B
Notes: 2, 5, 7, 9, 10, 11

## LAGUNA BEACH

### Eiler's Inn B&B

741 S. Coast Hwy., 92651
(714) 494-3004; FAX (714) 497-2215

Twelve rooms with private baths and a courtyard with gurgling fountain and colorful blooming plants are within walking distance of town and most restaurants; half block from the beach.

Host: Henk Wirtz
Rooms: 12 (PB) $100-130
Full Breakfast
Credit Cards: A, B, C, D
Notes: 2, 5, 8, 9, 10, 12

## LAKE ARROWHEAD

### Arrowhead Windermere Manor

263 S. State Hwy. 173, P.O. Box 2177, 92352
(909) 336-3292; (800) 429-BLUE

The cozy elegance of European decor in an alpine setting welcomes you to the Arrowhead Windermere Manor (formerly the Bluebell House). Guests appreciate immaculate housekeeping, exquisite breakfasts, warm hospitality, and relaxing by the fire or out on the deck. Walk to charming lakeside village, boating, swimming, and restaurants. Private beach club and ice skating are nearby; winter sports 30 minutes away. Ask about discounts!

Hosts: Paul and Tudee Evers
Rooms: 5 (PB) $105-150
Full Breakfast
Credit Cards: A, B
Notes: 2, 5, 9, 11

---

NOTES: Credit cards accepted: A Master Card; B Visa; C American Express; D Discover; E Diners Club; F Other; 2 Personal checks accepted; 3 Lunch available; 4 Dinner available;

## LONG BEACH

### Lord Mayor's Inn B&B

435 Cedar Avenue, 90802
(310) 436-0324 (voice and FAX)

An award-winning historical landmark, the 1904 home of the first mayor of Long Beach invites you to enjoy the ambiance of years gone by. Rooms have 10-foot ceilings and are decorated with period antiques. Each unique bedroom has its private bath and access to a large sundeck. Full breakfast is served in the dining room or on the deck overlooking the garden. Located near beaches, close to major attractions, within walking distance of convention and civic center and special events held downtown. The right touch for the business and vacation traveler.

Hosts: Laura and Reuben Brasser
Rooms: 5 (PB) $85-105
Full Breakfast
Credit Cards: A, B, C, D
Notes: 2, 5, 7, 9, 10, 12

## LOS ANGELES

### California Home Hospitality

P.O. Box 66662, 90066
(310) 390-1526 (voice and FAX)

Situated in a quiet residential area, this hilltop home enjoys a spectacular view of the Santa Monica Mountains and the entire northern portion of the city. Just 15 minutes from the beach at Santa Monica and adjacent to Mariuce del Key Yacht Harbor and Santa Monica Municipal Airport. For enthusiastic sight-seers, a rental car is suggested, although public transportation is within walking distance.

Hostess: Helen Hause
Rooms: 1 (PB) $45
Full Breakfast
Credit Cards: none
Notes: 2, 3, 4, 5, 8, 9, 10

## LOS OSOS

### Gerarda's Bed and Breakfast

1056 Bay Oaks Dr., 93402
(805) 534-0834

Gerarda's three bedroom ranch-style home is comfortably furnished and offers wonderful ocean and mountain views from the elaborate flower gardens in front and back. Gerarda, the hostess, speaks five languages and will welcome you warmly. She cooks a wonderful family-style breakfast. A few miles from state parks, Morro Bay, Hearst Castle, San Luis Obispo, universities, and shopping center.

Hostess: Gerarda Ondang
Rooms: 3 (1PB; 2SB) $28-45
Full Breakfast
Credit Cards: none
Notes: 2, 5, 7, 8, 9, 10

## MARIPOSA

### Finch Haven

4605 Triangle Road, 95338
(209) 966-4738 (voice and FAX)

A quiet country home on nine acres with panoramic mountain views. Birds, deer, and other abundant wildlife. Two

---

5 Open all year; 6 Pets welcome; 7 Children welcome; 8 Tennis nearby; 9 Swimming nearby; 10 Golf nearby; 11 Skiing nearby; 12 May be booked through travel agent.

rooms with private bath and private deck. Queen and twin beds. Nutritious breakfast. In the heart of the California Gold Rush Country near historic attractions. Convenient access to spectacular Yosemite Valley and Yosemite National Park. A restful place to practice Mark 6:31 and to enjoy Christian hospitality.

Hosts: Bruce and Carol Fincham
Rooms: 2 (PB) $75
Full Breakfast
Credit Cards: none
Notes: 2, 5, 7, 8, 9, 11, 12

## Oak Meadows, too Bed and Breakfast

5263 Hwy. 140 N., 95338
(209) 742-6161; FAX (209) 966-2320

Just a short drive to Yosemite National Park, Oak Meadows, is located in the historic Gold Rush town of Mariposa. Oak Meadows, too was built with New England Architecture and turn-of-the-century charm. A stone fireplace greets you upon arrival in the guest parlor, where a continental plus breakfast is served each morning. All rooms are furnished with handmade quilts, brass headboards, and charming wallpapers. Central heat and air-conditioning.

Hosts: Frank Ross and Kaaren Black
Rooms: 6 (PB) $69-89
Continental Plus Breakfast
Credit Cards: A, B
Notes: 2, 5, 11, 12 (10%)

## Shiloh Bed and Breakfast

3265 Triangle Park Rd., 95338
(209) 742-7200

Shiloh is an old peaceful farmhouse with a private guest house nestled among Ponderosa pines in the foothills of Yosemite National Park. Two quaint knotty pine bedrooms in the main house share a private bath. The pleasantly decorated guest house sleeps five or six and has a full kitchen, living room, and private deck. Playground for the children, plus a swimming pool and horse shoe pits. Historic gold rush country and Yosemite to explore. Christian hospitality.

Hosts: Ron and Joan Smith
Rooms: 3 (1PB; 2SB) $55-85
Extended Continental Breakfast
Credit Cards: A, B, C, D
Notes: 2, 5, 7, 9, 10

## Winsor Farms Bed and Breakfast

5636 Whitlock Rd., 95338
(209) 966-5592

A country home seven miles north of Mariposa, just off Highway 140 to Yosemite National Park. This peaceful hilltop retreat among majestic pines and

---

NOTES: Credit cards accepted: A Master Card; B Visa; C American Express; D Discover; E Diners Club; F Other; 2 Personal checks accepted; 3 Lunch available; 4 Dinner available;

rugged oaks offers two rooms decorated for your comfort and convenience. An extended continental breakfast is served. The town of Mariposa is the Gateway to the Mother Lode Gold Country, with famous court house, museums, and history center. Yosemite National Park, a scenic wonder of the world with waterfalls, granite cliffs, Sequoia Big Trees, birds, and animals.

Hosts: Donald and Janice Haag
Rooms: 2 (SB) $40-50
Extended Continental Breakfast
Credit Cards: none
Notes: 2, 5, 7 (restricted)

## MENDOCINO

### Antioch Ranch

39451 Comptche Rd., 95460
(707) 937-5570; FAX (707) 937-1757

Antioch Ranch, providing a Christian atmosphere of peace, is a place for refreshment and renewal. Located just five and a half miles inland from the picturesque town of Mendocino, the Ranch features four guest cottages on 20 acres of rolling hills, redwoods, and apple orchards. Each cottage has its own style and ambiance. Rustic, yet comfortable, they feature woodstoves, complete kitchens with a microwave, two bedrooms, a bath, and open living/dining room.

Hosts: Jerry and Pat Westfall
Rooms: 4 two bedroom cottages (PB) $55-75
Breakfast on request basis.
Credit Cards: none
Notes: 2, 5, 7, 8, 9 (beach), 10

### Mendocino Village Inn

44860 Main St., Box 626, 95460
(707) 937-0246; (800) 882-7029;
(e-mail) MendoInn@aol.com

An 1882 Queen Anne Victorian with gardens, frog pond, and sun deck. Many rooms with fireplaces and ocean views. Style is eclectic with emphasis on clean, comfortable, and welcoming. We are close to the beach and walking distance to all shops and restaurants. "Please come and play our pump organ."

Hosts: Kathleen and Bill Erwin
Rooms: 12 + 1 suite (11PB; 2SB) $75-175
Full Breakfast (two courses)
Credit Cards: none
Notes: 2, 5, 8, 9, 10

## MT. SHASTA

### Mt. Shasta Ranch Bed and Breakfast

1008 W. A. Barr Rd., 96067
(916) 926-3870; FAX (916) 926-6882

The inn is situated in a rural setting with a majestic view of Mt. Shasta and features a main lodge, carriage house, and cottage. Group accommodations are available.Our breakfast room is ideally suited for seminars and retreats with large seating capacity. The game room includes piano, ping-pong, pool table, and board games. Guests also enjoy an outdoor jacuzzi. Nearby recreational facilities include alpine and Nordic skiing, fishing, hiking, mountain bike

5 Open all year; 6 Pets welcome; 7 Children welcome; 8 Tennis nearby; 9 Swimming nearby; 10 Golf nearby; 11 Skiing nearby; 12 May be booked through travel agent.

rentals, surrey rides, and museums. Call for pastor's discount.

Hosts: Bill and Mary Larsen
Rooms: 9 + 1 cabin (5PB; 5SB) $55-80
Full breakfast
Credit Cards: A, B, C, D
Notes: 2, 5, 7, 8, 9, 10, 11, 12

## NAPA

## Blue Violet Mansion

443 Brown Street, 94559
(707) 253-2583; (800) 959-2583;
FAX (707) 257-8205

Cross the threshold of this graceful Queen Anne Victorian mansion and return to the elegance of the 1880s. Situated on a quiet street with an acre of private gardens in historic Old Town Napa and walking distance from downtown shops and restaurants. Winner of the prestigious Landmarks Preservation Award of Excellence in 1993, this lovingly restored inn is an intimate and romantic home offering large, cheerful rooms with fireplaces, balconies, and private baths or spas. Guests are encouraged to feel at home in the grand front rooms and enjoy the garden gazebo and grape arbored deck outside. Enjoy an evening of romantic elegance with a private candlelight champagne dinner, in room massages for two, flowers, and gift service. Picnic lunches. Bicycles. Hot air ballooning and golf packages available. Near Wine Train.

Hosts: Bob and Kathy Morris
Rooms: 10 (PB) $125-195 (amenity extra)
Full Breakfast
Credit Cards: A, B, C, E, F
Notes: 2, 3, 4, 5, 7, 8, 9, 10, 12

## Hennessey House

1727 Main Street, 94559
(707) 226-3774; FAX (707) 226-2975

Hennessey House, a beautiful Eastlake-style Queen Anne Victorian located in downtown Napa, is listed in the National Register of Historic Places. It features antique furnishings, fireplaces, whirlpools, patios, and a sauna. The dining room, where a sumptuous breakfast is served, features one of the finest examples of a hand-painted, stamped tin ceilings in California. Just a short walk to the Wine Train! Golf packages available.

Hostesses: Andrea Lamar and Lauriann Delay
Rooms: 10 (PB) $80-155
Full Breakfast
Credit Cards: A, B, C
Notes: 2, 5, 7, 10, 12

## La Belle Epoque

1386 Calistoga Ave., 94559
(707) 257-2161; (800) 238-8070;
FAX (707) 226-6314

Elaborate Queen Anne architecture and extensive use of stained glass are complimented by elegant period furnishings. This century-old Victorian boasts six tastefully decorated guest rooms, each with private bath and two with fireplaces. A generous, gourmet breakfast is offered each morning either by fireside in the formal dining room or in the more relaxed atmosphere of the inn's plant-filled sunroom. Complimentary evening wine and appetizers on the premises. Wine tasting room/cellar. Walk to Old Town, Wine Train, and

---

NOTES: Credit cards accepted: A Master Card; B Visa; C American Express; D Discover; E Diners Club; F Other; 2 Personal checks accepted; 3 Lunch available; 4 Dinner available;

Opera House. On-grounds parking and air-conditioned throughout.

Hosts: Merlin and Claudia Wedepohl (owners)
Rooms: 6 (PB) $110-155
Full Gourmet Breakfast
Credit Cards: A, B, C, D
Notes: 2, 5, 8, 9, 10, 12

## NEVADA CITY

### *Downey House Bed and Breakfast*
517 West Broad Street, 95959
(916) 265-2815; (800) 258-2815

1870 Eastlake Victorian, one block from downtown. Beautiful gardens surround the house with it's curved verandah; sunroom with a grand view of town. Sound proofed rooms with contemporary furnishings in guest rooms featuring excellent beds, comfort, and elegance. Fall, delicious breakfast. Business travelers and other mid week guests offered a discount Sun.-Thurs., Jan.-Nov.

Hostess: Miriam Wright
Rooms: 6 (PB) $75-100
Full Breakfast
Credit Cards: A, B
Notes: 2, 5, 7, 8, 9, 10, 11, 12

### *The Parsonage Bed and Breakfast Inn*
427 Broad St., 95959
(916) 265-9478; (916) 265-8147

History comes alive in this 125-year-old-home in Nevada City's Historic District. Cozy guest rooms, parlor, and dining and family rooms are all lovingly furnished with the innkeeper's pioneer family's antiques. Breakfast is served on the veranda or in the formal dining room.

Hosts: Peter and Barbara Franchine
Owner: Deborah Dane
Rooms: 6 (PB) $65-120
Expanded Continental Breakfast
Credit Cards: A, B
Notes: 2, 5, 7, 9, 10, 11, 12

The Parsonage Bed and Breakfast Inn

## PALM SPRINGS

### *Casa Cody Bed and Breakfast Country Inn*
175 S. Cahuilla Road, 92262
(619) 320-9346; (800) 231-CODY (2639);
FAX (619) 325-8610

A romantic, historic hideaway is nestled against the spectacular San Jacinto Mountains in the heart of Palm Springs Village. Completely redecorated in Santa Fe decor, it has 17 ground-level units consisting of hotel rooms, studio suites, and one- and two-bedroom suites with private patios, fireplaces, and fully equipped, tiled kitchens. Cable TV and

5 Open all year;  6 Pets welcome;  7 Children welcome;  8 Tennis nearby;  9 Swimming nearby;
10 Golf nearby;  11 Skiing nearby;  12 May be booked through travel agent.

private phones; two pools; secluded, tree-shaded whirlpool spa.

Hosts: Therese Hayes and Frank Tysen
Manager: Elissa Goforth
Rooms: 17 (PB) $49 summer - $185 (suite) winter
Continental Breakfast
Credit Cards: A, B, C
Notes: 2, 5, 6 and 7 (limited), 8, 9, 10, 11

## PALO ALTO

### *Adella Villa*

P.O. Box 4528, 94309-4528
(415) 321-5195; FAX (415) 325-5121

Luxurious '20s Italian villa on one acre of lovely manicured gardens with pool, fountains, antiques, and a music room featuring Steinway grand piano. Four-thousand square-foot inn with all the amenities! Pamper yourself in one of our jacuzzi tubs. Enjoy a full breakfast. Refreshments available throughout the day. Thirty minutes from San Francisco.

Hostess: Tricia Young
Rooms: 5 (PB) $99-110
Full Breakfast
Credit Cards: A, B, C, E
Notes: 2, 5, 8, 10, 12

## RED BLUFF (LASSEN VOLCANIC NATIONAL PARK)

### *Drakesbad Guest Ranch*

2150 N. Main St., Suite #5, 96080
(916) 529-1512; FAX (916) 529-4511

In the heart of Lassen Volcanic National Park, Drakesbad Guest Ranch is a beautiful, scenic area that offers a serene and peaceful getaway from the daily pressures of everyday life. Its beautiful meadows house an abundance of nature's wildlife including squirrels, chipmunks, raccoons, mule deer, hawks, owls, eagles, and even black bears and a cougar. At Drakesbad there is a lovely pool fed by the natural hot springs where guests can relax after a day of hiking, sightseeing, or many other activities. Come to Drakesbad for a chance to experience the quiet beauty of a California Ranch.

Hosts: John and Pam Koebfrer
Rooms: 19 (PB) $175-195 A.P.
Three Meals Included
Open June - October
Credit Cards: A, B
Notes: 2, 3 and 4 (included), 6, 7, 9, 12

Adella Villa

NOTES: Credit cards accepted: A Master Card; B Visa; C American Express; D Discover; E Diners Club; F Other; 2 Personal checks accepted; 3 Lunch available; 4 Dinner available;

## REDONDO BEACH

### Breeze Inn

122 S. Juanita Ave., 90277
(310) 316-5123

Located in a quiet, modest neighborhood. Large suite with private entrance, private bath with spa, antiques, Oriental carpet, California king bed, and breakfast area with microwave and toaster oven, and stocked refrigerator for continental breakfast. Good ventilation with skylight and ceiling fan. Outside patio. One room also available with twin beds and private bath. A brochure is available with map. Near Los Angeles, Disneyland, Universal City, and approximately five blocks to pier and beach.

Hosts: Norris and Betty Binding
Rooms: 2 (PB)
Continental Breakfast (extra charge for Full)
Credit Cards: none
Notes: 2, 5, 7 (over 5), 8, 9, 10

## RIDGECREST

### BevLen Haus Bed and Breakfast

809 N. Sanders Street, 93555
(619) 375-1988; (800) 375-1989;
FAX (619) 446-3220

"Once a guest, always a friend." Gracious, quiet, safe, and comfortable; your "secret high desert hideaway." Nearly 2,000 square feet, furnished with antiques, handmade quilts, and comforters in winter! Paved parking. Cooling air in summer. Old-fashioned kitchen has antique cast-iron cookstove, hand-hammered copper sink. In full-service community. Close to Sierra Nevada, Death Valley, Naval Air Warfare Center, China Lake, ghost towns, movie sites, and ancient Indian cultural sites. Wildflowers in spring. No smoking.

Hosts: Bev and Len de Geus
Rooms: 3 (1PB; 2SB) $40-60
Full Breakfast
Credit Cards: A, B, C, D
Notes: 2, 5, 8, 9, 10, 12

## ST. HELENA

### Hilltop House Bed and Breakfast

9550 St. Helena Rd., 94574
(707) 944-0880; FAX (707) 571-0263

Poised at the very top of the ridge that separates the famous wine regions of Napa and Sonoma, Hilltop House is a country retreat with all the comforts of home and a view that you must see to believe. Annette and Bill Gevarter built their contemporary home with this mountain panorama in mind, the vast deck allows you to enjoy it at your leisure with a glass of wine in the afternoon, with breakfast in the morning, or with a long soak in the hot tub. From this vantage point, sunrises and sunsets are simply amazing. You'll cherish the natural setting, the caring hospitality, and the prize location.

Hostess: Annette Gevarter
Rooms: 4 (PB) $105-175
Full Breakfast
Credit Cards: A, B, C
Notes: 2, 5, 7, 8, 9, 10, 12

---

5 Open all year; 6 Pets welcome; 7 Children welcome; 8 Tennis nearby; 9 Swimming nearby; 10 Golf nearby; 11 Skiing nearby; 12 May be booked through travel agent.

## SAN FRANCISCO

### *Amsterdam Hotel*

749 Taylor St., 94108
(415) 673-3277; (800) 637-3444;
FAX (415) 673-0453

Originally built in 1909, the hotel reflects the charm of a small European hotel. From our spacious lobby to our beautifully decorated rooms, we offer quality accomodations and friendly service. Every modern convenience is provided for the most discriminating business or pleasure traveler. The hotel is situated on Nob Hill just two blocks from the historic cable cars which connect you in minutes to Union Square, Chinatown, Fisherman's Wharf, the Suasalito Ferry, and much more.

Hostess: Marilyn
Rooms: 32 (29PB; 3SB); $50-89
Continental Breakfast
Credit Cards: A, B, C
Notes: 5, 7, 8, 9, 10, 12

### *Chateau Tivoli Bed and Breakfast Inn*

1057 Steiner St., 94115
(415) 776-5462; (800) 228-1647;
FAX (415) 776-0505

The Chateau is a landmark mansion built in 1892. Guests experience a time travel journey back to San Francisco's golden age of opulence. Choose from five rooms, two with fireplaces, and two suites; all with phones. Breakfast is served in guest rooms or in the dining room. Near shops, restaurants, opera, and symphony. Reservation deposit required.

Hosts: Rodney Karr and Willard Gersbach
Rooms: 7 (5PB; 2SB) $80-200
Full Breakfast; Continental (weekdays)
Credit Cards: A, B, C
Notes: 2, 5, 7, 8, 9, 10, 12

Chateau Tivoli Bed and Breakfast Inn

### *The Grove Inn*

890 Grove St., 94117
(415) 929-0780; (800) 829-0780;
FAX (415) 929-1037

The Grove Inn is a part of a historic Victorian setting, the Alamo Square. Centrally located, the Grove Inn is within reach of the Golden Gate Park, symphony, operas, and the Museum for Modern Arts. It is reasonably priced and managed by experienced innkeepers. This is the eleventh season for the Grove Inn.

Hosts: Klaus and Rosetta Zimmerman
Rooms: 20 (14PB; 6SB) $65-85
Continental Breakfast
Credit Cards: A, B, C
Notes: 2, 5, 7, 8, 9, 10, 12

---

NOTES: Credit cards accepted: A Master Card; B Visa; C American Express; D Discover; E Diners Club; F Other; 2 Personal checks accepted; 3 Lunch available; 4 Dinner available;

## The Monte Cristo

600 Prisido Ave., 94115
(415) 931-1875; FAX (415) 931-6005

The Monte Cristo has been part of San Francisco since 1875, located two blocks from the elegantly restored Victorian shops, restaurants, and antique stores on Sacramento Street. There is convenient transportation to downtown San Francisco and to the financial district. Each room is elegantly furnished with authentic period pieces.

Host: George Yuan
Rooms: 14 (11PB; 3SB) $63-108
Full Buffet Breakfast
Credit Cards: A, B, C, D, E
Notes: 5, 7, 12

## The Red Victorian

1665 Haight St., 94117
(415) 864-1978

Built in 1904, The Red Victorian Inn is a standing monument of history in the heart of San Francisco. The inn has 18 rooms which were designed by the current owner Sami Sunchild. Each of the rooms are tastefully furnished with unique decor and come in a variety of styles with private or shared baths. The Red Victorian is the perfect place for a three-day mini-vacation or just an overnight stay for a wonderful bed and breakfast experience.

Hostess: Sami Sunchild
Rooms: 18 (4PB; 14SB) $50-200
Continental Buffet Breakfast
Credit Cards: A, B, C
Notes: 5, 12

The Red Victorian

## SAN GREGORIO

## Rancho San Gregorio

5086 La Honda Rd. (Hwy. 84), 94074
(415) 747-0810; FAX (415) 747-0184

Five miles inland from the Pacific Ocean is an idyllic rural valley where Rancho San Gregorio welcomes travelers to share relaxed hospitality. Picnic, hike, or bike in wooded parks or on ocean beaches. Our country breakfast features local specialties. Located 45 minutes from San Francisco, Santa Cruz, and the Bay area.

Hosts: Bud and Lee Raynor
Rooms: 4 (PB) $70-145
Full Breakfast
Credit Cards: A, B, C, D
Notes: 2, 5, 7, 9, 10, 12 (10%)

## SAN LUIS OBISPO

## Garden Street Inn

1212 Garden St., 93401
(805) 545-9802; FAX (805) 781-7469

The grace and simplicity of yesteryear

---

5 Open all year; 6 Pets welcome; 7 Children welcome; 8 Tennis nearby; 9 Swimming nearby; 10 Golf nearby; 11 Skiing nearby; 12 May be booked through travel agent.

prevail at the 1887 Italiante Queen Anne home situated one block from a 1772 mission on the old-fashioned downtown in one of the nation's celebrated California communities. Classic Victorian decor in nine guest rooms and four suites appointed with antiques, fireplaces, jacuzzis, and historical, cultural, and personal memorabilia. Homemade full breakfasts, spacious outside decks, and well-stocked library. Close to Hearst Castle, Pismo Beach, Morro Bay, and Cambria.

Hosts: Dan and Kathy Smith
Rooms: 9 + 4 suites (PB) $90-160
Full Breakfast
Credit Cards: A, B, C
Notes: 2, 5, 8, 9, 10, 12

## SANTA BARBARA

## Long's Seaview Bed and Breakfast

317 Piedmont, 93105
(805) 687-2947

Overlooking the ocean and Channel Islands. Quiet neighborhood of lovely homes. Breakfast usually served on huge patio. Large bedroom with king-size bed. Private entrance, private bath. Convenient to all attractions and Solvang. Local information and maps. Fantastic views from patio.

Hostess: LaVerne Long
Rooms: 1 (PB) $75-79
Full Breakfast
Credit Cards: None
Notes: 12

## Montecito Bed and Breakfast

167 Olive Mill Rd., 93108
(805) 969-7992

Enjoy a spacious room with private bath, private entrance, TV, phone, desk, and eating area. Patio jacuzzi is available for your use. Includes homemade continental breakfast and coffee. Room has garden atmosphere and looks out on a vista of trees and mountains. Located close to Westmont College and just above coastal village shopping and restaurants. Approximately one-half mile to the beach.

Hostess: Linda Ryan
Rooms: 1 (PB) $50-60
Continental Breakfast
Credit Cards: none
Notes: 2, 5, 7, 8, 9, 10, 12

## The Old Yacht Club Inn

431 Corona Del Mar Dr., 93103
(805) 962-1277; (800) 676-1676 (reservations); FAX (805) 962-3989

The Inn at the beach! These 1912 California Craftsman and 1925 early California-style homes house nine individually decorated guest rooms furnished with antiques. Bicycles, beach chairs, and towels are included, and an evening social hour is provided. Gourmet dinner is available on Saturdays.

Hostesses: Nancy Donaldson and Sandy Hunt
Rooms: 9 (PB) $90-160
Full Breakfast
Credit Cards: A, B, C, D, E
Notes: 2, 4 (Saturdays), 5, 7, 8, 9, 10, 12

---

NOTES: Credit cards accepted: A Master Card; B Visa; C American Express; D Discover; E Diners Club; F Other; 2 Personal checks accepted; 3 Lunch available; 4 Dinner available;

Babbling Brook Inn

## SANTA CRUZ

## *Babbling Brook Inn*

1025 Laurel St., 95060
(408) 427-2437; (800) 866-1131;
FAX (408) 427-2457

The foundations of the Inn date back to the 1790s when padres from the local mission built a grist mill to take advantage of the stream to grind corn. In the 19th century, a water wheel generated power for a tannery. Then a few years later, a rustic log cabin was built which remains as the heart of the inn. Most of the rooms are chalets in the garden, surrounded by pines and redwoods, cascading waterfalls, and gardens.

Hostess: Helen King
Rooms: 12 (PB) $85-165
Full Breakfast
Credit Cards: A, B, C, D, E, F
Notes: 2, 5, 8, 9, 10, 12

## *Chateau Victorian*

118 First St., 95060
(408) 458-9458

Chateau Victorian was turned into an elegant B&B with a warm, friendly atmosphere in 1983. Built around 1885, the Inn is only one block from the beach. All seven rooms have a queen-size bed; a private, tiled bathroom, one of which has a clawfoot tub with shower; and a fireplace, with fire logs provided. Each room has its own heating system, controlled by the guest. Wine and cheeses are available for the guest in late afternoon. Chateau Victorian is within walking distance to downtown, the Municipal Wharf, the Boardwalk Amusement Park, and fine, as well as casual, dining.

Hostess: Alice June
Rooms: 7 (PB) $110-140 + tax
Expanded Continental Breakfast
Credit Cards: A, B, C
Notes: 2, 5, 8, 9, 10, 12 (no commissions)

## *Pleasure Point Inn and Boat Charters*

2-3665 E. Cliff Dr., 95062
(408) 475-4657

On the water overlooking the beautiful Monterey Bay. Fantastic views from three of our rooms. Fireplaces and whirlpool tubs. Boat charters are underway daily for fishing or cruising. Your host is an accomplished captain of the "Margaret Mary" and your hostess is more than willing to arrange dinner reservations at a fine, local restaurant or point you to historic landmarks in the area. Within walking distance to the beaches and shopping villages.

Hosts: Sal and Margaret Margo
Rooms: 4 (3PB; 1SB) $100-145
Full Breakfast
Credit Cards: A, B
Notes: 5, 7, 8, 9, 10, 12

5 Open all year; 6 Pets welcome; 7 Children welcome; 8 Tennis nearby; 9 Swimming nearby; 10 Golf nearby; 11 Skiing nearby; 12 May be booked through travel agent.

## SEAL BEACH

### *The Seal Beach Inn and Gardens*

212 5th St., 92740
(310) 493-2416; (800) HIDEAWAY;
FAX (310) 799-0483

Elegant, historic Southern California Inn, one block from ocean beach in a charming, prestigious, seaside town next to Long Beach. Lush gardens, lovely estate appearance. Exquisite rooms and suites. Pool, library, and kitchens available. Free full breakfast/social hour. Modern amenities. Short walk to restaurants, shops, and beach pier. Three freeways close by. Easy drive to Disneyland and other major Los Angeles attractions and business centers. Meeting rooms available (24 maximum). Convenient to LAX, Long Beach, and Orange County Airports.

Hostess: Marjorie Bettenhausen
Rooms: 23 (PB) $118-185
Full Breakfast
Credit Cards: A, B, C, D, F
Notes: 3, 4, 5, 8, 9, 10, 12

## SONOMA

### *Sonoma Hotel*

110 W. Spain St., 95476
(707) 996-2996; (800) 468-6016;
FAX (707) 996-7014

Sonoma Hotel is a wonderful place, an hours drive from San Francisco, but a hundred years away. On Sonoma's tree-lined plaza, this vintage hotel offers ac-commodations and dining to the discriminating guest. To spend an evening here is to step back into a romantic period in history. Each antique furnished room evokes a distinct feel of early California, the emphasis on comfort is decidedly European. Short walks to wineries, historic landmarks, art galleries, and unique shops.

Hosts: John and Dorene Musilli
Rooms: 17 (5PB; 12SB) $59-98 (Sun. - Thurs.)
$75-120 (off season)
Continental Breakfast
Credit Cards: A, B, C
Notes: 2, 3, 4, 5, 7 (over 13), 9, 10, 12 (5%)

Sonoma Hotel

### *Sparrow's Nest Inn*

424 Denmark St., 95476
(707) 996-3750

Sparrow's Nest Inn for a lovely stay away from it all. . . . A charming private, country cottage with English garden and courtyard in the heart of Sonoma Valley. One mile from the historic town square. Accommodations include fresh flowers, bedroom with Laura Ashley bedding, living room, cable TV/VCR, phone, air-condition-

---

NOTES: Credit cards accepted: A Master Card; B Visa; C American Express; D Discover; E Diners Club; F Other; 2 Personal checks accepted; 3 Lunch available; 4 Dinner available;

ing, bath, and kitchenette. We think all of our guests are special and do our best to make a visit to Sparrow's Nest enjoyable and memorable.

Hosts: Thomas and Kathleen Anderson
Rooms: 1 single cottage (PB) $85-105
Both Full and Continental Breakfast available
Credit Cards: A, B, C, D
Notes: 2, 5, 6 (special arrangements), 7, 8, 9, 10

Lavender Hill Bed and Breakfast Inn

## SONORA

## Lavender Hill Bed and Breakfast Inn

683 S. Barretta, 95370
(209) 532-9024; (800) 446-1333 ext. 290

Come home . . . to a 1900s Victorian home overlooking the historic gold rush town of Sonora. At sunset you can watch the world from a wraparound porch, enjoy a country walk through year round flower gardens, and a covered patio, ideal for a small wedding. In the morning, you wake to a home-cooked breakfast and have the opportunity to listen and share experiences with others, perhaps planning your day to include hiking in Yosemite, fishing,

biking, river rafting, or even a scenic steam train ride. Afternoons and evenings could include a stroll to downtown antique shops and boutiques, fine dining, and topped off with your enjoyment for one of the professional repertory theaters. We will be glad to plan a dinner theater package for your stay. Gift certificates also available. One visit will have you longing to return "home"—home to Lavender Hill.

Hosts: Jean and Charlie Marinelli
Rooms: 4 (2PB; 2SB) $70-90
Full Breakfast
Credit Cards: A, B, C
Notes: 2, 5, 7, 8, 9, 10, 11, 12

## SOQUEL

## Blue Spruce Inn

2815 Main St., 95073
(408) 464-1137; (800) 559-1137;
FAX (408) 475-0608

Spa tubs, fireplaces, quiet gardens, and original local art foster relaxation for our guests. The Blue Spruce is four miles south of Santa Cruz and one mile inland from Capitola Beach—an ideal location that blends the flavor of yesteryear with the comfort of today. Hike in the redwoods. Bike through country fields. Walk to fine dining. Relax in the outdoor hot tub. Professional, personal attention is our hallmark. Visit us soon!

Hosts: Pat and Tom O'Brien
Rooms: 5 (PB) $80-125
Full Breakfast
Credit Cards: A, B, C
Notes: 2

5 Open all year;  6 Pets welcome;  7 Children welcome;  8 Tennis nearby;  9 Swimming nearby;
10 Golf nearby;  11 Skiing nearby;  12 May be booked through travel agent.

## SUMMERLAND

### Inn on Summer Hill

2520 Lillie Ave., 93067
(805) 969-9998; (800) 845-5566;
FAX (805) 565-9946

One of America's Top Rated B&Bs awaits you with visually captivating English country decor and world class amenities. Set in the seaside village of Summerland, just five minutes south of Santa Barbara, this California Craftsman-styled award-winning inn, built in 1989, offers sixteen mini-suites with ocean views, fireplaces, jacuzzi tubs, canopy beds, video cassette players and original art and accessories. Sumptuous full gourmet breakfasts, hor d'oeuvres and desserts add to the uncompromising comfort and charm. Guests rooms provide a directory of local activities along with concierge service and special packages for the discerning traveler in the mood for something out of the ordinary. The Automobile Club and *Country Inns Magazine* have also rated the Inn one of the "Best in the Country."

Hostess: Verlinda Richardson
Rooms: 16 (PB) $160-295
Full Breakfast
Credit Cards: A, B, C, D
Notes: 3 (picnic only), 5, 8, 9, 10, 12

### Summerland Inn

2161 Ortega Hill Rd., P.O. Box 1209, 93067
(805) 969-5225

Located minutes from beautiful Santa Barbara, this newly built New England-style bed and breakfast is a must for Southern California travelers. Enjoy ocean views, fireplaced rooms, brass and four-poster beds, country folk art, biblical quotations, and Christian motifs. Christian reading material is available. All rooms include cable TV and free local calls.

Hosts: Jim Farned
Rooms: 11 (PB) $65-150 (10% discount to *Christian Bed and Breakfast Directory* patrons)
Continental Breakfast
Credit Cards: A, B, C, E
Notes: 2, 5, 7, 8, 9, 10

The Foxes in Sutter Creek

## SUTTER CREEK

### The Foxes in Sutter Creek

77 Main St., P.O. Box 159, 95685
(209) 267-5882; FAX (209) 267-0712

An award winning Inn offering seven large, elegant suites; private baths; queen beds; air-conditioning; wood burning fireplaces; covered parking; gourmet breakfasts, cooked to order and served to your room on silver service or in the garden with the morning newspaper. Downtown location near all the sites and shops. Three Star Mobile rated. Named "the very best" in *The Best of the Gold Country.* Named "the most elegant in the gold country" by AAA *Motorland Magazine.* Certified members of CABBI-CLIA and BBIAC.

Hosts: Pete and Min Fox
Rooms: 7 (PB) $100-145
Full Breakfast (cooked to order)
Credit Cards: A, B, D
Notes: 2, 5 (closed Dec. 24 and 25), 8, 9, 10, 11 (1½ hours), 12

## Sutter Creek Inn
75 Main St., Box 385, 95685
(209) 267-5606

The Inn is known for its fireplaces, hanging beds, and private patios. All rooms have private baths and electric blankets. All guests gather 'round the kitchen fireplace to enjoy a hot breakfast. A huge library in the living room invites guests to while away the time before afternoon refreshments.

Hostess: Jane Way
Rooms: 18 (PB) $50-135
Full Breakfast
Credit Cards: none
Notes: 2, 3 and 4 (nearby), 5, 8, 9, 10, 11, 12

## TRINIDAD

## Trinidad Bay Bed and Breakfast
560 Edwards St., P.O. Box 849, 95570
(707) 677-0840

Our Cape Cod style home overlooks beautiful Trinidad Bay and offers spectacular views of the rugged coastline and fishing harbor below. Two suites, one with fireplace, and two upstairs bedrooms are available. We are surrounded by dozens of beaches, trails, and Redwood National Parks; within walking distance of restaurants and shops. Breakfast delivered to guests staying in suites, while a family style breakfast is served to guests in rooms.

Hosts: Paul and Carol Kirk
Rooms: 4 (PB) $105-155
Expanded Continental Breakfast
Credit Cards: A, B
Closed December and January
Notes: 2, 8, 10

## UKIAH

## Vichy Hot Springs
2605 Vichy Springs Rd., 95482
(707) 462-9515; FAX (707) 462-9516

Vichy Springs is a delightful two-hour drive north of San Francisco. Historic cottages and rooms await with delightful vistas from all locations. Vichy Springs features naturally sparkling 90-degree mineral baths, a communal 104-degree pool, and olympic-size pool, along with 700 private acres with trails and roads for hiking, jogging, picnicing, and mountain bicycling. Vichy's idyllic setting is a quiet, healing environment.

Hosts: Gilbert and Marjorie Ashoff
Rooms: 14 (PB) $130-165
Full Breakfast
Credit Cards: A, B, C, D, E, F
Notes: 2, 3, 4, 5, 7, 8, 9, 10, 12

---

5 Open all year; 6 Pets welcome; 7 Children welcome; 8 Tennis nearby; 9 Swimming nearby; 10 Golf nearby; 11 Skiing nearby; 12 May be booked through travel agent.

## VENICE

### The Venice Beach House

#15 30th Ave., 90291
(310) 823-1966; FAX (310) 823-1842

The original founder of Venice, California, Abbot Kinney and his family, lived in the new historic landmark in 1911. Steps from the beach and all that makes Venice unlike anywhere in the world. The nine guestroom house is decorated with dark oak antiques, hardwood floors, and wood burning fireplaces. Rooms and suites are named for characters and events which reflect the colorful history of Venice.

Manager: Leslie Smith
Owners: Phillip and Vivian Boesch
Rooms: 9 (5PB; 4SB) $80-150
Full Breakfast
Credit Cards: A, B, C
Notes: 5, 7, 8, 9, 10, 12

## VENTURA

### Bella Maggiore Inn

67 S. California St., 93001
(805) 652-0277; (800) 523-8479

An intimate European-style B&B, one hour north of Los Angeles. Garden courtyard with fountain; lobby with fireplace and piano. Comfortable rooms with suites, some have fireplaces and spa tubs. Full breakfast served in our courtyard restaurant, Nona's. Special rates for business travelers and groups.

We are three blocks from the beach and walking distance to several fine restaurants.

Hosts: Tom and Cyndi Wood
Rooms: 24 (PB) $75-150
Full Breakfast
Credit Cards: A, B, C, D, E
Notes: 3, 4, 5, 7, 8, 9, 10, 12

### La Mer Gastehaus

411 Poli St., 93001
(805) 643-3600; FAX (805) 653-7329

Built in 1890, this is a romantic European getaway in a Victorian Cape Cod home. A historic landmark nestled on a green hillside overlooking the spectacular California coastline. The distinctive guest rooms, all with private entrances and baths, are each a European adventure, furnished in European antiques to capture the feeling of a specific country. Bavarian buffet-style breakfast and complimentary refreshments; midweek packages; antique horse carriage rides. AAA and Mobil approved.

Hosts: Gisela and Michael Baida
Rooms: 5 (PB) $85-155
Full Breakfast
Credit Cards: A, B, C
Notes: 2, 5, 8, 9, 10, 12

## WESTPORT

### Howard Creek Ranch

P.O. Box 121, 95488
(707) 964-6725 (voice and FAX)

Howard Creek Ranch is a historic 1867 oceanfront farm bordered by miles of beach and mountains in a wilderness area. Flower gardens, antiques, fire-places, redwoods, a 75-foot swinging foot bridge over Howard Creek, cabins, hot tub, sauna, cold pool, and nearby horseback riding are combined with comfort, hospitality, and good food.

Hosts: Charles and Sally Grigg
Rooms: 10 (8PB; 2SB) $55-145
Full Breakfast
Credit Cards: A, B
Notes: 2, 5, 6 and 7 (by arrangement)

Howard Creek Ranch

## WHITTIER

## *Coleen's California Casa*

P.O. Box 9302, 90608
(310) 699-8427

Outstanding view of the city and private hillside location mark some of the features of Coleen's California Casa. Enjoy comfortable king-size or twin beds, private baths, full breakfast and offstreet parking as a few features of this B&B. The location, just east of Los Angeles, is near the 605 freeway, with its proximity to the 605 and 60 freeways. Come to Los Angeles and enjoy sun and fun! Have breakfast on the balcony as we plan your day of sight-seeing!

Hostess: Coleen Davis
Rooms: 7 (5PB; 2SB) $65-85
Full Breakfast
Credit Cards: none
Notes: 2, 3, 4, 5, 7 (prior arrangement), 8, 9, 10

## YOSEMITE NATIONAL PARK (GROVELAND)

## *Lee's Middle Fork Resort*

11399 Cherry Oil Rd., **Groveland** 95321
(209) 962-7408; (800) 626-7408;
FAX (209) 962-7400

Conveniently located eleven miles from Big Oak Flat entrance to Yosemite National Park, Lee's Middle Fork Resort is the perfect place to stay for beautiful scenic landscapes while you vacation or simply pass through the charming Yosemite area. Relax and enjoy the restful atmosphere as you discover why Yosemite is so acclaimed for its beauty. While there, you can take the opportunity to gaze upon some of the most amazing rock formations and the most stunning waterfalls, or enjoy an afternoon of activities which include hiking, well-stocked river fishing, swimming, or white-water rafting. For winter guests there is downhill and cross-country skiing. Come and visit Lee's Middle Fork Resort and discover for yourself the real meaning of paradise.

Hosts: Lee and Nita L. Hilarides
Rooms: 20 (PB) $49-89
Continental Breakfast (May to Sept.)
Credit Cards: A, B, C, D, E
Notes: 2, 3, 5, 7, 9, 10, 11, 12

---

5 Open all year;  6 Pets welcome;  7 Children welcome;  8 Tennis nearby;  9 Swimming nearby;
10 Golf nearby;  11 Skiing nearby;  12 May be booked through travel agent.

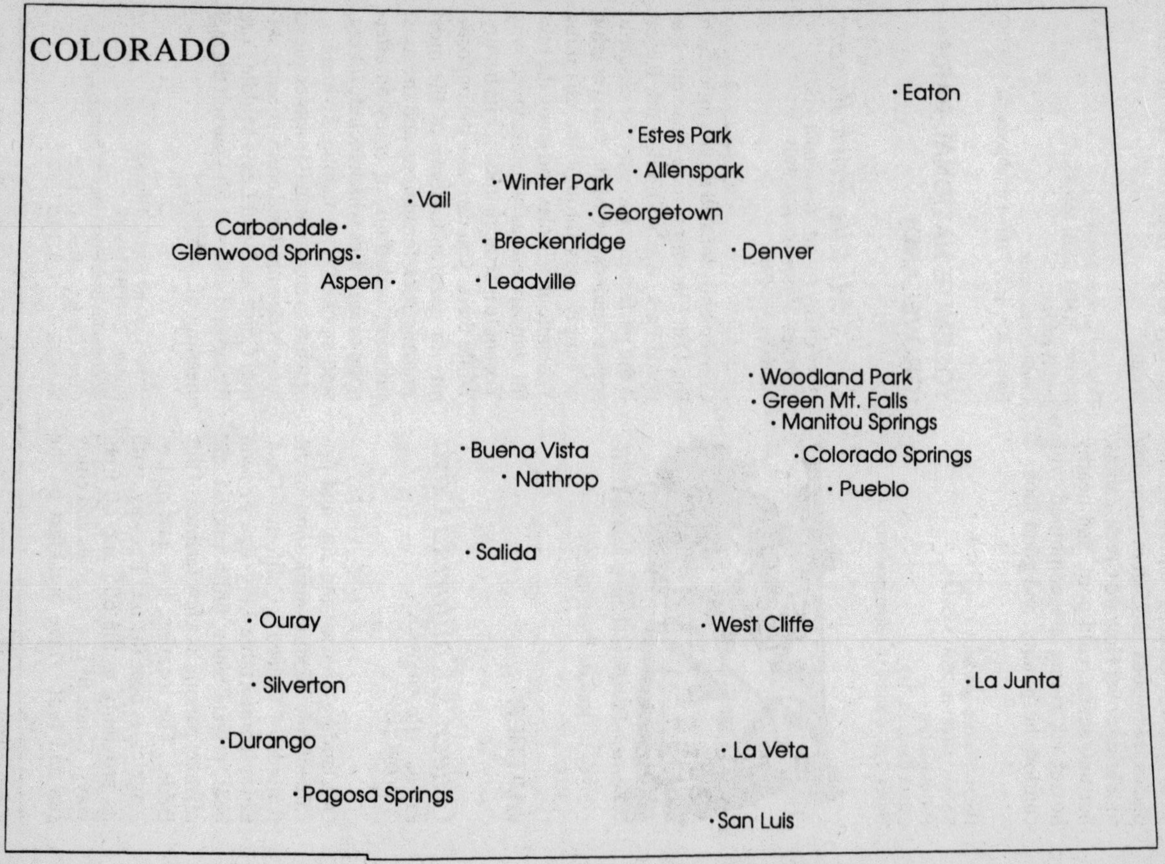

# COLORADO

- Eaton

- Estes Park
- Allenspark
- Winter Park
- Georgetown
- Denver

- Vail

- Breckenridge
- Leadville

Carbondale •
Glenwood Springs •
Aspen •

- Woodland Park
- Green Mt. Falls
- Manitou Springs
- Colorado Springs
- Pueblo

- Buena Vista
- Nathrop

- Salida

- West Cliffe

- La Veta

- San Luis

- La Junta

- Ouray

- Silverton

- Durango

- Pagosa Springs

# Colorado

## Bed and Breakfast Agency of Colorado at Vail

P.O. Box 491, **Vail** 81658
(970) 949-1212, (800) 748-2666

Come and enjoy the splendor of Colorado summer or winter. We are Colorado's only professional reservation service established in 1984, representing over 150 pre-approved and inspected private homes and inns, guest houses, and ranches statewide. From mountain ski retreats, centrally located Victorian properties in metro areas, to secluded ranches, each property is quite unique where warmth and charm abounds. Master Card and Visa accepted. Kathy Westerberg, coordinator.

## ALLENSPARK

### Allenspark Lodge

P.O. Box 247, 184 Main, 80510
(303) 747-2552; (800) 206-2552

A classic high mountain bed and breakfast, nestled in a flower-starred village. Comfortable rooms, warm hospitality and magnificent surroundings make our historic, cozy, beautifully remodeled lodge the ideal place for that vacation weekend, reception, reunion, or retreat. Let the magic begin! Hot tub, continental breakfast, hospitality, and game room; near Rocky Mountain National Park.

Hosts: Mike and Becky Osmun
Rooms: 14 (5PB; 9SB) $45-80
Continental Breakfast
Credit Cards: A, B
Notes: 2, 3, 5, 11

## ASPEN

### Little Red Ski Haus

118 E. Cooper Ave., 81611
(970) 925-3333; FAX (970) 925-4873

We are a quaint historic lodge that has had only one owner for 34 years. The 108 year old Victorian house has additional rooms for a total of 21 bedrooms. Christian hosts look forward to welcoming you to their lodge. Located in the center of Aspen and surrounded by impressive 14,000 ft. peaks of the Rocky

---

NOTES: Credit cards accepted: A Master Card; B Visa; C American Express; D Discover; E Diners Club; F Other; 2 Personal checks accepted; 3 Lunch available; 4 Dinner available; 5 Open all year; 6 Pets welcome; 7 Children welcome; 8 Tennis nearby; 9 Swimming nearby; 10 Golf nearby; 11 Skiing nearby; 12 May be booked through travel agent.

Mountains. Non-smoking lodge.

Hosts: Marjorie Babcock and Derek Brown
Rooms: 21 (4PB; 17SB) $52-118
Breakfast—Full (winter); Continental (summer)
Credit Cards: A, B
Notes: 7, 8, 9, 10, 11

## BRECKENRIDGE

### Allaire Timbers Inn

9511 Hwy. 9, S. Main St., P.O. Box 4653,
80424
(970) 453-7530; (800) 624-4904;
FAX (970) 453-8699

Distinctive Log Inn was named to "Top
10 New Inns of 1993" by *Inn Market-
ing Review*. Ten individually decorated
guest rooms have private baths and private deck. Romantic suites offer private hot tub and fireplace. The Inn provides gourmet breakfasts, afternoon
treats, and spectacular mountain views
from an outdoor spa. Close to historic
downtown and to ski slopes. Wheelchair accessible.

Hosts: Jack and Kathy Gumph
Rooms: 10 (PB) $115-250
Full Breakfast
Credit Cards: A, B, C, D
Notes: 2, 5, 10, 11, 12

## BUENA VISTA

### Meister House
### Bed and Breakfast

P.O. Box 1133, 414 E. Main St., 81211
(719) 395-9220; (800) 882-1821;
FAX (719) 395-9128

This historic landmark hotel was built
over 100 years ago as a small, first-class
hotel. Today it has been renovated to
its current state as an intimate five room
bed and breakfast. It is nestled near the
head waters of the world famous
whitewater Arkansas River and at the
base of the Collegiate Peaks Mountain
Range, part of the rugged Rocky Mountains. After your fresh, gourmet breakfast in our courtyard, there are many
recreational activities all within walking distance!

Hosts: Barbara and Frank Hofmeister
Rooms: 5 (SB) $65-80
Full Breakfast
Credit Cards: A, B, C, D
Notes: 2, 5, 7, 8, 9, 10, 11, 12

Mt. Sopris Inn

## CARBONDALE

### Mt. Sopris Inn

Box 126 (0165 Mt. Sopris Ranch Rd.), 81623
(970) 963-2209; (800) 437-8675 (reservations
only); FAX (970) 963-8975

At Mt. Sopris Inn, country elegance surrounds the visitor who appreciates our
extraordinary property. Central to Aspen, Redstone, and Glenwood Springs,
the inn offers 15 private rooms and
baths professionally decorated. All
rooms have king or queen beds, TV,

telephone, and include full breakfast, some have fireplaces, jacuzzis, and steam baths. Guest use of swimming pool, whirlpool, pool table, library, great rooms, and seven-foot grand piano. Open to all.

Hostess: Barbara Fasching
Rooms: 15 (PB) $ 85-250
Full Breakfast
Credit Cards: A, B
Notes: 2, 3, 4, 5, 8, 9, 10, 11, 12

## COLORADO SPRINGS

### Grand View Terrace

5720 Del Paz Drive, 80918
(719) 531-6979

No room at the Inn? Enjoy the sights of Colorado while staying at Grand View Terrace. Choose from a suite with two bedrooms, living area with queen sofa bed, dining area with microwave and refrigerator. Games, TV, VCR, books for your pleasure, new queen size beds. Washer-dryer. Breakfast can be served on the deck or patio viewing majestic Pikes Peak. Tables in rooms for business or writing, *"Wish you were here! Having a Great Time,"* letters. Convenient to shopping and tourist attractions. The hostess will make your reservations for the Cog Railway, Flying W. Ranch, tour of Navagator's Mansion, etc.

Hosts: Diane, Karl, and Ruby Lassen
Rooms: 4 (2SB) $50-130 (suite: $500 per week)
Full Breakfast
Credit Cards: none
Notes: 2, 3, 4, 5, 7 (over 7), 8, 9, 10

Holden House1902 Bed and Breakfast Inn

### Holden House 1902 Bed and Breakfast Inn

1102 W. Pikes Peak Ave., 80904
(719) 471-3980

Historic 1902 storybook Victorian and carriage house filled with antiques and family treasures. Guest rooms boast feather pillows, individual decor, period furnishings, and queen beds. One disabled access room available. Suites include fireplaces, "tubs for two," and more! Centrally located in residential area near historic Old Colorado City, shopping, restaurants, and attractions. "The Romance of the Past with the Comforts of Today." Two friendly resident cats—Muffin and Mingtoy. AAA/ Mobile approved. Full Gourmet breakfast.

Hosts: Sallie and Welling Clark
Rooms: 6 (PB) $75-110
Full Gourmet Breakfast
Credit Cards: A, B, C, D, E
Notes: 2, 5, 8, 9, 10, 12

### Room at the Inn B&B

618 N. Nevada Ave., 80903
(719) 442-1896; FAX (719) 442-6802

Experience a peek at the past in this

---

5 Open all year; 6 Pets welcome; 7 Children welcome; 8 Tennis nearby; 9 Swimming nearby;
10 Golf nearby; 11 Skiing nearby; 12 May be booked through travel agent.

recently restored Victorian B&B. Enjoy . . . the charm of a classic three story turreted Queen Anne furnished with period antiques . . . the romance of fireplaces, plush robes, whirlpool tubs for two. and cut flowers . . . and gracious hospitality featuring full breakfasts, afternoon tea, and turn down service. Conveniently located near downtown, Colorado College, and USOTC. Airconditioning, outdoor hot tub, retreat facilities and much more. Discount for church staff.

Hostesses: Jan, Chick, and Kelly McCormick
Rooms: 7 (PB) $85-115
Full Breakfast
Credit Cards: A, B, C, D
Notes: .2, 5, 7 (over 12), 8, 10, 12

## DENVER

## Castle Marne
## A Luxury Urban Inn
1572 Race St., 80206
(303) 331-0621; (800) 92 MARNE (reservations); FAX (303) 331-0623

Chosen by *Country Inns Magazine* as one of the "Top 12 Inns in North America." Come fall under the spell of one of Denver's grandest historic mansions. Your stay at the Castle Marne combines Old World elegance with modern day convenience and comfort. Each guest room is a unique experience in pampered luxury. All rooms have private baths. Two suites with jacuzzi tubs for two. Three rooms with private balconies and hot tubs. Afternoon tea and a full gourmet breakfast are served in the cherry-paneled dining room. Castle

Marne is a certified Denver Landmark and on the National Register of Historic Structures.

Hosts: The Peikers Family
Rooms: 9 (PB) $85-180
Full Breakfast
Credit Cards: A, B, C, D, E, F
Notes: 2, 3, 4, 5, 8, 9, 10, 11, 12

Castle Marne

## Queen Anne Bed
## and Breakfast Inn
2147 Tremont Pl., 80205
(303) 296-6666; (800) 432-4667;
FAX (303) 296-2151

Facing quiet Benedict Fountain Park in downtown Denver are two side-by-side National Register Victorian homes with fourteen guest rooms including four gallery suites. Fresh flowers, chamber music, period antiques, phone, and private baths are in all rooms. Six rooms have special tubs; one has a fireplace. The Inn is only walking distance to the Capital, 16th St. Pedestrian Mall, Convention Center, and Larimer Square. Among its many awards: Best 12 B&Bs nationally, Ten Most Romantic, Best of Denver, and Best 105 in Great American Cities. Inspected/approved by AAA, Mobile, ABBA, and Distinctive Inns of Colorado.

Hosts: Tom and Chris King
Rooms: 14 (PB) $75-155
Full Breakfast
Credit Cards: A, B, C, D, E
Notes: 2, 5, 8, 9, 10, 11, 12

## DURANGO

### Logwood Bed and Breakfast
35060 US Hwy 550, 81301
(970) 259-4396; (800) 367-1200

Built in 1988, this 4,800 square-foot red, cedar log home sits on 15 acres amid the beautiful San Juan Mountains and beside the Animas River. Guest rooms are decorated with a southwestern flair. Homemade country quilts adorn the country made queen-sized beds. Private baths in all guest rooms. A large, river rock fireplace warms the elegant living and dining areas in the winter season. Award-winning desserts are served in the evening. Pamper yourselves. Come home to LOGWOOD.

Hosts: Debby and Greg Verheyden
Rooms: 5 (PB) $70-125
Full Breakfast
Credit Cards: A, B
Notes: 2, 5, 7 (over eight), 9, 10, 11, 12

### Strater Hotel
699 Main Ave., 81301
(970) 247-4431; (800) 247-4431;
FAX (970) 259-2208 (FAX)

Strater Hotel has been around since 1887. Authentic Victorian walnut an-

tiques and architecture. Romance and charm. Cable TV, phones, private baths, jacuzzi, restaurant, and bar. Located in the heart of the historic downtown shopping and entertainment district. Two blocks from D&SNG RR depot. Free parking. Near historic sites and outdoor activities.

Host: Rod Barker
Rooms: 93 (PB) $78-170 ($115-170 summer)
No Breakfast
Credit Cards: A, B, C, D
Notes: 2, 4, 6, 7, 8, 9, 10, 11, 12

## EATON

### The Country Rose Inn
725 Fourth St., 80615
(970) 454-3915

Country, Victorian decorated inn. The master suite is decorated with white wicker, antiques, lace, and rose stencils. Amenities include private bath, cable TV, second bedroom, shared bath, queen bed, and self-serve tea with home-baked cookies. The full breakfast is served on the patio or in the dining room.

Hosts: Don and Donna Anderson
Rooms: 2 (1PB; 1SB) $45-60
Full Breakfast
Credit Cards: none
Notes: 2 (+ travelers'), 5, 8, 9, 10, 11

### The Victorian Veranda Bed and Breakfast
515 Cheyenne Ave., 80615
(970) 454-3890

We want to share with you our beautiful two-story Queen Anne home with a wraparound porch. It also has a view of the Rocky Mountains which are 45 minutes away. Our guests enjoy the spacious and comfortable rooms, balcony, fireplaces, bicycles-built-for-two, baby grand, player piano, and one room that has a private whirlpool bath. We are just 50 minutes from North Denver. A memorable and elegant stay for a moderate price.

Hostess: Nadine and Dick White
Rooms: 3 (1PB; 2SB) $45-60
Full Breakfast
Credit Cards: none
Notes: 2, 5, 7, 8, 9, 10, 11, 12

## ESTES PARK

## *The Quilt House Bed and Breakfast*

P.O. Box 399, 80517
(970) 586-0427

We have three bedrooms upstairs for our guests, plus a lounge where guests can read, look at the mountains, and have a cup of coffee or tea. A beautiful mountain view can be enjoyed from every window of this sturdy mountain home, yet it is just a 15 minute walk from downtown Estes Park. We are only four miles from the entrance of Rocky Mountain National Park. The hosts will help with information concerning hiking trails, car drives, wildlife viewing, shopping, etc.

Hosts: Hans and Miriam Graetzer
Rooms: 3 (1PB; 2SB) $50 ($30 single)
Full Breakfast
Credit Cards: none
Notes: 2, 5, 8, 9, 10

## GEORGETOWN

## *Hardy House B&B*

605 Brownell, P.O. Box 156, 80444
(303) 569-3388; (800) 490-4802

The Hardy House with its late 19th century charm invites you to relax in the parlor by the potbellied stove, sleep under feather comforters, and enjoy a candlelight breakfast. Georgetown is only 55 minutes from Denver and the airport. Surrounded by mountains, it boasts unique shopping, wonderful restaurants, and close proximity to seven ski areas.

Hosts: Carla and Mike Wagner
Rooms: 4 (PB) $73-82
Full Breakfast
Credit Cards: A, B
Notes: 2, 5, 7 (over 13), 11, 12

Back In Time

## GLENWOOD SPRINGS

## *Back In Time*

927 Cooper, 81601
(970) 945-6183

A spacious Victorian home filled with antiques, family quilts, and clocks. A full breakfast is served in the dining room: a hot dish accompanied by fresh hot muffins, fruit, and a specialty of June's mouth watering cinnamon rolls.

Hosts: June and Ron Robinson
Rooms: 3 (2PB; 2SB) $60-65
Full Breakfast
Credit Cards: A, B, C
Notes: 2, 5, 8, 9, 10, 11, 12

## GREEN MT. FALLS

## Outlook Lodge
## Bed and Breakfast

P.O. Box 5, 6975 Howard St., 80819
(719) 684-2303

A quaint lodge nestled at the foot of Pike's Peak. Built in 1889 as the parsonage for the Church of the Wildwood. Features stained-glass windows and hand-carved balustrades. Rooms furnished with brass beds and other antiques. Nearby swimming, hiking, tennis, fishing, horseback riding, restaurants, and shopping. Outlook Lodge provides nostalgia with a relaxing atmosphere.

Hosts: Hayley, Patrick, and Taylor Moran
Rooms: 7 (PB) $60-85
Full Breakfast
Credit Cards: A, B, D
Notes: 2, 5, 7, 8, 9, 10, 11, 12

## LAJUNTA

## My Wife's Inn
## Bed and Breakfast

801 Colorado Avenue, 81050
(719) 384-7911; (800) 616-3642

My Wife's Inn is located in a residential area near downtown LaJunta. It is a perfect starting point for sampling the many attractions of the Arkansas Valley such as Bent's Old Fort National Historic Site, Koshare Indian Museum and Kiva, and more. We feature sumptuous breakfasts and evening snacks, clean tastefully decorated rooms, complete with queen beds and private bathrooms in warm relaxed surroundings that welcome you home.

Hosts: Karen and Sheridan Moosman
Rooms: 3 (PB) $45; cottage $65
Full Breakfast
Credit Cards: A, B, D, E
Notes: 2, 5, 7 (at cottage), 8, 9, 10, 12

## LAVETA

## LaVeta Inn

103 W. Ryus 1, Box 129, 81055
(719) 742-3700; FAX (719) 742-3105

This charming turn-of-the-century, country inn features delightful rooms, an exceptional restaurant, an elegant bar and lobby, and banquet and meeting rooms. Unlimited adventures await all, including cycling, fishing, hiking, horseback riding, and cross-country skiing. Grandote Peaks Golf Course, located a few blocks away, was designated by *Golf Digest* as one of the three top courses in Colorado. Nearby Cuchara Valley Ski Resort provides family fun.

Hosts: Warren and Karen Scott
Rooms: 10 (9PB; 1SB) $62-125
Continental Breakfast
Credit Cards: A, B
Notes: 4, 5, 7, 10, 11

---

5 Open all year; 6 Pets welcome; 7 Children welcome; 8 Tennis nearby; 9 Swimming nearby; 10 Golf nearby; 11 Skiing nearby; 12 May be booked through travel agent.

## LEADVILLE

### The Ice Palace Inn and Antiques

813 Spruce St., 80461
(719) 486-8272

This gracious Victorian inn was built at the turn-of-the-century, using the lumber from the famous Leadville Ice Palace. Romantic guest rooms, elegantly decorated with antiques and quilts, each with an exquisite private bath, are named after the original rooms of the Ice Palace. Begin your day with a delicious gourmet breakfast served in this historic inn. Innkeepers are owners, Giles and Kami Kolakowski, welcome you!

Hosts: Giles and Kami Kolakowski
Rooms: 3 (PB) $79-119
Full Gourmet Breakfast
Credit Cards: F
Notes: 2, 5, 7, 8, 9, 10, 11, 12

### Wood Haven Manor

P.O. Box 1291, 809 Spruce, 80461
(719) 486-0109; (800)798-2570;
FAX (719) 486-0210

Enjoy the taste and style of Victorian Leadville by stepping back 100 years in this beautiful home located in this prestigious "Banker's Row." Each room is distinctively decorated in Victorian style with private bath. One suite with whirlpool tub. Spacious dining room; comfortable living room with fireplace. Historic city with a backdrop of Colorado's highest mountains. Enjoy snow-mobiling, biking, hiking, and more.

Hosts: Bobby and Jolene Wood
Rooms: 7 (PB) $59-99
Full Breakfast
Credit Cards: A, B, C, D
Notes: 2, 5, 7, 8, 9, 10, 11, 12

## MANITOU SPRINGS

### Ute Pass Motel

1132 Manitou Ave., 80829
(719) 685-5171; (800) 845-9702;
FAX (719) 685-0529

Surrounded by Fountain Creek, its location is serene and secluded. Each room is different and some are connected, making the Ute Pass Motel an ideal location for family reunions. Many of the units have kitchens and some offer covered porches, which are great for people-watching!

Hostess: Suzie Hawkins
Rooms: 17 (16PB; 2SB) $44-99
Credit Cards: A, B, C, E
Notes: 5, 7, 8, 9, 10, 12

## NATHROP

### Deer Valley Ranch

16825 C.R. 162, 81236
(719) 395-2353; FAX (719) 395-2394

Colorado's Christian family guest ranch welcomes you to the heart of the Rocky Mountains. The hosting ranch family provides the best of western hospitality in a unique Christian atmosphere. In summer, enjoy horseback riding, white water rafting, hiking, tennis, hot springs pools, four wheel drives, fishing, golf,

---

NOTES: Credit cards accepted: A Master Card; B Visa; C American Express; D Discover; E Diners Club; F Other; 2 Personal checks accepted; 3 Lunch available; 4 Dinner available;

and evening entertainment. In winter, enjoy snow-mobiling and Nordic and alpine skiing. Off-season rates available.

Hosts: Harold DeWalt / John Woolmington
Rooms: 23 (PB) $95
Full Breakfast
Credit Cards: none
Notes: 2, 3, 4, 5, 7, 8, 9, 10, 11, 12

## OURAY

### The Damn Yankee Country Inn

100 6th Ave., P.O. Box 709, 81427
(970) 325-4219; (800) OURAY CO; FAX (970) 325-0502

Relax your body. Ten uniquely appointed rooms await, each with a private bath and entrance. Cabins along the river will be available in 1996. Drift off to the soothing music of a mountain stream from your luxurious queen-size bed. Snuggle under a plush down comforter. Most rooms have fireplaces. Sit back and watch your favorite film on cable TV. Drink in the fresh mountain air. Relax in our hot tub. Or, gather around the parlor with friends and sing along to music from a baby grand piano. Feast your senses. You'll receive complimentary fresh fruit upon arrival. Enjoy afternoon snacks in our towering observatory. And savor a hearty, gourmet breakfast, as you watch the sun glint over the mountaintops.

Hosts: Mike and Marj Manley
Rooms: 10 (PB) $60-145
Full Hearty Gourmet Breakfast
Credit Cards: A, B, C, D
Notes: 2, 3, 4, 5, 8, 9, 10, 11, 12

### Ouray 1898 House

322 Main St., P.O. Box 641, 81427
(970) 325-4871

This 90-year-old house has been completely renovated and combines the elegance of the 19th century with the comfortable amenities of the 20th century. Each room features a TV and a spectacular view of the San Juan Mountains from its deck. Eat a health-conscious, full breakfast on antique china. Jeep rides, horseback riding, and the city's hot spring pool are a few of the local diversions.

Hosts: Lee and Kathy Bates
Rooms: 4 (PB) $65-85
Full Breakfast
Credit Cards: A, B
Notes: 2, 7, 8, 9, 10

## PAGOSA SPRINGS

### Davidson's Country Inn

P.O. Box 87, 81147
(303) 264-5863

Davidson's Country Inn is a three-story log house located at the foot of the Rocky Mountains on 32 acres. The inn provides a library, a playroom, a game room, and some outdoor activities. A two-bedroom cabin is also available. The Inn is tastefully decorated with family heirlooms and antiques, with a warm country touch to make you feel at home. Two miles east of Highway 160.

Host: Gilbert Davidson
Rooms: 8 (3PB; 5SB) $48-67
Full Breakfast
Credit Cards: A, B
Notes: 2, 5, 7, 8, 9, 10, 11, 12

5 Open all year; 6 Pets welcome; 7 Children welcome; 8 Tennis nearby; 9 Swimming nearby; 10 Golf nearby; 11 Skiing nearby; 12 May be booked through travel agent.

## PUEBLO

### Abriendo Inn

300 W. Abriendo Ave., 81004
(719) 544-2703; (719) 542-1806 FAX

Experience the elegance of an estate home as you delight in the pleasure of personal attention and hospitality. Antiques, crocheted bedspreads, and brass and four-poster beds take you to a get-away to yesterday with the conveniences you expect of today. Breakfast is always hearty, home-baked, and served in the oak wainscoted dining room or one of the picturesque porches. The inn is located within walking distance of restaurants, shops, and galleries . . . all in the heart of Pueblo. The Abriendo Inn is on the National Register of Historic Places.

Hostess: Kerrelyn Trent
Rooms: 10 (PB) $54-95
Full Breakfast
Credit Cards: A, B, C, E
Notes: 2, 5, 7 (over 7), 8, 9, 10, 12

## SALIDA

### Gazebo Country Inn

507 E. 3rd., 81201
(719) 539-7806

A 1901, restored Victorian home with magnificent deck and porch views. Gourmet breakfasts and private baths. Located in the heart of the Rockies. Whitewater rafting on the Arkansas River and skiing at the Monarch Mountain Lodge are a few of the amenities.

We are committed to your comfort and relaxation.

Hosts: Don and Bonnie Johannsen
Rooms: 3 (PB) $50-65
Full Breakfast
Credit Cards: A, B
Notes: 2, 5, 7 (over 8), 9, 10, 11, 12

## SAN LUIS

### Casa De Oro

P.O. Box 674, 81152
(719) 672-3608

The Casa De Oro Inn was built in 1906. Situated in San Luis, Colorado, the oldest town in the state, makes for a great get away. Nearby is the eighth Wonder of the World, Mt. Blanca as well as the Great Sand Dunes, Ski Rio, and much more! A great family get away! Call for your reservation now at (719) 672-3608.

Hostess: Katie Duncan
Rooms: 3 (SB);$50
Continental Breakfast
Credit Cards: F
Notes: 5, 7, 11

## SILVERTON

### Christopher House

P.O. Box 241, 821 Empire St., 81433
(970) 387-5857 (June-September);
(904) 567-7423 (October-May)

This charming 1894 Victorian home has the original, golden oak woodwork, parlor fireplace, and antiques through-

---

NOTES: Credit cards accepted: A Master Card; B Visa; C American Express; D Discover; E Diners Club; F Other; 2 Personal checks accepted; 3 Lunch available; 4 Dinner available;

out. All bedrooms offer comfortable mattresses, wall-to-wall carpeting, and a mountain view. Guests are warmly welcomed with mints and fresh wild-flowers. A full breakfast is served to Christian and Irish music. Conveniently located only four blocks from the town's narrow-gauge train depot, Old West shops, restaurants, and riding stables. Guest transportation to and from the train depot is available.

Hosts: Howard and Eileen Swonger
Rooms: 4 (1PB; 3SB) $42-52
Full Breakfast
Credit Cards: none
Notes: 2, 7, 8, 10, 12

## Wyman Hotel and Inn

1371 Greene St., 81433
(970) 387-5372; (800) 609-7845;
FAX (970) 387-5745

The Inn was built in 1902, and totally restored in 1987. The rooms are antique to modern, all with telephones, TV/VCRs, bathrooms, ceiling fans, and European down comforters for those crisp mountain nights. All hot water baseboard heat adds to the comfort. Over 400 free videos for our guests viewing pleasure. Located at 9,318 feet elevation, the Inn offers spectacular views of the San Juan Mountains which surround this National Historic Register listed town. AAA and Mobile rated.

Hosts: Frank and Candy Cross
Rooms: 19 (PB) $44-55 (off season);
$68-78 (in season)
Continental Breakfast
Credit Cards: A, B, C, D
Notes: 2, 5, 6, 7, 8, 9, 10, 11, 12

## VAIL

## Bed and Breakfast Agency of Colorado

P.O. Box 491, 81658
(970) 949-1212, (800) 748-2666

Come and enjoy the splendor of Colorado summer or winter. We are Colorado's only professional reservation service established in 1984, representing over 150 preapproved and inspected private homes and inns, guest houses, and ranches statewide. From mountain ski retreats, centrally located Victorian properties in metro areas, to secluded ranches, each property is quite unique where warmth and charm abounds. MasterCard and Visa accepted. Kathy Westerberg, coordinator.

## WEST CLIFFE

## Purnell's Rainbow Inn

104 Main St., 81252
(719) 783-2313

Purnell's Rainbow Inn comfortable, hospitable, western-style inn situated between the magnificent Sangre de Cristos and Wet Mountains in historic West Cliffe. Four bedrooms, uniquely decorated, provide genuine comfort. A great room offers big screen TV, game table, and books for reading pleasure. Full breakfast features freshly baked muffins, special entrees, and seasonal fruits. Mountain bike rentals, hiking supplies and maps, fly fishing pro shop with instruction, and cross-country ski-

---

5 Open all year; 6 Pets welcome; 7 Children welcome; 8 Tennis nearby; 9 Swimming nearby; 10 Golf nearby; 11 Skiing nearby; 12 May be booked through travel agent.

ing opportunities are readily available for a memorable Wet Mountain experience.

Hosts: David and Karen Purnell
Rooms: 4 (2PB; 2SB) $50-60
Full Breakfast
Credit Cards: A, B
Notes: 2, 5, 7, 9, 10, 11, 12

Candlelight Mountain Inn

## WINTER PARK

### Candlelight Mountain Inn

P.O. Box 600, 80482
(970) 887-2877; (800) KIM-4-TIM (546-4846)

Nestled on a mountainside among pine and aspen trees, the Candlelight Mountain Inn is located in Colorado's beautiful Fraser Valley. Married couples, retired folks, and families will enjoy the comfortable beds, full breakfasts, candlelit lane, game and toy room, hot tub under the stars, glider swings around the campfire, the beautiful view, and other surprises. Our inn is situated in the heart of a vacation paradise; it's just 15 minutes to the ski slopes, 30 minutes to the Rocky Mountain National Park, and only three minutes to the Pole Creek Golf Course and the YMCA of the Rockies . . . a fantastic family vacation spot.

Hosts: Kim and Tim Onnen
Rooms: 4 (2PB; 2SB) $40-80
Full Breakfast
Credit Cards: none
Notes: 2, 5, 7, 8, 9, 10, 11

## WOODLAND PARK

### Woodland Inn Bed and Breakfast

159 Trull Rd., 80863
(719) 687-8209; (800) 226-9565;
FAX (719) 687-3112

Guests enjoy the relaxing home-like atmosphere and fantastic views of Pikes Peak from this cozy country inn in the heart of the Rocky Mountains. Peacefully secluded on twelve private acres of woodlands, the Inn is convenient to a variety of attractions, some of which include limited stakes gambling in Cripple Creek, Pikes Peak, Cog Railway and highway; hiking; biking; golf; trail riding; and cross-country skiing. Hot air ballooning with host is also available! Expansions are planned that will add rooms, baths, comforts, and conveniences.

Hosts: Frank and Nancy O'Neil
Rooms: 4 (1PB; 3SB) $55-75
Full Breakfast
Credit Cards: A, B, C
Notes: 2, 5, 6, 7, 8, 10, 11, 12

---

NOTES: Credit cards accepted: A Master Card; B Visa; C American Express; D Discover; E Diners Club; F Other; 2 Personal checks accepted; 3 Lunch available; 4 Dinner available;

# Connecticut

## Bed and Breakfast, Ltd.

P.O. Box 216, **New Haven** 06513
(203) 469-3260

Bed and Breakfast, Ltd. Offers over 125 accommodations throughout **Connecticut, Massachusetts, and Rhode Island**—from elegantly simple to simply elegant. We offer incredible variety, both in home styles and in price ranges. A quick call assures accurate descriptions and availability. (Host homes nationwide are invited to join our growing network.)

Director: Jack M. Argenio
Rooms: 125+ (60PB, 65SB) $50-125
Credit Cards: (at some) A, B, C
Notes: 2 (at some), 5, 7 (at some), 8, 9, 10, 11

## CLINTON

## Captain Dibbell House

21 Commerce St., 06413
(860) 669-1646

Our 1886 Victorian, just two blocks from the shore, features a wisteria-covered century-old footbridge and gazebo on our half-acre of lawn and gardens. Spacious living rooms and bedrooms are comfortably furnished with antiques and family heirlooms, fresh flowers, fruit baskets, and home-baked treats. There are bicycles, nearby beaches, and marinas to enjoy.

Hosts: Helen and Ellis Adams
Rooms: 4 (PB) $75-95
Full Breakfast
Credit Cards: A, B, C, D
Notes: 2, 8, 9, 10, 12

## ESSEX

## The Griswold Inn

36 Main Street, 06426
(203) 767-1776; FAX (203) 767-0481

More than a country hotel. More than a comfortable bed, an extraordinary meal...The "Gris" is what Essex is all about. It embodies a spirit understood perhaps only as one warms up to its potbelly stove or is hypnotized by the magic of a crackling log in one of its many fireplaces. It is a kaleidoscope of nostalgic images: A lovely country

---

5 Open all year; 6 Pets welcome; 7 Children welcome; 8 Tennis nearby; 9 Swimming nearby; 10 Golf nearby; 11 Skiing nearby; 12 May be booked through travel agent.

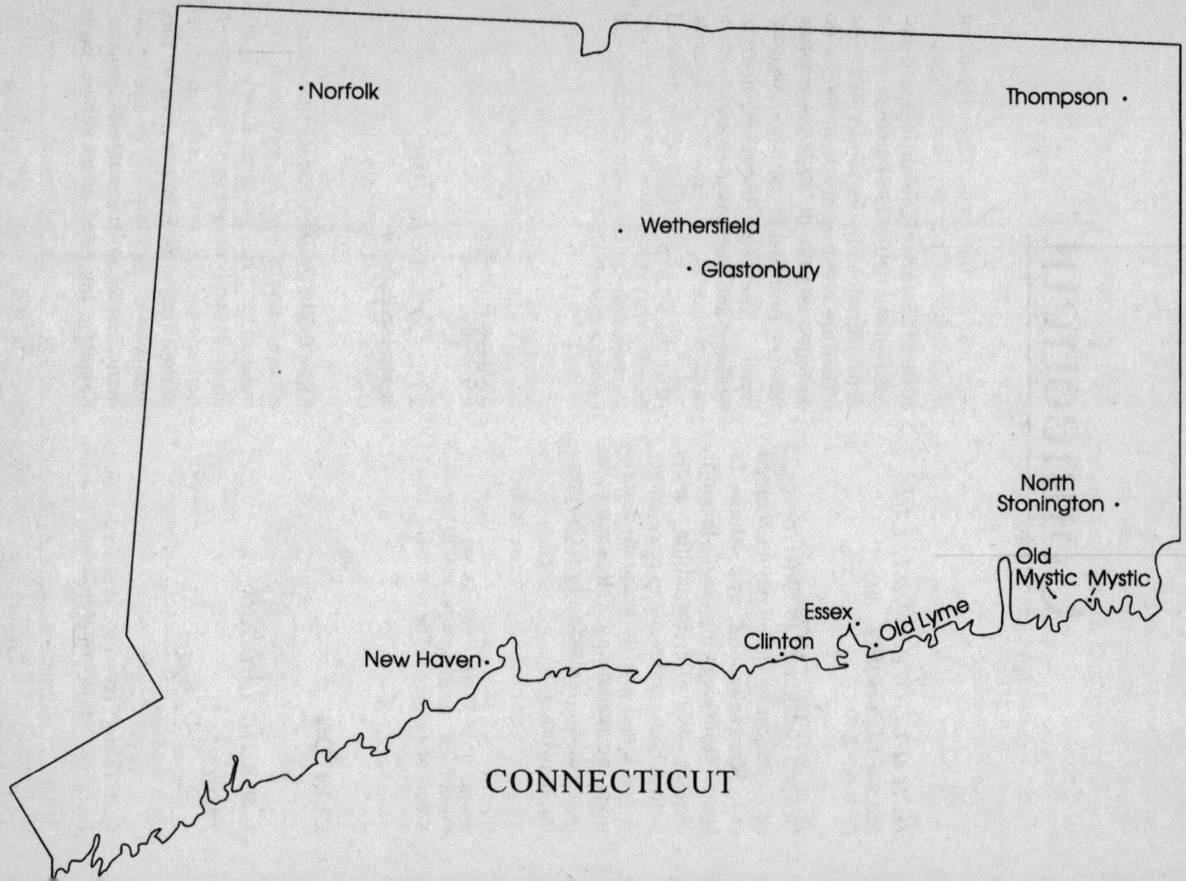

Thompson

North
Stonington

Old
Mystic  Mystic

Wethersfield
Glastonbury

Essex
Old Lyme

Clinton

New Haven

Norfolk

CONNECTICUT

place. An historic collection of Antonio Jacobsen marine art. A gentle smile and a helping hand from a waitress. A cuisine unmatched for its genuineness and purity.

Hosts: Victoria and William Winterer
Rooms: 26 (PB) $90-175
Continental Breakfast
Credit Cards: A, B, C
Notes: 2, 3, 4, 5, 6, 7, 8, 9, 10

## GLASTONBURY

## *Butternut Farm*

1654 Main St., 06033
(860) 633-7197 (voice and FAX)

This 18th century architectural jewel is furnished in period antiques. Prize-winning dairy goats, pigeons, and chickens roam in an estate setting with trees and herb gardens. The farm is located ten minutes from Hartford by expressway; one and one-half hours to any place in Connecticut. Private baths.

Host: Don Reid
Rooms: 3 + suite and apartment (PB) $68-88
Full Breakfast
Credit Cards: C
Notes: 2, 5, 7, 8, 9, 10, 11

Harbour Inne and Cottage

## MYSTIC

## *Harbour Inne and Cottage*

15 Edgemont St., 06355
(203) 572-9253

The Harbour Inne and cottage is located on the Mystic River two block from historic downtown Mystic. Six rooms and a cottage. Three-room cottage with a fireplace and two double beds in the bedroom. Sleep sofa and color TV in living room with glider doors opening onto deck with hot tub spa. Shower/lavatory facilities, kitchen and dining area. Guest house has five rooms, each with double bed, color TV, shower or bath, and air-conditioning. Equipped galley and dining area for guests' use as well as social area with fireplace and antique piano.

Host: Charles Lecouras, Jr.
Rooms: 6 and cottage (PB) $75-250
Self-catered Breakfast
Credit Cards: none
Notes: 5, 6, 7, 8, 9, 10

## NORFOLK

## *Greenwoods Gate Bed and Breakfast*

105 Greenwoods Rd. E., 06058
(203) 542-5439

Warm hospitality greets you in this beautifully restored 1797 Colonial home. Small and elegant with four exquisitely appointed guest suites, each

NOTES: Credit cards accepted: A Master Card; B Visa; C American Express; D Discover; E Diners Club; F Other; 2 Personal checks accepted; 3 Lunch available; 4 Dinner available; 5 Open all year; 6 Pets welcome; 7 Children welcome; 8 Tennis nearby; 9 Swimming nearby; 10 Golf nearby; 11 Skiing nearby; 12 May be booked through travel agent.

Old Lyme Inn

with private bath (one with jacuzzi). Fine antiques, fireplaces, and sumptuous breakfasts to indulge you. *Yankee Magazine*, calls this "New England's most romantic Bed and Breakfast." *Country Inns* Bed and Breakfast Magazine says: "A Connecticut Jewel." Home to Deanne Raymond's Romantic Cooking Classes. Call for details.

Hosts: George E. and Marian M. Schumaker
Rooms: 4 suites (PB) $165-225
Gourmet Breakfast (afternoon tea and refreshments before going out to dinner)
Credit Cards: A, B, C
Notes: 5, 7, 8, 9, 11, 12

## NORTH STONINGTON

## *Antiques and Accommodations*

32 Main St., 06359
(203) 535-1736; (800) 554-7829

Stroll through our well-tended gardens filled with edible flowers and herbs. Relax on our porches and patios. Our country retreat is located 2.5 miles from I-95, minutes from Mystic Seaport, Aquarium, and superb beaches. Gracious hospitality awaits you at our lovingly restored homes: antiques, canopy beds, fireplaces, private baths, air-conditioned rooms, and cable TV. Greet the day with our acclaimed four-course candlelight breakfast. Always an abundance of flowers. We welcome children who appreciate antiques.

Hosts: Thomas and Ann Gray
Rooms: 3 + 2 cottages (PB) $95-195
Full Breakfast
Credit Cards: A, B
Notes: 2, 5, 7, 8, 9, 10, 12

## OLD LYME

## *Old Lyme Inn*

85 Lyme St., 06371
(203) 434-2600; (800) 434-5352;
FAX (203) 434-5352

In the heart of a small Connecticut town, the Old Lyme Inn is a fine 19th century home restored to its full grandeur. A tree shaded-lawn leads up to the banistered front porch where each guest can relax and just watch the world go by. Built in the 1850s as a farmhouse, the Inn is now a lodging place with five guest rooms and eight suites. All rooms are handsomely furnished in Empire and Victorian with antiques and are equipped with air-conditioning, telephones, and TVs to make your stay even more enjoyable.

Hostess: Diana Field Atwood
Rooms: 13 (PB) $99-158
Country Continental Breakfast
Credit Cards: A, B, C, D, E
Notes: 2, 3, 4, 5, 6, 7, 8, 10, 12

## OLD MYSTIC

## Red Brook Inn

P.O. Box 237, 06372
(203) 572-0349 (voice and FAX)

Nestled on seven acres of old New England wooded countryside, bed and breakfast lodging is provided in two historic buildings. The Haley Tavern, circa 1770, is a Colonial built by sea captain Nathaniel Crary. Each room is appointed with period furnishings, including canopy beds, and there are many working fireplaces throughout the inn and guest rooms. A hearty breakfast is served family style in the ancient keeping room. Enjoy a quiet, colonial atmosphere near Mystic Seaport Museum, antique shops, Foxwoods Casino, and Aquarium. Colonial dinner weekends are also available November and December. No smoking.

Hostess: Ruth Keyes
Rooms: 9 (PB) $119-189
Full Breakfast
Credit Cards: A, B
Notes: 2, 5, 7, 8, 9, 10

## THOMPSON

## Hickory Ridge Bed and Breakfast

1084 Quaddick Town Farm Rd., 06277
(203) 928-9530

A 1990 Post and Beam house built on three wooded acres in a country garden setting. 325 feet of lake frontage. Also 17 private acres for hiking with access to unlimited state land. Two bikes, canoe, rowboat, swimming area, decks (four), picnic tables, gas grills, and refrigerator; also high chair/cribs/cots, TV, VCR, games, and book and video libraries. Children and pets welcome. No smoking. Open all year.

Hosts: Ken and Birdie Olson
Rooms: 3 (1PB; 2SB, a suite) $65-85 + CT tax
Full Gourmet Breakfast
Credit Cards: none
Notes: 2, 3 and 4 (available upon request and prior notice) 5, 6, 7, 8, 9, 10, 11 (cross-country), 12

Hickory Ridge Bed and Breakfast

---

5 Open all year; 6 Pets welcome; 7 Children welcome; 8 Tennis nearby; 9 Swimming nearby; 10 Golf nearby; 11 Skiing nearby; 12 May be booked through travel agent.

## A Taste of Ireland Bed and Breakfast

47 Quaddick Rd., 06277
(203) 923-2883 (voice and FAX)

Charming country cottage, circa 1780, on National Historic Register. Sitting room with fireplace. Home library of Irish literature and Celtic music. Hosts well-versed in assisting guests in genealogy research and travel planning to "the old sod." Authentic imported foods and beverages complete the full breakfast served in atrium room overlooking gardens and lovely stone walls. Home is located in quiet corner of NE Connecticut—a nature lover's retreat area.

Hosts: Elaine Chicoine and husband, Jean
Rooms: 3 (PB) $60-70
Full Irish Breakfast (Healthy also available)
Credit Cards: none
Notes: 2, 5, 6, 7, 9, 10, 11, 12

## WETHERSFIELD

## Chester Bulkley House Bed and Breakfast

184 Main St., 06109
(203) 563-4236

Nestled in the historic village of Old Wethersfield, this classic Greek Revival house has been lovingly restored by innkeepers Frank and Sophie Bottaro to provide a warm and gracious New England welcome to the vacationer, traveler, or businessperson. Built in 1830, the house boasts five delightfully airy guest rooms, each with a unique character and decorated with period antiques and vintage design details.

Hosts: Frank and Sophie Bottaro
Rooms: 5 (3PB; 2SB) $65-85
Full Breakfast
Credit Cards: A, B, C, D
Notes: 2, 5, 7, 8, 9, 10, 11, 12

---

NOTES: Credit cards accepted: A Master Card; B Visa; C American Express; D Discover; E Diners Club; F Other; 2 Personal checks accepted; 3 Lunch available; 4 Dinner available;

# Delaware

## Bed and Breakfast of Delaware

3650 Siverside Rd., Box 177, **Wilmington**
19810
(302) 479-9500 (voice and FAX)

Historic Landmark properties and private homes. In **Pennsylvania**—in Brandywine Valley, Cadds Ford, West Chester, New Hope, Landenberg, Oxford, and Kennett Square. In **Delaware**—Wilmington, New Castle, Newark, Odessa, Dover, Bridgeville, Laurel, Milford, Lewes, Dagsboro, Milton, and Selbyville. Near the University of Delaware in Newark and Del-Tech Campuses in Wilmington, Stanton, and Georgetown. Others are on the Eastern Shore of **Maryland,** and **Virginia's** Chesapeake Bay. Many are on the National Register. Near Winterthur, Longwood Gardens, and the Atlantic Ocean. Rates: $60-160. Surcharge for one-night stay. Short-term available/reduced rate.

## NEW CASTLE

### Armitage Inn

2 The Strand, 19720
(302) 328-6618

Built in 1732, the Armitage Inn is beautifully situated on the bank of the Delaware River in historic New Castle, Delaware. Elegantly furnished, air-conditioned guest rooms, all with private baths and most with whirlpool tubs, overlook the picturesque vistas of the grand Delaware River, the acres of parkland surrounding the Inn, and a peaceful walled garden. Gourmet buffet breakfast is served in the grand dining room or in the garden. The Inn is conveniently located in the heart of this historic town which was established in 1651 and functions today as a living museum, with buildings dating back to its founding years. New Castle is located in the heart of the Brandywine Valley with its numerous museums and attractions.

Hosts: Stephen and Rina Marks
Rooms: 5 (PB) $95-135
Breakfast Buffet
Credit Cards: A, B
Notes: 2, 5, 7 (over 12), 8, 12

### William Penn Guest House

206 Delaware St., 19720
(302) 328-7736

Visit historic New Castle and stay in a charmingly restored home, circa 1682,

---

5 Open all year; 6 Pets welcome; 7 Children welcome; 8 Tennis nearby; 9 Swimming nearby; 10 Golf nearby; 11 Skiing nearby; 12 May be booked through travel agent.

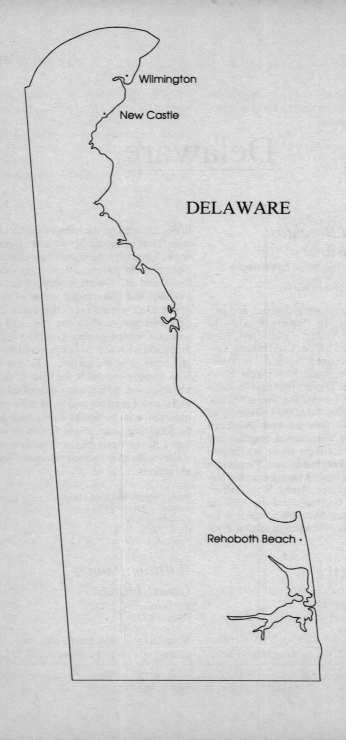

Wilmington

New Castle

DELAWARE

Rehoboth Beach

close to museums and major highways. Rates are $50 for shared baths and $75 for private baths.

Hosts: Richard and Irma Burwell
Rooms: 4 (1PB; 2SB) $50-75
Continental Breakfast
Credit Cards: none
Notes: 2, 7 (over 12), 8

## REHOBOTH BEACH

## The Royal Rose Inn Bed and Breakfast

41 Baltimore Ave., 19971
(302) 226-2535

A charming and relaxing 1920's beach cottage, this bed and breakfast is tastefully furnished with antiques and a romantic rose theme. A scrumptious breakfast of homemade bread, muffins, egg dishes, and much more is served on a large screened-in porch. Air-conditioned bedrooms, guest refrigerator, and off-street parking are real pluses for guests. Centrally located one and one half blocks from the ocean and boardwalk. Midweek specials, weekend packages, and gift certificates. Open May through October.

Hostess: Kenny and Cindy Vincent
Rooms: 7 (3PB; 4SB) $55-120
Continental Plus Breakfast
Credit Cards: none
Notes: 2, 7 (over 6), 8, 9, 10

## Tembo Bed and Breakfast

100 Laurel St., 19971
(302) 227-3360

Tembo, named after Gerry's elephant

collection, is a white frame beach cottage set among old shade trees in a quiet residential area just one block from the beach. Furnished with comfortable antique furniture, hand-braided rugs, paintings, and carvings by Delaware artists. A cozy ambiance pervades the casual, hospitable atmosphere.

Hosts: Don and Gerry Cooper
Rooms: 6 (1PB; 5SB)
Continental Breakfast
Credit Cards: none
Notes: 2, 6 (sometimes), 7 (12 and over; off season under 12), 8, 9, 10

## WILMINGTON

## The Boulevard Bed and Breakfast

1909 Baynard Boulevard, 19802
(302) 656-9700; FAX (302) 656-9700

This beautifully restored city mansion was originally built in 1913. Impressive foyer and magnificent staircase leading to a landing complete with window seat and large leaded-glass windows flanked by 15-foot columns. Full breakfast served on screened porch or formal dining room. Bedrooms furnished with antiques and family heirlooms. Close to business district and area attractions.

Hosts: Charles and Judy Powell
Rooms: 6 (4PB; 2SB) $60-75
Full Breakfast
Credit Cards: A, B, C
Notes: 2, 5, 7, 8, 10

NOTES: Credit cards accepted: A Master Card; B Visa; C American Express; D Discover; E Diners Club; F Other; 2 Personal checks accepted; 3 Lunch available; 4 Dinner available; 5 Open all year; 6 Pets welcome; 7 Children welcome; 8 Tennis nearby; 9 Swimming nearby; 10 Golf nearby; 11 Skiing nearby; 12 May be booked through travel agent.

# DISTRICT OF COLUMBIA

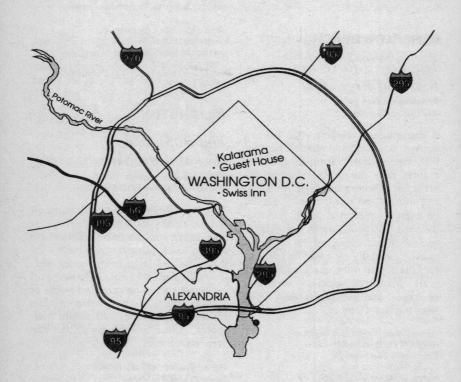

# District of Columbia

**NOTE: ALSO SEE LISTINGS UNDER MARYLAND AND VIRGINIA**

## Adams Inn

1744 Lanier Place NW, 20009
(202) 745-3600; (800) 578-6807;
FAX (202) 332-5867

This turn-of-the-century town house is in the Adams-Morgan neighborhood with over 40 ethnic restaurants. It has clean comfortable home-style furnishings. Adams Inn, located north of the White House and near the National Zoo, is convenient to transportation (Woodley Park Zoo Metro), convention sites, government buildings, and tourist attractions.

Host: Gene and Nancy Thompson with Anne Owens
Rooms: 25 (12PB; 13SB) $45-90
Expanded Continental Breakfast
Credit cards: A, B, C, D, E
Notes: 2, 5, 7, 12

## Bed and Breakfast Accommodations, Ltd.

P.O. Box 12011, 20005
(202) 328-3510; FAX (202) 332-3885

A reservation service representing over 80 properties in Washington, DC, and nearby Maryland and Northern Virginia. Unique accommodations include private home bed and breakfast, guest houses, inns and hotels, and unhosted one and two bedroom apartments. Many restored and historic Victorians, some with jacuzzi tubs and fireplaces. Children welcome. Major credit cards accepted. Personal Checks accepted if presented two weeks prior to arrival. Wendy Serpan, coordinator.

## Kalorama Guest House at Kalorama Park

1854 Mintwood Place NW, 20009
(202) 667-6369; FAX (202) 319-1262

Enjoy Washington, DC the right way! Try bed and breakfast in a charming Victorian townhouse. Lodge downtown, within an easy walk to the restaurants, clubs, and nightlife of Adams Morgan and Dupont Circle. Walk to the Metro (subway). Allow us to provide you with a complimentary continental breakfast when you awake, and an evening aperitif when you return to your "home-away-from-home." Most tourist

---

NOTES: Credit cards accepted: A Master Card; B Visa; C American Express; D Discover; E Diners Club; F Other; 2 Personal checks accepted; 3 Lunch available; 4 Dinner available; 5 Open all year; 6 Pets welcome; 7 Children welcome; 8 Tennis nearby; 9 Swimming nearby; 10 Golf nearby; 11 Skiing nearby; 12 May be booked through travel agent.

attractions are only 10 minutes away.

Hosts: Tami, Carlotta, John, and Mark
Rooms: 31 (12PB; 19SB) $50-95
Continental Plus Breakfast
Credit Cards: A, B, C, E
Notes: 2, 5, 7, 12

## Kalorama Guest House at Woodley Park

2700 Cathedral Ave. NW, 20008
(202) 328-0860; FAX (202) 319-1262

This charming Victorian inn provides a cozy home-away-from-home. Located on a quiet street in a lovely downtown residential neighborhood, the House is a stroll from the Metro (subway), neighborhood restaurants, and shops. Guest rooms are tastefully decorated in period. Enjoy your breakfast in a sun-filled room and relax with an aperitif at day's end. Our hospitality and personal service is nationally known. Most tourist attractions are only ten minutes away.

Hosts: Michael and Mary Anne
Rooms: 19 (12PB; 7SB) $50-95
Continental Plus Breakfast
Credit Cards: A, B, C, E
Notes: 2, 5, 7, 12

## The Reeds

P.O. Box 12011, 20005
(202) 328-3510; FAX (202) 332-3885

Built in the late 1800s, this large Victorian home features original wood paneling, including a unique oak staircase, stained glass, chandeliers, Victorian-style lattice porch, and art nouveau and Victorian antiques and decorations. It

is a double lot and it has a garden with fountains and an old-fashioned swing. The house has been featured in the *Washington Post* and the *Philadelphia Inquirer* and as part of "Christmas at the Smithsonian." It is located ten blocks from the White House at historic Logan Circle.

Hosts: Charles and Jackie Reed
Rooms: 6 (1PB; 5SB) $55-95
Continental Plus Breakfast
Credit Cards: A, B, C, E
Notes: 2 (2 weeks in advance), 5, 7, 8, 9

## Swiss Inn

1204 Massachusetts Ave. NW, 20005
(202) 371-1816; (800) 955-7947

The Swiss Inn is one of the last few turn-of-the-century townhouses located in Washington, DC. The small family-owned and operated inn is within walking distance of the White House, FBI, National Geographic, Chinatown, the Convention Center, the Smithsonian Museums, Ford's Theater, Women in the Arts Museum, and many other attractions. We are also just two blocks from the main business district. We do not serve breakfast but all of our rooms have kitchenettes. Many of our guests prepare their own breakfast, lunch, or dinner. Grocery stores are within walking distance.

Host: Ralph Nussbaumer
Rooms: 7 (PB) $58-98
Breakfast is not served
Credit Cards: A, B, C, D, E
Notes: 2, 5, 6, 7

NOTES:  Credit cards accepted:  A  Master Card;  B  Visa;  C  American Express;  D  Discover;  E  Diners Club;  F  Other;  2  Personal checks accepted;  3  Lunch available;  4  Dinner available;

# Florida

Bailey House

## AMELIA ISLAND/FERNANDINA BEACH

### *Bailey House*

28 S. 7th St., 32034
(904) 261-5390; (800) 251-5390;
FAX (904) 321-0103

Visit an elegant Queen Anne home furnished in Victorian period decor. The beautiful home, with magnificent stained glass windows, turrets, and a wraparound porch, was built in 1895 and is on the National Register of Historic Places. The recently renovated home offers the comfort of air conditioning and private baths. The location in Fernandina's historic district is within walking distance of excellent restaurants, antique shopping, and many historic churches. No smoking or pets please.

Hosts: Tom and Jenny Bishop
Rooms: 5 (PB) $75-115
Extended Continental Breakfast
Credit cards: A, B, C
Notes: 2, 5, 8, 9, 10, 12

## AMELIA ISLAND

### *Elizabeth Pointe Lodge*

98 S. Fletcher, 32034
(904) 277-4851; (800) 772-3359;
FAX (904) 277-6500

The main house of the lodge is constructed in an 1890s Nantucket shingle-style with a strong maritime theme, broad porches, rockers, sunshine, and lemonade. Located prominently by the Atlantic Ocean, the Lodge is only steps from often deserted beaches. Suites are available for families. A newspaper is delivered to your room in the morning and breakfast is served overlooking the ocean.

Hosts: David and Susan Caples
Rooms: 25 (PB) $100-175
Full Breakfast
Credit Cards: A, B, C
Notes: 2, 3, 4, 5, 7, 8, 9, 10, 12

---

5 Open all year; 6 Pets welcome; 7 Children welcome; 8 Tennis nearby; 9 Swimming nearby; 10 Golf nearby; 11 Skiing nearby; 12 May be booked through travel agent.

# FLORIDA

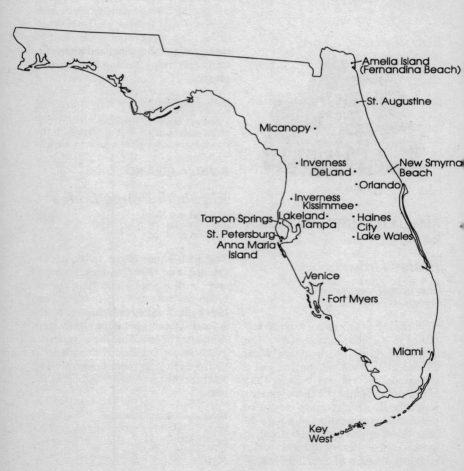

Amelia Island
(Fernandina Beach)

·St. Augustine

Micanopy ·

·Inverness
DeLand ·

New Smyrna
Beach

·Orlando

·Inverness
Kissimmee·

Tarpon Springs·
Lakeland·
Tampa

·Haines
City

·Lake Wales

St. Petersburg·
Anna Maria
Island

·Venice

·Fort Myers

Miami ·

Key
West

Florida House Inn

## Florida House Inn

22 S. 3rd St., P.O. Box 688, 32034
(904) 261-3300; (800) 258-3301 (reservations);
FAX (904) 277-3831

Located in the heart of our Victorian seaport village, Florida's oldest hotel dates from 1857. Recently restored, our award-winning inn is the perfect combination of historic charm and modern convenience. Each room is a comfortable blend of antiques and reproductions, vintage quilts, handmade rugs, and polished pine floors. Deluxe rooms offer fireplaces, jacuzzis, or original clawfoot tubs. A cozy English-style pub, original boardinghouse restaurants, and brick courtyard with gazebo are all a part of the Florida House experience.

Hosts: Bob and Karen Warner
Rooms: 11 (PB) $70-130
Full Breakfast each morning
Credit Cards: A, B, C, E
Notes: 2, 3, 4, 5, 7, 8, 9, 10, 12

## ANNA MARIA ISLAND

## Harrington House Beachfront B&B

5626 Gulf Dr., **Holmes Beach** 34217
(813) 778-5444; FAX (813) 778-0527

Centrally located on the Anna Maria Island, in the small city of Holmes Beach directly overlooking the Gulf of Mexico, Harrington House awaits your visit. The largest three-story home on the island was constructed in 1925 and was owned by the first mayor of Holmes Beach. Flower gardens, in-ground pool, and beachfront swimming are attractive features you'll find at Harrington House. Our great room lends itself to reading, watching TV, listening to music, or just sitting, talking, and creating new friends or getting acquainted with old ones. Christmas time is especially festive at Harrington House. Rooms are gorgeously decorated each with its own atmosphere. Breakfast is served on the porch overlooking the sea or in the formal dining room.

Hosts: Jo and Frank Davis
Rooms: 12 (PB) $79-195
Full Breakfast
Credit cards: A, B, C
Notes: 2, 5, 8, 9, 10, 12

## COLEMAN

## The Son's Shady Brook Bed and Breakfast

P.O. Box 551 (949 N. US 301), 33521
(904) PIT-STOP (748-7867)

Offering a refreshing change. Modern home, beautifully decorated rooms with comfortable beds and private baths. Overlooks springfed creek on 21 secluded, wooded acres. A relaxing retreat for elderly, handicapped, newlyweds, and others. Central air, heat, and sound system. Enjoy piano, library, fireplace and more. Solitude and tranquility with therapeutic, scenic, picturesque surroundings. Easy to find, rural setting within 50 miles from Central Florida attractions, Orlando, and Tampa.

Hostess: Jean Lake Martin
Rooms: 4 (PB) $50-60
Full Breakfast
Credit cards: A, B, C
Notes: 2, 5, 8, 9, 10

The Son's Shady Brook Bed and Breakfast

## DELAND

### Eastwood Terrace Inn

442 E. New York Ave., 32724
(904) 736-9902

Experience the legendary Eastwood Terrace Inn. . .elegant suites or inviting rooms all accompanied by private baths, most with original 1925 clawfoot tub. Spend your down time in this quiet, historic town only 30 minutes from New Symrna Beach and Daytona Beach and a short drive to all central Florida attractions. Shoppes and Cafe on premises for your convenience. Inn is only four blocks from Stetson University. Corporate and retreat groups welcome.

Rope Course close.

Hosts: Rene' and Lynn Jacoby
Rooms: 10 (PB) $59-115
Continental Breakfast
Credit cards: A, B
Notes: 2, 3, 4, 5, 9, 10

## FORT MYERS

### Windsong Garden and Art Gallery

5570-4 Woodrose Ct., 33907
(941) 936-6378

This town house-type home is designed to be your home away from home. The spacious accommodations include a bright and cheery suite with a large, private bath and dressing area. Located 15 minutes from the beaches, Sanibel and Captiva Islands, fine shopping, good restaurants, and the University of Florida. Resident Cat.

Hostess: Embe Burdick
Rooms: 1 (PB) $75
Continental Breakfast
Credit cards: none
Notes: 2, 5, 8, 9, 10

## HAINES CITY

### Holly Garden Inn

106 S. 1st Street, 33844
(941) 421-9867

Romantic Bed and Breakfast in historic small town in the heart of central Florida's citrus groves. This 1924 home has been lovingly restored to recapture the grand elegance of the old South. Just 20 miles from Disney World and most central Florida attractions, it's a perfect spot for that romantic getaway, family vacation, wedding, or small meeting. Escape to a place where true Southern hospitality is still a way of life.

Hosts: Camilla and Wes Donnelly
Rooms: 5 (PB) $79-89
Full Southern Breakfast
Credit cards: A, B, C
Notes: 2, 3, 5, 7, 8, 10, 12

## INVERNESS

### Crown Hotel

109 N. Seminole Ave., 34450
(904) 344-5555; FAX (904) 726-4040

Experience the elegance of authentic Victorian decor in one of our 34 individually styled rooms. Your choice of dining in Churchill's Grill or our British Fox and Hound Pub. Centrally located in the secluded hill of Inverness activities. Available activities within the area include canoeing, horseback riding, golfing, and bicycling trails. The perfect place for a quiet, relaxing getaway.

Hosts: Mr. and Mrs. Nigel Sumner
Rooms: 34 (PB) $55-70
Continental Breakfast
Credit cards: A, B, C, E
Notes: 2, 3, 4, 5, 6, 7, 8, 9, 10, 12

Crown Hotel

## KEY WEST

### Center Court—Historic Inn and Cottages

916 Center St., 33040
(305) 296-9292 (voice and FAX);
(800) 797-8787

Beautifully renovated Key West home from 1873, located one block from Duval and Truman Avenue. On quiet, historic lane, yet within walking distance of every Old Town attraction and beaches. This elegantly appointed and handicapped accessible inn has hair dryers, cable TV, telephones, air-conditioning, and fans in each room. One and two room cottages available. Common area has heated pools, jacuzzi, exercise pavilion, fish and lily pond, and lush, tropical gardens. AAA approved, three-diamonds. Winner of two Historic Preservation awards. French, German, Spanish and Italian spoken.

Hostess: Naomi Van Steelandt
Rooms: 7 (PB) $78-308
Expanded Continental Breakfast
Credit cards: A, B, C, D
Notes: 5, 6, 7, 8, 9, 10, 12

### Whispers Bed and Breakfast Inn

409 William St., 33040
(305) 294-5969; (800) 856-SHHH

Located in the heart of Old Town, Whispers, a 150-year-old Victorian-style house, offers its guest the luxury of a private resort (free use of lap pool, private beach, and health spa) yet the

---

5 Open all year; 6 Pets welcome; 7 Children welcome; 8 Tennis nearby; 9 Swimming nearby; 10 Golf nearby; 11 Skiing nearby; 12 May be booked through travel agent.

quaintness of a B&B. Whispers also offers its guests a full and varied gourmet breakfast. So come down and enjoy Key West—and come home to Whispers.

Host: John W. Marburg
Rooms: 7 (5PB; 2SB) $69-150
Full Gourmet Breakfast
Credit cards: A, B, C, D
Notes: 2, 5, 8, 9, 10, 12

Unicorn Inn

## KISSIMMEE

## *Unicorn Inn*

8 S. Orlando Ave., 34741
(407) 846-1200; FAX (407) 846-1773

The Unicorn—the only colonial style bed and breakfast in Kissimmee—is located in Historic Downtown off the Broadway. A safe, peaceful, relaxing district 300 yards from Lake Tohopekalegia (fishing boats and other boats can be rented), the Unicorn is close to golf courses, horseback riding, and other attractions like Disney World, Sea World, and Wet and Wild. Orlando Airport is a 25 minute drive. Amtrak and Greyhound stations are nearby. All rooms have TV, air-conditioning, kitchen facilities, and tea and coffee

machines. Restored to its full grandeur, the Unicorn Inn has antique pottery, prints, and furniture. Many churches located nearby. British owned and run by Fran and Don Williamson of Yorkshire, England. Our rule is: "Make Yourself At Home." Airport pick-ups available. AAA Approved.

Hostess: Don and Fran Williamson
Rooms: 8 (2 of which have space for children) (PB) $55-65
Full or Light Breakfast
Credit cards: A, B, C, D, E
Notes: 2, 5, 7, 8, 9, 10, 12

## LAKE WALES

## *Chalet Suzanne Country Inn and Restaurant*

3800 Chalet Suzanne Dr., 33853
(941) 676-6011; (800) 433-6011;
FAX (941) 676-1814

Listed on the National Register of Historic Places, Chalet Suzanne has been family owned and operated since 1931. It is on 100 acres in a fairy-tale setting. Thirty guest rooms have all the amenities. Our four-star restaurants serve breakfast, lunch, and dinner. We also have gift shops, a ceramic studio, swimming pool, soup cannery, and lighted airstrip. We are proud to say that our soups accompanied Jim Irwin to the moon on Apollo 15. Ask about our mini-vacation special.

Hosts: Carl and Vita Hinshaw
Rooms: 30 (PB) $125-185
Full Breakfast
Credit Cards: A, B, C, D, E, F
Notes: 2, 3, 4, 5, 6, 7, 8, 9, 10, 12

---

NOTES: Credit cards accepted: A Master Card; B Visa; C American Express; D Discover; E Diners Club; F Other; 2 Personal checks accepted; 3 Lunch available; 4 Dinner available;

## LAKELAND

### Sunset Motel

2301 New Tampa Hwy., 33801
(813) 683-6464

This tranquil oasis with birds, fish, flowering plants, pool, fountain, picnic areas, and clubhouse is central to major attractions of Florida. Walk to banks and shopping. TV, telephone, and refrigerators in all rooms. Microwaves and grills available. Many options from rooms to suites.

Hosts: Bill and Will
Rooms: 23 (PB) $35-89
Continental Breakfast
Credit cards: A, B, C
Notes: 5, 7, 9, 12

## MIAMI

### Banyon Treehouse B&B / Agency of Bed and Breakfast Hosts

7436 SW 117 Ave., P.O. Box 160, 33183
(305) 271-5422

Private, five-acre, equestrian estate. Safe, clean, and beautiful. Three guest rooms, two apartments, all private whirlpool baths. Wraparound decks, lush tropical foliage, therapeutic hot tubs, and a treehouse. Breakfast under giant orchid tree. Romantic. Five minutes to restaurants, great shopping, and movies. Fifteen minutes to zoo, Parrot Jungle, Monkey Jungle, and Orchid Jungle. Twenty-five minutes to Miami Beach and Art Deco Center. Thirty minutes to Florida Key for snorkeling, scuba diving, glass-bottom boats, and deep sea fishing. Twenty minutes to Everglades National Park, etc. Call for brochure.

Hostess: Ms. Beck
Rooms: 3 + 2 apartments (PB) $45-65
Continental Breakfast
Credit cards: none
Notes: 2, 5, 8, 9, 10, 12 (20% com.)

## MICANOPY

### Shady Oak Bed and Breakfast

P.O. Box 327., 32667
(904) 466-3476

The Shady Oak stands majestically in the center of historic downtown Micanopy. A marvelous canopy of old, live oaks; quiet, shaded streets; and many antique stores offer visitors a memorable connection to Florida's past. This three-story, 19th century-style mansion features five beautiful, spacious suites, private baths, porches, jacuzzi, Florida room, and widow's walk. Three lovely, historic churches within walking distance. Local activities include antiquing, bicycling, canoeing, bird watching, and much more. "Playfully elegant accommodations, where stained glass, antiques, and innkeeping go together as kindly as warm hugs with old friends."

Host: Frank James
Rooms: 5 suites (PB) $85-145
Full Breakfast
Credit cards: A, B, D
Notes: 2, 3, 4, 5, 7, 9, 10, 12

5 Open all year; 6 Pets welcome; 7 Children welcome; 8 Tennis nearby; 9 Swimming nearby; 10 Golf nearby; 11 Skiing nearby; 12 May be booked through travel agent.

## NEW SMYRNA BEACH

### Indian River Inn

1210 S. Riverside Dr., 32168
(904) 428-2491; (800) 541-4529 (reservations);
FAX (904) 426-2532

Built in 1916, this inn is the oldest extant hotel in Volusia County. It has been lovingly restored and remodeled to meet all current standard of security, comfort, and convenience without sacrificing its charm and character. A gracious atmosphere of warmth and friendliness, unsurpassed in today's often frantic lifestyle, can be found here. We are located on the Atlantic Intercoastal Waterway minutes from I-95 and I-4 between Daytona Beach and the Kennedy Space Center. Church groups and buses welcomed.

Hosts: Ed and Donna Ruby
Rooms: 27 + 15 suites (PB) $50-115
Continental Breakfast
Credit cards: A, B, D
Notes: 2, 3 and 4 (available Thanksgiving—
Easter), 5, 7, 8, 9 (on premises), 10, 12

### Night Swan Intracoastal Bed and Breakfast

512 S. Riverside Dr., 32168
(904) 423-4940 (voice and FAX)

Come watch the pelicans, dolphins, sailboats, and yachts along the Atlantic Intracoastal Waterway from our beautiful front room, our wraparound porch, our 140-foot dock, or your room. Our spacious three-story home has kept its character and charm of 1906 in the Historic District of New Smyrna Beach, with its central fireplace and its intricate natural wood in every room. We are located between Daytona Beach and Kennedy Space Center, on the Indian River, just two miles from the beach. AAA approved.

Hosts: Martha and Chuck Nighswonger
Rooms: 8 (PB) $59-129
Full or Continental Breakfast
Credit cards: A, B, C, D
Notes: 2, 5, 7, 8, 9, 10

Night Swan

## ORLANDO

### The Courtyard at Lake Lucerne

211 N. Lucerne Circle E., 32801
(407) 648-5188; (800) 444-5289;
FAX (407) 246-1368

A unique property made up of three historic buildings furnished with antiques and surrounding a tropically landscaped brick courtyard, this establishment is located in the historic district on the southern edge of downtown Orlando, convenient to everything central Florida has to offer. Rooms have phones and cable TV; two suites have double jacuzzis and steam showers. Selected by *Country Inns Magazine* as one of 1992's "Best Inn Buys" and by Herb Hillier for *The Miami Herald* as one of the ten best inns in Florida for 1992.

Hosts: Charles, Sam, and Eleanor Meiner and Paula Bowers
Rooms: 22 (PB) $65-150
Expanded Continental Breakfast
Credit cards: A, B, C, E
Notes: 2, 5, 7, 10, 12

## PerriHouse
## Bed and Breakfast

10417 State Rd., 32836
(407) 876-4830; (800) 780-4830;
FAX (407) 876-0241

PerriHouse is a quiet, private country estate inn secluded on 20 acres of land adjacent to the Walt Disney World complex. Because of its outstanding location, Disney Village and Pleasure Island are only three minutes away; EPCOT Center is only five minutes. It's the perfect vacation setting for families who desire a unique travel experience with a comfortable, convenient home away from home. An upscale continental breakfast awaits you each morning and a refreshing pool relaxes you after a full day of activities. Each guest room features its own private bath, entrance, TV, telephone, ceiling fan, and central air/heat. The PerriHouse grounds are being developed and landscaped to create a future bird sanctuary and wildlife preserve. Come bird watch on the peaceful, tranquil grounds of the PerriHouse Estate and wake up to the bird songs outside your window. Your hosts, Nick and Angi instinctively offer their guests

a unique blend of cordial hospitality, comfort, and friendship!

Hosts: Nick and Angi Perretti
Rooms: 6 (PB) $69-85
Continental Plus Breakfast
Credit cards: A, B, C, D
Notes: 2 (2 weeks ahead), 5, 7, 8, 9, 10, 12

## ST. AUGUSTINE

## Carriage Way
## Bed and Breakfast

70 Cuna St., 32084
(904) 829-2467; (800) 908-9832;
FAX (904) 826-1461

Built in 1833, a Victorian home located in the heart of the historic district amid unique and charming shops, museums, and historic sites. The atmosphere is leisurely and casual, in keeping with the general attitude and feeling of Old St. Augustine. All guest rooms have a private bath with a clawfoot tub or shower. Rooms are furnished with antiques and reproductions including brass, canopy, or four poster beds. A full home-baked breakfast is served.

Hosts: Bill and Diane Johnson
Rooms: 9 (PB) $59-115
Full Breakfast
Credit Cards: A, B, D
Notes: 2, 3 and 4 (picnic), 5, 7 (over 8), 8, 9, 10, 12

## Castle Garden B&B

15 Shenandoah St., 32084
(904) 829-3839

Stay at a Castle and be treated like royalty! Relax and enjoy the peace and quiet of "royal treatment" at our newly

---

restored, 100-year-old castle of the Moorish Revival design where the only sound you'll hear is the occasional roar of a cannon shot from the old fort 200 yards to the south or the creak of solid wood floors. Awaken to the aroma of freshly baked goodies as we prepare a full, mouth-watering, country breakfast just like "Mom used to make." The unusual coquina stone exterior remains virtually untouched while the interior of the former Castle Warden Carriage House boasts two beautiful bridal suites complete with soothing in-room jacuzzi, sunken bedrooms, and all of life's little pleasures! Amenities: complimentary wine, chocolates, bikes, and private parking. Packages and gift baskets available. We believe that every guest is a gift from God.

Hosts: Bruce Kloeckner and Kimmy VanKooten
Rooms: 6 (PB) $75-150
Full Breakfast
Credit cards: A, B, C, D
Notes: 2, 5, 7, 8, 9, 10, 12

Castle Garden Bed and Breakfast

## The Cedar House Inn

79 Cedar St., 32084
(904) 829-0079; (800) 233-2746

Capture romantic moments at our 1893 Victorian home in the heart of the an-

cient city. Escape into your antique filled bedroom with private whirlpool bath or clawfooted tub, enjoy the comfortable parlor with its fireplace, player piano and antique Victrola, or sit on the shady veranda and watch time stroll by. Elegant full breakfast, evening snack, on premises parking, jacuzzi spa, and bicycles. Walk to historical sites or bicycle to beach. AAA approved, 3 diamond rated. Smoke free home.

Hosts: Russ and Nina Thomas
Rooms: 5 + 1 suite (PB) $79-150
Full Breakfast
Credit cards: A, B, D
Notes: 2, 7 (over 10)

## Old Powder House Inn

38 Cordova St., 32084
(904) 824-4149; (800) 447-4149

Towering pecan and oak trees shade verandas with large rockers to watch the passing horse-drawn buggies. An introduction to a romantic escape in the charming turn-of-the-century Victorian inn. Amenities include high tea, hors d' oeuvres, jacuzzi, cable TV, parking, bicycles, family hospitality, picnics, special honeymoon packages, anniversaries, and birthdays.

Hosts: Al and Eunice Howes
Rooms: 9 (PB) $59-115
Full Gourmet Breakfast
Credit cards: A, B
Notes: 2, 5, 7, 8, 9, 10, 12

## St. Francis Inn

279 St. George St., 32084
(904) 824-6068; (800) 824-6062

Built in 1791, the Inn is a beautiful Spanish Colonial building. The courtyard garden provides a peaceful setting for traditional hospitality. Accommodations range from double rooms and suites to a five-room cottage—all private bath, cable TV, central air-conditioning and heat, and many have fireplaces. The Inn is centrally located in the historic district within easy walking to restaurants, shops, and historical sites.

Host: Joe Finnegan
Rooms: 14 (PB) $52-125
Continental Plus Breakfast
Credit cards: A, B
Notes: 2, 5, 7 (limited), 8, 9, 10, 12

St. Francis Inn

## ST. PETERSBURG

## *Island's End Resort*

1 Pass A Grille Way, 33706
(813) 360-5023; FAX (813) 367-7890

Six rental units; one three-bedroom with private pool. All other cottages equally as enjoyable with fully equipped, complete kitchens and color cable TV with VCR and HBO. Our fishing dock provides many hours of enjoyment. We provide a continental breakfast for guests three times a week in our gazebo. Croissants, freshly squeezed juice, and coffee are served to our guests by our friendly staff. We here at Island's End take pride in preserving genuine hospitality. Recommended by *Frommer's 1991 Guide to Florida, Atlantic Monthly, USA Today,* etc.

Hosts: Jone and Millard Gamble
Rooms: 6 (PB) $61-160
Continental served Tues., Thurs., and Saturday
Credit cards: A, B
Notes: 2, 5, 7, 8, 9, 10

## *Mansion House*

105 5th Ave. NE, 33701
(813) 821-9391 (voice and FAX)

Experience traditional Welsh hospitality at our double award winning bed and breakfast. Six guest bedrooms all private baths, two dining rooms, spacious guest areas for relaxation, excellent location. AAA and AB&BA inspected and approved, member of Florida Inn route.

Hosts: Alan and Suzanne Lucas
Rooms: 6 (PB) $80-110
Full English Breakfast
Credit Cards: A, B, C, D
Notes: 2 (deposit required), 5, 8, 9, 12

## TAMPA

## *Behind the Fence Bed and Breakfast Inn*

1400 Viola Dr. @ Countryside, **Brandon** 33511
(813) 685-8201

Retreat into the simplicity and tranquility of life in a bygone era with all the conveniences of today's world. Come to Florida and choose your accommo-

---

5 Open all year; 6 Pets welcome; 7 Children welcome; 8 Tennis nearby; 9 Swimming nearby; 10 Golf nearby; 11 Skiing nearby; 12 May be booked through travel agent.

dations from a cottage by our pool to a private room in our antique-filled New England Salt-Box house. Nearby parks and river canoeing offer lots of opportunities for family activities. Homemade, Amish sweet rolls are featured and "relaxing" is the word most guests use to refer to their stay "behind the fence." Country furniture for sale and tours available upon request. AAA and 3-star approved.

Hosts: Larry and Carolyn Yoss
Rooms: 5 (3PB; 2SB) $65-75
Expanded Continental Breakfast
Credit Cards: none
Notes: 2, 3, 5, 6 (some), 7, 8, 9, 10

Behind the FenceBed and Breakfast Inn

## TARPON SPRINGS

### East Lake Bed and Breakfast

421 Old East Lake Rd., 34689
(813) 937-5487

Private home on two and a half acres, situated on a quiet road along Lake Tar-

pon, close to the Gulf of Mexico. The hosts are retired business people who enjoy new friends and are well informed about the area. The room and adjoining bath are at the front of the house, away from the family quarters. The room has central air, color TV, and telephone. Breakfast includes fresh fruit, juice, entree, and homemade breads and jams. Close to many Florida attractions.

Hosts: Dick and Marie Fiorito
Rooms: 1 (PB) $40
Full Home-Cooked Breakfast
Credit Cards: none
Notes: 2, 5, 8, 9, 10

## VENICE

### The Banyon House

519 S. Harbor Dr., 34285
(941) 484-1385; FAX (941) 484-8032

Experience the Old World charm of one of Venice's historic Mediterranean homes, circa 1926, on the Gulf coast. Relax in the peaceful atmosphere of our lovely courtyard dominated by a huge banyon tree. This provides an unusual setting for the garden patio, pool, and jacuzzi. Central to shopping, beaches, restaurants, and golf. Complimentary bicycles. No smoking. Minimum two night stay.

Hosts: Chuck and Susan McCormick
Rooms: 9 (PB) $59-99
Deluxe Continental Breakfast
Credit Cards: none
Notes: 2, 5, 7 (over 12), 8, 9, 10

---

NOTES: Credit cards accepted: A Master Card; B Visa; C American Express; D Discover; E Diners Club; F Other; 2 Personal checks accepted; 3 Lunch available; 4 Dinner available;

# Georgia

## RSVP GRITS, INC.

541 Londonberry Rd. NE, Altlanta 30327
(404) 843-3933; (800) 823-7787
FAX (404) 252-8886

RSVP GRITS, INC. (Great Reservations in the South) represents a select group of very special B&Bs and Inns in the **Atlanta** area, within 100 miles of Atlanta, in **North Georgia**, as far east as **Augusta** plus a sampling in **Alabama** and in the **Chattanooga, TN** area. We provide personal service and are pleased to help plan get-away weekends, romantic retreats, or small business seminars or meetings. All properties are properly licensed and inspected. Free service. 40+ inns, all with private baths. Rates: $85-250. Credit cards and personal checks accepted.Marty Barnes, coordinator. Free brochure.

## AMERICUS

### The Pathway Inn B&B

501 S. Lee St., 31709
(912) 928-2078 (voice and FAX)
(800) 889-1466

Parlors, porches, whirlpools, down comforters, fireplaces, friends, muffins, and more await you at a 1906 Greek Revival style inn with stained glass and a sumptuous candlelit breakfast. Between Plains (Home of President Carter) and historic Civil War Andersonville. 30 minutes west of I-75 / 2½ hours south of Atlanta. Home of Habitat for Humanity. We spoil our business travelers the same as tourists and honeymooners. Attend and hear President Carter teach Sunday School.

Hosts: David and Sheila Judah
Rooms: 5 (PB) $67-107
Full Breakfast
Credit Cards: A, B, C, D
Notes: 2, 5, 6 (with permission), 7, 10, 12 (7%)

The Pathway Inn

## ATHENS

### The Nicholson House

6295 Jefferson Rd., 30607
(706) 353-2200

An 1820 tavern and stage coach stop,

---

5 Open all year; 6 Pets welcome; 7 Children welcome; 8 Tennis nearby; 9 Swimming nearby; 10 Golf nearby; 11 Skiing nearby; 12 May be booked through travel agent.

# GEORGIA

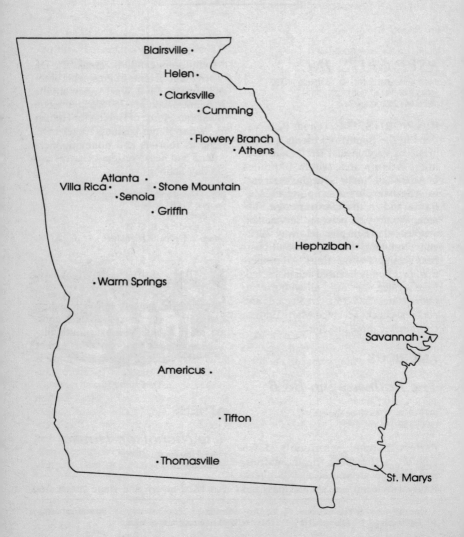

Nicholson House is now an ante-bellum home on six wooded acres. Spacious guestrooms include cable TV, king and queen beds, telephones, and clock radios. Rocking chair on porch. AAA approved. Four miles to center of Athens and UGA. Seventeen miles to I-85.

Host: Stuart J. Kelley
Rooms: 4 (PB)
Gourmet Continental Breakfast
Credit Cards: A, B, C, D
Notes: 5, 12

## Oakwood Bed and Breakfast

4959 Barnett Shoals Road, 30605
(706) 546-7886; (800) 546-7886
FAX (706) 546-0007

Oakwood is a place to enjoy the gracious Southern lifestyle of years gone by. The 1860 Victorian farmhouse has been gingerly restored and adapted into a lovely bed and breakfast which provides a comfortable environment offering warm hospitality and professional service. Three guestrooms, each traditionally appointed with fireplaces and ceiling fans, are in the main farmhouse. The cottage has two bedrooms, kitchen, washer, dryer, and a separate living room. Each morning enjoy a hearty breakfast complete with fresh brewed coffee and a morning paper in the formal dining room or on the front porch....Southern style!

Hosts: Bob and Gerri Tate
Rooms: 3(PB); 1(cottage; 2 bedroom, PB) $75-150
Full Breakfast
Credit Cards: A, B, C, D, E
Notes: 2, 6 (kennel nearby for pets)

## ATLANTA

NOTE: AREA CODE IS CHANGING TO 770 IN 1996.

## Beverly Hills Inn

65 Sheridan Dr., 30305
(404) 233-8520 (voice and FAX)
(800) 331-8520

A charming European-style hotel, with 18 suites uniquely decorated with period furnishings, offers fresh flowers, continental breakfast, and the little things that count. We're a morning star, not a constellation; a solitary path, not a highway. Only some will understand, but then, we don't have room for everybody.

Hosts: Bonnie and Lyle Klienhans
Rooms: 18 (PB) $80-450
Continental Breakfast
Credit Cards: A, B, C, E
Notes: 2, 5, 6, 7, 8, 9, 10, 12

## Oakwood House Bed and Breakfast

951 Edgewood Ave. NE, 30307
(404) 521-9320; FAX (404) 688-6034

Get away—in the city to our relaxing, small inn. Your hosts live next door. Located in Atlanta's oldest suburb, historic Inman park, just two miles east of downtown Atlanta, Oakwood House is perfect for business and pleasure travelers. Easy access via car and subway. There's lots to do in the city of Rhett and Scarlet, Coca Cola, Martin Luther King Jr., and Jimmy Carter. You'll enjoy our comfortable rooms which feel like a real home. New whirlpool suite. Free theater tickets (seasonal). Family

NOTES: Credit cards accepted: A Master Card; B Visa; C American Express; D Discover; E Diners Club; F Other; 2 Personal checks accepted; 3 Lunch available; 4 Dinner available; 5 Open all year; 6 Pets welcome; 7 Children welcome; 8 Tennis nearby; 9 Swimming nearby; 10 Golf nearby; 11 Skiing nearby; 12 May be booked through travel agent.

room features trundle bed for two children. Board your pet nearby. No smoking.

Hosts: Robert and Judy Hotchkiss
Rooms: 5 (PB) $65-150
Enhanced Continental Breakfast
Credit Cards: A, B, C
Notes: 2, 5, 7, 8, 9, 10, 12

Oakwood House Bed and Breakfast

## Shellmont Bed and Breakfast

821 Piedmont Ave. NE, 30308
(404) 872-9290; FAX (404) 872-5379

Built in 1891, Shellmont is on the National Register of Historic Places and is a city of Atlanta Landmark Building. A true Victorian treasure of carved woodwork, stained and leaded glass, and unique architecture located in Midtown Atlanta's restaurant, theater, and cultural district, one mile from downtown. It is furnished entirely with antiques.

Hosts: Ed and Debbie McCord
Rooms: 5 (PB) $79-109
Full Breakfast
Credit Cards: A, B, C, E
Notes: 2, 5, 7 (limited), 8, 10, 12

## The Woodruff Bed and Breakfast Inn

223 Ponce de Leon Ave., 30308
(404) 875-9449; (800) 473-9449
FAX (404) 875-2882

Prepare yourself for Southern charm, hospitality, and a full Southern breakfast. The Woodruff Bed and Breakfast Inn is conveniently located in Midtown Atlanta. It is a 1906 Victorian home built by a prominent Atlanta family and fully restored by the current owners. Each room has been meticulously decorated with antiques. The Woodruff has a very colorful past which lends to the charm and history of the building and the city. Close to everything. Ya'll come!

Hosts: Joan and Douglas Jones
Rooms: 13 (PB) $69-295
Full Breakfast
Credit Cards: A, B, D
Notes: 2, 5, 7, 8, 12

## BLAIRSVILLE

## Autumn Gold Lodge Christian B&B

5671 Praise the Lord Lane, 30512
(706) 745-3111

Constructed in the rustic thick and beam style, the Autumn Gold Lodge Christian B&B has beautiful wood floors and walls with skylights in the vaulted ceilings. The Lodge is on fourteen and one half acres with walking trails, fruit orchards, and flower gardens where guests are welcome to explore God's amazing creation. Also, on the premises there is a screened-in porch, wraparound deck,

NOTES: Credit cards accepted: A Master Card; B Visa; C American Express; D Discover; E Diners Club; F Other; 2 Personal checks accepted; 3 Lunch available; 4 Dinner available;

picnic tables, and swings. The Lodge is close to Brasstown Ball; Helen, GA; and the Georgia Mountain Resort. It is also near seven waterfalls and the Appalachian Trail and five minutes from Lake Nottely. No smoking or alcohol.

Hosts: Tommy and Drucilla Thomson
Rooms: 4 (1PB; 3SB) $30-50
Continental Breakfast
Credit Cards: none
Notes: 2 (and travelers'), 12

## CLARKSVILLE (HELEN)

### Habersham Hollow B&B and Cabins

Route 6, Box 6208, 30523
(706) 754-5147

Nestled in the northeast Georgia mountains, this elegant country B&B features king beds, fireplace, private baths, and TVs in each room. Nearby on the secluded wooded grounds are cozy fireplace cabins with fully equipped kitchens, TV, and deck with BBQ grills where well-mannered pets are welcome.

Hosts: C.J. and Maryann Gibbons
Rooms: 4 (PB) $85-145
Full Breakfast
Credit Cards: A, B
Notes: 2, 5, 6, 8, 9, 10, 11

## CUMMING

### The Fetzner's House

2861 Echols Rd., 30131
(770) 844-1238

Located 35 miles north of Atlanta, 45 miles south of Stone Mountain, and six miles from Lake Lanier, we are ready to serve you for the 1996 Olympics! We are surrounded by acres of beautiful pine trees and lots of fresh vegetables and fruits from the garden. We also make all our own breads, waffles, cinnamon rolls etc. with 100% whole grains which are milled fresh daily at home. Please come and share our Christian hospitality.

Hosts: Paul and Debbie Fetzner
Rooms: 4 (1 PB; 3 SB) $50-65
Full Breakfast
Credit Cards: none
Notes: 2, 3, 4, 5, 7, 9

## ETON

### Ivy Inn

245 Fifth Ave. E., P.O. Box 406, 30724
(706) 517-0526; (800) 201-5477

Historic 1908 country home was one of the first homes built in Eton. Rocking-chair porches offer a break from a busy day shopping for antiques, clothes or carpet; Eton is part of the carpet capital of the world. Hiking in Cohutta Wilderness or bicycling on the Inn's bikes refreshes the weary soul. In-room telephone and TV. Day trips to Atlanta, Chattanooga, and Ocoee River. Horses/stabling next door to inn. Restricted smoking.

Hosts: Gene and Juanita Twiggs
Rooms: 3 (PB) $87
Full Southern Breakfast
Credit Cards: A, B, C, D
Notes: 2, 5, 7, 9, 10, 11 (water)

---

5 Open all year; 6 Pets welcome; 7 Children welcome; 8 Tennis nearby; 9 Swimming nearby; 10 Golf nearby; 11 Skiing nearby; 12 May be booked through travel agent.

## FLOWERY BRANCH

### *Whitworth Inn*
6593 McEver Rd., 30542
(770) 967-2386; FAX (770) 967-2649

Contemporary country inn on five
wooded acres offers a relaxing atmosphere. Ten uniquely decorated guest
rooms with their own baths. Two guest
living rooms. Full, country breakfast
served in a large, sunlit dining room.
Meeting/party space available. Thirty
minutes northeast of Atlanta at Lake
Lanier. Nearby attractions and activities include boating, golf, beaches, and
water parks. Close to Road Atlanta and
Chateau Elen Winery/Golf Course. Easily accessible from major interstates.
Three diamond AAA rating.

Hosts: Ken and Christine Jonick
Rooms: 10 (PB) $55-70
Call for 1996 Olympic rates.
Full Breakfast
Credit Cards: A, B, C
Notes: 2, 5, 7, 8, 9, 10, 12

## GRIFFIN

### *Double Cabins Bed and Breakfast*
3335 Jackson Road, 30223
(770) 227-6611

This National Register home was built
in 1842 in the Greek Revival Style char-
acteristic of Southern country homes.
The five bedroom home features an
original walnut staircase and gold leaf
cornice boards in the living room as well
as numerous additional accents of the
period. The doors throughout have their
original knobs and locks with brass
keys. The property was part of the Great
1823-1825 land purchase from the
Creek Indians and lies on the McIntosh
Trail. The propery included two cabin-
like structures known as "Double Cabins." Group tours of the house, museum,
and property can also be arranged by
appointment.

Rooms: 3 (2PB; 1SB)
Full Breakfast
Credit Cards: none
Notes: 5, 7, 10

Whitworth Inn

# HELEN

## *Chattahoochee Ridge Lodge and Chalets*

P.O. Box 175, 500 Ridge Rd., 30545
(706) 878-3144; (800) 476-8331
FAX (706) 878-4032

Alone on a woodsy mountain above a waterfall, the Lodge has five new rooms and suites (kitchens and fireplaces) with private entrances, TV, air-conditioning, free phones, and jacuzzi; plus double insulation and back up solar for stewards of the earth. In the lodge and cabins you'll like the quiet seclusion, large windows, and deep-rock water. We'll help you plan great vacation days, including Bob's oom-pah band at a German restaurant. Decor includes wide-board knotty pine, brass beds, full carpeting, and paddle fans.

Hosts: Mary and Bob Swift
Rooms: 5 + cabins (PB) $50-85
Credit Cards: A, B, C, D
Notes: 2, 5, 7, 8, 9, 10

## *Dutch Cottage Bed and Breakfast*

P.O. Box 757, 114 Ridge Rd., 30545
(706) 878-3135

Located in a beautiful alpine village in the mountains of north Georgia, a tranquil waterfall and ivy-covered hillside lead to this European-style bed and breakfast located in an idyllic wooded setting. Choose from three comfortable rooms, each with private bath, air-conditioning, and TV, or a charming hilltop honeymoon chalet. Full Breakfast

buffet. Walk to town. Open May through October.

Hosts: Bill and Jane Vander Werf
Rooms: 3 (4) (3PB; 1SB) $65-75
Credit Cards: none
Notes: 2, 7, 9, 10

# HEPHZIBAH

## *Into the Woods Bed and Breakfast*

176 Longhorn Rd., 30815
**Office:** 11205 Country Club Rd., Waynesboro, PA 17268
(706) 554-1400; **Office** (717) 762-8525

Relax in a completely restored B&B built in the late 1800s. All guest rooms have firm, good beds to assure you a good, restful night. Guests can take a short drive to Augusta for a lovely Riverwalk along the Savannah River, or visit the restaurants and shops. You'll enjoy breakfast, in the morning, in our sunny dining room.

Hosts: Robert and Twila Risser
Rooms: 4 (2PB; 2SB) $65-85
Full Breakfast
Credit Cards: A, B, D
Notes: 2, 5, 7, 10, 12

Into the Woods Bed and Breakfast

---

5 Open all year; 6 Pets welcome; 7 Children welcome; 8 Tennis nearby; 9 Swimming nearby; 10 Golf nearby; 11 Skiing nearby; 12 May be booked through travel agent.

## ST. MARYS

### Goodbread Inn Bed and Breakfast

209 Osborne St., 31558
(912) 882-7490

This 1875 Victorian inn is in the historic district of a quaint fishing village nine miles east of I-95, halfway between Jacksonville, FL, and Brunswick, GA. Each antique-filled room has its own bath, fireplace, ceiling fan, and air-conditioning. Restaurants and Cumberland Island ferry are within walking distance.

Hosts: Betty and George Krauss
Rooms: 4 (PB) $55-65 + tax
Full Breakfast
Credit Cards: none
Notes: 2, 5, 10, 12

## SAUTEE

### The Stovall House

1526 Hwy. 225 N., 30571
(706) 878-3355

Our 1837 Victorian farmhouse, restored in 1983, is listed on the National Register of Historic Places. Located on 26 acres in the historic Sautee Valley, the Inn has views of the mountains in all directions. The recipient of several awards for its attentive restorations, the Inn is furnished with family antiques and decorated with hand-stenciling. The restaurant, open to the public, features regional cuisine prepared with a fresh difference and served in an intimate, yet informal, setting. It's a country experience!

Host: Ham Schwartz
Rooms: 5 (PB) $65-75
Continental Breakfast
Credit Cards: A, B
Notes: 2, 4, 5, 7, 8, 9, 10

The Stovall House

## SAVANNAH

### Jesse Mount House

209 W. Jones St., 31401
(912) 236-1774; (800) 347-1774
FAX (912) 236-2103

This elegant Georgian townhouse, built in 1856, is decorated with art and antiques from around the world. Located in the historic district, all rooms include fireplaces, private baths (some with whirlpools), TV, VCR, and telephones. Bicycles, off-street parking, and a private garden with fountains enhance your visit. Enjoy the charm, grace, and comfort that Savannah has possessed for centuries.

Hostess: Sue Dron
Rooms: 4 (PB) $135-160
Full Breakfast
Credit Cards: A, B, C, D
Notes: 2, 5, 6, 7, 8, 10, 12

---

NOTES: Credit cards accepted: A Master Card; B Visa; C American Express; D Discover; E Diners Club; F Other; 2 Personal checks accepted; 3 Lunch available; 4 Dinner available;

## Joan's on Jones Bed and Breakfast

17 W. Jones St., 31401
(912) 234-3863; (800) 407-3863
FAX (912) 234-1455

In the heart of the historic district, two charming bed and breakfast suites grace the garden level of this three-story Victorian, private home. Each suite has a private entry, off-street parking, bedroom, sitting room, kitchen, bath, private phone, and cable TV. Note the original heart pine floors, period furnishings, and Savannah brick walls. Innkeepers Joan and Gary Levy, restauranters, live upstairs and invite you for a tour of their home if you're staying two nights or more.

Hosts: Joan and Gary Levy
Rooms: 2 suites (PB) $95-110
Continental Breakfast
Credit Cards: none
Notes: 2, 5, 6 (dogs in garden suite only), 7, 8, 9, 10, 12

Joan's on Jones Bed and Breakfast

## Lion's Head Inn

120 E. Gaston St., 31401
(912) 232-4580; (800) 355-5466;
FAX (912) 232-7422

The stately 19th century mansion is situated in a quiet neighborhood just north of picturesque Forsyth Park. This lovely 9,200 square-foot home is exquisitely appointed with four-poster beds, private baths, period furnishings, fireplaces, TVs, and telephones. Each morning enjoy a deluxe continental breakfast, and in the evening enjoy wine and cheese on the sweeping veranda overlooking the marbled courtyard.

Hostess: Christy Dell'Orco
Rooms: 6 (PB) $85-125
Continental Deluxe Breakfast
Credit Cards: A, B, C
Notes: 2, 5, 7, 8, 9, 10, 12

## SENOIA

## Culpepper House B&B

35 Broad St., 30276
(404) 599-8182

Step back 120 years to casual Victorian elegance at the Culpepper House. Enjoy a four-poster canopy bed next to a fireplace, with sounds of the night coming through the window. . . . Wake to a gourmet breakfast then take a tandem bike ride through the historic town, visit area shops and picturesque countryside, or just sit on the porch and rock. Only 30 minutes from Atlanta.

Hostess: Maggie Armstrong
Rooms: 3 (1PB; 2SB) $75
Full Gourmet Breakfast
Credit Cards: A, B, C
Notes: 2, 5, 6 (limited), 8, 9, 10, 12

5 Open all year; 6 Pets welcome; 7 Children welcome; 8 Tennis nearby; 9 Swimming nearby; 10 Golf nearby; 11 Skiing nearby; 12 May be booked through travel agent.

## STONE MOUNTAIN

### The Village Inn B&B

992 Ridge Avenue, 30083
(770) 469-3459; (800) 214-8385

This c. 1850's inn is situated in the quaint historic village of Stone Mountain, just three-quarters mile from Stone Mountain Park. Fifteen miles east of Atlanta. Charming rooms, like Scarlett's with private entry or Rhett's with great balcony view, are warmly decorated with period antiques. Fireplaces, whirlpool tubs, ceiling fans, AC. Full Southern breakfast and turn-down treats. Walk to shops and restaurants. Come enjoy our Southern hospitality!

Hosts: Rob and Deandra Bailey
Rooms: 5 (PB) $80-130
Full, Sit-Down Breakfast
Credit Cards: A, B, C, D
Notes: 2, 5, 6 (boarding available), 7, 8, 9, 10, 12

## THOMASVILLE

### Deer Creek Bed and Breakfast

1304 Old Monticello Rd., 31792
(912) 226-7294

Visit the world renowned 19th century resort, Thomasville, GA, frequently visited by presidents and inhabited by business tycoons. Affordable luxury is offered at Deer Creek, nestled among pines and magnolias on beautiful grounds sloping to a stream. Suite with full breakfast served elegantly in private dining room. Beamed 16 foot Cathedral ceiling, large fireplace, and ceiling fans

in suite opening to treetop deck. Private bath. Window walls afford scenic views. Next to the South's second oldest golf course. Near historic tours, antique shops, and fine restaurants.

Hosts: Bill and Gladys Muggidge
Rooms: a 1600 square foot suite; $75-90
Full Breakfast
Credit Cards: none
Notes: 2, 5, 7, 10, 12 (min. 2 night stay)

## TIFTON

### Hummingbirds Perch Bed and Breakfast

305 Adams Rd., **Chula** 31733
(912) 382-5431

Hummingbird's Perch is a traditional modern brick home that has a large front porch with a porch swing and rocking chairs where weary guests can relax and enjoy the beauty that surrounds them. There on the porch, the fragrance, color, and splendor of the many flower beds greets each visitor from sunrise to sunset.

Hostess: Frances Wilson
Rooms: 3 (1PB; 2SB) $70 + tax
Full or Continental Breakfast
Credit Cards: A, B, C
Notes: 2, 5, 7, 9, 10

Hummingbirds Perch Bed and Breakfast

## VILLA RICA

### Twin Oaks Bed and Breakfast, Cottages, and Reservations
9565 E. Liberty Rd., 30180
(770) 459-4374; (800) 459-4374

A uniquely intimate bed and breakfast located on a 23-acre farm only thirty minutes from Atlanta. There are two exquisite guest cottages ideal for honeymoons or celebrating anniversaries. There are also two private suites on the property. All accommodations have hot tubs or jacuzzis, fireplaces, private bathrooms, queen size beds, TV, VCR, refrigerators, microwaves, and coffee makers. There is a swimming pool on the property, walking trails, horseback riding, and lots of exotic animals for feeding and viewing.

Hosts: Earl and Carol Turner
Rooms: 2 suites; 2 cottages (PB) $85-105
Full Breakfast
Credit Cards: C
Notes: 2, 5, 9, 10, 12

## WARM SPRINGS

### Hotel Warm Springs
17 Broad St., P.O. Box 351, 31830
(706) 655-2114; (800) 366-7616

Relive history and the Roosevelt Era in our 1907 hotel, ice cream parlor, and gift shops. Authentically restored and beautifully decorated with Roosevelt furniture and family antiques. Featuring our cozy honeymoon suite with king bed, suspended canopy, Victorian antiques, red heart tub, gold fixtures, breakfast in bed, flowers, champagne, and chocolates. Our large living and dining room with Queen Anne furniture, Oriental rugs, and crystal teardrop chandelier is ideal for group meetings. Nestled in quaint Warm Springs Village—a shopper's paradise, home of FDR's Little White House, 14 miles from Callaway Gardens, and one hour from Atlanta.

Hostess: Geraldine (Gerrie) Thompson
Rooms: 14 (PB) $60-160
Southern Breakfast Feast
Credit Cards: A, B, C, D
Notes: 2, 3, 4, 5, 7, 8, 9, 10, 11 (water), 12

---

5 Open all year; 6 Pets welcome; 7 Children welcome; 8 Tennis nearby; 9 Swimming nearby;
10 Golf nearby; 11 Skiing nearby; 12 May be booked through travel agent.

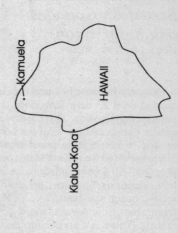

HAWAII

KAUAI
Princeville
Koloa

OAHU
Kaneohe
Kailua
Aiea  Kapaau

MAUI
Lahaina
Kula

HAWAII
Kamuela
Kialua-Kona

# Hawaii

## HAWAII—KAILUA

### Bed and Breakfast By the Sea

111 Haokea Drive, 96734
(808) 261-2644 (voice and FAX)

Bed and Breakfast By the Sea—Kailua/Lanikai—are beachside communities which boasts the best hiking, snorkeling, kayaking, and wind surfing. Enjoy white sandy beaches and sparkling turquoise waters. Studios, cottages, and oceanfront homes are available with kitchens and kitchenettes, TV's, and telephones. Many hosts offer information about local island accessories.

Hosts: Gabriel and Paulette Vigil
Studios, cottages, + oceanfront homes $69-250
Continental Breakfast
Credit Cards: none
Notes: 5, 7, 8, 9

## HAWAII—KAMUELA

### Kamuela Inn

P.O. Box 1994, 96743
(808) 885-4243; FAX (808) 885-8857

Comfortable, cozy rooms and suites with private baths, with or without kitchenettes, and all with cable, color television. Complimentary continental breakfast served in our coffee lanai every morning. Situated in a quiet, peaceful setting just off Highway 19. Conveniently located near shops, retail outlets, banks, theaters, parks, tennis courts, museums, restaurants, and post office. The big island's famous white sand beaches, golf courses, horseback rides, and valley and mountain tours are only minutes away.

Hostess: Carolyn Cascavilla
Rooms: 31 (PB) $54-165
Continental Breakfast
Credit Cards: A, B, C, D, E
Notes: 2, 5, 7, 8, 9, 10, 11, 12

## HAWAII—KANEOHE

### Aurora's Place

47-680 Hui Ulili St., 96744
(808) 239-1210

This house, 17 years old, is very comfortable with five bedrooms and three baths, family room, dining room, kitchen, swimming pool, etc. The guests

---

NOTES: Credit cards accepted: A Master Card; B Visa; C American Express; D Discover; E Diners Club; F Other; 2 Personal checks accepted; 3 Lunch available; 4 Dinner available; 5 Open all year; 6 Pets welcome; 7 Children welcome; 8 Tennis nearby; 9 Swimming nearby; 10 Golf nearby; 11 Skiing nearby; 12 May be booked through travel agent.

may use the swimming pool, washer and dryer, microwave, family room, and backyard. No smoking inside.

Hosts: Aurora and Steve
Rooms: 5 (2PB; 3SB) $38 ($25 single)
Continental Breakfast
Credit Cards: none
Notes: 2 (4 weeks in advance), 5, 7, 9

## HAWAII—KAPAÀU

### Big Sky Ranch

P.O. Box 1468, 96755
(808) 889-0500; (800) 277-0509
(808) 889-0564 (FAX)

The Big Sky Ranch, an exotic Hawaiian getaway, lies on the tip of the Kohala Gold Coast in northern Hawaii. This resort location is accessible to a variety of activities including horseback riding, tennis, golf, deep sea fishing, hiking, swimming, and even skiing in the mountains nearby. Late night strolls along the ocean are also a great way to relax and enjoy the true beauty of the islands. The actual ranch has one to two bedrooms with king-size beds, a complete kitchen and even a small TV room.

Hostess: Doris Reichert
Rooms: 1 bedroom (2 guests) = $135;
2 bedrooms (4 guests) = $175
Breakfast fixings included
Credit Cards: A, B
Notes: 2, 5, 7, 9, 10, 12

## KAILUA—KONA

### Hale Maluhai B&B

76-770 Hualalai Rd., 96740
(808) 329-5773; (800) 559-6627
FAX (808) 326-5487

Gracious up-country Kona plantation hide-a-way, off the beaten path, on a beautiful acre of Holualoa coffee land. Large rambling home with good beds, private baths, and plenty of room to have some time alone. Exceptional Japanese slate and tile spa, massage table, and beach/snorkel equipment. Full buffet breakfast with farm eggs, ham, daily fresh breads, local fruits and juices, and 100% pure Kona coffee. Also included is cable TV/VCR, first class video library, and games including Sega. Easy access to Kona airport and close to town. The discovery of Hale Maluhai, in the heart of the Kona recreational paradise, is the fulfillment of many who dream of experiencing a touch of old Hawaii. Please write or call for a free brochure.

Hosts: Ken and Ann Smith
Rooms: 5 + 2 cottages (PB) $45-126
Breakfast Lovers Buffet
Credit Cards: A, B, C, D
Notes: 2, 5, 6, 7, 8, 9, 10, 11, 12

## KAUAI—KOLOA

### Island Home

1707 Kelaukia St., 96756
(808) 742-2839; (800) 555-3881

Enjoy Kauai's sunny south shore at Island Home in Poipu. Just minutes to

---

NOTES: Credit cards accepted: A Master Card; B Visa; C American Express; D Discover; E Diners Club; F Other; 2 Personal checks accepted; 3 Lunch available; 4 Dinner available;

Island Home

walk to great snorkeling and swimming beaches, turtle watching, restaurants, and the beautiful Hyatt Regency. Our units offer private entrances, lanai or deck, TVs, VCRs, telephones, compact refrigerators, microwaves, beach and picnic gear with laundry facilities available. Queen- or king-size beds are offered. Inquire about special rates for those in ministry. Three night minimum.

Hosts: Michael and Gail Beeson
Rooms: 2 (PB) $65-75
Continental Breakfast
Credit Cards: none
Notes: 2 (and travelers'), 5, 8, 9, 10, 12

## KAUAI—PRINCEVILLE

## Hale 'Aha
## "House of Gathering"
3875 Kamehameha Dr., P.O. Box 3370, 96722
(808) 826-6733; (800) 826-6733
FAX (808) 826-9052

VACATION, HONEYMOON, or RETREAT in this peaceful resort setting on the golf course, overlooking the ocean and majestic mountains of the Garden Isle. On one side enjoy Hanalei, where "South Pacific" was filmed, with one beach after another leading you to the famous, lush, Napoli Coast hiking trails. Hale' Aha has been written about in many books and magazines, but only a brochure can tell it all. Enjoy bananas, papayas, and pineapple from your host's garden.

Hosts: Herb and Ruth Bockelman
Rooms: 2 + 2 suites (PB) $85-210
"More Than" Continental Breakfast
Credit Cards: A, B
Notes: 2, 5, 8, 9, 10, 12

## MAUI—KULA

## Elaine's Up Country Guest Rooms
2112 Noalae Rd., 96790
(808) 878-6623; FAX (808) 878-2619

Quiet country setting. Splendid ocean and mountain views. All rooms have private baths, full kitchens, and sitting room privileges. Guests are welcome to cook breakfast or whatever meals they like. Next to our main house is a delightful cottage made to order for a family. One bedroom with queen-size bed and twin beds in the loft. Large kitchen.

5 Open all year; 6 Pets welcome; 7 Children welcome; 8 Tennis nearby; 9 Swimming nearby; 10 Golf nearby; 11 Skiing nearby; 12 May be booked through travel agent.

We ask that our guests do not smoke or drink.

Hosts: Elaine and Murray Gildersleeve
Rooms: 3 + a cottage (PB) $55-110 + tax
No Breakfast served
Credit Cards: F
Notes: 2, 5, 7, 9, 10, 12

## MAUI—LAHAINA

### Blue Horizons

P.O. Box 10578, 96761
(808) 665-0054; (800) 669-1948

Want to mingle over breakfast, yet have all the privacy of your own one-bedroom apartment complete with private bath and kitchen? This spacious B&B offers it all! Just minutes north of Lahaina and with great views of Lanai and Molkai, choose one of our two guest rooms with private bath or one of three kitchen units. Feel right at home at poolside or while viewing spectacular ocean sunsets!

Hosts: Jim and Beverly Spence
Rooms: 5 (PB) $75-95
Continental Breakfast
Credit Cards: A, B, C
Notes: 2, 5, 9, 10, 12

### Old Lahaina House

P.O. Box 10355, 96761
(808) 667-4663; (800) 847-0761;
FAX (808) 667-5615

All rooms have air-conditioning, TV, phone, and other features. 27,000 gallon, specially treated pool and private tropical courtyard. Serene neighborhood beach. All rooms non-smoking. Two blocks from historic Lahaina town. Wonderful fellowship and aloha. Your "home" away from home. Excellent rental car rates. Call us, let us answer your questions. We hope to hear from you.

Hosts: John and Sherry Barbier
Rooms: 5 (2PB; 3SB) $50-95
Tropical Continental Breakfast
Credit Cards: A, B, C
Notes: 5, 7, 8, 9, 10, 12

Old Lahaina House

### Nelson Ohana

P.O. Box 5288, 87 S. Iwa Pl., 96761
(808) 661-3377; FAX (808) 667-5573

Relax at our luxurious family home overlooking Kaanapali Beach Resort. Bathe in the sun at poolside just steps away from your private entrance or ponder in the sweet fragrance and shade of our pristine gardens. Let us start your day with a health-minded breakfast and the inside on Maui's activities and places to dine. Immaculate surroundings and our guest accommodations are complete with TV, telephone, CD

NOTES: Credit cards accepted: A Master Card; B Visa; C American Express; D Discover; E Diners Club; F Other; 2 Personal checks accepted; 3 Lunch available; 4 Dinner available;

player, microwave, refrigerator, queen bed, and private bath.

Hosts: Sky and Cheyenne Nelson
Rooms: 1 PB $75
Continental Breakfast
Credit Cards: none
Notes: 2, 5, 8, 9, 10

## The Walkus House

1620 Ainakea Rd., 96761
(808) 661-8085; (800) 621-8942;
FAX (808) 661-1896

Visit Maui . . . from home to home. . . . Have the privacy of this entirely new four-bedroom, three bath home (the den can be used as a fifth bedroom). Sunbathe at poolside, relax in the jacuzzi, or take a short stroll to "Baby Beach" right in Lahaina. With central air conditioning, modern laundry facilities, and a kitchen that lacks nothing, you'll be right at home. Great for families or small groups.

Rooms: 4 + den (1PB; 4SB) $295
Self-serve Breakfast
Credit Cards: A, B, C, D
Notes: 2, 5, 7, 8, 9, 10

## OAHU—AIEA

## Above Pearl Harbor

899-442 KEKOA Place, 96701
(808) 487-1228, (800) 999-6026;
FAX (808) 261-6573 or (808) 487-1228

Lush tropical garden. Two bedrooms,

bath, living room, complete kitchen. Upstairs apartment in two-story private home. Sleeps up to five guests. Antique oriental furniture.

Hostess: Doris Reichert
Rooms: 1 two-bedroom apartment (PB) $65-75
Continental Breakfast
Credit Cards: A, B
Notes: 2, 5, 7, 12

## OAHU—KAILUA

## Auntie Barbara's

516-A N. Kainalu Dr., 96734
(808) 262-7420 (voice and FAX)

Located on the beautiful windward side of Oahu in Kailua, Auntie Barbara's is nestled between the awe inspiring Koolau Mountain range and the blue Pacific Ocean. A short, five-minute walk takes you to one of the most beautiful beaches on all of the islands, where you can enjoy four miles of uncrowded beach, spectacular sunrises, gentle waves, and wind surfing. The B&B is removed from the hectic activity of Waikiki, but close enough for those who want an evening of entertainment.

Hosts: Joseph and Barbara Carvalho
Rooms: 1 (PB) $55
Continental Breakfast
Credit Cards: none
Notes: 2, 5, 8, 9, 10

---

5 Open all year; 6 Pets welcome; 7 Children welcome; 8 Tennis nearby; 9 Swimming nearby; 10 Golf nearby; 11 Skiing nearby; 12 May be booked through travel agent.

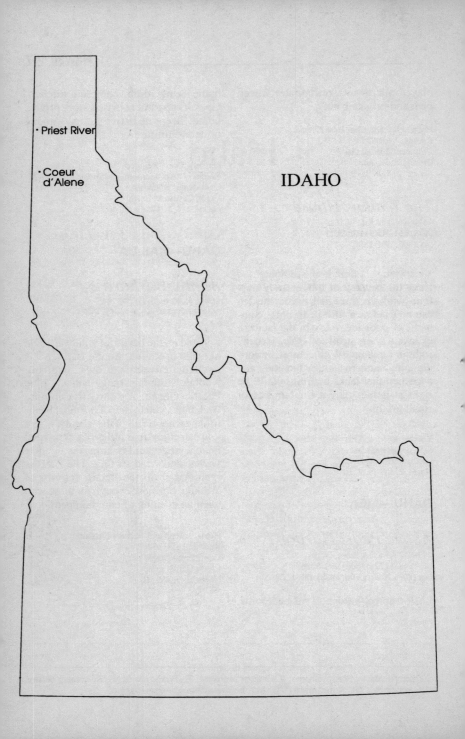

· Priest River

· Coeur
d'Alene

IDAHO

# Idaho

## COEUR D'ALENE

### Gregory's McFarland House Bed and Breakfast

601 Foster Ave., 83814
(208) 664-1232 (voice and FAX)

Surrender to the elegance of this award-winning historical home, circa 1905. The full breakfast is gourmet to the last crumb. Guests will be delighted by an ideal blending of beauty, comfort, and clean surroundings. Jerry Hulse, travel editor for *The Los Angeles Times* wrote, "Entering Gregory McFarland's House is like stepping back 100 years to an unhurried time when four posters were in fashion and lace curtains fluttered at the windows." Private baths, air-conditioning, non-smoking house. If planning a wedding, our resident minister and professional photographer are available to make your special day beautiful.

Hosts: Winifred, Carol, and Stephen Gregory
Rooms: 5 (PB) $75-125 + tax
Full Gourmet Breakfast
Credit Cards: A, B
Notes: 2, 5, 8, 9, 10, 11, 12

### Katie's Wild Rose Inn

E. 5150 Couer d'Alene Lake Dr., 83814
(208) 765-WISH (voice and FAX)

Looking through the pine trees to Lake Couer d'Alene, Katie's Wild Rose Inn is a haven for the weary traveler. Only ten miles from the public dock and beach, the inn has four cozy rooms, one with its own jacuzzi. Guests can relax in the family room beside the fireplace or enjoy a game of pool. A full breakfast is served on the deck or in the dining room where you can admire the view.

Hosts: Joisse and Lee Knowles
Rooms: 4 (2PB; 2SB) $55-95
Full Breakfast
Credit Cards: A, B
Notes: 5, 8, 9, 10, 11, 12

Katie's Wild Rose Inn

---

NOTES: Credit cards accepted: A Master Card; B Visa; C American Express; D Discover; E Diners Club; F Other; 2 Personal checks accepted; 3 Lunch available; 4 Dinner available; 5 Open all year; 6 Pets welcome; 7 Children welcome; 8 Tennis nearby; 9 Swimming nearby; 10 Golf nearby; 11 Skiing nearby; 12 May be booked through travel agent.

## PRIEST LAKE

### *Whispering Waters Bed and Breakfast*

HCR 5, Box 125 B, 83856
(208) 443-3229

Located on the secluded shores of Priest Lake's Outlet Bay. Just minutes away from golf course, hiking, cross-country skiing and snowmobiling trails, gift shops, resorts, and restaurants. Three guest rooms; each has private bath, sitting area with parlor stove, view, outside access, and covered patio. Early morning juice or coffee delivered to the rooms.

Hosts: Lana and Ray Feldman
Rooms: 3 (PB) $85
Full Breakfast
Credit Cards: A, B
Notes: 2, 5, 9, 10, 11 (cross country), 12

# Illinois

## ARCOLA

### Curly's Corner Bed and Breakfast

425 E. Country Rd. 200 N., 61910
(217) 268-3352

This ranch-style, centrally air-conditioned farmhouse is located in the heart of a prairie farmland, quiet Amish community. Your hosts Warren and Maxine are dedicated to cordial hospitality and will gladly share information about the area and provide a suggested tour of Amish businesses. Curly's Corner has four lovely and comfortable bedrooms, queen-size beds, TVs, etc. In the morning enjoy a wonderful breakfast of homemade biscuits, fresh country sausage, bacon, eggs, etc.! Curly's Corner is one-half mile north of beautiful Rockome Gardens; also close to three universities and historical sites.

Hosts: Warren and Maxine Arthur
Rooms: 3 (2PB; 1SB) $50-60
Full Breakfast
Credit Cards: none
Notes: 2, 5, 7 (over 10), 8, 9, 10

## CHICAGO

### Amber Creek's Chicago Connection

1260 N. Dearborn, Chicago
(Mail: P.O. Box 5, **Galena, IL** 61036)
(815) 777-9320; FAX (815) 777-9432

A delightful one-bedroom apartment on the Gold Coast of Chicago in a quiet, secure building. Tastefully decorated with antiques and comfortable furniture. Spacious, light-filled living room with nice views, including the lake. Full kitchen and full bath. Romantic bedroom with king bed, down quilts, and extra pillows. Linens and towels provided. Walk to lake, Water Tower, and Michigan Avenue shopping. Half block to airport limousine service, and public transportation. Parking garage next door. Ideal for one couple. Queen-sized futon provides sleeping for additional guests.

Hosts: Kate Freeman
Rooms: 1 (PB) $95-125
Continental Breakfast
Credit Cards: A, B, C, D, E
Notes: 2, 3, 4, 7, 9, 12

---

5 Open all year; 6 Pets welcome; 7 Children welcome; 8 Tennis nearby; 9 Swimming nearby; 10 Golf nearby; 11 Skiing nearby; 12 May be booked through travel agent.

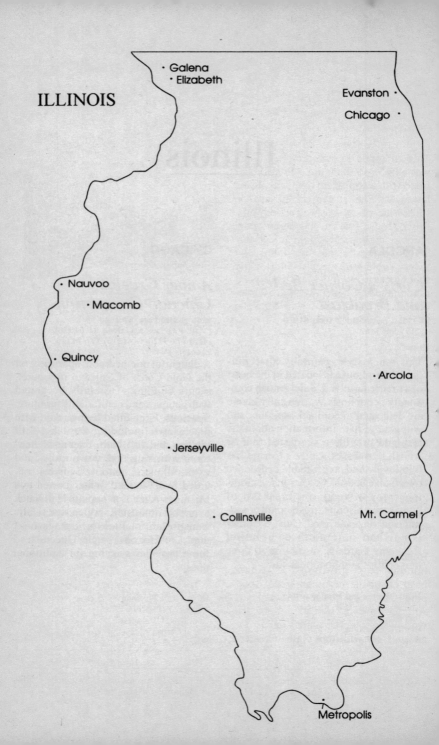

ILLINOIS

Galena
Elizabeth

Evanston
Chicago

Nauvoo
Macomb

Quincy

Arcola

Jerseyville

Collinsville

Mt. Carmel

Metropolis

## Chateau des Fleurs

552 Ridge Rd., Winnetka 60093
(708) 256-7272 (voice and FAX)

This authentic French, country home was built in 1936 on three-fourths acre filled with magnificent trees, expansive lawns, and English gardens. It's a home filled with antiques, as well as comforts. Private baths, jacuzzi, air-conditioning, hardwood floors, in-room telephone, TV, fireplaces in common rooms, and lovely views from every window. Only four blocks to Northwestern Train commuting to the Chicago loop in 30 minutes. Lake Michigan is 10 blocks and O'Hare Airport 30 minutes west.

Hostess: Sally Ward
Rooms: 3 (PB); $95
Full Breakfast
Credit Cards: none
Notes: 2, 5, 7 (over 11), 8, 9 (on grounds), 10, 11, 12

## COLLINSVILLE

## Maggie's Bed and Breakfast

2102 N. Keebler, 62234
(618) 344-8283

Beautiful, quiet, country setting just minutes from downtown St. Louis. Near hospitals, restaurants, and shopping. Cooking with natural ingredients. Antiques and art objects collected in worldwide travels. Games, cable TV, and hot tub with terrycloth robes and house slippers.

Hostess: Maggie Leyda
Rooms: 5 (4PB; 1SB) $35-70
Full Breakfast
Credit Cards: A, B
Notes: 2, 5, 6, 7 (by arrangement), 8, 9, 10, 12

Ridgeview Bed and Breakfast

## ELIZABETH/GALENA

## Ridgeview Bed and Breakfast

8833 S. Massbach Rd., 61028
(815) 598-3150

Experience a unique B&B in the hills of Galena/Jo Daviess County—a 1921 country school and the former residence of renowned artist Thomas Locker. Enjoy the fabulous ten-mile overview of Rush Creek Valley. Views formed by glacial intrusion. Full breakfast, private baths, color TV/VCR—50 movie video library, picnic tables. Kitchen privileges. Children and pets by special arrangements. Smoking limited to outside only.

Hosts: Elizabeth (Betty) Avaly
Rooms: 4 (PB) $79-99
Full Breakfast
Credit Cards: A, B
Notes: 2, 5, 6, 7, 9, 10, 11, 12

---

NOTES: Credit cards accepted: A Master Card; B Visa; C American Express; D Discover; E Diners Club; F Other; 2 Personal checks accepted; 3 Lunch available; 4 Dinner available; 5 Open all year; 6 Pets welcome; 7 Children welcome; 8 Tennis nearby; 9 Swimming nearby; 10 Golf nearby; 11 Skiing nearby; 12 May be booked through travel agent.

## EVANSTON

### The Margarita European Inn

1566 Oak Ave., 60201
(708) 869-2273; FAX (708) 869-2353

The romantic at heart will truly enjoy this charming European-style inn located next door to Chicago in Evanston, the home of Northwestern University. Relax in the grand parlor with breakfast and the morning paper or in the roof garden at sunset. Explore the numerous antique and specialty shops nearby. On rainy days, curl up with a novel from the wood-paneled English library, or indulge in a culinary creation from our award-winning regional Italian ristorante, Va Pensiero. Facilities for weddings and meetings are also available.

Hosts: Barbara and Tim Gorham
Rooms: 49 (16PB; 33SB) $60-100
Continental Breakfast
Credit Cards: A, B, C
Notes: 2, 3, 4, 5, 7, 8, 9, 10, 12

## GALENA

### Amber Creek's Eagle Nest

PO Box 5, 61036
(815) 777-9320

A quaint, charming Federal brick cottage built in 1842 and tucked into a private wooded hillside in Galena's historic district, within walking distance of shops and restaurants. It has been faithfully restored and furnished with antiques of the period. Living room with fireplace, master bedroom with queen bed, second bedroom with double bed. Fully equipped kitchen, bath with shower and double whirlpool, TV, stereo, deck, and grill. Crib available. Linens and towels provided. Perfect for history and antique buffs and those who appreciate authenticity. Ideal for one couple, but will also comfortably accommodate two couples or a small family.

Hosts: Kate Freeman
Rooms: $99-159 per night
Continental Breakfast
Credit Cards: A, B, C, D, E
Notes: 2, 5, 6, 7, 12

Avery Guest House

### Avery Guest House

606 S. Prospect St., 61036
(815) 777-3883

This Pre-Civil War home located near Galena's main shopping and historic buildings is a homey refuge after a day of exploring. Enjoy the view from our porch swing, feel free to watch TV, or join a table game. Sleep soundly on comfortable queen beds. Our delicious full breakfast is served in our sunny dining room with a bay window overlook-

NOTES: Credit cards accepted: A Master Card; B Visa; C American Express; D Discover; E Diners Club; F Other; 2 Personal checks accepted; 3 Lunch available; 4 Dinner available;

ing the valley. Mississippi riverboats nearby.

Hosts: Gerry and Armon Lamparelli
Rooms: 4 (SB) $65-75
Full Breakfast
Credit Cards: A, B, D
Notes: 2, 5, 8, 9, 10, 11

Belle Aire Mansion Guest House

# Belle Aire Mansion Guest House

11410 Route 20 W., 61036
(815) 777-0893

Belle Aire Mansion guest house is a pre-Civil War Federal home surrounded by eleven well-groomed acres that include extensive lawns, flowers, and a block-long, tree-lined driveway. We do our best to make our guests feel they are special friends.

Hosts: Jan and Lorraine Svec
Rooms: 5 (PB) $65-140
Full Breakfast
Credit Cards: A, B, D
Notes: 2, 7, 8, 10, 12

# Brierwreath Manor Bed and Breakfast

216 N. Bench St., 61036
(815) 777-0608

Brierwreath Manor, circa 1884, is just one block from Galena's Main Street and has a dramatic and inviting wrap-around porch that beckons to you after a hard day. The house is furnished in an eclectic blend of antique and early American. You'll not only relax but feel right at home. Two suites offer gas-log fireplaces. Central air-conditioning, ceiling fans, and cable TV add to your enjoyment.

Hosts: Mike and Lyn Cook
Rooms: 3 (PB) $85-95
Full Breakfast
Credit Cards: none
Notes: 2, 5, 8, 9, 10, 11

# Forget-Me-Not B&B

1467 N. Elizabeth Scales Mound Rd., Elizabeth 61028
(815) 858-3744 (voice and FAX)

Each guest room features a queen-size bed, private bath, patio, and air-conditioning and heat control. Rooms are spacious and romantically decorated to suit any occasion. . .birthdays, honeymoons, anniversaries, etc. Relax in a large comfortable great room decorated with imported German furnishings. Gaze at deer and turkeys from your guest room window overlooking miles of countryside. Fifteen minutes from historic Galena and Apple Canyon Lake. Five minutes from Eagle Ridge Territory. Very scenic routes.

Hosts: Christa and Richard Grunert
Rooms: 3 (PB) $65-85
Full Breakfast
Credit Cards: A, B
Notes: 2, 5, 7 (12 and older), 8, 9, 10, 11

5 Open all year; 6 Pets welcome; 7 Children welcome; 8 Tennis nearby; 9 Swimming nearby; 10 Golf nearby; 11 Skiing nearby; 12 May be booked through travel agent.

## Park Avenue Guest House

208 Park Ave., 61036
(815) 777-1075

1893 Queen Anne Painted Lady. Wrap-around screened porch, gardens, and gazebo for summer. Fireplace and opulent Victorian Christmas in winter. One suite sleeps three, and there are three antique-filled guest rooms, all with queen-size beds and fireplaces. Located in quiet residential area, it is only a short walk to Grant Park or across footbridge to Main Street shopping and restaurants.

Hosts: John and Sharon Fallbacher
Rooms: 4 (PB) $70-105
Hearty Continental Breakfast
Credit Cards: A, B, D
Notes: 2, 5, 8, 9, 10, 11

## Pine Hollow Inn

4700 N. Council Hill Rd., 61036
(815) 777-1071

Pine Hollow is located on a secluded 120 acre Christmas tree farm just one mile from Main Street Galena. Roam around the grounds and enjoy the wild-life or simply put your feet up, lean back and enjoy the country from our front porch. We provide all the comforts of home in a beautiful country setting. Each of our rooms is decorated in a country style with four poster queen-size beds, fireplaces, and private bath. Whirlpool bath suites are available.

Hosts: Sally and Larry Priske
Rooms: 5 (PB) $75-110
Continental Breakfast
Credit Cards: A, B, D
Notes: 2, 5, 8, 9, 10, 11, 12

The Homeridge Bed and Breakfast

## JERSEYVILLE

## The Homeridge B&B

1470 N. State St., 62052
(618) 498-3442

Beautiful, warm, brick 1867 Italianate Victorian private home on 18 acres in a comfortable, country atmosphere. Drive through stately iron gates and pine tree-lined driveway to 14-room historic estate of Senator Theodore Chapman. Expansive pillared front porch; hand-carved, curved stairway to spacious guest rooms and third floor. 20' by 40' swimming pool. Central air-conditioning. Located between Springfield, IL, and St. Louis, MO.

Hosts: Sue and Howard Landon
Rooms: 4 (SB) $65
Full Breakfast
Credit Cards: A, B
Notes: 2, 5, 7 (over 14), 8, 9 (on grounds), 10

## MACOMB

## The Pineapple Inn, Inc.

204 West Jefferson St., 61455
(309) 837-1914 (voice and FAX)

The Pineapple Inn, Inc., located in Old Town Macomb, Illinois, is within walk-

---

NOTES: Credit cards accepted: A Master Card; B Visa; C American Express; D Discover; E Diners Club; F Other; 2 Personal checks accepted; 3 Lunch available; 4 Dinner available;

ing distance of the central business district and the historic country courthouse. 45 miles from Nauvoo, IL. The Inn is a Queen Anne Victorian built in the late 1800's. It has central air-conditioning/ heating and all guest rooms have private baths. Traditionally, the pineapple has been used as a symbol of warmth and hospitality traced back to Colonial Williamsburg, Virginia. In keeping with the historic symbolism, the innkeepers seek to provide their guests with the same warmth and Southern hospitality as of bygone days.

Hosts: Dr. K Dale and Wanda Adkins
Rooms: 5 (PB) $49-99
Full Breakfast
Credit Cards: none
Notes: 2, 3, 4, 5, 7, 8, 9, 10, 12

Park Street House

## METROPOLIS

## *Park Street House*

310 Park St., 62960
(618) 524-5966; (800) 524-5916

Graced with original oak woodwork, antiques, and private collections, each room has unique character. This circa 1910 home is ideally located in a small rivertown within walking distance to shops, restaurants, riverfront and the Superman museum. Minutes away from Fort Massac State Park, the American Quilt Museum, antique shops, and many scenic parks with hiking trails. Enjoy breakfast in the dining room or on the veranda overlooking Washington Park. Resident, bent willow furniture craftsman.

Hosts: Ron and Melodee Thomas
Rooms: 2 (PB) $35-65
Full Breakfast
Credit Cards: A, B
Notes: 2, 5, 7, 8, 10

## MOUNT CARMEL

## *The Poor Farm Bed and Breakfast*

Poor Farm Rd., 62863
(618) 262-HOME (4663); (800) 646-FARM (3276); FAX (618) 262-8199

From 1857 to 1949 the Wabash Country Poor Farm served as home for the homeless. Today the Poor Farm B&B is a home for the traveler who enjoys a warm friendly atmosphere and a gracious glimpse of yesteryear. Located next to a 25-acre park with a well-stocked lake; within walking distance from perhaps the finest 18-hole municipal golf course in Illinois; and a 15-minute drive lands you in the spectacular 270-acre Beall Woods Conservation Area and Nature Preserve!

Hosts: Liz and John Stelzer
Rooms: 5 (2 suites and 3 doubles) (PB) $49-89
Full Country Breakfast
Credit Cards: A, B, C, D
Notes: 2, 3 and 4 (for groups of 10-30), 5, 7, 8, 9, 10, 12

---

5 Open all year; 6 Pets welcome; 7 Children welcome; 8 Tennis nearby; 9 Swimming nearby; 10 Golf nearby; 11 Skiing nearby; 12 May be booked through travel agent.

## NAUVOO

### Mississippi Memories Bed and Breakfast

1 Riverview Terrace, 62354
(217) 453-2771

Located on the banks of the Mississippi, this gracious home offers peaceful lodging and elegantly served, all homemade, full breakfast. Each room features fresh fruit and flowers. In quiet, wooded surroundings, it's just two miles from historic Nauvoo with 30 restored Mormon, era homes and shops. Two decks offer spectacular sunsets, drifting barges, bald eagle watching, piano, two fireplaces, and library. AAA three-diamond rated. No smoking, alcohol, or pets will interrupt you stay.

Hosts: Marge and Dean Starr
Rooms: 4 (2 PB; 2 SB) $59-89
Full Breakfast
Credit Cards: A, B
Notes: 2, 5, 9, 10, 12

## QUINCY

### The Kaufmann House

1641 Hampshire, 62301
(217) 223-2502

Heart-warming hospitality, that's what you feel as you are welcomed into the genuine Midwest charm and hospitality of Quincy, the twice-acclaimed "All-American City." Imagine yourself sleeping in an intimate Victorian bed chamber, freshly treated with flowers and light, or slumbering on a painted iron bed among brightly pieced quilts in the simplicity of early American atmosphere . . . then waking to the delicious aroma of piping hot, homemade rolls, coffee and tea, complemented by chilled, fresh fruit—served to you on the stone terraced patio or the antique-filled Ancestor Room. Come, indulge and pamper yourself.

Hosts: Emery and Bettie Kaufmann
Rooms: 3 (1PB; 2SB) $45-65
Gourmet Continental Breakfast
Credit Cards: none
Notes: 2, 5, 7, 8, 9, 10, 11 (cross country)

---

NOTES: Credit cards accepted: A Master Card; B Visa; C American Express; D Discover; E Diners Club; F Other; 2 Personal checks accepted; 3 Lunch available; 4 Dinner available;

# Indiana

## AUBURN

### Hill Top Country Inn
1733 Co. Rd. 28, 46706
(219) 281-2298

The Hill Top Country Inn offers a quiet and beautiful setting with country porches, wicker furniture, walking areas, small fish pond with fountain, and distinctive bed chambers and sitting room. Our rooms are decorated with a variety of quilts, stenciling, country antiques, a formal dining room, and farm kitchen with an old fashioned cook stove. Places to visit in the area include antique shops, car museum, lakes, and parks.

Hosts: Chuck and Becky Derrow
Rooms: 4 (1PB; 3SB) $45-60
Full Breakfast
Credit Cards: none
Notes: 2, 5, 7, 12

Hill Top Country Inn

### Yawn to Dawn B&B
211 W. 5th St., 46706
(219) 925-2583; FAX (219) 927-1202

Enjoy the friendly atmosphere of a 1900s home decorated with touches of antiques and collectibles. Within the Auburn area you'll find the Auburn Cord Duesenberg Museum, The National Auto and Trucks Railroad and Art Museums, shopping malls, theaters, Pokagon State Park, fine dining, golf courses, and a beautiful children's zoo, all located five to 30 minutes from Yawn to Dawn. Whether traveling I-69 or the IL/IN/OH toll road, Yawn to Dawn is your place to rest.

Hosts: Don and Shirley Quick
Rooms: 3 (SB) $45
Full Breakfast
Credit Cards: none
Notes: 2, 5, 8, 9, 10, 11

## BRISTOL

### Tyler's Place
19560 St. Rt. 120, 46507
(219) 848-7145

Tyler's Place is located in the heart of Amish country. On a 27-hole golf course, with five rooms available. You can relax on the deck, enjoying the outdoor water garden and the warm

5 Open all year; 6 Pets welcome; 7 Children welcome; 8 Tennis nearby; 9 Swimming nearby; 10 Golf nearby; 11 Skiing nearby; 12 May be booked through travel agent.

# INDIANA

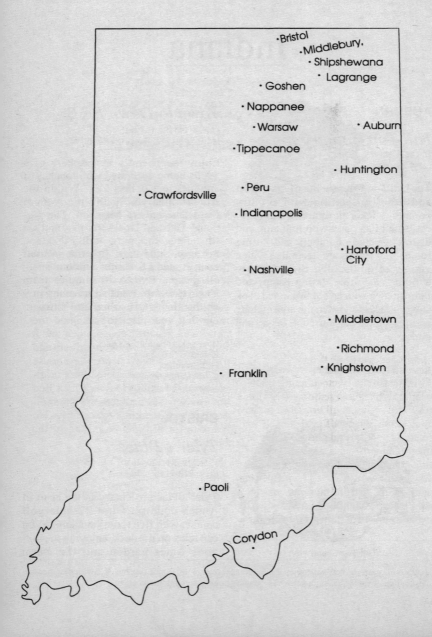

• Bristol
• Middlebury •
• Shipshewana
• Lagrange
• Goshen
• Nappanee
• Warsaw
• Auburn
• Tippecanoe
• Huntington
• Peru
• Crawfordsville
• Indianapolis
• Hartoford City
• Nashville
• Middletown
• Richmond
• Franklin
• Knightstown
• Paoli
Corydon
•

Hoosier hospitality. Full Breakfast. Enjoy a back-roads tour of Amish country. Three miles from I80-90 toll road.

Hosts: Ron and Esther Tyler
Rooms: 4 (2PB; 2SB) $50-75
Full Breakfast
Credit Cards: A, B
Notes: 2, 5, 7, 8, 9, 10, 11

Tyler's Place

## CORYDON

## *Kinter House Inn*

201 S. Capital Ave., 47112
(812) 738-2020; (812) 738-7430 (FAX)

AAA rated, this completely restored inn is furnished with Victorian and country antiques. The Inn features five fireplaces and serves a full breakfast in the dining room. The staff prides itself on personal attention and guests' comfort. Fifteen elegant rooms all with private baths and color TVs; five with fireplaces and seven with VCRs. Nearby are unique shops, fine restaurants, antique malls, historical buildings, art glass factory, and an excursion train. All this

within walking distance, as well as a Civil War battle site not far from town. A hideaway for romantics that is located in historical downtown Corydon, Indiana's first state capital.

Hosts: Blaine H. Wiseman
Rooms: 15 (PB) $39-89
Full Breakfast
Credit Cards: A, B, C, D, E
Notes: 2, 5, 8, 9, 10, 11

## CRAWFORDSVILLE

## *Sugar Creek Queen Anne Bed and Breakfast*

901 W. Market, Box 726, 47933
(317) 362-4095

Sugar Creek's decor is Victorian with a French Provincial touch. The turn-of-the-century home has two guest rooms with private baths and a honeymoon suite complete with a private sitting room and a private bath. Behind the house is a beautiful rose garden and a fourth guest room with private bath and a jacuzzi and fitness center. The house has been newly remodeled with originality and creativity. Sugar Creek Bed and Breakfast is a member of the Indiana Bed and Breakfast Association. No smoking or alcohol permitted in the building.

Hostess: Mary Alice Barbee
Rooms: 4 (PB) $55
Full Breakfast
Credit Cards: A, B
Notes: 2, 5, 7, 8, 9, 10, 12

---

NOTES: Credit cards accepted: A Master Card; B Visa; C American Express; D Discover; E Diners Club; F Other; 2 Personal checks accepted; 3 Lunch available; 4 Dinner available; 5 Open all year; 6 Pets welcome; 7 Children welcome; 8 Tennis nearby; 9 Swimming nearby; 10 Golf nearby; 11 Skiing nearby; 12 May be booked through travel agent.

## FRANKLIN

### Oak Haven B&B

Route #2, Box 57, 46131
(317) 535-9491

A 1913 home nestled among stately trees that give a feeling of tranquillity to our country setting. Beautifully decorated rooms, family keepsakes, and oak woodwork throughout our "haven." Play the player piano or relax on the old porch swing. Perfect get-away for those with romance in their hearts or peaceful seclusion on their minds. Full country breakfast is served. Easy to find and 25 minutes south of Indianapolis. Close to shopping and golf. Come experience our country hospitality!

Hosts: Alan and Brenda Smith with Bert and Chris Foster
Rooms: 4 (3PB; 1SB) $45-70
Full Breakfast
Credit Cards: A, B
Notes: 2, 5, 7, 10

Oak Haven Bed and Breakfast

## GOSHEN

### Indian Creek B&B

20300 Co. Rd. 18, 46526
(219) 875-6606

Come and enjoy our newly built country Victorian home in the middle of Amish country. It is decorated with family antiques. Walk back to the woods or sit on the deck to watch for deer. Also enjoy the great room, game room, and family room. Full breakfast. Children welcome. Handicap accessible.

Hosts: Herman and Shirley Hochstetler
Rooms: 4 (PB) $65
Full Breakfast
Credit Cards: A, B, D
Notes: 2, 5, 7, 9, 10

### Timberidge Bed and Breakfast

16801 St. Rt. #4, 46526
(219) 533-7133

The Austrian chalet, white pine log home is nestled in the beauty of the quiet woods, just two miles from Goshen and near many local points of interest. Our guests enjoy the privacy of a master suite. A path through the woods is frequented by birds, squirrels, and deer. Nearby are Amish farms where field work is done by horse drawn equipment. Timberidge offers the best of city and country—close to town, yet removed to the majestic beauty of the woods that evokes a love of nature and a reverence for God's creation. Air-conditioning and TV.

Hosts: Edward and Donita Brookmyer
Rooms: 1 (PB) $60-70
Continental Breakfast
Credit Cards: none
Notes: 2

NOTES: Credit cards accepted: A Master Card; B Visa; C American Express; D Discover; E Diners Club; F Other; 2 Personal checks accepted; 3 Lunch available; 4 Dinner available;

## HARTFORD CITY

### De'Coys' Bed and Breakfast

1546 W. 100 N., 47348
(317) 348-2164

Located just west of Hartford City, Indiana, De'Coys' Bed and Breakfast offers its clients extraordinary, attractive guest rooms with many special "Hoosier" touches. Guests enjoy a relaxed rural atmosphere in an old, restored, country home enriched with many amenities not customary to the typical hotel or motel setting. Each room demonstrates its own character, featuring antique furnishings and comfortable arrangements. An overnight stay includes a complimentary breakfast consisting of homemade specialties served from the thrasher kitchen.

Hosts: Chris and Tiann Coy
Rooms: 5 (1PB; 4SB) $44-50
Full Breakfast
Credit Cards: none
Notes: 2, 5, 7

## HUNTINGTON

### Purviance House Bed and Breakfast

326 South Jefferson St., 46750
(219) 356-4218

Built in 1859, this beautiful home is on the National Register of Historic Places.

It features a winding, cherry staircase, ornate ceilings, unique fireplaces; and parquet floors and has been lovingly restored and decorated with antiques and period furnishings to create a warm, inviting atmosphere. Amenities include TV in rooms, snacks, beverages, kitchen privileges, and library. Near recreational areas with swimming, boating, hiking, and bicycling. Historic tours available. One-half hour from Fort Wayne; two hours from Indianapolis.

Hosts: Bob and Jean Gernand
Rooms: 4 (2PB; 2SB) $40-65
Full Breakfast
Credit Cards: A, B, D
Notes: 2, 5, 7, 8, 9, 10, 12

## INDIANAPOLIS

### Carriage House Bed and Breakfast

6440 N. Michigan Rd., 46268
(317) 255-2276 or (317) 255-5658

Relax and enjoy all the comforts of home in your own private suite. Located within 10 to 15 minutes of most Indianapolis events. Can accommodate groups of six to eight. Upstairs suite includes large whirlpool bath. Our facilities are smoke free and, please, no alcohol on the premises.

Hosts: David and Sue Wilson
Rooms: 2 (PB) $60-200
Full Breakfast
Credit Cards: none
Notes: 2, 5, 10

---

5 Open all year; 6 Pets welcome; 7 Children welcome; 8 Tennis nearby; 9 Swimming nearby; 10 Golf nearby; 11 Skiing nearby; 12 May be booked through travel agent.

Old Hoosier House

## KNIGHTSTOWN

### Old Hoosier House B&B

7601 S. Greensboro Pike, 46148
(317) 345-2969; (800) 775-5315

Central Indiana's first and favorite country bed and breakfast located in historic Knightstown, midway between Indianapolis and Richmond. Ideally situated for sightseeing and shopping Indiana's "Antique Alley." Golf on the adjoining eighteen hole Royal Highlands golf course. Golf package available. Handicap accessible. Member of Indiana Bed and Breakfast Association and American Historic Inn, Inc.

Hosts: Tom Lewis and Jean Lewis
Rooms: 4 (PB) $60-70 + tax
Full Breakfast
Credit Cards: none
Notes: 2, 5, 7, 8, 10, 12

## LAGRANGE

### Weaver's Country Oaks Bed and Breakfast

0310 N. US 20, 46761
(219) 768-7191

This very comfortable two-level home is located just three miles from Shipshewana, amongst Amish farmland. Located on three and a half acres of well landscaped property. Tasteful country decor throughout the home with delicious country breakfast. Special rates for full-house reservations. Open all year. Nearby attractions include reknowned summer flea market, weekly auctions, golf courses, natural wildlife reserves, museums, many shops, and Amish stores.

Hosts: Cathy and Rocky Weaver
Rooms: 4 (PB) $65-75
Full Breakfast
Credit Cards: A, B
Notes: 2, 5, 8, 10

## MADISON

### Schussler House Bed and Breakfast

514 Jefferson St., 47250
(812) 273-2078; (800) 392-1931

Experience the quiet elegance of a circa 1849 Federal/Greek Revival home tastefully combined with today's modern amenities. In Madison's historic district, antique shops, historic sites, restaurants, and churches are within a pleasant walk. This gracious home offers spacious rooms decorated with antiques and reproductions and carefully selected fabrics and wall coverings. A sumptuous breakfast in the sun-filled dining room begins your day.

Hosts: Judy and Bill Gilbert
Rooms: 3 (PB) $90 + tax (10%)
Full Breakfast
Credit Cards: A, B, D
Notes: 2, 5, 8, 9, 10, 11, 12

NOTES: Credit cards accepted: A Master Card; B Visa; C American Express; D Discover; E Diners Club; F Other; 2 Personal checks accepted; 3 Lunch available; 4 Dinner available;

## METAMORA

### The Thorpe House Country Inn

P.O. Box 36, 19049 Clayborne St., 47030
(317) 932-2365 or (317) 647-5425

Visit the Thorpe House in historic Metamora where the steam engine still brings passenger cars and the grist mill still grinds cornmeal. Spend a relaxing evening in this 1840 canal town home. Rooms are tastefully furnished with antiques and country accessories. Enjoy a hearty breakfast before visiting more than 100 shops in this quaint village. Our family-style dining room is also open to the public.

Hosts: Mike and Jean Owens
Rooms: 4 + 2 room suite (PB) $70-125
Full Breakfast
Credit Cards: A, B, C, D
Notes: 2, 3, 4, 6, 7, 10, 12

The Thorpe House Country Inn

## MIDDLEBURY

### Bee Hive B&B

Box 1191, 46540
(219) 825-5023

Come visit Amish country and enjoy Hoosier hospitality. The Bee Hive is a two-story, open floor plan with ex-posed, hand-sawed, red oak beams and a loft. Enjoy our collection of antique farm machinery and other collectibles. Snuggle under handmade quilts and wake to the smell of freshly baked muffins. A guest cottage is available.

Hosts: Herb and Treva Swarm
Rooms: 4 (1PB; 3SB) $52-70
Full Breakfast
Credit Cards: A, B
Notes: 2, 5, 7, 8, 9, 10, 11

### The Country Victorian

435 S. Main St., 46540
(219) 825-2568

Come celebrate 100 years of lovely Victorian living. Our large home is a fully updated Victorian with lots of charm and original style. Located in the heart of Amish country, relax on the porch and watch buggies drive by or sit in the hot tub in our old fashioned garden. In colder months, sit by the fireplace to chat or curl up with a good book. We offer evening refreshments and full breakfasts. Get pampered and experience the loving family atmosphere where children are a pleasure! Hot tub and honeymoon suite with jacuzzi. Bicycle rental. Special packages available. Very accessible to Indiana's toll road (I-80/90) and close to Shipshewana. Other local attractions include Amish-style restaurants and crafters, community festivals, University of Notre Dame, and Goshen College.

Hosts: Mark and Becky Potterbaum
Rooms: 5 (PB) $60-95
Full Breakfast
Credit Cards: A, B, D
Notes: 5, 7, 8, 10, 11, 12

5 Open all year; 6 Pets welcome; 7 Children welcome; 8 Tennis nearby; 9 Swimming nearby; 10 Golf nearby; 11 Skiing nearby; 12 May be booked through travel agent.

## A Laber of Love Bed and Breakfast by Lori

11030 CR 10, 46540
(219) 825-7877

Cape Cod home located in northern Indiana Amish farm country on three acres, two of which are wooded. Screened-in gazebo in woods is ideal for quiet time or just relaxing. Queen-size beds and private baths. Common game/sitting room available for guests use. Air-conditioned. (Guest rooms are located upstairs.) Close to large flea market open from May to October on Tuesdays and Wednesdays. Lots of shopping in Middlebury and Shipshewana. Home-baked cinnamon rolls highlight continental breakfast. Smoke free.

Hostess: Lori Laber
Rooms: 2 (PB) $55
Continental Breakfast
Credit Cards: none
Notes: 2, 5, 10, 12

## Lookout Country Inn

14544 CR 12, 46540
(219) 825-9809

Located in the Amish country of northeast Indiana. Near the Menno-Hof (Amish-Mennonite Information Center); Shipshewana auction and flea market; antique, craft, and gift shops; famous restaurants; and the 1832 Bonneyville mill. Enjoy the spectacular view with a country-style breakfast in the sunroom. Swim in the private pool, or walk the wooded trails.

Hosts: Mary-Lou and Jim Wolfe
Rooms: 5 (3PB; 2SB) $50-70
Full Breakfast
Credit Cards: A, B
Notes: 2, 5, 7, 9, 10, 11, 12

## Patchwork Quilt Country Inn

11748 CR 2, 46540
(219) 825-2417; FAX (219) 825-5172

Relax and enjoy the simple grace and charm of our 100-year-old farmhouse. Sample our country cooking with home-made breads and desserts. Tour our back roads, and meet our Amish friends. Buy homemade articles, then return to the inn and rest in our quaint guest rooms.

Hostesses: Susan Thomas and Maxine Zook
Rooms: 15 (12PB; 3SB) $55.95-100
Full Breakfast
Credit Cards: A, B
Notes: 2, 3, 4, 8, 10, 11, 12

Yoder's Zimmer mit Frühstück Haus

## Yoder's Zimmer mit Frühstück Haus

P.O. Box 1396, 504 S. Main, 46540
(219) 825-2378

We enjoy sharing our Amish-Mennonite heritage in our spacious Crystal Valley home. The rooms feature handmade quilts and antiques. Antiques and collectibles can be seen throughout the home. Three of our rooms can accommodate families. There are several common rooms available for relaxing, reading, TV, games, or socializing. Facilities are also available for pastor-elder retreats. Air-conditioned, playground, swimming pool.

Hosts: Wilbur and Evelyn Yoder
Rooms: 5 (SB) $52.50
Full Breakfast
Credit Cards: A, B
Notes: 2, 5, 7, 8, 9, 10, 11, 12

## MIDDLETOWN

## Country Rose B&B

5098 N. Mechanicsburg Rd., 47356
(317) 779-4501; (800) 395-6449

A small town bed and breakfast looking out on berry patches and flower garden. Awake early or late to a delicious full breakfast. Fifty minutes to Indianapolis, twenty minutes to Anderson and Ball State Universities.

Hosts: Rose and Jack Lewis
Rooms: 2 (1 suite and 1SB) $45-65
Full Breakfast
Credit Cards: none
Notes: 2, 5, 7, 8, 10

## NAPPANEE

## Victorian Guest House

302 E. Market St., 46550
(219) 773-4383

Antiques, stained glass windows, and pocket doors highlight this 1887 Historical Register mansion. Nestled amongst the Amish Countryside where antique shops abound. A warm welcome awaits as you return to gracious living with all the ambiance of the 1800s. Everything has been designed to make your "Bed and Breakfast" stay a

memorable one. Close to Notre Dame and Shipshewana. Two hours from Chicago. Complimentary evening tea and sweets. "Prepare for a memory."

Hosts: Bruce and Vickie Hunsberger
Rooms: 6 (PB) $45-75
Full Breakfast
Credit Cards: A, B, D
Notes: 2, 5, 8, 9, 10

## NASHVILLE

## Day Star Inn

Box 361, 87 E. Main St., 47448
(812) 988-0430

Day Star Inn is in downtown Nashville in beautiful Brown County. There are over 200 shops and restaurants, art galleries, country music shows, drama theaters, and more. We are two miles from scenic Brown County State Park, and many churches for worship. We require no smoking, alcohol, or pets. All rooms have private baths and cable TV.

Host: Edwin K. Taggart
Rooms: 5 + parlor (PB) $80-95
Continental Plus Breakfast
Credit Cards: A, B, D
Notes: 2, 5, 7, 8, 9, 10, 11, 12

## Wraylyn Knoll B&B

2008 Greasy Creek Rd., P.O. Box 481, 47448
(812) 988-0733

Wraylyn Knoll B&B is a family-owned and operated, Brown County, hilltop country guest house. Five guest rooms with king or queen beds, private baths, and exceptional views. Lots of common areas. Romantic garden with fountain and awesome view of the stars.

---

5 Open all year; 6 Pets welcome; 7 Children welcome; 8 Tennis nearby; 9 Swimming nearby; 10 Golf nearby; 11 Skiing nearby; 12 May be booked through travel agent.

Plus swimming pool, fishing pond, 12 acres for hiking, croquet, and porch swing. Help yourself to evening refreshments, cool breezes, and warm welcomes! We welcome small groups, too.

Hosts: Marcia and Larry Wray
Rooms: 5 (PB) 2 persons $160 / 2 nights
(extra nights $50 each)
Full Breakfast (weekends); Continental (weekdays)
Credit Cards: A, B
Notes: 2, 5, 7, 8, 9, 10, 11, 12

## PAOLI

### Braxtan House Inn Bed and Breakfast
210 N. Gospel Street, 47454
(812) 723-4677; (800) 627-2982

The Inn is an 1893 Queen Anne Victorian listed on the National Register of Historic Places. The Braxtan family converted it into a hotel in the 1920's, and the house has been restored and furnished with antiques. Ski Paoli Peaks, enjoy Patoka Lake, explore the cave, and canoe the country nearby. Close to Louisville, KY, and Bloomington, IN.

Hosts: Duane and Kate Wilhelmi
Rooms: 6 (PB) $60-65
Full Breakfast
Credit Cards: A, B, C, D
Notes: 2, 5, 7, 8, 9, 10, 11, 12

## PERU

### Cole House B&B
27 E. Third St., 46970
(317) 472-2273

Cole House, known far and wide for its elaborate parquet wooden floors, magnificent fireplaces, and ornamental plaster ceilings is on the National Register of Historic Places. Staying at Cole House, the home of Cole Porter's grandfather, is like stepping back 100 years in history, but with all the modern conveniences. Each of the huge bedrooms is filled with period furniture and has air conditioning, cable TV, and a private bath.

Hosts: Miles and Peggy Straly
Rooms: 4 (PB) $60-75
Full Breakfast
Credit Cards: A, B, D
Notes: 2, 5, 7, 8, 9, 10, 12

Cole House Bed and Breakfast

### Rosewood Mansion Inn
54 N. Hood St., 46970
(317) 472-7151; FAX (317) 472-5575

The Rosewood is a lovely Victorian home in downtown Peru, IN. A welcome change from impersonal hotel accommodations, we offer the warmth and friendliness of a private home, with the privacy and elegance of a fine hotel, for a truly unique experience. Consider the Rosewood Mansion for your next romantic getaway, anniversary, party, business meeting, or corporate retreat. Whether business or pleasure brings you to Peru, the Rosewood rewards you with a wonderful experience at a moderate price.

Hosts: Lynn and Dave Hausner
Rooms: 8 (PB) $70-85
Full Breakfast
Credit Cards: A, B, C, D
Notes: 2, 5, 7, 8, 9, 10, 12

# RICHMOND

## Norwich Lodge and Conference Center

920 Earlham Dr., 47374
(317) 983-1575; FAX (317) 983-1576

Surrounded by 400 acres of woods and streams, Norwich Lodge is open year-round and provides the ideal getaway for anyone who wants to escape life's daily routine. Outside the Lodge a choice of paths can lead you on a fascinating escapade through one of nature's most scenic and beautiful playgrounds. You can hike along winding creeks, pause to watch the wildlife, or spot a variety of birds that inhabit the surrounding countryside.

Hostesses: Kim Mondices and Cathy Kight
Rooms: 15 (PB) $35-45
Continental Breakfast
Credit Cards: A, B
Notes: 2, 5, 7, 8

## Philip W. Smith B&B

2039 E. Main St., 47374
(800) 966-8972

Elegant Queen Anne Victorian family home located in East Main-Glen Miller Park Historic District, right on the IN-OH border off I-70. Built in 1890 by Philip W. Smith, the two and a half story brick has Romanesque details and features stained glass windows and ornate-carved wood. Four distinctive guest rooms: two with full-size beds, two with queen-size beds. Unwind in the evening with homemade snacks, coffee, and tea. Awaken to a breakfast highlighting fresh, regional ingredients. Stroll through four historic districts, listen to outdoor concerts in the park, hike Whitewater River Gorge, relax in the garden at the B&B, and shop the unique shops of Richmond and "Antique Alley." AAA and ABBA approved.

Hosts: Chip and Chartley Bondurant
Rooms: 4 (PB) $65-75
Full Breakfast
Credit Cards: A, B
Notes: 2, 5, 7, 8, 10, 11, 12

# ROCKPORT—SEE OWENSBORO, KENTUCKY

# SHIPSHEWANA

## Morton Street Bed and Breakfast, Inc.

P.O. Box 775, 46565
(219) 768-4391; (800) 447-6475;
FAX (219) 768-7468

Three old homes located on Morton Street, in the heart of Amish country in Shipshewana. Experience the comfort of country, antique, or Victorian stylings. You will find yourself within walking distance of the town's country quilt and craft shops and the famous Shipshewana flea market. Special win-

---

5 Open all year; 6 Pets welcome; 7 Children welcome; 8 Tennis nearby; 9 Swimming nearby; 10 Golf nearby; 11 Skiing nearby; 12 May be booked through travel agent.

ter and weekend rates available.

Hosts: Joel and Kim Mishler with Esther Mishler
Rooms: 10 (PB) (call for rates)
Full Breakfast (Continental on Sundays)
Credit Cards: A, B, D
Notes: 2, 5, 7, 10, 11, 12

## SWEDESBURG

## The Carlson House

105 Park St., 52652
(319) 254-2451

Accommodations have an Old World charm in this stylishly decorated home in a Swedish-American country village. Guests enjoy the candlelight breakfast with Swedish treats, historical mementos, and gracious hosts. Guest facilities include a sitting room with TV, extensive reading materials, and wide porches for relaxation. The pleasant grounds of the Carlson House are next to the buildings of the Swedish-American Museum of Swedesburg.

Hosts: Ruth and Ned Ratekin
Rooms: 2 (PB) $50
Full Breakfast
Credit Cards: A, B
Notes: 2, 5

## TIPPECANOE

## Bessinger's Hillfarm Wildlife Refuge B&B

4588 State Road 110, 46570
(219) 223-3288

This cozy log home overlooks 265 acres of rolling hills, woods, pasture fields, and marsh with 31 islands. It is ideal for geese and deer year-round. This farm features hiking trails with beautiful views, picnic areas, and benches tucked away in a quiet area. Varied seasons make it possible to canoe, swim, fish, bird watch, hike, and cross-country ski. Start with a country breakfast and be ready for an unforgettable table experience.

Hosts: Wayne and Betty Bessinger
Rooms: 3 (PB) $55-65
Full Breakfast
Credit Cards: none
Notes: 2, 5, 9, 10, 11

## WARSAW

## Candlelight Inn

503 E. Ft. Wayne St., 46580
(219) 267-2906; (800) 352-0640;
FAX (219) 269-4646

An 1860 Italiante home renovated by Bill and Debi Hambright. The Inn features eleven foot ceilings, natural woodwork, a grand stairway, marble fireplace, antique-filled rooms, and large porch. Whirlpool tubs available along with queen and king beds, phones, and cable TV in each room. Our Victorian home offers all the Old World charm with today's modern comforts.

Rooms: 11 (PB) $69-135
Full Home-cooked Breakfast
Credit Cards: A, B, C, E
Notes: 2, 5, 8, 9, 10, 12 (no commission)

---

NOTES: Credit cards accepted: A Master Card; B Visa; C American Express; D Discover; E Diners Club; F Other; 2 Personal checks accepted; 3 Lunch available; 4 Dinner available;

# Iowa

## BURLINGTON

### Lakeview Bed and Breakfast

11351 60th St., 52601
(319) 752-8735; (800) 753-8735;
FAX (319) 752-5126

Built from the ruins of the county's third oldest home, this elegant country home stands where stagecoach passengers once slept. Now your retreat to Lakeview is a mix of the old and the new on 30 acres of magnificent country charm. The house features crystal chandeliers, antiques, collectibles, and a circular staircase. Outdoors your can enjoy a swim in our pool; fishing in our three-acre lake stocked with catfish, bass, crappie, and bluegill; or just spend time making friends with our family of miniature horses. Guests can also take advantage of our large video library of noted Christian speakers. A video studio is available for recording and small conferences.

Hosts: Jack and Linda Rowley
Rooms: 4 (PB) $45-60
Expanded Continental Breakfast
Credit Cards: A, B
Notes: 2, 5, 8, 9, 10, 12

### The Schramm House B&B

616 Columbia St., 52601
(319) 754-0373 (voice and FAX)

Step into the past when you enter this restored 1870s Victorian in the heart of the historical district. High ceilings, parquet floors, original oak woodwork, wainscoting, and antique furnishings create the mood of an era past. Experience Burlington hospitality while having lemonade on the porch or tea by the fire with your gracious hosts. Walk to the Mississippi River, antique shops, restaurants, and more. An architectural masterpiece awaits you in the City of Steeples.

Hosts: Sandy and Bruce Morrison
Rooms: 2 (PB) $65-75
Full Breakfast
Credit Cards: A, B
Notes: 2, 5, 7, 8, 9, 10

The Schramm House

---

5 Open all year; 6 Pets welcome; 7 Children welcome; 8 Tennis nearby; 9 Swimming nearby; 10 Golf nearby; 11 Skiing nearby; 12 May be booked through travel agent.

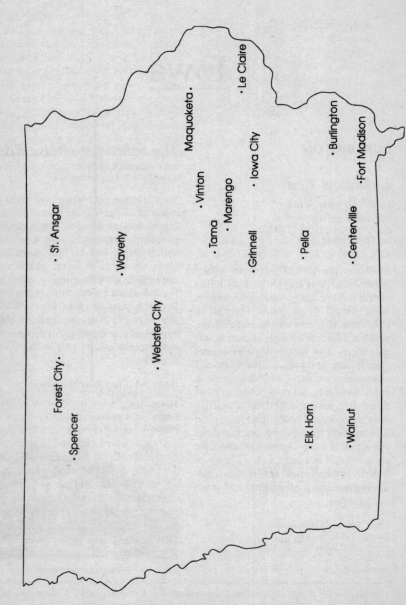

IOWA

Spencer ·

Forest City ·

· St. Ansgar

· Waverly

Webster City ·

Maquoketa ·

· Le Claire

· Vinton

· Tama    · Marengo

· Grinnell    · Iowa City

· Burlington

· Fort Madison

· Pella

· Centerville

Elk Horn ·

· Walnut

One of a Kind

## CENTERVILLE

### One of a Kind

314 W. State, 52544
(515) 437-4540 (voice and FAX)

One of a Kind is a stately three-story brick home built in 1867 and situated in one of Iowa's delightful small communities. You will be within walking distance of antique shops, the town square, city park with tennis courts, swimming pool, etc. Twelve-minute drive to Iowa's largest lake.

Hosts: Jack and Joyce Stufflebeem
Rooms: 5 (2PB; 3SB) $35-60
Full Breakfast
Credit Cards: A, B
Notes: 2, 3, 4, 5, 8, 9, 10, 11, 12

## ELK HORN

### Joy's Morning Glory Bed and Breakfast

4308 Main St., Box 12, 51531
(712) 764-5631

Be special guests in our beautiful, refurbished, 1912 home. As our guest, you will be greeted by an abundant array of flowers that line our walkways. Inside, your choice of floral decorated bedrooms await you as well. Breakfast is prepared on Joy's antique cookstove and served in the dining room, front porch, or flower-filled backyard. Elk Horn community is home to the largest rural Danish settlement in the United States. The town has a working windmill and is home to the National Danish Immigrant Museum and the Tivoli Festival.

Hosts: Joy and Merle Petersen
Rooms: 3 (SB) $45
Full Breakfast
Credit Cards: none
Notes: 2, 7 (over 10), 8, 9, 10

## FOREST CITY

### The 1897 Victorian House

306 S. Clark St., 50436
(515) 582-3613

Offering you hospitality in this turn-of-the-century Queen Anne Victorian home. As a guest in the 1897 Victorian House, you may choose from four beautifully decorated bedrooms, each with private bath. Breakfast, included in your room rate, is served every morning in our dining room, and we specialize in homemade food. An antique shop is located on premises. Gift certificates are available. Come play our 1923 baby grand player piano, play crochet in the yard, and relax in Forest City, a quiet

---

NOTES: Credit cards accepted: A Master Card; B Visa; C American Express; D Discover; E Diners Club; F Other; 2 Personal checks accepted; 3 Lunch available; 4 Dinner available; 5 Open all year; 6 Pets welcome; 7 Children welcome; 8 Tennis nearby; 9 Swimming nearby; 10 Golf nearby; 11 Skiing nearby; 12 May be booked through travel agent.

yet progressive rural community.

Hosts: Richard and Doris Johnson
Rooms: 4 (PB) $70-90
Full Breakfast
Credit Cards: A, B
Notes: 2, 3 and 4 (by reservation), 5, 9, 10, 12

Kingsley Inn

## FORT MADISON

### Kingsley Inn

707 Ave. H, 52627
(319) 372-7074; (800) 441-2327;
FAX (319) 372-7096

Experience complete relaxation in
1860's Victorian luxury. Fourteen spacious rooms are furnished in period antiques with today's modern comforts.
Awaken to the aroma of "Kingsley
Blend" coffee and enjoy the specialty
breakfast in the elegant Morning Room.
Stroll to replica of 1808 Fort, museum,
parks, shops, Catfish Bend Casino, and
antique malls. Fifteen minutes from historic Nauvoo, Illinois. Treat yourselves
to a unique lunch or dinner at Alpha's
on the Riverfront, right off our lobby.
Private baths (some whirlpools),
CATV, air-conditioning, and telephones. Non-smoking facility.

Hostess: Myrna M. Reinhard
Rooms: 14 (PB) $70-115
Continental Plus Breakfast
Credit Cards: A, B, C, D, E
Notes: 2, 3, 4, 5, 7 (limited), 9, 10, 12

## GRINNELL

### Carriage House B&B

1133 Broad Street, 50112
(515) 236-7520

Beautiful Queen Anne style Victorian
home with relaxing wicker furniture and
a swing seat on the front porch. Several
fireplaces to be enjoyed in the winter-
time. Gourmet breakfast with fresh fruit,
quiche, and Irish soda bread fresh from
the griddle. Local shopping, nearby lake
and hiking, excellent restaurants. One
block from Grinnell College, one hour
from Des Moines and Iowa City. Member of Iowa Bed and Breakfast Innkeepers Association, Iowa Lodging Association, and Grinnell Area Chamber of
Commerce.

Hostess: Dorothy Spriggs
Rooms: 4 (2PB; 2SB) $45-60
Full Breakfast
Credit Cards: none
Notes: 2, 5, 8, 9, 10, 11, 12

## IOWA CITY

### Bella Vista Place Bed and Breakfast

2 Bella Vista Place, 52245
(319) 338-4129

Daissy has furnished her lovely, air-con-

---

NOTES: Credit cards accepted: A Master Card; B Visa; C American Express; D Discover;
E Diners Club; F Other; 2 Personal checks accepted; 3 Lunch available; 4 Dinner available;

ditioned, 1920s home with antiques and artifacts she has acquired on her travels in Europe and Latin America. Conveniently located on Iowa City's historical northside with a beautiful view of the Iowa River. The Hoover Library, the Amana Colonies, and the Amish center of Kalona are all nearby. A full breakfast, with Daissy's famous coffee, is served in the dining room's unique setting. Daissy is fluent in Spanish and speaks some French. From I-80: take Dubuque St. Exit 244, turn left on Brown St., then first left on Linn St. one block to #2 Bella Vista Place.

Hosts: Daissy P. Owen
Rooms: 4 (2PB; 2SB) $45-75
Full Breakfast
Credit Cards: none
Notes: 2, 5, 7 (over 10), 8, 9, 12

Bella Vista Place Bed and Breakfast

## Haverkamps' Linn Street Homestage Bed and Breakfast

619 N. Linn St., 52245
(319) 337-4363

Enjoy the warmth and hospitality in our

1908 Edwardian home filled with heirlooms and collectibles. Only a short walk to downtown Iowa City and the University of Iowa main campus, and a short drive to the Hoover Library in West Branch, to the Amish in Kalona, and to seven Amama Colonies.

Hosts: Clarence and Dorothy Haverkamp
Rooms: 3 (SB) $35-45
Full Breakfast
Credit Cards: none
Notes: 2, 5, 7, 8, 9, 12

## LECLAIRE

## Monarch B&B Inn and McCaffrey House B&B

303 S. 2nd St., 52753
(319) 289-3011; (800) 772-7724 (reservations)

The Monarch B&B Inn (late 1850s) and the McCaffrey House B&B (1870) are working together to provide you with ideal settings for relaxation, meetings, and retreats. Wooden floors, high ceilings, and antique furniture help the homes retain their original charm while air conditioning, enclosed porches, open decks, and off street parking provide modern-day comforts. Magnificent Mississippi River views, antique shopping, and Buffalo Bill Museum await you in LeClaire, IA.

Hosts: David and Emilie Oltman and Jean Duncan
Rooms: 7 (4PB; 2SB) $40-55
Full or Continental Breakfast
Credit Cards: none
Notes: 2, 5, 7, 10, 12

5 Open all year; 6 Pets welcome; 7 Children welcome; 8 Tennis nearby; 9 Swimming nearby; 10 Golf nearby; 11 Skiing nearby; 12 May be booked through travel agent.

## MAQUOKETA

### Squiers Manor B&B

418 W. Pleasant, 52060
(319) 652-6961

Squiers Manor Bed and Breakfast is located in the West Pleasant Street Historic District. This 1882 Queen Anne mansion features walnut, cherry, and butternut woods throughout. Enjoy period furnishings, queen-size beds, in-room phone and TV, private baths, as well as single and double jacuzzis. Come hungry and enjoy delicious, candlelight evening desserts and breakfast (more like brunch) served in the elegant dining room. Virl's and Kathy's goal is to make your stay as pleasant and enjoyable as possible. Give us a call today!

Hosts: Virl and Kathy Banowetz
Rooms: 8 (PB) $75-195
Full Breakfast
Credit Cards: A, B, C
Notes: 2, 5, 7, 8, 9, 10, 11, 12

## MARENGO

### Loy's Farm Bed and Breakfast

2077 KK Ave., I-80 Exit 216 N., 52301
(319) 642-7787

This beautiful, modern home is on a working grain and hog farm with quiet and pleasant views of rolling countryside. A farm tour is offered with friendly hospitality. Pheasant hunting can be enjoyed. The large reception room includes a pool table, table tennis, and shuffleboard. Swing set and sand pile are in the large yard. Close to the Amana Colonies, Tanger Mall, Kalona, Iowa City, West Branch, and Cedar Rapids. I-80, Exit 216 North one mile.

Hosts: Loy and Robert Walker
Rooms: 3 (1PB; 2SB) $50-60
Full Breakfast
Credit Cards: none
Notes: 2, 4 (by reservation), 5, 6 (caged), 7, 8, 9, 10 (4 courses), 12

## PELLA

### Heritage House Bed and Breakfast

1345 Highway 163, **Leighton** 50143
(515) 626-3092

"Great hospitality, cleanliness, beautiful home, and wonderful breakfast," are just a few of the comments we've received from our guests. This lovely 1918 country home has TV's and central air-conditioning. The rooms were redecorated and newly carpeted in 1993. The Victorian suite has antique furniture, an old pump organ, TV, VCR, and private bath. The Blue Room is furnished with 1915 family heirloom furniture, TV, and private bath. Enjoy complimentary popcorn, snacks, and drinks provided by the wonderful hospitality. Catered services to honeymooners and other celebrations are available. There are special facilities available for pheasant hunters and their dogs. Enjoy a gourmet breakfast served in the formal dining room with crystal and lace. Member IBBIA and ILA. We

---

NOTES: Credit cards accepted: A Master Card; B Visa; C American Express; D Discover; E Diners Club; F Other; 2 Personal checks accepted; 3 Lunch available; 4 Dinner available;

are located near Knoxville, Iowa—the sprint car racing capital. Smoking is permitted in screen enclosed porch.

Hosts: The Vander Wilt Family
Rooms: 2 (PB) $45-55
Full Breakfast
Credit Cards: none
Notes: 2, 7, 8, 9, 10, 11, 12

The Woodlands

## PRINCETON

### The Woodlands

P.O. Box 127, 52768
(800) 257-3177

A secluded woodland escape that can be as private or social as you wish. The Woodlands Bed and Breakfast is nestled among pines on 26 acres of forest and meadows in a private wildlife refuge. Guests delight in an elegant breakfast by the swimming pool or by a cozy fireplace, while viewing the outdoor wildlife activity. Perfect for intimate weddings!

Hosts: The Wallace Family
Rooms: 2 (PB) $60-115
Full Breakfast
Credit Cards: none
Notes: 2, 3, 4, 5, 6 (limited), 7, 8, 9, 10, 11, 1

## ST. ANSGAR

### Blue Belle Inn Bed and Breakfast

P.O. Box 205, 513 W. 4th St., 50472
(515) 736-2225

Rediscover the romance of the 1890s while enjoying the comfort and convenience of the 1990s in one of six distinctively decorated guest rooms at the Blue Belle Inn. The festive Victorian Painted Lady features air conditioning, fireplaces, and Jacuzzis. Lofty tin ceilings, gleaming maple woodwork, stained glass, and crystal chandeliers set in bay and curved window pockets create a shimmering interplay of light and color. Enjoy breakfast on the balcony or gourmet dining by candlelight.

Hostess: Sherrie C. Hansen
Rooms: 6 (5PB; 1SB) $40-120
Full Breakfast
Credit Cards: A, B, D
Notes: 2, 3, 4, 5, 7, 8, 9, 10, 12

## SPENCER

### Hannah Marie Country Inn

4070 Hwy. 71, 51301
(712) 262-1286; (800) 792-1286;
FAX (712) 262-3294

The Romance of Country: claw foot tubs and whirlpools, central air, softened water, bubble bath by lantern light in our romantic Lamplighter Room, or in the oasis in the Enchanting Safari Room. Herb gardens, Wedding Garden,

5 Open all year; 6 Pets welcome; 7 Children welcome; 8 Tennis nearby; 9 Swimming nearby; 10 Golf nearby; 11 Skiing nearby; 12 May be booked through travel agent.

croquet on the lawn. "Best B&B in Iowa 1990," *Des Moines* Register Readers. "One of the Top 50 Inns in America," by *Inn Times,* 1991. Lunch/dinner at our Carl Gustav House Bistro. (Weds.-Sat. 11am-2pm) Iowa Great Lakes area, West Bend, and Grotto nearby.

Hostess: Mary Nichols
Rooms: 5 (PB) $50-89
Full Breakfast ending with cappuccinos
Credit Cards: A, B, C, D
Notes: 2, 3, 4, 6 (outside), 7, 8, 9, 10, 12 (10%)

The Lion and The Lamb

## TAMA

### *Hummingbird Haven A Bed and Breakfast*

1201 Harding Street, 52339
(515) 484-2022

We hope you will join us at Hummingbird Haven and get a taste of Central Iowa's hospitality. The B&B offers two guest rooms with a large shared bath. Guests have use of the home, laundry services are available, and the home has central air and heat. Tama's central location makes our B&B a perfect home base for seeing many of Iowa's attractions. Ten minutes from Tama County Museum and Mesquaki Bingo and Casino; 30 minutes from Mashalltown, County Lake with water sports, Opera House in Brooklyn, and Grinnell College and Museum. One hour from much more. Please no pets or smoking.

Hostess: Bernita Thomsen
Rooms: 2 (SB) $38-50
Full Breakfast
Credit Cards: none
Notes: 2, 3, 4, 5, 7, 9, 10

## VINTON

### *The Lion and The Lamb*

913 2nd Avenue, 52349
(319) 472-5086; (800) 808-LAMB (5262); FAX (319) 472-9115

Experience elegant accommodations in this newly restored 1892 Queen Anne Victorian Mansion. This "Painted Lady" features elaborate woodwork, seven fireplaces, stained glass windows, parquet floors, and a dusting porch. Each of our guest rooms have air-conditioning, queen-size beds, and TV. One room has a private bath. We're located between Cedar Rapids and Waterloo. Evening dessert is also provided.

Hosts: Richard and Rachel Waterbury
Rooms: 3 (1PB; 2SB) $55-75
Full Breakfast
Credit Cards: A, B
Notes: 2, 5, 7, 8, 9, 10, 12

NOTES: Credit cards accepted: A Master Card; B Visa; C American Express; D Discover; E Diners Club; F Other; 2 Personal checks accepted; 3 Lunch available; 4 Dinner available;

## WALNUT

### Antique City Inn B&B

400 Antique City Dr., P.O. Box 584, 51577
(712) 784-3722; (800) 714-3722

This 1911 Victorian home has been restored and furnished to its original state. Enjoy a nostalgic experience of simplicity of life, craftsmanship of yesterday, quiet living, and small town hospitality. One block from malls and stores with 250 antique dealers. Home has beautiful woods, dumb waiter icebox, French doors, and wraparound porch.

Hostess: Sylvia Reddie
Rooms: 5 (1PB; 4SB) $42 (includes tax)
Full Breakfast
Credit Cards: A, B, C
Notes: 2, 3, 4, 5

### Clark's Country Inn Bed and Breakfast

701 Walnut St., P.O. Box 533, 51577
(712) 784-3010

Iowa's antique capital, one mile south of I-80 between Omaha and Des Moines. Six malls, individual shops, over 200 dealers, open all year. 1912 two-story home with oak interior, antiques, newly remodeled guest rooms, private baths, king/queen beds, central air, and full breakfast. Mastercard/Visa deposit required. No smoking.

Host: Ron and Mary Lou Clark
Rooms: 3 (PB) $52
Full Breakfast
Credit Cards: A, B
Notes: 2, 5, 7 (over 12), 8, 9, 10, 12

## WAVERLY

### Villa Fairfield

401 2nd Ave. SW, 50677
(319) 352-0739

Built in 1876, this totally restored Italianate Victorian bed and breakfast is designed as the perfect get-away spot. The house is furnished with many family antiques and keepsakes, as well as with various articles collected by innkeeper Inez Boevers-Christensen during the years which she presided in Brazil. All rooms are uniquely decorated with their own charm and character and have ceiling fans, air-conditioning, and queen-size beds. Come to the Villa Fairfield to enjoy the rest and relaxation of a bygone era.

Hostess: Inez Boevers-Christensen
Rooms: 4 (2PB; 2SB) $55-75
Full Breakfast
Credit Cards: A, B
Notes: 2, 5, 10, 12

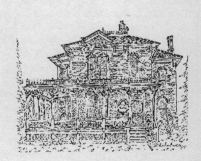

Villa Fairfield

---

5 Open all year; 6 Pets welcome; 7 Children welcome; 8 Tennis nearby; 9 Swimming nearby; 10 Golf nearby; 11 Skiing nearby; 12 May be booked through travel agent.

## WEBSTER CITY

### Centennial Farm Bed and Breakfast

1091 220th St., 50595
(515) 832-3050

Hosts: Tom and Shirley Yungclas
Rooms: 2 (SB) $35
Full Breakfast
Credit Cards: none
Notes: 2, 5, 7, 8, 9, 10

Centennial Farm is a bed and breakfast homestay located on a farm that has been in the family since 1869. Tom was born in the house. Guests may take a ride in the 1929 Model A pickup truck, if desired. In a quiet location near several good antique shops. Member of Iowa Bed and Breakfast Innkeepers Association, Inc. Air-conditioned. Twenty-two miles west of I-35 at Exit 142 or Exit 144.

Centennial Farm Bed and Breakfast

---

NOTES: Credit cards accepted: A Master Card; B Visa; C American Express; D Discover; E Diners Club; F Other; 2 Personal checks accepted; 3 Lunch available; 4 Dinner available;

# Kansas

## ABILENE

### Victorian Reflections Bed and Breakfast Inn

820 NW Third, 67410
(913) 263-7774

Enjoy the Victorian splendor of one of Abilene's finest historic homes. Victorian Reflections is located on beautiful Third Street in the historic Hurd House. Relax in the parlors or on one of the home's many porches. The city park, pool, and tennis courts are adjacent to the home which is also within walking distance of Abilene's many attractions.

Hosts: Don and Diana McBride
Rooms: 4 (PB) $45-65
Full Breakfast
Credit Cards: A, B
Notes: 2, 5, 7 (over 9), 8, 9, 10, 12

Victorian Reflections Bed and Breakfast Inn

## GREAT BEND

### Peaceful Acres Bed and Breakfast

Route 5, Box 153, 67530
(316) 793-7527

Enjoy a mini-farm and sprawling, tree-shaded, old farmhouse furnished with some antiques. If you like quiet and peace, chickens, goats, guineas, kittens in the springs, and old-fashioned hospitality, you need to come and visit us. Breakfast will be fixed from home-grown products. We are near historical areas: Sante Fe Trail, Ft. Larned, Cheyenne Bottoms, zoo, and tennis courts. Member of the Kansas Bed and Breakfast Association.

Hosts: Dale and Doris Nitzel
Rooms: 3 (1 PB; 2 SB) $30
Full Breakfast
Credit Cards: none
Notes: 2, 3, 4, 5, 7, 8, 9, 10, 12

## MELVERN

### Schoolhouse Inn

106 E. Beck, 66510
(913) 549-3473

Two-story, limestone building built in

---

5  Open all year;  6  Pets welcome;  7  Children welcome;  8  Tennis nearby;  9  Swimming nearby;
10  Golf nearby;  11  Skiing nearby;  12  May be booked through travel agent.

KANSAS

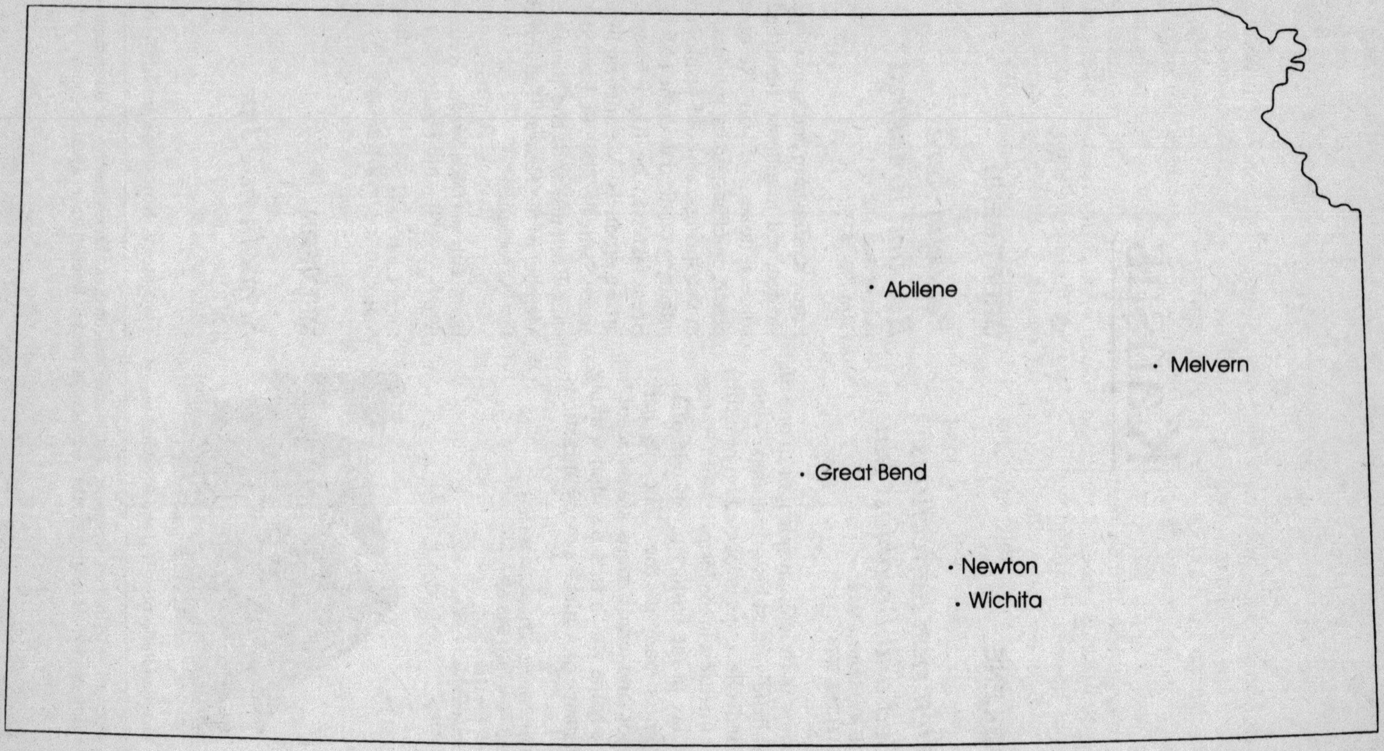

- Melvern
- Abilene
- Great Bend
- Newton
- Wichita

1870 sets on a one-and-a-half acre lawn. In 1986 it was entered in Kansas Historic Places. The Inn is a place you need to come visit. The guests can visit in a parlor with antique furniture or sit around a large table in the dining room and enjoy playing games. Four large bedrooms upstairs furnished with antiques and contemporary furnishings where guests can relax while reading a good book or looking at magazines. Enjoy this B&B for celebrating your anniversary or just a quiet getaway to our small town of Melvern.

Hosts: Rudy and Alice White
Rooms: 4 (2PB; 2SB) $50-55
Full Breakfast
Credit Cards: A, B
Notes: 2, 5, 7, 9

Schoolhouse Inn

# NEWTON

## Hawk House Bed and Breakfast

307 W. Broadway, 67114
(316) 283-2045; (800) 500-2045

This elegant 1914 home has original light fixtures, wallpaper from Europe, and stained glass windows awaiting your arrival. Three blocks from downtown, where quaint shops and antiques can be found. Close to bike paths, historical sites, and good restaurants. Guest rooms offer queen-size beds and antique furniture. Facility is available for meetings, retreats, weddings, and receptions. Member Kansas B&B Association.

Hosts: Lon and Carol Buller
Rooms: 4 (1PB; 3SB) $50-60
Full Breakfast
Credit Cards: A, B
Notes: 2, 5, 7, 8, 9, 10

# WELLS

## Trader's Lodge

1392 210th Rd., 67488
(913) 488-3930

Join us for a "taste of the Wild West" and experience the history of the fur trade era in our newly built lodge of fir and limestone, decorated with antiques, furs, and Indian artifacts. Choose from the Trapper's Room, Plains Indian Room, Southwest Room, or Renaissance Room, each individually climate-controlled with private bath. Fitness room and hot tub downstairs. Quiet country setting near a state lake. No alcohol or tobacco please.

Hosts: Neal and Kathy Kindall
Rooms: 4 (PB) $65-85
Full Breakfast
Credit Cards: A, B, D
Notes: 2, 3, 4, 5, 7

NOTES: Credit cards accepted: A Master Card; B Visa; C American Express; D Discover; E Diners Club; F Other; 2 Personal checks accepted; 3 Lunch available; 4 Dinner available; 5 Open all year; 6 Pets welcome; 7 Children welcome; 8 Tennis nearby; 9 Swimming nearby; 10 Golf nearby; 11 Skiing nearby; 12 May be booked through travel agent.

## WICHITA

### *The Castle Inn Riverside*

1155 N. River Blvd., 67203
(316) 263-9300; (316) 263-6219 (messages)

Hosts: Terry and Paula Lowry
Rooms: 14 (PB) $125-225
Full Breakfast
Credit Cards: A, B, C, D
Notes: 2, 5, 8, 10

Listed on the Local, State, and National Registers of Historic Places, the Castle is of Richardsonian Romanesque architectural style. Fourteen uniquely appointed rooms with baths and fireplaces, five sitting areas, coffee bar, gift shop, seminar rooms, business amenities, and exercise facility. Amenities include gourmet breakfast, wine and cheese, dessert, coffee, and more. We tailor our services to our guests needs and will go out of our way to make any occasion special.

The Castle Inn Riverside

---

# Kentucky

## AUGUSTA

### Augusta Ayre Bed and Breakfast

201 West Second St., 41002
(606) 756-3228

Built in 1840, this Federal house (a designated Kentucky landmark) takes you back to a simpler time. Located one block from antique and gift shops, art galleries, restaurants, parks, and the Ohio River. Amenities include fireplaces, ceiling fans, central air/heat, and a sitting room with cable TV/VCR. Children and pets are welcome. Gift certificates and deluxe packages are available.

Hostess: Maynard Krum
Rooms: 2 (SB) $50-90
Full Breakfast
Credit Cards: none
Notes: 2, 5, 6, 7, 8, 9, 10 (20 miles)

### Augusta Bed and Breakfast Association

P.O. Box 31, 41002
FAX (606) 756-2168; also see individual inn's numbers

Steeped in history, Augusta is the quint-essential river town. Stroll along the river and tree lined streets as you leave the hustle and bustle of the big city behind. Ride the ferry and view the varied architectural styles as you step back in time.

Explore the antique and gift shops and art galleries as you hunt for that special find. Then dine in one of Augusta's fine restaurants before retiring for the evening at a cozy bed and breakfast.

Each B&B is unique in architecture, ambiance, and furnishings. All are located in the heart of Augusta, Kentucky. Located only one hour from both Cincinnati, Ohio, and Lexington, Kentucky, Augusta is easily accessible to Interstate-75. Augusta hospitality is without equal and your visit is welcome!

| | |
|---|---|
| *Augusta Ayre*<br>201 West Second St.<br>(606) 756-3228 | *Doniphan House*<br>302 East Fourth St.<br>(606) 756-2409 |
| *Augusta Landing*<br>206 East Riverside Dr.<br>(606) 756-2510 | *The Lamplighter Inn*<br>103 West Second St.<br>(606) 756-2603 |
| *Augusta White*<br>*House Inn*<br>307 Main St.<br>(606) 756-2004 | *Mains Family Home*<br>201 Riverside Dr.<br>(606) 756-3125 |

---

5 Open all year; 6 Pets welcome; 7 Children welcome; 8 Tennis nearby; 9 Swimming nearby; 10 Golf nearby; 11 Skiing nearby; 12 May be booked through travel agent.

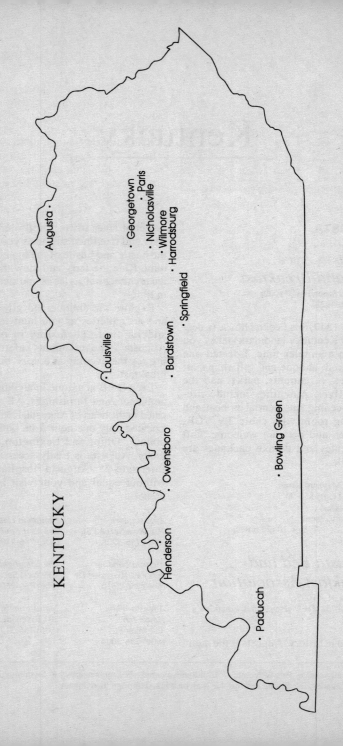

KENTUCKY

Augusta •

Georgetown •
Paris •
Nicholasville •
Wilmore •
Harrodsburg

Springfield •

Louisville •

Bardstown •

Owensboro •

Bowling Green •

Henderson •

Paducah •

Beautiful Dreamer Bed and Breakfast

## BARDSTOWN

### Beautiful Dreamer B&B

440 E. Stephen Foster Ave., 40004
(502) 348-4004

Federal design home (circa 1995) in historic district. Fully A/C rooms. Cherry furniture, antiques, and all rooms available with queen-sized beds: Beautiful Dreamer (w/double jacuzzi), Stephen Foster (handicapped accessible), and Captain's (fireplace-single jacuzzi). Enjoy a hearty breakfast then relax on our porches with a beautiful view of my Old Kentucky Home.

Hostess: Lynell Ginter
Rooms: 3 (PB) $79-99
Full Breakfast
Credit Cards: A, B
Notes: 2, 5, 7 (over 8), 10, 12

### Jailer's Inn

111 W. Stephen Foster Ave., 40004
(502) 348-5551; (800) 948-5551;
FAX (502) 348-1852

We pamper our "prisoners!" Come "spend time" in jail and unlock an ad-venture in history. Large, spacious rooms, beautifully decorated in antiques and heirlooms. All rooms have private baths so "escape" to our Victorian, Colonial, Library, Garden, or 1819 room. The 1819 room has a double jacuzzi. Deluxe continental breakfast served in lovely courtyard in summertime. Located in center of Historic Bardstown. Rated AAA, Mobile Oil, American B&B Association. The Jailer's Inn is a "captivating experience."

Host: Paul McCoy
Rooms: 6 (PB) $65-95
Full Breakfast
Credit Cards: A, B, C, D
Notes: 2, 7, 8, 9, 10, 12

### Kenmore Farms B&B

1050 Bloomfield Rd., 40004
(502) 348-8023; (800) 831-6159

Drop your hurried ways and enjoy the charm and warmth of days gone by. Beautiful 1860's Victorian home features antiques, Oriental rugs, gleaming poplar floors, and cherry stairway. Air-conditioned guest rooms are decorated with four poster beds or Lincoln beds and lovely linens, including period antiques. Large, private baths and spacious vanities. Full country breakfast—all home cooked—a real treat. The decor and our brand of hospitality create a relaxing and enjoyable atmosphere. AAA approved.

Hosts: Dorothy and Bernie Keene
Rooms: 4 (PB) $80-90
Full Breakfast
Credit Cards: none
Notes: 2, 5, 7 (over 12), 8, 9, 10

---

NOTES: Credit cards accepted: A Master Card; B Visa; C American Express; D Discover; E Diners Club; F Other; 2 Personal checks accepted; 3 Lunch available; 4 Dinner available; 5 Open all year; 6 Pets welcome; 7 Children welcome; 8 Tennis nearby; 9 Swimming nearby; 10 Golf nearby; 11 Skiing nearby; 12 May be booked through travel agent.

## BOWLING GREEN

### Alpine Lodge

5310 Morgantown Rd., 42101
(502) 843-4846

Alpine Lodge is a spacious, Swiss chalet-style home that has over 6,000 square feet and is located on eleven and a half acres. The furnishings are mostly antiques. A typical Southern breakfast of eggs, sausage, biscuits, gravy, fried apples, grits, coffee cake, coffee, and orange juice starts your day. There are grounds and nature trails to stroll through. We also have a swimming pool, gazebo, and outdoor spa. All the rooms have phones and cable TV (three movie channels). The Lodge is near many popular attractions. Your hosts are retired musicians who might be persuaded to play something for the guests.

Hosts: Dr. and Mrs. Livingston
Rooms: 5 (3PB; 2SB) $45-65; suites $75-90
Full Breakfast
Credit Cards: A, B, C, D, E
Notes: 2, 5, 8, 9, 10, 12

## FRANKFORT

### Country Morning Bed and Breakfast

1220 Deerwood Drive, 40601
(502) 695-4325; FAX (502) 223-4900

Reminiscent of the old country farmhouse, Country Morning Bed and Breakfast is located in Frankfort, KY. We are within driving distance to most of KY's attractions, horse farms, historical homes and sites. We are nestled in the woods where peace and quiet abound. Traditional country breakfast. Open Spring 1996.

Hostess: Jackie Hillyer
Rooms: 2 (SB) $45-65
Full Country Breakfast
Credit Cards: A, B, D
Notes: 2, 8, 9, 10

## GEORGETOWN

### Pineapple Inn Bed and Breakfast

645 S. Broadway, 40324
(502) 868-5453

Located in beautiful Georgetown, Kentucky, our beautiful home, built in 1876, is on the National Register. Country, French dining room, and large living room. Three bedrooms with private baths upstairs: Grandma's Country Room with full bed, Victorian Room also with full bed, and Americana Room with twin beds. Main Floor Derby Room with queen-sized, canopied bed and private bath with hot tub. The home is furnished with antiques and very beautifully decorated. Full breakfast is served.

Hosts: Muriel and Les
Rooms: 4 (3PB; 1SB) $60-75 + tax
Full Breakfast
Credit Cards: A, B
Notes: 2, 5, 7, 8, 9, 10, 12

## HARRODSBURG

### Canaan Land Farm B&B

4355 Lexington Road, 40330
(606) 734-3984; (800) 450-7307, pin # 0307

Step back in time to a house nearly 200

---

NOTES: Credit cards accepted: A Master Card; B Visa; C American Express; D Discover; E Diners Club; F Other; 2 Personal checks accepted; 3 Lunch available; 4 Dinner available;

years old. Canaan Land B&B is a historic home, c.1795. Rooms feature antiques, collectibles, and feather beds. Full breakfast and true Southern hospitality. This is a working sheep farm with lambing. Your host is a shepherd/attorney, and you hostess is a handspinner/artist. Farm is secluded and peaceful. Close to Shaker Village. Also, an historic log cabin with three additional rooms, including private baths, opens September of 1995. This is a nonsmoking B&B.

Hosts: Theo and Fred Bee
Rooms: 7 (6PB;1SB) $75-125
Full Breakfast
Credit Cards: none
Notes: 2, 5, 7 (12 and older), 9 (on premises), 10, 12

L&N Bed and Breakfast

# HENDERSON

## *L&N Bed and Breakfast*

327 North Main, 42420
(502) 831-1100; FAX (502) 826-0075

Two-story, Victorian home located in downtown Henderson, near the Ohio River and within walking distance of three city parks. Rooms are comfortable and beautifully decorated. Home has central heat and air. Guests can be lulled to sleep by passing trains.

Hosts: Mary Elizabeth and Norris Priest
Rooms: 2 (PB) $65-75
Continental Breakfast
Credit Cards: none
Notes: 2, 5, 8, 10

The Sandusky House

# NICHOLASVILLE

## *Sandusky House and The O'neal Cabin B&B*

1626 Delaney Ferry Road, 40356
(606) 223-4730

A tree-lined drive to the Sandusky House is just a prelude to a wonderful visit to the Bluegrass. A quiet ten-acre country setting amid horse farms yet close to downtown Lexington, Kentucky, Horse Par, and Shakertown. The Greek Revival Sandusky House was built circa 1850 from bricks fired on the farm. A 1780, one-thousand-acre land grant from Patrick Henry, governor of Virginia, given to Revolutionary War soldier, Jacob Sandusky. In addtition to the Sandusky House we also have an 1820s, reconstructed, two-story, two-bedroom, authentic log cabin with full kitchen and whirlpool bath. Large stone

---

5 Open all year; 6 Pets welcome; 7 Children welcome; 8 Tennis nearby; 9 Swimming nearby; 10 Golf nearby; 11 Skiing nearby; 12 May be booked through travel agent.

fireplace, AC, and located in a wooded area close to main house. A get-a-way that is ideal for the entire family! Please call for a brochure.

Hosts: Jim and Linda Humphrey
Rooms: 3 (PB) $69
Full Breakfast
Credit Cards: A, B
Notes: 2, 5, 7 (over 12)

## OLD LOUISVILLE

### The Victorian Secret Bed and Breakfast

1132 S. First St., 40203
(502) 581-1914; (800) 449-4691 pin #0604

"Step inside and step back 100 years in time" describes this three-story, Victorian brick mansion in historic Louisville. Recently restored to its former elegance, the 100-year-old structure offers spacious accommodations, high ceilings, and original woodwork. The Louisville area, rich in historic homes, will also tempt railbirds and would-be jockeys to make a pilgrimage to the famous tack at Churchill Downs, Home of the Kentucky Derby.

Hosts: Nan and Steve Roosa
Rooms: 6 (2PB, 4SB) $58-89
Continental Breakfast
Credit Cards: none
Notes: 5, 7, 8, 9, 10, 11, 12

## OWENSBORO

### Trails End B&B

5931 Hwy. 56, 42301
(502) 771-5590; FAX (502) 771-4723

Trails End offers two comfortable cottages within 20 minutes of each other across state lines. Red House in Kentucky is adjacent to an indoor tennis club where Ramey Tennis School camps are held in season. It sits next to an apple orchard and has horses in the pasture field behind. It has three bedrooms, one queen and two with two bunk beds and it has an outdoor pool and tennis courts. A former tenant house the quaint country cottage has in addition a sitting room, a laundry room, and bath with shower and separate tub. Breakfast is served in the clubhouse. Barn Cottage is named for its location next to the Ramey Riding Stables in **Rockport, IN** which offers trail riding and lessons. The lovely country condo cottage is finely appointed with antiques and furnished patio overlooking the countryside and horse pastures. It has three bedrooms and laundry room with separate tub. Refrigerator is stocked with breakfast "fixins." Only 45 minutes to Holiday World.

Hostess: Joan G. Ramey
Cottages: 2 (PB) $55-85
Full Southern Breakfast
Credit Cards: A, B
Notes: 2, 5, 6, 7, 8, 9 (outdoor)

## PADUCAH

### The 1857's Bed and Breakfast

127 Market House Sq., 42001
(Mail: P.O. Box 7771, 42002)
(502) 444-3960 (voice and FAX);
(800) 264-5607

The 1857's Bed and Breakfast is in the

---

NOTES: Credit cards accepted: A Master Card; B Visa; C American Express; D Discover; E Diners Club; F Other; 2 Personal checks accepted; 3 Lunch available; 4 Dinner available;

center of Paducah's historic downtown on Market House Square. The three-story building was built in 1857 and is on the National Register of Historic Places. The first floor is Cynthia's Ristorante. The second floor guest rooms have been renovated in Victorian Era-style and period furnishings abound. Also available for guest enjoyment on the third floor is a game room with a view of the Ohio River. The game room features an elegant mahogany billiards table. Hot tub also on the third floor. Advance reservations advised.

Hostess: Deborah Bohnert
Rooms: 3 (1PB; 2SB) $55-65
Continental Plus Breakfast
Credit Cards: A, B
Notes: 2, 5, 8, 9, 10, 11, 12

## Ehrhardt's Bed and Breakfast

285 Springwell Lane, 42001
(502) 554-0644

Our brick Colonial ranch home is located just one mile off I-24, which is noted for its lovely scenery. We hope to make you feel at home in antique-filled bedrooms and a cozy den with a fireplace. Nearby are the beautiful Kentucky and Barkley Lakes and the famous Land Between the Lakes area.

Hosts: Eileen and Phil Ehrhardt
Rooms: 2 (SB) $45
Full Breakfast
Credit Cards: none
Notes: 2, 7 (over 6), 8, 9, 10

## Paducah Harbor Plaza Bed and Breakfast

201 Broadway, 42001
(502) 442-2698 (voice and FAX);
(800) 719-7799

Paducah Harbor Plaza B&B guests thrive on the attention and hospitality of their innkeeper. On the first floor, guests will find the buildings' original copper ceilings, marble columns, ceramic tile floors, and stained glass windows restored to their original beauty. Four guest rooms are located on the second floor. Each is comfortably furnished with early 20th century antique furniture and warm, handmade quilts. The air-conditioned rooms feature ten foot ceilings, original windows, ceiling fans, and tongue-and-groove painted floors. Historic downtown Paducah offers many attractions, fine restaurants, and cultural events.

Hostess: Beverly McKinley
Rooms: 4 (SB) $65-125
Continental Plus Breakfast
Credit Cards: A, B, C
Notes: 2, 5, 7, 8, 9, 10, 11, 12

## PARIS

## Rosedale Bed and Breakfast

1917 Cypress St., 40361
(606) 987-1845

Tucked into three secluded acres in Paris, KY, Rosedale invites you to take time for yourself and to leave the cares of the world at the end of the driveway.

Listed on the Historic Register, the 14-room, Italiante, brick home, furnished in antiques, was built in 1862 and was the home of Civil War General John Croxton. Guests will enjoy a social parlor, complete with games, TV, VCR, and small library. Across the foyer, the living room provides the perfect place for quiet reading and reflection. Both rooms feature beautiful, working fireplaces. Voted the 1994 best B&B in the five-county Bluegrass region.

Hosts: Katie and Jim Haag
Rooms: 4 (2PB; 2SB) $65-85
Full Breakfast
Credit Cards: A, B
Notes: 2, 5, 6 (kennel close), 7 (over 11), 8, 9, 10

## SPRINGFIELD

## Maple Hill Manor Bed and Breakfast

2941 Perryville Rd., 40069
(606) 366-3075

Listed on the National Register of Historic Places, we are located on 14 tranquil acres in the scenic Bluegrass region. It took three years to build, circa 1851, has ten-foot doors, 13½-foot ceilings, nine-foot windows, cherry spiral staircase, stenciling in foyer, three brass and crystal chandeliers, and nine fireplaces. The honeymoon hideaway has canopy bed and jacuzzi. One hour from Louisville and Lexington. No smoking.

Hosts: Bob and Kay Carroll
Rooms: 7 (PB) $60-80
Full Breakfast
Credit Cards: A, B
Notes: 2, 5, 7, 8, 9, 10, 12

## WILMORE

## Scott Station Inn

305 E. Main St., 40390
(606) 858-0121; (800) SCOTT-10

The Scott Station Inn is located in downtown, historic Wilmore, Kentucky, just three blocks from famous Asbury College, and Asbury Seminary, and only minutes from Shakertown, Fort Harrod, and Lexington, Kentucky. Beautifully refurbished in 1990, this 100-year-old farmhouse has kept the charm of an old Kentucky home. Our inn has four rental rooms with private baths. We welcome pastor-staff and Sunday school retreats, family reunions, and wedding parties.

Hosts: Jennifer, Annette and John Fitch
Rooms: 6 (4PB; 2SB) $39.95-49.95
Full Breakfast
Credit Cards: A, B
Notes: 2, 5, 7

Scott Station Inn

# Louisiana

**ALSO SEE RESERVATION
SERVICES UNDER
MISSISSIPPI**

Milbank Historic House

## JACKSON

### Milbank Historic House

P.O. Box 1000, 3045 Bank St., 70748
(504) 634-5901

Located in the beautiful Felicianas of
Louisiana, Milbank is a massive, romantic antebellum mansion. It has a
varied and interesting history. Rooms
are furnished with authentic antique furniture of the late 1800s. Persian rugs,
ormolu clocks, carved settees, poster
beds, armoires, and much more. Upstairs galleries to stand on and enjoy
scenic large backyard. Delicious breakfast; friendly hosts. Owners are Mr. and
Mrs. M. L. Harvey.

Hosts: Paul and Margurite Carter
Rooms: 3 (PB) $75
Full Breakfast (Continental available on request)
Credit Cards: A, B
Notes: 5 (except holidays), 7 (12 and up), 10

## NEW ORLEANS

### The Dusty Mansion

2231 Gen Pershing, 70115
(504) 895-4576; FAX (504) 891-0049

Charming turn-of-the-century home,
cozy and affordable. Sundeck, game
room, hot tub. Close to St. Charles Ave.
Street Car, easy access to French Quarter, Aquarium, Zoo, and Botanical Gardens.

Hostess: Cynthia Tomlin Riggs
Rooms: 4 (2PB; 2SB) $50-75
Continental Breakfast
Credit Cards: none
Notes: 2, 5, 7, 10, 12

### La Maison

608 Kerlerec St., 70116
(504) 271-0228 (voice and FAX)

La Maison was built in 1805 in the Historic Faurbourg Marigny area. It is
within walking distance of the French

---

5 Open all year;  6 Pets welcome;  7 Children welcome;  8 Tennis nearby;  9 Swimming nearby;
10 Golf nearby;  11 Skiing nearby;  12 May be booked through travel agent.

# LOUISIANA

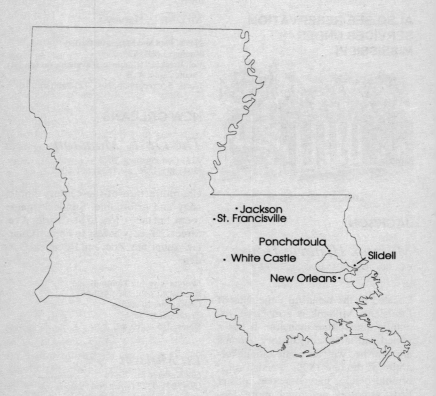

Quarter (three blocks) and many restaurants. Each mini-suite has queen and double beds, sitting room, phone, color TV, and lovely courtyard. Parking is available across from the cottage. Reservations are required.

Hostess: Alma Hulin
Rooms: 7 (PB) $65-165
Continental Breakfast
Credit Cards: none
Notes: 2, 5, 7, 8, 12

La Maison

## Madam Julia's Boarding House

941 Julia St., 70130
(504) 529-2952

A unique "old town" experience in historic Fauburg St. Marie, heart of downtown. Walking distance to Amtrak, Superdome, Convention Center, French Quarter, mall shopping, Streetcar line, and Art galleries. 150 year old buildings, court yards, and gathering rooms. Unique in all of downtown.

Hosts: Joanne and Dennis Hilton
Rooms: 32 (SB) $45-75
Continental Breakfast
Credit Cards: A, B, C
Notes: 2 (in advance), 5, 7, 8, 9

## New Orleans Bed and Breakfast Accommodations

671 Rosa Ave., Suite 208, **Metairie** 70005
(504) 838-0071; FAX (504) 838-0140

If you appreciate crystal chandeliers, hardwood floors, antiques, Oriental rugs, interesting architecture, or simple traditional elegance, call us. If you want private hide-aways, condominiums, private apartments, or cozy rooms in New Orleans neighborhoods, call us. Whatever your choice, you will find gracious hospitality, knowledgeable hosts who are concerned about your safety, comfort, and pleasure. We are also familiar with bed and breakfast plantations, homes, or cottages throughout Louisiana. Call us, too, for referrals to other states, England, Isreal, or a villa in Mallorca. Sarah-Margaret Brown, owner.

## St. Charles Guest House

1748 Prytania St., 70130
(504) 523-6556

A simple and affordable pension in the Lower Garden District on the streetcar line is just ten minutes to downtown and the French Quarter. Continental breakfast is served overlooking a charming pool and patio complete with banana trees. Tours are available from our lobby. Antique, cozy, quintessentially

NOTES: Credit cards accepted: A Master Card; B Visa; C American Express; D Discover; E Diners Club; F Other; 2 Personal checks accepted; 3 Lunch available; 4 Dinner available; 5 Open all year; 6 Pets welcome; 7 Children welcome; 8 Tennis nearby; 9 Swimming nearby; 10 Golf nearby; 11 Skiing nearby; 12 May be booked through travel agent.

"Old New Orleans."

Hosts: Joanne and Dennis Hilton
Rooms: 30 (26PB; 4SB) $30-85
Continental Breakfast
Credit Cards: A, B, C
Notes: 2 (in advance), 5, 7, 8, 9

## PONCHATOULA

### The Bella Rose Mansion

255 N. Eighth St., 70454
(504) 386-3857 (voice and FAX)

The Bella Rose Mansion

"When only the best will do." Bella
Rose is on the National Historical Register in the heart of America's Antique
City and Plantations. Thirty five minutes from New Orleans International
Airport and 45 minutes from Baton
Rouge. Romantic heart-shaped jacuzzi
suites and unique rooms; exquisite
hand-carved mahogany, spiral staircase
crowned with a stained glass dome is
the finest in the South. Guests enjoy a
silver service breakfast of eggs
Benedict, Banana Foster crepes, Mimo-
sas, and New Orleans blend coffee in a
marble walled solarium with a fountain
of Bacchus. Georgian in style, the mansion consists of over 12,000 square feet.
Indoor terrazzo shuffleboard court, an
extensive library, and a heated Olympia style swimming pool are only a few
of the magnificent features the await
you at the Bella Rose Mansion. Available for functions.

Hostess: Rose James
Rooms: 2 jacuzzi suites + 4 rooms (PB)
Full Breakfast
Credit Cards: A, B
Notes: 5, 8, 9, 10, 12

## ST. FRANCISVILLE

### Dogwood Plantation

4363 LA Hwy. 966, Box 81, 70775
(800) 635-4790; FAX (800) 767-5831

An 1803 log core building located on
five acres with a pond. Furnished in period antiques, all rooms have private
facilities.

Hosts: Pat and Roland Bahan
Rooms: 2 (PB) $85-95
Continental Breakfast
Credit Cards: A, B, C, D, E
Notes: 5, 9, 10, 12

## SLIDELL

### Salmen-Fritchie House Bed and Breakfast

127 Cleveland Ave., 70458
(504) 643-1405; (800) 235-4168;
FAX (504) 643-2251

This magnificent 1895 Victorian home
is listed in the "*The Best Places to Stay
in the South.*" Just 30 minutes from
New Orleans famous French Quarter or
the Mississippi Gulf Coast. Easy access from I-10 Expressway. Family

---

NOTES: Credit cards accepted: A Master Card; B Visa; C American Express; D Discover;
E Diners Club; F Other; 2 Personal checks accepted; 3 Lunch available; 4 Dinner available;

owned for 100 years, it now offers comfortable lodging for personal and business travelers. Home sits on a four and one half acre city block with 300 year old live oaks, and is listed on the National Historic Register. Home has five guest rooms in the main house and one cottage with a living room, kitchen combo, laundry facility, private bedroom, screened porch with courtyard, and marble jacuzzi for two.

Hosts: Sharon and Homer Fritchie
Rooms: 5 (PB) $85-95; cottage $225
Full Breakfast
Credit Cards: A, B, C
Notes: 2, 5, 7 (over 10), 8, 9, 10, 11, 12

Salmen-Fritchie House Bed and Breakfast

## WHITE CASTLE

### *Nottoway Plantation Inn and Restaurant*
30970 Hwy. 405, 70788
(504) 545-2730 or (504) 545-9167;
FAX (504) 545-8632

Built in 1859 by John Randolph, a wealthy sugar cane planter, Nottoway is a blend of Italianate and Greek Revival styles. Nottoway is the largest remaining plantation home in the South. Its guest rooms are individually decorated with period furnishings. Wake up with juice, coffee, and homemade muffins served to your room.

Hostesses: Cindy Hidalgo and Faye Russell
Rooms: 10 +, 3 suites (PB) $125-250
Full Breakfast
Credit Cards: A, B, C, D
Notes: 2, 3, 4, 5, 7, 8, 9, 10, 12

---

5 Open all year; 6 Pets welcome; 7 Children welcome; 8 Tennis nearby; 9 Swimming nearby; 10 Golf nearby; 11 Skiing nearby; 12 May be booked through travel agent.

# MAINE

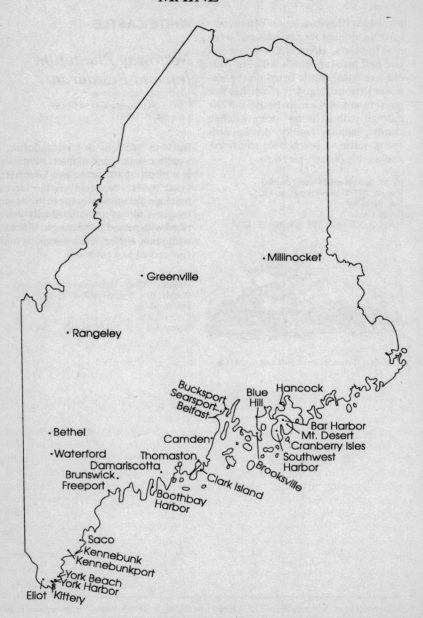

- Millinocket

- Greenville

- Rangeley

Bucksport
Searsport
Belfast
Blue Hill
Hancock

- Bethel

Camden
Bar Harbor
Mt. Desert
Cranberry Isles
Southwest Harbor

- Waterford
Thomaston
Damariscotta
Brunswick
Freeport
Clark Island
Brooksville

Boothbay Harbor

- Saco
Kennebunk
Kennebunkport
York Beach
York Harbor
Eliot  Kittery

# Maine

**BAR HARBOR**

## The Atlantic Oakes
## The Willows

P.O. Box 3, Eden St., 04609
(207) 288-5801; (800) 33 MAINE;
FAX (207) 288-5802

We have restored the Sir Harry Oakes mansion/summer cottage on our grounds. This charming house was named *The Willows* after the willow trees on the entrance drive. About 200 summer cottages were built in Bar Harbor from 1880 to 1890. *The Willows* was built in 1913, one of the last estates built. The large wooden hotels (now gone) were built from 1865-1885.

No matter how large and ostentatious the summer homes were, they were always called "cottages." *The Willows* is located on the ground of the Atlantic Oakes By-The-Sea. There are four tennis courts and indoor and outdoor pools available for use by B&B guests.

Hosts: The Coughs
Rooms: 9 (PB) $55-180
Continental or Full Breakfast
Credit Cards: A, B, C
Notes: 5, 8, 9, 10, 12

## Black Friar Inn

10 Summer St., 04609
(207) 288-5091

Black Friar Inn is a completely rebuilt and restored inn incorporating beautiful woodwork, mantels, windows, and bookcases from old mansions and churches on Mount Desert Island. Gourmet breakfast includes homemade breads, pastry, and muffins; fresh fruit; eggs du jour; etc. Afternoon refreshments are provided. All rooms have queen beds; the suite has a king bed. Within walking distance of the waterfront, restaurants, and shops, with ample

---

NOTES: Credit cards accepted: A Master Card; B Visa; C American Express; D Discover; E Diners Club; F Other; 2 Personal checks accepted; 3 Lunch available; 4 Dinner available; 5 Open all year; 6 Pets welcome; 7 Children welcome; 8 Tennis nearby; 9 Swimming nearby; 10 Golf nearby; 11 Skiing nearby; 12 May be booked through travel agent.

parking available. Short drive to Acadia National Park.

Hosts: Perry and Sharon, Risley and Falke
Rooms: 7 (PB) $90-140
Full Breakfast
Credit Cards: A, B
Notes: 2, 5, 7 (over 11), 8, 9, 10, 11 (cross-country)

## Hearthside Bed and Breakfast

7 High St., 04609
(207) 288-4533

Built in 1907 as a private residence, the inn features a blend of country and Victorian furnishings. All rooms have queen beds, some have a private porch, fireplace, whirlpool bath, and/or air-conditioning. We serve a homemade full breakfast, afternoon tea and home-made cookies, and evening refreshments. Located on a quiet side street in town, we are five minutes from Acadia National Park.

Hosts: Barry and Susan Schwartz
Rooms: 9 (PB) $55-75 (off season)
$85-125 (in season)
Full Breakfast
Credit Cards: A, B
Notes: 2, 5, 8, 9, 10, 11

## Wayside Inn

11 Atlantic Ave., 04609
(207) 288-5703 (voice and FAX);
(800) 722-6671

A beautiful English Tudor building decorated in early Victorian offering private and semi-private rooms with fireplaces. Full gourmet breakfast served. Located on a quiet side street

in historic district within walking distance to all in-town activities. Open all year. Lower rates off season.

Hosts: Steve and Sandi Straubel
Rooms: 8 (6PB; 2SB) $95-140
Full Breakfast
Credit Cards: A, B
Notes: 2, 5, 7, 9, 10, 12

## BATH

## Fairhaven Inn

RR 2, Box 85, N. Bath Rd., 04530
(207) 443-4391

A 1790 Colonial nestled on the hillside overlooking the Kennebec River on 20 acres of country sights and sounds. Beaches, golf, and maritime museum nearby, plus cross-country ski trails and wood fires. Gourmet breakfast is served year-round. Candlelight dinners available in winter.

Hosts: Susie and Dave Reed
Rooms: 8 (6PB; 2SB) $60-90
Full Breakfast
Credit Cards: A, B
Notes: 4 (weekend package), 5, 6 and 7 (by arrangement), 8, 9, 10, 11 (cross country)

## BELFAST

## The Jeweled Turret Inn

16 Pearl St., 04915
(207) 338-2304; (800) 696-2304 (Maine only)

This grand lady of the Victorian era, circa 1898, offers many unique architectural features and is on the National Register of Historic Places. The Inn is named for the grand staircase that winds

---

NOTES: Credit cards accepted: A Master Card; B Visa; C American Express; D Discover; E Diners Club; F Other; 2 Personal checks accepted; 3 Lunch available; 4 Dinner available;

up the turret, lighted by stained and leaded glass panels with jewel-like embellishments. Each guest room is filled with Victoriana and has its own bath. A gourmet breakfast is served. Shops, restaurants, and waterfront are a stroll away.

Hosts: Carl and Cathy Heffentrager
Rooms: 7 (PB) $60-95
Full Breakfast
Credit Cards: A, B
Notes: 2, 5, 8, 9, 10, 11,12

The Jeweled Turret Inn

## BELGRADE LAKES

## Wings Hill

Rt. 27, P.O. Box 386, 04918
(207) 495-2400; (800) 50 WINGS

The ultimate stop in central Maine. In a class by itself, the Inn is powerfully decorated with oriental, art, and antiques. Large guest rooms with private baths. A great base for all vacation needs. Sensational food and accommodations. Quiet, adult, refined luxury.

Renovated 200 year old farm house. Wonderful grounds in a scenic area.

Hosts: The Hofmann Family (Dick, Sharon, Brett, Jason, Scott, and Sarah)
Rooms: 8 (PB) $95
Full Breakfast
Credit Cards: A, B, C
Notes: 2, 5, 7, 9, 10, 11, 12

## BETHEL

## Sunday River Inn and Cross Country Ski Center

R.R. 2, Box 1688, 04217
(207) 824-2410; FAX (207) 824-3181

Sunday River Inn is a small country resort built around winter sports. A nationally renowned cross-country ski center is adjacent to the Inn, and Sunday River Ski Resort with eight mountains of alpine skiing is one-half mile away. A wood-fired sauna and hot tub, a skating rink, snowshoe trails, and dogsledding are also available. With all this the guests still return for the *food!*

Hosts: Steve and Peggy Wight
Rooms: 17 (2PB; 15SB) $65-78 prepaid
Full Breakfast and Dinner
Credit Cards: A, B, C, D
Notes: 2, 4, 7, 8, 9, 10, 11, 12

## BLUE HILL

## Mountain Road House

R.R. 1, Box 2040 Mountain Rd., 04614
(207) 374-2794

Located on the only road that traverses the face of Blue Hill Mountain, our 1890s farmhouse offers views of the

5 Open all year; 6 Pets welcome; 7 Children welcome; 8 Tennis nearby; 9 Swimming nearby; 10 Golf nearby; 11 Skiing nearby; 12 May be booked through travel agent.

Bay while only one mile from the village. Choose twin, double, or queen-size bedrooms, each with private bath. Early bird coffee/tea available at 7 AM, the breakfast includes a hot entree, fresh fruit, and coffee cake. Enjoy antiquing, galleries, craft shops, bookstores, musical events, fine dining, hiking, coastal villages, and of course Acadia National Park. No smoking.

Hosts: Carol and John McCulloch
Rooms: 3 (PB) $55-85
Full Breakfast
Credit Cards: A, B
Notes: 2, 5, 7, 12

Mountain Road House

## BOOTHBAY HARBOR

### Anchor Watch
### Bed and Breakfast
5 Eames Dr., 04538
(207) 633-7565

Our seaside, captain's house welcomes you to Boothbay Region. It's a pleasant walk to unique shops, fine dining, and scenic boat trips. A delicious homemade breakfast is served in the sunny breakfast nook looking out to the sea. Quilts, stenciling, and nautical decor

make our four bedrooms comfortable and cozy. Enjoy your afternoon tea in the attractive sitting room facing the ocean. Your host captains the Monhegan and Squirrel Island ferries from nearby Pier 8.

Hostess: Diane Campbell
Rooms: 4 (PB) $75-105
Full Breakfast
Credit Cards: A, B
Notes: 2, 5, 8, 9, 10, 12

### Harbour Towne Inn
### on the Waterfront
71 Townsend Ave., 04538
(207) 633-4300 (voice and FAX);
(800) 722-4240

THE FINEST B&B ON THE WATER-FRONT. Our refurbished Victorian Inn retains turn-of-the-century ambiance while providing all modern amenities. The colorful gardens and quiet, tree-shaded location slopes right to the edge of the beautiful New England harbor. Choose an Inn room with or without an outside deck for scenic views or a Carriage House room with waterfront decks. Our luxurious penthouse is a modern and spacious home that sleeps six people in absolute luxury and privacy. Come stay with us just once and you will know why our guests return year after year. No smoking.

Hosts: George Thomas (owner) and Jill (manager)
Rooms: 12 (PB) $59-150 ($79-225 in season)
Continental Breakfast
Credit Cards: A, B, C, D
Notes: 2, 5, 7 (well behaved), 8, 9, 10, 11, 12

NOTES: Credit cards accepted: A Master Card; B Visa; C American Express; D Discover; E Diners Club; F Other; 2 Personal checks accepted; 3 Lunch available; 4 Dinner available;

Oakland House–Shore Oaks Seaside Inn

## BROOKSVILLE

## Oakland House—Shore Oaks Seaside Inn

RR 1, Box 400, Herrick Rd., 04617
(800) 359-RELAX; FAX can be arranged

The Inn was built in 1907 as a private Craftsman / Mission style summer cottage. Victorian pieces are tastefully blended in. There is a living room with stone fireplace, library, dining room, porch, and gazebo / deck extending out onto the water. See loons, seals, and windjammers right off shore. Relax, dream. . . , breakfast, dine (in season). Use Oakland House's dock, rowboats, firewood, salt / freshwater beaches, and climb to grand vistas. Bar Harbor, Acadia National Park, Stonington, Blue Hill, Isle au Haut, and the "Mailboat" are nearby.

Hosts: Jim and Sally Littlefield
Rooms: 10 (7PB; 3SB) $41-172
Seasonal Full or Continental Breakfast
Credit Cards: none
Notes: 2, 3, 4, 9, 10, 12

## BRUNSWICK

## Harborgate B&B

R.D. 2, Box 2260, 04011
(207) 725-5894

This contemporary redwood home is 40 feet from the ocean. Flower gardens and wooded landscape provide gracious relaxation. Two ocean-facing, first floor bedrooms are separated by a guest living room with patio. Dock for swimming and sunbathing. Close to Bowdoin College, L.L. Bean, and sandy beaches. Wide selection of stores, gift shops, and steak and seafood restaurants. Summer theater, college art museum, Perry McMillan Museum, and historical society buildings and events.

Hostess: Carolyn Bolles
Rooms: 2 (SB) $60
Continental Breakfast
Credit Cards: none
Closed November through April
Notes: 2, 9

## BUCKSPORT

## Old Parsonage Inn

P.O. Box 1577, 04416
(207) 469-6477

The Clough family invites you to share their historic Federal home, formerly the Methodist parsonage, located one half mile from coastal Route 1. All rooms are tastefully decorated and retain original architectural features. The third floor houses an 1809 Masonic Hall. Private guest entrance, kitchenette in the breakfast/sitting room. Short walk to waterfront and restaurants. Convenient for

---

5 Open all year; 6 Pets welcome; 7 Children welcome; 8 Tennis nearby; 9 Swimming nearby; 10 Golf nearby; 11 Skiing nearby; 12 May be booked through travel agent.

day trips to Acadia, both sides of Penobscot Bay, and historic Fort Knox.

Hosts: Judith and Brian Clough
Rooms: 3 (1PB; 2SB) $45
No Breakfast
Credit Cards: A, B
Notes: 2, 5, 7, 8, 9, 10

## CAMDEN

### The Owl and Turtle View Harbor Guest Rooms

8 Bay View, 04843
(207) 236-9014

Two of the three rooms immediately overlook the harbor. Air conditioning, TV, electric heat, phone, private bath, private parking. Continental breakfast served on tray to room. Downstairs is one of the states best book shops. Surrounded by good restaurants and shops. No smoking.

Hosts: The Conrad Family
Rooms: 3 (PB) $50-55 (off season)
$75-85 (in season) + tax
Continental Breakfast
Credit Cards: A, B
Notes: 2, 5, 7, 8, 9, 10, 11, 12

## CLARK ISLAND

### Craignair Inn

Clark Island Rd. Box 533, 04859
(207) 594-7644; FAX (207) 596-7124

Located on the water, the Inn is near great hiking trails along the shore or through the forests. The Inn was formerly a boardinghouse for stonecutters from the nearby quarries that provide great swimming. The annex was once

the village chapel. A peaceful and secluded setting located 10 miles south of Rockland in St. George.

Hosts: Norman E. and Theresa E. Smith
Rooms: 24 (8PB; 16SB) $64-93
Full Breakfast
Credit Cards: A, B, C
Notes: 2, 5, 7, 8, 9, 10, 11, 12

## CRANBERRY ISLES

### The Red House

Main Rd., 04625
(207) 288-4250

Enjoy the breathtaking beauty of Maine, while experiencing the relaxing, quiet atmosphere of The Red House on Great Cranberry Island. Situated on a large saltwater inlet, guests need only look outside for beautiful scenery and extraordinary ocean views. At The Red House there are six guest rooms and each is distinctively decorated in traditional style; some with shared baths and some private with baths. Come and share your hosts' island home and experience the tranquil peace of God's creation.

Hosts: Dorothy and John Towns
Rooms: 6 (3PB; 3SB) $50-75
Full Breakfast
Credit Cards: A, B
Notes: 2, 3, 4, 8, 9, 12

## DAMARISCOTTA

### Brannon-Bunker Inn

H.C.R. 64, Box 045, 04543
(207) 563-5941

Brannon-Bunker Inn is an intimate and

---

NOTES: Credit cards accepted: A Master Card; B Visa; C American Express; D Discover; E Diners Club; F Other; 2 Personal checks accepted; 3 Lunch available; 4 Dinner available;

relaxed country bed and breakfast situated minutes from sandy beach, lighthouse, and historic fort in Maine's mid-coastal region. Located in a 1920s Cape, converted barn and carriage house, the guest rooms are furnished in themes regarding the charm of yesterday and the comforts of today. Antique shops, too!

Hosts: Jeanne and Joe Hovance
Rooms: 7 (5PB; 2SB) $55-65
Expanded Continental Breakfast
Credit Cards: A, B, C
Notes: 2, 5, 7, 8, 9, 10, 12

Brannon-Bunker Inn

## Down Easter Inn

Bristol Rd., Routes 129 and 130, 04543
(207) 563-5332; winter (201) 267-1697

The Down Easter Inn, one mile from downtown Damariscotta, is in the heart of the rocky coast of Maine. On the National Register of Historic Places, it features a two-story porch framed by Corintian columns. Minutes from golfing, lakes, and the ocean. Nearby are lobster wharves for local fare and boat trips around Muscongus Bay and to Mohegan Island. The Inn features 22 lovely rooms with TVs.

Hosts: Mary and Robert Colquhoun
Rooms: 22 (PB) $70-80
Continental Breakfast
Credit Cards: A, B
Notes: 2, 7, 9, 10

## ELIOT

## Farmstead Bed and Breakfast

379 Goodwin Rd., 03903
(207) 748-3145

Lovely country inn on three acres. Warm, friendly atmosphere exemplifies farm life of the late 1800s. Guest rooms are Victorian in style. Each has mini-refrigerator and microwave for late evening snacks or those special diets. Full breakfast may include blueberry pancakes or french toast, homemade syrup, fruit, and juice. Handicap accessible. Minutes from Kittery Factory Outlets, York Beaches, and Portsmouth, NH, historic sites. One hour from Boston.

Hosts: Meb and John Lippincott
Rooms: 6 (PB) $48
Full Breakfast
Credit Cards: A, B, C
Notes: 2, 5, 6, 7, 12

## FREEPORT

## Captain Josiah Mitchell House Bed and Breakfast

188 Main St., 04032
(207) 865-3289

Two blocks from L.L. Bean, this house is a few minutes walk past centuries-old sea captains' homes and shady trees to over 120 factory outlet discount shops in town. After exploring, relax on our beautiful, peaceful veranda with antique wicker furniture and "remember when" porch swing. State inspected

---

5 Open all year; 6 Pets welcome; 7 Children welcome; 8 Tennis nearby; 9 Swimming nearby; 10 Golf nearby; 11 Skiing nearby; 12 May be booked through travel agent.

White Cedar Inn

and approved. Family owned and operated.

Hosts: Loretta and Alan Bradley
Rooms: 7 (PB) $68-85 (lower winter rates)
Full Breakfast
Credit Cards: A, B
Notes: 2, 5, 8, 9, 10, 11, 12

## Country at Heart Bed and Breakfast

37 Bow St., 04032
(207) 865-0512

Our cozy 1870s home is located off Main Street and only two blocks from L.L. Bean. Park your car and walk to the restaurants and many outlet stores. Stay in one of three country decorated rooms: the Shaker Room, Quilt Room, or the Teddy Bear Room. Our rooms have hand-stenciled borders, handmade crafts, and either antique or reproduction furnishings. There is also a gift shop for guests.

Hosts: Roger and Kim Dubay
Rooms: 3 (PB) $65-85
Full Breakfast
Credit Cards: none
Notes: 2, 5, 7, 9, 10, 11, 12

## White Cedar Inn

178 Main St., 04032
(207) 865-9099; (800) 853-1269

The White Cedar Inn is a century old historic Victorian Inn located just two blocks north of L.L. Bean and most of Freeport's luxury outlets. Our six air-conditioned bedrooms, all with private baths, are spacious and furnished with antiques. Most rooms have queen-size beds while some offer separate beds. We serve a full country breakfast in the sun room over looking our beautifully landscaped grounds. A common room with TV and library is also available to our guests.

Hosts: Phil and Carla Kerber
Rooms: 6 (PB) $80-100
Full Breakfast
Credit Cards: A, B, C, D
Notes: 5, 8, 9, 10, 11, 12

## GREENVILLE

## Greenville Inn

P.O. Box 1194 Norris St., 04441
(207) 695-2206

Restored 1895 lumber baron's mansion

---

NOTES: Credit cards accepted: A Master Card; B Visa; C American Express; D Discover; E Diners Club; F Other; 2 Personal checks accepted; 3 Lunch available; 4 Dinner available;

on a hillside overlooking Moosehead Lake and the Squaw Mountains. A large leaded glass window decorated with a painted spruce tree, gas lights, embossed wall coverings, and carved fireplace mantles grace the Inn. A sumptuous continental breakfast buffet is included with the room. In the evening our restaurant is open to the public. Open year round.

Hosts: Effie, Michael, and Susie Schnetzer
Rooms: 13 (11PB; 2SB) $85-115
Continental Plus Breakfast
Credit Cards: A, B, D
Notes: 2, 4, 7, 8, 9, 10, 11, 12

The Crocker House Country Inn

## HANCOCK

## *The Crocker House Country Inn*

H.C. 77, Box 171, 04640
(207) 422-6806

Sequestered on Hancock Point, this restored 111 year old inn is a three-minute walk from Frenchman Bay. Each of the eleven guest rooms is individually appointed and has a private bath. The carriage house, converted in 1992, provides an additional common room and a spa, available to all guests. The restaurant, open to the public, continues to draw guests from distant places for its extraordinary cuisine and live jazz piano on Friday and Saturday nights.

Hosts: Richard and Elizabeth Malaby
Rooms: 11 (PB) $75-120
Full Breakfast
Credit Cards: A, B, C, D
Notes: 2, 4, 6, 7, 8, 10

## KENNEBUNK

## *Sundial Inn*

P.O. Box 1147, 48 Beach Ave., 04043
(207) 967-3850; FAX (207) 967-4719

Unique oceanfront inn furnished with turn-of-the-century Victorian antiques. Each of the 34 guest rooms has a private bath, phone, color TV, and air-conditioning. Several rooms also offer ocean views and whirlpool baths. Visit Kennebunkport's art galleries and studios. museums, and gift shops. Go whale-watching, deep-sea fishing, or hiking at the nearby wildlife refuge and estuary. Golf and tennis are nearby. Continental breakfast features muffins and coffee cakes. Wheelchair accessible. No Smoking.

Hosts: Larry and Pat Kenny
Rooms: 34 (PB) $65-155
Continental Breakfast
Credit Cards: A, B, C, E
Notes: 5, 8, 9, 10

---

5  Open all year;  6  Pets welcome;  7  Children welcome;  8  Tennis nearby;  9  Swimming nearby;
10  Golf nearby;  11  Skiing nearby;  12  May be booked through travel agent.

## KENNEBUNKPORT

### The Captain Lord Mansion

P.O. Box 800, 04046
(207) 967-3141; FAX (207) 967-3172

The Captain Lord Mansion is an intimate and stylish inn situated at the head of a large village green, overlooking the Kennebunk River. Built during the War of 1812 as an elegant, private residence, it is now listed on the National Historic Register. The large, luxurious guest rooms are furnished with rich fabrics, European paintings, and fine period antiques, yet have modern creature comforts such as private baths and working fireplaces. Christians, as well as gracious hosts and innkeepers, Bev Davis, husband Rick Litchfield and their friendly, helpful staff are eager to make your visit enjoyable. Family style breakfasts are served in an atmospheric, country kitchen. A conference room is also available.

Hosts: Bev Davis and Rick Litchfield
Rooms: 16 (PB) $79-149 Jan.-May;
$149-199 June-Dec.
Full Breakfast
Credit Cards: A, B, D
Notes: 2, 5, 8, 9, 10, 11 (cross-country)

### The Green Heron Inn

126 Ocean Ave., P.O. Box 2578, 04046
(207) 967-3315

Comfortable, clean, and cozy ten-room bed and breakfast. Each guest room has private bath, air conditioning, and color TV. A full breakfast from a menu is served. "Serving the best breakfast in the Port."

Hosts: Charles and Elizabeth Reid
Manager: Carol Stahl
Rooms: 10 (PB) $85-133
Full Breakfast
Credit Cards: none
Notes: 2, 5, 6 (restricted), 7, 8, 9, 10

The Inn on South Street

### The Inn on South Street

P.O. Box 478A, 04046
(207) 967-5151; (800) 963-5151

Now approaching its 200th year, this stately Greek Revival house is in Kennebunkport's historic district. Located on a quiet street, the Inn is within walking distance of restaurants, shops, and the water. There are three beautifully decorated guest rooms and one luxury apartment/suite. Private baths, queen-size beds, fireplaces, a common room, afternoon refreshments, and early morning coffee. Breakfast is always special and is served in the large country kitchen with views of the river and ocean. Rated A and Excellent by ABBA.

Hosts: Jaques and Eva Downs
Rooms: 3 + 1 suite (PB) $85-125;
$155-185 suite
Full Breakfast
Credit Cards: A, B
Notes: 2, 8, 9, 10, 11, 12

NOTES: Credit cards accepted: A Master Card; B Visa; C American Express; D Discover; E Diners Club; F Other; 2 Personal checks accepted; 3 Lunch available; 4 Dinner available;

## Kennebunkport Inn

One Dock Sq., P.O. Box 111, 04046
(207) 967-2621; (800) 248-2621;
FAX (207) 967-3705

Classic country inn located in the heart
of Kennebunkport near shops and historic district, beaches, boating, and golf.
Originally a Sea Captain's home, the
Inn maintains its charm with antiques
furnishings, two elegant dining rooms,
Victorian pub, and piano bar. Serving
breakfast and dinner, May through October, the Inn is recognized for its fine
food. Rooms are available year-round.

Hosts: Rick and Martha Griffin
Rooms: 34 (PB) $69.50-189
Full Breakfast (dinner available in restaurant)
Credit Cards: A, B, C
Notes: 4, 5, 8, 9, 10, 12

## KENTS HILL

## Home-Nest Farm

Rt. 1, Box 2350, 04349
(207) 897-4125

Off the beaten track, on a foothill of the
Longfellow Mountains of West Central
Maine's lake district, Home-Nest Farm
offers a 60 mile panoramic view of the
White Mountains. A place for all seasons, it includes four historic homes,
furnished with period antiques: the main
house (1784), Lilac Cottage (c. 1800),
and the Red Schoolhouse (c. 1830).
Local activities include sheep tending,
berry picking, Living History Farm
Museum, exploring many trails (maintained for snowmobiling and skiing in
the winter), swimming, fishing, and

boating (boats provided). Two day
minimum stay.

Hosts: Arn and Leda Sturtevant
Rooms: 4 (PB) $50-95
Closed in March and April
Full Breakfast
Credit Cards: none
Notes: 2, 7, 9, 10, 11

## KITTERY

## Enchanted Nights Bed and Breakfast

29 Wentworth St., 03904
(207) 439-1489

Affordable luxury 75 minutes north of
Boston, Coastal Maine. Fanciful and
whimsical for the romantic at heart.
French and Victorian furnishings with
CATVs. Three minutes to historic Portsmouth dining, dancing, concerts in the
park, historic homes, theater, harbor
cruises, cliff walks, scenic ocean drives,
beaches, charming neighboring resorts,
water park, and outlet malls. Whirlpool
tub for two. Full breakfast, or $12 less,
and enjoy a Portsmouth cafe. Pets welcome. No smoking indoors.

Hosts: Nancy Bogenberger and Peter Lamandia
Rooms: 6 (5PB; 2SB) $47-135
Full Breakfast
Credit Cards: A, B, C, D
Notes: 2, 5, 6, 7, 8, 9, 10, 12

## MILLINOCKET

## Katahdin Area B&B

94-96 Oxford St., 04462
(207) 723-5220

Katahdin Area B&B is located 17 miles

5 Open all year; 6 Pets welcome; 7 Children welcome; 8 Tennis nearby; 9 Swimming nearby;
10 Golf nearby; 11 Skiing nearby; 12 May be booked through travel agent.

south of Baxter State Park, the gateway to Katahdin, Maine's highest peak and the Appalachian Trail Access. Millinocket is a friendly town with fewer than 6,500 population. The spectacular "Grand Canyon of the East" at Gulf Hagas is 30 miles south on Route 11. Hiking the many groomed trails, whitewater rafting, canoeing, and seaplane rides are just a few of the many outdoor attractions around Millinocket, a tourist attraction "To see a moose" might top your list. Winter snowmobiling, cross-country skiing, and ice fishing top the winter activities. KABB is located within walking distance to our "downtown" shops, Main Street, restaurants, and places to worship.

Hosts: Rodney and Mary Lou Corriveau
Rooms: 5 (1PB; 4SB) $40-50
Full Breakfast
Credit Cards: none
Notes: 2, 5, 7, 8, 9, 10, 11

## MT. DESERT

## *Long Pond Inn*

Box 120, 04660
(207) 244-5854

Conveniently located in historic Somesville, the heart of Mt. Desert Island, the Inn offers a peaceful retreat within 15 minutes of all island activities. Our Inn offers warmth and hospitality that reflects an admired tradition associated with New England inns. The Inn was built with dismantled vintage materials from summer estates, country stores, hotels, and cottages. Four guest bedrooms are uniquely furnished

featuring a cozy two-room suite with king-size bed, private deck and bath, and jacuzzi tub. We also have three rooms with queen-size beds, private baths, and one additional jacuzzi. Your stay includes a hearty, continental breakfast of fresh seasonal fruit and homemade muffins. After breakfast take a stroll in our gardens or paddle one of our rental canoes on Long Pond.

Hosts: Lois and Brian Hamor
Rooms: 4 (PB) $75-125
Continental Plus Breakfast
Credit Cards: A, B
Notes: 2, 8, 9, 10

Northwoods Bed and Breakfast

## RANGELEY

## *Northwoods Bed and Breakfast*

P.O. Box 79, Main St., 04970
(207) 864-2440

An historic 1912 home of rare charm and easy elegance, Northwoods is centrally located in Rangeley Village with spacious rooms, a lakefront porch, expansive grounds, and private boat dock. Northwoods provides superb accommodations. Golf, tennis, water sports, hiking, and skiing are a few of the many

---

NOTES: Credit cards accepted: A Master Card; B Visa; C American Express; D Discover; E Diners Club; F Other; 2 Personal checks accepted; 3 Lunch available; 4 Dinner available;

activities offered by the region.

Hosts: Carol and Robert Scofield
Rooms: 4 (3PB; 1SB) $60-75
Full Breakfast
Credit Cards: A, B
Notes: 2, 8, 9, 10, 11, 12

## SACO

### Crown 'N' Anchor Inn

P.O. Box 228, 121 N. St., 04072-0228
(207) 282-3829

Our North Street location places the Crown 'N' Anchor Inn at the hub of local attractions. Delight in this Greek revival two-story house with ornate Victorian furnishings, period antiques, and many collectibles. Guests desiring to take time out from their busy schedules are invited to socialize in our parlor, curl up with a good book in our library, or just relax and enjoy the garden views from the comfort of our front porch. Just minutes from Kennebunkport, Wells, Ogunquit, Kittery, and more.

Hosts: John Barclay and Martha Forester
Rooms: 6 (PB) $60-95
Full Breakfast
Credit Cards: A, B
Notes: 2, 5, 6, 7 (by arrangement), 8, 9, 10, 11, 12

Crown 'N' Anchor Inn

## SEARSPORT

### Brass Lantern Inn

P.O. Box 407, 81 W. Main St. (US Rt. 1), 04974
(207) 548-0150; (800) 691-0150

Nestled at the edge of the woods, this gracious Victorian inn, built in 1850 by a sea captain, overlooks Penobscot Bay. Features include an ornate tin ceiling in the dining room, antiques, an extensive doll collection, and a shop on premises specializing in collectible trains. Each guest room has a private bath and is designed for a comfortable stay. Near Penobscot Marine Museum. Open all year, The Brass Lantern will be lit to welcome you!

Hosts: Pat Gatto, Dan and Lee Anne Lee
Rooms: 4 (PB) $65-75
Full Breakfast
Credit Cards: A, B
Notes: 2, 5, 7, 8, 9, 10, 11, 12

### Homeport Inn

E. Main St., Box 647, 04974
(207) 548-2259; (800) 742-5814

Enjoy the unusual with a restful stop at this fine example of a New England sea captain's mansion, listed in the Historic Register and appointed with period antiques and family heirlooms. Enjoy the many mid-coast attractions such as nearby Acadia National Park, sailing, cruises, local museums and galleries, antique shops, golf, and the Maine coast. Weekly rental, oceanfront, Victorian cottages on estate.

Hosts: Edith and George Johnson
Rooms: 10 (6PB; 4SB) $55-75
Full Breakfast
Credit Cards: A, B, C, D, F (Enroute)
Notes: 2, 5, 7 (3 and over), 8, 9, 10, 11, 12

5 Open all year; 6 Pets welcome; 7 Children welcome; 8 Tennis nearby; 9 Swimming nearby; 10 Golf nearby; 11 Skiing nearby; 12 May be booked through travel agent.

## Thurston House Bed and Breakfast Inn

P.O. Box 686, 04974
(207) 548-2213, (800) 240-2213

This beautiful colonial home, circa 1830, with ell and carriage house was built as a parsonage house for Stephen Thurston, uncle of Winslow Homer, who visited often. Now you can visit in a casual environment. The quiet village setting is steps away from Penobscot Marine Museum, beach park of Penobscot Bay, restaurants, churches, galleries, antiques, and more. Relax in one of four guest rooms, one with a bay view, two great for kids, and enjoy the "forget about lunch" breakfasts.

Hosts: Carl and Beverly Eppig
Rooms: 4 (2PB; 2SB) $50-65
Full Breakfast
Credit Cards: A, B
Notes: 2, 5, 7, 8, 9, 10, 11, 12

The Island House

## SOUTHWEST HARBOR

## The Island House

P.O. Box 1006, Clark Point Rd., 04679
(207) 244-5180

Relax in a gracious, restful seacoast home on the quiet side of Mt. Desert Island. We serve such Island House favorites as blueberry scones and fresh fruit crepes. A charming, private loft apartment is available. Acadia National Park is only a five-minute drive away. Located across the street from the harbor, near swimming, sailing, biking, and hiking.

Hosts: Ann and Charles Bradford
Rooms: 4 (SB; PB off season) $50-95
Full Breakfast
Credit Cards: A, B
Notes: 2, 5, 7 (over 11), 9, 11

## Lambs Ear Inn

Clark Point Rd., P.O. Box 30, 04679
(207) 244-9828

Our old Maine house was built in 1857. It is comfortable and scenic, away from the hustle and bustle. Private baths, comfortable beds with crisp, fresh linens. Sparkling harbor views and a breakfast to remember. Come and be a part of this special village and of Mt. Desert Island surrounded by Acadia National Park.

Hostess: Elizabeth Hoke
Rooms: 6 (PB) $75-125
Full Breakfast
Credit Cards: A, B
Notes: 2 (restricted), 7 (limited), 8, 9, 10, 12

## THOMASTON

## Cap'n Frost Bed and Breakfast

241 Main St., 04861
(207) 354-8217

Our 1840 Cape is furnished with country antiques, some of which are for sale.

NOTES: Credit cards accepted: A Master Card; B Visa; C American Express; D Discover; E Diners Club; F Other; 2 Personal checks accepted; 3 Lunch available; 4 Dinner available;

If you are visiting our mid-coastal area, we are a comfortable overnight stay, close to Mohegan Island and a two-hour drive to Acadia National Park. Reservations are helpful.

Hosts: Arlene and Harold Frost
Rooms: 3 (1PB; 2SB) $45-50
Full Breakfast
Credit Cards: none
Notes: 2, 5, 9, 11

## WATERFORD

### *Kedarburn Inn*

Rt. 35, Box 61, 04088
(207) 583-6182

Located in historic Waterford Village, a place to step back in time while you enjoy the comforts of today. Charming bedrooms decorated with warm country touches, including handmade quilts by Margaret, will add pleasure to your visit. Each day will start with a hearty breakfast. In the evening one can relax and enjoy an elegant dinner served daily. Whether you come for outdoor activities or simply to enjoy the countryside, let us pamper you in our relaxed and friendly atmosphere.

Hosts: Margaret and Derek Gibson
Rooms: 6 (4PB; 2SB) $69-88
Full Breakfast
Credit Cards: A, B
Notes: 2, 5, 6, 7, 9, 10, 11, 12

### *The Parsonage House Bed and Breakfast*

Rice Rd., P.O. Box 116, 04088
(207) 583-4115

Built in 1870 for the Waterford Church, this restored historic home overlooks Waterford Village, Keoka Lake, and Mt. Tirem. It is located in a four-season area providing a variety of opportunities for the outdoor enthusiast. The Parsonage is a haven of peace where Christ is honored. Three double guest rooms are tastefully furnished. Weather permitting, we feature a full breakfast on the screened porch. Guests love our large New England farm kitchen and its glowing wood-burning stove.

Hosts: Joe and Gail St. Hilaire
Rooms: 3 (1PB; 2SB) $60-85
Full Breakfast
Credit Cards: none
Notes: 2, 3, 5, 7, 9, 10, 11

Homestead Inn Bed and Breakfast

## YORK BEACH

### *Homestead Inn Bed and Breakfast*

P.O. Box 15, 03910
(207) 363-8952

Friendly, quiet, and homey—four rooms in an old (1905) boardinghouse connected to our home in 1969. Panoramic view of ocean and shore hills. Walk to two beaches, shops, and

5 Open all year; 6 Pets welcome; 7 Children welcome; 8 Tennis nearby; 9 Swimming nearby; 10 Golf nearby; 11 Skiing nearby; 12 May be booked through travel agent.

Nubble Lighthouse. Great for small, adult groups. Fireplace in living room. Breakfast served in barn board dining room and outside on private sun deck.

Hosts: Dan and Danielle Duffy
Rooms: 4 (SB) $49-59
Continental Plus Breakfast
Credit Cards: none
Notes: 2, 8, 9, 10, 12

## YORK HARBOR

### *Bell Buoy Bed and Breakfast*

570 York St., P.O. Box 445, 03911
(207) 363-7264

At the Bell Buoy, there are no strangers, only friends who have never met. Located minutes from I-95 and US 1, minutes from Kittery outlet malls, or a short walk to sandy beaches or you may want to stroll the marginal way along the ocean shore just minutes away. Fireplace and cable TV. Homemade bread or muffins are served with breakfast in the dining room each morning or on the front porch.

Hosts: Wes and Kathie Cook
Rooms: 5 (2PB; 3SB) $65-85
Full Breakfast
Credit Cards: none
Notes: 2, 5, 7 (over 6), 8, 9, 10

**BELL BUOY**

# Maryland

**ALSO SEE RESERVATION SERVICES UNDER DELAWARE AND LISTINGS UNDER DISTRICT OF COLUMBIA.**

## ANNAPOLIS

### The Barn on Howard's Cove
500 Wilson Rd., 21401
(410) 266-6840; FAX (410) 266-7293

The Barn on Howard's Cove welcomes you with warm hospitality to a restored 1850's horse barn overlooking a beautiful cove off the Severn River. You will be convenient to both Washington, D.C., and Baltimore and very close to historic Annapolis. Begin the day with choice of full breakfast served in dining area overlooking river or in our new solarium or on the deck which is also on the river. Beautiful gardens, rural setting, antiques, quilts, charming Noah's ark collection. Two guest rooms await you. One room has a loft and private deck on the river. Docking in deep water provided and canoe available.

Hosts: Graham and Libbie Gutsche
Rooms: 2 (2P½B; shared shower/tub) $70
Full Breakfast
Credit Cards: none
Notes: 2, 5, 7, 8, 10, 12 (10%)

### Chesapeake B&B
408 Cranes Roost, 21401
(410) 757-7599 (voice and FAX)

Comfortable, English country town home nestled in wooded community near Chesapeake Bay and Magothy River. Furnished in antiques, Orientals, and contemporaries. Bedroom choices include a king, queen, and a single. Perfect for family vacation or couple's getaway. Guest space has private living room. Marked nature trail. Hostess was local restaurant critic and can recommend dining choices. Only ten minutes from historic Annapolis, the U.S. Naval Academy, St. John's College, boating, and other marine adventures. Prefer a two night minimum.

Hostess: Carolyn Curtis
Rooms: 3 (1PB; 2SB) $60-80
Continental Breakfast
Credit Cards: none
Notes: 2, 5, 7, 8, 10

### Chez Amis B&B
85 East St., 21401
(410) 263-6631; (800) 474-6631

Around 1900 Chez Amis "House of Friends" was a grocery store. Still evident are the original oak display cabinet, tin ceiling, and pine floors. One

---

5 Open all year; 6 Pets welcome; 7 Children welcome; 8 Tennis nearby; 9 Swimming nearby; 10 Golf nearby; 11 Skiing nearby; 12 May be booked through travel agent.

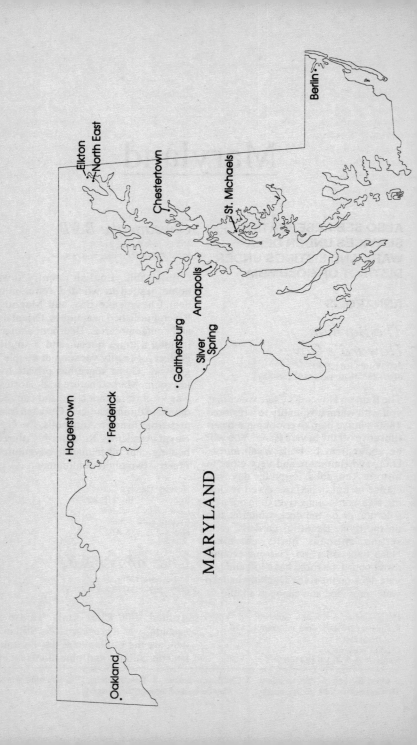

half block from Capital, one block from the harbor, and minutes by foot to the Naval Academy. "European Country" decor with antiques and quilts. Four guest rooms with two private baths. King and queen brass beds, TVs, central air-conditioning, terry robes, coffee service, and down comforters in every room. Don is a retired Army lawyer; Mickie a former D.C. tour guide. They welcome you with true "Southern" Christian hospitality!

Hosts: Don and Mickie Deline
Rooms: 4 (2PB; 2SB) $75-95 + tax
Full Breakfast
Credit Cards: A, B
Notes: 2, 5, 12

## *Duke and Duchess Bed and Breakfast*

151 Duke of Gloucester St., 21401
(401) 268-6323

A beautifully renovated 1850 home located in the Historic District of Annapolis. Just a short walk to the US Naval Academy, City Dock, restaurants, and shops. Furnished tastefully with antiques and artwork, guests can relax and enjoy an atmosphere of cozy elegance. The B&B offers clean, comfortable accommodations with modern conveniences, including central air-conditioning. A full, complimentary breakfast is served. Advance reservations by phone. Special weekday and off-season rates.

Hostess: Doris Marsh
Rooms: 2 (PB) $100-150
Full Breakfast
Credit Cards: A, B
Notes: 2, 5, 6, 7

## BERLIN

## *Merry Sherwood Plantation*

8909 Worcester Hwy., 21811
(410) 641-2112; (800) 660-0358;
FAX (410) 641-9528

This 1859, pre-Civil War mansion allows the visitor to experience a glorious step back in time. Recently restored, this elegant and opulent home is furnished throughout with authentic Vic-

Merry Sherwood Plantation

NOTES: Credit cards accepted: A Master Card; B Visa; C American Express; D Discover; E Diners Club; F Other; 2 Personal checks accepted; 3 Lunch available; 4 Dinner available; 5 Open all year; 6 Pets welcome; 7 Children welcome; 8 Tennis nearby; 9 Swimming nearby; 10 Golf nearby; 11 Skiing nearby; 12 May be booked through travel agent.

torian antiques. Situated on 19 acres of beautiful 19th century landscaping. Upon entering the main gates, you definitely begin your very special getaway. Enjoy formal ballroom, stately dining room, warm fireplaces, superb breakfast, and loving hospitality. Just minutes to Assateague national seashore. Listed on the Register of Historic Places. We are just minutes to the resort of Ocean City.

Host: Kirk Burbage
Rooms: 8 (6PB; 2SB) $95-150
Full Gourmet Breakfast
Credit Cards: A, B
Notes: 2, 5, 8, 9, 10, 12

## CHESTERTOWN

### Claddaugh Farm Bed and Breakfast

160 Claddaugh Lane, 21620
(410) 778-4894 (voice and FAX);
(800) 328-4894

Claddaugh Farm B&B is located two miles south of historic Chestertown on Route 213. It is a Victorian style home with rooms on the second and third floors. We have three-and-a-half acres of ground with three kennels for your pets. We welcome children of all ages. We serve a delightful, full continental breakfast.

Hosts: Florence and David Bustard
Rooms: 4 + 1 suite (2PB; 4SB) $65-150
Full Continental Breakfast
Credit Cards: A, B
Notes: 2, 5, 6 (kennel), 7, 9, 10

## ELKTON

### Garden Cottage at Sinking Springs Herb Farm

234 Blair Shore Rd., 21921
(410) 398-5566; FAX (410) 392-2389

With an early plantation house, including a 400 year old sycamore, the garden cottage nestles at the edge of a meadow flanked by herb gardens and a historic barn with a gift shop. It has a sitting room with fireplace, bedroom, bath, air-conditioning, and electric heat. Freshly ground coffee and herbal teas are offered with the country breakfast. Longwood Gardens and Winterthur Museum are 50 minutes away. Historic Chesapeake City is nearby with excellent restaurants. Sleeps three in two rooms. Third person pays only $25. Entrance at Elk Forest Road.

Hosts: Bill and Ann Stubbs
Rooms: 1 (PB) $85
Full Breakfast
Credit Cards: A, B
Notes: 2, 5, 7, 8, 10, 12

## FREDERICK

### Middle Plantation Inn

9549 Liberty Rd., 21701
(301) 898-7128

From this rustic inn built of stone and log, drive through horse country to the village of Mt. Pleasant. The Inn is located several miles east of Frederick on 26 acres. Each room is furnished with antiques and has a private bath, air-conditioning, and TV. The keeping room,

NOTES: Credit cards accepted: A Master Card; B Visa; C American Express; D Discover; E Diners Club; F Other; 2 Personal checks accepted; 3 Lunch available; 4 Dinner available;

a common room, has stained glass and a stone fireplace. Nearby are antique shops, museums, and many historic attractions. Located within 40 minutes of Gettysburg, Pennsylvania, Antietam Battlefield, and Harper's Ferry.

Hosts: Shirley and Dwight Mullican
Rooms: 4 (PB) $90-105
Continental Breakfast
Credit Cards: A, B
Notes: 2, 5, 8, 9, 10, 12

Middle Plantation Inn

## GAITHERSBURG

## Gaithersburg Hospitality Bed and Breakfast

18908 Chimney Place, 20879
(301) 977-7377

This luxury host home just off I-270 with all amenities, including private parking, is located in the beautifully planned community of Montgomery Village, near churches, restaurants, and shops, and is ten minutes from D.C. Metro Station or a convenient drive south to Washington, D.C., and north to historic Gettysburg, PA, and Harper's Ferry. This spacious bed and breakfast has two rooms with private baths, one has a queen bed. Also offered are a large, sunny third room with twin beds, and a fourth room with a single bed.

Hosts delight in serving full, home cooked breakfasts with your pleasure and comfort in mind.

Hosts: Suzanne and Joe Danilowicz
Rooms: 4 (2PB; 2SB) $45-55
Full Breakfast
Credit Cards: none
Notes: 2, 7, 8, 9, 10, 12

## HAGERSTOWN

## Lewrene Farm Bed and Breakfast

9738 Downsville Pike, 21740
(301) 582-1735

Enjoy our quiet, Colonial country home on 125 acres near I-70 and I-81, a home away from home for tourists, business people, and families. We have room for family celebrations. Sit by the fireplace or enjoy the great outdoors. Antietam Battlefield and Harper's Ferry are nearby; Washington, DC, and Baltimore are one and one half hours away. Quilts for sale.

Hosts: Irene and Lewis Lehman
Rooms: 5 (3PB; 2SB) $55-95
Full Breakfast
Credit Cards: A, B
Notes: 2, 5, 7, 8, 9, 10, 11

## Sunday's Bed and Breakfast

39 Broadway, 21740
(301) 797-4331; (800) 221-4828

This elegant 1890 Queen Anne Victorian home is situated in the historic north end of Hagerstown. Relax in any of the many public rooms and porches or ex-

---

5 Open all year; 6 Pets welcome; 7 Children welcome; 8 Tennis nearby; 9 Swimming nearby; 10 Golf nearby; 11 Skiing nearby; 12 May be booked through travel agent.

plore the many historic attractions, antique shops, golf courses, museums, shopping outlets, and ski areas that are nearby. You'll experience special hospitality and many personal touches at Sunday's. A full breakfast, afternoon tea and desserts, evening refreshments, fruit baskets, fresh flowers, special toiletries, and late night cordial and chocolate are just some of the offerings at Sunday's. We are located less than 90 minutes from Baltimore and Washington, D.C.

Host: Bob Ferrino
Rooms: 3 (PB) $95
Full Breakfast
Credit Cards: none
Notes: 2, 4, 5, 6, 7, 8, 9, 10, 11, 12

Sunday's Bed and Breakfast

## NORTH EAST

### Chesapeake Lodge at Sandy Cove

P.O. Box B, 21901
(800) 234-COVE (2683); FAX (410) 287-3196

Peaceful, relaxing, and breathtaking is how guests describe Sandy Cove.

Nestled among 200 acres of unspoiled woodland, overlooking the headwaters of the Chesapeake Bay, and located only one hour from Baltimore and Philadelphia. Discounts are available for Sunday through Thursday stays. Our self contained seven year old lodge and conference center includes 152 deluxe guest rooms, twelve air-conditioned meeting rooms with largest meeting room seating 1,100, banquet capacity of 550. Call for a list of Christian conferences held at Sandy Cove.

Host: Sandy Cove Ministries
Rooms: 152 (PB) $49-89
Full Breakfast
Credit Cards: A, B, D
Notes: 2, 3, 4, 5, 7, 8, 9, 10

## OAKLAND

### The Oak and Apple Bed and Breakfast

208 N. Second St., 21550
(301) 334-9265

Circa 1915, this restored Colonial Revival sits on a beautiful large lawn with mature trees and includes a large, columned front porch, enclosed sun porch, parlor with fireplace, and cozy gathering room with television. Awaken to fresh continental breakfast served fireside in the dining room or on the sun porch. The quaint town of Oakland offers a wonderful small-town atmosphere, Deep Creek Lake, Wisp Ski Resort, and state parks with hiking, fishing, swimming, bicycling, boating, and skiing are nearby.

Hostess: Jana Kight
Rooms: 5 (3PB; 2SB) $55-80
Expanded Continental Breakfast
Credit Cards: A, B
Notes: 2, 5, 8, 9, 10, 11, 12

## ST. MICHAELS

## *Kemp House Inn*

412 Talbot St., P.O. Box 638, 21663
(410) 745-2243

Built in 1807 by Colonel Joseph Kemp, a commander in the War of 1812, this superbly crafted home is one of a collection of large Federal period brick structures in St. Michaels. Each of the rooms are tastefully furnished with period decor. Cozy, antique, four poster, rope beds with patchwork quilts and down pillows, wing-back chairs, low-light sconces, candles, and working fireplaces create an ambiance of the early 19th century.

Hosts: Diane and Steve Cooper
Rooms: 8 (6PB; 2SB) $65-105
Continental Breakfast
Credit Cards: A, B, D
Notes: 2, 5, 7, 8, 9, 10, 12

## *Parsonage Inn*

210 N. Talbot St., 21663
(410) 745-5519; (800) 394-5519

This late Victorian, circa 1883, was lavishly restored in 1985 with seven guest rooms, private baths, and brass beds with Laura Ashley linens. Fireplaces in three rooms. The parlor and dining room are in the European tradition. Striking

architecture! Two blocks to the maritime museum, shops, and restaurants. Mobile three-star rated.

Hosts: Anthony and Jodi Deyesu
Rooms: 8 (PB) $80-130
Full Breakfast
Credit Cards: A, B
Notes: 2, 5, 7, 8, 10, 12

## *Wades Point Inn on the Bay*

P.O. Box 7, 21663
(410) 745-2500

For those seeking the serenity of the country and the splendor of the bay, we invite you to charming Wades Point Inn, just a few miles from St. Michaels. Complemented by the ever-changing view of boats, birds, and water lapping the shoreline, our 120 acres of fields and woodlands, with one mile walking or jogging trail, provide a peaceful setting for relaxation and recreation on Maryland's eastern shore.

Hosts: Betsy and John Feiler
Rooms: 15 winter, 24 summer (16PB; 8SB)
$80-175
Expanded Continental Breakfast
Credit Cards: A, B
Closed February through March
Notes: 2, 7, 8, 10

Wades Point Inn on the Bay

## SILVER SPRINGS

### The Carpenter's House
P.O. Box 10103, 20905
(800) 796-4679; FAX (301) 989-3493

Private garden apartment for two to seven people in smoke-free, air-conditioned comfort with three bedrooms, two baths, living/dining room, kitchen, and private laundry room. Computerized home office has modem and FAX. Relax with cable TV, VCR, stereo, and a video and reading libraries. Also enjoy local tennis, golf, fishing, hiking, and jogging. Ample free parking; easy access to shopping, restaurants, and subway connections. Minutes from downtown Washington, DC, the U of MD, and Baltimore. Only one to three hours to Annapolis, Gettysburg, Richmond, and Williamsburg.

Hosts: The Carpenter Family
Rooms: 3 (1PB; 2SB) $45-55
Kitchen available for self-serve breakfast
Credit Cards: A, B
Notes: 2, 5, 6 and 7 (prior arrangement), 8, 10

### Varborg Bed and Breakfast
2620 Briggs Chaney Rd., 20905
(301) 384-2842

This suburban, Colonial home in the countryside is convenient to Washington, DC, and Baltimore, MD, just off Route 29 and close to Route 95. Three guest rooms with a shared bath are available. Hosts are happy to share their knowledge of good nearby restaurants.

Hosts: Bob and Pat Johnson
Rooms: 3 (SB) $30-50
Full Breakfast (Continental if desired)
Credit Cards: none
Notes: 5, 7, 8

# Massachusetts

## American Country Collection of Bed and Breakfasts

4 Greenwood Ln., **Delmar, NY** 12054
(518) 439-7001 (information and reservations);
FAX (518) 439-4301

This reservation service provides reservations for eastern **New York**, western **Massachusetts**, all of **Vermont**, and **St. Thomas/St. John, U.S.V.I.** Just one call does it all. Relax and unwind at any of our 120 immaculate, personally inspected bed and breakfasts and country inns. Many include fireplace, jacuzzi, and/or Modified American Plan. We cater to the budget-minded, yet also offer luxurious accommodations in older Colonial homes and inns. Urban, suburban, and rural locations available. $35-180. Carol Matos, coordinator.

## Golden Slumber Accommodations B&B/Inn Reservation Service

640 Revere Beach Blvd., **Revere** 02151
(617) 289-1053; (800) 892-3231;
FAX (617) 289-9112

Golden Slumber features an unrivaled array of screened accommodations on the seacoast of Massachusetts including Cape Cod, the North and South Shores, and Greater Boston. From sprawling, ocean-front villas to quaint, romantic, country road retreats, our gracious historic residences and unique contemporary properties offer the paramount in revered Yankee hospitality. All boast the finest amenities and several feature incomparable water views, canopy beds, jacuzzis, fireplaces, private entrances, and swimming pools. No reservation fee! Children welcome. Limousine and gift service. Free brochure/directory.

Coordinator: Leah A. Schmidt
Rooms: 150 (90%PB; 10%SB) $55-220
Full and Continental Breakfast
Credit Cards: A, B
Notes: 2, 3, 4, 5, 6, 7, 8, 9, 10, 12

## BARNSTABLE (CAPE COD)

### Beechwood

2839 Main St. (Rt. 6A), 02630
(508) 362-6618; (800) 609-6618;
FAX (508) 362-0298

Beechwood is a romantic Victorian Inn with six large guest rooms, some with fireplaces or water views. All rooms are

---

5 Open all year; 6 Pets welcome; 7 Children welcome; 8 Tennis nearby; 9 Swimming nearby; 10 Golf nearby; 11 Skiing nearby; 12 May be booked through travel agent.

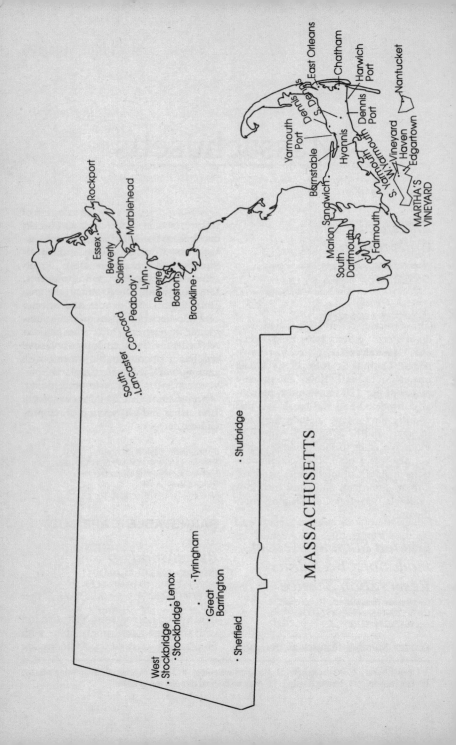

MASSACHUSETTS

Rockport
Essex •
Beverly
Salem •
Marblehead
Peabody •
Lynn •
Revere
Boston •
Brookline •

South
Lancaster •
Concord •

Sturbridge

West
Stockbridge •
Stockbridge • Lenox
• Tyringham
• Great
Barrington
• Sheffield

Barnstable
Marion Sandwich •
South
Dartmouth
Falmouth •

Yarmouth
Port
Dennis
S. Dennis
Dennis
Port
Hyannis
W. Yarmouth
S. Yarmouth

East Orleans
Chatham
Harwich
Port
Nantucket

Vineyard
Haven
Edgartown
MARTHA'S
VINEYARD

furnished with period antiques and have private baths. Gourmet breakfasts are served in the paneled dining room, and afternoon tea and sweets by the parlor fireplace in winter. In summer, iced tea and lemonade are served on the wraparound veranda, overlooking one-and-a-half acres of beautifully landscaped lawns and gardens.

Hosts: Debbie and Ken Traugot
Rooms: 6 (PB) $115-150
Full Breakfast
Credit Cards: A, B, C
Notes: 2, 5, 7 (over 12; only one room to accommodate under 12), 8, 9, 10, 12

## BEVERLY FARMS

## Jon Larcom House Bed and Breakfast

28 Hart Street, 01915
(508) 922-6074

Enjoy an authentic antique Colonial with beams, fireplaces, and Indian shutters, decorated with down comforters and Oriental rugs. Situated 1 ½ miles from Gorden College; ten-minute walk to beautiful prestine beach. Continental breakfast served in our smoke-free home. Many subtle touches that reflect the innkeepers total commitment to quality and comfort await your arrival.

Hosts: Steve and Peg Powers
Rooms: 3 (1PB; 3SB) $65-90
Continental Breakfast
Credit Cards: none
Notes: 2, 5, 8, 9, 10

## BOSTON

## A B&B Agency of Boston (and Boston Harbor Bed and Breakfast)

47 Commercial Wharf, 02110
(617) 720-3540; (800) 248-9262;
FAX (617) 523-5761

Downtown Boston's largest selection of guest rooms in historic bed and breakfast homes including Federal and Victorian town houses and beautifully restored 1840s waterfront lofts. Available, nightly, weekly, and/or monthly. Or, choose from the loveliest selection of fully furnished, private studios, one- and two-bedroom condominiums, corporate suites and lofts with all the amenities, including fully furnished kitchens, private baths (some with jacuzzis), TV, and telephones. Exclusive locations include waterfront, Faneuil Hall/Quincy Market, North End, Back Bay, Beacon Hill, Copley Square, and Cambridge.

Hosts: Ferne Mintz
Rooms: 120 (80PB; 40SB) $65-120
Continental Breakfast
Credit Cards: A, B
Notes: 2, 5, 7, 12

## Beacon Hill Bed and Breakfast

27 Brimmer Street, 02108
(617) 523-7376

Be a guest in my historic home...first three floors of six-story, brick, 1869 Victorian row house in Boston's most

---

NOTES: Credit cards accepted: A Master Card; B Visa; C American Express; D Discover; E Diners Club; F Other; 2 Personal checks accepted; 3 Lunch available; 4 Dinner available; 5 Open all year; 6 Pets welcome; 7 Children welcome; 8 Tennis nearby; 9 Swimming nearby; 10 Golf nearby; 11 Skiing nearby; 12 May be booked through travel agent.

elegant and convenient, gas-lit, residential neighborhood. Easy walk to tourist attractions: Freedom Trail, Quincy Market, convention center, Boston Common, "Cheers," shops, restaurants, subway, and parking. Spacious rooms with double or queen beds, fireplaces, Oriental rugs, TV, and A/C, elevator for luggage. Hostess, a caterer, speaks French and enjoys sharing her home of 27 years and her knowledge of Boston.

Hosts: Susan Butterworth
Rooms: 3 (PB) $125-160
Full Breakfast
Credit Cards: none
Notes: 2 (for deposit), 5, 7, 12

## BROOKLINE

### The Beacon Inn
1087 and 1750 Beacon St., 02146
(617) 566-0088; (800) 726-0088;
FAX (617) 397-9267

These turn-of-the-century town houses have been converted into two of Brookline's most charming guest houses. The original woodwork is reminiscent of their 19th century construction, and the lobby fireplace offers a friendly welcome to travelers. Large, comfortably furnished, sunny rooms provide pleasant accommodations at a reasonable price. The Beacon Inn is minutes away from downtown Boston. The area offers a wide variety of restaurants, shops, museums, theater, and other tourist attractions.

Hosts: Fulton W. Gaylord and Colleen Carrigan
Rooms: 24 (14PB; 9SB) $49-99 + tax
Continental Breakfast
Credit Cards: A, B, C
Notes: 5, 7, 8, 9, 10, 12

### Beacon Plaza
1459 Beacon St., 02146
(617) 232-6550

The Beacon Plaza has been family owned and operated for approximately 40 years. We are conveniently located on the Greenline which stops across the street from us. We are 15 minutes from downtown Boston and 20 minutes from Logan Airport. Our rooms are clean and neat and we offer the use of our community kitchens to our guests. Some rooms are available with TV and/or air-conditioning.

Hosts: The Pappas Family
Rooms: 40 (20PB; 20SB) $45-85
No Breakfast
Credit Cards: none
Notes: 5, 7, 9, 12

## CHATHAM

### The Cyrus Kent House Inn
63 Cross St., 02633
(508) 945-9104 (voice and FAX);
(800) 338-5368

A 19th century sea captain's house reborn and now a gracious inn! Built in 1877, the Inn has been completely restored and furnished in period antiques and reproductions. Enjoy the subtle mingling of past and present; found within our quiet informal inn. Our fireplace suites make a special retreat! Walking distance to beaches, shops, and restaurants.

Hostess: Sharon Mitchell Juan
Rooms: 9 (PB) $125-165
Continental Breakfast
Credit Cards: A, B
Notes: 2, 5, 7 (over 9), 8, 9, 10, 12

NOTES: Credit cards accepted: A Master Card; B Visa; C American Express; D Discover; E Diners Club; F Other; 2 Personal checks accepted; 3 Lunch available; 4 Dinner available;

# CONCORD

## Hawthorne Inn

462 Lexington Rd., 01742
(508) 369-5610; FAX (508) 287-4949

Fast by the ancient way; that the Minute Men trod to first face the British Regulars, rests this most colorful inn where history and literature gracefully entwine. On earth once claimed by Emerson, Hawthorne, and the Alcotts, the Hawthorne Inn beckons the traveler to refresh the spirit in a winsome atmosphere abounding with antique furnishings and delight the eye exploring rooms festooned with handmade quilts, original artwork, and archaic artifacts.

Host: G. Burch
Rooms: 7 (PB) $100-160
Continental Plus Breakfast
Credit Cards: A, B, C, D
Notes: 2, 5, 7, 8, 9, 11

Hawthorne Inn

# DENNIS

## Isaiah Hall B&B Inn

P.O. Box 1007, 152 Whig St., 02638
(508) 385-9928; (800) 736-0160;
FAX (508) 385-5879

Enjoy country ambiance and hospital-ity in the heart of Cape Cod. Tucked away on a quiet historic side street, this lovely 1857 farmhouse is within walking distance of the beach, restaurants, shops, and playhouse. Delightful gardens surround the Inn with country antiques, Oriental rugs, and quilts within. Most rooms have private baths and queen-size beds. Some have balconies or fireplaces. Near biking, golf, and tennis. AAA three-diamond rating and ABBA three crown award.

Hostess: Marie Brophy
Rooms: 11 (10PB; 1SB) $62-112
Expanded Continental Breakfast
Credit Cards: A, B, C
Notes: 2, 7 (over 7), 8, 9, 10, 12

# DENNIS PORT

## The Rose Petal B&B

P.O. Box 974, 152 Sea St., 02639
(508) 398-8470

A picturesque, traditional New England home, complete with picket fence, invites guests to share this historic 1872 residence in a delightful seaside resort neighborhood. Stroll past century-old homes to a sandy beach. Home-baked pastries highlight a full breakfast. A comfortable parlor offers TV, piano, and reading. Enjoy queen-size beds, antiques, hand-stitched quilts, and spacious and bright baths. Convenient to all Cape Cod's attractions. Open all year. AAA-three Diamonds; ABBA-three Crowns.

Hosts: Dan and Gayle Kelly
Rooms: 3 (2PB; 1SB) $49-89
Full Breakfast
Credit Cards: A, B, C
Notes: 5, 7, 8, 9, 10, 12

5 Open all year; 6 Pets welcome; 7 Children welcome; 8 Tennis nearby; 9 Swimming nearby; 10 Golf nearby; 11 Skiing nearby; 12 May be booked through travel agent.

## EAST ORLEANS

### Ivy Lodge

194 Main St., Box 1195, 02643
(508) 255-0119

A guest house since 1910, this smoke-free 1864 Greek Revival home is graced with family photos and antiques. A morning wake-up breakfast basket is found outside each guest room door, to be enjoyed in your room or under a shade tree on the spacious grounds. Located midway between ocean and bay beaches in beautiful, historic Orleans at the elbow of Cape Cod. Walking distance to shops and restaurants. Other amenities close by.

Hosts: David and Barbara McCormack
Rooms: 3 + apartment (1PB; 2SB) $55-65
Continental Breakfast
Credit Cards: none
Notes: 2, 5, 7 (in apartment), 8, 9, 10

### Nauset House Inn

143 Beach Rd., Box 774, 02643
(508) 255-2195

A real, old fashioned, country inn farmhouse, circa 1810, is located on three acres with an apple orchard, one half mile from Nauset Beach. A quiet romantic getaway. Large common room with fireplace and a brick-floored dining room where breakfast is served. Cozily furnished with antiques, eclectic—a true fantasy.

Hosts: Diane and Al Johnson; John and Cindy Vessella
Rooms: 14 (8PB; 6SB) $55-105
Full ($5) or Continental ($3) Breakfast
Credit Cards: A, B
Notes: 2, 8, 9, 10

### Ship's Knees Inn

186 Beach Rd., P.O. Box 756, 02643
(508) 255-1312; FAX (508) 240-1351

This 170-year-old restored sea captain's home is a three minute walk to beautiful sand-duned Nauset Beach. Inside the warm, lantern-lit doorways are 19 rooms individually appointed with special Colonial color schemes and authentic antiques. Some rooms feature authentic ship's knees, hand painted trunks, old clipper ship models, braided rugs, and four-poster beds. Tennis and swimming are available on the premises. Three miles away overlooking Orleans Cove, the Cove House property offers three rooms, a one-bedroom efficiency apartment, and two cottages.

Hosts: Jean and Ken Pitchford
Rooms: 22, 1 efficiency apt., 2 cottages (11PB; 14SB) $50-100
Continental Breakfast
Credit Cards: A, B
Notes: 2, 5, 7 (Cove House), 8 and 9 (on premises), 10, 12

## EDGARTOWN—MARTHA'S VINEYARD

### The Arbor

222 Upper Main St., P.O. Box 1228, 02539
(508) 627-8137

This charming Victorian home was originally built on the island of Chappaquiddick and moved by barge to its present location; a short stroll to the village shops, fine restaurants, and the bustling activity of the Edgartown harbor. The rooms are typically New England, furnished with antiques, and filled with the fragrance of fresh flow-

---

NOTES: Credit cards accepted: A Master Card; B Visa; C American Express; D Discover; E Diners Club; F Other; 2 Personal checks accepted; 3 Lunch available; 4 Dinner available;

ers. Peggy will gladly direct you to unspoiled beaches, walking trails, fishing, and all the delights of Martha's Vineyard.

Hostess: Peggy Hall
Rooms: 10 (8PB; 2SB) $85-135 (off season rates available)
Continental Breakfast
Credit Cards: A, B
Notes: 2, 7 (over 12), 8, 9, 10, 12

The Arbor

## Captain Dexter House of Edgartown

35 Pease's Point Way, P.O. Box 2798, 02539
(508) 627-7289; FAX (508) 693-8448

Our historic inn offers both charm and hospitality. Enjoy beautiful gardens. Savor a home-baked continental breakfast and evening aperitif. Relax in a four-poster, lace canopied bed in a room with a working fireplace. Stroll to the harbor, town, and restaurants. Bicycle or walk to the beach. Let our innkeepers make your vacation something special!

Hosts: Eric and Pamela
Rooms: 11 (PB) $65-195
Continental Plus Breakfast
Credit Cards: A, B, C, E
Notes: 2, 8, 9, 10, 12

## The Shiretown Inn on the Island of Martha's Vineyard

21 North Water Street, P.O. Box 921, 02539
(508) 627-3353; (800) 541-0090;
FAX (508) 627-8478

Shiretown Inn on the island of Martha's Vineyard is listed in the National Register of Historic Places. In the center of Edgartown, one block from the Chappaquiddick Ferry and yacht harbor. 1700s whaling captain's houses, carriage houses, cottage, all with private baths. Some rooms have canopy bed, harbor and garden views, deck, cable color television, telephone, and/or air-conditioning. Lovely Garden Terrace Restaurant and Pub. Call us toll free.

Hostess: Sonya Lima
Rooms: 33 (PB) $49-259
Continental Breakfast
Credit Cards: A, B, D
Notes: 2, 4, 7, 8, 9, 10, 12

## ESSEX

## George Fuller House

148 Main Street, 01929
(508) 768-7766

Built in 1830, this handsome Federalist-style home retains much of its 19th century charm, including Indian shutters and a captain's staircase. Three of the guest rooms have working fireplaces. Decorations include handmade quilts, braided rugs, and caned Boston rockers. A full breakfast might include such features as Cindy's French toast drizzled with brandy lemon butter.

5 Open all year;  6 Pets welcome;  7 Children welcome;  8 Tennis nearby;  9 Swimming nearby;
10 Golf nearby;  11 Skiing nearby;  12 May be booked through travel agent.

Gordon College and Gordon Conwall Seminary are close by.

Hosts: Cindy and Bob Cameron
Rooms: 5 + 2 suites (PB) $75-135
Full Breakfast
Credit Cards: A, B, C, D, E
Notes: 2, 5, 7, 8, 9, 10, 12

## FALMOUTH

## Captain Tom Lawrence House Inn

75 Locust Street, 02540
(508) 540-1445; FAX (508) 457-1790

1861 whaling captain's residence in historic village close to beach, bikeway, ferries, bus station, ships, and restaurants. Explore entire Cape, Vineyard, and Plymouth by day trips. Six beautiful guest rooms have private baths and firm beds, some with canopies. Fully furnished apartment with kitchenette and air-conditioning sleeps two to four people. Antiques, a Steinway piano, fireplace in sitting room. Homemade, delicious breakfasts include specialties from organic grain. German spoken. All rooms have central air-conditioning. No smoking! AAA and Mobile rated.

Hostess: Barbara Sabo-Feller
Rooms: 6 (PB) $75-115
Full Breakfast
Credit Cards: A, B
Closed January
Notes: 2, 7 (over 12), 8, 9, 10

## Inn on the Sound

313 Grand Ave., 02540
(508) 457-9666; (800) 564-9668

This oceanfront bed and breakfast of-
fers ten spacious rooms, fireplaces, country charm, and comfort. Enjoy the breathtaking view, sample our deluxe full breakfast, then spend your day touring year-round attractions. We are within walking distance of the island ferry, shops, and restaurants. Reservations suggested.

Hosts: Renee Ross and David Ross
Rooms: 10 (PB) $95-140
Full Breakfast
Credit Cards: A, B, C, D
Notes: 2, 5, 8, 9, 10, 12

Inn on the Sound

## The Palmer House Inn

81 Palmer Avenue, 02540
(508) 548-1230; (800) 472-2632 (reservations only); FAX (508) 540-1878

"High Victorian" in style, The Palmer House Inn has rich woodwork and floors, period furniture, stained glass windows, and old photos, books, and memorabilia everywhere. The main inn has eight guest rooms; the guest house features four large corner rooms, two with whirlpool tubs; and the cottage suite has a large bedroom with whirlpool tub, separate parlor, and kitchenette. All accommodations feature romantic laces, plump pillows, fine linens, and firm posture-pedic mattresses

NOTES: Credit cards accepted: A Master Card; B Visa; C American Express; D Discover; E Diners Club; F Other; 2 Personal checks accepted; 3 Lunch available; 4 Dinner available;

blending today's comfort with yesterday's elegance.

Hosts: Ken and Joanne Baker
Rooms: 13 (PB) $64-150
Full Gourmet Breakfast
Credit Cards: A, B, C, D, E
Notes: 2 (deposit only), 5, 7 (10 and over), 8, 9, 10, 12

## Village Green Inn

40 W. Main Street, 02540
(508) 548-5621

Gracious, old, 1804 Colonial-Victorian is ideally located on Falmouth's historic village green. Walk to fine shops and restaurants; bike to beaches and picturesque Woods Hole along the Shining Ski Bike Path. Enjoy 19th-century charm and warm hospitality amidst elegant surroundings. Four lovely guest rooms and one romantic suite all have private baths and unique fireplaces (two are working). A full gourmet breakfast is served featuring delicious house specialties. Many thoughtful amenities are included.

Hosts: Diane and Don Crosby
Rooms: 5 (PB) $90-140
Full Breakfast
Credit Cards: A, B, C
Notes: 2, 8, 9, 10

## FALMOUTH HEIGHTS (CAPE COD)

## Grafton Inn

261 Grand Avenue S., 02540
(508) 540-8688; (800) 642-4069;
FAX (508) 540-1861

Oceanfront Victorian, 30 steps to sandy beach, with breathtaking views of Martha's Vineyard. Eleven air-conditioned guest rooms with private baths are furnished with comfortable queen beds and period antiques. Sumptuous, full, gourmet breakfast served at private tables overlooking Nantucket Sound. Thoughtful amenities include, fresh flowers and homemade chocolates. Bicycles, beach chairs, and towels. Late afternoon wine and cheese. Walk to Island Ferry, restaurants, and shops. No smoking. Open all year. AAA and Mobil rated.

Hosts: Liz and Rudy Cvitan
Rooms: 11 (PB) $65-145
Full Breakfast
Credit Cards: A, B, C
Notes: 2, 5, 8, 9, 10

Grafton Inn

## The Moorings Lodge

207 Grand Ave. S., 02540
(508) 540-2370

Captain Frank Spencer built this large, lovely Victorian home in 1905. It is directly across from a sandy beach with lifeguard safety and it is within walking distance of good restaurants and the island ferry. Your homemade, buffet breakfast is served on a glassed-in porch overlooking the island, Martha's Vineyard. Your airy rooms with private baths

5 Open all year; 6 Pets welcome; 7 Children welcome; 8 Tennis nearby; 9 Swimming nearby; 10 Golf nearby; 11 Skiing nearby; 12 May be booked through travel agent.

add to your comfort. Call us home while you tour the Cape!

Hosts: Ernie and Shirley Benard
Rooms: 8 (PB) $75-95
Full Breakfast
Credit Cards: A, B
Notes: 2, 7, 8, 9, 10, 12

## GT. BARRINGTON

### Thornewood Inn
453 Stockbridge Rd, 01230
(413) 528-3828; (800) 854-1008;
FAX (413) 528-3307

Our beautiful accommodations all have private baths. Some rooms have fireplaces and/or canopy beds. Antiques throughout the Inn add to the charm of your New England stay. We are a family run establishment. A delicious, full country breakfast is included with your room. The Thornewood Inn also has a public restaurant, serving the finest in country, continental cuisine, and our library Tap Room. Pool on-site, rooms are air conditioned. We are minutes to great water skiing, summer plays, Tanglewood music festival, and the Norman Rockwell Museum.

Hosts: Terry and David Thorne
Rooms: 10 (PB) $65-165
Full Breakfast
Credit Cards: A, B, C, D
Notes: 2, 4, 5, 7 (over 10), 8, 9 (on-site), 10, 11, 12

## HARWICH PORT (CAPE COD)

### Harbor Walk
6 Freeman St., 02646
(508) 432-1675

This Victorian summer guest house was originally built in 1880 and is furnished with eclectic charm. A few steps from the house will bring you into view of Wychmere Harbor and further along to one of the fine beaches of Nantucket sound. The village of Harwich Port is only one half mile from the Inn and contains interesting shops and some of the finest restaurants on Cape Cod. Harbor Walk offers six comfortable rooms with twin or queen beds. An attractive garden and porch are available for sitting, lounging, and reading. Open May through October.

Hosts: Preston and Marilyn Barry
Rooms: 6 (4PB; 2SB) $45-60
Full Breakfast
Credit Cards: none
Notes: 6 (limited), 7, 8, 9, 10, 12

## HYANNIS

### Sea Breeze Inn
397 Sea St., 02601
(508) 771-7213

Sea Breeze is a fourteen room quaint bed and breakfast. It is just a three minute walk to the beach and 20 minutes to the island ferries. Restaurants, night-life, shopping, golf and tennis are within a ten minute drive. Some rooms have ocean views. An expanded continental breakfast is served between 7:30 and 9:30 each morning. All rooms are air conditioned.

Hosts: Patricia and Martin Battle
Rooms: 14 (PB) $55-115
Expanded Continental Breakfast
Credit Cards: A, B, C, D
Notes: 2, 5, 7, 8, 9, 10, 12

NOTES: Credit cards accepted: A Master Card; B Visa; C American Express; D Discover; E Diners Club; F Other; 2 Personal checks accepted; 3 Lunch available; 4 Dinner available;

## LENOX

### Garden Gables Inn

135 Main St., P.O. Box 52, 01240
(413) 637-0193; FAX (413) 637-4554

220-year-old charming and quiet inn located in historic Lenox on five wooded acres dotted with gardens. 72-foot swimming pool. Some rooms have fireplaces, and sitting rooms are furnished with antiques and a Steinway grand piano. All rooms have private baths, and some also have whirlpool tubs and private porches. Breakfast is included. In-room phones are provided and the famous Tanglewood festival is only one mile away. Restaurants are all within walking distance.

Hosts: Mario and Lynn Mekinda
Rooms: 18 (PB) $70-200
Full Breakfast
Credit Cards: A, B, C, D
Notes: 2, 5, 7 (over 12), 8, 10, 11

### Seven Hills Country Inn and Restaurant

40 Plunkett St., 01240
(413) 637-0060; (800) 869-6518;
FAX (413) 637-3651

Lovely 27-acre country property featuring beautiful terraced lawns and gardens, huge swimming pool, two hard surface tennis courts, banquet and meeting facilities, and outstanding restaurant with wonderful and creative cuisine. Many rooms furnished with antiques, all have private bath and include shower. We are a romantic spot and do weddings like no one else can. Also popular resort and vacation destination, but business travelers love us, too. Lodging/food packages and tie-in discounts available. Near Tanglewood, summer home of the Boston Symphony Orchestra, and Jacob's Pillow, featuring the world's finest dance troupes. Lose yourself in time and come visit!!!

Hosts: Patricia and Jim Eder
Rooms: 52 (PB) $101-299
Full High Season Breakfast (Continental off season)
Credit Cards: A, B, C, D, E
Notes: 4, 5, 7, 10, 11, 12

## LYNN

### Diamond District Bed and Breakfast

142 Ocean St., 01902
(617) 599-5122; (800) 666-3076;
FAX (617) 599-4470

This 17 room Architect designed clapboard mansion was built in 1911 by a Lynn shoe manufacturer. Features include a gracious foyer and a grand staircase winding up the three floors, a spacious fireplace living room with ocean view finished in Mexican mahogany, French doors leading to an adjacent large 36x14 veranda that overlooks the gardens and ocean, and a banquet-size dining room. The 44 page architect specifications permitted only the best of materials. Antiques and Oriental rugs fill the house. Other furnishings include an 1895 rosewood Knabe concert grand piano and custom Chippendale dining room table and chairs signed by Joseph Gerty, a 1940's Boston custom furniture maker. Bedrooms offer a custom 1870s Victorian bed and a twin bed by

5 Open all year; 6 Pets welcome; 7 Children welcome; 8 Tennis nearby; 9 Swimming nearby; 10 Golf nearby; 11 Skiing nearby; 12 May be booked through travel agent.

Charak, yet another Boston custom furniture maker. Each room boasts the elegance of yesteryear.

Hosts: Sandra and Jerry Caron
Rooms: 8 (4PB; 4SB) $58-105
Full Home-cooked Breakfast
Credit Cards: A, B, C, D, E, F
Notes: 2, 5, 6 (some), 9, 10, 12

Diamond District Bed and Breakfast

## MARBLEHEAD

## *Harborside House*

23 Gregory St., 01945
(617) 631-1032

An 1850 Colonial overlooks picturesque Marblehead Harbor, with water views from the paneled living room with a cozy fireplace, period dining room, sunny breakfast porch, and third-story deck. A generous breakfast includes juice, fresh fruit, home-baked goods, and cereals. Antique shops, gourmet restaurants, historic sites, and beaches are a pleasant stroll away. The owner is a professional dressmaker and a nationally ranked competitive swimmer. No smoking.

Hostess: Susan Livingston
Rooms: 2 (SB) $60-75
Expanded Continental Breakfast
Credit Cards: none
Notes: 2, 5, 7 (over 10), 8, 9

## MARION

## *Pineywood Farm B&B*

599 Front St., P.O. Box 322, 02738
(508) 748-3925

A charming, 1815 farmhouse with carriage house, which has been completely restored, yet retains the warmth and ambiance of a bygone era. . .complete with wide plank, white pine floors; four working fireplaces; a large screened porch; and a "good morning" staircase. We offer spacious rooms with air-conditioning, cable TV, paddle fans, and private jacuzzi bath, overlooking a lovely perennial garden and private swimming pool. Located on a three-acre estate within walking distance of the town village or borrow a bike and ride to the town beach. We are open year round and are handicap accessible.

Hosts: Beverly and George McTurk
Rooms: 5 (3PB; 2SB) $85-125
Gourmet Continental Breakfast
Credit Cards: none
Notes: 2, 5, 8, 9, 10

## NANTUCKET

## *Eighteen Gardner Street Inn*

18 Gardner St., 02554
(508) 228-1155; (800) 435-1450

The Gardner Street Inn was built by Captain Robert Joy during the prosperous whaling era. Today his home has been carefully restored and **voted the Best Bed and Breakfast on Nantucket** for the past two years. Your accommodations will include our wonderful Nan-

---

NOTES: Credit cards accepted: A Master Card; B Visa; C American Express; D Discover; E Diners Club; F Other; 2 Personal checks accepted; 3 Lunch available; 4 Dinner available;

tucket breakfast served in the dining room each morning and comfortable air-conditioned guest rooms in the summer. Roaring fireplaces will warm your heart and fresh-baked cookies will fill your senses during the quiet season. For your enjoyment, the Inn provides complimentary bicycles, beach towels, and guest refrigerators. Whatever time of year, you will find our courteous staff happy to assist you with all your holiday planning.

Hosts: Roger and Mary Schmidt
Rooms: 17 (15PB; 2SB)
Continental "Nantucket" Breakfast
Credit Cards: A, B, C, D
Notes: 2, 5, 7, 8, 9, 10, 12

Eighteen Gardner Street Inn

## Martin House Inn
61 Centre St., P.O. Box 743, 02554
(508) 228-0678

In a stately 1803 mariner's home in Nantucket's historic district, a romantic sojourn awaits you a glowing fire in a spacious, charming living/dining room; large, airy guest rooms, three with fireplaces, with authentic period pieces and four-poster beds; a lovely yard and veranda for peaceful summer afternoons. Our complimentary breakfast includes inn-baked breads and muffins,

fresh fruit, and homemade granola.

Hosts: Channing and Ceci Moore
Rooms: 13 (9PB; 4SB) $60-145
Expanded Continental Breakfast
Credit Cards: A, B, C
Notes: 2, 5, 7 (over 5), 8, 9, 10

The Woodbox Inn

## The Woodbox Inn
29 Fair St., 02554
(508) 228-0587

The Woodbox is Nantucket's oldest inn, built in 1709. It is one and one half blocks from the center of town, serves "the best breakfast on the island," and offers gourmet dinners by candlelight. There are nine units, queen-size beds, private baths, including one and two bedroom suites with working fireplaces.

Host: Dexter Tutein
Rooms: 9 (PB) $125-200
Full Breakfast Available
Credit Cards: none
Notes: 2, 4, 7, 8, 9, 10, 12

## PEABODY

## Joan's Bed and Breakfast
R 210 Lynn St., 01960
(508) 536-2667

Located 25 miles from Boston, 10 miles

---

5 Open all year; 6 Pets welcome; 7 Children welcome; 8 Tennis nearby; 9 Swimming nearby; 10 Golf nearby; 11 Skiing nearby; 12 May be booked through travel agent.

from historic Salem, and 25 miles from quaint Rockport. We have wonderful restaurants in the area, also two large shopping malls and a terrific summer theater. Also enjoy our in-ground pool!

Hostess: Joan Hetherington
Rooms: 3 (1PB; 2SB) $50-65
Continental Plus Breakfast and afternoon tea
Credit Cards: none
Notes: 2, 5, 7, 9 (on-site), 10, 12

## REHOBOTH

### Gilbert's Tree Farm Bed and Breakfast

30 Spring St., 02769
(508) 252-6416

Our 150-year-old home is special in all seasons. The in-ground pool refreshes weary travelers, and the quiet walks through our 100 acres give food for the soul. Guests also enjoy the horses. We praise God for being allowed to enjoy the beauty with others. No smoking inside the house.

Hosts: Jeanne and Martin Gilbert
Rooms: 3 (SB) $45-50
Full Breakfast
Credit Cards: none
Notes: 2, 5, 6 (horses only), 7, 8, 9, 10, 12 (10%)

## ROCKPORT

### Lantana Guest House

22 Broadway, 01966
(508) 546-3535; (800) 291-3535

An intimate guest house in heart of historic Rockport, Lantana House is close to Main Street, the T-Wharf, and the beaches. There is a large sundeck reserved for guests, as well as, TV, games, magazine, and books, a guest refrigerator, and ice service. Nearby you will find a golf course, tennis courts, picnic areas, rocky bays, and inlets. Boston is one hour away by car. No smoking.

Hostess: Cynthia A. Sewell
Rooms: 7 (5PB; 2SB) $60-75
Continental Plus Breakfast
Credit Cards: None
Notes: 2, 5, 7, 8, 9, 10

## SALEM

### Amelia Payson House

16 Winter St., 01970
(508) 744-8304

Built in 1845, 16 Winter Street is one of Salem's finest examples of Greek Revival architecture. Elegantly restored and beautifully decorated, each room is furnished with period antiques and warmed by a personal touch. Comfort amenities include private baths, air-conditioning, and cable TV. Located in the heart of Salem's historic district, a five-minute stroll finds downtown shopping, historic houses, museums, and Pickering Wharf's water-front dining. The seaside towns of Rockport and Gloucester are a short drive up the coast; downtown Boston is only 30 minutes away by car or easily reached by train or bus. Color brochure available. No smoking.

Hosts: Ada and Donald Roberts
Rooms: 4 (PB) $65-95
Continental Plus Breakfast
Credit Cards: A, B, C
Notes: 5, 9, 10

NOTES: Credit cards accepted: A Master Card; B Visa; C American Express; D Discover; E Diners Club; F Other; 2 Personal checks accepted; 3 Lunch available; 4 Dinner available;

## The Salem Inn

7 Summer St., 01970
(508) 741-0680; (800) 446-2995;
FAX (508) 744-8924

The Salem Inn is an upscale thirty one room inn which is located in the heart of the downtown McIntire Historic District. The Inn comprises two renovated and restored sea captain's homes on the National Register: the West House and the Curwen House. The ambiance in this unique setting includes working fireplaces, canopy beds, antique furnishings, and period details, as well as the modern day convenience of whirlpool baths, cable TV, telephones, in-room coffee makers, and air-conditioning. This full service inn features an excellent on-site restaurant and a unique gift shop, The Enchanted Forest. Special Packages! For a corporate meeting or special functions the perfect choice is The Salem Inn. The Inn offers private, exclusive meeting space, full catering, on-site parking, deluxe guest rooms, complete line of audio visual equipment, FAX machine, and computer hook ups. We supply the staff, service, and the spirit for the most successful meeting and special occasions.

Hosts: Diane and Richard Pabich
Rooms: 31 (PB) $99-150
Continental Breakfast
Credit Cards: A, B, C, D, E
Notes: 2, 4, 5, 6, 7, 9, 10, 12

## SANDWICH

## Bay Beach B&B

1-3 Bay Beach Ln., Box 151, 02563
(508) 888-8813; FAX (508) 888-5416

Located on a secluded and private beach, Bay Beach offers five ocean front suites. Each room has a dramatic view of Cape Cod Bay and surrounding areas. Some rooms include the ultimate in luxury amenities with jacuzzi tubs, private decks, and paddle fans. Of course, all rooms include private baths, air conditioning, telephones, CD players, cable TV, and refrigerators. Relaxation and privacy defines Bay Beach. Your stay begins with a complimentary wine and cheese spread welcoming each arrival. Every amenity has been personally selected to make your stay a memorable one. Begin each day with an extensive continental breakfast served in our dining are, which can be enjoyed on our ocean front decks. Also experience Bay Beach's exercise room, touring bikes, and all that historic Sandwich and Cape Cod have to offer.

Hosts: Emily and Reale J Lemieux
Rooms: 5 (PB) $125-195
Continental Breakfast
Credit Cards: A, B
Notes: 2, 8, 9, 10, 12

Captain Ezra Nye House

## Captain Ezra Nye House

152 Main St., 02563
(800) 388-CAPT; FAX (508) 933-2897

Whether you come to enjoy summer on Cape Cod, a fall foliage trip, or a quiet winter vacation, the Captain Ezra Nye

House is a great place to start. Located 60 miles from Boston, 20 miles from Hyannis, and within walking distance of many noteworthy attractions, including Heritage Plantation, Sandwich Glass Museum, and the Cape Cod Canal. Award winning Readers Choice, Best B&B Upper Cape, *Cape Cod Life* magazine, and named one of the Top Fifty Inns in America by *Inn Times*.

Hosts: Elaine and Harry Dickson
Rooms: 7 (PB) $65-95
Full Breakfast
Credit Cards: A, B, C, D
Notes: 2, 5, 7 (over 6), 8, 9, 10, 12

## The Summer House

158 Main St., 02563
(508) 888-4991

This exquisite 1835 Greek Revival home, featured in *Country Living* magazine, is located in the heart of historic Sandwich village and features antiques, working fireplaces, hand-stitched quilts, flowers, large sunny rooms, and English-style gardens. We are within strolling distance of dining, museums, shops, pond, and the boardwalk to the beach. Bountiful breakfasts and elegant afternoon tea in the garden.

Hosts: David and Kay Merrell
Rooms: 5 (1PB; 4SB) $55-75
Full Breakfast
Credit Cards: A, B, C, D
Notes: 2, 5, 7 (over 5), 8, 9, 10, 12

## SHEFFIELD

## Ramblewood Inn

P.O. Box 729, 400 S. Undermountain Rd., 01257
(413) 229-3363

This stylish country house, furnished for comfort and romance, is located in a beautiful natural setting of mountains, pine forest, and serene private lake for swimming and canoeing. Private baths, fireplaces, central air, lovely gardens, gourmet breakfasts. Convenient to all Berkshire attractions: Tanglewood, drama/dance festivals, antiques, Lime Rock Racing, skiing, and hiking.

Hosts: June and Martin Ederer
Rooms: 6 + suite with kitchen
(4PB; 2SB) $85-110
Full Breakfast
Credit Cards: A, B
Notes: 2, 5, 7, 8, 9, 10, 11

Ramblewood Inn

## SOUTH DARTMOUTH

## The Little Red House

631 Elm St., 02748
(508) 996-4554

A charming gambrel Colonial home located in the lovely coastal village of Padanaram. This home is beautifully furnished with country accents, antiques, lovely living room with fireplace, and luxuriously comfortable four-poster or brass-and-iron beds. A full homemade breakfast in the romantic, candlelit dining room is a delectable treat. Close to the harbor, beaches and historic sites; a short distance to New Bedford, Newport, Plymouth, Boston,

NOTES: Credit cards accepted: A Master Card; B Visa; C American Express; D Discover; E Diners Club; F Other; 2 Personal checks accepted; 3 Lunch available; 4 Dinner available;

and Cape Cod. Martha Vineyard's ferry is just 10 minutes away.

Hostess: Meryl Zwirblis
Rooms: 2 (PB) $65-75
Full Breakfast
Credit Cards: none
Notes: 2, 5, 8, 9, 10, 12

## SOUTH DENNIS

## *Captain Nickerson Inn*
333 Main St., 02660
(508) 398-5966; (800) 282-1619

Delightful, Victorian sea captain's home built in 1828 and changed to its present Queen Anne style in 1879. Comfortable front porch is lined with white wicker rockers and tables. Five guest rooms decorated with period four poster or white iron queen beds and Oriental or hand woven rugs. The living and dining rooms have fireplaces and stained glass windows. The Inn, which is situated on a bike path, offers bicycles to guests for a small fee. The Cape Cod 20-plus-mile bike Rail Trail is only one half mile from the Inn. Area attractions include championship public golf courses, world class beaches, paddle boats, horseback riding, museums, Cape Playhouse, fishing, craft and antique shops, and a local church which houses the oldest working pipe organ in the country. Full Breakfast is satisfying with homemade muffins and a hot entree. Smoking is restricted to the front porch.

Hosts: Pat and Dave York
Rooms: 5 (3PB; 2SB) $60-90
Full Breakfast
Credit Cards: A, B, D
Notes: 2, 4 (weekends only), 5, 7, 9, 10, 12

College Town Inn

## SOUTH LANCASTER

## *College Town Inn*
12 Old Common Rd., Box 876, 01561
(508) 368-7000

A beautiful, contemporary retreat set in the heart of scenic apple country and surrounded by many historical sites. Each room has its own private deck or balcony. Full breakfast served on our trellised, flower-filled patio in the summer. Vacationing families and business travelers equally welcome. Access to FAX and copier. No smoking.

Hosts: Jack and Charlotte Creighton
Rooms: 3 (PB) $50-80
Full Breakfast
Credit Cards: A, B, D
Notes: 2, 3 (with notice), 7, 9, 10, 11, 12

## STOCKBRIDGE

## *Arbor Rose Bed and Breakfast*
Box 114, 8 Yale Hill, 01262
(413) 298-4744

Lovely, old, New England mill house with pond, gardens, and mountain view. Walk to Berkshire Theater and

5 Open all year; 6 Pets welcome; 7 Children welcome; 8 Tennis nearby; 9 Swimming nearby; 10 Golf nearby; 11 Skiing nearby; 12 May be booked through travel agent.

The Colonel Ebenezer Crafts Inn

Stockbridge Center. Beautiful rooms, comfy, good beds, antiques, paintings, and sunshine. Fireplace and TV in common room. Home-baked mmm . . . breakfast.

Hostess: Christina Alsop
Rooms: 4 (2PB; 2SB) $55-150
Home-baked Continental; Full Breakfast on weekends
Credit Cards: A, B, C
Notes: 2, 5, 7, 8, 9, 10, 11, 12

## *The Inn at Stockbridge*

P.O. Box 618, 01262
(413) 298-3337; FAX (413) 298-3406

This eight-room inn is situated on a 12-acre plot one mile north of the village of Stockbridge. This Gregorian Colonial, built in the early 20th century as a country estate, has retained its features of elegance and comfort. Located in the heart of the four season Berkshire Hills, it is close to all local attractions including the Norman Rockwell museum, Tanglewood, Berkshire Theater, and several ski areas. A memorable full breakfast and gracious hospitality are the highlights.

Hosts: Allie and Lenny Schiller
Rooms: 8 (PB) $80-245
Full Breakfast
Credit Cards: A, B, C
Notes: 2, 5, 7 (over 11), 8, 9, 10, 11, 12

## STURBRIDGE

## *The Colonel Ebenezer Crafts Inn*

Fiske Hill Rd., 01566
(508) 347-3313; (800) PUBLICK;
FAX (508) 347-5073

The Colonel Ebenezer's Crafts Inn built in 1786 on the summit of Fiske Hill, offers a sensational panoramic view. Accommodations at the magnificently restored inn are enchanting and historically captivating. There are canopy beds, as well as poster beds. Guests may relax by the pool or unwind in the sunroom, take afternoon tea, or simply enjoy sweeping views of the

NOTES: Credit cards accepted: A Master Card; B Visa; C American Express; D Discover; E Diners Club; F Other; 2 Personal checks accepted; 3 Lunch available; 4 Dinner available;

countryside.

Hostess: Mary Stocum
Rooms: 8 (PB) $65-155
Continental Breakfast
Credit Cards: A, B, C, E, F
Notes: 2, 5, 7, 8, 9, 10

## Sturbridge Country Inn

530 Main St., 01566
(508) 347-5503; FAX (508) 347-5319

At this historic 1840s inn each room has a fireplace and private whirlpool tub. It is close to Old Sturbridge Village and within walking distance of restaurants, shops, and antiques. Breakfast available in room. Repertory theater nightly in barn July 1 through October 25.

Host: Mr. MacConnel
Rooms: 9 (PB) $69-149
Continental Breakfast
Credit Cards: A, B, C, D
Notes: 2, 4, 5, 7, 8, 9, 10, 11, 12

## STURBRIDGE - WARE

## Antique 1880 Bed and Breakfast

14 Pleasant St., Ware 01082
(413) 967-7847

Built in 1876, this Colonial style has pumpkin and maple hardwood floors, beamed ceilings, six fireplaces, and antique furnishings. Afternoon tea is served by the fireplace; breakfast is served in the dining room or on the porch, weather permitting. It is a short, pretty, country ride to historic Old Sturbridge Village and Old Deerfield Village; hiking and fishing are nearby. Midpoint between Boston and the Berk-

shires, this is a very comfortable bed and breakfast.

Hostess: Margaret Skutnik
Rooms: 5 (2PB; 3SB) $40-65
Full Breakfast
Credit Cards: none
Notes: 2, 5, 8, 9, 10, 11, 12

## TYRINGHAM

## The Golden Goose

123 Main Rd., Box 336, 01264
(413) 243-3008

Warm, friendly, circa 1800 bed and breakfast nestled in a secluded valley. Near to Tanglewood, Stockbridge, skiing, and hiking. All homemade jams, applesauce, and biscuits, fresh fruit in season, and hot and cold cereals. Open all year.

Hosts: Lilja and Joseph Rizzo
Rooms: 7 (5PB; 2SB) $65-125
Semi-Full Breakfast
Credit Cards: A, B, C, D
Notes: 2, 5, 7, 8, 9, 10, 11, 12

## VINEYARD HAVEN (MARTHA'S VINEYARD)

## Captain Dexter House of Vineyard Haven

100 Main St., P.O. Box 2457, 02568
(508) 693-6564; (508) 693-8448

Your perfect country inn! Built in 1840, the house has been meticulously restored and exquisitely furnished to reflect the charm of that period. You will be surrounded by flowers from our garden and pampered by innkeepers who

---

5 Open all year; 6 Pets welcome; 7 Children welcome; 8 Tennis nearby; 9 Swimming nearby; 10 Golf nearby; 11 Skiing nearby; 12 May be booked through travel agent.

believe in old-fashioned hospitality. The inn's eight romantic guest rooms are distinctively decorated. Several rooms have working fireplaces (as does the parlor) and four-poster canopy beds. Stroll to town and harbor.

Hosts: Michael and Colleen
Rooms: 8 (PB) $55-170
Continental Plus Breakfast
Credit Cards: A, B, C, E
Notes: 2, 8, 9, 10, 12

## Crocker House Inn

4 Crocker Ave., P.O. Box 1658, 02568
(508) 698-1151; (800) 772-0206

A cozy, casually elegant, adult oriented eight bedroom bed and breakfast. All with private baths. Each room is decorated uniquely, lacy touches, white wicker, with brass, oak, and cherry furnishings. Homemade continental breakfast is buffet style and held in common room. The Inn is a short walk to ferry, beaches, shops, restaurants, golf, tennis, and bike paths. No smoking.

Hostess: Darlene Stavens
Rooms: 8 (PB) $75-155
Continental Breakfast
Credit Cards: A, B, C
Notes: 8, 9, 10

The Hanover House

## The Hanover House

10 Edgartown Rd., P.O. Box 2107
(508) 693-1066; (800) 339-1066;
(508) 696-6099

Non-smoking and located just a short five minute walk to town and the ferry. The Hanover House offers immaculate rooms with a homey, country feeling. All rroms have private baths, cable TV, and air-conditioning. In addition, there are charming suites in a separate carriage house; some have kitchenettes. All have private decks or patios. The Hanover House can be your home on the Vineyard any season of the year. No smoking.

Hosts: Ron and Kay Nelson
Rooms: 15 (PB) $68-188
Continental Breakfast
Credit Cards: A, B, C, D
Notes: 2, 5, 7, 8, 9, 10, 12

## WEST STOCKBRIDGE

## Caro Lake Inn

29 Main St., 01266
(413) 232-0272 (voice and FAX)

Minutes from Tanglewood, the Norman Rockwell museum, and the Butternut Ski Area. Fine dining and lodging at reasonable prices. Rooms are Colonially furnished, many with brass beds. Fully air-conditioned. Restaurant and rooms are smoke-free.

Hosts: Ed and Lisa Robbins
Rooms: 7 (5PB; 2SB) $45-135
Continental Breakfast
Credit Cards: A, B, C, D
Notes: 2, 3, 4, 5, 7, 9, 10, 11, 12

NOTES: Credit cards accepted: A Master Card; B Visa; C American Express; D Discover; E Diners Club; F Other; 2 Personal checks accepted; 3 Lunch available; 4 Dinner available;

## WEST YARMOUTH

## *The Manor House*
57 Maine Ave., 02673
(508) 771-3433; (800) 9-MANOR-9

The Manor House is a lovely, 1920s, six-bedroom, Dutch Colonial bed and breakfast overlooking Lewis Bay. Each room has a private bath and all are decorated differently and named after special little touches of Cape Cod. We are ideally located mid-Cape on the southern side, with easy access to virtually everything the Cape has to offer. We offer a bountiful breakfast, afternoon tea and friendly hospitality.

Hosts: Rick and Liz Latshaw
Rooms: 6 (PB) $74-98
Continental Breakfast
Credit Cards: A, B, C
Notes: 2, 5, 8, 9, 10

## WORTHINGTON

## *The Hill Gallery*
137 E. Windsor Rd., 01098
(413) 238-5914

Relax in an artist/owner designed, eight room, multi-level home built to insure privacy. We are secluded yet easily accessible, just over two miles off Route 9. Our home showcases original art works and pottery by Massachusetts artists. Two rooms with private baths (cots available). American breakfast.

Rates on request for a self contained cottage.

Hosts: Walter and Ellen Korzec
Rooms: 2 (PB) $60
Full Breakfast
Credit Cards: none
Notes: 2, 5, 7, 8, 9, 10, 11

## YARMOUTH PORT

## *The Colonial House Inn*
277 Main St., Rt. 6A, 02675
(508) 362-4348; (800) 999-3416;
FAX (508) 362-8034

This registered historical landmark has antique appointed guest rooms, private baths, and air-conditioning. It features gracious hospitality, old world charm, and traditional New England cuisine. Full liquor license, fine wines, and an indoor heated swimming pool. Lovely grounds, large deck, TV room, and Victorian living room. Close to nature trails, golf, tennis, antique shops, beaches, and shopping.

Host: Malcolm J. Perna
Rooms: 21 (PB) $50-85
Continental Breakfast
Credit Cards: A, B, C, D
Notes: 2, 3, 4, 5, 6, 7, 8, 9, 10, 11, 12

The Colonial House Inn

---

5 Open all year; 6 Pets welcome; 7 Children welcome; 8 Tennis nearby; 9 Swimming nearby; 10 Golf nearby; 11 Skiing nearby; 12 May be booked through travel agent.

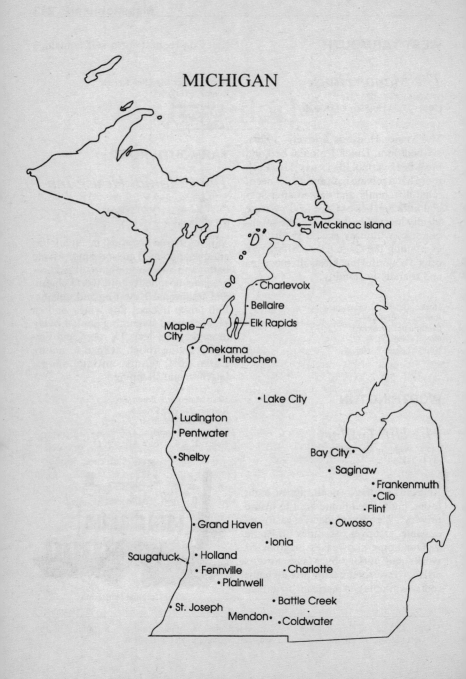

# MICHIGAN

- Mackinac Island
- Charlevoix
- Bellaire
- Elk Rapids
- Maple City
- Onekama
- Interlochen
- Lake City
- Ludington
- Pentwater
- Shelby
- Bay City
- Saginaw
- Frankenmuth
- Clio
- Flint
- Owosso
- Grand Haven
- Ionia
- Saugatuck
- Holland
- Fennville
- Charlotte
- Plainwell
- St. Joseph
- Battle Creek
- Mendon
- Coldwater

# Michigan

## BATTLE CREEK

### Greencrest Manor

6174 Halbert Rd., 49017
(616) 962-8633; FAX (616) 962-7254

To experience Greencrest is to step back in time to a way of life that is rare today. From the moment you enter the iron gates, you will be mesmerized. This French Normandy mansion situated on the highest elevation of St. Mary's Lake is constructed of sandstone, slate, and copper. Three levels of formal gardens include fountains, stone walls, iron rails, and cut sandstone urns. Air-conditioned. Featured "inn of the Month" in *Country Inns* magazine, August 1992 edition, and chosen as one of their top twelve inns in the nation for 1992.

Hosts: Kathy and Tom Van Daff
Rooms: 8 (6PB; 2SB) $75-170
Expanded Continental Breakfast
Credit Cards: A, B, C, E
Notes: 2, 5, 7, 8, 10, 11

Clements Inn

## BAY CITY

### Clements Inn

1712 Center Ave., 48708
(517) 894-4600; (800) 442-4605;
FAX (517) 895-8535

This 1886 Queen Anne-style Victorian home features six fireplaces, magnificent woodwork, oak staircase, amber-colored glass windows, working gas lamps, organ pipes, two clawfoot tubs, and a third floor Ballroom. Each of the seven bedrooms includes cable TV, telephone, private bath, and air-conditioning. Special features include in-room gas fireplaces, in-room whirlpool

---

NOTES: Credit cards accepted: A Master Card; B Visa; C American Express; D Discover; E Diners Club; F Other; 2 Personal checks accepted; 3 Lunch available; 4 Dinner available; 5 Open all year; 6 Pets welcome; 7 Children welcome; 8 Tennis nearby; 9 Swimming nearby; 10 Golf nearby; 11 Skiing nearby; 12 May be booked through travel agent.

tubs, and the 1,200 square foot, fully furnished (including kitchen) Alfred Lord Tennyson suite.

Hosts: Brian and Karen Hepp
Rooms: 7 (PB) $70-140
Continental Breakfast
Credit Cards: A, B, C, D, E
Notes: 2, 5, 7, 8, 10, 11, 12 (10%)

## Stonehedge Inn Bed and Breakfast

924 Center Ave. (M-25), 48708
(517) 894-4342

With stained glass windows and nine fireplaces, this 1889 English Tudor home is indeed an elegant journey into the past. The magnificent open foyer and staircase lead to large, beautiful bedrooms on the upper floors. Original features include speaking tubes, a warming oven, chandeliers, and a fireplace picturing Bible stories and passages on Blue Delft tiles. In the historic district; Frankenmuth is 20 miles away. Biech Run Manufacturer's Marketplace is 35 miles away.

Hostess: Ruth Koerber
Rooms: 7 (SB) $75-85
Expanded Continental Breakfast
Credit Cards: A, B, C, D
Notes: 2, 5, 7, 8, 9, 10, 11, 12

## BELLAIRE

## Grand Victorian Bed and Breakfast Inn

402 N. Bridge St., 49615
(616) 533-6111; (800) 336-3860;
FAX (616) 533-8197

1895 Victorian gingerbread mansion built by lumber baron Henri Richardi. Listed on National Register, the Inn features antiques throughout, three fireplaces, etched glass, exquisite woodwork, and wicker-filled front porch/balconies overlooking a park. Minutes to golf/skiing (Shanty/Schuss). Tandem town bike for shopping. Elegant breakfast experience. No smoking. Four rooms each with private bath. Featured on *June Midwest Living* cover.

Hosts: George and Jill Watson
Rooms: 4 (PB) $85-108
Full Breakfast
Credit Cards: A, B, C
Notes: 2, 8, 9, 10, 11, 12

Grand Victorian Bed and Breakfast Inn

## CHARLEVOIX

## Aaron's Windy Hill B&B

202 Michigan, 49720
(616) 547-2804; (616) 547-6100

Victorian-style home with huge riverstone porch where you can enjoy a homemade, buffet-style breakfast. Each of the eight spacious rooms are individually decorated and each has its own bath. Three rooms can accommodate up to five guests. One block north of drawbridge, shops, and restaurants, and one block east of Lake Michigan's swimming and sunsets.

Hosts: Nancy DeHollanden
Rooms: 8 (PB) $65-95
Full Breakfast
Open May 15 through October 30
Credit Cards: none
Notes: 2, 7, 8, 9, 10

Aaron's Windy Hill Bed and Breakfast

## CHARLOTTE

## Schatze Manor Bed and Breakfast

1281 W. Kinsel Hwy., 48813
(517) 543-4170; (800) 425-2244

Come, stay, and enjoy quiet elegance in our Victorian Oak Suite with red Oriental Soaking Tub, or enjoy sleeping in our 1948 Chevy Woody Room, or feel like a celebrity and relax in our Movie Star Room. All with private baths, distinctive hand carved woodwork, unique decorating, full breakfast, evening dessert, central air, and a non-smoking atmosphere.

Hosts: Donna and Paul Dunning
Rooms: 3 (PB) $60-85
Full Breakfast
Credit Cards: C
Notes: 2, 5, 8, 9, 10

## CLIO

## Chandelier Guest House

1567 Morgan Rd., 48420
(810) 687-6061

Relax in our country home. Enjoy bed and breakfast comforts including choice of rooms with twin, full, or queen beds. You may wish to be served full breakfast in bed, beneath the beautiful crystal chandelier, or on the sun porch with a view of surrounding woods. Located minutes from Clio Amphitheater, Flint Crossroad Village, Birch Run Manufacturer's Marketplace, Frankenmuth, and Chesaning. Senior citizen discount. Call for directions. Hospitality Award Winner in Flint and Genesee County, Michigan.

Hosts: Alfred and Clara Bielert
Rooms: 2 (1SB) $50-55
Full Country Breakfast
Credit Cards: none
Notes: 2, 5, 7, 10, 12

## Cinnamon Stick Bed and Breakfast

12364 N. Genesee Rd., 48420
(810) 686-8391

Large, country home on 50 acres. Nature trails, stocked pond for fishing, and tennis court on site. Guest facilities includes four bedrooms, great room, dining room and patio flower-garden area. Minutes to Frankenmuth, Birch Run Outlet Mall, Crossroads, and Genesee

---

5 Open all year; 6 Pets welcome; 7 Children welcome; 8 Tennis nearby; 9 Swimming nearby; 10 Golf nearby; 11 Skiing nearby; 12 May be booked through travel agent.

Bell paddle boat. Open all year.

Hosts: Brian and Carol Powell
Rooms: 4 (2PB; 2SB) $50-80
Full Breakfast
Credit Cards: A, B
Notes: 2, 5, 7, 8 (on-site), 9, 10

## COLDWATER

### Bativa Inn Bed and Breakfast

1824 W. Chicago Rd., US 12, 49036
(517) 278-5146

This 1872 Italiante, country inn has original massive woodwork, high ceilings, and restful charm. Seasonal decorations are a specialty. Christmas festival of trees. Located near recreation and discount shopping. In-ground pool, cross-country skiing, and 15 acres of wildlife trails. Guest pampering is the innkeepers' goal with treats and homemade breakfast. Perfect for small retreats.

Host: Fred Marquardt
Rooms: 5 (PB) $64-79
Full Breakfast
Credit Cards: A, B, D
Notes: 2, 5, 8, 9, 11

## ELK RAPIDS

### Cairn House Bed and Breakfast

8160 Cairn Hwy., 49629
(616) 264-8994

Elegant Colonial style home in beautifully landscaped surroundings, 15 miles north of Traverse City. Minutes from the bay. Delicious full breakfasts. Excellent area for year-round sports, gourmet dining, and shopping. Available for family celebrations and retreats. Children welcome. Boat parking available. Your comfort is our priority. Special midweek prices.

Host: Roger Vandervort
Rooms: 3 (PB) $60
Full Breakfast
Credit Cards: none
Notes: 2, 5, 7, 8, 9, 10, 11, 12

## FENNVILLE

### The Kingsley House Bed and Breakfast

626 W. Main St., 49408
(616) 561-6425

This elegant, Queen Anne Victorian was built by the prominent Kingsley family in 1886 and selected by *Inn Times* as one of the 50 best bed and breakfasts in America. It was also featured in *Insider* magazine. Near Holland, Saugatuck, Allegan State Forest, sandy beaches, and cross-country skiing. Bicycles available, three rooms with whirlpool baths and fireplaces, and a getaway honeymoon suite. Enjoy the beautiful surroundings and family antiques. Breakfast is served in the formal dining room.

Hosts: Gary and Kari King
Rooms: 8 (PB) $75-150
Full Breakfast (weekends); Continental Plus (weekdays)
Credit Cards: A, B, C, D
Notes: 2, 5, 8, 9, 10, 11, 12

---

## The Witt House

2354 Eagle Point Dr., 49508
(616) 561-2206

Enjoy the peaceful atmosphere of one of our lovely suites on the clear waters of Hutchins Lake. The suites are a decorators' delight, with fireplace, jacuzzi, and sitting area. Sit on the bench at the end of the dock and watch the sunset, or explore God's creation as you glide along in one of our canoes. Your private balcony is surrounded by tall oaks and pine trees. Sweet dreams in the queen canopy beds. Near Holland and Saugatuck.

Hosts: David and Shirley Witt
Rooms: 2 (PB) $95-125
Full Breakfast
Credit Cards: A, B, C, D
Notes: 2, 5, 8, 9, 10, 11, 12

## FLINT AND FRANKENMUTH— SEE CLIO

## FRANKENMUTH

## Bavarian Town Bedand Breakfast

206 Beyerlein St., 48734
(517) 652-8057

Beautifully decorated Cape Cod dwelling with central air-conditioning and private half baths in a peaceful, residential district of Michigan's most popular tourist town, just three blocks from Main Street. Bilingual hosts are descendants of original German settlers. Will serve as tour guide of area, including historic St. Lorenz Lutheran Church.

Color TV with comfortable sitting area in each room. Shared kitchenette. Leisurely served full breakfasts with home-made, baked food. Shared recipes. Superb hospitality.

Hosts: Louie and Kathy Weiss
Rooms: 2 (P½B, shower is shared) $50-55
Full Breakfast
Credit Cards: none
Notes: 2, 5, 7, 8, 9, 10

Bavarian Town Bed and Breakfast

## Bed and Breakfast at the Pines

327 Ardussi St., 48374
(517) 652-9019

Welcome to our friendly, "non-smoking," ranch-style home in a quiet residential neighborhood within walking distance of main tourist areas and famous restaurants. Hosts offer sightseeing ideas and suggestions of the area, along with Michigan travel tips. Bedrooms furnished with heirloom quilts, ceiling fans, and fresh flowers; shared shower with terry robes provided. A family-style breakfast of house specialties served in the dining area. Favorite recipes shared with guests.

Hosts: Richard and Donna Hodge
Rooms: 2 (1PB; 1SB) $40-45
Expanded Continental Breakfast
Credit Cards: none
Notes: 2, 5, 6, 7

5 Open all year; 6 Pets welcome; 7 Children welcome; 8 Tennis nearby; 9 Swimming nearby; 10 Golf nearby; 11 Skiing nearby; 12 May be booked through travel agent.

## GRAND HAVEN

### *Boyden House Inn Bed and Breakfast*

301 S. 5th, 49417
(616) 846-3538

Built in 1874, our charming Victorian inn is decorated with treasures from far-away places, antiques, and original art. Enjoy the comfort of air-conditioned rooms with private baths and two whirl-pool baths. Some rooms feature fire-places or balconies. Relax in our common room and veranda surrounded by a beautiful perennial garden. Full, homemade breakfast served in our lovely dining room. Walking distance to board walk beaches, shopping, and restaurants.

Hosts: Carrie and Berend Snoeyer
Rooms: 6 (PB) $65-110
Full Breakfast
Credit Cards: A, B, C
Notes: 2, 5, 7, 8, 9, 10, 11, 12

### *Seascape Bed and Breakfast*

20009 Breton, **Spring Lake** 49456
(616) 842-8409

On a private, Lake Michigan beach. Relaxing lakefront rooms. Enjoy the warm hospitality and "Country Living" ambiance of our nautical lakeshore home. Full, homemade breakfast served in gathering room with fieldstone fireplace or on the sun deck. Either offers a pan-oramic view of Grand Haven Harbor. Stroll or cross-country ski on dune land

nature trails. Open all year around, of-fering a kaleidoscope of scenes with the changing of the seasons. Stay Sunday-Thursday and get one night free!

Hostess: Susan Meyer
Rooms: 3 (PB) $75-105
Full Breakfast
Credit Cards: A, B
Notes: 2, 5, 8, 9, 10, 11, 12 (no commission)

Seascape Bed and Breakfast

### *Village Park Bed and Breakfast*

60 W. Park St., **Fruitport** 49415
(616) 865-6289

Overlooking the welcoming waters of Spring Lake and Village Park where guests can picnic, play tennis, or use pedestrian bike paths and boat launch. Spring Lake has access to Lake Michigan. Relaxing common area with fire-place; guests may also relax on decks or in outdoor hot tub. Historic setting of Mineral Springs Health Resort. Tra-dition continues with "Wellness Week" special package; also Romantic Get-away and B&B Vacation Week pack-ages available. Serving Grand Haven and Muskegon areas; Huffmaster Park with Gullette Sand Dune Nature Cen-

NOTES: Credit cards accepted: A Master Card; B Visa; C American Express; D Discover; E Diners Club; F Other; 2 Personal checks accepted; 3 Lunch available; 4 Dinner available;

ter nearby; also close to Maranatha Bible Conference Center.

Hosts: John Hewett and (B&B angel) Virginia
Rooms: 6 (PB) $60-90
Full Breakfast
Credit Cards: A, B
Notes: 2, 5, 7, 8, 9, 10, 11 (cross-country), 12

Village Park Bed and Breakfast

## HOLLAND

## *Dutch Colonial Inn*

560 Central Ave., 49423
(616) 396-3664; FAX (616) 396-0461

Relax and enjoy a gracious 1928 Dutch Colonial. Your hosts have elegantly decorated their home with family heirloom antiques and furnishings from the 1930s. Guests enjoy the cheery sun porch, honeymoon suites, fireplaces, or rooms with whirlpool tubs for two. Festive touches are everywhere during the Christmas holiday season. Nearby are Windmill Island, wooden shoe factory, Delftware factory, tulip festival, Hope College, Michigan's finest beaches, bike paths, and cross-country ski trails. Corporate rates are available

for business travelers.

Hosts: Bob and Pat Elenbaas, Ellen Moes
Rooms: 5 (PB) $75-150
Full Breakfast
Credit Cards: A, B, C, D
Notes: 2, 5, 8, 9, 10, 11, 12

## INTERLOCHEN

## *Sandy Shores B&B*

4487 State Park Hwy., 49643
(616) 276-9763

Your "home away from home." Large living room, glassed-in porch, decking. Rooms tastefully furnished. Guests have access to all facilities including yard and private, sandy beach on Duck Lake. Convenient to summer/winter activities, shopping, and dining. Within walking distance of Interlochen Arts Academy. 17 miles SW of Traverse City.

Hostess: Sandra E. Svec
Rooms: 3 (SB) $70-80
Continental Plus Breakfast
Credit Cards: none
Notes: 2, 5, 9, 10, 11, 12

## IONIA

## *Union Hill Inn*

306 Union St., 48846
(616) 527-0955

Enjoy a peaceful and romantic getaway amongst pre-Victorian splendor. Elegant historic 1868 Italiante home noted for its expansive veranda and panoramic view. Only two blocks from downtown. Rooms tastefully decorated with antiques. Each room has a TV and clock

radio. Central air. Union Hill Inn—
*Where love and peace abide.*

Hosts: Tom and Mary Kay Moular
Rooms: 5 (SB) $50-65
Full Breakfast
Credit Cards: none
Notes: 2, 5, 7, 8, 9, 10, 11, 12

Bed and Breakfast in the Pines

## LAKE CITY

### Bed and Breakfast in the Pines
1940 S. Schneider St., 49651
(616) 839-4876

A quaint chalet nestled among the pines on shimmering Sapphire Lake. Each bedroom has its own outside door leading to its own deck facing the lake. Enjoy our large fireplace and warm hospitality. Handicap ramp. Thirteen miles east of Cadillac. No alcohol, smoking, or pets. Enjoy downhill or cross-country skiing, fishing, swimming, hiking, biking, and boating. By reservation only.

Hostess: Reggie Ray
Rooms: 2 (1PB; 1SB) $65
Full Breakfast
Credit Cards: none
Notes: 2, 5, 8, 9, 10, 11

## LUDINGTON

### Doll House Inn Historical B&B
709 E. Ludington Ave., 49431
(616) 843-2286; (800) 275-4616

Gracious 1900 American Foursquare, seven rooms including bridal suite with whirlpool tub for two. Enclosed porch. Smoke and pet free adult accommodations. Full, heart-smart breakfast. Air-conditioning, corporate rates, bicycles, cross-country skiing, walk to beach and town, and special weekend and murder/mystery packages fall and winter. Transportation to and from car ferry/airport.

Hosts: Joe and Barb Gerovac
Rooms: 7 (PB) $60-110
Closed Dec 20-Jan 3
Full Breakfast
Credit Cards: A, B
Notes: 2, 5, 8, 9, 10

### The Inn at Ludington
701 E. Ludington Ave., 49431
(616) 845-7055; (800) 845-9170

Comfort and elegance are yours to enjoy in our historic 1889 Queen Anne Victorian. Ludington's only "painted lady" inn is conveniently located "on the avenue," within walking distance of shops, restaurants, beach, and car ferry. Six rooms, all with private baths, are lovingly decorated with treasured antiques and cherished collectibles. Our bountiful breakfast features locally grown and made-in-Michigan products. Special event weekends include Murder Mysteries, Dickens Christmas, Harvest Festival, and more!

Hostess: Diane Shields
Rooms: 6 (PB) $65-85
Full Buffet Breakfast
Credit Cards: A, B, C
Notes: 2, 3 (picnic), 5, 7, 8, 9, 10, 11, 12

The Inn at Ludington

## MACKINAC ISLAND

### Haan's 1830 Inn

P.O. Box 123, 49757
(906) 847-6244; winter (847) 526-2662

The earliest Greek Revival home in the Northwest Territory, this inn is on the Michigan Historic Registry and is completely restored. It is in a quiet neighborhood three blocks around Haldiman Bay from bustling 1800s downtown and Old Fort Mackinac. It is also adjacent to historic St. Anne's Church and gardens. Guest rooms are furnished with antiques. Enjoy the island's 19th century ambiance of horse drawn buggies and wagons.

Hosts: Nicholas and Nancy Haan; Vernon and Joy Haan
Rooms: 7 (5PB; 2SB) $80-128
Closed late October to mid May
Deluxe Continental Breakfast
Credit Cards: none
Notes: 2, 7, 8, 9, 10, 12

### Pine Cottage Bed and Breakfast

P.O. Box 1890, 49757
(906) 847-3820; (800) 510-1890

Constructed in 1890 forever preserving the Victorian era, Pine Cottage B&B is a quaint getaway for those that want to remember a time gone by. This bed and breakfast offers private and semi-private baths, cable TV, and an abundance of warm hospitality. Come relax and enjoy the quiet, friendly atmosphere of mystical Mackinac Island which offers indoor and outdoor fun for everyone.

Hosts: Greg and Peggy Woodard
Rooms: 15 (5PB; 10SB)
$50 (winter), $74-125 (in season)
Continental Breakfast
Credit Cards: A, B
Notes: 2, 5, 6, 7, 8, 10, 11 (cross-country), 12

## MAPLE CITY

### Leelanau Country Inn

149 E. Harbor Hwy., 49664
(616) 228-5060

For over 100 years, the Inn has stood ready to be of service. We feature six country appointed guest rooms and a 150-seat, award-winning restaurant specializing in fresh seafood flown directly to us from Boston, choice steaks, homemade pasta, and a large array of desserts. All items are made from scratch. Eight miles south of Leland on M-22. Surrounded by churches of all faiths.

Hosts: John and Linda Sisson
Rooms: 6 (SB) $35-45
Continental Breakfast
Credit Cards: A, B, C
Notes: 2, 4, 5, 6, 7, 8, 9, 10, 11

---

5 Open all year; 6 Pets welcome; 7 Children welcome; 8 Tennis nearby; 9 Swimming nearby; 10 Golf nearby; 11 Skiing nearby; 12 May be booked through travel agent.

## MENDON

### Mendon Country Inn
440 W. Main, 49072
(616) 496-8132; FAX (616) 496-8403

Overlooking the St. Joseph River, this romantic stage coach inn has eleven antique guest rooms with private baths. Free canoeing, bicycles built for two, fifteen acres of woods and water, restaurants, and Amish tour guides. Featured in *Country Living* and *Country Home* magazines. Nine jacuzzi suites with fireplaces.

Hosts: Dick and Dolly Buerkle
Rooms: 18 (PB) $59-159
Expanded Continental Breakfast
Credit Cards: A, B, C, D
Notes: 2, 5, 7, 8, 9, 10, 11, 12

## ONEKAMA

### Lake Breeze House
5089 Main St., 49675
(616) 889-4969

Our two-story frame house on Portage Lake is yours with a shared bath, living room, and breakfast room. Each room has its own special charm with family antiques. Come, relax, and enjoy our back porch and the sounds of the babbling creek. By reservation only. Boating and charter service available.

Hosts: Bill and Donna Erickson
Rooms: 3 (1P½B; 2SB) $55
Full Breakfast
Credit Cards: none
Notes: 2, 5, 8, 9, 10, 11

## OWOSSO

### R & R Ranch
308 E. Hibbard Rd., 48867
(517) 723-2553

A newly remodeled farmhouse from the 1900s, the ranch sits on 130 acres overlooking the Maple River Valley. A large concrete, circle drive with white board fences leads to stables of horses and cattle. The area's wildlife includes deer, fox, rabbits, pheasant, quail, and songbirds. Observe and explore from the farm lane, river walk, or outside deck. Country-like accents adorn the interior of the farmhouse, and guests are welcome to use the family parlor, garden, game room, and fireplace. Newly installed central air-conditioning.

Hosts: Carl and Jeanne Rossman
Rooms: 3 (SB) $45
Continental Breakfast
Credit Cards: none
Notes: 2, 5, 6, 7, 10

## PENTWATER

### Historic Nickerson Inn
262 Lowell, P.O. Box 986, 49449
(616) 869-6731

The Historic Nickerson Inn has been serving guests with "special hospitality" since 1914. Our inn was totally renovated in 1991. All our rooms have private baths and air-conditioning. We have two jacuzzi suites with fireplaces

---

NOTES: Credit cards accepted: A Master Card; B Visa; C American Express; D Discover; E Diners Club; F Other; 2 Personal checks accepted; 3 Lunch available; 4 Dinner available;

and balconies overlooking Lake Michigan. Two short blocks to Lake Michigan beach, and three blocks to shopping district. New ownership. Open all year. Casual, fine dining in our 80-seat restaurant. Excellent for retreats, workshops, and year-round recreation.

Hosts: Gretchen and Harry Shiparski
Rooms: 12 (PB) (10 rooms $75-95;
2 suites $150-175)
Full Breakfast
Credit Cards: A, B
Notes: 2, 4, 5, 7 (over 12), 8, 9, 10, 11 (cross-country), 12

Historic Nickerson Inn

## PLAINWELL

### The 1882 John Crispe House Bed and Breakfast

404 E. Bridge St., 49080
(616) 685-1293

Enjoy museum-quality Victorian elegance on the Kalamazoo River just off US 131 on Michigan 89, the John Crispe House is close to some of western Michigan's finest gourmet dining, golf, skiing, and antique shops. Air-

conditioned. No smoking or alcohol. Gift certificates are available.

Hosts: Nancy E. Lefever and Joel T. Lefever
Rooms: 5 (3PB; 2SB) $55-95
Full Breakfast
Credit Cards: A, B
Notes: 2, 5, 7, 8, 10, 11

## ST. JOSEPH

### South Cliff Inn Bed and Breakfast

1900 Lakeshore Dr., 49085
(616) 983-4881; (616) 983-7391

South Cliff Inn B&B is an English country home overlooking Lake Michigan. Beautiful decor with many antiques and custom designed furnishings. Homemade breakfast served in the lakeside sunroom. Private beach is only a five-minute walk. Shops, restaurants, beaches, antiques and many attractions nearby. Downtown is only one mile away. Voted best Bed and Breakfast in Southwestern Michigan in 1994.

Host: Bill Swisher
Rooms: 7 (PB) $60-115
Continental Plus Breakfast (sometimes Full)
Credit Cards: A, B, C, D
Notes: 5, 8, 9, 10, 11, 12

South Cliff Inn Bed and Breakfast

---

5 Open all year; 6 Pets welcome; 7 Children welcome; 8 Tennis nearby; 9 Swimming nearby; 10 Golf nearby; 11 Skiing nearby; 12 May be booked through travel agent.

## SAGINAW

## *Brockway House Bed and Breakfast*

1631 Brockway St., 48602
(517) 792-0746; (800) 531-5697

Brockway House has been completely restored using a mixture of primitive antiques, reproduction wallpaper, and Victorian touches. On the National Register of Historic Homes this B&B is only two and a half hours from the U.P. Land never more than 85 miles from a great lake. A short 25-minute drive will get you to Frankenmuth, Brick Run, the Outlet Mall, and Saginaw Bay with great fishing.

Hosts: Dick Zuehlke and Zoe
Rooms: 4-5 (4PB; 2SB) $85-175
Full Gourmet Breakfast
Credit Cards: A, B
Notes: 5, 7, 8, 9, 10, 11, 12

## SAUGATUCK

## *The Maplewood Hotel*

P.O. Box 1059, 428 Butler St., 49423
(616) 857-1771; FAX (616) 857-1773

The Maplewood Hotel architecture is unmistakably Greek Revival. Some rooms have fireplaces and double jacuzzi tubs. Other areas include a library, a glass enclosed porch where you can enjoy a gourmet breakfast, and a full-sized lap pool. Situated in down-town Saugatuck, within walking distance to all shops and restaurants.

Hosts: Catherine Simon and Sam Burnell
Rooms: 15 (PB) $65-155
Full Gourmet Breakfast
Credit Cards: A, B, C
Notes: 2, 3 (in season), 5, 7, 8, 9, 10, 11, 12

## *The "Porches" B&B*

2297 Lakeshore Dr., 49408
(616) 543-4162

Built in 1897, "The Porches" offers five guest rooms each with private bath. Located three miles south of Saugatuck, we have a private beach and hiking trails. The large common room has a TV. We overlook Lake Michigan with beautiful sunsets from the front porch.

Hosts: Bob and Ellen Johnson
Rooms: 5 (PB) $69-79
Continental Plus Breakfast (Full on Sundays)
Credit Cards: A, B
Notes: 2, 7 (Sun.-Thurs.), 8, 9, 10

## SHELBY

## *The Shepherd's Place Bed and Breakfast*

2200 32nd Ave., 49455
(616) 861-4298

Enjoy a peaceful retreat in a country atmosphere yet close to Lake Michigan beaches, dunes, fishing, golfing, and

---

NOTES: Credit cards accepted: A Master Card; B Visa; C American Express; D Discover; E Diners Club; F Other; 2 Personal checks accepted; 3 Lunch available; 4 Dinner available;

horseback riding. Choose between our comfortable and cozy accommodations with queen-size bed or twin beds, both with private baths. Full breakfast is served in our dining room or porch over-looking bird haven. No smoking al-lowed.

Hosts: Hans and Diane Oehring
Rooms: 2 (PB) $55-60
Open May through October
Full Breakfast
Credit Cards: none
Notes: 2, 9, 10

The Shepherd's Place Bed and Breakfast

- Ray
- Crookston
Lutsen •
- Detroit Lakes
Duluth •
- Fergus Falls

Stillwater •
• Hendricks
Minneapolis • — St. Paul
• Tyler    • Sanborn        St. Charles
• Kenyon
Owatonna •    • Dodge
Center    • Chatfield    Houston
• Sherburn
• Albert Lea

MINNESOTA

# Minnesota

## ALBERT LEA

### Victorian Rose Inn

609 W. Fountain St., 56007
(507) 373-7602; (800) 252-6558

Queen Anne Victorian home (1898) in virtually original condition, with fine woodwork, stained glass, gingerbread, and antique light fixtures. Antique furnishings, down comforters. Spacious rooms, one with fireplace. Air-conditioned. Full Breakfast. Business/extended-stay rates; gift certificates. Children by arrangement; no pets; no smoking.

Hosts: Darrel and Linda Roemmich
Rooms: 4 (PB) $40-70
Full Breakfast
Credit Cards: A, B
Notes: 2, 5, 7, 8, 10, 12

Victorian Rose Inn

## CHATFIELD

### Lund's Guest Houses

218 S.E. Winona St., 55923
(507) 867-4003

These charming 1920s homes are decorated in the 1920s and 1930s style and located only 20 minutes from Rochester, at the gateway to beautiful Bluff country. Personalized service includes kitchens, living and dinning rooms, two screened porches, TV, piano, and organ.

Hosts: Shelby and Marion Lund
Rooms: 8 (PB) $65
Continental Breakfast
Credit Cards: none
Notes: 2, 6 and 7 (restricted), 8, 9, 10, 11

## CROOKSTON

### Elm Street Inn

422 Elm St., 56716
(218) 281-2343; (800) 568-4476;
FAX (218) 281-1756

Georgian Revival (1910) home with antiques, hardwood floors, and stained and beveled glass. Wicker-filled sun porch, old fashioned beds, quilts, fresh flowers. Memorable candlelight full

---

NOTES: Credit cards accepted: A Master Card; B Visa; C American Express; D Discover; E Diners Club; F Other; 2 Personal checks accepted; 3 Lunch available; 4 Dinner available; 5 Open all year; 6 Pets welcome; 7 Children welcome; 8 Tennis nearby; 9 Swimming nearby; 10 Golf nearby; 11 Skiing nearby; 12 May be booked through travel agent.

breakfast; intimate dinners available. Bicycles, limo to casino. Community pool next door. Special anniversary and honey-moon packages. Children by arrangement; no pets; no smoking.

Hosts: John and Sherry Winters
Rooms: 4 (PB) $65
Full Breakfast
Credit Cards: A, B, C
Notes: 2, 3, 4, 5, 7, 8, 9, 10, 12

## DETROIT LAKES

### Idlewood by the Lake

1106 W. Lake Dr., 56501
(218) 847-1229

A charming, Colonial style, lake home set on a hill overlooking sparkling Little Detroit Lake. Stroll down the beach or take a walk on our wooded path. From our private access to the lake enjoy swimming, fishing, boating, and peaceful vistas of the lake in all seasons. Breathe the fresh air and enjoy the relaxed atmosphere. Stay in one of our five guest rooms, all with private baths, queen-size beds, and outdoor hot tub.

Hosts: John and Cheryl Kippen
Rooms: 5 (PB) $65
Full Breakfast
Credit Cards: A, B, D
Notes: 2, 5, 7, 8, 9, 10, 11

Pfeifer's Eden Bed and Breakfast

## DODGE CENTER

### Pfeifer's Eden Bed and Breakfast

R.R. 1, Box 215, 55927
(507) 527-2021

An 1898 Victorian home with peaceful surroundings just a few miles from the historic town of Mantorville and 25 miles from the Mayo Clinic in Rochester. Many antique furnishings are yours to enjoy. Guests are intrigued by old-fashioned pastimes: playing the eight-foot pump organ, touring the world in stereographic cards, pedaling the player piano, or just relaxing on the open and screened porches on mild days or by the fireplace in autumn and winter.

Hosts: Mike and Debbie Pfeifer
Rooms: 4 (2 PB, 2SB) $45-55
Full Breakfast
Credit Cards: none
Notes: 2, 5, 7, 8, 9, 10, 11

## DULUTH

### The Mansion

3600 London Rd., 55804
(218) 724-0739

This magnificent home was built in 1928. The seven-acre estate is nestled on 525 feet of Lake Superior beach with manicured lawns, woods, and gardens. Guests are encouraged to make themselves at home on the grounds and inside the mansion. The common rooms include the library, living room, three season porch, gallery, dinning room, and trophy room. Come and let us share our home with you.

Hosts: Warren, Sue and Andrea Monson
Rooms: 11 (7PB; 4SB) $95-195
Credit Cards: A, B
Notes: 2, 5

## FERGUS FALLS

### Bakketopp Hus

R.R. 2, Box 187 A, 56537
(218) 739-2915; (800) 739-2915

Quiet, spacious, lake home with vaulted ceilings, fireplaces, private spa, flower garden patio, and lakeside decks. Antique furnishings from family homestead; four poster, draped, French canopy bed; and private baths. Here you can listen as loons call to each other across the lake in the still of dusk, witness the falling foliage splendor, relax by the crackling fire, or sink into the warmth of the spa after a day of hiking or skiing. Near antique shops and Maplewood State Park. Ten minutes off I-94. Gift certificates available. Reservation with deposit.

Hosts: Dennis and Judy Nims
Rooms: 3 + loft area (PB) $65-95
Full Breakfast
Credit Cards: A, B, D
Notes: 2, 5, 7, 8, 9, 10, 11

Bakketopp Hus

Triple L Farm

## HENDRICKS

### Triple L Farm B&B

Route 1, Box 141, 56136
(507) 275-3740

Large, country home built in 1890, with upgraded facilities. On a working family farm with comfort, adventure, and open space. A mixture of antiques with locally hand-crafted and casual furnishings make up the country farm, home decor. A bunkhouse is available for those wanting to experience rustic living. Area attractions include ethnic villages, museums, antiques, wind turbans, concerts, plays, wild life, The Pipestone National Monument, Hiawatha and Laura Ingles Wilder pageants.

Hosts: Lanford and Joan Larson
Rooms: 3 (1PB; 2SB) $35-45
Full Breakfast
Credit Cards: A, B
Notes: 5, 6 (unlimited), 7, 8, 9, 10, 11, 12

## HOUSTON

### Addie's Attic B&B

117 S. Jackson, 55943
(507) 896-3010

Beautiful turn-of-the century home,

---

5 Open all year; 6 Pets welcome; 7 Children welcome; 8 Tennis nearby; 9 Swimming nearby; 10 Golf nearby; 11 Skiing nearby; 12 May be booked through travel agent.

circa 1903; cozy front parlor with curved glass window. Games, TV, and player piano available. Guest rooms decorated and furnished with "attic finds." Hearty, country breakfast served in dining room. Near hiking, biking, cross-country skiing trails, canoeing, and antique shops. Week-day rates.

Hosts: Fred and Marilyn Huhn
Rooms: 4 (SB) $45-50
Full Breakfast
Credit Cards: none
Notes: 2, 5, 8, 10, 11

## KENYON

### Grandfather's Woods Bed and Breakfast

3640 450th Street, 55946
(507) 789-6414

"Grandfather's Woods" fifth generation, working farm, charming 1860's home showcases family antiques and old-fashioned comfort. Hearty breakfast; private or shared baths. Horse-drawn hay/sleigh rides, hiking, cross-country skiing through 65 wooded acres to river. Near, and an integral part of the history, of Holden Lutheran Church, "birthplace" of St. Olaf College founded in 1860 by Rev. B.J. Muus. Near state park and bike trail. Half-way between Rochester and St. Paul/Minneapolis. Reservations preferred. No smoking.

Hosts: Judy and George Langemo
Rooms: 3 (2PB; 2SB) $60-99
Full and/or Continental Breakfast
Credit Cards: none
Notes: 2, 4, 5, 7 (supervised), 9, 10, 11

Lindgren's Bed and Breakfast

## LUTSEN

### Lindgren's Bed and Breakfast

C.R. 35, P.O. Box 56, 55612
(218) 663-7450

1920s log home in Superior National Forest on walkable shoreline of Lake Superior. Knotty cedar interior decorated with wildlife trophies. Massive stone fireplaces, Finnish sauna, whirlpool, baby grand piano, and TV's/VCR's/CD. In center of area known for skiing, golf, stream and lake fishing, skyride, mountain biking, snowmobiling, horseback riding, alpine slide, fall colors, Superior Hiking Trail, and near Boundary Waters Canoe Area entry point. Spacious, manicured grounds. One-half mile off Highway 61 on the Lake Superior Circle Tour.

Hostess: Shirley Lindgren
Rooms: 4 (PB) $85-125
Full Hearty Breakfast
Credit Cards: A, B
Notes: 2, 5, 7 (over 12), 8, 9, 10, 11, 12

---

NOTES: Credit cards accepted: A Master Card; B Visa; C American Express; D Discover; E Diners Club; F Other; 2 Personal checks accepted; 3 Lunch available; 4 Dinner available;

# OWATONNA

## The Northrop-Oftedahl House Bed and Breakfast

358 E. Main St., 55060
(507) 451-4040

This 1898 Victorian with stained glass is three blocks from downtown. It has pleasant porches, grand piano, six-foot footed bathtub and souvenirs (antiques and collectibles from the estate). Northrop, family-owned and operated, is one of twelve historical homes in the area, rich in local history with an extensive reading library, backgammon, croquet, badminton, bocce, and more. Near hiking and biking trails, tennis, parks, snowmobiling, and 35 miles to Mayo Clinic. Special group rates for retreats. NEW- Bikers' Bunks.

Hosts: Jean and Darrell Stewart
Rooms: 5 (SB) $25-59
Continental Breakfast; Full Breakfast on request
Credit Cards: none
Notes: 2, 3 and 4 (by arrangement), 5, 6 (by arrangement), 7, 8, 9, 10, 11

# RAY

## Bunt's Bed and Breakfast Inns

Lake Kabetogama, 12497 Burma Rd., 56669
(218) 875-2691; FAX (218) 875-3008

Three inns one-half mile apart. One is on the shores of Lake Kabetogama and Voyagers National Park. Another is on 300 secluded acres. The third is in a converted school/church building. Features include private baths, full kitchens, fireplaces, whirlpool, jacuzzi's, saunas, decks, beach, dock satellite, color TV's, VCR's, washer, and dryers. Truly, three touches of class in the midst of the wilderness.

Host: Bob Buntrock
Rooms: 10 (6 PB; 4SB) $65-130
Continental Breakfast
Credit Cards: A, B, C, D
Notes: 2, 3, 4, 5, 7, 8, 9, 10, 11, 12

Bunt's Bed and Breakfast Inns

# ST. CHARLES

## Thoreson's Carriage House Bed and Breakfast

606 Wabasha Ave., 55972
(507) 932-3479

Located at the of beautiful Whitewater State Park with its swimming, trails, and demonstrations by the park naturalist. We are also in Amish territory and minutes from the world-famous Mayo Clinic. Piano and organ are available for added enjoyment. Please write for free brochure.

Hostess: Moneta Thoreson
Rooms: 2 (SB) $40-45
Full Breakfast
Credit Cards: none
Notes: 2, 5, 7, 8, 9, 10

---

## SANBORN

### Sod House on the Prairie
Route 2, Box 75, 56083
(507) 723-5138

A unique opportunity to step back in time, retreat from life's hustle and bustle, and be a sod house pioneer for the night. The 36' by 21' sod house has two-feet thick sod walls and was built in the tradition of the prairie homesteaders. It is surrounded by restored prairie grasses and is furnished authentically with furnishings of the era. Just like in the 1880s, oil lamps will be your lighting. . .an old-fashioned pitcher and bowl on a washstand will be your sink. There is no running water. The outhouse is also built of sod and sits nearby. The sod house is heated by wood-burning stoves and wool blankets, quilts, and buffalo robes are provided. There is no air-conditioning for summer, but the thick walls keep it cool inside. From May to Labor Day the exhibit is open for touring. A gift shop features handmade items by Native Americans, as well as pioneer crafts by local crafters.

Hosts: McCone Family
Rooms: 1 unit (with 2 double beds) (PB)
Reservations only
Full Breakfast
Credit Cards: none
Notes: 2, 5, 6 (with approval), 7, 9, 10

## SHERBURN

### Four Columns Inn
Route 2, Box 75, 56171
(507) 764-8861

Enjoy Scandinavian hospitality in an antique-filled, loving remodeled, Greek revival inn. Four antique-filled bedrooms, clawfoot tubs, and working fireplaces welcome guests. A library, circular stairway, living room with a grand piano, and a solarium with jacuzzi make a stay here memorable. A hideaway bridal suite has access to a roof deck with a super view of the countryside is perfect for honeymooners or anniversary couples. A hearty breakfast is served in the formal dining room, on the balcony, in the gazebo, or in the kitchen by the fireplace. Near lakes, antiques, amusement park, and live summer theater. Two miles north of I-90 between Chicago and the Black Hills. Call for brochure. No Smoking. Children by arrangement.

Hosts: Norman and Pennie Kittleson
Rooms: 4 (3PB) $50-70
Full Breakfast
Credit Cards: none
Notes: 2, 5, 7 (by arrangement), 9, 10, 11, 12

Four Columns Inn

NOTES: Credit cards accepted: A Master Card; B Visa; C American Express; D Discover; E Diners Club; F Other; 2 Personal checks accepted; 3 Lunch available; 4 Dinner available;

Anchor Inn

## SPRING LAKE

## *Anchor Inn*

HCD 1, Box 260, 56680
(218) 798-2718

Lodge in the Chippewa National Forest on the Bigfork Canoe Trail; built in the early 1920s and originally used by duck hunters. Decorated with antique furniture and memorabilia. Shared bath. Delicious breakfast. State parks, historic sites, and restaurants nearby. Boats and motors available. Reservations. Open May through October. No smoking!

Hosts: Charles and Virginia Kitterman
Rooms: 4 (SB) $30-55
Full Breakfast
Credit Cards: A, B
Notes: 2, 7, 8, 9, 10

## STILLWATER

## *James A. Mulvey Residence Inn*

622 W. Churchill St., 55082
(612) 430-8008

This is an enchanting place. Built in 1878 by lumberman, James A. Mulvey, the Italianate residence and stone carriage house grace the most visited historic rivertown in the upper Midwest. Exclusively for you are the grand parlor, formal dining room, Victorian sun porch, and five fabulously decorated guest rooms filled with art and antiques. Four-course breakfast, double-whirlpools, fireplaces, mountain bikes, and air-conditioning. Welcome refreshments. Grace-filled service from innkeepers who care.

Hosts: Rev. Truett and Jill Lawson
Rooms: 5 (PB) $80-149
Full 4-Course Breakfast
Credit Cards: A, B
Notes: 2, 5, 8, 9, 10, 11, 12

## TYLER

## *Babette's Inn*

308 S. Tyler Street, 56178
(507) 247-3962; (800) 466-7067

Well known for great breakfasts, Babette's welcomes guests in style. The 1914 red brick, historic home offers three suites, gorgeously decorated and filled with guest comforts. Guests have use of whole house, plus film and book libraries, bicycles, antique shop, porches, and gardens. A very good value in luxury accommodations. "4-star" *Venture Magazine*.

Hosts: Jim and Alicia Johnson
Rooms: 3 suites (PB) (2 with fireplace) $55-65
Full Breakfast
Credit Cards: A, B
Notes: 2, 5, 7 (with approval), 8, 9, 10, 11, 12

---

5 Open all year; 6 Pets welcome; 7 Children welcome; 8 Tennis nearby; 9 Swimming nearby; 10 Golf nearby; 11 Skiing nearby; 12 May be booked through travel agent.

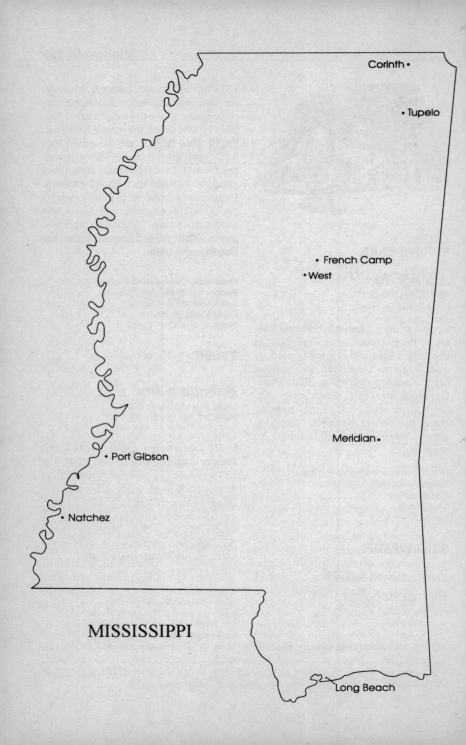

Corinth •

• Tupelo

• French Camp
• West

Meridian •

• Port Gibson

• Natchez

MISSISSIPPI

Long Beach

# Mississippi

## CORINTH

### The Generals' Quarters
924 Fillmore St., 38834
(601) 286-3325

The General's Quarters is a beautifully restored, Victorian home located in the historic district of the old Civil War town. The rooms are decorated with period antiques and contemporary pieces; and all rooms have private baths, cable TV and telephones; and the suite boasts a 140-year-old, four poster canopy bed. There is a second floor lounge with veranda, beautiful parlor and porch on the first floor, and lovely gardens to relax in after a day of sightseeing, antiquing, playing golf, or touring the various Civil War sights in Corinth and the outlaying areas. Our resident chef prepares a delicious full breakfast and evening snack. We are close to Shiloh National Military Park and the Tennessee-Tombigbee Waterway. The General's Quarters provides some of the best hospitality that the South has to offer.

Hosts: Luke Doehner and Charlotte Brandt
Rooms: 4 + 1 suite (PB) $75-85
Full Breakfast
Credit Cards: A, B, D
Notes: 5, 8, 10, 12

## FRENCH CAMP

### French Camp Bed and Breakfast Inn
1 Bluebird Ln., P.O. Box 120, 39745
(601) 547-6482; FAX (601) 547-6790

The Inn is located on the historic Natchez Trace National Parkway halfway between Jackson and Tupelo, Mississippi. It has been constructed from two restored, authentic hand-hewn log cabins, each more than 100 years old. Indulge in Southern cooking at its finest: sorghum-soaked "scratch" muffins, creamy grits, skillet fried apples, fresh cheese, scrambled eggs, crisp slab bacon, and lean sausage, with two kinds

---

NOTES: Credit cards accepted: A Master Card; B Visa; C American Express; D Discover; E Diners Club; F Other; 2 Personal checks accepted; 3 Lunch available; 4 Dinner available; 5 Open all year; 6 Pets welcome; 7 Children welcome; 8 Tennis nearby; 9 Swimming nearby; 10 Golf nearby; 11 Skiing nearby; 12 May be booked through travel agent.

of homemade bread and three kinds of homemade jellies. Life doesn't get any better!

Hosts: Ed and Sallie Williford
Rooms: 4 (PB) $60
Full Breakfast
Credit Cards: B
Notes: 2, 3, 4, 5, 6, 7, 8, 9, 12

French Camp Bed and Breakfast Inn

## LONG BEACH

### Red Creek Colonial Inn Bed and Breakfast

7416 Red Creek Rd., 39560
(601) 452-3080 (voice and FAX);
(800) 729-9670

Raised French cottage built in 1899 by a retired, Italian sea captain to entice his young bride away from her parents' home in New Orleans. Red Creek Colonial Inn is situated on eleven acres with ancient live oaks and fragrant magnolias, and delights itself in peaceful comforts. With a 64-foot porch, including porch swings, our inn is furnished in antiques for our guests' enjoyment. Ministerial discount of 10%.

Hosts: Karl and Toni Mertz
Rooms: 5 (3PB; 2SB) $49-79
Continental Plus Breakfast
Credit Cards: none
Notes: 2, 3 and 4 (advance request only), 5, 7, 9, 10, 12 (10%)

## MERIDIAN

### Lincoln Ltd./Travel

P.O. Box 3479, 39303
(601) 482-5483; (800) 633-MISS
FAX (601) 693-7447

Service offers B&B accommodations in historic homes and inns in the whole state of **Mississippi**, also southeast **Louisiana**, **Western Tennessee**, and **Alabama**. One phone call convenience for your B&B reservations and trip planning through Mississippi. Experience history from Natchez to Memphis, including the Gulf Coast and the Natchez Trace Parkway. We offer antebellum mansions, historic log houses, and contemporary homes. Also, there is a B&B suite on the premises. Call for details and brochure. $65-175; major credit cards welcome. Barbara Lincoln Hall, coordinator.

## NATCHEZ

### The Bed and Breakfast Mansions of Natchez

P.O. Box 347, 200 State St., 39121
(601) 446-6631; (800) 647-6742;
FAX (601) 446-8687

Over 30 magnificent B&B inns offer exquisite accommodations in pre-Civil War mansions, country plantations, and charming Victorian elegance. Situated on high buffs overlooking the Mississippi River, historic Natchez offers visitors year-round tours of historic homes, horse-drawn carriage tours, plus the fa-

NOTES: Credit cards accepted: A Master Card; B Visa; C American Express; D Discover; E Diners Club; F Other; 2 Personal checks accepted; 3 Lunch available; 4 Dinner available;

mous spring and fall pilgrimages featuring some of America's most splendid historic homes.

Hosts: Natchez Pilgrimage Tours
Rooms: Over 100 (PB) starting at $75
Full Southern Style Breakfast (at most inns)
Credit Cards: A, B, C, D
Notes: 2, 12

## Dunleith

84 Homochitto, 39120
(601) 446-8500; (800) 433-2445;
FAX (601) 446-6094

Dunleith is listed on the National Register of Historic Places and is a national landmark. It is located on 40 acres near downtown Natchez. Eleven rooms, three in main house and eight in courtyard wing. Full Southern breakfast served in Poultry House. All rooms have private baths and working fireplaces. No children. Reservations required.

Owner: W.F. Heins, III
Rooms: 11 (PB) $85-130
Full Breakfast
Credit Cards: A, B, C, D
Notes: none

Dunleith

## Monmouth Plantation

36 Melrose Ave., 39120
(601) 442-5852; FAX (601) 446-7762

Monmouth Plantation, circa 1818, is located on 27 acres of manicured grounds, virtually bursting with Southern charm, complete with magnolias and moss-draped oaks, a pond, gazebo, and rose garden. Rooms and suites (some with jacuzzi tubs) are situated throughout the grounds. A five-course, candlelight dinner is served Tuesday through Saturday in the main mansion. Monmouth is located approximately five minutes from the historic district and the Mississippi River.

Hostess: Lani Riches (owner)
Rooms: 25 (PB) $105-160
Full Breakfast
Credit Cards: A, B, C, D
Notes: 2, 4, 5, 8, 10, 12

## NATCHEZ TRACE AREA

## Natchez Trace Bed and Breakfast Reservation Service

P.O. Box 193, Hampshire, TN 38461
(615) 285-2777; (800) 377-2770

This reservation service is unusual in that all the homes listed are close to the Natchez Trace, the delightful National Parkway running from Nashville, Tennessee, to Natchez, Mississippi. Kay can help you plan your trip along the Trace, with homestays in interesting and

---

5 Open all year; 6 Pets welcome; 7 Children welcome; 8 Tennis nearby; 9 Swimming nearby;
10 Golf nearby; 11 Skiing nearby; 12 May be booked through travel agent.

historic homes along the way. Locations of homes include Ashland City, FairView, Leipers Fork, Coumbia, Hohenwald, Culleoka, Nashville, Franklin, and Hampshire, **Tennessee;** Florence, and Cherokee, **Alabama**; and Port Gibson, Corinth, French Camp, Kosciusko, Vicksburg, Loeman, Church Hill, and Natchez, **Mississippi.** Rates $60-125.

## PORT GIBSON

### Oak Square Plantation

1207 Church St., 39150
(601) 437-4350; (800) 729-0240;
FAX (601) 437-5768

This restored antebellum mansion of the Old South is in the town General U.S. Grant said was "too beautiful to burn." On the National Register of Historic Places, it has family heirloom antiques and canopied beds and is air-conditioned. Oak Square is home to the 1800's Spring Festival, "A top 20 event" in the Southeast held the last weekend in March. Your hosts' families have been in Mississippi for 200 years. Christ is the Lord of this house. "But as for me and my house, we will serve the Lord," Joshua 24:15. On U.S. Highway 61, adjacent to the Natchez Trace Parkway. Four-diamond rated by AAA.

Hosts: Mr. and Mrs. William Lum
Rooms: 12 (PB) $75-95; (special family rates)
Full Breakfast
Credit Cards: A, B, C, D
Notes: 2, 5, 7

## TUPELO

### The Mockingbird Inn Bed and Breakfast

305 N. Gloster, 38801
(601) 841-0286; FAX (601) 840-4158

Discover the romance of a different place and time in an enchanting getaway within the convenient confines of the city. Each guest room represents the decor from a different era in time. Delicious, hearty breakfast and evening refreshment included and two upscale restaurants in lovely old homes across the street. A health club is also nearby ($5 per visit).

Hosts: Jim and Sandy Gilmer
Rooms: 7 (PB) $65-110
Full Breakfast
Credit Cards: A, B, C, D
Notes: 2, 5, 6, 7 (over 13), 8, 9, 10, 12

## WEST

### The Alexander House

210 Green St., P.O. Box 187, 39192
(601) 967-2266; (800) 350-8034

Step inside the front door of the Alexander House Bed and Breakfast and go back in time to a more leisurely and gracious way of life. Victorian decor at its prettiest and country hospitality at its best is guaranteed to please your senses. Captain Alexander, Dr.

---

NOTES: Credit cards accepted: A Master Card; B Visa; C American Express; D Discover; E Diners Club; F Other; 2 Personal checks accepted; 3 Lunch available; 4 Dinner available;

Joe, Ulrich, Annie, and Miss Bealle are all rooms waiting to cast their spell over those who visit. Day trips to historic or recreational areas may be charted or chartered.

Hosts: Ruth Ray and Woody Dinstel
Rooms: 5 (3PB; 2SB) $65
Full Breakfast
Credit Cards: A, B, C, D
Notes: 2, 4, 5, 12

The Alexander House

- St. Joseph
- Hannibal
- Platte City
- Kansas City
- Boonville
- Warrensburg
- Hermann
- Defiance
- St. Louis
- Bonne Terre
- Nevada
- St. Genevieve
- Marshfield
- Jackson
- Carthage
- Springfield
- Joplin
- Branson
- Lampe

# MISSOURI

# Missouri

## Ozark Mountain Country B&B Service

P.O. Box 295, **Branson**, 65615
(417) 335-8134; (800) 695-1546

Ozark Mountain Country has been arranging accommodations for guests in **southwest Missouri** and **northwest Arkansas** since 1982. Our services are free. In the current list of over 100 homes and small inns, some locations offer private entrances, fantastic views, guest sitting areas, swimming pools, jacuzzis, and/or fireplaces. Most locations are available all year. Personal checks accepted. Some homes welcome children; a few welcome pets (even horses). Write for complimentary host brochure describing B&Bs available, listing, and discount coupons. Coordinator: Kay Cameron. $35-145; major credit cards welcomed.

## BONNE TERRE

### Victorian Veranda

207 E. School St., 63628
(314) 358-1134; (800) 343-1134

Return to the Victorian era as you step through this two-story, blue, Queen Anne-style home. Stay the night in one of the three lovely furnished guest rooms, all with private bath. Enjoy a full breakfast. On the main floor, guests enjoy full use of the parlor, gathering room with TV, dining room, and large wraparound veranda. Walking tour of Bonne Terre is nearby, three golf courses, tennis, and antique shops.

Hosts: Galen and Karen Forney
Rooms: 3 (PB) $60-75
Full Breakfast
Credit Cards: A, B
Notes: 2, 5, 7, 8, 9, 10

Victorian Veranda

---

NOTES: Credit cards accepted: A Master Card; B Visa; C American Express; D Discover; E Diners Club; F Other; 2 Personal checks accepted; 3 Lunch available; 4 Dinner available; 5 Open all year; 6 Pets welcome; 7 Children welcome; 8 Tennis nearby; 9 Swimming nearby; 10 Golf nearby; 11 Skiing nearby; 12 May be booked through travel agent.

## BOONVILLE

### Morgan Street Repose Bed and Breakfast

611 E. Morgan St., 65233
(816) 882-7195; (800) 248-5061

1869 national historic registered Home delightfully restored for a romantic, gracious, and hospitable stay. Filled with heirlooms, antiques, books, games, and curiosities to delight you. Our extravagant breakfasts are formally served in one of three dining rooms or Secret Garden. Situated one block to antique/specialty shops, restaurants, and Katy biking/hiking trail. Rental bikes available. Afternoon tea served.

Hostess: Doris Shenk
Rooms: 3 (PB) $55-95
Full Gourmet Breakfast
Credit Cards: none
Notes: 2, 5, 7 (older), 12

## BRANSON

### Cameron's CRAG

P.O. Box 526, **Pt. Lookout**, 65726
(417) 335-8134 (voice and FAX);
(800) 933-8529

Located high on a bluff overlooking Lake Taneycomo and the valley, three miles south of Branson, enjoy a spectacular view from a new spacious, detached, private suite with whirlpool tub, kitchen, living, and bedroom area. Two room suite with indoor hot tub and private bath. A third room has a great view of the lake and a private hot tub on the deck. All rooms have king-size beds, hot tubs, private entrances, TV/VCR's,

and a video library.

Hosts: Glen and Kay Cameron
Rooms: 3 (PB) $75-95
Full Breakfast
Credit Cards: A, B, C, D
Notes: 2, 4, 5, 12

## CARTHAGE

### Brewer's Maple Lane Farm Bed and Breakfast

Route 1, 64836
(417) 358-6312

Listed on the National Register of Historic Places, this Victorian home has 20 rooms furnished mostly with family heirlooms; four guest rooms. Our 240-acre farm is ideal for family vacations and campers. We have a playground, picnic area, hunting, and fishing in our 22-acre lake. Nearby are artist Lowell Davis' farm and Sam Butcher's Precious Moments Chapel.

Hosts: Arch and Renee Brewer
Rooms: 4 (SB) $50
Expanded Continental Breakfast
Credit Cards: none
Notes: 2, 5, 7, 8, 10, 12

Brewer's Maple Lane Farm B&B

---

NOTES: Credit cards accepted: A Master Card; B Visa; C American Express; D Discover; E Diners Club; F Other; 2 Personal checks accepted; 3 Lunch available; 4 Dinner available;

# DEFIANCE

## The Parsons House Bed and Breakfast

211 Lee St., P.O. Box 38, 63341
(314) 798-2222; FAX (314) 798-2220

This restored, 1842 Federal-style home overlooks the Missouri River Valley. Listed in the Historic Survey, it features fireplaces, a walnut staircase, and many antiques. For your enjoyment: an organ, piano, books, and games of bygone times. Closeby are the Katy Bicycle Trail, the Daniel Boone Home, and Missouri wineries, yet downtown St. Louis is only 35 miles away. Breakfast in the parlor, gardens, or on one of the porches. Resident dog, cat, computer consultant, and artist.

Hosts: Al and Carol Keyes
Rooms: 2 (SB) $60-80
Full Breakfast
Credit Cards: A, B
Notes: 2, 5 (except Christmas), 7 (limited), 10

# HANNIBAL

## Fifth St. Mansion Bed and Breakfast Inn

213 South Fifth Street, 63401
(314) 221-0445; (800) 874-5661;
FAX (314) 221-3335

Built in 1858 in Italianate style by friends of Mark Twain, antique furnishings complement the stained glass, ceramic fireplaces, and original gaslight fixtures of the house. Two parlors, din-

ing room, and library with hand-grained walnut paneling, plus wraparound porches provide space for conversation, reading, TV, games. Walk to Mark Twain historic district, shops, restaurants, riverfront. The mansion blends Victorian charm with plenty of old-fashioned hospitality. The whole house is available for reunions and weddings.

Hosts: Mike and Donalene Andreotti
Rooms: 7 (PB) $65-90
Full Breakfast
Credit Cards: A, B, C, D
Notes: 2, 5, 7, 8, 9, 10, 12

"A Little Log Cabin in the Woods"

# HERMANN

## "A Little Log Cabin in the Woods"

RR 1, Box 471, **New Florence,** 63363
(314) 252-4301

Enjoy a secluded, modern log house in the woods (owners live nearby). 270 acres, near Hermann, with central air, fireplace, full kitchen, dining room, living room with TV (satellite dish, VCR, videos), two bedrooms with king-size beds, one with full-size bed, two bath-

---

5 Open all year;  6 Pets welcome;  7 Children welcome;  8 Tennis nearby;  9 Swimming nearby;  10 Golf nearby;  11 Skiing nearby;  12 May be booked through travel agent.

rooms, porch, trails, 1900 one-room schoolhouse to tour, fantastic bird-watching opportunities, creekbeds for fossil hunting, and dark country nights for star-gazing! Nightshirts and full breakfast.

Hosts: Clyde and Ellen Waldo
Rooms: 1 cabin (3 rooms) (2SB) $65
Full Breakfast
Credit Cards: none
Notes: 2, 5, 7 (by arrangement), 10

## Die Gillig Heimat (Homestead)

HCR 62, Box 30, 65041
(314) 943-6942

Capture the beauty of country living on this farm located on beautiful rolling hills. The original Gillig home was built as a log cabin in 1842 and has been enlarged several times. Awake in the morning to beautiful views in every direction, and enjoy a hearty breakfast in the large, country kitchen. Stroll the pastures and hills of the working cattle farm while watching nature at its best. Historic Hermann is nearby.

Hosts: Ann and Armin Gillig
Rooms: 2 (PB) $55-65
Full Breakfast
Credit Cards: none
Notes: 2, 5, 7 (by arrangement)

## JACKSON

## Trisha's B&B, Tea Room, and Gifts

203 Bellevue, 63755
(314) 243-7427; (800) 651-0408

Innkeepers Gus and Trisha welcome guests to their 1905 Victorian home in Jackson, Cape Girardeau's county seat. The Wischmann home is located only three blocks from an excursion steam train. Smiles abound as vintage lingerie collections are discovered in the lovely guest rooms. Four bedrooms are available, three with private baths, with the fourth having a private half bath and shared shower. Breakfast is a gourmet delight as visitors feast on home-baked goodies, home-grown and hand-picked fresh fruit, and delicious entrees. Tea room open Wednesday, Thursday, and Friday.

Hosts: Gus and Trisha Wischmann
Rooms: 4 (3PB; 1SB) $65-75
Full Breakfast
Credit Cards: A, B
Notes: 2, 3, 4, 5, 7 (over 5), 8, 9, 10, 12

Visages

## JOPLIN

## Visages

327 N. Jackson, 64801
(417) 624-1397; (800) 896-1397

Just like coming home! Arrive as strangers, but depart as friends! Experience the turn-of-the-century ambiance of Visages, an 1898 Dutch Colonial house. Enjoy the concrete faces on masonry walls and artwork and ingenuity within. Never pretentious, always comfortable, Visages offers a unique bed and breakfast experience. Whether your visit is business or personal it will be a refreshing step back in time.

Hosts: Bill and Marge Meeker
Rooms: 3 (PB) $40-65
Full Breakfast
Credit Cards: C, D
Notes: 2, 5, 6 (sometimes), 7, 8, 9, 10, 12

## KANSAS CITY

## *Bed and Breakfast Reservations for Kansas City*

P.O. Box 14781, **Lenexa, KS** 66285
(913) 888-3636

This reservation service can arrange your accommodations in **Kansas City** or the **St. Louis, Missouri** area. From an 1857 plantation mansion on the river to a geodesic dome in the woods with hot tub, there is a price and style for everyone. Victorian, turn-of-the-century, English Tudor, and contemporary are available. Double, queen, or king beds; most with private baths. The service represents 35 inns and homes. $40-125.

## *Southmoreland on the Plaza*

116 E. 46th St., 64112
(816) 531-7979; FAX (816) 531-2407

Classic New England Colonial mansion located between renowned Country Club Plaza (shopping / entertainment district) and Nelson-Atkins and Kemper Museums of Art. Elegant B&B ambiance with small hotel amenities. Rooms with private decks, fireplaces, or jacuzzi baths. Special services for business travelers. Sport / dining privileges at nearby historic private club. Mobile Travel Guide Four-star winner since 1993. Only B&B to receive Midwest Travel Writers' "Gem of the Midwest" award.

Hostesses: Penni Johnson and Susan Moehl
Rooms: 12 (PB) $100-145
Full Breakfast
Credit Cards: A, B, C
Notes: 2, 5, 8, 9, 10, 12

Southmoreland on the Plaza

## LAMPE

## *Grandpa's Farm*

Box 476, HCR 1, 65681
(417) 779-5106; (800) 280-5106

A real old-time, 16-acre Ozark Mountain farm with plenty of friendly animal life. Luxurious Honeymoon suite with spa, Red Bud suite with large whirlpool tub, Dogwood suite with kitchenette, and Mother Hen room.

5 Open all year; 6 Pets welcome; 7 Children welcome; 8 Tennis nearby; 9 Swimming nearby; 10 Golf nearby; 11 Skiing nearby; 12 May be booked through travel agent.

Near Branson , MO and Eureka Springs, AR. Big, country breakfast served on screened in porch. Secret hideout lofts for children.

Hosts: Keith and Pat Lamb
Rooms: 4 (PB) $65-85
Full Breakfast
Credit Cards: A, B, D
Notes: 2, 5, 7, 9, 12

Dickey House Bed and Breakfast Inn

## MARSHFIELD

## Dickey House Bed and Breakfast Inn

331 South Clay Street, 65706
(417) 468-3000; FAX (417) 859-5478

The stately, three-story Ante-bellum Mansion situated on one acre of park-like grounds, is one of Missouri's finest bed and breakfast inns. Four antique-filled guest rooms with private baths, plus two spectacular suites with luxuriously appointed decor, double jacuzzi, fireplace, and cable TV. The Inn and dining room are enhanced by a display of fine American and European art and antiques. A gourmet breakfast is served

in true Victorian style, amid fine china, silver, and crystal.

Hosts: William and Dorothy Buesgen
Rooms: 6 (PB) $55-95
Full Breakfast
Credit Cards: A, B, D
Notes: 2, 5, 7 (well behaved), 8, 9, 10, 12

## NEVADA

## Red Horse Inn B&B

217 S. Main, 64772
(417) 667-7796; (800) 245-3685

Experience the friendly hospitality of the Red Horse Inn, a turn-of-the-century home furnished in antiques. Guests can walk to the town square or relax on the front porch, deck, or shaded backyard. We are located in historic Nevada, MO, between Kansas City and Joplin. Come stay with us on your visit to Cottey College or on your way to Branson. Come as a guest and leave as a friend.

Hosts: Victor and Sharon McCullough
Rooms: 5 (3PB; 2SB) $40-45
Full Breakfast
Credit Cards: A, B, C
Notes: 2, 5, 6 (prior notice), 7, 8, 9, 10

## PLATTE CITY

## Basswood Country Inn Resort

15880 Interurban Rd., 64079
(816) 858-5556 (voice and FAX);
(800) 242-2775

Country at Kansas City's doorstep . Enjoy Country French suites, lakeside cottages, or a condominium at Farmer

---

NOTES: Credit cards accepted: A Master Card; B Visa; C American Express; D Discover; E Diners Club; F Other; 2 Personal checks accepted; 3 Lunch available; 4 Dinner available;

Millionaire's estate. Fishing, walking trails, and outdoor pool available. Write or call for a brochure. Reservations only.

Hosts: Don and Betty Soper
Rooms: 8 (PB) $66-128
Continental Breakfast
Credit Cards: A, B, D
Notes: 2, 5, 7, 9, 10, 11, 12

## ST. GENEVIEVE

### Inn at St. Gemme Beauvais

78 N. Main, 63670
(314) 883-5744; (800) 818-5744

Jacuzzis, hors d'oeuvres, and private suites filled with antiques only begin your pampering stay in Missouri's oldest, continually operating bed and breakfast. The romantic dining room, complete with working fireplace, is the perfect setting for an intimate breakfast. The Inn has been recently redecorated and is walking distance to many shops and historical sites. Packages available for that special occasion, as well as picnics to take on hiking trails.

Hostess: Janet Joggerst
Rooms: 7 (PB) $69-125
Full Breakfast
Credit Cards: A, B
Notes: 2, 3, 5, 7, 8, 9, 10

## ST. JOSEPH

### Harding House B&B and Miss Annie's B&B

219 N. 20th St., 64501
(816) 232-7020

Gracious turn-of-the-century home.

Elegant, oak woodwork and pocket doors. Antiques and beveled, leaded glass windows. Historic area near museums, churches, and antique shops. Four unique guest rooms. Eastlake has a romantic wood-burning fireplace and queen-size bed; Blue room has an antique baby crib. Children welcome. Full breakfast with homemade pastry.

Hosts: Glen and Mary Harding
Rooms: 2 + 1 suite (1PB; 3SB) $45-55
Full Breakfast
Credit Cards: A, B, C, D
Notes: 2, 5, 7, 8, 10, 12

## ST. LOUIS

### Lafayette House B&B

2156 Lafayette Ave., 63104
(314) 772-4429

This 1876 Victorian mansion with modern amenities is in the center of things to do in St. Louis and on a direct bus line to downtown. It is air-conditioned and furnished with antiques and traditional furniture. Many collectibles and large, varied library to enjoy. Families welcome. Resident cats and dog.

Hosts: Bill, Nancy, and Anna
Rooms: 4 + 1 suite (2PB; 3SB) $50-75
Full Breakfast
Credit Cards: A, B
Notes: 2, 5, 7, 8, 9, 10, 12

## SPRINGFIELD

### Virginia Rose B&B

317 E. Glenwood, 65807
(417) 883-0693

This two-story farmhouse, built in 1906,

5 Open all year; 6 Pets welcome; 7 Children welcome; 8 Tennis nearby; 9 Swimming nearby; 10 Golf nearby; 11 Skiing nearby; 12 May be booked through travel agent.

offers country hospitality right in town. Situated in a tree-covered acre, our home is furnished with early 1900 antiques, quilts on queen-sized beds, and rockers on the porch. Relax in the parlor with a book, puzzle, or game, or watch a movie on the TV/VCR. Only minutes from BASS Pro Outdoor World, restaurants, shopping, antique shops, and miniature golf, and only 40 miles from Branson.

Hosts: Jackie and Virginia Buck
Rooms: 3 + 2 suites (PB) $50-100
Full Breakfast
Credit Cards: A, B
Notes: 2, 5, 7, 9, 10, 12

The Camel Crossing Bed and Breakfast

## WARRENSBURG

### *The Camel Crossing Bed and Breakfast*

210 East Gay, 64093
(816) 429-2973

Take a magic carpet to this bed and breakfast that is homey in atmosphere but museum-like in its decor. Brass, copper, hand tied carpets, and furnishings from the Far East will captivate your imaginations. An oasis for mind and body, if you come a stranger, you'll leave as a friend.

Hosts: Ed and Joyce Barnes
Rooms: 4 (2PB; 2SB) $55-65
Full Breakfast
Credit Cards: A, B
Notes: 2, 5, 7, 8, 9, 10

Virginia Rose Bed and Breakfast

---

# Montana

## BOZEMAN

### The Fox Hollow Bed and Breakfast at Baxter Creek

545 Mary Rd., 59715
(406) 582-8440 (voice and FAX);
(800) 431-5010

Our country setting is in the heart of the Gallatin River Valley. Enjoy panoramic views of majestic mountain ranges from the hot tubs on our wrap-around deck. Our 1993, country style home offers spacious guest rooms, all with private baths. Wake to full country breakfasts every morning. Easy access from interstate and minutes from airport or town.

Hosts: Nancy and Michael Dawson
Rooms: 3 (PB) $90-105
Full Breakfast
Credit Cards: A, B
Notes: 2, 5, 8, 9, 10, 11, 12

### Lindley House

202 Lindley Place, 59715
(406) 587-8403; (800) 787-8404;
(406) 582-8112

A unique and elegant Victorian inn featuring antiques, artwork, and period wall coverings to make your stay warm and comfortable. University town has much to offer. Within walking distance to theaters, galleries, fine restaurants, and specialty shopping. In the heart of fly-fishing country, close to Bridger Bowl ski area, and numerous outdoor recreational attractions. Personal attention, good food, and privacy are our specialties. No smoking.

Hostess: Stephanie Volz
Rooms: 4 with 2 suites (PB) $75-195
Full Breakfast
Credit Cards: A, B
Notes: 2, 3, 5, 8, 9, 10, 11

Lindley House

---

5  Open all year;  6  Pets welcome;  7  Children welcome;  8  Tennis nearby;  9  Swimming nearby;
10  Golf nearby;  11  Skiing nearby;  12  May be booked through travel agent.

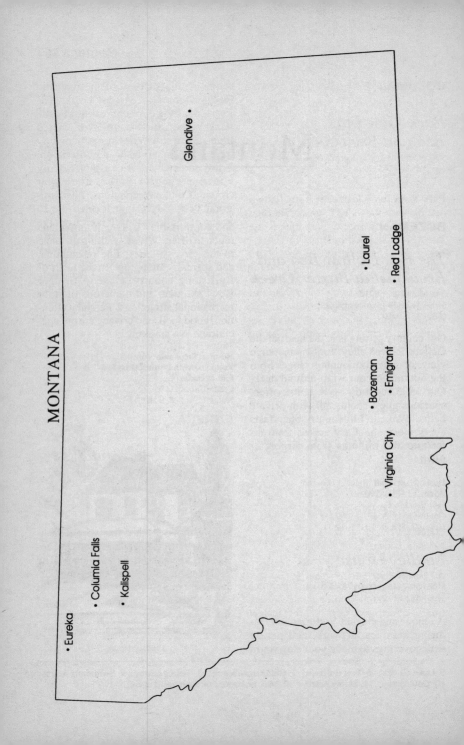

## COLUMBIA FALLS

### Park View Inn
### Bed and Breakfast

904 Fourth Ave. W., Box 567, 59912
(406) 892-(7275) Park

Park View Inn is located in a small town setting with views of Glacier National Park and our own city park across the street, which is complete with swimming pool, basketball court, and children's play area, as well as beautiful trees and picnic areas. We know you'll enjoy our two-story Victorian home with two suites and two luxury rooms or one of our three cabins, especially our honeymoon cabin featuring jacuzzi and four-poster bed.

Hosts: Gary and Jayne Hall
Rooms: 7 (3PB; 4SB) $45-95
Full and Continental Breakfast available
Credit Cards: A, B
Notes: 2, 5, 6 (prearranged), 7, 8, 9, 10, 11

## EMIGRANT (YELLOWSTONE NATIONAL PARK)

### Paradise Gateway
### Bed and Breakfast
### and Cabin

P.O. Box 84, 59027
(406) 333-4063; (800) 541-4113

Paradise Gateway B&B, just minutes from Yellowstone National Park, offers quiet, charming, comfortable guest rooms in the shadow of the majestic Rocky Mountains. As day breaks, enjoy a country, gourmet breakfast by the banks of the Yellowstone River, a noted blue ribbon trout stream. A "cowboy treat tray" is served in the afternoon. Enjoy summer and winter sports. Only entrance open to Yellowstone year 'round. Call for reservations. Plus Emigrant Peak Log Cabin located on 25 acres of Yellowstone River frontage next to the bed and breakfast. Modern two-bedroom log cabin with laundry services and complete kitchen. Decorated in country charm and extremely private. $125 a night for two—additional $20 per person above two—sleeps six. Continental breakfast served.

Hosts: Pete and Carol Reed
Rooms: 3 + 2-room cabin $125 (PB) $85-95
Full Country Gourmet Breakfast
Credit Cards: A, B
Notes: 2, 5, 8, 9, 10, 11, 12

## EUREKA

### Huckleberry Hannah's
### Montana B&B

3100 Sophie Lake Rd., 59917
(406) 889-3381 (voice and FAX)

Nearly 6,000 square feet of old-fashioned, country-sweet charm, it is the answer to vacationing in Montana. The B&B sits on 50 wooded acres, and bordering a fabulous trout-filled lake with glorious views of the Rockies. This bed and breakfast depicts a quieter time in

---

NOTES: Credit cards accepted: A Master Card; B Visa; C American Express; D Discover; E Diners Club; F Other; 2 Personal checks accepted; 3 Lunch available; 4 Dinner available; 5 Open all year; 6 Pets welcome; 7 Children welcome; 8 Tennis nearby; 9 Swimming nearby; 10 Golf nearby; 11 Skiing nearby; 12 May be booked through travel agent.

our history when the true pleasures of life represented a walk in the woods or a moonlight swim. Or maybe just a little early morning relaxation in a porch swing, sipping a fresh cup of coffee, and watching a colorful sunrise. The surrounding area is 91% public lands, perfect for hiking, biking, hunting, fishing, and swimming. It's a cross-country skiers dream in winter, also easy driving distance to downhill skiing in Whitefish. And, don't forget those comfortable sunny rooms and all that wonderful home-cooked food. The B&B is owned and operated by the author of one of the Northwest's Best-Selling Cookbooks "Huckleberry Hannah's Country Cooking Sampler." Questions cheerfully answered. Ask about kids and pets and Senior Discounts! Local airport nearby. Free brochure.

Hosts: Jack and Deanna Doying
Rooms: 5 + lake cottage (PB) $50-75
Full Breakfast (Continental upon request)
Credit Cards: A, B, D
Notes: 2, 3, 4, 5, 6 (some), 7, 8, 9, 11, 12

## GLENDIVE

## *The Hostetler House Bed and Breakfast*

113 N. Douglas St., 59330
(406) 365-4505; FAX (406) 365-8456

Located two blocks from downtown shopping and restaurants, The Hostetler House is a charming, 1912 historic home with two comfortable guest rooms, sitting room, sun porch, deck, gazebo, and hot tub. Full gourmet breakfast is served on Grandma's china.

On I-94 and the Yellowstone River, we are close to parks, swimming pool, tennis courts, golf course, antique shops, and churches. Craig and Dea invite you to "Arrive as a guest and leave as a friend."

Hosts: Craig and Dea Hostetler
Rooms: 2 (SB) $50
Full Gourmet Breakfast
Credit Cards: A, B, D
Notes: 2, 5, 8, 9, 10, 11 (cross-country), 12

The Hostetler House Bed and Breakfast

## KALISPELL

## *Stillwater Inn*

206 Fourth Ave. E., 59901
(406) 755-7080; (800) 398-7024;
FAX (416) 756-0020

Relax in this lovely, historic home built in 1900, decorated to fit the period, and furnished with turn-of-the-century antiques. Four guest bedrooms, two with private baths. Full gourmet breakfast. Walking distance to churches, shopping, dining, art galleries, antique shops, Woodland Park, and the Conrad Mansion. Short drive to Glacier National Park, Big Mountain skiing, six golf courses, excellent fishing, and

---

NOTES: Credit cards accepted: A Master Card; B Visa; C American Express; D Discover; E Diners Club; F Other; 2 Personal checks accepted; 3 Lunch available; 4 Dinner available;

hunting. Please, no smoking in the house. Come, enjoy our hospitality.

Hosts: Pat and Jane Morison
Rooms: 4 (2PB; 2SB) $60-85
Full Breakfast
Credit Cards: A, B
Notes: 2, 5, 7, 8, 9, 10, 11, 12

## LAUREL

## Riverside Bed and Breakfast

2231 Theil Rd., 59044
(406) 628-7890; (800) 768-1580;
FAX (406) 656-8306

Just off I-90, fifteen minutes from Billings, on a main route to skiing and Yellowstone National Park. Fly fish the Yellowstone from our backyard; soak away stress in the hot tub; llinger and llook at the lloveable llamas; take a spin on our bicycle built for two; enjoy a peaceful sleep, a friendly visit, and a fantastic breakfast.

Hosts: Lynn and Nancy Perey
Rooms: 2 (PB) $60
Full Breakfast
Credit Cards: A, B
Notes: 2, 5, 7 (over 10), 10, 11, 12

## RED LODGE

## Willows Inn

224 S. Platt Ave., P.O. Box 886, 59068
(406) 446-3913

Nestled beneath the majestic Beartooth Mountains in a quaint historic town, this delightful turn-of-the-century Victorian, complete with picket fence and porch swing, awaits you. A light and airy atmosphere with warm, cheerful decor greets the happy wanderer. Five charming guest rooms, each unique, are in the main inn. Two delightfully nostalgic cottages with kitchen and laundry are also available. Home-baked pastries are a specialty. Videos, books, games, afternoon refreshments, and sun deck.

Hosts: Kerry, Carolyn, and Elven Boggio
Rooms: 5 + 2 cottages (3PB; 2SB) $50-75
Continental Plus Breakfast
Credit Cards: A, B, D
Notes: 2, 5, 7 (restricted), 8, 9, 10, 11, 12

## VIRGINIA CITY

## Stonehouse Inn

Box 202, 306 E. Idaho, 59755
(406) 843-5504

Located on a quiet street only blocks away from the historic section of Virginia City, this Victorian stone home is listed on the National Register of Historic Places. Brass beds and antiques in every room give the Inn a romantic touch. Five bedrooms share two baths. Full breakfasts are served each morning, and smoking is allowed on our porches. Skiing, snowmobiling, golfing, hunting, and fly fishing nearby.

Hosts: John and Linda Hamilton
Rooms: 5 (SB) $50 + tax
Full Breakfast
Credit Cards: A, B
Notes: 2, 4, 5, 7, 8, 10, 12

---

5 Open all year; 6 Pets welcome; 7 Children welcome; 8 Tennis nearby; 9 Swimming nearby;
10 Golf nearby; 11 Skiing nearby; 12 May be booked through travel agent.

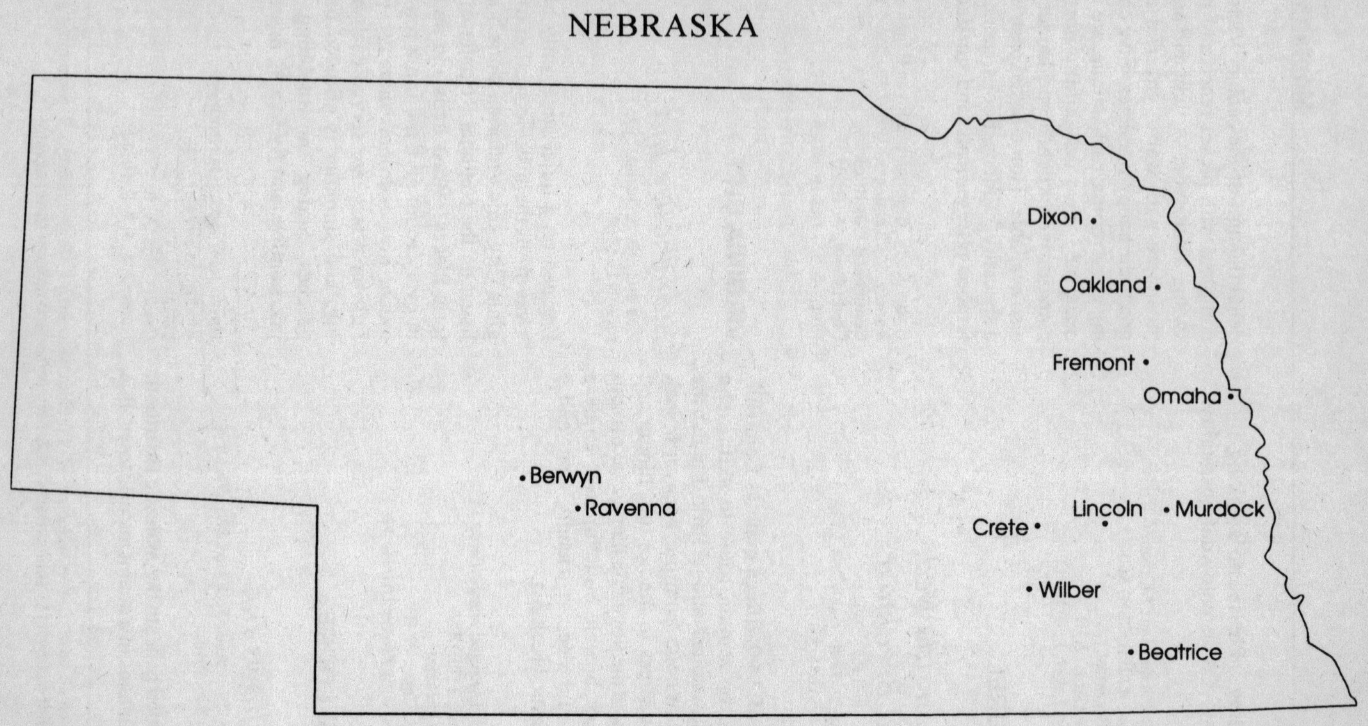

NEBRASKA

Dixon •

Oakland •

Fremont •

Omaha •

Murdock •

Lincoln •

Crete •

Wilber •

Beatrice •

Benwyn •

Ravenna •

# Nebraska

## BEATRICE

### The Carriage House B&B

Box 136 "B", RR 1, 68310
(402) 228-0356

Nestled in the quiet countryside on the edge of Beatrice, you will find a beautiful 18-room Georgian mansion filled with 1800's antiques. Enjoy a ride through the countryside in a horse drawn carriage; tour the shop and experience the craft of restoring carriages. View the crimson sunset from the swing on the porch or unwind with a stroll through the garden to the gazebo. Awake to the aroma of a delicious home- cooked breakfast after spending a restful night in one of six guest rooms, some with private baths.

Hosts: Jody and Floyd Forke
Rooms: 6 (1PB; 3SB)
$49.28-65.70 tax included
Full Breakfast
Credit Cards: A, B
Notes: 2, 5 (except Dec. 24-26), 7 (over 10), 8, 9, 10, 12

## BERWYN

### 1909 Heritage House at Berwyn

P.O. Box 196, 101 Curran, 68819
(308) 935-1136

A warm welcome awaits you in this lovely three-story Victorian/Country home with air-conditioned rooms. Heritage House is located in Central Nebraska, on Highway Two, which is one of the most scenic highways in America. Enjoy a country breakfast served in an elegant dining room, country kitchen, or sunroom.

Hosts: Meriam and Dale Thomas
Rooms: 5 (1PB; 4SB) $40-85
Full Breakfast
Credit Cards: none
Notes: 2, 5, 8, 9, 10, 12

## CRETE

### The Parson's House

638 Forest Ave., 68333
(402) 826-2634

Enjoy warm hospitality in a restored four square home built at the turn of the

---

NOTES: Credit cards accepted: A Master Card; B Visa; C American Express; D Discover; E Diners Club; F Other; 2 Personal checks accepted; 3 Lunch available; 4 Dinner available; 5 Open all year; 6 Pets welcome; 7 Children welcome; 8 Tennis nearby; 9 Swimming nearby; 10 Golf nearby; 11 Skiing nearby; 12 May be booked through travel agent.

century, furnished with many antiques and a modern whirlpool bathtub. Located near Doane College and its beautiful campus. A full breakfast is served in the formal dining room.

Hostess: Sandy Richardson
Rooms: 2 (SB) $35
Full Breakfast
Credit Cards: none
Notes: 2, 5, 8, 9

The Parson's House

## DIXON

### Country Bed and Breakfast

Rt. 2, Box 28A, 68732
(402) 584-2214

Our modern ranch style home in a quiet country setting is surrounded by beautiful flowers and trees. The queen-size bed in the large bedroom is covered with a beautiful log cabin quilt. Located 40 miles west of Sioux City, IA, 50 miles from Yankton, SD, 25 miles from Ponca State Park, and 15 miles from Wayne, NE. Your hosts enjoy cooking, gardening, birds, crafts, and traveling. No smoking or alcohol. Will serve an evening snack.

Hosts: Kenneth and Muriel Kardell
Rooms: 2 (SB) $30-40
Full Breakfast
Credit Cards: none
Notes: 2, 5, 9, 10

## FREMONT

### Bed and Breakfast of Fremont

1624 E. 25th St., 68025
(402) 727-9534

The B&B of Fremont is a two-story Colonial home situated on four and one half acres. Guest facilities include four private bedrooms, sitting room, upper balcony, and lower-level Garden room. One main floor bedroom with queen bed and private bath; four upstairs bedrooms with king, queen, or two double beds, and shared baths. Great for small retreats and family reunions! Group rates and senior citizen discounts.

Hosts: Dr. Paul and Linda VonBehren
Rooms: 5 (1PB; 4SB) $49-69
Full Breakfast
Credit Cards: none
Notes: 2, 5, 7, 8, 9, 10, 12

## MURDOCK

### Farm House

32617 Church Rd., 68407
(402) 867-2062

Originally built in 1896, The Farm House provides a glimpse back to country life of the past, complete with expansive ten-foot ceilings, wood floors, an oak spindle staircase, antiques, and even a front porch swing. Room decor and furnishings throughout provide a feeling of comfortable, country elegance. Air-conditioned. Half hour from Lincoln and Omaha.

Hosts: Mike and Pat Meierhenry
Rooms: 3 (1PB; 2SB) $35-45
Full Breakfast
Credit Cards: none
Notes: 2, 5, 6, 7, 8, 10

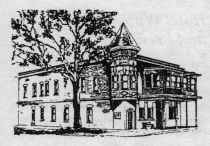

Benson Bed and Breakfast

## OAKLAND

# Benson Bed and Breakfast

402 N. Oakland Ave., 68045
(402) 685-6051

Located in the center of a small town. Benson B&B is beautifully decorated with a breakfast you won't soon forget, served in a dining room with all its finery. Large collection of soft drink collectibles, a library full of books, beautiful garden to relax in, and a large whirlpool tub with color TV on the wall. All rooms are on the second level. Craft and gift shops on the main floor. Three

blocks west of Highway 77. No smoking!

Hosts: Stan and Norma Anderson
Rooms: 3 (SB) $50-55
Full, Elegant Breakfast
Credit Cards: none
Notes: 2, 5, 8, 9, 10, 12

## OMAHA

# The Jones'

1617 S. 90th St., 68129
(402) 397-0721

Large, private residence with large deck and gazebo in the back. Fresh cinnamon rolls are served for breakfast. Your hosts' interests include golf, travel, needlework, and meeting other people. Located five minutes from I-80.

Hosts: Don and Theo Jones
Rooms: 3 (1PB; 2SB) $25
Continental Breakfast
Credit Cards: none
Notes: 2, 5, 6, 7, 8, 10

## RAVENNA

# Aunt Betty's Bed and Breakfast

804 Grand Avenue, 68864
(308) 452-3739

Enjoy the peacefulness of a small, central Nebraska town while staying at Aunt Betty's three-story Victorian Bed and Breakfast. Four bedrooms furnished in antiques and decorated with attention to detail. Relax in the sitting room while awaiting a delicious, full

5 Open all year; 6 Pets welcome; 7 Children welcome; 8 Tennis nearby; 9 Swimming nearby; 10 Golf nearby; 11 Skiing nearby; 12 May be booked through travel agent.

breakfast including Aunt Betty's "Sticky Buns" and homemade goodies. Flower garden area with fish pond for relaxing. Accommodations for hunters in the hunter's loft. Antique shop part of the B&B. Golf and tennis nearby. One-half hour from I-80.

Hosts: Harvey and Betty Shrader
Rooms: 4 (SB) $45-55
Full Breakfast
Credit Cards: A, B
Notes: 2, 3 and 4 (by appointment), 5, 7, 8, 9, 10

Aunt Betty's Bed and Breakfast

## TABLE ROCK

## *Hill Haven Lodge*

RR 1, Box 5AA, 68447
(402) 839-2023

A 126-year-old rock house filled with

antique bedroom furniture, a sitting room and a sitting room with TV, VCR, and tapes. One bathroom. Full breakfast of meat, eggs, muffins, and fruit.

Hostess: Jo Ann Kalina
Rooms: 3 (SB) $30-35
Full Breakfast
Credit Cards: none
Notes: 2, 5, 6, 7

## WILBER

## *Hotel Wilber Bed and Breakfast Inn*

W. Second and S. Wilson Streets.,
P.O. Box 641, 68465
(402) 821-2020; (800) 609-4663

Escape to tranquility at this 1895 hotel turned B&B in nostalgic Wilber, NE, Czech Capital of the USA, just forty minutes southwest from Lincoln, ninety from Omaha. Soothing country and Victorian style antique rooms await, each with cable TV and personally controlled heating and air. Relax in the charming pub, lobby, garden, or dining room where sumptuous breakfasts are served each morning and traditional Czech and American cuisine is offered weekends and by appointment.

Hostess: Frances L. Erb
Rooms: 10 (SB) $42.95-69.95
Full Breakfast
Credit Cards: A, B
Notes: 2, 3, 4, 5, 7, 8, 9, 10

NOTES: Credit cards accepted: A Master Card; B Visa; C American Express; D Discover; E Diners Club; F Other; 2 Personal checks accepted; 3 Lunch available; 4 Dinner available;

# Nevada

## INCLINE VILLAGE

### Haus Bavaria
593 N. Dyer Circle, P.O. Box 3308, 89450
(702) 831-6122; (800) 731-6222;
FAX (702) 831-1238

This European-style residence in the heart of the Sierra Nevadas, is within walking distance of Lake Tahoe. Each of the five guest rooms open onto a balcony, offering lovely views of the mountains. Breakfast, prepared by your host Bick Hewitt, includes a selection of home-baked goods, fresh fruit, juices, freshly ground coffee, and teas. A private beach and swimming pool are available to guests. Ski at Diamond Peak, Mt. Rose, Heavenly Valley, and other nearby areas.

Host: Bick Hewitt
Rooms: 5 (PB) $125
Full Breakfast
Credit Cards: A, B, C, D
Notes: 2, 5, 8, 9, 10, 11, 12

●Incline Village

---

5 Open all year; 6 Pets welcome; 7 Children welcome; 8 Tennis nearby; 9 Swimming nearby; 10 Golf nearby; 11 Skiing nearby; 12 May be booked through travel agent.

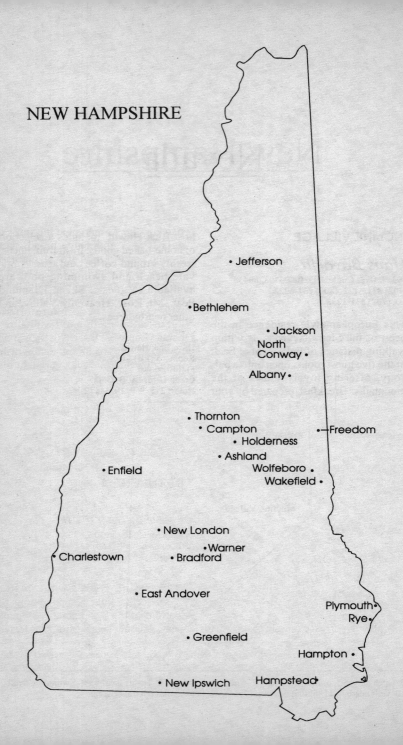

NEW HAMPSHIRE

• Jefferson

• Bethlehem

• Jackson

North
Conway •

Albany •

• Thornton
• Campton
• Holderness
• Ashland
Wolfeboro
Wakefield •

• Enfield

—• Freedom

• New London
• Warner
• Bradford

• Charlestown

• East Andover

Plymouth •
Rye •

• Greenfield

Hampton •

• New Ipswich    Hampstead

# New Hampshire

## ALBANY

### Kancamagus Swift River Inn

Rt. 112 Kancamagus Hwy., 03818
(603) 447-2332

This is a quality inn with that Old World flavor in a stress-free environment. Located in the White Mountains of New Hampshire in the Mt. Washington Valley on the most beautiful highway in the state, the Kancamagus Highway, one and a half miles off Route 16. We are only minutes from all factory outlets, attractions, and fine restaurants.

Hosts: Joseph and Janet Beckenbach
Rooms: 10 (PB) $40-90
Continental Breakfast
Credit Cards: none
Notes: 5, 7, 8, 9, 10, 11, 12

## ASHLAND

### Glynn House Victorian Inn

43 Highland St., P.O. Box 719, 03217
(603) 968-3775; (800) 637-9599

A picture perfect example of the Victorian era, guests marvel at the Inn's cupola towers and gingerbread, wraparound porch. Upon arrival, guests are greeted by a magnificent foyer accented with carved oak woodwork and pocket doors. The Inn is beautifully furnished with Queen Anne furniture offering guests the warmth and hospitality of being "home" in the 1890s! Each bedroom has its own mood, distinguished by unique interior decor, period furnishings, and amenities.

Hosts: Karol and Betsy Paterman
Rooms: 6 (PB) $75-125
Full Breakfast
Credit Cards: A, B, C, E
Notes: 2, 3, 5, 8, 9, 10, 11, 12

## BETHLEHEM

### The Mulburn Inn

Main Street, Route 302, 03574
(603) 869-3389; (800) 457-9440;
FAX (603) 869-5633

A charming B&B on the historic Woolworth Estate, hosted by four generations of the Skeels family. Open all year. Seven warm and comfortable

---

NOTES: Credit cards accepted: A Master Card; B Visa; C American Express; D Discover; E Diners Club; F Other; 2 Personal checks accepted; 3 Lunch available; 4 Dinner available; 5 Open all year; 6 Pets welcome; 7 Children welcome; 8 Tennis nearby; 9 Swimming nearby; 10 Golf nearby; 11 Skiing nearby; 12 May be booked through travel agent.

rooms, all with private bath. King-, queen-, and full-size beds available. Port-a-cribs provided on request. Complimentary full breakfast by the fire. Cheery common rooms with easy chairs for reading and relaxing. Cable TV and guest telephone in the common room. Spacious grounds for children to play. Four season attractions; hiking, biking, golfing on two local PGA rated courses, fishing, swimming, Storyland, Santa's Village, and Six-Gun City. Minutes away from the scenic beauty of Franconia Notch, Crawford Notch, and Mt. Washington. Children welcome. No smoking. No pets. AAA and Mobile approved and rated.

Hosts: The Skeels Family
Rooms: 7 (PB) $55-80
Full Breakfast
Credit Cards: A, B, C, D
Notes: 2, 4, 5, 7, 8, 9, 10, 11, 12

## *Wayside Inn and Motel*

Rt. 302 at Pierce Bridge, P.O. Box 480, 03574
(603) 869-3364; (800) 448-9557

Wonderful location by the Ammonoosuc River in the heart of the White Mountains. Classic New England inn encircled by many trees and native flowers. Cozy to spacious with connecting rooms; some with AC, CCTV, and balconies. Excellent meals in our Riverview Restaurant. Award winning European trained chef and innkeepers. Children's menu available. Secluded sandy beach by river. Common rooms, game room, lounge. Great value packages. Close to all attractions.

Hosts: The Hofmann Family
Rooms: 28 (22PB; 6SB) $48-58
Full/Continental Breakfast (not included in above rates)
Credit Cards: A, B, C, D
Notes: 4, 6, 7, 8 (on premises), 9, 10, 11, 12

## BRADFORD

## *The Bradford Inn*

11 W. Main St., 03221
(603) 938-5309; (800) 669-5309

The Bradford Inn was built as a small hotel in the 1890s. It has two parlors for guest use, one with a fireplace and one with a TV. J. Albert's Restaurant features Old World style cuisine spe-

Wayside Inn and Motel

cializing in German, Austrian, and Polish dishes. "Well worth the trip," says M. DePauld. The area abounds in outdoor activities in all seasons and offers craft and antique shops, auctions, summer theater, local fairs, and festivals. We can accommodate small groups (28-34) for retreats, family parties, or church outings.

Hosts: Tom and Connie Mazol
Rooms: 12 (PB) $59-79
Full Breakfast
Credit Cards: A, B, C, D, E, F
Notes: 2, 4, 5, 6, 7, 8, 9, 10, 11, 12

## Candlelite Inn Bed and Breakfast

5 Greenhouse Ln., 03221
(603) 938-5571

An 1857 country Victorian inn nestled on three acres in the Lake Sunapee Region. All of our guest rooms are tastefully decorated and have queen beds, private baths, and mountain views. A gazebo porch is there for your enjoyment on a lazy summer day, and in the parlor is a corner fireplace for those chilly evenings. A full breakfast is served in our lovely dining room or in the sun room overlooking a babbling brook and pond. Within minutes to skiing, hiking, antiquing, and restaurants. We are a non-smoking inn.

Hosts: Marilyn and Les Gordon
Rooms: 6 (PB) $65-75
Full Breakfast
Credit Cards: A, B, D
Notes: 2, 5, 7, 8, 9, 10, 11, 12

## CAMPTON

## Mountain-Fare Inn

Mad River Road, P.O. Box 553, 03223
(603) 726-4283

In New Hampshire's White Mountains. Lovely 1840's village home with the antiques, fabrics, and feel of country cottage living. Gardens in summer; foliage in fall; a true skier's lodge in winter. Accessible, peaceful, warm, friendly, affordable. Hearty breakfasts. Unspoiled beauty from Franconia Notch to Squam Lake. Four-season sports, soccer field, music, and theater. Wonderful family vacationing.

Hosts: Susan and Nick Preston
Rooms: 10 (7 PB; 3 SB) $50-90
Full Breakfast
Credit Cards: A, B, D, E
Notes: 2, 5, 7, 8, 9, 10, 11, 12

## CHARLESTOWN

## MapleHedge Bed and Breakfast Inn

Main St., Route 12, 03603
(603) 826-5237; (800) 9 MAPLE 9;
FAX (603) 826-3543

Rather than just touring homes two-and-a-half centuries old, make one your "home away from home" while visiting western New Hampshire or Eastern Vermont. MapleHedge offers five distinctly different bedrooms with private baths and antiques chosen to compliment the individual decor. It has very

---

5 Open all year; 6 Pets welcome; 7 Children welcome; 8 Tennis nearby; 9 Swimming nearby; 10 Golf nearby; 11 Skiing nearby; 12 May be booked through travel agent.

tastefully added all modern day amenities such as central air-conditioning, fire sprinkler system, and queen beds. Enjoy a gourmet breakfast in the grand dining room of this magnificent home on the National Register and situated among 200 year old maples and lovely gardens.

Hosts: Joan and Dick DeBrine
Rooms: 5 (PB) $80-90
Full three-Course Breakfast
Credit Cards: A, B
Notes: 2, 5, 7 (over 12), 8, 9, 10, 11, 12

Highland Lake Inn

## EAST ANDOVER

## Highland Lake Inn

P.O. Box 164, Maple St., 03231
(603) 735-6426; FAX (603) 735-5355

A 1767 classic building on twelve acres in a Currier and Ives setting with lake and mountain views. Secluded beach, fishing, boating, hiking, downhill and cross-country skiing, ice-skating, championship golf, and antiquing. Spacious guest rooms, private baths, elegantly decorated with antiques, fine bedding,

and fireplaces. Full sumptuous breakfasts.

Hosts: Chrys and Mary Petras
Rooms: 10 (PB) $85-100
Full Breakfast
Credit Cards: A, B, C, D
Notes: 2, 5, 8, 9, 10, 11, 12

## ENFIELD

## Boulder Cottage on Crystal Lake

RR 1, Box 257, 03748
(603) 632-7355

A turn-of-the-century Victorian cottage owned by our family for 72 years. Our home faces beautiful Crystal Lake, a small, private lake centrally located in the Dartmouth-Sunapee Region.

Hosts: Harry and Barbara Reed
Rooms: 4 (2PB; 2SB) $50-60
Full Country Breakfast
Credit Cards: none
Notes: 2, 7, 9, 10, 12

## FREEDOM

## Freedom House Bed and Breakfast

1 Maple St., P.O. Box 478, 03836
(603) 539-4815

Located in a quiet country village. 20 minutes from the Conway's Shopping Outlets and ski slopes. King Pine Ski Resort is five minutes away. Lake Ossipee and Loon Lakes nearby. One church is located in the village; others are 15 minutes away. Smoke-free environment.

Hosts: Marjorie and Bob Daly
Rooms: 5 (SB) $50 + tax
Full Breakfast
Credit Cards: A, B
Notes: 2, 5, 7, 8, 9, 10, 11

Freedom House Bed and Breakfast

# GREENFIELD

## The Greenfield Bed and Breakfast Inn

Box 400, Forest Rd., 03047
(603) 597-6327; FAX (603) 597-2418 (call first)

Bob Hope and his wife, Dolores have visited twice because it is romance in Victorian splendor. The Inn offers a sleep-six hayloft suite with kitchen, a sleep-six cottage with kitchen and three bathrooms, plus a sleep two to three suit with kitchen. Breakfast with crystal, china, and Mozart. In a quiet valley surrounded by mountains and big veranda views. Only 90 minutes from Boston or 40 minutes from Manchester airports.

Hosts: Barbara and Vic Mangini
Rooms: 9 (7PB; 2SB) $49-99; + 2 suites and a cottage
Full Breakfast
Credit Cards: A, B, C
Notes: 2 (preferred), 5, 7 (restrictions), 8, 9, 10, 11, 12

# HAMPSTEAD

## Stillmeadow Bed and Breakfast at Hampstead

P.O. Box 565, 545 Main St., 03841
(603) 329-8381; FAX (603) 329-4075

Historic home built in 1850 with five chimneys, three staircases, hardwood floors, Oriental rugs, and wood stoves. Set on rolling meadows adjacent to professional croquet courts. Single, doubles, and suites, all with private baths. Families are welcome, with amenities such as fenced-in play yard and children's playroom. Easy commute to Manchester, NH, and Boston, MA. Complimentary refreshments and the cookie jar is always full. Formal dining and living rooms; expanded Continental breakfast.

Hosts: Lori and Randy Offord
Rooms: 4½ (4PB) $60-90
Expanded Continental Breakfast
Credit Cards: A, B, C
Notes: 2, 5, 6 (with advance approval), 7, 8, 9, 10, 11, 12 (non-commissionable)

# HAMPTON

## The Curtis Field House

735 Exeter Rd., 03842
(603) 929-0082

A restored custom cape located on five country acres on Route 27 just over the Exeter Line which was established in 1638. Seven miles from the Atlantic Ocean. Our large rooms have air-conditioning and are decorated with antiques and many lovely reproductions crafted by a descendant of Darby Field.

---

5 Open all year; 6 Pets welcome; 7 Children welcome; 8 Tennis nearby; 9 Swimming nearby; 10 Golf nearby; 11 Skiing nearby; 12 May be booked through travel agent.

A New England lobster dinner can be ordered in advance. Limited smoking area. Reservations required. AAA 3-star. ABBA.

Hosts: Mary and Daniel Houston
Rooms: 3 (2PB; 1SB) $65 includes tax
Full Breakfast
Credit Cards: A, B (to hold a room)
Notes: 2, 7 (limited), 8, 9, 10, 11, 12

## HOLDERNESS

### The Inn on Golden Pond

Rt. 3, P.O. Box 680, 03245
(603) 968-7269

An 1879 Colonial home is nestled on 50 wooded acres offering guests a traditional New England setting where you can escape and enjoy warm hospitality and personal service of the resident hosts. Rooms are individually decorated with braided rugs and country curtains and bedspreads. Hearty, home-cooked breakfast features farm fresh eggs, muffins, homemade bread, and Bonnie's most requested rhubarb jam.

Hosts: Bonnie and Bill Webb
Rooms: 8 (PB) $95-130
Full Breakfast
Credit Cards: A, B, C
Notes: 2, 5, 8, 9, 10, 11, 12

## HOPKINTON

### The Country Porch Bed and Breakfast

281 Moran Rd., 03229
(603) 746-6391

Situated on 15 peaceful acres of lawn, pasture, and forest, this B&B is a reproduction of an 18th century Colonial. Sit on the wraparound porch and gaze out over the meadow, bask in the sun, and then cool off in the pool. The comfortably appointed rooms have a Colonial, Amish, or Shaker theme and have king or twin beds. Summer and winter activities are plentiful and fine country dining is a short drive away. "Come and sit a spell." No smoking.

Hosts: Tom and Wendy Solomon
Rooms: 3 (PB) $75-80
Full Breakfast
Credit Cards: A, B
Notes: 2, 5, 9, 10, 11

Ellis River House

## JACKSON

### Ellis River House

Rt. 16, P.O. Box 656, 03846
(603) 383-9339; (800) 233-8309;
FAX (603) 383-4142

Sample true New England hospitality at this enchanting, small hotel and country inn within a short stroll of the village. The Ellis River House has eighteen comfortable king-and queen-size guest rooms decorated with Laura Ashley prints, some with fireplaces and

---

NOTES: Credit cards accepted: A Master Card; B Visa; C American Express; D Discover; E Diners Club; F Other; 2 Personal checks accepted; 3 Lunch available; 4 Dinner available;

two person jacuzzis, cable TV, scenic balconies, and period antiques, all with individually controlled heat and air-conditioning. Two-room and family suites, river front cottage, hot tub, sauna, and heated pool, siting and game rooms, delightful sundeck overlooking the pristine Ellis River. Enjoy a full country breakfast with homemade breads, or a delicious trout dinner. Afterwards relax with libations and billiards in the pub.

Hosts: Barry and Barbara Lubao
Rooms: 18 (15PB; 3SB) $59-229
Full Country Breakfast
Credit Cards: A, B, C, D, E
Notes: 2, 4, 5, 6 (limited), 7, 8, 10, 11, 12

## *Mountainside Farm*

Carter Notch Rd., 03846
(603) 383-6531

The Mountainside Farm offers a wonderful family retreat for guests of all ages. The farm is filled with different animals which adds unique experiences for its visitors and it is surrounded by the White Mountain National Forest where wild animals abound throughout nature. The house, built in 1926, offers breathtaking views of the valley and mountains through charming picture windows. While staying, guest enjoy

Applebrook

endless opportunities of different things to do.

Hosts: Joany Alden, David and Orly White
Rooms: 2 suites (PB) $50-140
Full Country Breakfast
Credit Cards: A, B
Notes: 2, 5, 6 (including horses), 7 (free), 8, 9, 10, 11

## JEFFERSON

## *Applebrook*

Route 115A, 03583
(603) 586-7713; (800) 545-6504

Taste our mid-summer raspberries while enjoying spectacular mountain views. Applebrook is a comfortable, casual bed and breakfast in a large Victorian farmhouse with a peaceful, rural setting. After a restful night's sleep, you will enjoy a hearty breakfast before venturing out for a day of hiking, fishing, antique hunting, golfing, swimming, or skiing. Near Santa's Village and Six-Gun City. Dormitory available for groups. Brochures available. Hot tub under the stars.

Hosts: Sandra Conley and Martin Kelly
Rooms: 12 + dormitory (5PB; 7SB) $40-65
Full Breakfast
Credit Cards: A, B
Notes: 2, 5, 6, 7, 8, 9, 10, 11

## *The Jefferson Inn*

Route 2, 03583
(603) 586-7998; (800) 729-7908;
FAX (603) 586-7808

A warm, romantic, 1896 renovated Victorian home nestled in the Northern White Mountains. There are mountain views in all directions. Each of the nine

---

5 Open all year; 6 Pets welcome; 7 Children welcome; 8 Tennis nearby; 9 Swimming nearby; 10 Golf nearby; 11 Skiing nearby; 12 May be booked through travel agent.

unique rooms and two family suites has a private bath and distinctive decor. Wake up each morning to a gourmet breakfast. Spend the day hiking, cycling, or swimming in the summer and skiing, ice skating, or snow-mobiling in the winter. The outdoor opportunities and attractions abound. Afternoon tea and homemade baked goods are served at the end of the day before you return to the comfort of your well-appointed room for another restful night. No smoking in the Inn.

Hosts: Marla Mason and Don Garretson
Rooms: 11 (PB) $62-120
Full Breakfast
Credit Cards: A, B, C, D
Notes: 2, 7, 8, 9, 10, 11, 12

## NEW IPSWICH

### The Inn at New Ipswich

11 Porter Hill Rd., P.O. Box 208, 03071
(603) 878-3711

Relax a while in a graceful 1790 Colonial amid stone walls and fruit trees. With cozy fireplaces, front porch rockers, and large guest rooms furnished country-style, you'll feel right at home. Breakfasts are bountiful! Situated in New Hampshire's Monadnock Region, activities abound: hiking, band concerts, antique auctions, maple sugaring, apple picking, unsurpassed autumn color, and cross-country and downhill skiing. No smoking. Children over 8 welcome.

Hosts: Ginney and Steve Bankuti
Rooms: 6 (PB) $65
Full Breakfast
Credit Cards: A, B
Notes: 2, 5, 7 (over 8), 10, 11, 12

## NEW LONDON

### Pleasant Lake Inn

125 Pleasant St., P.O. Box 1030, 03257
(603) 526-6271; (800) 626-4907

Our 1790, lakeside, country inn is nestled on the shore of Pleasant Lake with Mt. Kearsarge as its backdrop. The panoramic location is only one of the many reasons to visit. All four seasons offer activities from our doorway: lake swimming, fishing, hiking, skiing, or just plain relaxing. Dinner is available. Call or write for brochure.

Hosts: Margaret and Grant Rich
Rooms: 11 (PB) $75-95
Full Breakfast
Credit Cards: A, B
Notes: 2, 4, 5, 7 (over 7), 8, 9, 10, 11, 12

## NORTH CONWAY

### The 1785 Inn and Restaurant

P.O. Box 1785, 03860
(603) 356-9025; (800) 421-1785;
FAX (603) 356-6081

The 1785 Inn is a relaxing place to vacation at any time of the year. The 1785 Inn is famous for its views and food. Located at the Scenic Vista, popularized by the White Mountain School of Art, its famous scene of Mt. Washington is virtually unchanged from when the Inn was built over 200 years ago. The Inn's homey atmosphere will make you feel right at home, and the food and service will make you eagerly await your return.

Hosts: Becky and Charlie Mallar
Rooms: 17 (12PB; 5SB) $59-159
Full Breakfast
Credit Cards: A, B, C, D, E
Notes: 2, 4, 5, 7, 8, 9, 10, 11, 12

## Buttonwood Inn

P.O. Box 1817, Mt. Surprise Rd., 03860
(603) 356-2625; (800) 258-2625 (U.S.A.);
FAX (603) 356-3140

Tucked away on Mt. Surprise and only two miles from North Conway Village, experience New England hospitality at its best. Whether it's our four course candlelight dinner in winter, or our complete breakfast, you'll always feel like you've just "come home." Enjoy one of our nine guest rooms, generous common space, pool, and 65K of groomed cross-country ski trails.

Hosts: Claudia and Peter Needham
Rooms: 9 (5PB; 4SB) $60-125
Full Breakfast
Credit Cards: A, B, C, D, E
Notes: 2, 5, 7, 8, 9, 10, 11, 12

The Center Chimney—1787

## The Center Chimney— 1787

107 River Road, P.O. Box 1220, 03860
(603) 356-6788

Cozy, affordable cape with beautiful early fireplace in living room over 200 years old. The Center Chimney is located in a quiet, wooded area just off the Saco River with swimming, canoeing, and fishing, but only a short walk to Main Street. North Conway Village with summer theatre, free cross-country skiing and ice skating, shops, restaurants, etc. Package plans available.

Hosts: Farley Ames Whitley
Rooms: 4 (SB) $44-55
Continental Breakfast
Credit Cards: none
Notes: 2, 5, 7, 8, 9, 10, 11

## Merrill Farm Resort

428 White Mountain Hwy., 03860
(603) 447-3866; (800) 445-1017;
FAX (603) 447-3867

100 year old accommodation with modern amenities and country warmth and hospitality. Fireplaced units and whirlpool units. Free rise and shine breakfast. Children 12 and under stay free (up to two per room). Heated outdoor pool and recreation. Handy to 10 major ski areas. Right on Saco River free canoeing. Fully air-conditioned. Canadian cash at par most of year. Senior discounts. AAA Rated, 10% discount.

Innkeeper: Lynn McArdle
Rooms: 60 (PB) $39-144
Rise and Shine Breakfast
Credit Cards: A, B, C, D, E
Notes: 5, 7, 8, 10, 11, 12

Merrill Farm Resort

5 Open all year; 6 Pets welcome; 7 Children welcome; 8 Tennis nearby; 9 Swimming nearby; 10 Golf nearby; 11 Skiing nearby; 12 May be booked through travel agent.

## Neverledge Inn

River Rd. (off Main St.), 03860
(603) 356-2831; FAX (603) 356-7085

Enjoy the charm, hospitality, and relaxation of a small 1787 bed and breakfast inn overlooking Cathedral Ledge. Walk to river or village. Close to all activities. Comfortable, casual, non-smoking atmosphere. Rates include delicious breakfast with warm apple pie.

Hosts: Valerie and Dave Halpin
Rooms: 11 (6PB; 5SB) $59-99
Full Breakfast
Credit Cards: A, B, C
Notes: 2, 5, 7, 8, 9, 10, 11

## The Victorian Harvest Inn

28 Locust Ln. P.O. Box 1763,
(just off White Mt. Hwy.), 03860
(603) 356-3548; (800) 642-0749;
FAX (603) 356-8430

Non-smokers delight in your comfortable elegant B&B home at the edge of quaint North Conway Village. Explore unique shoppes, outlets, and the AMC trails. Our 1850s multi-gabled Victorian find comes with six large comfy rooms, all with mountain views. Start your romantic adventure with a bounteous dining experience and classic New England hospitality. Relax by the fireplace or snuggle with a literary treasure in our elegant library. Private baths, lovely in-ground pool, and full air conditioning to add to your comfort. AAA three-diamond award. American Bed and Breakfast Association: rated "A" three-crowns. Cross-country skiing from the door, and 3-10 minutes to downhill skiing. "We welcome all God's people."

Hosts: Linda and Robert Dahlberg (and Tuckerman)
Rooms: 4 + 1 two-room suite (4PB; 2SB)
$65-105
Full Breakfast
Credit Cards: A, B, C, D
Notes: 2, 4 (Sat. night group only), 5, 7 (over 6), 8, 9, 11, 12

## PLYMOUTH

## Northway House

R.F.D. 1, Box 71, 03264
(603) 536-2838

Located in the heart of New Hampshire in the beautiful Pemigewasset River Valley, the Northway House is near Newfound, Squam, and Winnepesaukee Lakes, as well as the ski areas of Waterville Valley, Loon, and Cannon. Hospitality-plus awaits the traveler in this charming Colonial house that is homey, comfortable, and reasonably priced.

Hosts: Micheline and Norman McWilliams
Rooms: 3 (SB) $30-45
Full Breakfast
Credit Cards: none
Notes: 2, 5, 6, 7, 9, 10, 11

## RYE

## Rock Ledge Manor Bed and Breakfast

1413 Ocean Blvd., Rt. 1-A, 03870
(603) 431-1413

A gracious, traditional, seaside, manor home with an excellent location that offers an ocean view from all rooms. It is central to all New Hampshire and southern Maine seacoast activities; six minutes to historic Portsmouth and Hampton; 20 minutes to the University of New Hampshire; 15 minutes to Exeter Academy. Reservations are advised.

Hosts: Norman and Janice Marineau
Rooms: 4 (2PB; 2SB) $70-90
Full Breakfast
Credit Cards: none
Notes: 2, 5, 7, 8, 9, 10, 11

## THORNTON

### *Amber Lights Inn Bed and Breakfast*

Route 3, 03223
(603) 726-4077

Amber Lights Inn B&B is a beautifully restored, 1815 Colonial in the heart of the White Mountains in Thornton, NH, a quiet country setting. We have five meticulously clean guest rooms, all appointed with luxurious queen-size beds, handmade quilts, and antiques. In the early evening, join in a conversation with the innkeepers over nightly hors d'oeuvres and beverages. We are conveniently located between Loon Mountain and Waterville Valley, close to all White Mountains attractions. Ask about our murder mystery weekends.

Hosts: Paul Sears and Carola Warnsman
Rooms: 5 (1PB; 4SB) $45-60 (Continental Breakfast); $60-75 (Full Breakfast and hors d'oeuvres)
Full or Continental Breakfast
Credit Cards: A, B, C, D
Notes: 2, 5, 6, 7, 8, 9, 10, 11, 12

Amber Lights Inn

## WAKEFIELD

### *Jon Gilman Homestead*

Governor's Rd., 03872
(603) 522-3102

200-plus-old New England Colonial in a country setting. Built by the town's first settlers. In the lakes region of New Hampshire, handy to skiing, golfing, and tax free shopping. A step back in time awaits the weary traveler.

Hosts: Cliff and Barbara Singelais
Rooms: 5 (SB) $40
Continental Breakfast
Credit Cards: none
Notes: 2, 5, 7, 9, 10, 11

## WARNER

### *Jacob's Ladder Bed and Breakfast*

69 E. Main St., 03278
(603) 456-3494

Situated in the quaint village of Warner, Jacob's Ladder is conveniently located between exits 8 and 9 off I-89. The

5 Open all year; 6 Pets welcome; 7 Children welcome; 8 Tennis nearby; 9 Swimming nearby; 10 Golf nearby; 11 Skiing nearby; 12 May be booked through travel agent.

early 1800s home is furnished predominantly with antiques, creating a tasteful country atmosphere. Cross-country ski and snowmobile trail on site with three downhill ski areas within 20 miles. Lakes, mountains, covered bridges, arts and crafts, and more nearby. No smoking.

Hosts: Marlon and Deb Baese
Rooms: 3 (1PB; 2SB) $40-50
Full Breakfast
Credit Cards: D
Notes: 2, 5, 7, 8, 9, 10, 11

## WOLFEBORO

### The Tuc' Me Inn Bed and Breakfast

118 N. Main St., P.O. Box 657, 03894
(603) 569-5702

Our 1850, Colonial, Federal is located within walking distance of the lake and the quaint village of Wolfeboro, "The oldest summer resort in America." Family antiques in country, Victorian style. Relax in our music room, parlor, screened-in porches, or our cozy reading room. Complimentary full breakfast. We are a non-smoking inn. For your comfort, all bedrooms are air-conditioned.

Hosts: Ernie, Terry, and Tina Foultz
and Idabel Evans
Rooms: 7 (3PB; 4SB) $60-80
Full Breakfast
Credit Cards: A, B
Notes: 2, 5, 7, 8, 9, 10, 11, 12

The Tuc' Me Inn Bed and Breakfast

# New Jersey

## Amanda's Bed and Breakfast Reservation Service

21 S. Woodland Ave., **East Brunswick** 08816
(908) 249-4944; FAX (908) 246-1961

Listing approximately 70 inns, in and about **New Jersey, Pennsylvania,** and **New York.** Andover, Stewartsville, Stockton, Lambertville, Alloway, Cape May, Spring Lake, Princeton, and many more New Jersey towns. In PA: Washington's Crossing, Milford, Manheim, Kempton, Emmaus, Chalfont, Kennett Square, Delaware Water Gap, and the Poconos. Mastercard and Visa accepted. Children over 12 welcome. Orie Barr, coordinator.

The Avon Manor Inn

## AVON-BY-THE-SEA

### The Avon Manor Inn

109 Sylvania Ave., 07717
(908) 774-0110

The Avon Manor Inn is a gracious turn-of-the-century home (circa 1907) built in the Colonial Revival style. Enjoy breakfast in our sunny dining room, ocean breezes on our full wraparound veranda, and the charm of this small seaside town. Eight air-conditioned bedrooms and only one block to beach and boardwalk. The large living room has a cozy fireplace for winter nights. Rediscover romance at this charming seaside inn.

Hosts: Jim and Kathleen Curley
Rooms: 8 (6PB; 2SB) $70-110
Full Breakfast
Credit Cards: A, B, C
Notes: 5, 7, 8, 9, 10, 12

### Cashelmara Inn

22 Lakeside Ave., 07717
(908) 776-8727; (800) 821-2976

A tastefully restored turn-of-the-century inn rests on the bank of a swan lake and the Atlantic Ocean. This desirable set-

---

5 Open all year; 6 Pets welcome; 7 Children welcome; 8 Tennis nearby; 9 Swimming nearby; 10 Golf nearby; 11 Skiing nearby; 12 May be booked through travel agent.

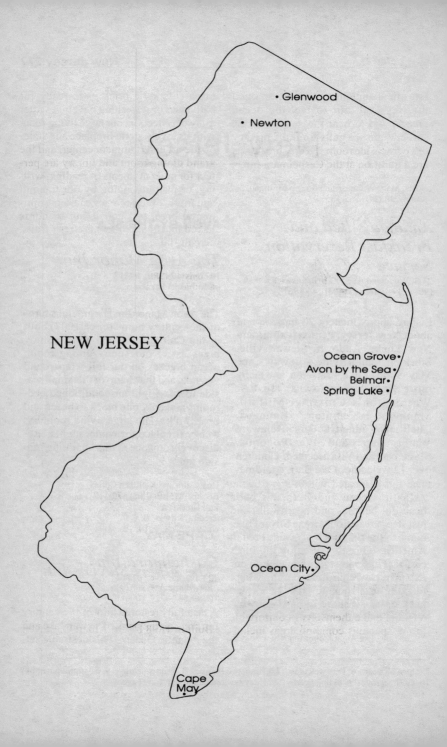

NEW JERSEY

• Glenwood

• Newton

Ocean Grove •
Avon by the Sea •
Belmar •
Spring Lake •

Ocean City •

Cape
May •

ting offers a unique opportunity to smell the fresh salt air, to feel the ocean breeze, and to hear the sounds of the surf and the sea gulls from the privacy of your seaside room. Hearty breakfasts are a tradition at the Cashelmara Inn.

Hosts: Mary Wiernasz and Martin Mulligan
Rooms: 13 (PB) $65-165
Full Breakfast
Credit Cards: A, B, C, D
Notes: 2, 5, 7, 8, 9, 10

The Inn at the Square

## BELMAR

## *The Inn at the Shore*

301 Fourth Ave., 07719
(908) 681-3762; FAX (201) 945-2944

The Inn is located within sight of the Atlantic Ocean and Belmar's wide beautiful beaches and boardwalk, and just steps away from serene Silver Lake, home to the first flock of swans bred in America. Guests will enjoy the Inn's casual, Victorian-style ambiance on our expansive wraparound porch, where relaxing in a rocking chair takes you back to the seashore of days gone by. Visitors make themselves comfortable in our spacious common areas includ-

ing a cafe style brick patio ready for barbecues or refreshing beverages after a day of reflection, our large living room with its lovely stone fireplace and state-of-the-art entertainment center, and the grand dining room and library are perfect for quiet moments of reading, writing, or just unwinding by our tranquil aquarium. We serve a generous continental breakfast consisting of home baked muffins, croissants, fresh fruits, cereals, juices, etc.

Hosts: Rosemary and Tom Volker
Rooms: 12 (3PB; 9SB) $45-95
Continental Breakfast
Credit Cards: A, B, C, D, E
Notes: 5, 7, 8, 9, 10, 12

The Albert Stevens Inn

## CAPE MAY

## *The Albert Stevens Inn*

127 Myrtle Ave., 08204
(609) 884-4717; (800) 890-CATS

Built in 1898 by Dr. Albert G. Stevens

---

NOTES: Credit cards accepted: A Master Card; B Visa; C American Express; D Discover; E Diners Club; F Other; 2 Personal checks accepted; 3 Lunch available; 4 Dinner available; 5 Open all year; 6 Pets welcome; 7 Children welcome; 8 Tennis nearby; 9 Swimming nearby; 10 Golf nearby; 11 Skiing nearby; 12 May be booked through travel agent.

as a wedding gift for his bride, Bessie, the Inn is just a ten minute walk to the beach and two blocks from Victorian shopping. The guest rooms are furnished with antiques and have private baths and air-conditioning. A 102-degree, six-person jacuzzi is privately scheduled for guests' comfort. Home of the original Cat's Garden Tea and Tour, the Inn is known for its comfort, privacy, and gourmet breakfasts. Resident pet cats.

Hosts: Curt and Diane Rangen
Rooms: 9 (PB) $85-165
Full Breakfast
Credit Cards: A, B, C, D
Notes: 2, 4, 8, 9, 10, 12

## Captain Mey's Inn

202 Ocean St., 08204
(609) 884-7793 or; (609) 884-9637

The Inn is an 1890 Colonial Revival Victorian named after the Dutch explorer, Captain Cornelius Mey. The Dutch heritage is evident from the Persian rugs on the tabletops to the Delft Blue china collection. The wraparound veranda is furnished with wicker furniture, hanging ferns, and Victorian wind curtains. A full breakfast is served by candlelight with classical music in the formal dining room; in the summer breakfast is served on the veranda.

Hosts: George and Kathleen Blinn
Rooms: 8 (PB) $75-210 (deluxe)
Full Breakfast
Credit Cards: A, B, C
Notes: 5, 7 (over 8), 8, 9, 10, 12 (off season and midweek only)

## Duke of Windsor Inn

817 Washington St., 08204
(609) 884-1355

This grand 1890 Victorian home offers gracious, relaxing accommodations furnished with period antiques, high-backed beds, and marble-topped tables and dressers. Two octagon rooms in our 40-foot turret are particularly fun and romantic. The dining room has five chandeliers and an elaborate plaster ceiling. We are within walking distance of the beach, historical attractions, tennis, and shopping.

Hosts: Bruce and Fran Prichard
Rooms: 9 (8PB; 1SB) $65-165
Full Breakfast
Credit Cards: A, B (for deposit only)
Open February to December.
Notes: 2, 8, 9, 10

## The Inn on Ocean

25 Ocean St., 08204
(609) 884-7070; (800) 304-4477;
FAX (609) 884-1384

An intimate, elegant, Victorian inn. Fanciful Second Empire style with an exuberant personality. Beautifully restored. King and queen beds. Private baths. Fireplaces. Fully air-conditioned. Full breakfasts. Wicker-filled ocean view porches. Billiard room. Open all seasons. Free on-site parking. Guest says, "A magical place!," "Second visit is as lovely as first!," and "Compliments to the chef!"

Hosts: Jack and Katha Davis
Rooms: 5 (PB) $99-175
Full Breakfast
Credit Cards: A, B, C, E
Notes: 2, 5, 8, 9, 10, 12

---

NOTES: Credit cards accepted: A Master Card; B Visa; C American Express; D Discover; E Diners Club; F Other; 2 Personal checks accepted; 3 Lunch available; 4 Dinner available;

## The Kings Cottage

9 Perry St., 08204
(609) 884-0415

This three-story "Stick Style" Victorian Cottage is an exquisite example of the work done by noted architect Frank Furness. Taking full advantage of its location, the rooms, all with private baths and the two wicker-filled verandas optimize the ocean views. The interior has been lovingly restored and furnished in true Victorian fashion to reflect the grandeur of that period. Antiques abound, especially in the parlor and formal dining room where a full breakfast is served utilizing fine china, crystal, and silver, all the trappings that make life that much more enjoyable. You may enjoy afternoon tea on the veranda or in the formal garden.

Hosts: Pat and Tony Marino
Rooms: 9 (PB) $95-195
Full Breakfast
Credit Cards: A, B
Notes: 2, 5, 8, 9, 10, 12

## The Mason Cottage

625 Columbia Ave., 08204
(609) 884-3358; (800) 716-2766

Built in 1871 for a wealthy Philadelphia businessman, the inn is in the French Empire style. The Mason family purchased the house in 1945 and started welcoming guests in 1946. The curved wood-shingle mansard roof was built by the local shipyard carpenters, and restored original furniture remains in the house. The house endured the 1878 Cape May fire and several hurricanes. Honeymoon packages and gift certificates available. The inn is one block from the ocean and all rooms and suites are air-conditioned.

Hosts: Dave and Joan Mason
Rooms: 5(PB) $95-165
Suites: 4 (PB) $145-265
Full Gourmet Breakfast
Credit Cards: A, B, C
Closed January - February
Notes: 2 (and travelers'), 7 (over 2), 8, 9, 10, 12

The Mason Cottage

## The Queen Victoria®

102 Ocean St., 08204
(609) 884-8702

The Queen Victoria includes three 1800s homes the have been restored and furnished with antiques. There are two parlors, one with a fireplace and one with TV and games. Two dining rooms serve a hearty, country breakfast and afternoon tea. Special services include free bicycles, beach showers and towels, and turned down beds with a special chocolate on your pillow. All rooms are air conditioned, and have private baths, many with whirlpool tubs.

Hosts: Joan and Dane Wells
Rooms: 23 (PB) $90-275
Full Breakfast
Credit Cards: A, B
Notes: 2, 5, 7, 8, 9, 10

---

5 Open all year; 6 Pets welcome; 7 Children welcome; 8 Tennis nearby; 9 Swimming nearby; 10 Golf nearby; 11 Skiing nearby; 12 May be booked through travel agent.

## Windward House

24 Jackson St., 08204
(609) 884-3368

An elegant, Edwardian, seaside inn has an entry room and staircase that are perhaps the prettiest in town. Spacious, antique-filled guest rooms have queen beds and air-conditioners. With three sun-and-shade porches, cozy parlor fireplace, and Christmas finery, the Inn is located in the historic district, one-half block from the beach and shopping mall. Rates include homemade breakfast, beach passes, parking, and bicycles. Midweek discounts September to June; off-season weekend packages.

Hosts: Sandy and Owen Miller
Rooms: 8 (PB) $80-150
Full Breakfast
Credit Cards: A, B (deposit only)
Notes: 2, 5, 7 (over 12), 8, 9, 10

Windward House

## The Wooden Rabbit Inn

609 Hughes St., 08204
(609) 884-7293

Charming country inn in the heart of Cape May, surrounded by Victorian cottages. Cool, shady street, the prettiest in Cape May. Two blocks to beautiful, sandy beaches, one block to shops and fine restaurants. Guest rooms are air-conditioned, have private baths, TV, and comfortably sleep two to four. Decor is country, with relaxed family atmosphere. Delicious breakfasts and afternoon tea time. Three pet cats to fill your laps. Open year round. Families welcome.

Hosts: Greg and Debby Burow
Rooms: 4 (PB) $155-185
Breakfast
Credit Cards: A, B, D
Notes: 2, 5, 7, 8, 9, 10, 12

## GLENWOOD

## Apple Valley Inn

Corner of Rt. 517 and Rt. 565, P.O. Box 302, 07418
(210) 764-3735

Elegantly appointed B&B in the early American tradition. Colonial mansion circa 1831. Pool, trout stream, apple orchard, antique shop, Old Grist Mill, skiing, water-park, Appalachian Trail, West Point, NJ, Botanical Gardens, two state parks, and Hudson Valley attractions within a short drive. Holidays. Two night minimum. Reduced rates for six plus day stay. Special events weekends.

Hostess: Mitzi Durham
Rooms: 7 (2PB; 5SB) $65-100
Full Breakfast
Credit Cards: none
Notes: 2, 3 (picnic), 5, 7 (over 13), 8, 9 (on-site), 10, 11, 12

---

NOTES: Credit cards accepted: A Master Card; B Visa; C American Express; D Discover; E Diners Club; F Other; 2 Personal checks accepted; 3 Lunch available; 4 Dinner available;

The Wooden Duck

# NEWTON

## *The Wooden Duck*

140 Goodale Rd., 07860
(201) 300-0395; FAX (201) 300-0141

The Wooden Duck is a secluded, 17-acre mini-estate about an hour's drive from New York City. Located on a country road in rural Sussex County, it is close to antiques, golf, the Delaware Water Gap, Waterloo Village, and winter sports. The rooms are spacious with private baths, television, VCR, phone, and desks. There is central air-conditioning, an in-ground pool, game room, and living room with see-through fireplaces. Antique furnishings and reproductions. Biking and hiking are at the doorstep with a 1,000-acre state park across the street and a "Rails to Trails" (abandoned railway maintained for hiking and biking) running behind the property. Wildlife abounds in the area.

Hosts: Bob and Barbara Hadden
Rooms: 5 (3PB; 2SB) $85-100
Full Breakfast
Credit Cards: A, B, C
Notes: 2, 5, 8, 9, 10, 11

# OCEAN CITY

## *Barna Gate B&B*

637 Wesley Avenue, 08228
(609) 391-9366

Enjoy the small, intimate accommodations of our 1895 seashore Victorian. The cozy rooms are decorated in country style with quilts on the antique beds and paddle fans to keep you cool. All rooms are named for flowers. Guests use our common area or front porch under burgundy awnings with white wicker rockers. Near Cape May, Atlantic City, county zoo, and antique shops. We've got everything—beach, boardwalk, and ocean. Hospitality is our specialty. Open year-round.

Hosts: Frank and Lois Barna
Rooms: 5 (1PB, 2SB) $75-130 suite
Full Breakfast; Continental in summer
Credit Cards: A, B, C
Notes: 2, 5, 7, 8, 9, 10

## *Delancey Manor*

869 Delancey Pl., 08226
(609) 398-9831

A turn-of-the-century summer house just 100 yards to a great beach and our 2.45 mile boardwalk. Summer fun for families and friends at "America's greatest family resort." Two breezy porches with ocean view. Walk to restaurants, boardwalk fun, and the Tabernacle with its renowned speakers. Located in a residential neighborhood in a dry town. Larger family rooms available. Breakfast optional for a small

---

5 Open all year; 6 Pets welcome; 7 Children welcome; 8 Tennis nearby; 9 Swimming nearby; 10 Golf nearby; 11 Skiing nearby; 12 May be booked through travel agent.

charge. Advance reservations recommended.

Hosts: Stewart and Pam Heisler
Rooms: 7 (3PB; 4SB) $40-70
Expanded Continental Breakfast
Credit Cards: none
Notes: 2, 7, 8, 9, 10

## New Brighton Inn

519 Fifth St., 08226
(609) 399-2829

This charming 1880 Queen Anne Victorian has been magnificently restored to its original beauty. All rooms and common areas (living room, library and, sun porch) are elegantly and comfortably furnished with antiques. The front veranda is furnished with rockers and a large swing. Rates include beach tags and use of bicycles.

Hosts: Daniel and Donna Hand
Rooms: 6 (PB) $90-100
Full Breakfast
Credit Cards: A, B, C, D
Notes: 2, 5, 8, 9, 10

## Ocean City Guest and Apartment House Referral Service

P.O. Box 356, 08226
(609) 399-8894 (9am to 9pm)

An association of 30 apartment, B&B, and guest home owners will provide you with a free brochure or our telephone referral service. A wide range of accommodations throughout Ocean City, NJ, "America's greatest family resort," from the beach to the bay to the boardwalk. Call or write us for information.

Scarborough Inn

## Scarborough Inn "An 1895 Bed and Breakfast"

720 Ocean Ave., 08226
(609) 399-1558; (800) 258-1558;
FAX (609) 399-4472

The Scarborough Inn, invitingly adorned in colors of wedgewood, rose, and soft creme, lends its special character to the neighborhood where it stands, just one and one half short blocks from the Atlantic Ocean. The Scarborough affords visitors a vacation residence reminiscent of an old-fashioned European-style inn—small enough to be intimate, yet large enough to offer privacy. Featured in *Country Inns* magazine.

Hosts: Gus and Carol Bruno
Rooms: 26 (PB) $70-120
Continental Plus Breakfast
Credit Cards: A, B, C, D
Notes: 7, 8, 9, 10, 12

NOTES: Credit cards accepted: A Master Card; B Visa; C American Express; D Discover; E Diners Club; F Other; 2 Personal checks accepted; 3 Lunch available; 4 Dinner available;

## OCEAN GROVE

### *Cordova*

26 Webb Ave., 07756
(908) 774-3084 (summer); (212) 751-9577
(winter); FAX (212) 207-4720

Ocean Grove was founded as a religious retreat center at the turn of the century. This flavor has lasted in the quiet, peaceful atmosphere. Constant religious programs for the family are arranged in the 7,000 seat Great Auditorium. The Cordova has "Old World" charm. Rooms are furnished with antiques. Friendliness, hospitality, cleanliness, and quiet one block from the magnificent white sand beach and boardwalk. The Cordova was recently featured in the travel guide, "O' New Jersey." Also listed in the *New Jersey* magazine as one of the "Seven best on the Jersey shore." The porches have a splendid ocean view. Midweek specials; also seven nights for the price of five. Saturday night refreshments.

Hostess: Doris Chernik
Rooms: 15 (5PB; 10SB) $45-80
Continental Breakfast
Credit Cards: none
Notes: 2, 7, 8, 9, 12

Cordova

Sea Crest by the Sea

## SPRING LAKE

### *Sea Crest by the Sea*

19 Tuttle Ave., 07762
(201) 449-9031; (800) 803-9031

Your romantic fantasy escape. A Spring Lake bed and breakfast inn just for the two of you. Lovingly restored, 1885 Queen Anne Victorian for ladies and gentleman on a seaside holiday. Ocean views, open fireplaces, luxurious linens, feather beds, antique-filled rooms, sumptuous breakfast, and afternoon tea. A *Gourmet Magazine* "top choice." John and Carol welcome you with old-fashioned hospitality to an atmosphere that will soothe your weary body and soul.

Hosts: John and Carol Kirby
Rooms: 11 + 1 suite (PB) $110-239
Full Breakfast
Credit Cards: A, B, C
Notes: 2, 5, 8, 9, 10

---

5 Open all year; 6 Pets welcome; 7 Children welcome; 8 Tennis nearby; 9 Swimming nearby; 10 Golf nearby; 11 Skiing nearby; 12 May be booked through travel agent.

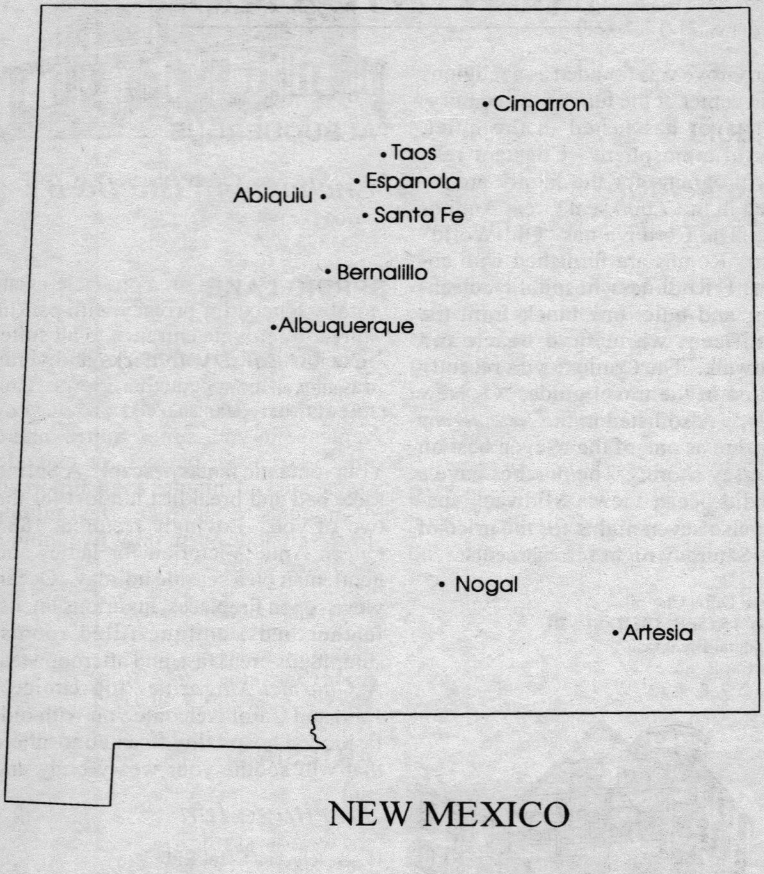

- Cimarron

- Taos
- Espanola
Abiquiu •
- Santa Fe

- Bernalillo

- Albuquerque

- Nogal

- Artesia

**NEW MEXICO**

# New Mexico

## ABIQUIU

### Casa del Rio

P.O. Box 702, 87532
(505) 753-2035

Casa del Rio is a micro-mini, southwestern ranch with Arabian horses, fine wool sheep, and authentic adobe construction. Set against a magnificent cliff, locally known as Los Palacios, at the base of which runs the Chama River. It is furnished with hand carved, traditional, Spanish Colonial furniture and crafts. A coffee or tea tray is delivered to each room as a wake-up. Gold Medallion certified and a three-diamond rating.

Hosts: Eileen and Mel Vigil
Rooms: 2 (PB) $85-105
Full Breakfast
Credit Cards: none
Notes: 2, 5, 6 (horses), 7 (inquire), 9, 11, 12

Casa del Rio

## ALBUQUERQUE

### Enchanted Vista B&B

10700 Del Rey NE, 87122
(505) 823-1301

A southwest villa on a one-acre estate, totally fenced for privacy with parking in rear by private entrance to all suites. Spacious suites with decks and verandas that offer spectacular views. Continental breakfast served at your convenience in your suite. Suites include micro-kitchens, perfect for extended stays. Just 20 minutes from airport and 45 minutes to Sante Fe. Just minutes from ski slopes, and only five minutes from the "tram."

Hosts: Tillie and Al Gonzales
Rooms: 2 (PB) $62-74
Continental Breakfast
Credit Cards: none
Notes: 2, 3, 5, 6, 7, 8, 9, 10, 11, 12

## ARTESIA

### Heritage Inn

209 W. Main, 88210
(505) 748-2552; (800) 594-7392;
FAX (505) 746-3407

New country/Victorian atmosphere will

---

NOTES: Credit cards accepted: A Master Card; B Visa; C American Express; D Discover; E Diners Club; F Other; 2 Personal checks accepted; 3 Lunch available; 4 Dinner available; 5 Open all year; 6 Pets welcome; 7 Children welcome; 8 Tennis nearby; 9 Swimming nearby; 10 Golf nearby; 11 Skiing nearby; 12 May be booked through travel agent.

take you back in time and warm your heart and soul. Spacious rooms with private baths, room phones, color TV, continental breakfast, computer modem hookups for business travelers and outside patio and deck for relaxation. Very secure second floor, downtown location convenient to excellent restaurants. Smoke free. No pets.

Hosts: James and Wanda Maupin
Rooms: 8 (PB) $55
Continental Breakfast
Credit Cards: A, B, C, D
Notes: 2, 5, 7, 10

La Hacienda Grande

## BERNALILLO

## *La Hacienda Grande*

21 Baros Ln., 87004
(505) 867-1887; (800) 353-1887;
FAX (505) 867-4621

At La Hacienda Grande we offer Southwestern casual elegance in a magnificent 250 year old Spanish hacienda built around a central courtyard. Originally it was part of a Spanish land-grant of 100 square miles given to Elena Gallegos in 1711. It later became one of the first stagecoach stops between Albuquerque and Sante Fe. Today it has been fully restored while maintaining all the charm of two-foot thick adobe walls, wood ceilings, and floors of tile, stone, or brick. The guest rooms are very well appointed with handmade furnishings and original artwork. We offer a full gourmet breakfast, and coffee is served to your room at wake up. Afternoon refreshments are available. We offer romance packages with intimate dinners for two by pre-arrangement, and massage therapy by appointment. We are available for weddings, family reunions, retreats, business meetings, parties, and special luncheons, picnics, receptions and company Christmas parties.

Hostess: Shoshana Zimmerman
Rooms: 6 (PB) $89-99 (subject to change)
Full Breakfast
Credit Cards: A, B, C
Notes: 4 (by arrangement), 5, 6 (limited), 7, 9, 10, 11, 12

## CIMARRON

## *Casa Del Gavilan*

PO Box 518, 87714
(505) 376-2246; FAX (505) 376-2247

Hunting, fishing, cross-country skiing, outdoor recreation, and sight-seeing abound the Cimarron area. The romance of the Santa Fe Trail, the Old West ambiance of the St. James Hotel of Cimarron and Kit Carson's home at Rayado, the magnificence of Cimarron Canyon, the tranquillity of Eagle Nest

Lake, the excitement of Angel Fire and Red River ski resorts, and the enchantment of Taos are all less than two hours away.

Hosts: Carl and Joyce Nelson
Rooms: 7 (5 PB; 2 SB) $ 70-100
Full Breakfast
Credit Cards: A, B, C, D
Notes: 5, 7, 8, 10, 11, 12

Casa Del Gavilan

## ESPANOLA

### The Inn of La Mesilla

Rt. 1, Box 368A, 87532
(505) 753-5368 (voice and FAX)

Beautiful Pueblo style home, the Inn is rural elegance in the heart of the Eight Northern Indian Pueblos and high on a hill with fabulous views. Quiet. Full breakfast and afternoon tea. Hot tub jacuzzi on large redwood deck with views. Two rooms both with private full bath, color TVs, and ceiling fans. 23 miles to downtown Sante Fe. Two English Springer Spaniels; Pork Chop and Te-Bon!!

Hostess: Yolanda F. Hoemann (Pork Chop and Te-Bon)
Rooms: 2 (PB) $80 (include tax)
Full Breakfast
Credit Cards: none
Notes: 2

## NOGAL

### Monjeau Shadows

HC 67, Box 87, 88341
(505) 336-4191

Four-level Victorian farmhouse located on ten acres of beautiful, landscaped grounds. Picnic area, nature trails. King and queen beds. Furnished with antiques. Just minutes from Lincoln National Park and White Mountain Wilderness. Cross-country skiing, fishing, and horseback riding. For fun or just relaxing. Enjoy the year-round comfort of Monjeau Shadows.

Hosts: J.R. and Kay Newton
Rooms: 6 (4PB; 2SB) $65-75
Full Breakfast
Credit Cards: A, B
Notes: 2, 5, 7, 9, 10, 11

## SANTE FE

### Canyon Road Casitas

652 Canyon Rd., 87501
(505) 988-5888; (800) 279-0755

Luxury accommodations are featured in this 100 year old historic Territorial adobe within walking distance of distinctive art galleries, numerous museums, unique shops, and historic landmarks. Both guest rooms have kitchenettes, down quilts and pillows, feather beds, separate entrances, and private patios. This is truly a four season retreat.

Hostess: Trisha Ambrose
Rooms: 2 (PB) $85-165
Continental Breakfast
Credit Cards: A, B, C, D
Notes: 2, 5, 7, 11, 12

---

5  Open all year;  6  Pets welcome;  7  Children welcome;  8  Tennis nearby;  9  Swimming nearby;
10  Golf nearby;  11  Skiing nearby;  12  May be booked through travel agent.

## Temple of Light

2407 Camino Capitan, 87505
(505) 471-4053

Simple and affordable. Loving and peaceful. Private home minutes from plaza. Car recommended. No smoking or drinking.

Hostess: Jean Gosse
Rooms: 1 (SB) $40
Continental Breakfast
Credit Cards: none
Notes: 2, 5

The Willows Inn

## TAOS

## The Willows Inn

NDCBU 4558 (Corner of Kit Carson Rd. and Dolan St.,) 87571
(505) 758-2558; (505) 758-5445

The Willows Inn is a B&B located on a secluded acre lot just a short walk to the Taos Plaza. Listed on the National Historic Registry, the property was the home and studio of E. Martin Hennings. Hennings was a member of the revered Taos Society of Artists, the group that established Taos as an artist colony in the 1920s. Scrumptious, full breakfasts are served family style in the dining rooms. Guests enjoy homemade snacks and beverages in the late afternoon on the flagstone courtyard in summer or by the fire in the cooler seasons. Each guest room has smooth adobe walls with *kiva* fireplaces, open beam (*viga*) ceilings, and Douglas Fir floors with various decor themes which highlight cultures significant to the Taos area. The grounds and courtyards form a park-like oasis with flowers, fountains, and two of America's largest living willow trees.

Hosts: Doug and Janet Camp
Rooms: 5 (PB) $95-130 + tax
Full Breakfast
Credit Cards: A, B
Notes: 2, 5, 7, 9, 10, 11, 12

## Orinda Bed and Breakfast

461 Valverde, 87571
(505) 758-8581; (800) 847-1837

A 50 year old adobe home, dramatic pastoral setting on two acres. View of Taos Mountains; surrounded by elm and cottonwood trees. Decorated southwestern design. Original art presented in rooms and common areas. Kiva fireplaces in suites. Quiet, on a private road, but only 15 minute walk to galleries, plaza, and restaurants.

Hosts: Cary and George Pratt
Rooms: 4 (3PB; 1SB) $65-85
Full Breakfast
Credit Cards: A, B, D
Notes: 2, 5, 7, 8, 9, 10, 11, 12

NOTES: Credit cards accepted: A Master Card; B Visa; C American Express; D Discover; E Diners Club; F Other; 2 Personal checks accepted; 3 Lunch available; 4 Dinner available;

# New York

**ALSO SEE RESERVATION
SERVICES UNDER NEW JERSEY**

## American Country Collection of B&B

4 Greenwood Ln., **Delmar,** 12054
(518) 439-7001 (information and reservations);
FAX (518) 439-4301

This reservation service provides reservations for eastern **New York,** western **Massachusetts,** all of **Vermont,** and **St. Thomas/St. John, U.S.V.I.** Just one call does it all. Relax and unwind at any of our 120 immaculate, personally inspected bed and breakfasts and country inns. Many include fireplace, jacuzzi, and/or Modified American Plan. We cater to the budget-minded, yet also offer luxurious accommodations in older Colonial homes and inns. Urban, suburban, and rural locations available. $35-180. Carol Metos, coordinator.

## ALBION

## Friendship Manor

349 S. Main St., 14411
(716) 589-7973

This historic house, dating back to 1880, is surrounded by lovely roses, an herb garden, and lots of shade trees. A swimming and tennis courts are provided for your pleasure. The intimate interior is an artful blend of Victorian-style furnishings with antiques throughout. Enjoy a breakfast of muffins, breads, fruit, juice, coffee, or tea in the formal dining room served buffet style for your convenience. Friendship Manor is central to Niagara Falls, Buffalo, or Rochester. For traveling through or just a getaway.

Hosts: John and Marylin Baker
Rooms: 4 (2PB; 2SB) $55 + tax
Continental Breakfast
Credit Cards: none
Notes: 2, 5, 7, 10

## BAINBRIDGE

## Berry Hill Gardens Bed and Breakfast

RD 1, Box 128, Ward-Loomis Rd., 13733
(607) 967-8745 (voice and FAX);
(800) 497-8745

This restored 1820s farmhouse on a hilltop is surrounded by extensive herb and perennial gardens and 180 acres where you can hike, swim, bird-watch, skate,

---

5 Open all year; 6 Pets welcome; 7 Children welcome; 8 Tennis nearby; 9 Swimming nearby; 10 Golf nearby; 11 Skiing nearby; 12 May be booked through travel agent.

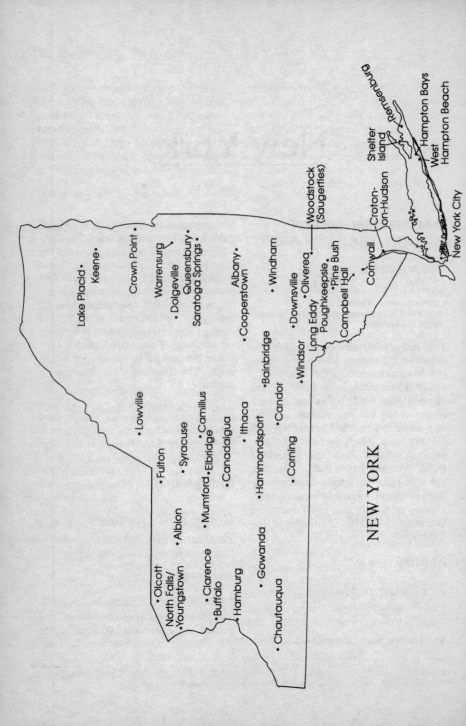

NEW YORK

cross-country ski, or sit on the wrap-around porch and watch nature parade. Our rooms are furnished with comfortable antiques. A ten-minute drive takes you to restaurants, golf, tennis, auctions, and antique centers. You can also buy plants, dried flowers, and wreaths grown and hand-crafted on the farm to take home with you. Cooperstown and most local colleges are only 45 minutes away. Three hours to New York City.

Hosts: Jean Fowler and Cecilio Rios
Rooms: 4 (SB) $60-70
Full Breakfast
Credit Cards: A, B, C
Notes: 2, 5, 7, 8, 9, 10, 11, 12

Berry Hill Gardens Bed and Breakfast

## BURDETT

## *The Red House Country Inn*

4586 Picnic Area Rd., 14818
(607) 546-8566

The Inn is located in the beautiful 13,000-acre Finger Lakes National Forest with 28 miles of maintained hiking and cross-country ski trails. Six award winning wineries are within ten minutes

from the completely restored 1840s farmstead on five acres of groomed lawns and flower gardens. Enjoy beautifully appointed rooms, country breakfasts, in-ground pool, and a fully equipped kitchen. Twelve minutes from Ithaca; 30 minutes from Corning.

Hostesses: Joan Martin and Sandy Schmanke
Rooms: 5 (SB) $60-85
Full Breakfast
Credit Cards: A, B, C, D
Notes: 2, 4 (Nov-Apr), 5, 7 (over 2), 8, 9 (on premises), 10, 11, 12

## CAMILLUS

## *The Re Family Bed and Breakfast*

4166 Split Rock Rd., 13031
(315) 468-2039

100 year old early American farmhouse featuring log-style den, country kitchen, side deck utilized for fair weather breakfasts, 40' pool, lawns, two guest rooms with queen-size brass beds and orthopedic mattresses, and pedestal sink in each room. Next to garden-style bathroom with walk-in tile shower, vanity with double sinks, and full-mirrored back wall. Also one room with full bed and captain's bed for two singles or for children. Stress-free environment close to Syracuse.

Hosts: Joseph and Terry Re
Rooms: 3 (SB) $55-75
Full or Continental Breakfast
Credit Cards: none
Notes: 2, 5, 7, 8, 9, 10, 11, 12

---

NOTES: Credit cards accepted: A Master Card; B Visa; C American Express; D Discover; E Diners Club; F Other; 2 Personal checks accepted; 3 Lunch available; 4 Dinner available; 5 Open all year; 6 Pets welcome; 7 Children welcome; 8 Tennis nearby; 9 Swimming nearby; 10 Golf nearby; 11 Skiing nearby; 12 May be booked through travel agent.

## CAMPBELL HALL

### *Point of View Bed and Breakfast*

RR 2, Box 766H Ridge Rd., 10916
(914) 294-6259; (800) 294-6259

Enjoy peace and tranquillity in a country setting with spectacular views of rolling hills and farmland. Modern conveniences with back-home comfort. One hour from New York City, 20 minutes from Stewart Airport, and three miles from the quaint, historic village of Goshen. Spacious rooms, private baths, and guest sitting room.

Hosts: Rev. Bill and Elaine Frankle
Rooms: 2 (PB) $55-65
Full Breakfast
Credit Cards: A, B
Notes: 2, 5, 10, 11

## CANANDAIGUA

### *Acorn Inn*

4508 Rt. 64 S. Bristol Center, 14424
(716) 229-2834; FAX (718) 229-5046

Antique-filled 1795 Stage Coach inn. Large, comfortable rooms, canopy beds, luxury linens, and private baths, one with a whirlpool. Relax before a cheery fire, stroll in our private gardens, or browse in our libraries. Full country breakfasts. Minutes to Bristol Mountains Ski Center, golf, and lake. Central air-conditioning. Rated Excellent American B&B Association. AAA–

three diamonds. Off season, week night, and ski packages available.

Hosts: Joan and Louis Clark
Rooms: 4 (PB) $75-140
Full Breakfast
Credit Cards: A, B, D
Notes: 2, 5, 9, 10, 11, 12

Acorn Inn

## CANDOR

### *The Edge of Thyme, A Bed and Breakfast Inn*

6 Main St., P.O. Box 48, 13743
(607) 659-5155; (800) 722-7365 (out of NY)

Featured in Historic Inns of the Northeast. Located in this quiet rural village is a large gracious Georgian home– leaded glass windowed porch, marble fireplaces, period sitting rooms, gardens, and pergola. Epicurean breakfast served in genteel manner. Central to Cornell, Ithaca College, Corning, Elmira, Watkins Glen, and wineries. Gift Shoppe; High Tea by appointment.

Hosts: Eva Mae and Frank Musgrave
Rooms: 4 (2PB; 2SB) $65-75
Full Breakfast
Credit Cards: A, B
Notes: 2, 5, 7 (well-behaved), 8, 9, 10, 11 (cross-country), 12

NOTES: Credit cards accepted: A Master Card; B Visa; C American Express; D Discover; E Diners Club; F Other; 2 Personal checks accepted; 3 Lunch available; 4 Dinner available;

## CHAUTAUQUA

### Plumbush, A Victorian Bed and Breakfast

P.O. Box 864, 14722
(716) 789-5309

Restored, circa 1865, Italian villa hill-top, country home surrounded by 125 acres. Chautauqua Institution less than one mile from our doorstep, offers lectures, study groups, symphony orchestra, opera, and dance summer school. Bluebirds and wildlife abound; bicycles available; cross-country ski trail. Sunny rooms, wicker, antiques, and a touch of elegant charm are all yours at Plumbush.

Hosts: George and Sandy Green
Rooms: 5 (PB) $85-100
Full Breakfast
Credit Cards: A, B, D
Notes: 2, 5, 8, 9, 10, 11, 12

## CLARENCE

### Asa Ransom House

10529 Main St., (Rt. 5), 14031
(716) 759-2315; FAX (716) 759-2791

Warmth, comfort, and hospitality are our main attractions. Nine guest rooms have antique and period furnishings, seven of these have fireplaces. Many rooms have a porch or balcony. We also have a library, gift shop, and herb garden on a two acre lot in the village. The original building housing the library, gift shop, and tap room dates back to 1853, built by Asa Ransom who received the land from the Holland Land Company in 1799.

Hosts: Robert Lenz; Judy Lenz
Rooms: 9 (PB) $85-145
Full Breakfast
Credit Cards: A, B, D
Closed January
Notes: 2, 4, 7, 8, 9, 10

Berrywick II

## COOPERSTOWN

### Berrywick II

RD 2, Box 486, 13326
(607) 547-2052

Located six miles from Cooperstown, home of the Baseball Hall of Fame, the Farmer's Museum, and the New York State Historical Association—Fenimore House and the Glimmerglass Opera House. All beautifully situated around nine mile long Otsego Lake. Berrywick II is a renovated 19th century farmhouse with separate entrance for guests to converted, two-bedroom apartment. Queen, double, and twin-bedded rooms with kitchen/sitting room and bath perfectly suitable for families with well-behaved children. Sorry, no pets and no smoking.

Hosts: Helen and Jack Weber
Rooms: 3 (1SB) $75
Continental or Full Breakfast
Credit Cards: none
Notes: 2, 5, 7, 9, 10

## CORNING

## 1865 White Birch Bed and Breakfast

69 E. First St., 14830
(607) 962-6355

The White Birch, Victorian in structure but decorated in country, has a been refurbished to show off its winding staircase, hardwood floors, and wall window in the dining room that overlooks the backyards. We are located in a residential area, two blocks from restored historic Market Street and six blocks from the Corning Museum of Glass. A warm fire during the colder months welcomes guests in the common room where TV and great conversation are available. A full, gourmet breakfast is served each morning.

Hosts: Kathy and Joe Donahue
Rooms: 4 (2PB; 2SB) $65-75
Full Breakfast
Credit Cards: A, B, C
Notes: 2, 5, 7, 8, 9, 10, 11

## Delevan House

188 Delevan Ave., 14830
(607) 962-2347

This Southern Colonial house sits on a hill overlooking Corning. It is charm-

ing, graceful, and warm in quiet surroundings. Delicious breakfast served from 8-9 am. Check-in time 3 pm, check-out time 10:30 am. Free transportation from airport. Two minutes from Market Street and Glass Center by car. TV in all rooms. Very private. Enjoy a cool refreshment on lovely screened-in porch.

Hostess: Mary M. De Pumpo
Rooms: 3 (1PB; 1½SB) $65-85
Full Breakfast
Credit Cards: none
Notes: 2, 5, 7 (over 10), 10, 11, 12

## CORNWALL

## Cromwell Manor Inn

Angola Rd., 12518
(914) 534-7136

Built in 1820, Cromwell Manor Inn is a fully-restored, romantic, country estate. Set on seven landscaped acres overlooking a 4,000-acre, mountain, forest preserve. The 6,000 square foot manor is fully furnished with period antiques and fine furnishings. Enjoy a full breakfast served on the veranda, or in our country breakfast room, at your own private table. 1764 restored cottage is also available for larger groups; sleeps eight. We are located 55 minutes north of New York City and five miles from historic West Point. Fireplaces and romance.

Hosts: Dale and Brenda Ohara
Rooms: 13 (12PB; 1SB) $120-150;
Suites $220-250
Full-Served Breakfast
Credit Cards: A, B
Notes: 2, 5, 8, 9, 10, 11, 12

---

NOTES: Credit cards accepted: A Master Card; B Visa; C American Express; D Discover; E Diners Club; F Other; 2 Personal checks accepted; 3 Lunch available; 4 Dinner available;

## CROTON-ON-HUDSON

### Alexander Hamilton House

49 Van Wyck St., 10520
(914) 271-6737

The Alexander Hamilton House, circa 1889, is a sprawling Victorian home situated on a cliff overlooking the Hudson. The home has many period antiques and collections and offers a queen bedded suite with fireplaced sitting room, two large rooms with queen beds (one with an additional daybed), and a bridal chamber with king bed, jacuzzi, entertainment center, pink marble fireplace, and lots of skylights. The master suite, with queen bed, fireplace, picture windows, stained glass, full entertainment center, jacuzzi, skylight, and winding river views was furnished last year. A one bedroom apartment with double bed, living room and kitchen on one wall, private bath, and separate entrance is also available for longer stays. Nearby attractions include West Point, the Sleepy Hollow Restorations, Lyndhurst, Boscobel, the Rockefeller mansion, hiking, biking, and sailing. New York City under an hour away by train or car. No smoking or pets. All rooms have air conditioning, private bath, cable TV, and phone. Off-street parking. Weekly and monthly rates available on request. Credit card guarantee required. Seven day cancellation policy.

Hostess: Barbara Notarius
Rooms: 7 (PB) $95-250
Full Breakfast
Credit Cards: A, B, C, D
Notes: 2, 5, 7, 9, 10, 12

Crown Point Bed and Breakfast

## CROWN POINT

### Crown Point B&B (The Wyman House)

Rt. 9N, Main St., P.O. Box 490, 12928
(518) 597-3651

The "Wyman House" is an elegant "painted lady," Victorian Manor house on five and one half acres. Its gracious interior is filled with period antiques. Each of five bed chambers is distinctively decorated and has its own ambiance and private bath. The house boasts woodwork panels of six types of wood. Outside there are three porches and a fountain amidst blooming gardens. Breakfast is all homemade. Near Lake Champlain, the area has museums, historical sites, and antiques.

Hosts: Hugh and Sandy Johnson
Rooms: 5(PB) $55-70; Suite for 4 $105
Continental Plus Breakfast
Credit Cards: A, B
Notes: 2, 5, 7, 8, 9, 10, 11, 12

## DOLGEVILLE

### Adrianna B&B

44 Stewart St., 13329
(315) 429-3249; (800) 335-4233

Rural, Little Falls area near I-90 exit

---

5 Open all year; 6 Pets welcome; 7 Children welcome; 8 Tennis nearby; 9 Swimming nearby; 10 Golf nearby; 11 Skiing nearby; 12 May be booked through travel agent.

29A. Cozy residence blending antique and contemporary furnishings. Convenient to Saratoga, Cooperstown, historic sites, and snowmobile, cross-country and hiking trails. Four guest rooms, two with private bath; full breakfast. Smoking restricted. Air-conditioning.

Hostess: Adrianna Naizby
Rooms: 4 (2PB; 2SB) $40-65 + tax
Full Breakfast
Credit Cards: A, B
Notes: 2, 5, 6 (well-behaved), 7 (over 5), 9, 10, 11, 12

## DOWNSVILLE

### Adam's Elegant Farmhouse Bed and Breakfast

P.O. Box 18, Upper Main St., 13755
(607) 363-2757

Come let us pamper you in our beautiful old farmhouse, full of antiques, and surrounded by majestic Catskill Mountains. Nestled in a small, friendly town, full of good things to do—canoeing, swimming, horseback riding, trailing in our Bear Spring State Park, antiquing, golfing, and much more. Enjoy just sitting and relaxing on the front porch. A feast awaits you. Afternoon sweets. Near Binghamton, Cooperstown, and Oneonta.

Hosts: Nancy and Harry Adams
Rooms: 3 (1PB; 2SB) $50
Full Breakfast
Credit Cards: none
Notes: 2, 7, 8, 9, 10, 12

## FOSTERDALE

### Fosterdale Heights House

205 Mueller Rd., 12726
(914) 482-3369

The historic, 1840, European-style, country estate in the Catskill Mountains is less than two hours from New York City. It is gentle and quiet with a bountiful breakfast. Enjoy the mountain view overlooking the pond, acres of Christmas trees (cut your own in season), and natural forest. Informal evenings of chamber music and parlor games break out frequently.

Hosts: Roy Singer
Rooms: 1(5PB; 6SB) $58-117
Full Breakfast
Credit Cards: A, B, C
Notes: 4, 5, 8, 9, 10, 11

## FULTON

### Battle Island Inn

RR #1, Box 176, 13069
(315) 593-3699

Battle Island Inn is a pre-Civil War farm estate that has been restored and furnished with period antiques. The Inn is across the road from a golf course that also provides cross-country skiing. Guest rooms are elegantly furnished with imposing high back beds, TVs, phones, and private baths. Breakfast is phones, and private baths. Breakfast is always special in the 1840s dining room.

Hosts: Richard and Joyce Rice
Rooms: 5 (PB) $60-85
Full Breakfast
Credit Cards: A, B, C, D
Notes: 2, 5, 7, 10, 11

## GOWANDA

## The TEEPEE

14396 Four Mile Level Rd., 14070
(716) 532-2168

The TEEPEE is operated by full-blooded Seneca Indians on the Cattaraugus Indian Reservation. Max is of the Turtle Clan and Phyllis is of the Wolf Clan. Tours of the reservation are available and also tours of the nearby Amish community. Good base when visiting Niagara Falls.

Hosts: Phyllis and Max Lay
Rooms: 4 (SB) $45
Full Breakfast
Credit Cards: none
Notes: 2, 5, 7, 8, 9, 10, 11

## HAMBURG

## Sharon's Lake House Bed and Breakfast

4862 Lakeshore Rd., 14075
(716) 627-7561

Built on the shore of Lake Erie, both rooms and sitting room offer a magnifi-

cent view of Buffalo city skyline and the Canadian border only fifteen minutes west of the city. Rooms are new and beautifully decorated with waterfront view. All prepared food is gourmet quality style. New hot tub room and widow's watch overlooking Lake Erie available. Reservations and two night minimum stay required.

Hostess: Sharon DiMaria
Rooms: 2 (1PB; 1SB) $55-110
Full Gourmet Breakfast
Credit Cards: none
Notes: 2, 3, 4, 5, 7 (by reservation), 9, 10, 11

## HAMMONDSPORT

## Gone With the Wind on Keuka Lake

453 W. Lake Rd., **Branchport**, 14418
(607) 868-4603

The name paints the picture—1887 stone Victorian, on 14 acres overlooking our quiet lake cove adorned by an inviting picnic gazebo. Feel the magic of total relaxation and peace of mind in the solarium hot tub; gather your gifts of imagination on our nature trails; unlock your creative powers to see your dreams accomplished. Fireplaces, delectable breakfasts, private beach and dock. Reserve "The Sequel," a log ,for small retreats, gatherings, or business meetings. One hour south of Rochester in the Fingerlakes on New York.

Hosts: Linda and Robert Lewis
Rooms: 6; $75-125
Full Breakfast
Credit Cards: none
Notes: 2, 5, 8, 9, 10, 11

---

## HAMPTON BAYS

## *House on the Water*

Box 106; 11946
(516) 728-3560

Quiet waterfront residence in Hampton Bays surrounded by two acres of gardens on Shinnecock Bay. A pleasant neighborhood on a peninsula, good for jogging and walking. Two miles to ocean beaches. Seven miles to Southampton. Kitchen facilities, bicycles, boats, lounges, and umbrellas. A full breakfast from 8 am to 12 pm is served on the terrace overlooking the water. Watch the boats and swans go by. Adults only. No pets. Rooms have water views and private baths and entrances. German, French, and Spanish spoken.

Hostess: Mrs. UTE
Rooms: 3 (2PB; 1SB) $75-95 (less off-season, midweek, and specials)
Full Breakfast
Credit Cards: none
Notes: 2, 8, 9, 10, 12 (10%)

## HOBART

## *Breezy Acres Farm Bed and Breakfast*

R.D. 1, Box 191, 13788
(607) 538-9338

For a respite from your busy, stressful lives, come visit us. We offer cozy accommodations with private bath in our circa 1830's farmhouse. You'll awaken refreshed to wonderful aromas from the kitchen. A full, homemade breakfast will be served to you while you plan your day. You'll could spend a week here leisurely exploring the museums, Howe Caverns, and Baseball Hall of Fame; leaving some time each day to roam our 300 acres, or to sit in a wicker swing on our old-fashioned pillared porches soaking in the view of meadows, pastures, and rolling hills. Or make use of golfing, tennis, fishing, and skiing facilities; all nearby.

Hosts: Joyce and David Barber
Rooms: 3 (PB) $50-60
Full Homemade Breakfast
Credit Cards: A, B, C
Notes: 2, 5, 7 (some restrictions), 8, 9, 10, 11

## ITHACA

## *A Slice of Home*

178 N. Main St., **Spencer,** 14883
(607) 589-6073

Newly remodeled,150-year old farmhouse with four bedrooms. Country cooking with hearty breakfasts. Located in the Fingerlakes Winery area just 20 minutes to Ithaca and Watkins Glen. Hiking, tenting, bicycle tours, and cross-country skiing. Hospitality is our specialty.

Hosts: Beatrice Brownell
Rooms: 4 (1PB; 2SB) $45-75
Full Breakfast
Credit Cards: none
Notes: 2, 5, 6 (outside), 7 (over 12), 12

NOTES: Credit cards accepted: A Master Card; B Visa; C American Express; D Discover; E Diners Club; F Other; 2 Personal checks accepted; 3 Lunch available; 4 Dinner available;

## Log Country Inn

P.O. Box 581, **Ithaca**, 14851
(607) 589-4771; (800) 274-4771;
FAX (607) 589-6151

Rustic charm of a log house at the edge of 7,000 acres of state forest; eleven miles south from Ithaca, off 96B. Modern accommodations provided in the spirit of international hospitality. Home atmosphere. Sauna and afternoon tea. Full Eastern European breakfast. Convenient to Cornell, Ithaca College, Corning Glass Center, Watkins Glen, wineries, and antique stores. Open year round.

Hostess: Wanda Grunberg
Rooms: 3 (1PB; 2SB) $45-65
Full Breakfast
Credit Cards: A, B
Notes: 2, 5, 6, 7, 9, 11, 12

## KEENE

## The Bark Eater Inn

Box 139; 12942
(518) 576-2221 (voice and FAX)

Originally a stagecoach stopover, the Inn is located on an old farm nestled in the famous Adirondack mountains minutes from the Olympic village of Lake Placid. The Inn is filled with antiques and all rooms are graciously appointed. Famous for it's food, the style is a refreshing country gourmet. The Inn has an extensive horseback riding program, including polo, and offers wonderful cross-country skiing in winter. In addition to spectacular views and great sightseeing in the Olympic area, summer and winter sports activities abound for both the participant and the viewer.

Host: Joe-Pete Wilson
Rooms: 16 (6PB; 10SB) $90-110
Full Breakfast
Credit Cards: A, B, C
Notes: 2, 3, 4, 5, 7, 8, 9, 10, 11, 12

Highland House Inn

## LAKE PLACID

## Highland House Inn

3 Highland Place, 12946
(518) 523-2377; (800) 342-8101;
FAX (518) 523-1863

The Highland House Inn is centrally located in a lovely residential setting just above Main Street in the village of Lake Placid. Seven tastefully decorated rooms are available, along with a darling, fully efficient, country cottage. A full breakfast is served in our year-round garden dining room. Outdoor hot tub spa, ceiling fans, and TV in all rooms.

Hosts: Ted and Cathy Blazer
Rooms: 7 + cottage (PB) $65-105
Full Breakfast
Credit Cards: A, B
Notes: 2, 5, 7, 8, 9, 10, 11, 12

---

5 Open all year; 6 Pets welcome; 7 Children welcome; 8 Tennis nearby; 9 Swimming nearby; 10 Golf nearby; 11 Skiing nearby; 12 May be booked through travel agent.

## LONG EDDY

### The Rolling Marble Guest House

P.O. Box 33, 12760
(914) 887-6016

Stay right on the beautiful Delaware River in this charming three-story Victorian with colorful details and wrap-around porches. 107-years-old and recently restored, the house is an elegant reminder of Long Eddy's historic past. Small and secluded, you will find this is a marvelous place to hole up and do nothing, enjoy the river and property, or explore the possibilities of many nearby activities. Casual comfort and a bountiful breakfast buffet are part of the magical atmosphere created by the innkeepers.

Hosts: Karen Gibbons and Peter Reich
Rooms: 4 (SB) $65
Full Breakfast
Credit Cards: A, B
Notes: 2, 7, 8, 9, 10, 11

The Rolling Marble Guest House

## LOWVILLE

### The Victoria Guest House

7700 North State Street, 13367
(315) 376-8502

A magnificently styled Victorian house of the late 1800's awaits your arrival in a quaint town nestled in the foothills of the Adirondack Mountains where winter recreation (downhill and cross-country skiing; snowmobiling) and summer fun (fishing, biking, hiking, rafting, etc.) abounds. Also awaiting you is a warm and gracious welcome. A full, hearty breakfast is served in the formal dining room featuring your hostess' home cooking and baking expertise which has been fostered by her Amish and Mennonite background. Come to enjoy a place of yesteryear's beauty and "old-fashioned" hospitality. No smoking or alcohol, please.

Hosts: Phyllis and Norman Lyndaker
Rooms: 4 (1PB; 3SB) $45-60
Full Breakfast
Credit Cards: none
Notes: 2, 5, 7, 8, 9, 10, 11

## MUMFORD

### The Genesee Country Inn

948 George St., 14511
(716) 538-2500; (800) NYSTAYS (reservations only); FAX (716) 538-4565

Let us share our magic, quiet, and hospitality. Storybook stone mill, circa 1883, chosen by *Country Inns Magazine* among Top Ten Inns USA 1992.

---

NOTES: Credit cards accepted: A Master Card; B Visa; C American Express; D Discover; E Diners Club; F Other; 2 Personal checks accepted; 3 Lunch available; 4 Dinner available;

Nine country, elegant guest rooms; seven secluded, wooded acres; and waterfalls. Gourmet breakfast, tea, fireplaces, canopy beds, balconies, and antiques. Flyfish; visit nearby Genesee Country museum, Rochester, Letchworth Park, and "Grand Canyon of the East;" or go birding, biking, or hiking. Take your coffee out to the falls and watch mink, blue heron, and ducks. AAA, Mobile, and FODORS. No smoking. Pets in residence.

Hostess: Glenda Barcklow, proprietor; Kim Rasmussen, innkeeper
Rooms: 9 (PB) $85-130
Full Breakfast
Credit Cards: A, B, D, E
Notes: 2, 5, 8, 9, 10, 11

## NIAGARA FALLS/ YOUNGSTOWN

## *The Cameo Manor North*
3881 Lower River Rd., 14174
(716) 745-3034

Located just seven miles north of Niagara Falls, our English manor house is the perfect spot for that quiet getaway you have been dreaming about. Situated on three secluded acres, the manor offers a great room with fireplaces, solarium, library, and an outdoor terrace for your enjoyment. Our beautifully appointed guest rooms include suites with private sun rooms and cable TV. A breakfast buffet is served daily.

Hosts: Greg and Carolyn Fisher
Rooms: 5 (3PB; 2SB) $65-130
Full Breakfast
Credit Cards: A, B, D
Notes: 5, 7, 8, 9, 10, 11, 12

## OLCOTT

## *Bit-O-Country*
6053 E. Lake Rd., P.O. Box 147, 14126
(716) 778-8161

We have a cozy, 200-year-old, updated, one and a half-story, private home located on Lake Ontario and bordered on two sides by lovely Krull Park. Our guests are invited to share our home for reading, relaxation, conversation, or TV viewing at their leisure. We have a large screened, electrified, and carpeted gazebo that we encourage guests to use. Our policy is to make you comfortable. We are a non-smoking establishment. We provide all information requested about the area.

Hosts: Judy and Howie Diez
Rooms: 2 with 3 single beds each (SB) $40
($20 each person)
Continental Plus Breakfast
Credit Cards: none
Notes: 2 (reservations only), 5, 7 (carefully supervised by parents), 8, 9, 10

## OLIVEREA

## *Slide Mountain Forest House*
805 Oliverea Rd., 12410
(914) 254-5365

Nestled in the Catskill Mountains State Park, our inn offers the flavor and charm of the old country. Come and enjoy our beautiful country setting, superb lodging, fine dining, and chalet rentals. Family-run for over 60 years, we strive to give you a pleasant and enjoyable stay. German and continental cuisine, lounge, pool, tennis, hiking, fishing, antiquing, and more available for your pleasure.

Hosts: Ursula and Ralph Combe
Rooms: 21 (17PB; 4SB) $50-70
Full Breakfast
Credit Cards: A, B, D
Notes: 4, 5 (chalets only), 7, 8, 9, 10, 11

## PINE BUSH

### The Milton Bull House

1065 Rt. 302, 12566
(914) 361-4770

The Milton Bull House is located in the foothills of the Shawangunk Ridge and has stood for over 200 years. Two rooms are available: one with a double bed, the other with two double beds. A full bath is shared by the two rooms. Our home is large, airy, and furnished with antiques. Breakfast is served at our guests' convenience, catering to special dietary needs; fresh fruit and home-baked goods served. The house is surrounded by shady lawns and gardens. An in-ground swimming pool is available to our guests. We are conveniently located near major highways.

Hosts: Graham and Ellen Jamison
Rooms: 2 (1PB; 2SB) $59
Full Breakfast
Credit Cards: none
Notes: 2, 5, 8, 9, 10, 11

## POUGHKEEPSIE

### Inn at the Falls

50 Red Oaks Mill Rd., 12603
(914) 462-5770; (800) 344-1466;
FAX (914) 462-5943

Inn at the Falls in Dutchess County combines the most luxurious elements of a modern hotel with the ambiance and personal attention of a country home. Complimentary European-style breakfast delivered to your room each morning. Twenty-two hotel rooms and fourteen suites all individually decorated for those who demand the finest in overnight accommodations.

Hosts: Arnold and Barbara Sheer
Rooms: 36 (PB) $110-150
Continental Breakfast
Credit Cards: A, B, C, D, E
Notes: 5, 7, 8, 9, 10, 11, 12

Inn at the Falls

## QUEENSBURY

### Crislip's Bed and Breakfast

693 Ridge Rd., 12804
(518) 793-6869

Located in the Adirondack area just minutes from Saratoga Springs and Lake George, this landmark Federal home provides spacious accommodations complete with period antiques, four-poster beds, and down comforters. The country breakfast menu features buttermilk pancakes, scrambled eggs, and sausages. Your hosts invite you to relax on their porches and enjoy the mountain view of Vermont.

Hosts: Ned and Joyce Crislip
Rooms: 3 (PB) $55-75
Full Breakfast
Credit Cards: A, B, C
Notes: 2, 5, 7, 8, 9, 10, 11

## REMSENBURG

## *Pear Tree Farm Bed and Breakfast*

96 S. Country Rd., P.O. Box 268, 11960
(516) 325-1443

Pear Tree Farm, a 200 year old charming farm house nestled among many historic homes, offers a romantic getaway with gracious, warm hospitality. Surrounded by beautiful flower/herb gardens, this country estate on two acres, offers warmth and beauty, filled with antiques and country charm. There is a pool, outdoor sauna, and two private guest cottages. Fully air-conditioned. A short drive to the Atlantic Ocean. The Hamptons and Montauk Pt. are some of the nearby attractions.

Hostess: Barbara Genco
Rooms: 3 (2PB; 1SB) $95-150 (off season $65-110)
Continental Gourmet Breakfast
Credit Cards: A, B
Notes: 2, 3, 5, 6, 7, 8, 9, 10

## SARATOGA SPRINGS

## *The Inn on Bacon Hill*

P.O. Box 1462, 12866
(518) 695-3693

Relax in the peacefulness of elegant living in this spacious, recently restored,

1862 Victorian just twelve minutes from historic Saratoga Springs and its racetracks. Four air-conditioned bedrooms overlook fertile farmland. A baby grand piano adorns the Victorian Parlor Suite. Enjoy our lovely gardens, extensive library, comfortable guest parlor, and many architectural features unique to the Inn. An inn where you come as strangers and leave as friends! Off season, a comprehensive innkeeping course is offered.

Hostess: Andrea Collins-Breslin
Rooms: 4 (2PB; 2SB) $65-85 (seasonal rates)
Full Breakfast
Credit Cards: A, B
Notes: 2, 5, 7 (over 12), 8, 9, 10, 11, 12

c. 1880

Six Sisters Bed and Breakfast

## *Six Sisters Bed and Breakfast*

149 Union Ave., 12866
(518) 583-1173; FAX (518) 587-2470

1880 Victorian beckons you with its relaxing veranda. Within walking distance of museums, city park, downtown, specialty shops, antiques, and restaurants. Spacious rooms, private baths, king/queen beds, and a full home-cooked breakfast. Mineral bath and

5 Open all year; 6 Pets welcome; 7 Children welcome; 8 Tennis nearby; 9 Swimming nearby;
10 Golf nearby; 11 Skiing nearby; 12 May be booked through travel agent.

massage package: November-May. Rec. by *NY Times* and *Gourmet*.

Hosts: Kate Benton; Steve Ramirez
Rooms: 4 (PB) $60-125 (except racing season)
Full Breakfast
Credit Cards: A, B, C
Notes: 2, 5, 7 (over 10), 8, 9, 10, 11, 12

## SHELTER ISLAND

### The Bayberry B&B

36 S. Menantic Rd., P.O. Box 538, 11964
(516) 749-3375

Experience an island accessible only by ferry with a simple, peaceful, life-style, and a third of it is a nature conservancy. Activities include hiking, bird-watching, biking, beaches, boating, fishing, winery tours, and antiquing. Our home is in a setting abounding with wildlife, and it has exceptionally large king-size bedrooms, cozy living room with piano and fireplace, antique furnishings, hammocks, and swimming pool.

Hosts: Suzanne and Richard Boland
Rooms: 2 (PB) $105-125 (seasonal rates avail.)
Full Breakfast
Credit Cards: none
Notes: 2, 5, 7 (over 12), 8, 9, 10

### Belle Crest Inn

P.O. Box 891, Shelter Island Heights, 11965
(516) 749-2041

The Belle Crest Inn is a unique bed and breakfast getaway with the charm of a warm atmosphere and friendly hosts. The home, located on Shelter Island, is furnished with antiques and offers an escape for visitors who want a break from day to day life. The Inn has delicious food which offers an excellent

opportunity to enjoy true American homemade cooking.

Hostess: Yvonne Loinig
Rooms: 10 (5PB; 5SB) $75-165
Full American Breakfast
Credit Cards: A, B
Notes: 2, 4, 5

## STEPHENTOWN

### Kirkmead Bed and Breakfast

RR 1, Box 169A, 12168
(413) 738-5420

Former stagecoach inn begun in 1767, the B&B is convenient to Jiminy Peak, Hancock Shaker Village, and Tanglewood. Easy access to a beautiful 30-acre mountain location. Walk along our tree-lined lane or wander on our nature trail beside our babbling brook. Full homemade breakfast featuring family recipes. Each guest room is air-conditioned and has its own private bath. No smoking, please.

Hosts: Don and Pat Bowman
Rooms: 7 (PB) $60
Full Homemade Breakfast
Credit Cards: none
Notes: 2, 5, 7, 11

## SYRACUSE

### Bed and Breakfast Wellington

707 Danforth St., 13208
(315) 474-3641; (800) 724-5006;
FAX (315) 474-2557

SALT CITY'S FINEST. Historic 1914 brick and stucco Tudor style home designed by the prolific arts and crafts ar-

---

NOTES: Credit cards accepted: A Master Card; B Visa; C American Express; D Discover; E Diners Club; F Other; 2 Personal checks accepted; 3 Lunch available; 4 Dinner available;

chitect, Ward Wellington Ward. Contains rich wood interiors, ample interior glass, tiled fireplaces and cozy porches. Antiques abound. Location central to downtown, medical centers, the Carousel Center, and Universities. Short drive to Finger Lakes Outlet Center. Spacious suites and private rooms available. Professional B&B consulting services/ classes for present and future innkeepers.

Hosts: Wendy Wilber and Ray Borg (owners)
Rooms: 5 (PB) $65-105
Continental Plus Breakfast (Weekend Gourmet)
Credit Cards: A, B, C
Notes: 2, 3 (on request), 4 (special), 5

## SYRACUSE AREA— ELBRIDGE

### Elaine's Bed and Breakfast Selections

4987 Kingston Rd., **Elbridge** 13060-9773
(315) 689-2082 (after 10AM)

Presently listing B&Bs in **New York** State in the following towns: Apulia, Baldwinsville, Cleveland and Constantia on Oneida Lake, DeWitt, Durhamville, Edmeston (near Cooperstown), Elbridge, Fayetteville, Geneva, Glen Haven, Gorham, Groton, Homer, Jamesville, Lafayette, Liverpool, Lyons, Marathon (near Binghamton and Ithaca), Marcellus, Naples, Ovid, Owasco Lake, Pompey, Port Ontario, Pulaski, Rome, Sheldrake-on-Cayuga, Skaneateles, Sodus Bay (on Lake Ontario), Spencer, Syracuse, Tully, Vernon, Vesper, Waterloo, and Watertown. Elaine N. Samuels, Director.

## WARRENSBURG

### White House Lodge

53 Main St., 12885
(518) 623-3640

An 1847 Victorian home in the heart of the queen village of the Adirondacks, an antiquer's paradise. The home is furnished with many Victorian antiques which send you back in time. Five minutes to Lake George, Fort William Henry, and Great Escape. Walk to restaurants and shopping. Enjoy air conditioned TV lounge for guests only. Wicker rockers and chairs on front porch. Window and Casablanca fans.

Hosts: Jim and Ruth Gibson
Rooms: 3 (SB) $85
Continental Breakfast
Credit Cards: A, B
Notes: 5, 7 (over 8), 9, 10, 11

## WESTHAMPTON BEACH

### 1880 House Bed and Breakfast

2 Seafield Lane, P.O. Box 648, 11978
(516) 288-1559; (800) 346-3290;
FAX (516) 288-0721

The Seafield House is a hidden, 100-year-old country retreat perfect for a romantic hideaway, a weekend of privacy, or just a change of pace from city life. Only 90 minutes from Manhattan,

5 Open all year; 6 Pets welcome; 7 Children welcome; 8 Tennis nearby; 9 Swimming nearby; 10 Golf nearby; 11 Skiing nearby; 12 May be booked through travel agent.

Seafield House is ideally situated on Westhampton Beach's exclusive Seafield Lane. The estate includes a swimming pool and a tennis court and is a short, brisk walk to the ocean beach. The areas offers outstanding restaurants, shops, and opportunities for antique hunting. Indoor tennis, Guerney's International Health Spa, and Montauk Point are nearby.

Hostess: Elsie Collins
Rooms: 3 suites (PB) $100-195
Full Breakfast
Credit Cards: A, B, C
Notes: 2, 5, 8, 9, 10, 12

1880 House Bed and Breakfast

## WINDHAM

### *Country Suite Bed and Breakfast*

P.O. Box 700, 12496
(518) 734-4079

Lovely 100-year-old farmhouse, furnished with family heirlooms and antiques, nestled in the Catskill Mountains on 10.5 acres of land. Renovated by current owners to accommodate guests seeking the quiet charm and ambiance of country life and relaxation. Open year-round for those who need "to get away."

Hostesses: Sandra Clark and Lorraine Seidel
Rooms: 9 (3PB; 6SB) $55-75
Full Complimentary Breakfast
Credit Cards: C
Notes: 2, 5, 7 (well-behaved), 8, 9, 10, 11, 12

## WINDSOR

### *Country Haven*

66 Garrett Rd., 13865
(607) 655-1204

A restored 1800s farmhouse in a quiet country setting on 350 acres. A haven for today's weary traveler and a weekend hideaway where warm hospitality awaits you. Craft shops with 70 artisans. Six mile Volkssport Hiking Trail. Located one mile from Rt. 17 East, Exit 78, 12 miles east of Binghamton, and seven miles from Rt. 81.

Hostess: Rita Saunders
Rooms: 4 (1PB; 2SB) $45-55
Full Breakfast
Credit Cards: A, B, D
Notes: 2, 5, 7, 8, 9, 10

## WOODSTOCK

### *Bed by the Stream*

9 George Sickle Rd., **Saugerties** 12477
(914) 246-2979

Five-acre farm, stream-side property with in-ground pool. Breakfast is served on the sun porch overlooking the stream.

Located seven miles from Woodstock. Three miles from exit 20 NY S. Thruway. Air conditioned. Hiking trails nearby and biking available.

Hosts: Odette and Bill Reinhardt
Rooms: 3 (PB) $60-75
Full Breakfast
Credit Cards: none
Notes: 2, 5, 7, 8, 9, 10, 11

**YOUNGSTOWN**

## *The Mill Glen Inn*
1102 Pletcher Rd., 14174
(716) 754-4085

You will enjoy a relaxing stay in a quiet country home with fresh flowers and early morning trays in each guest room. Breakfast is served in the Wagner Dining Room or, in season, on the covered porch with a view of our lovely gardens. Our renovated farmhouse was built in

1886 and has been designated a historic property by the town of Lewiston's Historic Society. Great shopping and restaurants nearby.

Hosts: Peter and Milly Brass
Rooms: 3 (1PB; 2SB) $45-65
Continental Plus Breakfast
Credit Cards: none
Notes: 2, 5, 7, 8, 9, 10, 11

The Mill Glen Inn

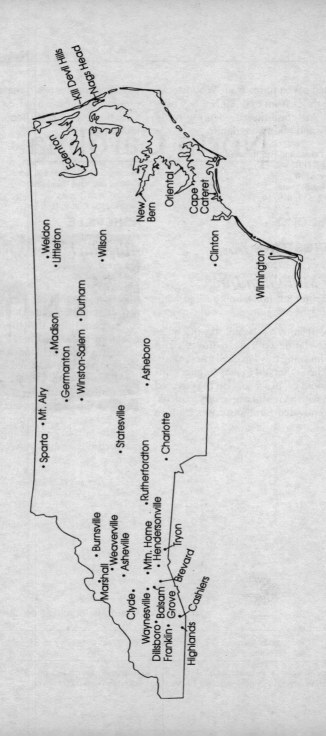

# North Carolina

## ASHEBORO

### The Doctor's Inn
716 S. Park St., 27203
(910) 625-4916 or (910) 625-4822

The Doctor's Inn is a home filled with antiques. It offers its guests the utmost in personal accommodations. Amenities include a gourmet breakfast served on fine china and silver, fresh flowers, terry-cloth robes and slippers, and ice cream parfaits. Nearby are over 60 potteries, and the North Carolina Zoo (five miles).

Hosts: Marion and Beth Griffin
Rooms: 2 (1PB; 1SB) $75-85
Full Breakfast
Credit Cards: none
Notes: 2, 5, 8, 9, 10

Albemarle Inn

## ASHEVILLE

### Albemarle Inn
86 Edgemont, 28801
(704) 255-0027

A distinguished Greek Revival mansion with exquisite carved oak staircase, balcony, paneling, and high ceilings. Beautiful residential area. On the National Register of Historic Places. Spacious, tastefully decorated, comfortable guest rooms with TV, telephones, air-conditioning, and private baths with clawfoot tubs and showers. Delicious full breakfast served in our dining room and sun porch. Swimming pool. Unmatched hospitality. AAA 3-Diamond rated.

Hosts: Kathy and Dick Hemes
Rooms: 11 (PB) $85-140
Full Breakfast
Credit Cards: A, B, D
Notes: 2, 5, 7 (over 13), 8, 9, 10, 12

### Cairn Brae
217 Patton Mountain Rd., 28804
(704) 252-9219

A mountain retreat on three secluded

---

NOTES: Credit cards accepted: A Master Card; B Visa; C American Express; D Discover; E Diners Club; F Other; 2 Personal checks accepted; 3 Lunch available; 4 Dinner available; 5 Open all year; 6 Pets welcome; 7 Children welcome; 8 Tennis nearby; 9 Swimming nearby; 10 Golf nearby; 11 Skiing nearby; 12 May be booked through travel agent.

acres above Asheville features beautiful views, walking trails, and a large terrace overlooking Beaver Dam Valley. Homemade full breakfast. Quiet, away from traffic, and only minutes from downtown.

Hosts: Edward and Milli Adams
Rooms: 3 (PB) $90-105
Full Breakfast
Credit Cards: A, B
Open April through Nov.
Notes: 2, 3, 7 (over 10), 8, 9, 10

Cairn Brae

## Reed House

119 Dodge St., 28803
(704) 274-1604

This comfortable Queen Anne Victorian with rocking chairs and swings on the porch also has a rocking chair in every room. Breakfast features homemade muffins, rolls, and jams and is served on the porch. Listed on the National Register of Historic Places; near Biltmore Estate. Open May 1 through November 1.

Hostess: Marge Turcot
Rooms: 2 (SB) $50; 2BR family cottage $95;
Suite: 1 (PB) $70
Continental Breakfast
Credit Cards: A, B
Notes: 2, 7, 8, 9, 10, 11

## BALSAM

## Balsam Lodge B&B

Valley Rd., 28707
(704) 456-6528; (800) 699-6528

Balsam Lodge main house was built in 1904. The Depot was built in 1908. In 1960 it was moved to its current location and has four efficient rooms with kitchenettes and private baths. In front we have a pond with a water wheel, fish, ducks, and chickens. Great country getaway one mile from Blue Ridge parkway and many nearby attractions.

Hosts: Marti S. Shaver and Frank S. Shaver
Rooms: 4 (PB) $60
Full Breakfast
Credit Cards: A, B, C, D
Notes: 2, 3, 5, 6, 7, 8, 9, 10, 11, 12

## BREVARD

## The Red House Inn

412 Probart St., 28712
(704) 884-9349

The Red House was built in 1851 and has served as a trading post, a railroad station, the county's first courthouse, and the first post office. It has been lovingly restored and is now open to the public. Charmingly furnished with turn-of-the-century antiques. Convenient to the Blue Ridge Parkway, Brevard Music Center, and Asheville's Biltmore Estate.

Hostess: Marilyn Ong
Rooms: 6 (4PB; 2SB) + 1 cottage (PB) $45-79
Full Breakfast
Credit Cards: A, B
Closed January through March
Notes: 2, 8, 9, 10, 12

NOTES: Credit cards accepted: A Master Card; B Visa; C American Express; D Discover; E Diners Club; F Other; 2 Personal checks accepted; 3 Lunch available; 4 Dinner available;

## BURNSVILLE

### *A Little Bit of Heaven Bed and Breakfast*

937 Bear Wallow Rd., 28714
(704) 675-5379

Getaway from the day to day routine for awhile and enjoy "A Little Bit of Heaven." This B&B offers a charming home with spectacular mountain views all around. The four guests rooms are beautifully decorated and furnished with queen or twin beds and private baths. While guests visit they can enjoy an abundance of activities in the area or just relax around the house and be pampered by the warm hospitality of their hosts.

Hosts: John and Shelley Johnson
Rooms: 4 (PB) $55-65
Full Breakfast
Credit Cards: none
Notes: 2, 5, 7, 8, 9, 10, 11

### *The NuWray Inn*

P.O. Box 156, Town Square, 28714
(704) 682-2329; (800) 368-9729

Historic country inn . . . since 1833. Nestled in the Blue Ridge Mountains in a quaint town square setting. Thirty miles northeast of Asheville. Close to Mt. Mitchell, Blue Ridge Parkway, Grandfather Mountain, antiques, golf, crafts, hiking, fishing, or just relaxing on the porch. Room rates include a hearty country breakfast and afternoon refreshments, with our nationally famous family style dinners also available.

Hosts: Chris and Pam Strickland
Rooms: 26 (PB) $70-110
Full Breakfast
Credit Cards: A, B, C
Notes: 2, 4, 5, 7, 8, 9, 10, 11, 12

## CAPE CATERET

### *Harborlight Guest House Bed and Breakfast*

332 Live Oak Dr., 28584
(919) 393-6868; (800) 624-VIEW;
FAX (919) 393-6868

The Harborlight is situated on a peninsula with water on three sides; thus, all suites offer panoramic vistas that are simply spectacular. All suites also offer private entrances and private baths; luxury suites feature two-person jacuzzis, fireplaces, and in-room breakfast. The guest house is minutes from area beaches, secluded island excursions, and the outdoor drama "Worthy is the Lamb"—a passion play that depicts the life of Christ.

Hosts: Bobby and Anita Gill
Rooms: 7 (PB) $75-155
Full Breakfast
Credit Cards: A, B, C
Notes: 5, 8, 9, 10

## CASHIERS

### *Millstone Inn*

Hwy. 64. W., P.O. Box 949, 28717
(704) 743-2737; FAX (704) 743-0208

Selected by *Country Inns* magazine as

---

5 Open all year; 6 Pets welcome; 7 Children welcome; 8 Tennis nearby; 9 Swimming nearby; 10 Golf nearby; 11 Skiing nearby; 12 May be booked through travel agent.

one of the best twelve inns, Millstone Inn has breathtaking views of the Nantahala forest. The exposed beams are complemented by the carefully selected antiques and artwork. Enjoy a gourmet breakfast in our glass enclosed dining room overlooking Whiteside Mountain. Located at 3,500 feet, it's always cool for a hike to the nearby Silver Slip Falls, or enjoy the nearby golf, tennis, restaurants, and antique shops.

Hosts: Paul and Patricia Collins
Rooms: 11 (PB) $95-139
Full Breakfast
Credit Cards: A, B, C, D
Notes: 2, 8, 9, 10, 11, 12

Millstone Inn

## CHARLOTTE

## The Elizabeth Bed and Breakfast

2145 E. 5th St., 28204
(704) 358-1368

This 1927 lavender "lady" is located in historic Elizabeth, Charlotte's second oldest neighborhood. European country-style rooms are beautifully appointed with antiques, ceiling fans, decorator linens, and unique collections. A guest cottage offers a private retreat

in elegant southwestern style. All rooms have central air and private baths; some have TV and phones. Enjoy a generous full or continental breakfast, then relax in our garden courtyard, complete with charming gazebo, or stroll beneath giant oak trees to convenient restaurants and shopping. Nearby attractions include the Mint Museum of Art, Blumenthal Performing Arts Center, Discovery Place, and professional sporting events.

Hostess: Joan Mastny
Rooms: 4 (PB) $55-88
Full or Continental Breakfast
Credit Cards: A, B
Notes: 2, 5, 9, 12

## The Homeplace Bed and Breakfast

5901 Sardis Road, 28270
(704) 365-1936; FAX (704) 366-2729

Restored 1902 country Victorian with wraparound porch and tin roof is nestled among two and one-half wooded acres. Secluded "cottage style" gardens with a gazebo, brick walkways, and a 1930's log barn further enhance this nostalgic oasis in southeast Charlotte. Experienced innkeepers offer a full breakfast and a Victorian Garden Room for small meetings and special occasions. Opened in 1984, the Homeplace is a "reflection of the true bed and breakfast."

Hosts: Peggy and Frank Dearien
Rooms: 2 + 1 suite with sitting room (PB) $93-120
Full Breakfast
Credit Cards: A, B, C
Notes: 2, 5, 7 (over 10), 12 (10%)

---

NOTES: Credit cards accepted: A Master Card; B Visa; C American Express; D Discover; E Diners Club; F Other; 2 Personal checks accepted; 3 Lunch available; 4 Dinner available;

## McElhinney House

10533 Fairway Ridge, 28277
(704) 846-0783 (voice and FAX)

A two-story, traditional home located in popular southeast Charlotte, 15 minutes from Charlotte-Douglas Airport. Close to fine restaurants, museums, Carowinds Park, and many golf courses. A lounge area with cable TV, a hot tub, laundry facilities, and barbecue are available. Families are welcome. A continental breakfast is served in the lounge or on the deck.

Hosts: Mary and Jim McElhinney
Rooms: 2 (PB) $55-65
Continental Breakfast
Credit Cards: A, B
Notes: 2, 5, 7, 8, 9, 10

Courthouse Inn

## CLINTON

## The Shield House Inn and Courthouse Inn

216 Sampson St., 28328
(910) 592-2634; (800) 462-9817 (reservations only); call for FAX #

The Shield House Inn consists of two estates. The Shield House, circa 1916, is reminiscent of "Gone with the Wind." Courthouse Inn, circa 1818, is a charmingly restored courthouse which was once described as the most glorious courthouse in North Carolina. Both are listed on the National Register of Historic Places and have spacious rooms, Victorian furniture, wraparound porches, and rockers for your enjoyment.

Hostesses: Anita Green and Juanita McLamb
Rooms: 15 + 2 suites (PB) $50-100 + 6% tax
Continental Plus Breakfast
Credit Cards: A, B, C, D, E
Notes: 2, 5, 7 (prior arrangement), 8, 10, 12

## CLYDE

## Windsong— A Mountain Inn

120 Ferguson Ridge, 28721
(704) 627-6111; FAX (704) 627-8080

A romantic, contemporary, log inn high in the breathtaking Smoky Mountains. Intimate rooms are large and bright with high beamed ceilings, pine log walls, and Mexican tile floors. Fireplaces, tubs for two, separate showers, and private decks or patios. Billiards, swimming, tennis, hiking, and llama trekking. Also, a new deluxe two-bedroom guest house, tub for two, and woodstove.

Hosts: Donna and Gale Livengood
Rooms: 5 + 1 guest house with 2 bedrooms (PB) $90-150
Full Breakfast (Continental in Guest House)
Credit Cards: A, B, D
Notes: 2, 5, 7 (over 8), 8, 9, 10, 11, 12 (10%)

Windsong—A Mountain Inn

5 Open all year; 6 Pets welcome; 7 Children welcome; 8 Tennis nearby; 9 Swimming nearby; 10 Golf nearby; 11 Skiing nearby; 12 May be booked through travel agent.

## DILLSBORO

### Applegate Inn

163 Hemlock St., 28725
(704) 586-2397

The "Gateway" to country charm, relaxation, and Southern hospitality at it's best. Situated in the village of Dillsboro, we are located on Scott's Creek, a footbridge from the Great Smoky Mountain Depot and Dillsboro's 50 unique shops. A quaint country home—families and seniors appreciate our one level. Private baths and queen beds. Full country breakfast. Let us make you the apple of our eye! Proverbs 3:24, 26.

Hosts: Emil and Judy Milkey
Rooms: 6 (5PB; 1SB) $55-75
Full Breakfast
Credit Cards: A, B, D
Notes: 2, 5, 7, 8, 12

Applegate Inn

## DURHAM

### Arrowhead Inn

106 Mason Rd., 27712
(919) 477-8430 (voice and FAX);
(800) 528-2207

The 1775 Colonial manor house is filled with antiques, quilts, samplers, and warmth. Located on four rural acres, Arrowhead features fireplaces, original architectural details, air-conditioning and homemade breakfasts. A two-room log cabin is also available. Easy access to restaurants, Duke University, University of North Carolina-Chapel Hill, Raleigh, and historic sites, including Duke Homestead Tobacco Museum and Bennett Place. Near I-85.

Hosts: Barb, Jerry, and Cathy Ryan
Rooms: 8 (6PB; 2SB) $75-160
Full Breakfast
Credit Cards: A, B, C, E
Notes: 2, 5, 7, 8, 9, 10, 12

## EDENTON

### Captain's Quarters Inn

202 W. Queen St., 27932
(919) 482-8945

The Inn is a seventeen-room, circa 1907 home in the Edenton historic district with a 65-foot wraparound front porch (swings and rockers). Eight charming bedrooms with modern, private baths (seven queen beds, one twin bed). We serve plenty of gourmet food, including welcome refreshments, continental breakfast, and a full three-course breakfast, as well as gourmet dinner on weekends. Sailing offered spring, summer, and fall; mystery weekends in fall, winter, and spring.

Hosts: Bill and Phyllis Pepper
Rooms: 8 (PB) $80-95
Continental and Full Breakfast
Credit Cards: A, B
Notes: 2, 5, 7, 8, 9, 10, 12

---

NOTES: Credit cards accepted: A Master Card; B Visa; C American Express; D Discover; E Diners Club; F Other; 2 Personal checks accepted; 3 Lunch available; 4 Dinner available;

## The Lords Proprietors' Inn

300 N. Broad St., 27932
(919) 482-3641; FAX (919) 482-2432

The Lords Proprietor's Inn, full-service Village Inn in the heart of Historic Edenton has twenty spacious rooms furnished with antiques and exquisite reproductions made by a local cabinet maker, and the finest dining in Eastern North Carolina. The Inn offers guests an opportunity to enjoy this beautiful waterfront town in a truly wonderful way.

Hosts: Arch and Jane Edwards
Rooms: 20 (PB) $165-215 MAP (includes dinner)
Full Breakfast and Dinner
Credit Cards: none
Notes: 2, 4, 5, 7 (additional rate), 8, 9, 10, 12

## EMERALD ISLE

## Emerald Isle Inn B&B

502 Ocean Dr., 28594
(919) 354-3222

Located at the ocean, this jewel of a Crystal Coast inn is truly a treasure to be discovered. A peaceful haven to all who seek a quiet, restful, and sun-filled getaway. Your stay includes a full gourmet breakfast and other tempting samplings. Suites include Victorian, French country, and tropical decor. Swings and porches with ocean and sound views add to your enjoyment. With direct beach access, you are only steps away from discovering the gentle shoreline treasures. We are only minutes from antiquing, fine restaurants, historic sites

and the outdoor drama passion play "Worthy is the Lamb." Come to your home away from home for a visit you'll always remember!

Hosts: A.K. and Marilyn Detwills
Rooms: 5 (3PB; 2SB) $50-105
Full Gourmet Breakfast
Credit Cards: none
Notes: 2, 5, 7, 8, 9, 10

## FRANKLIN

## Lullwater Retreat

88 Lullwater Rd., 28734
(704) 524-6532

The 120 year old farmhouse and cabins are located on a river and creek in a peaceful mountain cove. Hiking trails, river swimming, tubing, and other outdoor activities are on the premises. It serves as a retreat center for church groups and family reunions. Guests cook their own meals or visit nearby restaurants. Chapel, rocking chairs, wonderful views, and indoor and outdoor games. Christian videos and reading materials are supplied.

Hosts: Robert and Virginia Smith
Rooms: 10 (5PB; 5SB) $39-50
Self-serve Breakfast
Credit Cards: none
Notes: 2, 7, 8, 9, 10, 11

## GERMANTON

## MeadowHaven Bed and Breakfast

NC Hwy. 8, P.O. Box 222, 27019
(910) 593-3996; FAX (910) 593-3138

A contemporary retreat on 25 acres

---

5 Open all year; 6 Pets welcome; 7 Children welcome; 8 Tennis nearby; 9 Swimming nearby; 10 Golf nearby; 11 Skiing nearby; 12 May be booked through travel agent.

along Sauratown Mountain. Convenient to Winston-Salem, Hanging Rock and Pilot Mountain State Parks, and the Dan River. Heated indoor pool, hot tub, game room, guest pantry, fishing pond, fireplaces, TV/VCR, and movies. "Luv Tubs" and sauna available. Hiking, canoeing, horseback riding, golf, winery, art gallery, fresco, and dining nearby. Plan a "Lovebirds' Retreat" to MeadowHaven!

Hosts: Sam and Darlene Fain
Rooms: 3 + 1 luxury cabin (PB) $65-150
Full Breakfast
Credit Cards: A, B, C, D
Notes: 2, 5, 8, 9, 10, 12

## HENDERSONVILLE

## The Claddagh Inn
755 N. Main St., 28792
(704) 697-7778; (800) 225-4700;
FAX (704) 697-8664

The Claddagh Inn at Hendersonville is a recently renovated, meticulously clean bed and breakfast that is eclectically furnished with antiques and a variety of collectibles. The Inn is located two blocks from the main shopping promenade of beautiful, historic downtown Hendersonville. The friendly, homelike atmosphere is complemented by a safe and secure feeling guests experience while at this lovely inn. The Claddagh Inn is listed on the National Register of Historic Places. No smoking rooms available.

Hosts: Vicki and Dennis Pacilio
Rooms: 14 (PB) $69-99
Full Breakfast
Credit Cards: A, B, C, D, E
Notes: 2, 5, 7, 8, 9, 10, 12

## The Waverly Inn
783 N. Main, 28792
(704) 693-9193; (800) 537-8195;
FAX (704) 692-1010
Internet: JSHEIRY@AOL.COM

Listed on the National Register, this is the oldest inn in Hendersonville. Recently renovated, there is something for everyone including claw foot tubs, king and queen canopy beds, a suite, telephones, rocking chairs, sitting rooms, and all rooms have private baths. Enjoy our complimentary soft drinks and fresh baked goods. Walk to exceptional restaurants, antique stores, and shopping. Biltmore Estate, Blue Ridge Parkway, and Connemara are nearby. Full country breakfast included in rates. Rated as one of 1993s top ten bed and breakfasts in the USA by *INNovations*.

Hosts: John and Diane Sheiry, Darla Olmstead
Rooms: 15 (PB) $79-139
Full Breakfast
Credit Cards: A, B, C, D
Notes: 2, 5, 7, 8, 9, 10, 12

## HIGHLANDS

## Long House B&B
P.O. Box 2078, 28741
(704) 526-4394; (800) 833-0020

Long House B&B offers a comfortable retreat in the scenic mountains of western North Carolina. Guests enjoy the beauty and charm of the quaint town and scenic wonders of the Nentahala National Forest. This rustic mountain B&B offers all the comforts with country charm and warm hospitality. A hearty breakfast is served family-style

---

NOTES: Credit cards accepted: A Master Card; B Visa; C American Express; D Discover; E Diners Club; F Other; 2 Personal checks accepted; 3 Lunch available; 4 Dinner available;

and is one of the many highlights of everyone's visit!

Hosts: Lynn and Valerie Long
Rooms: 4 (PB) $55-95
Very Full Breakfast
Credit Cards: A, B
Notes: 2, 7, 8, 9, 10, 11

## KILL DEVIL HILLS

## *Cherokee Inn Bed and Breakfast*

500 N. Virginia Dare Trail, 27948
(919) 441-6127; (800) 554-2764;
FAX (919) 441-1072

Our beach house, located at Nags Head Beach on the outer banks of North Carolina, is 600 feet from the ocean. Fine food, history, sports, and adventure galore. We welcome you for a restful, active, or romantic getaway. Enjoy the cypress walls, white ruffled curtains, and wraparound porch.

Hosts: Bob and Kaye Combs
Rooms: 6 (PB) $60-90
Continental Breakfast
Credit Cards: A, B, C
Notes: 2, 8, 9, 10, 12

## LITTLETON

## *Littleton's Maplewood Manor*

120 College Street, P.O. Box 116527850
(919) 586-4682

Littleton's Manor is a small hometown B&B, offering you a nice clean, spacious room with a king or twin beds, shared bath, and a full breakfast. There are books, games, videos, CD's, and tapes, all for you to enjoy. There will be tea in the afternoon and wine and crackers in the evening. The grounds are park-like and for you to enjoy. There are also benches and chairs placed around for the use of our guests. The screened porch is another great place for relaxation.

Hosts: Helen and Alan Burtchell
Rooms: 2 (SB) $55
Full Breakfast
Credit Cards: A, B
Notes: 5, 9, 10

Littleton's Maplewood Manor

## MADISON

## *The Boxley B&B*

117 E. Hunter Street, 27025
(910) 427-0453; (800) 429-3516

The Greek, Federal-style home, built in

5 Open all year; 6 Pets welcome; 7 Children welcome; 8 Tennis nearby; 9 Swimming nearby; 10 Golf nearby; 11 Skiing nearby; 12 May be booked through travel agent.

1825, is located in the historic district of Madison. Boxwoods adorn the long front walk and the gardens in the rear. The porch, connecting the main house to the dining room and kitchen, is a wonderful place to sit in and relax, and enjoy the peacefulness and serenity the 19th century setting. JoAnn and Monte want you to make yourself at home.

Hosts: JoAnn and Monte McIntosh
Rooms: 4 (PB) $70
Full Breakfast
Credit Cards: A, B, C
Notes: 2, 5, 8, 10

The Boxley Bed and Breakfast

## MANSON

### Kimball Oaks

Route 1, Box 158, 27553
(919) 456-2004 (voice and FAX)

1800's home on Kerr Lake—800 mile shore line an hour north of Research Triangle, two hours south of Richmond, and 3½ hours south of Washington. Comfortable home tastefully decorated in a quiet nature-filled setting near Kimball Point. Lawn games and comfortable chairs under massive oaks. Modern baths. Home-baked breads. Refreshments on arrival. Proprietors hosting skills honed by years of military and diplomatic living in Brussels, Geneva, Verona, Rome, and Washington. Italian and French spoken.

Hosts: Colonel and Mrs. Allen Kimball
Rooms: 3 (1PB; 2 SB) $60-100
Full Breakfast
Credit Cards: A, B
Notes: 2, 3, 4, 5 (closed Christmas), 7(over 12), 9, 10

## MARSHALL

### Marshall House Bed and Breakfast

5 Hill Street, P.O. Box 865, 28753
(704) 649-9205; FAX (704) 649-2999

Built in 1903, the inn overlooks the peaceful town of Marshall and the waters of the French Broad River. This country inn, listed on the National Historic Register, is decorated with fancy chandeliers, antiques, and pictures. Four fireplaces, formal dining room, parlor, and upstairs TV/reading room. Storytelling about the house, the town, the people, and the history. Loving house pets, the toot of a choo-choo train, and good service make your visit a unique experience.

Hosts: Ruth and Jim Boylan
Rooms: 9 (2PB; 7SB) $39.50-75
Continental Plus Breakfast
Credit Cards: A, B, C, D, E
Notes: 3, 4, 5, 6, 7, 9, 10, 11, 12

NOTES: Credit cards accepted: A Master Card; B Visa; C American Express; D Discover; E Diners Club; F Other; 2 Personal checks accepted; 3 Lunch available; 4 Dinner available;

## MT. AIRY

### *Pine Ridge Inn*
2893 W. Pine St., 27030
(910) 789-5034; FAX (910) 786-9039

An English Manor mansion on eight acres. Located in the foothills near Blue Ridge Parkway. Golfing, swimming, tennis, and horseback riding. AAA and Mobile approved. Remote controlled TV, touch tone phones, and clock radios in every room. FAX available. Full breakfast. Limited smoking.

Hosts: Ellen and Manford Haxton
Rooms: 8 (6PB; 2SB) $60-100
Full Breakfast
Credit Cards: A, B, C
Notes: 2, 5, 7, 8, 9, 10, 12

## MOUNTAIN HOME

### *Mountain Home Bed and Breakfast*
P.O. Box 234, 10 Courtland Blvd., 28758
(704) 697-9090; (800) 397-0066

Between Asheville and Hendersonville, and near the airport, antiques and Oriental-style rugs grace this English-style home. Large, Tennessee, pink marble porch and rocking chairs to relax the day or night away. Cable TV and telephones in all rooms. Some rooms with private entrance. Full candlelight breakfast. Convenient to Biltmore Estate (on their preferred lodging list), Chimney Rock, Pisgah National Forest, Carl Sandburg Home, and much more. Wheelchair accessible ramp to front and one room.

Hosts: Bob and Donna Marriott
Rooms: 7 (5PB; 2SB) $70-95
Full Breakfast
Credit Cards: A, B
Notes: 2, 5, 8, 10, 12

## NAGS HEAD

### *First Colony Inn*
6720 S. Virginia Dare Trail, 27959
(919) 441-2343; (800) 368-9390;
FAX (919) 441-9234

Enjoy Southern hospitality at the only historic B&B inn on the Outer Banks (National Register). Enjoy our individual rooms, continental breakfast buffet and afternoon tea, private walk to the beach, pool, and croquet. Or visit the Wright Brothers Memorial, lighthouses, and Fort Raleigh (site of the Lost Colony). The only AAA Four Diamond rating in Eastern North Carolina.

Hosts: The Lawrences
Rooms: 26 (PB) $ 75 (winter)-225 (summer)
Continental Plus Buffet Breakfast
Credit Cards: A, B, D
Notes: 2 (30 days in advance), 5, 7, 8, 9, 10, 12

---

5 Open all year; 6 Pets welcome; 7 Children welcome; 8 Tennis nearby; 9 Swimming nearby; 10 Golf nearby; 11 Skiing nearby; 12 May be booked through travel agent.

## NEW BERN

### The Aerie

509 Pollock St., 28562
(919) 636-5553 (voice and FAX); (800) 849-5553

Just one block from the Tryon Palace in the heart of the historic district, the Aerie offers the closest accommodations to all of New Bern's historic attractions. The Victorian inn is furnished with antiques and reproductions, yet each of the seven, individually decorated guest rooms has a modern private bathroom, telephone, and color TV. Complimentary beverages are offered throughout your stay, and generous breakfasts await you each morning served in the dining room.

Hosts: Howard and Dee Smith
Rooms: 7 (PB) $79-89
Full Breakfast
Credit Cards: A, B, C, D
Notes: 2, 5, 7, 8, 9, 10, 12

### Harmony House Inn

215 Pollock St., 28560
(919) 636-3810; (800) 636-3113;
FAX (919) 636-3810

Enjoy comfortable elegance in an unusually spacious Greek Revival inn built circa 1850 with final additions circa 1900. Guests enjoy a parlor, front porch with rocking chairs and swings, antiques and reproductions, plus a full breakfast in the dining room. Soft drinks and juice available throughout stay. All rooms have fully private,

modern bathrooms. Located in the historic district near Tryon Palace, shops, and restaurants. No smoking!

Hosts: Ed and Sooki Kirkpatrick
Rooms: 10 (PB) $85-95
Full Breakfast
Credit Cards: A, B, C, D
Notes: 2, 5, 7, 8, 10, 12

### King's Arms Colonial Inn

212 Pollock St., 28560
(919) 638-4409; (800) 872-9306;
FAX (919) 638-2191

The King's Arms Inn, named for an old New Bern tavern said to have hosted members of the First Continental Congress, upholds a heritage of hospitality as New Bern's winner of the "Best of the Best" award for bed and breakfast accommodations. Spacious rooms with comfortable four-poster, canopied, or brass beds; all modern amenities; and elegant decor harbor travelers who want to escape the present and steep themselves in Colonial history. Home-baked breakfasts feature piping hot specialty ham and cheese and seasonal fruit muf-

---

NOTES: Credit cards accepted: A Master Card; B Visa; C American Express; D Discover; E Diners Club; F Other; 2 Personal checks accepted; 3 Lunch available; 4 Dinner available;

fins from our exclusive recipe; fresh fruit, juice, and coffee or tea delivered to your room with the morning paper. The inviting third floor Mansard Suite offers a view of the Neuse River and features unique open gables and the tongue and groove paneling added to this 1848 Greek Revival during the last part of the 19th century.

Hosts: Richard and Pat Gulley
Rooms: 7 + 1 suite (PB) $85-125
Continental Plus Breakfast
Credit Cards: A, B, C
Notes: 2, 5, 7, 8, 9, 10, 12

## ORIENTAL

## Tar Heel Inn
205 Church St., P.O. Box 176, 28571
(919) 249-1078

The Tar Heel Inn is over 100 years old and has been restored to capture the atmosphere of an English country inn. Guest rooms have four-poster or canopy king and queen beds. Patios and bicycles are for guest use. Five churches are within walking distance. Tennis, fishing, and golf are nearby. This quiet fishing village is known as the sailing capital of the Carolinas. Sailing cruises can be arranged, and there are great restaurants. Smoking on porch and patios only. Three-diamond AAA rating.

Hosts: Shawna and Robert Hyde
Rooms: 8 (PB) $65-85
Full Breakfast
Credit Cards: A, B
Notes: 2, 7 (by arrangement), 8, 9, 10, 12

## RUTHERFORDTON

## The Carrier Houses Bed and Breakfast
423 N. Main, Hwy 221, 28139
(704) 287-4222

National register houses side-by-side in the historic district of downtown Rutherfordton, NC. The Carrier House Bed and Breakfast offers a unique atmosphere of being at home, whether you are on your way to a fun-packed ski trip, touring all the great sites of NC, or just passing through. Facilities available for meetings, receptions, and formal gatherings. Private baths, suite style rooms, cable TV, and antique furnished rooms (some with feather mattresses).

Hosts: Boyce and Barbara Hodge
Rooms: 8 (PB) call for rates
Full Breakfast
Credit Cards: A, B, D
Notes: 2, 5, 7, 8, 9, 10, 11

## SPARTA

## Turby Villa
E. Whitehead St., Star Rt. 1, Box 48, 28675
(910) 372-8490

At an altitude of 3,000 feet, this contemporary two-story home is the centerpiece of a 20-acre farm located two miles from town. The house is surrounded by an acre of trees and manicured lawn with a lovely view of the Blue Ridge Mountains. Breakfast is served either on the enclosed porch with white wicker furnishings or in the more formal dining room with Early Ameri-

---

5 Open all year; 6 Pets welcome; 7 Children welcome; 8 Tennis nearby; 9 Swimming nearby; 10 Golf nearby; 11 Skiing nearby; 12 May be booked through travel agent.

can furnishings. Mrs. Mimi Turbiville takes justifiable pride in her attractive, well-maintained bed and breakfast.

Hostess: Maybelline R. Turbiville
Rooms: 3 (PB) $35 (single) $50 + tax
Full Breakfast
Credit Cards: none
Notes: 2, 5, 7, 8, 10

## STATESVILLE

### Aunt Mae's B&B

532 East Broad Street, 28677
(704) 873-9525

Aunt Mae's century-old home is filled with nostalgia, and located just one mile off I-40/I-77 convenient for the traveler or for an extended stay. Stroll to quaint shops and fine restaurants, retreat to our lower lawn and the serenity of nature in action, and browse through 90 years of collections. Special amenities for special occasions. Welcome to Aunt Mae's! Call or write for information on Special Romantic Weekend Packages.

Hostess: Sue Rowland
Rooms: 3 (PB) $60
Full Breakfast
Credit Cards: A, B
Notes: 2, 5, 8, 9, 10, 12

### Cedar Hill Farm B&B

778 Elmwood Road, 28677
(704) 873-4332; (800) 948-4423

An 1840 farmhouse and private cottage on a 32-acre sheep farm in the rolling hills of North Carolina. Antique furnishings, air-conditioning, cable TV, and phones in rooms. After your full country breakfast, swim, play badminton, or relax in a porch rocker or hammock. For a busier day, visit two lovely towns with historic districts, Old Salem, or two larger cities in a 45-mile radius. Convenient to restaurants, shopping, and three interstate highways.

Hosts: Brenda and Jim Vernon
Rooms: 2 (PB) $60-75
Full Breakfast
Credit Cards: A, B
Notes: 2, 5, 6 (limited), 7, 9, 10, 12

### Madelyn's B&B

514 Carrol St., 28677
(704) 872-3973; (800) 948-4473;
FAX (704) 881-0713

Relax on one of the most peaceful streets in Statesville, the crossroads of the Carolinas. When you arrive, fresh fruit, candy, and a plate of homemade cookies await. Take a short walk down tree-lined streets, and shop and eat in historic downtown Statesville. Truly a charming home where John and Madelyn will greet you with a smile. A full gourmet breakfast is served.

Hosts: Madelyn and John Hill
Rooms: 3 (PB) $65-75
Full Gourmet Breakfast
Credit Cards: A, B
Notes: 2, 5, 8, 9, 10, 12

## TRYON

### Fox Trot Inn

P.O. Box 1561, 800 Lynn Rd., (Rt. #108), 28782
(704) 859-9706

This lovingly restored residence, circa

---

NOTES: Credit cards accepted: A Master Card; B Visa; C American Express; D Discover; E Diners Club; F Other; 2 Personal checks accepted; 3 Lunch available; 4 Dinner available;

1915, is situated on six wooded acres within the city limits. It is convenient to everything, yet secluded with a quietly elegant atmosphere. Full gourmet breakfast, afternoon refreshments, heated swimming pool, fully furnished guest house with two bedrooms, kitchen, living room, and deck with mountain views. Two guest rooms have sitting rooms.

Host: Wim Woody
Rooms: 4 (PB) $80-125; Guest House: $550 weekly
Full Breakfast
Credit Cards: none
Notes: 2, 5, 6 and 7 (in guest house), 8, 9, 10

## WAYNESVILLE

## Wynne's Creekside Lodge Bed and Breakfast

Rt. 2, Box 365, 28786
(704) 926-8300

Situated on trout-stocked Jonathan Creek in the scenic western North Carolina mountains, Wynne's Creekside Lodge lies on two and a fourth country acres five minutes outside Maggie Valley. The Inn, a 1926 two-story farmhouse, was recently raised and set upon a wood and stone contemporary addition. A full country breakfast includes homemade bread, jams, or pastry. Complimentary cappuccino or refreshments served. Three rooms and one suite in a Christian atmosphere.

Hosts: Les and Gail Wynne
Rooms: 4 (PB) $55-60
Full Breakfast
Credit Cards: A, B
Notes: 2, 5, 6 (separate facilities), 7, 8, 9, 10, 11

Wynne's CreeksideLodge Bed and Breakfast

## WEAVERVILLE

## Dry Ridge Inn

26 Brown St., 28787
(704) 658-3899; (800) 839-3899

This casually elegant bed and breakfast is quietly removed ten minutes north of Asheville's many attractions. Country-style antiques and contemporary art enhance this unique 1800s village farmhouse. A full breakfast is served with individual seating. Relax in our outdoor spa or with quality, spiritual reading after enjoying a day of mountain adventure.

Hosts: Paul and Mary Lou Gibson
Rooms: 7 (PB) $65-85
Full Breakfast
Credit Cards: A, B, C, D
Notes: 2, 5, 7, 10, 11, 12

## Weaverville Featherbed and Breakfast

3 Le Perrion Dr., 28787
(704) 645-7594; FAX (704) 658-3905

Our "romantic revival" mountain-top home was built at the turn-of-the-century in an era when true comfort was the mark of excellence. Enjoy the awe-

5 Open all year; 6 Pets welcome; 7 Children welcome; 8 Tennis nearby; 9 Swimming nearby; 10 Golf nearby; 11 Skiing nearby; 12 May be booked through travel agent.

some mountain view from every room! Majestic sunsets and fluffy featherbeds ensure the "ultimate" peaceful nights rest. Wake to crisp mountain air and a full "mountain-size" breakfast! Just seven miles north of Asheville and all its attractions. Honeymoon suite available!

Hostesses: Sharon Ballas and Shelly Burtt
Rooms: 6 (PB) $85-195
Full Breakfast
Credit Cards: A, B
Notes: 2, 5, 7, 10, 11, 12

## WELDON

### Weldon Place Inn

500 Washington Ave., 27890
(919) 536-4582; (800) 831-4470

Your home away from home is only two miles from I-95 Exit 173 halfway between New York and Florida. Sleep in canopy beds, wake to singing sparrows, stroll through our cozy historic hometown, and savor a gourmet breakfast. At the Weldon Place Inn, your peace of mind begins with antiques and country elegance. Personal attention is provided to ensure you the ultimate in solitude and relaxation. Select the Romantic Retreat Package and you'll enjoy flowers, sparkling cider, a whirlpool tub and breakfast in bed. Local sinclude state historic site, early canal system, river overlook of the rapids, and the railroad.

Hosts: Angel and Andy Whitby
Rooms: 4 (PB) $49-85
Full Breakfast
Credit Cards: A, B, C
Notes: 5, 8, 12

Weldon Place Inn

## WILMINGTON

### James Place B&B

9 S. Fourth St., 28401
(910) 251-0999; (800) 303-9444

Our inn is located in Wilmington's Historic District minutes from some of Carolina's finest beaches. A carefully restored turn-of-the-century "Four Square" style home with a large front porch for rocking and reminiscing. The Renewal Room has a special intimacy with jacuzzi bathroom, queen bed, and personal balcony. The Nesting Suite has a queen canopy nesting bed, sitting area, and private bath. The Shaker Room has a queen bed, twin bed, and a private bath.

Hosts: Tony and Maureen Spataro
Rooms: 3 (PB) $70-95
Full Breakfast
Credit Cards: A, B
Notes: 2, 5, 7, 8, 9, 10, 12

### Taylor House Inn

14 N. Seventh St., 28401
(910) 763-7581; (800) 382-9982

Neoclassic built in 1905 in Historic District and blessed with vast ceilings, enormous rooms, rich oak woodwork, parquet floors, stained glass windows, and a magnificent open staircase. Guest rooms are artfully appointed with antiques, hand-decorated furniture, canopies, ceiling fans, and beautiful linens. A full gourmet breakfast is served on Blue China.

Hosts: Glenda Moreadith
Rooms: 4 (PB) $95-110
Full Breakfast
Credit Cards: A, B, C
Notes: 2, 5, 8, 9, 10, 12

Taylor House Inn

## WILSON

## *Miss Betty's B&B Inn*

600 W. Nash St., 27893
(919) 243-4447; (800) 258-2058

Selected as one of the **"best places to stay in the South"** Miss Betty's is ideally located midway between Maine and Florida along the main North-South route, I-95. Comprised of three beautifully restored structures in the downtown historic section; the National Registered Davis-Whitehead-Harriss House (circa 1858), the adjacent Riley House (circa 1900), and Rosebud (circa 1942) are a recapture of the elegance and style of days gone by and where quiet Victorian charm abounds in an atmosphere of all modern-day conveniences. Guests can browse for antiques in the Inn or visit any of the numerous antique shops that have given Wilson the title "Antique Capital of North Carolina." A quiet eastern North Carolina town known for its famous barbecue, Wilson also has four beautiful golf courses and numerous tennis courts.

Hosts: Betty and Fred Spitz
Rooms: 10 + 3 king suites (PB) $60-75
Full Breakfast
Credit Cards: A, B, C, D, E
Notes: 2, 5, 8, 9, 10

## WINSTON-SALEM

## *Lady Anne's Victorian Bed and Breakfast*

612 Summit St., 27101
(910) 724-1074

Warm, southern hospitality surrounds you in this 1890 Victorian home, listed on the National Register of Historic Places. An aura of romance touches each suite or room, all individually decorated with period antiques, treasures, and modern luxuries. Some rooms have two-person whirlpools, cable TV, HBO, stereo, telephone, coffee, refrigerator, private entrances, and balconies. An evening dessert and full breakfast are served. Lady Anne's is ideally located near downtown attractions, performances, restaurants, shops, and Old Salem Historic Village. Smoking only on the porch!

Hostess: Shelley Kirby
Rooms: 4 (PB) $55-155
Full Breakfast
Credit Cards: A, B, C
Notes: 5, 8, 9, 10, 12 (no commission)

5 Open all year; 6 Pets welcome; 7 Children welcome; 8 Tennis nearby; 9 Swimming nearby; 10 Golf nearby; 11 Skiing nearby; 12 May be booked through travel agent.

# NORTH DAKOTA

●Luverne

●McClusky

# North Dakota

## LUVERNE

### Volden Farm
### Bed and Breakfast
R.R. 2, Box 50, 58056
(701) 769-2275

This weathered redwood farmhouse is a 1926/1978 built home—two in one—if you please. Relaxation is the theme. Hiking through the native prairie down to the Sheyenne River is an option, along with reading in a comfortable spot on the porch or deck. Antiques and collectibles surround you and the food is good!

Hosts: Jim and JoAnne Wold
Rooms: 4 + cottage (2PB; 2SB) $50-95
Full Breakfast
Credit Cards: none
Notes: 2, 3, 4, 5, 7, 8, 9, 10, 11, 12

Volden Farm Bed and Breakfast

## MCCLUSKY

### Midstate B&B
Route 3, Box 28, 58463
(701) 363-2520 (voice & FAX); (800) 573-2520

In the center of North Dakota, this country home built in 1980 operates under the banner of "The beauty of the house is order, the blessing of the house is contentment, and the glory of the house is hospitality." The guest entrance opens the way to a complete and private lower level with your bedroom, bath, large TV lounge with fireplace, and kitchenette. Three upstairs bedrooms share a bath. Breakfast in your choice of locations: your room, formal dining room, the plant-filled atrium, or on the patio. Very easy to locate: mile marker 232 on ND 200. In an area of great hunting of deer, waterfowl, and upland game, our guests are allowed hunting privileges on over 4,000 acres. Special rates and provisions for hunting parties. Air conditioned. Children welcome.

Hosts: Allen and Grace Faul
Rooms: 4 (1PB, 3SB) $30 ($25 single)
Full or Continental Breakfast
Credit Cards: none
Notes: 2, 3, 4, 5, 6, 7, 8, 9

---

NOTES: Credit cards accepted: A Master Card; B Visa; C American Express; D Discover; E Diners Club; F Other; 2 Personal checks accepted; 3 Lunch available; 4 Dinner available; 5 Open all year; 6 Pets welcome; 7 Children welcome; 8 Tennis nearby; 9 Swimming nearby; 10 Golf nearby; 11 Skiing nearby; 12 May be booked through travel agent.

- Geneva-On-The-Lake
- Marblehead
- Sandusky
- Bowling Green
- Wakeman
- Hiram
- Defiance
- Tiffin
- Orrville
- Wooster
- Wilmot
- Berlin
- Strasburg
- Millersburg
- Marion
- Charm
- Dellroy
- Sidney
- Dover
- Delaware
- Fresno
- Urbana
- Plain City
- Martins Ferry
- Tipp City
- Columbus
- Dayton
- E. Fultonham
- Camden
- Sugar Grove
- Blue Rock
- Oxford
- Lebanon
- Caldwell
- Hamilton
- Albany
- Waverly
- Bethel
- Lucasville
- Georgetown
- Ripley

OHIO

# Ohio

## ALBANY

### The Albany House B&B
9 Clinton Street
(614) 698-6311; (800) 600-4941

Enjoy today's comfort in yesterday's atmosphere at The Albany House. A 150-year-old house, renovated for a B&B in the village of Albany, seven miles west of Athens and Ohio University. Enjoy antiques, quilts, Oriental rugs, and family heirlooms, plus modern amenities of air-conditioning, indoor heated pool, fireplace, and guest living room with TV/VCR. Resident cat.

Hosts: Sarah and Ted Hutchins
Rooms: 8 (PB) $75-100
Continental Plus Breakfast
Credit Cards: A, B, C, D
Notes: 2, 5, 7 (over 8), 8, 9 (indoors), 10, 12

## BERLIN

### Donna's Country Bed and Breakfast
East Street
(216) 893-3068

Featuring Honeymoon/Anniversary cottages with heart-shaped waterfall jacuzzi, cathedral wood ceiling with skylights, gas log fireplace, stereo, cable TV, VCR, kitchenette, deck, and full breakfast served to your cottage. Country-decor rooms with kitchenette, cable TV, VCR, plush carpet, and wallpapering. Featured on TV channel 27 out of Youngstown and TV channel 8 out of Cleveland. Call for brochure package.

Hosts: Johannes and Donna Marie Schlabach
Rooms: 4 (PB) $65-149.95
Full breakfast to honeymoon/anniversary cottages
Continental Breakfast delivered to rooms
Credit Cards: A, B, D
Notes: 2, 5, 7, 8, 9, 10, 12

Donna's Country Bed and Breakfast

---

NOTES:  Credit cards accepted:  A  Master Card;  B  Visa;  C  American Express;  D  Discover; E  Diners Club;  F  Other;  2  Personal checks accepted;  3  Lunch available;  4  Dinner available; 5  Open all year;  6  Pets welcome;  7  Children welcome;  8  Tennis nearby;  9  Swimming nearby; 10  Golf nearby;  11  Skiing nearby;  12  May be booked through travel agent.

## BETHEL

### Dorothea's Bed and Breakfast

562 S. Charity St., 45106
(513) 734-7696

This bed and breakfast is an old-fashioned farmhouse built in 1905. It is near several churches and has off-street parking available. East Fork State Lake is only three miles away. The B&B is furnished with antiques and old dolls. Dorothea's has also hosted family reunions.

Hostess: Dorothy
Rooms: 3 (1PB, 1SB) $25 per person
Full Breakfast
Credit Cards: none
Notes: 2, 3, 4 (inquire), 5, 7, 8, 9, 10

## BLUE ROCK

### McNutt Farm II / Outdoorsman Lodge

6120 Cutler Lake Rd., 43720
(614) 674-4555

Country bed and breakfast for overnight travelers in rustic quarters on a working farm in the quiet of the Blue Rock hill country. Only eleven miles from I-70, 35 miles from I-77, and 60 miles from I-71. B&B guests enjoy their own private kitchen, living room with fireplace or woodburner, private bath, porch with swing, and a beautiful view with forests and pastured livestock. Choose either the log cabin or the carriage house. For those who want more than an overnight stay, please ask about our log cabin by the week or weekend. A cellar-house cabin is also available, although it is somewhat primitive. Sleep to the sounds of the whippoorwills and tree frogs. Awake to the ever-crowing rooster, the wild turkey calling, and sometimes the bleating of a newborn fawn can be heard. We welcome you by reservation and deposit.

Hosts: Don R. and Patty L. McNutt
Rooms: 2 suites (PB) $40-100
Continental Breakfast
Credit Cards: none
Notes: 2 (deposit, cash for balance), 5, 6 and 7 (prearranged), 9, 10

Pine Ridge Bed and Breakfast

## BOWLING GREEN

### Pine Ridge Bed and Breakfast

14543 Sand Ridge Rd., 43402
(419) 352-2064

Pine Ridge offers comfortable accommodations and warm hospitality in a Victorian style farmhouse dating from 1878. Two guest rooms and bath on the second floor overlook woods, well kept lawn and gardens, and fertile farms. Breakfast is served in the spacious living/dining room or sunny porch, and often includes homemade breads or coffee cakes and fruits from the orchard or garden.

Hosts: Bill and Sue Rock
Rooms: 2 (SB) $40
Full Breakfast
Credit Cards: none
Notes: 2, 7

## CALDWELL

## *The Harkins House Inn*

715 W. Street, 43724
(614) 732-7347

When passing through the beautiful countryside of southeastern Ohio take a moment to relax in the comfort of the Harkins House, a newly restored 1905 home. The home was built by V.E. Harkings. His son, Donald and his wife Bea lived there until 1991. Jeff and Stacey are their descendants. There are presently two guest rooms with private baths. One in country blue and sunny yellow floral wallpaper. The other in red rose buds with touches of green and ivory.

Hosts: Jeff and Stacey Lucas
Rooms: 2 (PB) $53
Full Breakfast
Credit Cards: A, B, C
Notes: 2, 5, 7, 8, 9, 10

## CAMDEN

## *Pleasant Valley Bed and Breakfast*

7343 Pleasant Valley Rd., 45311
(513) 787-3800

Our bed and breakfast is a sixteen room

Victorian brick with a center hall design, matching pocket doors, rich woodwork, fireplaces, and a third floor attic ballroom. There is also a summer kitchen and carriage house. We have a billiard room as well as a game room for puzzles, reading, board games, or card playing. Fishing, volleyball, horse shoes, or a leisurely stroll are a welcome pastime on our ten acres with colorful birds, butterflies, herbs, and wildflowers.

Hosts: Tim and Peg Lowman
Rooms: 4 (2PB; 2SB) $50-60
Full Breakfast
Credit Cards: none
Notes: 2, 3, 4, 6, 7, 8, 9, 10, 11 (water)

## CHARM

## *Charm Countryview Inn*

P.O. Box 100, 44617
(216) 893-3003

Traveling on State Route 557 past Amish buggies and farms on your way to the Charm Countryview Inn, you'll notice the calm atmosphere, the lovely trees and meadows, the winding drive over our bridge, and up the hill to the Inn's peaceful setting at the edge of the woods. Each guest room is individually decorated and has been named after members of our family. The comfortably furnished rooms feature handmade quilts on queen-size beds and beautiful solid oak furniture. There's no limit to the amount of time you may spend relaxing in a rocker on our spa-

---

5 Open all year;  6 Pets welcome;  7 Children welcome;  8 Tennis nearby;  9 Swimming nearby;
10 Golf nearby;  11 Skiing nearby;  12 May be booked through travel agent.

cious front porch simply enjoying the beautiful view and the fresh country air.

Innkeepers: Paul and Naomi Miller
Rooms: 15 (PB) $65-95
Full Breakfast; (Sunday) Continental
Credit Cards: A, B
Notes: 2, 5

## Guggisberg Swiss Inn

5025 S.R. 557, PO Box 1, 44617
(216) 893-3600

New quaint, peaceful, little inn, nestled snuggly in the hills of the world's largest Amish settlement—close to shops and attractions. Each room has two double beds with all the comforts of home; local TV channels plus HBO, TNT, etc. Enjoy a horse-drawn carriage or sleigh ride (seasonal—at small additional charge) or sit outside and watch the farmers work their fields. Enjoy visiting with the other guests in front of the fireplace in the lobby. Swiss breakfast includes cheese, meat, bread, cereal, fruit, danish, coffee, and orange juice.

Hosts: Eric and Julia Guggisberg
Rooms: 23 + 1 suite (PB) $79-129
Credit Cards: A, B, C, D, E
Notes: 2, 5, 7 (no children on top floor), 8, 9, 10, 11

Guggisberg Swiss Inn

## Miller Haus Bed and Breakfast

P.O. Box 126, 44617
(216) 893-3602

Our B&B is not only cozy it radiates the joy and love we have for our home. We collect antiques and quilts, so our decor is a reminder of a home from generations before us. We have nine guest rooms. They each have private bath and ample free space for reading or relaxing. We are situated on one of the highest elevations in Holmes County. The sights of the surrounding farmland are spectacular!

Hosts: Daryl and Lee Ann Miller
Rooms: 9 (PB) $85-105
Full, Cooked Breakfast
Credit Cards: A, B
Notes: 2, 5, 7 (5 and over), 10, 12

## COLUMBUS

## The House of the Seven Goebels Bed and Breakfast

4975 Hayden Run Rd., 43221
(614) 761-9595

From the pineapple sign to the warmth of the fireplaces, the House of the Seven Goebels beckons those who enjoy the past. A reproduction of a 1780 Connecticut River Valley farmhouse. Situated on two acres with brook near Northwest Columbus, Dublin, and Hilliard. Many flower beds and quiet places to sit and read. Fine dining in the area.

Hosts: Pat and Frank Goebel
Rooms: 2 (PB) $65
Full Breakfast (before 9AM); Continental (after)
Credit Cards: A, B
Notes: 2, 5

The House of the Seven Goebels

## Shamrock B&B

5657 Sunbury Rd., 43230
(614) 337-9849

The Shamrock B&B is one half mile from I-270, close to the airport, and 15 minutes from downtown. The B&B is handicapped accessible and it is all on one floor. There are one and one fourth acres of landscaped gardens, trees, patio, and arbor for enjoyment. For entertainment guests can choose from the large library of books, videos, and CDs or just relax in front of the fireplace. There is easy access to downtown activities like Polaris Amphitheater, shopping, parks, gardens, galleries, and country. Entirely air-conditioned and special smoking rooms available.

Host: Tom McLaughlin
Rooms: 2 (PB) $45-55 (discount for 3 or more days)
Full Irish Breakfast with menu
Credit Cards: none
Notes: 2, 3, 5, 7, 8, 9, 10, 11

## DAYTON

## Candlewick Bed and Breakfast

4991 Bath Rd., 45424
(513) 233-9297

This tranquil Dutch Colonial home sits atop a hill on five rolling acres. George, a retired engineer, and Nancy, a retired teacher, invite you to spend a peaceful night in comfortable rooms containing a blend of antiques and Colonial and country furnishings. Full breakfast includes fresh fruit and juice, choice homemade pastries, and freshly brewed coffee. Weather permitting, enjoy breakfast on the screened porch often visited by wild ducks and geese. Convenient to the Air Force Museum and major universities, Candlewick is a perfect retreat for either business or pleasure.

Hosts: Nancy and George Thompson
Rooms: 2 (SB) $55-60 (includes tax)
Full Breakfast
Credit Cards: none
Notes: 2, 5

## DEFIANCE

## Sanctuary Ministries

20277 Schick Rd., 43512
(419) 658-2069

Sanctuary Ministries is a quiet getaway in a Christian atmosphere. A two-story cedar-sided home with air-conditioning, a six-acre lake, a pond, and five acres of woods make for a peaceful getaway. This is a favorite fishing hole for many

5 Open all year; 6 Pets welcome; 7 Children welcome; 8 Tennis nearby; 9 Swimming nearby; 10 Golf nearby; 11 Skiing nearby; 12 May be booked through travel agent.

with row boat and canoe. Picnicking and bird-watching from porch swings add to the tranquil atmosphere.

Hosts: Emil and Barbara Schoch
Rooms: 2 (SB) $35-50
Full Breakfast
Credit Cards: none
Notes: 2, 5, 7, 9, 10

## DELAWARE

### Miracle House Bed and Breakfast

P.O. Box 1496, 585 Magnolia Dr., 43015
(614) 369-4017 (voice and FAX)

A magnificent stone home with over 12,000 square feet, consisting of seven rooms, four private dining rooms, a commercial kitchen, and banquet space for 120 people. A life-size miracle picture of "Jesus" is painted on one wall in a round sunken living room, furniture from yesteryear, and a huge roof skylight. Watch this painted picture move as you change directions.

Hosts: Dick and Rita Boyen
Rooms: 7 (PB) $87-117
Full Breakfast
Credit Cards: A, B, C
Notes: 2, 3, 4, 5, 8, 9, 10, 12

Candleglow Bed and Breakfast

## DELLROY

### Candleglow Bed and Breakfast

4247 Roswell Rd. SW, 44620
(216) 735-2407

Spacious Victorian built in 1868. Romantic; elegantly casual. Three guest rooms; private baths; king, queen, and twin beds; clawfoot and whirlpool tubs. Full breakfasts; Atwood Lake Resort area. Swimming, boating, hiking, horseback riding, and golf are in the area.

Hostess: Audrey Genova (innkeeper)
Rooms: 3 (PB) $90 (summer call for winter rates)
Full Breakfast
Credit Cards: none
Notes: 2, 5, 8, 9, 10

## DOVER

### Little House B&B at Home Again Farm

5108 Winfield-Strasburg Rd. NW, 44622
(216) 343-6279

We welcome travelers and business people to the detached guest house on our hillside farm. Peace and quiet are our specialty. Well-behaved children are welcome! Amish Country is four miles away, as well as Warthers Museum and Moravian sites. Come enjoy the privacy of our two-bedroom Little House. Your own kitchen will be stocked with home baked rolls and all you need for a private breakfast. Sleep

---

NOTES: Credit cards accepted: A Master Card; B Visa; C American Express; D Discover; E Diners Club; F Other; 2 Personal checks accepted; 3 Lunch available; 4 Dinner available;

on line dried sheets, walk down a country road, and open your senses to evening birdsong and the "*morning chorus*". We are located only four miles from the I-77/St. Rte. 39 exit.

Hosts: Kathy and Eric Riley
Guesthouse: 1(PB; 2 bedrooms) $70
Continental Breakfast
Credit Cards: none
Notes: 2, 5, 7, 8, 9, 10, 12

## Olde World Bed and Breakfast

2982 SR 516 NW, 44622
(216) 343-1333; (800) 447-1273

The Olde World Bed and Breakfast is a one-of-a-kind restored 1880's Victorian home nestled among the hills of Tuscarawas Valley, home of historic sites and old-fashioned culture. Our five suites are uniquely decorated to include Victorian,-Parisian,-Oriental,-Alpine, and Mediterranean. All suites include private baths, use of hot tub, full breakfast, and air-conditioning. The parlor is equipped with game table and TV.

Hostess: Jonna Sigrist
Rooms: 5 (PB) $65-75
Full Breakfast
Credit Cards: A, B, D
Notes: 2, 3, 5, 9, 10, 12

Olde World Bed and Breakfast

## EAST FULTONHAM

## Hill View Acres

7320 Old Town Rd., 43735
(614) 849-2728

Old World hospitality and comfort await each of our guests. During your visit, wander over the 21 acres, relax on the deck or patio, use the pool and year-round spa, or cuddle up by the fireplace in cooler months. A hearty, country breakfast with homemade breads, jams, and jellies is served. We are located ten miles southwest of Zanesville.

Hosts: Jim and Dawn Graham
Rooms: 2 (SB) $40.25-45.50 (including tax)
Full Breakfast
Credit Cards: A, B, C
Notes: 2, 3, 4 (by arrangement), 5, 7, 9, 10

## FREDERICKSBURG

## Gilead's Balm Manor Bed and Breakfast

8690 CR 201, 44627
(216) 695-3881

Nestled among the Amish farms of Holmes County, 12 minutes north of Berlin, Ohio, you will find five landscaped acres of Amish country elegance. We have added four luxurious and spacious suites with 12-foot ceilings to our Manor House. Each suite includes two-person jacuzzi, fireplace/gas logs, kitchen, private bath, satellite TV, air-conditioner, and double French doors with round top windows overlooking our 2 1/2 acre lake. Just minutes from shops and restaurants. Our

---

5 Open all year; 6 Pets welcome; 7 Children welcome; 8 Tennis nearby; 9 Swimming nearby; 10 Golf nearby; 11 Skiing nearby; 12 May be booked through travel agent.

guests say, it's like experiencing the luxurious accommodations of an estate in Europe overlooking a lake. Your hosts, David and Sara Mae Stutzman are both from Amish and Mennonite backgrounds.

Hosts: David and Sara Mae Stutzman
Rooms: 4 (PB) $125 (summer)
Continental (fresh fruit + pastry bar) Breakfast
Credit Cards: A, B
Notes: 2, 5, 7, 8, 9, 10, 12

## FRESNO

## *Valley View Inn of New Bedford*
32327 SR 643, 43824
(216) 897-3232; (800) 331-8439

The panoramic view from the back of the Inn is nothing short of breathtaking and is enhanced only by the changing seasons. Guests can enjoy the coziness of the fireplace in the living room or relax in the family room. A player piano, checkers, ping-pong table, chess, or a comfortable Lazy Boy chair await you. No TVs to interrupt the serenity that abounds as one enjoys gazing at the surrounding fields and farms, woods, and wildlife. The Inn is located between Roscoe Village and Sugarcreek and within minutes from all Amish shopping places. We're in the heart of Amish Country and in the service of God's people. No smoking. Handicap accessible.

Hosts: Dan and Nancy Lembke
Rooms: 10 (PB) $75-105
Full Breakfast; Continental (Sun.)
Credit Cards: A, B
Notes: 2, 5, 7 (over 2), 10

## GENEVA-ON-THE-LAKE

## *The Otto Court B&B*
5653 Lake Rd., 44041
(216) 466-8668; FAX (216) 466-0106

Otto Court B&B is a family-run business situated on two acres of lakefront property. There are eight cottages and a 19-room hotel overlooking Lake Erie. Besides a small game room, there is a horse shoe pit, a volleyball court, picnic tables, and beach with area for a bonfire. Within walking distance is the Geneva State Park and Marina. The Old Firehouse winery, Geneva-on-the-Lake Amusement Center, and the Jennie Munger Museum are also nearby.

Hosts: Joyce Otto and Dan Otto (son)
Rooms: 12 (8PB; 4SB) $48-63
Full Breakfast
Credit Cards: A, B, D, F
Notes: 2, 4, 5, 7, 8, 9, 10, 11, 12

## GEORGETOWN

## *Log Cabin B&B*
350 N. Broadway, 40324
(502) 863-3514

This authentic log cabin has two bedrooms, fireplace, kitchen/family room, and air-conditioning. Georgetown is a quiet historic town five miles north of the Kentucky Horse Park and 12 miles north of Lexington. Facilities are completely private.

Hosts: Clay and Janis McKnight
Rooms: 1 (PB) $64
Expanded Continental Breakfast
Credit Cards: none
Notes: 2, 5, 6, 7, 8, 9, 12

---

NOTES: Credit cards accepted: A Master Card; B Visa; C American Express; D Discover; E Diners Club; F Other; 2 Personal checks accepted; 3 Lunch available; 4 Dinner available;

## HAMILTON

### *Eaton Hill Bed and Breakfast*

1951 Eaton Rd., 45013
(513) 856-9552

Eaton Hill has a country feel although it is officially part of Hamilton. The white Colonial home is surrounded by fields, trees, and flower beds. Only ten miles from the Miami University campus and conveniently situated for parents, guests, and friends of the University and Butler County residents. Two double bedrooms with shared bath will provide you with a quiet night's rest amid antique furnishings. Children welcome ($10 each). A portable crib and high chair are available.

Hostess: Mrs. Pauline K. Zink
Rooms: 2 (SB) $50 + tax
Full Breakfast
Credit Cards: none
Notes: 2, 5, 6 (caged), 7, 8, 9, 10

Eaton Hill Bed and Breakfast

## HIRAM

### *The Lily Ponds Bed and Breakfast*

P.O. Box 322, 6720 Wakefield Rd., 44234
(216) 569-3222; (800) 325-5087;
FAX (216) 569-3223

Spacious house with antiques and Es-

kimo art. One level; living room with cathedral ceiling and wood-burning fireplace; 20 acres of woods and streams to explore; large screened porch; quiet, peaceful atmosphere in small college village. Fifteen minutes to Sea World and Geauga Lake Park, one hour to Cleveland, Akron, and Youngstown.

Hostess: Marilane B. Spencer
Rooms: 3 (PB) $55-75
Full Breakfast
Credit Cards: none
Notes: 2, 5, 7, 8, 9, 10, 11, 12

## HOLMES COUNTY (AMISH COUNTRY) SEE ALSO—BERLIN, CHARM, DOVER, FREDERICKSBURG, FRESNO, MILLERSBURG, ORRVILLE, STRASBURG, SUGARCREEK, WILMOT, AND WOOSTER

## LEBANON

### *Hexagon House*

419 Cincinnati Ave., 45036
(513) 932-9655

Built in the mid 1850s, Hexagon House is located 30 miles north of Cincinnati in Lebanon, Ohio; easy to reach from interstates and convenient to local attractions. The house is listed on the National Register of Historic Places due to its unique six-sided exterior and its interesting interior floor plan. Rooms are spacious, comfortable, and tastefully decorated. The objective of your full time hostess is to provide each guest with a pleasantly memorable experience.

Hosts: Lois Duncan Hart and husband Ron
Rooms: 3 (1PB: 2SB) $55-70
Full Breakfast
Credit Cards: none
Notes: 2, 5, 7 (over 12), 10

Hexagon House

## LUCASVILLE

### The Olde Lamplighter

P.O. Box 820, (9 West St.), 45648
(614) 259-3002

Nestled in the hills of Southern Ohio, this 1939 brick home has been recently restored and redecorated. Furnished with antiques and air-conditioned with a deck. Gift shop serves as a showcase for local crafters. Manufactured gifts at discounted prices. Scenic views.

Many points of interest nearby. Ten miles north of Portsmouth; 80 miles south of Columbus.

Hosts: Gaylord and Marilyn Liles
Rooms: 4 (SB) $48
Continental Breakfast
Credit Cards: A, B
Notes: 2, 5, 7 (teenagers), 8, 9, 10, 12

## MARBLEHEAD

### The Ivy House

504 Ottawa Dr., 43440
(419) 798-4944

A quiet unpretentious retreat in a grove of oak trees at lakeside with beaches nearby. Near Vacationland attractions with Cedar Point only 25 minutes away. Just outside the Christian community of Lakeside with public parks and island ferries within walking distance. Off-street parking available. Water side screened porch.

Hosts: Ray and Susan Lawyer
Rooms: 4 + suite (SB) $25-55
Full Breakfast
Credit Cards: A, B, C
Notes: 2, 3 and 4 (on order), 5, 6 (by arrangement), 7, 8, 9, 10

## MARION

### Olde Towne Manor

245 St. James St., 43302
(614) 382-2402; (800) 341-6163

The elegant stone home nestles on a beautiful acre of land on a quiet street

---

NOTES: Credit cards accepted: A Master Card; B Visa; C American Express; D Discover; E Diners Club; F Other; 2 Personal checks accepted; 3 Lunch available; 4 Dinner available;

in Marion's historic district. Enjoy a quiet setting in the gazebo, the soothing sauna, or relax reading one of the more than 1,000 books available in the library. A pool table is also available for your enjoyment. A leisurely stroll will take you to the home of President Warren G. Harding and the Harding Memorial. Awarded the 1990 Marion's Beautifications Most Attractive Building.

Hostess: Mary Louisa Rimbach
Rooms: 4 (PB) $55-65
Full Breakfast
Credit Cards: A, B, C
Notes: 2, 5, 8, 9, 10

Olde Towne Manor

## MARTINS FERRY

### Mulberry Inn Bed and Breakfast

53 N. 4th St., 43935
(614) 633-6058

Victorian frame house built in 1868 by Dr. Ong, the thirteen room home was used as his office. In 1911 Dr. Blackford bought the house and also used three rooms for his practice. The Probsts pur-

chased the home in 1971. It became a bed and breakfast in 1987. The guest rooms are done in different periods. The Roosevelt (1930s) and Country Rooms have queen beds; all others have double beds. Guests have a beautiful parlor in which to relax and a private dining room. There is a wood-burning fireplace, for cold winter nights. Homemade quilts, up-down lights, pocket doors, antiques, three stairways. Five minutes from Olgebay Park, famous for its Festival of Lights November through February.

Hosts: Charles and Shirley Probst
Rooms: 3 (1PB; 1SB) $45-55
Full Breakfast
Credit Cards: A, B, D
Notes: 2, 5, 7 (over 5), 8, 9, 10, 11, 12

## MILAN

### Gastier Farm Bed and Breakfast

1902 Strecker Road, 44846
(419) 499-2985

The farm homestead has been in the family for over 100 years. Now the farmhouse is available for sharing with travelers. Located two miles west of the Ohio Turnpike exit 7, next to the Norfolk Southern Railroad between Toledo and Cleveland. No pets or smoking. Reservations required.

Hosts: Ted and Donna Gastier
Rooms: 3 (SB) $50
Continental Plus Breakfast
Credit Cards: A, B
Notes: 2, 5, 7, 8, 9, 10

---

5 Open all year; 6 Pets welcome; 7 Children welcome; 8 Tennis nearby; 9 Swimming nearby; 10 Golf nearby; 11 Skiing nearby; 12 May be booked through travel agent.

## MILLERSBURG

### Bigham House Bed and Breakfast and English Tea Room

151 S. Washington St., 44654
(216) 674-2337; (800) 689-6950

A 19th century B&B is located on a quiet street in the historic district of Millersburg, Ohio in the heart of the largest Amish settlement in the world. All rooms with private baths, queen-size beds, air-conditioning, and cable TV. Guest rooms are furnished with a mix of antiques and reproductions. Price includes a full, hearty breakfast.

Hosts: John and Janice Ellis
Rooms: 4 (PB) $55-75
Full Breakfast
Credit Cards: A, B, C, D
Notes: 2, 3, 5, 7, 9, 10, 12

### Indiantree Farm Bed and Breakfast

5488 S.R. 515, 44654
(216) 893-2497

Peaceful lodging a in guest house on a picturesque hilltop farm in the heart of Amish Country, a mile from Walnut Creek. Large front porch, farming with horses, hiking trails. Apartments, with kitchen and bath, for the price of a room. An oasis where time slows and the mood is conversation, not television.

Hosts: Larry D. Miller
Rooms: 3 (PB) $50-60
Continental Breakfast
Credit Cards: none
Notes: 2, 5, 11

## ORRVILLE

### Grandma's House Bed and Breakfast

5598 Chippewa Rd., 44667
(216) 682-5112

Peace and quiet prevail at this 1860s farmhouse with comfortable beds, antiques, and handmade quilts. Located in the heart of Wayne County's rolling farm land, planted in alternating strips of corn, wheat, and soybeans. Several hiking trails meander through the large woods on the hill. Hickory rockers grace the front porch for relaxing and watching the world go by. Few minutes from Amish country.

Hosts: Marilyn and Dave Farver
Rooms: 5 (3PB; 2SB) $55-90
Continental Breakfast
Credit Cards: none
Notes: 2, 5, 7, 8, 9, 10

## OXFORD

### The Duck Pond Bed and Breakfast

6391 Morning Sun Rd., S.R. 732 N., 54056
(513) 523-8914

An 1863 farmhouse situated three miles north of Miami University and uptown Oxford, and two miles south of Hueston Woods State Park, which has an 18-hole golf course, nature trails, boating, swimming, and fishing. Antiquing is just 15 miles away. Come and enjoy the quaintness that only a bed and break-

---

NOTES:  Credit cards accepted:  A  Master Card;  B  Visa;  C  American Express;  D  Discover;
E  Diners Club;  F  Other;  2  Personal checks accepted;  3  Lunch available;  4  Dinner available;

fast can offer. Be our guest and enjoy our famous Hawaiian French toast. Reservations are required, so please call in advance. Cat in residence. The Duck Pond is a member of OBBA (Ohio Bed and Breakfast Association) and has met OBBA standards inspection.

Hosts: Don and Toni Kohlstedt
Rooms: 4 (1PB; 3SB) $50-70 ($10 for extra person)
Full Country Breakfast
Credit Cards: none
Notes: 2, 5, 7 (over 12), 8, 9, 10

The Duck Pond Bed and Breakfast

## PLAIN CITY

## Yoder's Bed and Breakfast

8144 Cemetery Pike, 43064
(614) 873-4489

Located on a 107-acre farm northwest of Columbus. Big Darby Creek runs along the front yard. Excellent bird-watching and fishing in the creek. The house is air-conditioned. Rooms have king and queen beds. No smoking. We are within minutes of two Amish restaurants, gift shops, cheese house, chocolate house, Amish furniture store,

bookstores, and antiques shops. Only about 30 minutes from downtown Columbus.

Hosts: Claribel and Loyd Yoder
Rooms: 4 (1PB; 3SB) $55-65
Full Breakfast
Credit Cards: none
Notes: 2, 5, 9, 10

## RIPLEY

## The Baird House Bed and Breakfast

201 N. Second St., 45167
(513) 392-4918

Built in 1825, the house is on the Historical Register. It is within view of the Ohio River and has three porches, swings, rockers, fireplaces, tea at 4pm, music, relaxation at its best, air-conditioning, king beds, library with books and games, and two bicycles. Our gourmet-style breakfast is served in our formal dining room.

Hosts: Glenn A. and Patricia A. Kittles
Rooms: 3 (1PB; 2SB) $75-90
Full Gourmet Breakfast
Credit Cards: none
Notes: 2, 5, 8, 10

## SANDUSKY

## The 1890 Queen Anne Bed and Breakfast

714 Wayne St., 44870
(419) 626-0391

Spacious accommodations with charm and elegance await guests at the 1890

---

5 Open all year; 6 Pets welcome; 7 Children welcome; 8 Tennis nearby; 9 Swimming nearby; 10 Golf nearby; 11 Skiing nearby; 12 May be booked through travel agent.

Queen Anne B&B in downtown Sandusky. Built of native limestone, this 100-year-old Victorian homelands ambiance and romance for its guests. Three large air-conditioned rooms offer tranquil luxury for relaxation. Beauty abounds in the regal outdoors as viewed from a screened-in porch where continental plus breakfasts are enjoyed. Easy access abounds to beaches, Lake Erie island boat trips, Cedar Point, shopping, and other recreational opportunities. Brochure available upon request.

Hosts: Robert and Joan Kromer
Rooms: 3 (PB) $70-80
Continental Plus Breakfast
Credit Cards: A, B, D
Notes: 2, 5, 8, 9, 10

The 1890 Queen Anne Bed and Breakfast

## SHARON CENTER

### Hart and Mather Guest House

1343 Sharon Copley Rd., P.O. Box 93, 44274
(216) 239-2801

This 1840's home and the Sharon Center circle where it resides are both on the National Register of Historic Places. Lavishly furnished with traditional antiques and reproductions, Hart and Mather Guest House has three guest rooms, all with private baths, and one suite with adjoining sitting room, fireplace, and private bath. All guest rooms have color televisions with VCR and full cable TV.

Hosts: Thomas and Sally Thompson
Rooms: 4 (PB) $69-89 to $99-119
Continental Breakfast (full for additional charge)
Credit Cards: A, B, C, D
Notes: 2, 5, 7, 8, 9, 10, 11

## SIDNEY

### GreatStone Castle

429 N. Ohio Ave., 45365
(513) 498-4728; FAX (513) 498-9950

Great Stone Castle, registered with the National Historical Society, is a 100-year-old mansion on two beautiful acres. The Castle is constructed of 18-inch limestone with three turrets and is finished with rare, imported hardwood. Antique furniture, fireplaces, and fine furnishings help complete the elegant setting. Deluxe continental breakfast served in conservatory.

Hosts: Frederick and Victoria Keller
Rooms: 5 (3PB; 2SB) $60-90
Deluxe Continental Breakfast
Credit Cards: A, B, C
Notes: 2, 5, 6, 10

Great Stone Castle

NOTES: Credit cards accepted: A Master Card; B Visa; C American Express; D Discover; E Diners Club; F Other; 2 Personal checks accepted; 3 Lunch available; 4 Dinner available;

## STRASBURG

### Ellis's Bed and Breakfast

104 4th St. SW, 44680
(216) 878-7863

Our turn-of-the-century home is comfortably furnished for your "home away from home." A big screen TV in the sunken living room and a secluded patio are for your relaxation. A tasty, complete breakfast, different each morning, is served in the dining room using our best china, silver, etc. We are conveniently located for Zoar, Amish Country, Dover/New Philadelphia, and Canton. Antiques, flea markets, gift shops, and restaurants abound. No smoking, please.

Hosts: Tom and Grace Ellis
Rooms: 3 (SB) $50 ($35 single)
Full Breakfast
Credit Cards: none
Notes: 2, 5, 7

## SUGARCREEK

### Marbeyo B&B

2370 CR 144, 44681
(216) 852-4533

Hosted by an Amish/Mennonite family. Four rooms, private bath, complimentary continental breakfast. 100 acre farm with freedom to enjoy pets and walking at you leisure. Families welcome. One mile east of Walnut Creek on County Road 144.

Hosts: Mark and Betty Yoder
Rooms: 4 (PB) $55
Continental Breakfast
Credit Cards: A, B
Notes: 2, 5, 7, 10

## SUGAR GROVE

### Hickory Bend Bed and Breakfast

7541 Dupler Rd. SE, 43155
(614) 746-8381

Nestled in the Hocking Hills of southeastern Ohio on ten wooded acres. "So peaceful, we got out to watch the car go by on Sunday afternoon," says Pat. Patty is a spinner and a weaver. The cozy, private room with private bath is located outside the home in the midst of dogwood, poplar, and oak trees. Guests come to the home for breakfast and conversation. Heated in the winter and cooled in the summer. Write for brochure.

Hosts: Pat and Patty Peery
Rooms: 1 (PB) $50
Full Breakfast
Credit Cards: none
Notes: 2, 10

## TIFFIN

### Mad River Railroad Bed and Breakfast

107 W. Perry St., 44883
(419) 477-2222 or (419) 477-0665

Relax in the comfort of the Colonial Revival home built in the late 1890s. Three guest rooms are provided in the historically registered home, decorated with antiques and period furnishings. The house is situated beside the former site of the first railroad in the area which now has been transformed into a tree and flower adorned walk and bike path

---

5 Open all year; 6 Pets welcome; 7 Children welcome; 8 Tennis nearby; 9 Swimming nearby; 10 Golf nearby; 11 Skiing nearby; 12 May be booked through travel agent.

for your enjoyment. Cedar Point and Lake Erie attractions within one hour. Our home is open for your pleasure while you visit us.

Hosts: Bill and Nancy Cook
Rooms: 3 (2PB; 1SB) $55-65
Full Breakfast
Credit Cards: none
Notes: 2; 7

The Willowtree Inn

## TIPP CITY

### The Willowtree Inn
1900 West St. Route 571, 45371
(513) 667-2957

Nestled on five country acres and surrounded by rolling fields. The WILLOWTREE INN is the perfect getaway. An ancient willow tree drowses by a spring-fed pond while ducks lazily paddle by. It's a place to relax, kick your shoes off, and enjoy good old-fashioned hospitality. Built in 1830, our 6,000 square foot historic estate has been fully restored. The original wide plank, ash floors and built-in book-

shelves add elegance to the front parlor, where guests gather for complimentary evening refreshments.

Hosts: Charles H. Sell, II and Jolene K. Sell
Rooms: 3 (PB) $69-89
Full Breakfast
Credit Cards: A, B
Notes: 2, 5, 7, 8, 9, 10

## URBANA

### At Home in Urbana Bed and Breakfast
301 Scioto St., 43078
(513) 653-8595; (800) 800-0970;
FAX (513) 652-4400

Restored 1842 home in historic district. Furnished in Victorian period pieces and family antiques. Two blocks away from downtown shops and restaurants. All rooms are air-conditioned and have private baths. Non-smoking guests only.

Hosts: Grant and Shirley Ingersoll
Rooms: 3 + 1 suite (PB) $60-90
Full Breakfast
Credit Cards: A, B, C, D
Notes: 2, 5, 10, 11

## WAKEMAN

### Melrose Farm
727 Vesta Rd., 44889
(419) 929-1867

Situated halfway between Ashland and Oberlin, Melrose Farm is a peaceful country retreat. Each of the three lovely guestrooms in the 125-year-old brick house has its own private bath. Guests will enjoy the tennis court, stocked pond, perennial gardens, and quiet rural setting. Thirty miles from Cedar Point, one hours drive from Cleveland or Toledo, and two hours from Columbus. Old-fashioned relaxed hospitality.

Hosts: Abe and Eleanor Klassen
Rooms: 3 (PB) $75
Full Breakfast
Credit Cards: none
Notes: 2, 3, 5, 7, 8 (on-site), 9, 10

Melrose Farm

## WAVERLY

### *Governor's Lodge*
171 Gregg Rd., 45690
(614) 947-2266

Governor's Lodge is a place like no other. Imagine a beautiful, shimmering lake and an iridescent sunset. A quiet calm in the friendly atmosphere of an eight room bed and breakfast open all year and situated on a peninsula on Lake White. Every room has a mag-

nificent view. An affiliate of Bristol Village Retirement Community, we offer a meeting room and group rates for gatherings using the whole lodge. Now approved by AAA.

Hosts: David and Jeannie James
Rooms: 8 + 1 cottage (PB) $44-68
Continental Plus Breakfast
Credit Cards: A, B
Notes: 2, 7, 9, 11

## WILMOT

### *Raber's Tri County View*
P.O. Box 155, 44689
(216) 359-5189

Located in the world's largest Amish settlement, with lots of rolling hills and fields all around. Each room has its own unique, peaceful atmosphere and decor, with a private bath, queen-size beds, central heating and air, microwave, refigerator, and coffee pot. A garden swing where you can relax and enjoy the view of three different counties. No smoking inside. One mile from Wilmot, ten miles from Berlin, Walnut Creek, and Kidron. Lots of quilts, antiques, and craft shops, cheese houses, furniture stores, and the best restaurants in the state.

Hosts: Ed and Esther Raber
Rooms: 3 + 1 suite (PB) $55-85
Full Breakfast
Credit Cards: A, B
Notes: 2, 5, 7, 8, 9, 10

5 Open all year; 6 Pets welcome; 7 Children welcome; 8 Tennis nearby; 9 Swimming nearby; 10 Golf nearby; 11 Skiing nearby; 12 May be booked through travel agent.

## WOOSTER

### Historic Overholt House Bed and Breakfast

1473 Beall Ave., 44691
(216) 263-6300; (800) 992-0643

Millennium Classic Bed and Breakfast

Elegantly decorated, "Stick Style Victorian," historic home with a rare solid walnut "flying staircase," is located at the gateway to Amish Country. Romantic packages, mystery evening, and gift certificates available. Enjoy a full breakfast with homemade breads and goodies. AAA approved.

Hostesses: Sandy Pohalski and Bobbie Walton
Rooms: 3 (PB) $63-70
Full Breakfast
Credit Cards: A, B, D
Notes: 2, 5, 8, 9, 10

### Millenium Classic Bed and Breakfast

1626 Beall Avenue, 44691
(216) 264-6005; (800) 937-4199;
FAX (216) 264-5008

Millennium Classic Bed and Breakfast is centrally located right in the heart of Wooster. Close to College of Wooster, hospital, shopping mall, restaurants, grocery store, and the bus stops in front of house. A Post Victorian architectural style exterior home, following traditional, classic theme in the interior. Lots of decks, porches, quiet sitting areas, and shade trees. A friendly, homelike atmosphere.

Historic Overholt House Bed and Breakfast

Innkeeper: John Byler
Rooms: 6 (3PB; 1SB) $55-65
Continental Breakfast
Credit Cards: A, B
Notes: 2, 5, 7, 8, 10, 12

NOTES: Credit cards accepted: A Master Card; B Visa; C American Express; D Discover; E Diners Club; F Other; 2 Personal checks accepted; 3 Lunch available; 4 Dinner available;

# Oklahoma

Heritage Manor

Close to Salenite Crystal digging area and several other attractions.

Hosts: A.J. and Carolyn Rexroat
Rooms: 4 (3SB) $50 + tax
Full Breakfast
Credit Cards: none
Notes: 2, 3 and 4 (by reservation), 5, 6 and 7 (by arrangement), 9, 10 (30 miles)

## ALPINE

### Heritage Manor
R.R. 2, Box 33, 73716
(405) 463-2563 or (405) 463-2566;
(800) 295-2563

Heritage Manor is a country getaway on 80 acres that was settled in the 1893 Land Run in northwest Oklahoma. Two pre-statehood homes have been joined together and restored by innkeepers using a Victorian theme. Beautiful sunrises, sunsets, and stargazing from rooftop deck and relaxing in the hot tub or reading a book from the 5,000-volume library. Ostriches, donkeys, and Scotch Highland cattle roam a fenced area.

## EDMOND

### The Arcadian Inn
328 E. First St., 73003
(405) 348-6347; (800) 299-6347

With angels watching over you, you are ministered peace and relaxation. The Arcadian Inn is a step back in time to the era of Christian love, hospitality, and family values. The historical home of Dr. Ruhl, the inn has five luxurious Victorian guests rooms with tubs, fireplaces, canopy beds, and sunrooms. Sumptuous homemade breakfast served in the sunny dining room beneath cherub paintings. Perfect for romantic getaways, business travelers, or old-fashioned family gatherings. Jacuzzi

---

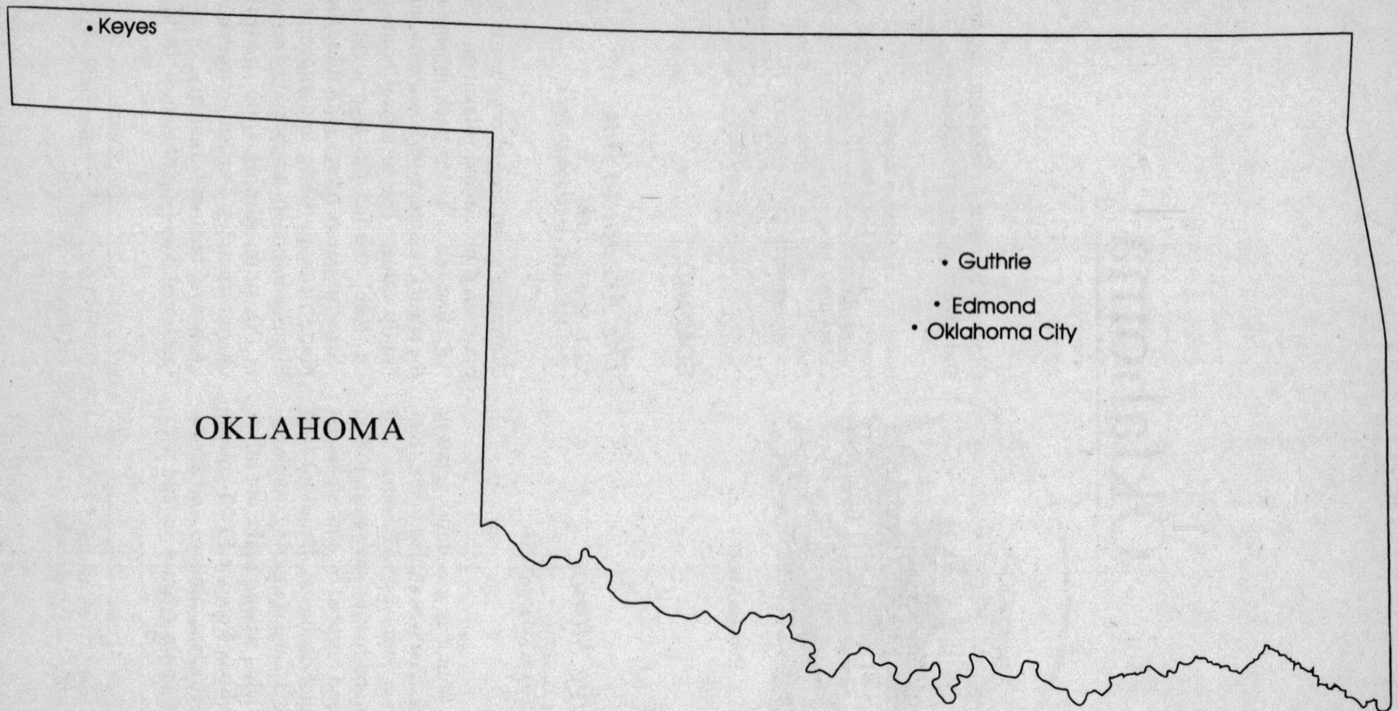

OKLAHOMA

• Keyes

• Guthrie
• Edmond
• Oklahoma City

and outdoor spa available.

Hosts: Martha and Gary Hall
Rooms: 6 (PB) $85-195
Full Breakfast
Credit Cards: A, B, C, D
Notes: 2, 4 (by reservation), 5, 8, 9, 10

The Arcadian Inn

## GUTHRIE

### Victorian Rose B&B

415 E. Cleveland, 73044
(405) 282-3928

The 100-year-old Queen Anne-style home, built in 1894, mixes the charm of the past with the comforts of the present. Located on a brick street and features a wraparound porch with gingerbread accents, with porch swing and garden area. Lovely restoration with quality workmanship are displayed with beautiful oak floors, exquisite original beveled windows, gleaming brass light fixtures, and antiques. Located three blocks from historic downtown (the largest urban historical fistrict in the U.S.). Three beautiful Victorian guest rooms offer queen-size beds and private

baths. Full, complementary, gourmet breakfast. Family rates and gift certificates available.

Hosts: Linda and Foy Shahan
Rooms: 3 (PB) $69-79
Full Gourmet Breakfast
Credit Cards: A, B, D
Notes: 2, 5, 7, 8, 9, 10, 12

Victorian Rose Bed and Breakfast

## KEYES

### Cattle Country Inn

HCR 1, Box 34, 73947
(405) 543-6458

We are truly country located. If you like wide open spaces where you can see for miles and not be in hearing distance of any highway traffic, you are welcome to stay with us. Located in the panhandle between Guymon and Boise City, the Inn is a nice stopping place on the way to or from the Rockies. Come experience the hospitality and hearty cookin' served up by your host in the beautiful, spacious, and very modern ranch-style home. Located 38 miles

---

NOTES: Credit cards accepted: A Master Card; B Visa; C American Express; D Discover; E Diners Club; F Other; 2 Personal checks accepted; 3 Lunch available; 4 Dinner available; 5 Open all year; 6 Pets welcome; 7 Children welcome; 8 Tennis nearby; 9 Swimming nearby; 10 Golf nearby; 11 Skiing nearby; 12 May be booked through travel agent.

west of Guymon on Hwy. 64 then eight and one half miles south on dirt roads. Cimaron County, the last county west, has many points of interest, as well as plenty of good prairie dog and pheasant hunting.

Hosts: Lane and Karen Sparkman
Rooms: 6 (3SB) $45-65
Full Breakfast
Credit Cards: A, B, C
Notes: 2, 3, 4, 5, and 7 (all by reservation)

## OKLAHOMA CITY

## *The Grandison B&B*

1841 NW 15th, 73106
(405) 521-0011 (voice and FAX);
(800) 240-INNS

This three-story, country Victorian sits on a large double lot with beautifully landscaped gardens, trees taller than the house, and a gazebo. Built in 1912, the home has all the original brass and crystal chandeliers and stained glass windows. It is furnished throughout with antiques from the turn-of-the-century. There is a jacuzzi in the third-floor suite. Just ten minutes from Myriad Gardens and Convention Center, State Fairgrounds, Remington Park Raceway, Oklahoma City Zoo, The National Cowboy Hall of Fame, and many wonderful restaurants and shopping facilities.

Hosts: Claudia and Bob Wright
Rooms: 5 (PB) $55-125
Full Breakfast
Credit Cards: A, B, C, D
Notes: 2, 3, 4, 5, 6 and 7 (by reservation)

NOTES: Credit cards accepted: A Master Card; B Visa; C American Express; D Discover; E Diners Club; F Other; 2 Personal checks accepted; 3 Lunch available; 4 Dinner available;

# Oregon

## ASHLAND

### Cowslip's Belle
### Bed and Breakfast

159 N. Main St., 97520
(503) 488-2901; (800) 888-6819

Teddy Bears and chocolate truffles, roses, antiques, cozy down comforters, and scrumptious breakfasts. Just three blocks to restaurants, shops, and theaters. Nestled in Ashland's historic district, this beautiful 1913 Craftsman bungalow and carriage house is featured in "Northwest Best Places," "The Best Places to Kiss in the Pacific Northwest," and "Weekends for Two in the Pacific Northwest—50 Romantic Getaways."

Hosts: Jon and Carmen Reinhardt
Rooms: 4 (PB) $75-120
Full Breakfast
Credit Cards: A, B
Notes: 2, 5, 8, 9, 10, 11, 12

### The Redwing
### Bed and Breakfast

115 N. Main St., 97520
(503) 482-1807; (800) 461-6743

The Redwing, nestled in Ashland's charming historic district, is a 1911 craftsman-style home with its original lighting fixtures, beautiful wood, and comfortable decor. Each of our inviting guest rooms enjoy its own distinctive intimacy, queen-size beds, and private bath. We are located one city block from the Shakespeare Festival, Lithia Park, restaurants, and gift shops. In addition, downhill and cross-country skiing, river rafting, and fishing are nearby. Full breakfasts are offered.

Hosts: Mike and Judi Cook
Rooms: 3 (PB) $70-97
Full Breakfast
Credit Cards: A, B, D
Notes: 2, 5, 8, 9, 10, 11

## ASTORIA

### Columbia River Inn
### Bed and Breakfast

1681 Franklin Ave., 97103
(503) 325-5044; (800) 953-5044

Columbia River Inn Bed and Breakfast is charming in every way. Built in 1870, this beautiful "Painted Lady" Victorian now has a gazebo for weddings and parties. Come see the unique gardens

---

5 Open all year;  6 Pets welcome;  7 Children welcome;  8 Tennis nearby;  9 Swimming nearby;
10 Golf nearby;  11 Skiing nearby;  12 May be booked through travel agent.

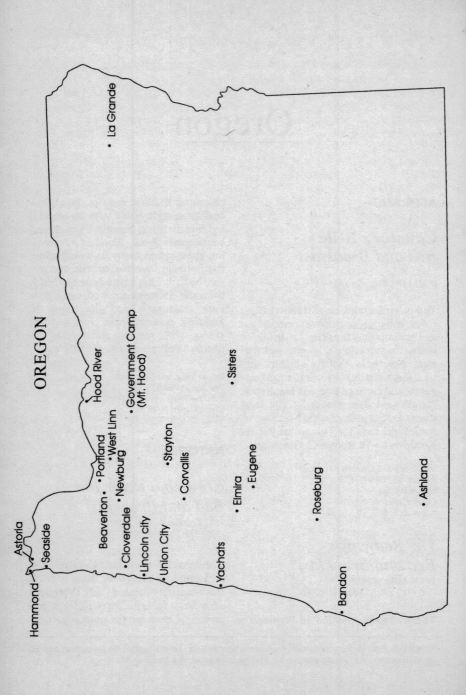

and "stairway to the stars." Many memories are discovered and the experience will last forever. My specialty is hospitality, "Home is where the heart is." Off-street parking available.

Hostess: Mrs. Karen N. Nelson
Rooms: 5 (PB) $70-100
Full Breakfast
Credit Cards: A, B
Notes: 2, 5, 7, 10

## Grandview
## Bed and Breakfast

1574 Grand Ave., 97103
(503) 325-5555; (800) 488-3250

Antiques and white wicker furnishings grace this Victorian home, born in 1896. Ivy and alders grow profusely on west side, sheltering birds and birdhouses. Most rooms have bird cages for decoration. Some rooms overlook the Columbia River. Breakfast, served in the tower of bullet turret, may include smoked salmon, cream cheese, and bagels. Astoria was established in 1811. Fur trading, then salmon and logging gave this town its start.

Hostess: Charleen Maxwell
Rooms: 9 (7PB; 2SB) $39-92
Full Breakfast
Credit Cards: A, B, D
Notes: 5, 7 (over 6), 8, 9, 10

## Inn-Chanted
## Bed and Breakfast

707 Eighth St., 97103
(503) 325-5223; (800) 455-7018

The historic Fulton House, built in 1883, is beautifully decorated with silk brocade wallpaper, crystal chandeliers, and ornately painted medallions and columns. Guest rooms have magnificent views of the Columbia River, private baths, queen-size beds, and TVs. Full gourmet breakfasts. Dolls and trains displayed. Within walking distance to historic buildings, town, and antique shops.

Hosts: Richard and Dixie Swart
Rooms: 3 (PB) $70-100
Full Breakfast
Credit Cards: A, B, C, D
Notes: 2, 5, 7, 8, 12

Inn-Chanted Bed and Breakfast

## BANDON

## Sea Star Guesthouse

370 First St., 97411
(503) 347-9632; FAX (503) 347-9533

A uniquely designed coastal getaway in historic Old Town Bawdon, located right in the harbor with an incredible view of the water and beach from each unit and deck. Our in-season rates are affordable and we offer special off-sea-

---

NOTES: Credit cards accepted: A Master Card; B Visa; C American Express; D Discover; E Diners Club; F Other; 2 Personal checks accepted; 3 Lunch available; 4 Dinner available; 5 Open all year; 6 Pets welcome; 7 Children welcome; 8 Tennis nearby; 9 Swimming nearby; 10 Golf nearby; 11 Skiing nearby; 12 May be booked through travel agent.

son rates. Sleeping rooms and full suites have private baths, cable TV, and queen beds. Wonderful meals are available in our award-winning Bistro.

Hostess: Eileen Sexton
Rooms: 4 (PB) $40-85
Full or Continental Breakfast
Credit Cards: A, B
Notes: 3, 4, 5, 7, 9, 10

## BEAVERTON

## The Yankee Tinker Bed and Breakfast

5480 SW 183rd Ave., 97007
(503) 649-0932 (voice and FAX)

"A hand-crafted New England experience in the heart of Northwest Oregon." Located ten miles west of Portland in a peaceful residential neighborhood. From here, visit wineries, farmers' markets, historical sites as well as the dramatic Columbia River Gorge and grand Oregon beaches. Three distinctive guest rooms with comfortable beds are graced by a fireplace and TV; private yard has spacious deck and gardens. Memorable breakfasts, served alfresco weather permitting, are designed to accommodate special dietary needs and your schedule. The mouthwatering choices might include blueberry pancakes or muffins, peaches 'n cream French toast, or herbed omelets. The traditional Yankee offering of pie for breakfast is available for a hearty eater. Benefit from "all the extras" that make your business or leisure travel successful. The *Yankee Tinker's* warmth and hospitality will convince you to linger an extra day or

two as well as to plan a return visit.

Hosts: Jan and Ralph Wadleigh
Rooms: 3 (2PB; 2SB) $60-70
Full Breakfast
Credit Cards: A, B, C, D, E
Notes: 2, 5, 9, 10, 12

## CLOVERDALE

## Sandlake Country Inn

8505 Galloway Rd., 97112
(503) 965-6745; FAX (503) 965-7425

Sshhh. . .we're a secret hideaway on the awesome Oregon Coast, a private, peaceful place for making memories. This 1894 shipwreck-timbered farmhouse on the Oregon Historic Registry is tucked into a bower of old roses. Hummingbirds, Mozart, cookies at midnight, marble fireplaces, whirlpools for two, honeymoon cottage, breakfast "en suite," vintage movies, "green" rooms, no smoking, wheelchair accessible, closed-captioned TV.

Hosts: Femke and David Durham
Rooms: 4 (PB) $80-125
Full Breakfast
Credit Cards: A, B, D
Notes: 2, 5, 12

Sandlake Country Inn

NOTES: Credit cards accepted: A Master Card; B Visa; C American Express; D Discover; E Diners Club; F Other; 2 Personal checks accepted; 3 Lunch available; 4 Dinner available;

Abed and Breakfast at Spark's Hearth

## CORVALLIS

### Abed and Breakfast at Spark's Hearth

2515 SW 45th St., 97333
(503) 757-7321

Our country home of 22 years is on the Corvallis Country Club golf course in the midst of peace, quiet, and serenity. Three miles to downtown and OSU. Guest amenities include outdoor spa, luxurious robes, wraparound porch, large decks, spacious living room, and warm hospitality. King beds in king-size rooms. Sumptuous breakfasts feature a fruit compote, hot entree, and homemade pie. Coffee and soft drinks anytime—help yourself!

Hosts: Neoma and Herb Sparks
Rooms: 4 (2PB; 2SB) $65-85
Full Breakfast
Credit Cards: A, B, C, D
Notes: 2, 5, 7 (over 8), 8, 9, 10

## ELMIRA

### McGillivray's Log Home Bed and Breakfast

88680 Evers Rd., 97437
(503) 935-3564

Fourteen miles west of Eugene, on the way to the coast, you will find the best of yesterday and the comforts of today. King beds, air-conditioning, and quiet. Old-fashioned breakfasts are usually prepared on an antique, wood-burning cookstove. This built-from-scratch 1982 log home is near Fern Ridge Lake.

Hostess: Evelyn McGillivray
Rooms: 2 (PB) $50-70
Full Breakfast
Credit Cards: A, B
Notes: 2, 5

## EUGENE

### Camille's Bed and Breakfast

3277 Onyx Place, 97405
(503) 344-9576; FAX (503) 345-9970

Camille's Bed and Breakfast is a 60s contemporary home in quiet, woodsy neighborhood furnished with American country antiques. Rooms are wonderfully comfortable queen beds, with work space. Cozy guest sitting room with phone and TV. Full hearty breakfast. Located just over a mile south of the University of Oregon, downtown is just minutes away. Bike path and park with major jogging path nearby. Excellent restaurant within walking distance. One hour drive to Oregon coast.

Hosts: Bill and Camille Kievith
Rooms: 2 (1PB; 2SB) $55-70
Full Breakfast
Credit Cards: none
Notes: 2, 5, 8, 9, 10

---

5 Open all year; 6 Pets welcome; 7 Children welcome; 8 Tennis nearby; 9 Swimming nearby; 10 Golf nearby; 11 Skiing nearby; 12 May be booked through travel agent.

## The Campbell House, A City Inn

252 Pearl, 97401
(503) 343-1119; (800) 264-2519;
FAX (503) 343-2258

Splendor and romance in the tradition of a fine European hotel. Each of the elegant rooms feature private bath, TV/VCR, telephone, and robes. Selected rooms feature a four-poster bed, fireplace, and jetted or clawfoot tub. Take pleasure from the Old World ambiance of the parlor and library with a fine selection of books and videos to choose from. Walking distance to restaurants, theaters, museums, and shops. Two blocks from nine miles of riverside bike paths and jogging trails.

Hostesses: Mrya Plant and Sonja Cruthers
Rooms: 14 (PB) $80-225
Full Breakfast
Credit Cards: A, B, C
Notes: 5, 7, 10, 12

## Kjaer's House in the Woods Bed and Breakfast

814 Lorane Hwy., 97405
(503) 343-3234

This 1910 Craftsman home in a park-like setting provides urban convenience and suburban tranquillity. The grounds have both wildflowers and landscaped shrubs, colorful in the spring but peaceful throughout the year; wildlife is abundant. The home is furnished with antiques, Oriental carpets, a square rosewood grand piano, an extensive music library, and a plate collection. A full

breakfast is served featuring local cheeses, nuts, and fruits. In operation since 1984 this B&B is inspected by the Eugene Area B&B Association and the Oregon B&B Guild. Hosts are long time Eugene residents who take pleasure in sharing their knowledge of the area with guests.

Hosts: George and Eunice Kjaer
Rooms: 2 (PB) $55-75
Full Breakfast
Credit Cards: none
Notes: 2, 5, 7, 8, 9, 10, 12

Kjaer's House in the Woods Bed and Breakfast

## HAMMOND

## Officers' Inn Bed and Breakfast

540 Russell Place; 97121
(503) 861-0884; (800) 377-2524

Once the guardian of the mighty Columbia River, Officers' Inn is located in quiet Fort Stevens, Hammond, Oregon (between Astoria and Seaside). The Inn is a spacious 8,000 square-foot duplex originally built in 1905 to house Army Officers, and now is on the Register of National Historic Places. In the foyers of the Inn, one can view the grand staircases leading to the eight spacious

---

NOTES: Credit cards accepted: A Master Card; B Visa; C American Express; D Discover; E Diners Club; F Other; 2 Personal checks accepted; 3 Lunch available; 4 Dinner available;

Victorian guest rooms.

Hosts: Trent and Pat Townley
Rooms: 9 (PB) $65-95
Full Breakfast
Credit Cards: A, B, C, D, E
Notes: 2, 4 (for groups), 7, 9

## HOOD RIVER

## *The Upper Rooms on Avalon*

3444 Avalon Drive, 97031
(503) 386-2560

Down home charm in our renovated Avalon farmhouse on the Heights in Hood River. Just minutes from skiing, windsurfing, and other outdoor recreation. Cozy neighborhood with little traffic noise and yet just bordering city limits. Deck and large upstairs bedrooms with views of Mt. Adams. Relaxed friendly atmosphere. Family style breakfast. Barbeque available. Reasonable rates.

Hosts: Jim and Dorothy Tollen
Rooms: 2 (SB) $65
Full Breakfast
Credit Cards: A, B
Notes: 5, 7, 8, 9, 10, 11

The Upper Rooms on Avalon

## LA GRANDE

## *Stang Manor Inn*

1612 Walnut, 97850
(503) 963-2400 (voice and FAX)

Capturing the romance and elegance of a former era, Stang Manor is a lovingly preserved, Georgian Colonial home which beckons even the casual traveler to bask in its comfort and hospitality. One of the rooms adjoins a balcony overlooking the rose garden. The suite features a large fireplace in its comfortable sitting room. Extraordinary woodwork throughout the house serves as a reminder that the original owner, August Stange, spared no expense to make this 1920s mansion a masterpiece. Full breakfast in the formal dining room sparkles with silver, crystal, candles, and conversation.

Hosts: Marjorie and Pat McClure
Rooms: 4 (PB) $70-90 (includes tax)
Full Breakfast
Credit Cards: A, B, D
Notes: 2, 5, 10, 11, 12

## LINCOLN CITY

## *Brey House "OCEAN VIEW" Bed and Breakfast Inn*

3725 NW Keel Ave., 97365
(503) 994-7123

The ocean awaits you just across the street. Enjoy whale-watching, storm-

---

5 Open all year; 6 Pets welcome; 7 Children welcome; 8 Tennis nearby; 9 Swimming nearby;
10 Golf nearby; 11 Skiing nearby; 12 May be booked through travel agent.

watching, or just beach-combing. We are conveniently located a short walking distance away from local restaurants and retail shops. Four beautiful rooms to choose from, all with private baths and queen beds. Flannel sheets and electric blankets in all rooms. Enjoy Milt and Shirley's talked-about breakfast. Three-story, Cape Code style house.

Hosts: Milt and Shirley Brey
Rooms: 4 (PB) $65-125
Full Breakfast
Credit Cards: A, B, D
Notes 2, 5, 9, 10, 12

Falcon's Crest Inn

## MOUNT HOOD AREA

## *Falcon's Crest Inn*

P.O. Box 185, 87287 Government Camp Loop Hwy., **Government Camp** 97028
(503) 272-3403; (800) 624-7384 (reservations);
FAX (503) 272-3454

Falcon's Crest Inn is a beautiful mountain lodge/chalet-style house, architecturally designed to fit into the quiet natural forest and majestic setting of the Cascades. Conveniently located at the intersection of Highway 26 and the Government Camp Loop Highway, it is within walking distance to Ski Bowl, a year-round playground featuring downhill skiing in the winter and the Alpine Slide in the summer! The Inn has five suites, all with private baths. Each guest room is individually decorated with interesting and unique collectibles and views of mountains and forest. Telephones are available for guest use in each suite. Smoking restricted. Fine dining restaurant on premises and ski packages available!

Hosts: B.J. and Melody Johnson
Rooms: 5 (PB) $85-179
Full Breakfast
Credit Cards: A, B, C, D
Notes: 2, 4, 5, 9, 10, 11, 12

## NEWBERG

## *Secluded Bed and Breakfast*

19719 NE Williamson Rd., 97132
(503) 538-2635

This secluded, beautiful, country home on ten acres is an ideal retreat in a wooded setting for hiking, walking in the country, and observing wildlife. Located near Newberg behind the beautiful Red Hills of Dundee, it is convenient to George Fox College. McMinnville is a 20-minute drive, and the Oregon coast is one hour away. A delectable breakfast varies for your pleasure, tempting you with succulent fresh, farm fruit from the famous Willamette Valley of Oregon. The home has many antiques, collectibles and

---

NOTES: Credit cards accepted: A Master Card; B Visa; C American Express; D Discover; E Diners Club; F Other; 2 Personal checks accepted; 3 Lunch available; 4 Dinner available;

stained glass in each room.

Hosts: Del and Durell Belanger
Rooms: 2 (1PB; 1SB) $50-60
Full Gourmet Breakfast
Credit Cards: none
Notes: 2, 5, 7, 8, 9, 10, 11, 12

Secluded Bed and Breakfast

## PORTLAND

## John Palmer House

4314 N. Mississippi Ave., 97217
(503) 284-5893; FAX (503) 284-7789

This Victorian inn is run by three generations of the same family, and you
become one of the family the moment
you enter the door. We are told we serve
the best breakfast in town. Close to the
ocean and the mountains. Make this
your home away from home whether on
business or vacation.

Rooms: 7 (2PB; 6SB) $45-125
Full Breakfast
Credit Cards: A, B, C, D
Notes: 2, 5, 7 (by arrangement), 8, 9, 10, 11, 12
(with restrictions)

## ROSEBURG

## Hokanson's Guest House

848 SE Jackson, 97470
(503) 672-2632; FAX (503) 673-5253

Gracefully standing on land once owned
by Roseberg's founding father, Aaron
Rose, the Guest House is Douglas
County's only B&B on the National
Historic Register. The Gothic Revival
style house was built in 1882. Close to
downtown shops. No pets and no children under 12. Phone service and TV
available. Smoking on porches only.
Two rooms with private baths. Full
Breakfast and dinner upon request. Discounts available.

Hosts: John and Victoria Hokanson
Rooms: 2 (PB) $65-85
Full or Continental Breakfast
Credit Cards: A, B
Notes: 2, 4, 5, 7 (over 12), 8, 9, 10

## SEASIDE

## 10th Avenue Inn Bed and Breakfast

125 10th Ave., 97138
(503) 738-0643 (voice and FAX);
(800) 569-1114

Enjoy this 1908 ocean view home just
steps from the beach and a short walk
on the promenade to restaurants and
shopping. Light, airy guest rooms are
decorated in soft colors, sprinkled in
antiques, and include TVs. Full break-

---

5 Open all year; 6 Pets welcome; 7 Children welcome; 8 Tennis nearby; 9 Swimming nearby;
10 Golf nearby; 11 Skiing nearby; 12 May be booked through travel agent.

fast. Please no smoking or pets. Vacation rental available; sleeps seven.

Hosts: Francie and Vern Starkey
Rooms: 4 (PB) $55-70 + tax
Full Breakfast
Credit Cards: A, B
Notes: 2, 5, 7 (over 9), 8, 9, 10

10th Avenue Inn Bed and Breakfast

## SISTERS

## Cascade Country Inn

15870 Barclay Dr., 97759
(503) 549-4666; (800) 316-0089

With a panoramic view of the snow-capped Cascades, Cascade Country Inn is an elegant, yet homey retreat for those who are looking for the best. Antiques, hand-painted murals, delicate stenciling and custom stained glass greet you from sun-filled rooms. Handmade quilts, overstuffed sofas, and afghans throughout create the feeling of coming home.

Celebrate weddings, honeymoons, anniversaries, birthdays, family reunions, or just "time away." Fly in and taxi to an open door of country charm; or drive in. Come create a memory with us!

Hostesses: Judy and Victoria Tolonen
Rooms: 6 (PB) $100-125
Full Breakfast
Credit Cards: none
Notes: 2, 5, 7, 8, 10, 11

Conklin's Guest House

## Conklin's Guest House

69013 Camp Polk Rd., 97759
(503) 549-0123; (800) 549-4262

Conklin's Guest House is surrounded by a sprawling meadow with a panoramic backdrop of snow-capped peaks. Rich in history, the near century-old homesite gives evidence that early settlers chose the most beautiful sites first! Modern conveniences and attention to detail ensure a comfortable and restful stay. The house offers guests a truly peaceful environment within walking distance of the bustling shops and restaurants of Sisters. Guests are welcome to use the barbecue, swimming pool, laundry facilities, and to otherwise *be at home!* The ponds are stocked with trout for catch and release fishing. The

NOTES: Credit cards accepted: A Master Card; B Visa; C American Express; D Discover; E Diners Club; F Other; 2 Personal checks accepted; 3 Lunch available; 4 Dinner available;

Sisters area has something for everyone from rafting and rock climbing to dining and shopping and much more, all the time!

Hosts: Marie and Frank Conklin
Rooms: 5 (2PB; 3SB) $70-110
Full Breakfast
Credit Cards: none
Notes: 2, 5, 7 (over 5), 8, 9, 10, 11

## STAYTON

### Gardner House
### Bed and Breakfast

633 North Third Ave., 97383
(503) 769-6331

Well house suite! This extraordinary suite has coordinated decor, a separate entrance, kitchen, dining room, large bathroom, sitting room, queen size bed, telephone, CATV, and VCR. The Madonna Room is in the main house and has much the same as the Well Suite. The dining room is on the same floor in a glassed-in porch. A bright room on any day.

Host: Richard Jungwirth
Rooms: 2 (PB) $55-65
Full Breakfast
Credit Cards: A, B, C, D, E
Notes: 2, 3, 4, 5, 6, 7, 8, 9, 10, 11

Gardner House Bed and Breakfast

## WELCHES

### Doublegate Inn
### Bed and Breakfast

26711 E. Welches Rd., 97067
(503) 622-4859

The house, which has now become the Doublegate Inn B&B, has been a landmark in the Mt. Hood area since it was built in the 1920s. Commonly referred to as "the house with the rock wall" and located just one block from a golf course, the B&B sits serenely atop a cedar treed knoll with a view of the Salmon River behind. The beautifully decorated Inn filled with crafts and antiques, features four distinctly styled guest rooms, each with private baths and some with spa tubs. The Doublegate Inn is quietly yet conveniently located near the many diverse activities found on and around scenic Mt. Hood. Be spoiled and refreshed and find the romance in "God's Country" just off the Oregon Trail! Sumptuous "no lunch" breakfasts served "en suite" on the deck or fireside in the dining room.

Hosts: Gary and Charlene Poston
Rooms: 4 (PB) $80-115
Full Breakfast
Credit Cards: none
Notes: 2, 5, 7 (over 12), 8, 9, 10, 11

## WEST LINN

### Swift Shore Chalet

1190 Swift Shore, 97068
(503) 650-3853 (voice and FAX)

"The perfect getaway...a time to relax in the quietness of a beautiful home, surrounded by a panoramic view of hillsides covered with trees, a garden filled with the fragrance of flowers, and songs of birds. A full breakfast, beautifully served on the deck or in the dining room, includes warm scones, cinnamon rolls, fruit sorbets, waffles, pancakes, quiches, and much more. Let yourself be pampered and served with quiet attention to detail. Just minutes to downtown Portland or many outlying attractions."

Hosts: Nancy and Horace Duke
Rooms: 2 (SB) $70 + tax
Full Breakfast
Credit Cards: A, B, C, D
Notes: 2, 5, 7, 10, 11

## YACHATS

### Serenity Bed and Breakfast

5985 Yachats River Rd., 97498
(503) 547-3813

Wholesome retreat nestled in the lush Yachats Valley. Gentle place to relax after countryside, forest, and tide pool exploration or bird-watching. Minutes from Cape Perpetua, Sea Lion Caves, and the Oregon Coast Aquarium. Elegant European comfort with private two-person jacuzzi tubs. Centrally located between Newport and Florence, Yachats is the gem of the Oregon Coast. German cooking at its best. Featured in "The Best Places to Kiss in the Northwest."

Hosts: Sam and Baerbel Morgan
Rooms: 4 (PB) $75-145
Full German Breakfast
Credit Cards: A, B
Notes: 2, 5, 8, 9, 10

---

NOTES: Credit cards accepted: A Master Card; B Visa; C American Express; D Discover; E Diners Club; F Other; 2 Personal checks accepted; 3 Lunch available; 4 Dinner available;

# Pennsylvania

**ALSO SEE RESERVATION
SERVICES UNDER
DELAWARE AND NEW JERSEY**

## A Bed and Breakfast Connection (B&B of Philadelphia)

P.O. Box 21, **Devon** 19333
(610) 687-3565; (800) 448-3619;
FAX (610) 995-9524

From elegant townhouses in history-filled **Center-City** to a manor house in scenic **Bucks County**; from an elegant home-within-a-barn in the **suburbs** to charming Victorian inns in **York**, Bed and Breakfast Connections/Bed and Breakfast of Philadelphia offers a wide variety of styles and locations in its scores of inspected homes, guesthouses and inns. For example—choose from accommodations just three blocks from "America's most historic square mile," **Independence National Historical Park**; or within easy distance of **Valley Forge Park**; or in the heart of the **Brandywine Valley** area with its magnificent historic estates and museums. Stay on a working farm in the Amish country of **Lancaster County**. Our accommodations range in price from $30 to $200 per night; we offer houses with one guest room and inns with many rooms. We cover seven counties in the southeastern corner of Pennsylvania. Peggy Gregg and Mary Alice Hamilton, owners. Major credit cards accepted.

## ADAMSTOWN

## Adamstown Inn

62 W. Main St., 19501
(717) 484-0800; (800) 594-4808

Experience simple elegance in a Victorian home resplendent with leaded-glass windows and door, magnificent chestnut woodwork, and Oriental rugs. All four guest rooms are decorated with family heirlooms, handmade quilts, lace curtains, fresh flowers, and many distinctive touches. Accommodations range from antique to king beds. Two rooms have jacuzzis for two. The Inn is located in a small town brimming with antique dealers and only minutes from Reading and Lancaster.

Hosts: Tom and Wanda Berman
Rooms: 4 (PB) $65-95
Expanded Continental Breakfast
Credit Cards: A, B
Notes: 2, 5, 8, 9, 10, 12

---

5 Open all year; 6 Pets welcome; 7 Children welcome; 8 Tennis nearby; 9 Swimming nearby; 10 Golf nearby; 11 Skiing nearby; 12 May be booked through travel agent.

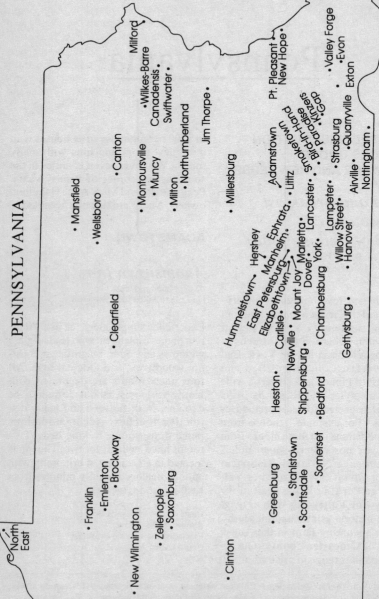

PENNSYLVANIA

North East

Franklin
Emlenton
Brockway

New Wilmington

Zelienople
Saxonburg

Clinton

Greenburg
Stahlstown
Scottsdale
Somerset

Hesston

Shippensburg
Bedford
Newville
Carlisle

Clearfield

Mansfield
Wellsboro

Canton

Montoursville
Muncy
Milton
Northumberland

Millersburg

Jim Thorpe

Milford

Wilkes-Barre
Canadensis
Swiftwater

Hummelstown
Hershey
East Petersburg
Manheim
Elizabethtown
Ephrata
Adamstown
Lititz
Mount Joy
Marietta
Lancaster
Dover
York
Chambersburg
Willow Street
Hanover
Lampeter
Gettysburg

Pt. Pleasant
New Hope

Valley Forge
Evon
Exton

Smoketown
Intercourse
Bird-in-Hand
Paradise
Kinzers
Gap
Strasburg
Quarryville
Alnville
Nottingham

## AIRVILLE

## *Spring House*

1264 Muddy Creek Forks Rd., 17302
(717) 927-6906

Built in 1798 of warm fieldstone, Spring House is a fine example of Colonial architecture with original stenciling that overlooks a river valley. Now on the National Registry of Historic Places, the House has welcomed guests from around the world who seek a historic setting, tranquillity, and access to Amish Country and Gettysburg with scenic railroad soon to be open to the public. Regional breakfast specialties and Amish cheeses welcome the traveler. Country luxuries abound: featherbeds and woodstoves in the winter, large porch with porch swing for summer breezes. Also, creek swimming and horseback riding nearby.

Hosts: Ray Constance Hearne and Michael Schuster
Rooms: 4 (3PB; 1SB) $60-95
Full Breakfast
Credit Cards: none
Notes: 2, 5, 7, 8, 9, 10, 12

## BEDFORD

## *Conifer Ridge Farm*

R.D. #2, Box 202 A, **Clearville** 15535
(814) 784-3342

Conifer Ridge Farm has 126 acres of woodland, pasture, Christmas trees, and crops. There is a one-acre pond with a pier for swimming, fishing, and boat-ing. The home's rustic exterior opens to a spacious contemporary design of exceptional beauty. You'll feel its country character in the old barn beams and brick walls that collect the sun's warmth for solar heat. Near Bedford, Bedford Village, Raystown Lake, and Rocky Gap State Park in Maryland.

Hosts: Dan and Myrtle Haldeman
Rooms: 2 (PB) $55; cabin for 4 people $30
Full Breakfast
Credit Cards: none
Notes: 2, 4, 5, 7, 9, 10, 11

The Village Inn of Bird-in-Hand

## BIRD-IN-HAND

## *The Village Inn of Bird-in-Hand*

2695 Old Philadelphia Pike, P.O. Box 253, 17505
(717) 293-8369; FAX (717) 768-1117

Listed on the National Historic Register, our inn is located on Route 340, five miles east of Lancaster in the heart of the Pennsylvania Dutch Country. Each room features its own private bath and includes a continental plus breakfast, free use of indoor and outdoor pools,

---

NOTES: Credit cards accepted: A Master Card; B Visa; C American Express; D Discover; E Diners Club; F Other; 2 Personal checks accepted; 3 Lunch available; 4 Dinner available; 5 Open all year; 6 Pets welcome; 7 Children welcome; 8 Tennis nearby; 9 Swimming nearby; 10 Golf nearby; 11 Skiing nearby; 12 May be booked through travel agent.

tennis courts located within walking distance, and a complimentary two-hour tour of the surrounding Amish farmlands. Reservations suggested. Package available.

Hosts: Richmond and Janice Young
Rooms: 11 (PB) $75-144
Continental Breakfast
Credit Cards: A, B, C, D
Notes: 2, 5, 7, 8, 9, 12

## BROCKWAY

### Humphreys Homestead

Rd. 2, Box 335, 15824
(814) 265-0162

Come, rest, relax, and renew your spirit in our 100-year-old home, filled with country elegance and genuine hospitality. Take a walk thru the garden paths to the brook on our 30-acre estate. Enjoy the variety of quilts and antiques available throughout our home and nearby shops. We are located 5.5 miles north off I-80 DuBois Exit 16. Our belief reflects Proverbs 3:5-6.

Hosts:  Harry and Ruth Martz
Rooms:  4 (2PB; 2SB) $45-65
Full Breakfast
Credit Cards:  A, B, C
Notes:  2, 5, 7, 8, 9, 10, 11, 12

## CANADENSIS

### Brookview Manor Bed and Breakfast

Route 447, R.R. #1, Box 365, 18325
(717) 595-2451

Situated on four picturesque acres, the inn offers the traveler an ideal retreat from the workaday world.  Enjoy the simple pleasures of hiking trails or a cozy porch glider on a spacious wraparound porch.  Each room offers a panoramic view of the forest, mountains, and stream, and all have private baths. Breakfast is served in our cheery dining room and includes fruits, juices, fresh muffins, and a hearty main entree.

Hosts: Patty and David DeMaria
Rooms: 8 (PB) $70-145
Full Breakfast
Credit Cards: A, B, C, D, E
Notes: 2, 5, 7 (over 12), 8, 9, 10, 11, 12

### Dreamy Acres

Route 447 and Seese Hill Rd., Box 7, 18325
(717) 595-7115

Esther and Bill Pickett started Dreamy Acres as a bed and breakfast inn in 1959, doing bed and breakfast before it was in style. Situated on three acres with a stream and a pond, Dreamy Acres is in the heart of the Pocono Mountains vacationland, close to stores, churches, gift shops, and recreational facilities. Guest rooms have air-conditioning and color cable TV, and some have VCRs.

Hosts: Esther and Bill Pickett
Rooms: 6 (4PB; 2SB) $38-50
Expanded Continental Breakfast
Credit Cards: none
Notes: 2, 5, 8, 9, 10, 11

## CANTON

### M-mm Good B&B

R.D. 1, Box 71, 17724
(717) 673-8153

Located along Route 414, three miles

---

NOTES:  Credit cards accepted:  A  Master Card;  B  Visa;  C  American Express;  D  Discover;  E  Diners Club;  F  Other;  2  Personal checks accepted;  3  Lunch available;  4  Dinner available;

from Canton, in a quiet country setting in the center of the Endless Mountains. Clean, comfortable rooms. Enjoy hiking, fishing, or picnicing under the maple trees in the large lawn.

Hosts: Melvin and Irene Good
Rooms: 3 (SB) $23.50
Full Breakfast
Credit Cards: none
Notes: 2, 5, 7

## CARLISLE

### Line Limousin Farmhouse Bed and Breakfast

2070 Ritner Hwy., 17013
(717) 243-1281

Relax and unwind in an 1864 brick and stone farmhouse on 100 acres, two miles off I-81, Exit 12. French Limousin cattle are raised here. Enjoy antiques, including a player piano, and the use of a golf driving range. Join us for worship at our historic First Presbyterian Church. Two rooms having comfortable king beds and private bath. Two rooms with shared bath. Non-smokers, please.

Hosts: Bob and Joan Line
Rooms: 4 (2PB; 2SB) $53.00-68.90
Full Breakfast
Credit Cards: none
Notes: 2, 5, 7 (over 8), 10

Line Limousin Farmhouse Bed and Breakfast

### Pheasant Field Bed and Breakfast

150 Hickorytown Rd., 17013
(717) 258-0717 (voice and FAX)

Stay in a homey, old, brick farmhouse in quiet surroundings. Wake up to a full, cooked breakfast including homemade bread or muffins. We have four air conditioned guest rooms, two with private bath. There is a tennis court on the grounds and overnight horse boarding is available. "Come Home to the Country." AAA—three star rating.

Hosts: Denise (Dee) Fegan and Chuck DeMarco
Rooms: 4 (2PB; 2SB) $65-95
Full Breakfast
Credit Cards: A, B, C
Notes: 2, 5, 7 (over 8), 8 (on-site), 9, 10, 11, 12

## CHAMBERSBURG

### Falling Spring Inn

1838 Falling Spring Rd., 17201
(717) 267-3654; FAX (717) 267-2584

Enjoy country living only two miles from I-81, Exit 6 and Route 30, on a working farm with animals and Falling Spring, a nationally renowned, freshwater trout stream. A large pond, lawns, meadows, ducks, and birds all make a pleasant stay. Historic Gettysburg is only 25 miles away. Relax in our air conditioned rooms with queen beds. One room with spa. One room wheelchair accessible.

Hosts: Adin and Janet Frey
Rooms: 5 (PB) $49-89
Full Breakfast
Credit Cards: A, B
Notes: 2, 5, 7, 8, 9, 10, 11, 12

5 Open all year; 6 Pets welcome; 7 Children welcome; 8 Tennis nearby; 9 Swimming nearby; 10 Golf nearby; 11 Skiing nearby; 12 May be booked through travel agent.

## CLEARFIELD

### Victorian Loft Bed and Breakfast

216 S. Front St., 16830
(814) 765-4805; (800) 798-0456;
FAX (814) 765-9596

Elegant 1894 Victorian, riverfront home in historic district. Amenities include a memorable breakfast, air-conditioned rooms with skylights, private kitchen and dining, guest entertainment center, family movies, and whirlpool bath. Weaving/sewing studio; spinning demonstrations by request. Hosts are Bible college graduates. Perfect stop on I-80; three miles off Exit 19 in rural West Central PA. Also, completely equipped three-bedroom cabin on eight forested acres, two miles from Parker Dam and Elliot State Parks with swimming, fishing, boating, and numerous outdoor activities.

Hosts: Tim and Peggy Durant
Rooms: 2 (SB) $45-60; suite (PB) $85-100;
cabin $60-100
Full Breakfast
Credit Cards: A, B, C
Notes: 2, 5 (call ahead), 6 (limited), 7, 8, 9, 11, 12

## CLINTON

### Country Road Bed and Breakfast

Moody Rd., Box 265, 15026
(412) 899-2528

A peaceful, quiet, farm setting just five miles from Gr. Pittsburgh Airport with pick-up service available, and 20 minutes from downtown. A restored 100-year-old farmhouse with trout pond, in-ground pool, and screened-in front porch. Recently a cottage, once a springhouse, and 200-year-old log cabin were restored and made available to guests. Golf course within walking distance, and air tours available in vintage, Piper restored aircraft.

Hosts: Janice and David Cornell
Rooms: 5 (4PB; 1SB) $55-100
Full Breakfast
Credit Cards: A, B
Notes: 2, 5, 7, 9, 10

## CRESCO

### LaAnna Guest House

RR 2, Box 1051, 18326
(717) 676-4225

The 111-year-old Victorian is furnished with Victorian and Empire antiques and has spacious rooms, quiet surroundings, and a trout pond. Walk to waterfalls, mountain views, and wildlife.

Hostess: Kay Swingle
Rooms: 32 (SB) $25-40
Continental Breakfast
Credit Cards: none
Notes: 2, 5, 7, 8, 9, 10, 11

## DOVER

### Detter's Acres Bed and Breakfast

6631 Old Carlisle Rd., 17315
(717) 292-3172

This is a 76-acre working farm with Colonial type home. Raise beef cattle. Social room with fireplace. All rooms

---

NOTES: Credit cards accepted: A Master Card; B Visa; C American Express; D Discover; E Diners Club; F Other; 2 Personal checks accepted; 3 Lunch available; 4 Dinner available;

air-conditioned and have TV. Full home-cooked breakfast. Short driving distance to Lancaster Amish, Gettysburg Military Park, Hershey Amusement Park, and York Interstate Fairgrounds. Lorne is a salesman, farmer and entertainer. Ailean is an artist and has an art gallery on the premises. Horse and Amish buggy rides available at nominal fee. Golf cart for guests to use on farm.

Hosts: Lorne and Ailean Detter
Rooms: 3 (1PB; 2SB) $55-60
Full Breakfast
Credit Cards: none
Notes: 2, 5, 9, 10, 11

## EAGLES MERE

### Shady Lane,
### A Bed and Breakfast Inn

P.O. Box 314, Allegheny Ave., 17731
(717) 525-3394; (800) 524-1248

Surrounded by tall trees on a mountaintop with a mesmerizing view of the Endless Mountains. A five minute walk to swimming, boating, canoeing, and fishing on the gorgeous mile-long, springfed lake (with groomed path around the perimeter). Minutes' walk to craft and gift shops in small village. All in a Victorian "town that time forgot," a resort town since the late 1800s, with summer theater and winter cross-country skiing, ice-skating, and famous toboggan slide.

Hosts: Pat and Dennis Dougherty
Rooms: 7 (PB) $75
Full Breakfast
Credit Cards: none
Notes: 2, 5, 8, 9, 10, 11, 12

## EAST BERLIN

### The Copper Lantern Inn

213 W. King St., 17316
(717) 259-0745

Located in historic East Berlin, the Copper Lantern graciously took its name from the works of a local coppersmith, Mr. Eisinhart. From the open staircase in the foyer to the French doors which open into the living room, a tour through the house is sure to be a charming experience. Rich in heritage, the Copper Lantern Inn is conveniently located just minutes away from some of the most impressive tourist attractions in Pennsylvania. New Oxford, known as "a town of antiques," is only ten minutes away. Area attractions: antique shops, Pennsylvania Dutch Country, Hershey Park, golfing, Adams County Orchards, outlet malls, farmers' markets, Gettysburg Battlefield, State Capitol, restaurants, and museums.

Hosts: Yvonne and John Myers
Rooms: 3 (1PB; 2SB) $49-69
Full, Hearty Breakfast
Credit Cards: none
Notes: 2, 5, 8, 10

## EAST PETERSBURG

### George·Zahm House
### Bed and Breakfast

6070 Main Street, 17520
(717) 569-6026

The George Zahm House, built in 1854, is a restored Federal period home in beautiful Lancaster County, Pennsylvania. The inn features three bedrooms

---

5 Open all year;  6 Pets welcome;  7 Children welcome;  8 Tennis nearby;  9 Swimming nearby;
10 Golf nearby;  11 Skiing nearby;  12 May be booked through travel agent.

with private baths and a first floor suite that includes a sitting room, bedroom, and private bath. The inn has ten-foot ceilings throughout and is furnished with an eclectic collection of antiques. Breakfast is served in the dining room and features homemade muffins, breads, Belgian waffles, granolas, and seasonal fresh fruit.

Hosts: Robyn Kemple-Keeports, Jeff Keeports, and Daneen Kemple
Rooms: 4 (PB) $65-85
Continental Plus Breakfast
Credit Cards: A, B
Notes: 2, 5, 7 (over12), 8, 9, 10

George Zahm House Bed and Breakfast

## ELIZABETHTOWN

## *Apples Abound Inn Bed and Breakfast*

518 S. Market St., 17022
(717) 367-3018

A refreshing bite of hospitality, rest, and romance in a 1907 Victorian home in Lancaster County centrally located near Hershey, York, and Lancaster. The three guest rooms are a delightful treat to simple elegance and understated

charm. Your stay will be like biting into a crisp red apple; refreshing, delicious, and appetite quenching. A visit will fill all your senses. Come and be tempted among our apples.

Hosts: Jennifer and Jon Sheppard
Rooms: 3 (1-2PB; 2SB) $65-75
Full Breakfast
Credit Cards: A, B
Notes: 2, 5, 7, 8, 10, 11, 12

Apples Abound Inn Bed and Breakfast

## *West Ridge Guest House*

1285 West Ridge Rd., 17022
(717) 367-7783

Tucked midway between Harrisburg and Lancaster, this European manor can be found four miles off Route 283 at Rheems-Elizabethtown exit. Nine guest rooms with private baths, phones, and TV. Some rooms have fireplaces and whirlpool tubs. Two are two-room suites. An exercise room with hot tub and large great room is in an adjacent guest house. You may relax on one of the decks or gazebo and enjoy the restful view and quiet country setting. Twenty to forty minutes to local attractions, including Hershey Park, Lancaster County Amish Community, outlet shopping malls, Masonic homes, and Harrisburg, the state capital.

Hostess: Alice P. Heisey
Rooms: 9 (PB) $60-100
Full Breakfast
Credit Cards: A, B, C, D
Notes: 2, 5, 7, 8, 12

## EMLENTON

## Whippletree Inn and Farm

RD 3, Box 285, 16373
(412) 867-9543

The inn is a restored, turn-of-the-century home on a cattle farm. The house, barns, and 100 acres of pasture sit on a hill above the Allegheny River. A pleasant trail leads down to the river. Guests are welcome to use the one-half mile racetrack for horses and carriages. Hiking, biking, cross-country skiing, canoeing, hunting, and fishing are nearby. Emlenton offers antique and craft shopping in the restored Old Mill. Air-conditioned.

Hosts: Warren and Joey Simmons
Rooms: 4 (2PB; 2SB) $50-60
Full Breakfast
Credit Cards: B
Notes: 2, 5, 7, 10

The Inns at Doneckers

## EPHRATA

## The Inns at Doneckers

318-324 N. State St., 17522
(717) 738-9502; FAX (717) 738-9554

Relax in country elegance in historic Lancaster County. Four inns of 40 distinctive rooms, decorated in fine antiques, some fireplace/jacuzzi suites. A few steps from The Doneckers Community, a 34-year-old family owned business of exceptional fashion store for the family and the home, award-winning gourmet restaurant, art/craft/quilt galleries and artists' studios, and farmers' market. Minutes from antique and collectible markets. "An oasis of sophistication in PA Dutch Country"—*Country Inns* magazine.

Host: H. William Donecker (owner)
Rooms: 40 (38PB; 2SB) $59-185
Continental Breakfast
Credit Cards: A, B, C, D, E, F
Notes: 2, 3, 4, 5, 7, 8, 9, 10

## Historic Smithton Inn

900 W. Main St., 17522
(717) 733-6094

Smithton Inn originated prior to the Revolutionary War. The Inn is a romantic and picturesque place located in Lancaster County. Its big, square rooms are bright and sunny. Each room has its own working fireplace and can be candlelighted during evening hours. There is a sitting room in each guest room with comfortable leather upholstered chairs, reading lamps, soft goose down pillows, and bright, handmade Pennsylvania Dutch quilts. Smithton's Dahlia Gardens feature a striking dis-

---

5 Open all year; 6 Pets welcome; 7 Children welcome; 8 Tennis nearby; 9 Swimming nearby; 10 Golf nearby; 11 Skiing nearby; 12 May be booked through travel agent.

play of blossoms that are grown from tubers that were all winners in American Dahlia Society competitions. Mannerly children and pets are welcome, but please make prior arrangements. Smoking is prohibited.

Hostess: Dorthy R. Graybill
Rooms: 8 (PB) $65-150; suites $140-170
Full Breakfast
Credit Cards: A, B, C
Notes: 2, 5, 6 (prior arrangement), 7, 8, 9, 10, 12

## Martin House

265 Ridge Avenue, 17522
(717) 733-6804

The curving driveway leads to our contemporary home which has a spacious deck overlooking the tranquil semi-secluded grounds. Located in Pennsylvania Dutch Country, close to antique markets, shopping malls, Hershey Park, and golf courses. For your comfort we offer king- and queen-size beds in tastefully decorated rooms. The master bedroom comes with a hot tub for your enjoyment.

Hosts: Moses and Vera Martin
Rooms: 3 (2PB; 1-2SB) $49-110
Full Breakfast
Credit Cards: none
Notes: 2, 5, 7, 9, 10

## EXTON

## Duling-Kurtz House and Country Inn

146 S. Whitford Rd., 19341
(610) 524-1830; FAX (610) 524-6258

Built in 1830, the interiors of the Inn

and Restaurant have been artfully restored. Viennese-born restauranter, Michael Person, oversees the details of the comfortable 15-room inn and a series of seven elegant dining rooms in the adjacent restaurant. Guests register in a narrow, rustic parlor. Tiny chirping birds, a gas fireplace, patterned furniture, Oriental rugs, and prints of Philadelphia architecture add homeyness. Access to fresh fruit, cookies, and local newspapers add a welcoming touch!

Rooms: 15 (PB) $55-120
Continental Breakfast
Credit Cards: A, B, C, D, E
Notes: 3, 4, 5, 8, 10, 12

## FRANKLIN

## Quo Vadis Bed and Breakfast

1501 Liberty St., 16323
(814) 432-4208; (800) 360-6598

A stately home, accented with terra cotta tile, Quo Vadis is an 1867, eclectic, Queen Anne house. It is located in an historic district listed on the National Register with a walking tour. The high-ceilinged, spacious rooms, parquet floors, detailed woodworking, moldings, and friezes are from a time of caring craftsmanship and Victorian elegance. The furniture is mahogany, rosewood, oak, walnut, and wicker and has been acquired by the same family for four generations. The quilts, embroidery, and lacework are the handiwork of two beloved ladies. Restaurants, museums, antiques, Barrow-Civic Theater, DeBonce Antique Music

---

NOTES: Credit cards accepted: A Master Card; B Visa; C American Express; D Discover; E Diners Club; F Other; 2 Personal checks accepted; 3 Lunch available; 4 Dinner available;

World, bicycle paths, train trip, fishing, Allegheny River Valley are all nearby to enjoy. Smoking allowed only on the porch.

Hosts: Erin and Jerry Cassady
Rooms: 6 (PB) $60-80
Full Breakfast
Credit Cards: A, B, C
Notes: 2, 5, 7 (over 9), 8, 9, 10, 11, 12

## GAP

## Ben Mar Farm Bed and Breakfast

5721 Old Phila Pike, 17527
(717) 768-3309

Come stay with us on our working dairy farm. We are located in the heart of famous "Amish Country." Experience quiet country life while staying in the large, beautifully decorated rooms of our 200 year old farmhouse. Our efficiency apartment is a favorite including a full kitchen and queen and double beds with private bath. Enjoy a fresh continental breakfast brought to your room. Air-conditioned.

Hosts: Herb and Melanie Benner
Rooms: 2 (PB) $40-50
Continental Plus Breakfast
Credit Cards: none
Notes: 2, 5, 7

## GETTYSBURG

## The Brafferton Inn

44 York St., 17325
(717) 337-3423

In the town of historic Gettysburg the Brafferton Inn is one of its gracious

landmarks. The elegant 1786 fieldstone home, listed on the National Registry of Historic Places, has been fully restored to include a private bath for each of the ten guestrooms. Featured in *Country Living*, the Inn has exquisite antiques and original artistry throughout. The Inn combines elegance and ease. Warm colored Orientals, comfortable wingbacks, and a tall 1800 grandfather clock grace the living room. The dining room boasts a stunning folk art mural. Other surprising nooks and crannies, a deck and in-town garden provide getaway spots. The spirit of an earlier time pervades.

Hosts: Jane and Sam Back
Rooms: 10 (PB) $75-120
Full Breakfast
Credit Cards: A, B
Notes: 2, 5, 7 (over 7), 8, 9, 10, 11, 12

The Doubleday Inn

## The Doubleday Inn

104 Doubleday Ave., 17325
(717) 334-9119

Located directly on the Gettysburg Battlefield, this beautifully restored Colonial country inn enjoys splendid views of historic Gettysburg and the

---

battlefield. Guests enjoy candlelight country breakfasts, afternoon refreshments, and the cozy comfort of a centrally air-conditioned inn surrounded by lovely antiques and Civil War memorabilia. Free presentations by battlefield historians on selected evenings.

Hosts: Ruth Anne and Charles Wilcox
Rooms: 9 (5PB; 4SB) $84-105
Full Breakfast
Credit Cards: A, B
Notes: 2, 5, 8, 10, 11, 12

### Keystone Inn B&B

231 Hanover St., 17325
(717) 337-3888

The Keystone Inn is a large, brick, Victorian home built in 1913. The high-ceilinged rooms are decorated with lace and flowers, and a handsome chestnut staircase rises to the third floor. The guest rooms are bright, cheerful, and air-conditioned. Each has a reading nook and writing desk. Choose your own breakfast from our full breakfast menu. One suite available.

Hosts: Wilmer and Doris Martin
Rooms: 5 + 1 suite (3PB; 2SB) $59-100
Full Breakfast
Credit Cards: A, B
Notes: 2, 5, 7, 8, 9, 10, 11

Keystone Inn Bed and Breakfast

## GREENBURG

### Huntland Farm Bed and Breakfast

RD 9, Box 21, 15601
(412) 834-8483; FAX (412) 838-8253

Nestled in the foothills of the Allegheny Mountains, the 100-acre Huntland Farm is three miles northeast of Greensburg. The house, built in 1848 and listed in *Historic Places in Western PA*, is furnished with antiques. A large living room, as well as porches and gardens are available for guests' use. Four, large, corner bedrooms make it comfortable for up to eight people. Nearby are many scenic and historical places, walking trails, hot air ballooning, and shops.

Hosts: Robert and Elizabeth Weidlein
Rooms: 4 (SB) $70
Full Breakfast
Credit Cards: A, B
Notes: 2, 5, 7 (over 12), 10, 12

## HANOVER

### Beechmont Inn

315 Broadway, 17331
(717) 632-3013; (800) 553-7009

An elegant, 1834 Federal period inn with seven guest rooms, all private baths, fireplaces, air-conditioning, afternoon refreshments, and gourmet breakfast. One large suite has a private whirlpool tub, canopy beds, and fireplaces. Gettysburg Battlefield, Lake Marburg, golf, and great antiquing nearby. Convenient location for visits to Hershey, York, or Lancaster. Weekend and golf

NOTES: Credit cards accepted: A Master Card; B Visa; C American Express; D Discover; E Diners Club; F Other; 2 Personal checks accepted; 3 Lunch available; 4 Dinner available;

packages and romantic honeymoon or anniversary packages offered. Picnic baskets available. Great area for biking and hiking. AAA and Mobil approved.

Hosts: William and Susan Day
Rooms: 7 (PB) $80-135
Full Breakfast
Credit Cards: A, B
Notes: 2, 5, 7, 8, 9, 10, 12

## HERSHEY

## *Pinehurst Inn*
## *Bed and Breakfast*

50 Northeast Dr., 17033
(717) 533-2603; (800) 743-9140;
FAX (717) 534-2639

Spacious brick home surrounded by lawns and countryside. There is a warm, welcoming, many-windowed living room and old-fashioned porch swing. All this within walking distance of all Hershey attractions: Hershey Museums, Rose Gardens, Hersheypark, and Chocolate World. Less than one hour's drive to Gettysburg and Lancaster County. Each room welcomes you with a queen-size bed and a Hershey Kiss on each pillow.

Hosts: Roger and Phyllis Ingold
Rooms: 15 (2PB; 13SB) $45-62
Complete Breakfast
Credit Cards: A, B
Notes: 2, 5, 7, 8, 9, 10, 12

## *Shepherd's Acres*
## *Bed and Breakfast*

R.D. 3, Box 370 Bell Road, **Palmyra** 17078
(717) 838-3899

Welcome to the Hershey-Lancaster area! You'll enjoy it more if you stay on our 20-acre farmette overlooking the scenic Lebanon Valley. Our new and spacious Cape-Cod home is filled with Margy's hand-sewn quilts and wall-hangings, with some antique furniture accenting the "country theme" as well. The eat-in enclosed porch area is a great place to enjoy both beauty and tranquillity as you watch the sheep in the pasture or the deer in the fields.

Hosts: Jerry and Margy Allebach
Rooms: 3 (1PB; 2SB) $45-60
Full Breakfast
Credit Cards: none
Notes: 2, 5, 8, 9, 10, 11

## HESSTON

## *Aunt Susie's*
## *Country Vacations*

R.D. 1, Box 225, 16647
(814) 658-3638

Experience Raystown country living in a warm friendly atmosphere with antiques and oil paintings. Our country inn is an old general store and post office built in the 1860's beautifully restored as a bed and breakfast. Rest comfortably in one of our five large, air-conditioned bedrooms or relax in our large living room. Breakfast is always alive with conversation and new friendships. We are two miles from beautiful Lake Raystown in the heart of the Central Pennsylvanian Mountains.

Hosts: Paul and Betty Bonfiglio
Rooms: 5 (1PB; 4SB) $55-60
Full Breakfast
Credit Cards: A, B, C, D
Notes: 2, 5, 7, 8, 9, 10, 11, 12

---

5 Open all year; 6 Pets welcome; 7 Children welcome; 8 Tennis nearby; 9 Swimming nearby; 10 Golf nearby; 11 Skiing nearby; 12 May be booked through travel agent.

## HUMMELSTOWN

### Mottern's Bed and Breakfast

28 East Main St., 17036
(717) 566-3840; FAX (717) 566-3780

Enjoy small town hospitality only five minutes from Hershey. Private apartment is a restored 1860s limestone home can be your "home away from home". Bedroom with queen-sized bed, living room with sofa bed, kitchen, dining room, bath with shower, central air, color cable TV, large patio, and yard. Private parking. We are located in the center of our small town and walking distance to shops, restaurants, banks, and the local public park. There are United Methodist, United Church of Christ, and Lutheran Churches within three blocks.

Hostesss: Susan Mottern
Rooms: 1 (5-room apartment) $75
(Additional $10 per person over five years old)
Continental Breakfast
Credit Cards: A, B
Notes: 2, 5, 7, 8, 9, 11

## JIM THORPE

### The Inn at Jim Thorpe

24 Broadway, 18229
(717) 325-2599; (800) 329-2599;
FAX (717) 325-9145

The Inn rests in a unique and picturesque setting in the heart of historic Jim Thorpe. Our elegant, restored guest rooms are complete with private baths, color TV/HBO, and air-conditioning. Our stunning Victorian suite is available for that very special occasion.

While in town take in the sights including mansion tours, museum, art galleries, and quaint shops, or go mountain biking and whitewater rafting. It's all right outside our doors!

Host: David Drury
Rooms: 22 + 1 suite (PB) $65-100
Continental Breakfast
Credit Cards: A, B, C, D, E
Notes: 3, 4, 5, 7, 9, 11, 12

## KINZERS

### Sycamore Haven Farm

35 S. Kinzer Rd., 17535
(717) 442-4901

We have approximately 40 milking cows and many young cattle and cats for children to enjoy. Our farmhouse has three guest rooms, all with double beds and one single. We also have cots and a playpen. Located 15 miles east of Lancaster on Route 30.

Hosts: Charles and Janet Groff
Rooms: 3 (SB) $30-40
Continental Breakfast
Credit Cards: none
Notes: 2, 5, 6, 7, 8, 9, 10

## LAMPETER (LANCASTER)

### Australian Walkabout Inn

837 Village Rd., P.O. Box 294, 17537
(717) 464-0707; FAX (717) 464-2678

This 1925 brick, Mennonite farmhouse features large wraparound porches, balconies, English gardens, and antique furnishings. The Inn takes its name from the Australian word which means to go out and discover new places. Australian born host Richard will help you explore

NOTES: Credit cards accepted: A Master Card; B Visa; C American Express; D Discover; E Diners Club; F Other; 2 Personal checks accepted; 3 Lunch available; 4 Dinner available;

the Amish country surrounding the home. An elegant, full breakfast is served by candlelight. The honeymoon and anniversary rooms/suites are beautiful. AAA—three-diamonds.

Hosts: Richard and Margaret Mason
Rooms: 4 (PB) $89-149; 2 suites $169-199
Full Breakfast
Credit Cards: A, B, C, D
Notes: 2, 3, 4, 5, 7, 8, 9, 10, 12

## Bed and Breakfast— The Manor

830 Village Rd., P.O. Box 416, 17537
(717) 464-9564; (800) 461-6BED

This cozy farmhouse is minutes away from Lancaster's historical sites and attractions. Guests delight in Mary Lou's homemade breakfasts featuring Eggs Mornay, crepes, stratas, fruit cobblers, and homemade breads and jams. A swim in the pool and a nap under a shade tree is the perfect way to cap your day of touring. Dinner, an overnight stay, and a buggy ride with an Old Order Amish family can be arranged. Amish waitresses. Children welcome.

Hostesses: Mary Lou Paolini and Jackie Curtis
Rooms: 6 (4PB; 2SB) $79-99
Gourmet Buffet-style Breakfast
Credit Cards: A, B
Notes: 2, 3, 4, 5, 7, 8, 9, 10

## LANCASTER

## Country Living Inn

2406 Old Phila. Pike, 17602
(717) 295-7295

Just like "HOME!" Warm inviting hospitality. Country decor with quilts on the beds. The front porch is filled with rocking chairs and benches for viewing the Amish buggies passing by or social visits with other guests. One romantic suite with a whirlpool for two. Amish farms on the North and West side. Two floors. Non-smoking available.

Hosts: Bill and Judy Harnish
Rooms: 34 (PB) $43-125
Continental Breakfast
Credit Cards: A, B
Notes: 5, 10, 12

Flowers and Thyme Bed and Breakfast

## Flowers and Thyme Bed and Breakfast

238 Strasburg Pike, 17602
(717) 393-1460

Charming brick, Colonial home in a country setting amid flowers, herbs, and perennials. Oak, brass, or Shaker poster beds, country decor; TV;, ceiling fans, one room with jacuzzi; and air-conditioned for your comfort. Warm hospitality and marvelous breakfasts await you. Dinner with Amish family available. Located in the heart of the Pennsylvania Dutch Country, five minutes from the Pennsylvania Dutch Visitors Bureau, one mile from Tanger Outlet Center at Millstream, and two miles

---

5 Open all year; 6 Pets welcome; 7 Children welcome; 8 Tennis nearby; 9 Swimming nearby; 10 Golf nearby; 11 Skiing nearby; 12 May be booked through travel agent.

from Rockvale Square outlets.

Hosts: Don and Ruth Harnish
Rooms: 3 (2PB; 1SB) $60-95
Full Breakfast
Credit Cards: none
Notes: 2, 5, 7 (over 12), 8, 9, 10

## Gardens of Eden B&B

1894 Eden Rd., 17601
(717) 393-5179

Victorian iron master's home built circa 1860 on the banks of the Conestoga River is three miles northeast of Lancaster. Antiques and family collections of quilts and coverlets fill the three guest rooms, all with private baths. The adjoining guest cottage (restored summer kitchen) features a walk-in fireplace, dining room, bedroom, and bath on second floor. Marilyn's floral designs are featured and for sale. The three acres of gardens feature herbs, perennials, and wildflowers among the woodsy trails. Local attractions are personalized by a tour guide service and dinner in a young Amish couple's home. Canoe and row boat available. Two bike trails pass the house.

Hosts: Marilyn and Bill Ebel
Rooms: 4 (PB) $75
Full Breakfast
Credit Cards: A, B
Notes: 2, 5, 7 (in guest house), 8, 9, 10, 12

Gardens of Eden Bed and Breakfast

## The King's Cottage, A Bed and Breakfast Inn

1049 E. King St., 17602
(717) 397-1017; (800) 747-8717;
FAX (717) 397-3447

Traditionally-styled elegance, modern comfort, and warm hospitality in Amish Ccountry. King and queen beds, private baths, gourmet breakfasts, and personal service create a gracious friendly atmosphere at this award-winning Spanish-style mansion. The Inn's newly restored Carriage House is an oasis of private elegance. Relax by the fire and enjoy afternoon tea in the library while chatting with innkeepers about directions to restaurants and attractions. Special Amish dinners or personal tours arranged. No pets, please. Near farmers' markets, Gettysburg, and Hershey. On National Register, AAA, and Mobile listed EXCELLENT!

Hosts: Karen and Jim Owens
Rooms: 9 (PB) $80-160
Full Breakfast
Credit Cards: A, B, D
Notes: 2, 5, 7 (12 and over), 8, 9, 10, 12

## Lincoln Haus Inn Bed and Breakfast

1687 Lincoln Hwy. E., 17602
(717) 392-9412

Lincoln Haus Inn is the only inn in Lancaster County with a distinctive hip roof. It is furnished with antiques and rugs on gleaming, hardwood floors, and it has natural oak woodwork. I am a member of the Old Amish Church, serving family-style breakfast with a homey atmosphere. Convenient location, close

NOTES: Credit cards accepted: A Master Card; B Visa; C American Express; D Discover; E Diners Club; F Other; 2 Personal checks accepted; 3 Lunch available; 4 Dinner available;

to Amish farmlands, malls, historic Lancaster; five minutes from Route 30 and Pennsylvania Dutch Visitors' Bureau.

Hostess: Mary K. Zook
Rooms: 6 (PB) $48-75; 2 apartments (PB)
Full Breakfast
Credit Cards: none
Notes: 2, 4, 5, 7, 8, 9, 10, 12

## Meadowview Guest House

2169 New Holland Pike, 17601
(717) 299-4017

Large contemporary home located in the heart of the Pennsylvania Dutch Amish area. Three guest rooms and kitchen on the second floor. There is a stove, refrigerator, sink, and dishes. A breakfast tray is put in the kitchen in the morning for our guests. Close to many historical sites, farmers and antique markets, excellent restaurants, and many attractions to help guests enjoy the beautiful county. Personalized maps are provided.

Hosts: Edward and Sheila Christie
Rooms: 3 (1PB; 2SB) $30-45
Continental Breakfast
Credit Cards: none
Notes: 2 (for deposit), 5, 7 (over 6), 8, 9, 10

## New Life Homestead Bed and Breakfast

1400 E. King St. (Rt. 462), 17602
(717) 396-8928

In the heart of the Amish area is a stately, brick Victorian close to all attractions, markets, farms, and outlets.

Each room is decorated with family heirlooms and antiques. Full breakfast and evening refreshments are served. Tours and meals are arranged with local families. Worship with us in our Mennonite church. Private baths and air-conditioning.

Hosts: Carol and Bill Giersch
Rooms: (PB) $50-75
Fulll Breakfast
Credit Cards: none
Notes: 2, 5, 7, 8, 9, 10, 12

O'Flaherty's Dingeldein House

## O'Flaherty's Dingeldein House Bed and Breakfast

1105 East King Street, 17602
(717) 293-1723; (800) 779-7765;
FAX (717) 293-1947

Enjoy genuine warmth and hospitality in the friendly atmosphere of our home. Our Dutch Colonial home is traditionally appointed for your comfort, two fireplaces in the fall and winter and A/C when needed to provide a restful, relaxing stay in beautiful Lancaster County. Conveniently located near downtown Lancaster attractions and just a short, scenic ride to the Amish farmland, outlet shopping, and antique area. Amish dining arranged. Personalized

5 Open all year; 6 Pets welcome; 7 Children welcome; 8 Tennis nearby; 9 Swimming nearby; 10 Golf nearby; 11 Skiing nearby; 12 May be booked through travel agent.

maps prepared. Our breakfast guarantees you won't go away hungry.

Hosts: Jack and Sue Flatley
Rooms: 4 (2PB; 2SB) $68-78
Full Breakfast
Credit Cards: A, B, D
Notes: 2, 5, 7, 8, 9, 10

**LANCASTER COUNTY (SEE ALSO**—Bird-in-Hand, East Petersburg, Elizabethtown, Ephrata, Gap, Kinzers, Lampeter, Lancaster, Lititz, Manheim, Marietta, Mount Joy, Nottingham, Paradise, Peach Bottom, Quarryville, and Willow Street**)**

## Carriage Corner Bed and Breakfast

3705 E. Newport Rd., P.O. Box 371,
**Intercourse** 17534
(717) 768-3059

"A comfortable bed, a hearty breakfast, a charming village, and friendly hosts" has been used to describe our B&B. We have four comfortable rooms, two with private baths and two with a shared bath. Our bed and breakfast offers a relaxing country atmosphere with handcrafted touches of folk-art and country. Rooms are air conditioned. We are centered in the heart of beautiful farms and a culture which draws many to nearby villages of Intercourse, Bird-in-Hand, and Paradise. Amish dinners arranged. There is much to learn from these calm

and gentle people.

Hosts: Gordon and Gwen Schuit
Rooms: 4 (2PB; 2SB) $45-70
Full Breakfast
Credit Cards: A, B
Notes: 2, 5, 7, 12

## The Colombian, A Bed and Breakfast Inn

360 Chestnut St., **Columbia** 17512
(717) 684-5869; (800) 422-5869

A restored turn-of-the-century Colonial Revival mansion, featuring an ornate stained glass window and magnificent tiered staircase. Decorated with antiques in Victorian or country style, large, air-conditioned rooms offer queen-size beds, private baths, and TV. Breakfast here consists of a hearty buffet offering a variety of fresh fruit, hot main dishes, and homemade breads. Guests may relax on the wraparound porch or in the sitting room which has a fireplace.

Hosts: Becky and Chris Will
Rooms: 6 (SB) $70-85
Full Breakfast
Credit Cards: A, B
Notes: 2, 5, 7, 8, 9, 10, 11

## Old Leacock Road Bed and Breakfast

244 Old Leacock Rd., **Gordonville** 17529
(717) 768-3824

Welcome to Lancaster County. A complimentary rumble seat ride in our 1929 Model "A" Ford awaits all our guests. You will experience the lush Lancaster County farmland and travel through a

NOTES: Credit cards accepted: A Master Card; B Visa; C American Express; D Discover; E Diners Club; F Other; 2 Personal checks accepted; 3 Lunch available; 4 Dinner available;

covered bridge. Arrangements for dinner with an Amish family are available. Our rooms are furnished in period antiques. We are close to all attractions and shopping, yet surrounded by the serene Amish farms.

Hosts: Richard and Sandee Hughes
Rooms: 3 (1PB; 2SB) $50-65
Full Breakfast
Credit Cards: none
Notes: 2, 5, 6, 7, 10

## LANDENBERG

### Cornerstone B&B

300 Buttonwood Rd., 19350
(610) 274-2143; FAX (610) 274-0734

Cornerstone dates back to 1704, the time when early records document a land grant from William Penn of England to William Penn's son in Philadelphia. The original house was built in the early 1700s with additions constructed at three later times. Then, in 1820, Cornerstone was completed as the proud, gracious structure that will soon welcome you. Each bedroom's quaint decor is surrounded by a sense of timeless romance, bringing together the unhurried pace of the past and the conveniences of today. For long-term guests, Cornerstone's renovated barn is the home of six furnished guest cottages. Come to your home in the country. Call today for reservations or information. It's a place with a long history of pampered guests.

Hosts: Linda Chamberlin and Marty Mulligan
Rooms: 7 (PB) $75-150
Full Breakfast
Credit Cards: A, B, D
Notes: 2, 5, 7, 8, 9, 10, 12

Cornerstone Bed and Breakfast

## LITITZ

### Swiss Woods Bed and Breakfast

500 Blantz Rd., 17543
(717) 627-3358; (800) 594-8018;
FAX (717) 627-3483

A visit to Swiss Woods is reminiscent of a trip to one of Switzerland's quaint, charming guest houses. Located in beautiful Lancaster County, this inn was designed with comfort in mind. Breakfast is a memorable experience of inn specialties. The gardens have a unique variety of flowering perennials and annuals. A massive sandstone fireplace dominates the sunny common room. Rooms feature natural woodwork and queen beds with down comforters, and some have jacuzzis, patios, and balconies. Enjoy our spectacular view and special touches. German spoken.

Hosts: Debrah and Werner Mosimann
Rooms: 7 (PB) $75-130
Full Breakfast
Credit Cards: A, B, D
Closed December 24 - 26
Notes: 2, 8, 9, 10, 12

---

5  Open all year;  6  Pets welcome;  7  Children welcome;  8  Tennis nearby;  9  Swimming nearby;
10  Golf nearby;  11  Skiing nearby;  12  May be booked through travel agent.

## MANHEIM

### Herr Farmhouse Inn

2256 Huber Dr., 17545
(717) 653-9852; (800) 584-0743

Historic, circa 1750, stone farmhouse nestled on 11.5 acres of scenic farmland. The Inn has been fully restored and retains original trim, random width flooring and doors. Two of the six working fireplaces are located in guest rooms and a walk-in country kitchen. Take a step into yesteryear amidst period antiques. Enjoy breakfast on the sun porch. Amish, antiques, quilts, golf, tennis, Hershey, Gettysburg, and excellent dining nearby. Nine miles west of Lancaster outside of Mt. Joy.

Host: Barry Herr
Rooms: 4 (2PB; 2SB) $75-90
Suite (4 persons) $100
Full Breakfast
Credit Cards: A, B
Notes: 2, 5, 7 (over 12), 8, 10, 11

### The Inn at Mt. Hope

2232 E Mt. Hope Rd., 17545
(717) 664-4708

An 1850s stone home with high ceilings and magnificent pine floors. The Inn sits on four and one half acres of woodland and grass bordered by a stream. Convenient to all Lancaster County attractions as well as Hershey and adjacent to the Mt. Hope Winery and Pennsylvania Renaissance Faire. Ideal setting for a small couples retreat or getaway. Screened porch and family TV room are available for relaxation.

Hosts: Bob and Nancy Ladd
Rooms: 5 (2PB; 3SB) $50-115
Full Breakfast
Credit Cards: A, B
Notes: 2, 5, 7, 9, 10

### Wenger's Bed and Breakfast

571 Hossler Rd., 17545
(717) 665-3862

Relax and enjoy your stay in the quiet countryside of Lancaster County. Our ranch-style house is within walking distance of our son's 100 acre dairy farm. The spacious rooms will accommodate families. You can get a guided tour through the Amish farmland. Hershey, the chocolate town, Pennsylvania's state capital at Harrisburg, and the Gettysburg battlefield are all within one hour's drive.

Hosts: Arthur D. and Mary K. Wenger
Rooms: 2 (PB) $40-45
Full Breakfast
Credit Cards: none
Notes: 2, 5, 7

## MANSFIELD

### Crossroads Bed and Breakfast

131 S. Main St., 16933
(717) 662-7008

Enjoy a peaceful Victorian spot in Mansfield, PA. Warm hospitality; rooms enhanced with quilts, lace, an-

---

NOTES: Credit cards accepted: A Master Card; B Visa; C American Express; D Discover; E Diners Club; F Other; 2 Personal checks accepted; 3 Lunch available; 4 Dinner available;

tiques, and special touches, along with gourmet breakfast are just a few of the delights our guests experience. Our quaint gift shop specializes in gourmet coffees, braided rugs, bath capitals and potpourri sprays. Rooms are air-conditioned and provide cozy comforts with remote control TV, European duvet coverlets and jacuzzi in the shared bath. Walk to dinner.

Hosts: Rob and Cindy Fitzgerald
Rooms: 5 (1PB; 4SB) $56-76
Full Gourmet Breakfast
Credit Cards: A, B
Notes: 2, 5, 7, 8, 9, 10, 11

Historic Linden House

## MARIETTA

### *Historic Linden House*

606 E. Market St., 17547
(717) 426-4697; (800) 416-4697;
FAX (717) 426-4136

The Historic Linden House is a Federal style home built in 1806 and listed on the National Historic Register. When they built it, it was considered one of the finest mansions in south-central PA, costing between $16,000 and $17,000

to build. A charming town situated along the Susquehanna River, which TIME HAS FORGOTTEN with 48% of its buildings in the historic district. The home historically is known for its staircase, being the longest, original preserved continuous handrail staircase in Lancaster County. Guests enjoy queen-size beds and private baths. Fresh flowers in seasons. Spend a relaxing evening in the parlor by the two crackling fireplaces. The house contains a total of sixteen fireplaces. Special packages and discounts available.

Hosts: Henry, Jeanene, and David Hill
Rooms: 6 (PB) $50-75
Expanded Continental Breakfast (weekdays);
Full (weekends)
Credit Cards: A, B
Notes: 2, 5, 7

## MILFORD

### *Cliff Park Inn and Golf Course*

RR 4, Box 7200, 18337
(717) 296-6491; (800) 225-6535;
FAX (717) 296-3982

Historic country inn on secluded 600-acre estate. Spacious rooms with private bath, telephone and climate control. Victorian-style furnishings. Fireplaces. Golf at the door on one of America's oldest golf courses (1913). Hike or cross-country ski on seven miles of marked trails. Golf and ski equipment rentals. Golf school. Full service restaurant rated three stars by Mobil Guide. MAP or B&B plans available. Specialists in business conferences and

---

5 Open all year; 6 Pets welcome; 7 Children welcome; 8 Tennis nearby; 9 Swimming nearby; 10 Golf nearby; 11 Skiing nearby; 12 May be booked through travel agent.

country weddings.

Host: Harry W. Buchanan III
Rooms: 18 (PB) $90-155
Full Breakfast
Credit Cards: A, B, C, D, E
Notes: 2, 3, 4, 5, 7, 8, 9, 10, 11, 12

## MILLERSBURG

### Victorian Manor Inn

312 Market St., 17061
(717) 692-3511

Victorian Manor Inn is located on Route 147 between Harrisburg and Sunbury, one block from the picturesque river and historic Millersburg Ferry. The elegantly restored, second Empire home is furnished with period antiques and collectibles. Enjoy wicker-furnished porches, gazebo, and courtyard, or relax in the spacious parlor. Whether visiting during the holiday season amid the exquisite Christmas decorations or in the summer with the quaint gardens in bloom, breakfast is always a treat.

Hosts: Skip and Sue Wingard
Rooms: 4 (2PB; 2SB) $60-75
Full Breakfast
Credit Cards: A, B, C
Notes: 2, 5, 7, 8, 9, 10, 11

Victorian Manor Inn

Pau-Lyn's Country Bed and Breakfast

## MILTON

### Pau-Lyn's Country Bed and Breakfast (A Restful Haven)

RD 3, Box 676, 17847
(717) 742-4110

The beautiful Susquehanna Valley of Central PA is unique. Truly a variety of pleasant experience await persons who desire being in touch with God's handiwork and observing agriculture, scenic mountains, rivers and valleys. Recreational activities also abound. Guests experience "a Restful Haven" as the innkeepers with their generous hospitality provide nostalgic memories throughout the antique furnished, 1850 Victorian brick house, two miles from I-80. Comfortable air-conditioned bedrooms and birds, add to the relaxing atmosphere.

Hosts: Paul and Evelyn Landis
Rooms: 7 (4PB; 3SB) $45-55
Full Breakfast
Credit Cards: none
Notes: 2, 5, 7, 8, 9, 10, 11, 12

NOTES: Credit cards accepted: A Master Card; B Visa; C American Express; D Discover; E Diners Club; F Other; 2 Personal checks accepted; 3 Lunch available; 4 Dinner available;

## Teneriff Farm Bed and Breakfast

RD 1, Box 314, 17847
(717) 742-9061

The house, with a screened-in porch, was built in 1891 and it has fields all around for exploring and hiking. This B&B is a comfortable, clean home away from home with many area activities indoor and outdoor alike. Certificate valid year round except College weekends.

Hosts: Soenke and Christa Haseloff
Rooms: 3 (SB) $50
Full Country Breakfast
Credit Cards: none
Notes: 2, 5, 7, 9, 10, 11, 12

Teneriff Farm Bed and Breakfast

## MONTOURSVILLE

## The Carriage House at Stonegate

RR 1, Box 11A, 17754
(717) 433-4340; (717) 433-4653

The Carriage House at Stonegate is the original carriage house for one of the oldest farms in the beautiful Loyalsock Valley. It offers 1,400 square feet of space on two levels and is totally self-contained and separate from the main house. It is located within easy access to I-80, I-180, and U.S. 15 and on the edge of extensive forests offering a wide range of outdoor activities in all seasons.

Hosts: Harold and Dena Mesaris
Rooms: 2 (SB) $50
Continental Breakfast
Credit Cards: none
Notes: 2, 5, 6, 7, 8, 9, 10, 11

## MOUNT JOY

## Cedar Hill Farm

305 Longenecker Rd., 17552
(717) 653-4655

This 1817 stone farmhouse overlooks a peaceful stream and was the birthplace of the host. Stroll the acreage or relax on the wicker rockers on the large front porch. Enjoy the singing of the birds and serene countryside. A winding staircase leads to the comfortable rooms, each with a private and centrally air conditioned. A room for honeymooners offers a private balcony. Breakfast is served daily by a walk-in fireplace. Located midway between the Lancaster and Hershey areas where farmers' markets, antique shops, and good restaurants abound. Gift certificates for anniversary or holiday giving. Open all seasons.

Hosts: Russel and Gladys Swarr
Rooms: 5 (PB) $65-70
Continental Plus Breakfast
Credit Cards: A, B, C, D
Notes: 2, 5, 7, 8, 10

5 Open all year; 6 Pets welcome; 7 Children welcome; 8 Tennis nearby; 9 Swimming nearby; 10 Golf nearby; 11 Skiing nearby; 12 May be booked through travel agent.

## Green Acres Farm Bed and Breakfast

1382 Pinkerton Rd., 17552
(717) 653-4028; FAX (717) 653-2840

Our 1830 farmhouse is furnished with antiques and offers a peaceful haven for your getaway. The rooster, chickens, Pigmy goats, lots of kittens, pony, and 1,000 hogs give a real farm atmosphere on this 160-acre grain farm. Children love the pony cart rides and the 8' x 10' playhouse, and everyone enjoys the trampoline and swings. We offer tour information about the Amish Country.

Hosts: Wayne and Yvonne Miller
Rooms: 7 (PB) $60 (+ $6 per child)
Full Breakfast
Credit Cards: A, B
Notes: 2, 5, 6, 7, 8, 9, 10

The Bodine House

## MUNCY

## The Bodine House

307 S. Main St., 17756
(717) 546-8949

The Bodine House, featured in the December 1991 issue of *Colonial Homes*

magazine, is located on tree-lined Main Street in the historic district. Built in 1805, the House has been authentically restored and is listed on the National Register of Historic Places. Most of the furnishings are antiques. The center of Muncy, with its shops, restaurants, library, and churches, is a short walk down the street. No smoking.

Hosts: David and Marie Louise Smith
Rooms : 4 (PB) $55-70
Full Breakfast
Credit Cards: A, B, C
Notes: 2, 5, 7 (over 6), 8, 9, 10, 11, 12

## NEW BERLIN

## The Inn at Olde New Berlin

321 Market St., 17855
(717) 966-0321; FAX (717) 966-9557

"A luxurious base for indulging in a clutch of quiet pleasures" is *The Philadelphia Inquirer's* most apt description for this elegantly appointed Victorian inn. The superb dining opportunities at Gabiel's Restaurant (on-site) coupled with the antique-filled lodging accommodations provide romance and ambiance. An upscale experience in a rural setting. Guests relay that they depart feeling nurtured, relaxed, yet, most of all, inspired. Gifts, herb garden, air-conditioning. AAA approved.

Hosts: Nancy and John Showers
Rooms: 6 (PB) $75-85
Full Breakfast
Credit Cards: A, B
Notes: 2, 3, 4, 5, 7, 8, 9, 10

NOTES: Credit cards accepted: A Master Card; B Visa; C American Express; D Discover; E Diners Club; F Other; 2 Personal checks accepted; 3 Lunch available; 4 Dinner available;

## NEW HOPE

### The Whitehall Inn

1370 Pineville Rd., 18938
(215) 598-7945

Join us at The Whitehall, our c. 1794 Bucks County Inn. Afternoon tea begins your stay. We will help you make plans to enjoy chamber music concerts, special summer picnics, and more. You will indulge yourself in the romance of a candlelit, fireplaced room which features such amenities as Whitehall's chocolate truffles, velour robes, and bath salts. Our four course breakfast, called "Sumptuous" by *Bon Appetit*, will set the mood for the rest of your day—nothing less than perfect!

Hosts: Mike and Suella Wass
Rooms: 6 (4PB; 2SB) $130-190
Full, Four-Course Candlelight Breakfast
Credit Cards: A, B, C, D, E
Notes: 2, 5, 8, 9 (on-site), 10, 12

## NEW WILMINGTON

### Behm's Bed and Breakfast

166 Waugh Ave., 16142
(412) 946-8641; (800) 932-3315

Located but one block from Westminster College campus, Behm's 100 year old B&B is comfortably furnished with family, primitive, and collected antiques. Located within walking distance of shops and restaurants, Behm's is surrounded by rural, Old Or-

der Amish. Nationally recognized watercolorist Nancy Behm's gallery on site.

Hosts: Bob and Nancy Behm
Rooms: 5 (1PB; 4SB) $50
Full Hearty Breakfast
Credit Cards: A, B
Notes: 2, 5, 7, 8, 9, 10

## NEWVILLE

### Nature's Nook Farm

740 Shed Road, 17241
(717) 776-5619

Nature's Nook Farm is located in a quiet, peaceful setting along the Blue Mountains. Warm Mennonite hospitality and clean, comfortable lodging await you. Enjoy freshly brewed, garden tea and fresh fruit in season. Homemade cinnamon rolls, muffins, or coffee cake are a specialty. Perennial flower garden. Close to Colonel Denning State Park with hiking trails, fishing, and swimming. Two hours to Lancaster, one hour to Harrisburg, anf one and a half hours to Gettysburg and Hershey. Wheelchair accessible.

Hosts: Don and Lois Leatherman
Rooms: 1 (PB) $50
Continental Breakfast
Credit Cards: none
Notes: 2, 5, 7, 8, 9, 10

Nature's Nook Farm

---

5 Open all year; 6 Pets welcome; 7 Children welcome; 8 Tennis nearby; 9 Swimming nearby; 10 Golf nearby; 11 Skiing nearby; 12 May be booked through travel agent.

## NORTH EAST

### Vineyard Bed and Breakfast

10757 Sidehill Rd., 16428
(814) 725-5307

Your hosts would like to welcome you to the "Heart of Grape Country" on the shores of Lake Erie where you are surrounded by vineyards and orchards. Our turn-of-the-century farmhouse is quiet and peaceful with rooms furnished with queen or king beds and tastefully decorated to complement our home.

Hosts: Clyde and Judy Burnham
Rooms: 4 (2PB; 2SB) $55
Full Breakfast
Credit Cards: A, B
Notes: 2, 5, 7, 9, 10, 11

## NORTHUMBERLAND

### Campbell's Bed and Breakfast

707 Duke St., 17857
(717) 473-3276

Campbell's Bed and Breakfast, a turn-of-the-century inn built in 1859, has three large bedrooms await your occupancy. Enjoy a refreshing swim in the large in-ground pool surrounded by the rose garden, or relax by the fire in the spacious living room during the cool months.

Hosts: Bob and Millie Campbell
Rooms: 3 (2PB; 1SB) $50-60
Full Breakfast
Credit Cards: none
Notes: 2, 5, 7 (cal first), 8, 9 (on-site), 10, 12

Little Britain Manor

## NOTTINGHAM

### Little Britain Manor

20 Brawn Rd., (Village of Little Britain), 19362
(717) 529-2862

We are a farm B&B surrounded by Amish and Mennonite farms in beautiful Southern Lancaster County. Relax in our quiet, restful, country home away from noise, busy crowds, and city traffic. Gather in the large farm kitchen to enjoy a full country breakfast and experience the warmth of heartfelt hospitality. Nicely located to do Lancaster Amish attractions, antiques, crafts, Longwood Gardens, and Baltimore Inner Harbor.

Hosts: Fred and Evelyn Crider
Rooms: 4 (SB) $50
Full Country Breakfast
Credit Cards: none
Notes: 2, 7

## ORRTENNA

### Hickory Bridge Farm

96 Hickory Bridge Rd., 17353
(717) 642-5261

Only eight miles west of historical

---

NOTES: Credit cards accepted: A Master Card; B Visa; C American Express; D Discover; E Diners Club; F Other; 2 Personal checks accepted; 3 Lunch available; 4 Dinner available;

Gettysburg. Unique country dining and B&B. Cozy cottages with wood stoves and private baths located in secluded wooded settings along a stream. Full, farm breakfast served at the farmhouse which was built in the late 1700s. Country dining offered on Fridays, Saturdays, and Sundays in a 130-year-old barn decorated with many antiques. Family owned and operated for over 15 years.

Hosts: Dr. and Nancy Jean Hammett
Rooms: 7 (6PB; 1SB) $79-89
Full Breakfast
Credit Cards: A, B
Notes: 2, 4 (on weekends), 5, 7, 8, 9, 10, 11

## PARADISE

## Maple Lane Farm Bed and Breakfast
505 Paradise Lane, 17562
(717) 687-7479

This 200-acre, family owned dairy farm is situated in the heart of Amish Country with nearby quilt and craft shops, museums, farmers' markets, antique shops, outlets, and auctions. The large front porch overlooks spacious lawn, green meadows, and rolling hills with no busy highways. Pleasantly furnished rooms have quilts, crafts, canopy and poster beds, TV, and air-conditioning. Victorian parlor for guest use. Breakfast served daily. Featured in several national magazines.

Hosts: Ed and Marion Rohrer
Rooms: 4 (2PB; 2SB) $45-58
Continental Plus Breakfast
Credit Cards: none
Notes: 2, 5, 7, 8, 9, 10, 12

## Parson's Place in Pardise B&B
37 Leacock Road, 17562
(717) 687-8529

Mid 1700s stone house with stone house with stone patio overlooking flower gardens and picturesque road traveled by horse-drawn buggies to the Amsh village-mecca of "Intercourse" (the tourist center of Lancaster county) three miles to the East. Share this charming home furnished with country decor with former pastor and wife.

Hosts: Parson Bob and Margaret Bell
Rooms: 3 (2PB; 1SB) $50-70
Full Menu Breakfast
Credit Cards: none
Notes: 2, 5

## PEACH BOTTOM

## Inn-Between
177 Riverview Rd., 17563
(717) 548-2141

Our century-old farmhouse sits in the rolling hills of Lancaster County. From the enclosed second floor porch you can look out over the beautiful countryside. We offer a peaceful, comfortable stay after a day of sight-seeing or shopping, or a quiet getaway for a weekend. A full breakfast is provided including specially prepared dishes along with homemade breads and pastries.

Hosts: Bob and Miriam Dempsey
Rooms: 3 (1PB; 2SB) $50-60
Full Breakfast
Credit Cards: none
Notes: 2, 5, 7, 10

---

5 Open all year; 6 Pets welcome; 7 Children welcome; 8 Tennis nearby; 9 Swimming nearby; 10 Golf nearby; 11 Skiing nearby; 12 May be booked through travel agent.

## Pleasant Grove Farm Bed and Breakfast

368 Pilottown Rd., 17563
(717) 548-3100

Located in beautiful, historic Lancaster County, this 160 acre dairy farm has been a family run operation for 110 years, earning the title of Century Farm by the Pennsylvania Department of Agriculture. As a working farm, it provides guests the opportunity to experience daily life in a rural setting. Built in 1814, 1818, and 1820, the house once served as a country store and post office. Full country breakfast served by candlelight.

Hosts: Charles and Labertha Tindall
Rooms: 4 (SB) $45-60
Full Breakfast
Credit Cards: none
Notes: 2, 5, 7, 9

## POCONO MOUNTAINS
## (SEE ALSO—CANADENSIS, CRESCO, AND SWIFTWATER)

## Eagle Rock Lodge Bed and Breakfast

P.O .Box 265, River Rd., **Shawnee on Deleware** 18356
(717) 421-2139

This century-old, seven-room inn is located on 10.5 Delaware River acres adjacent to the scenic Delaware Water Gap National Recreation Area and the Pocono Mountains. Breakfast is served on an 80-foot Screened porch overlooking the river. Enjoy a step back in time to a more relaxed by-gone era. Consider group rentals.

Hosts: Jane and Jim Cox
Rooms: 8 (1PB; 6SB) $60-95
Full Breakfast
Credit Cards: C
Notes: 2, 5, 7, 8, 9, 10, 11, 12

## POINT PLEASANT (NEW HOPE)

## Tattersall Inn

P.O. Box 569, Cafferty and River Rd., 18950
(215) 297-8233

This 18th century, plastered, fieldstone home with its broad porches and manicured lawns resembles the unhurried atmosphere of a bygone era. Enjoy the richly wainscoted entry hall, formal dining room with marble fireplace, and a collection of vintage phonographs. Step back in time when you enter the Colonial common room with beamed ceiling and walk-in fireplace. The spacious, antique-furnished guest rooms are a joy. Air-conditioned. Private baths.

Hosts: Gerry and Herb Moss
Rooms: 6 (PB) $70-109
Continental Breakfast
Credit Cards: A, B, C, D
Notes: 2, 5, 7, 8, 9, 12

## QUARRYVILLE

## Runnymede Farm Guest House Bed and Breakfast

1030 Robert Fulton Highway, 17566
(717) 786-3625

Enjoy our comfortable farmhouse in southern Lancaster County. The rooms are clean and air-conditioned, and the

---

NOTES: Credit cards accepted: A Master Card; B Visa; C American Express; D Discover; E Diners Club; F Other; 2 Personal checks accepted; 3 Lunch available; 4 Dinner available;

lounge has a TV. Close to tourist attractions, but not in the mainstream. Country breakfast is optional.

Hosts: Herb and Sara Hess
Rooms: 3 (SB) $35-40
Full Breakfast
Credit Cards: none
Notes: 2, 5, 7, 8, 9, 10

## SAXONBURG

### The Main Stay B&B

P.O. Box 507, 214 Main St., 16056
(412) 352-9363

This 150-year-old country home is located in Saxonburg, in the heart of farm country in southern Butler County of Pennsylvania, about 30 miles from Pittsburgh. Its a fine place to get away from the stress and strains of everyday life or to spend the night enroute east or west. Saxonburg is not a large place but it boasts some fine shops to browse and an excellent restaurant to enjoy.

Hosts: Barbara and Ivan Franson
Rooms: 4 (PB) $60 (includes tax)
Full Breakfast
Credit Cards: A, B, C
Notes: 2, 5, 7, 10

The Main Stay Bed and Breakfast

## SCOTTDALE

### Pine Wood Acres Bed and Breakfast

Route 1, Box 634, 15683
(412) 887-5404

A country home surrounded by four acres of woods, wildflowers, and herb and flower gardens. Ten miles from the Pennsylvania Turnpike and I-70, New Stanton exits; 22 miles from Frank Lloyd Wright's Fallingwater. Full breakfasts and warm hospitality are yours to enjoy at Pine Wood Acres. Hosts are members of the Mennonite Church.

Hostess: Ruth A. Horsch
Rooms: 3 (2PB; 1SB) $68.90-79.50
Full Breakfast
Credit Cards: none
Notes: 2, 5, 6, 7, 8, 9, 10, 11, 12

## SHIPPENSBURG

### Field and Pine Bed and Breakfast

2155 Ritner Hwy., 17257
(717) 776-7179

Surrounded by stately pine trees, Field and Pine is a family owned B&B with the charm of an Early American stone house on an 80-acre gentleman's farm. Built in 1790, the house has seven working fireplaces, original wide-pine floors, and stenciled walls. Bedrooms are furnished with antiques, quilts, and comforters. A gourmet breakfast is served

5 Open all year; 6 Pets welcome; 7 Children welcome; 8 Tennis nearby; 9 Swimming nearby; 10 Golf nearby; 11 Skiing nearby; 12 May be booked through travel agent.

in the formal dining room. Three miles from I-81 between Carlisle and Shippensburg.

Hosts: Mary Ellen and Allan Williams
Rooms: 3 (1PB; 2SB) $65-75
Full Breakfast
Credit Cards: A, B
Notes: 2, 5, 8, 9, 10, 12

## Wilmar Manor Bed and Breakfast

303 West King Street, 17257
(717) 532-3784

A beautiful Victorian mansion built in 1898 in the heart of Shippensburg. You can stroll down Main Street of our historic village or enjoy the serenity of our spacious landscaped gardens. The air-conditioned guest rooms are comfortably furnished with antiques. Your choice of private or shared baths at reasonable rates. Enjoy a delicious breakfast served in our formal Victorian dining room.

Hosts:  Marise and Wilton Banks
Rooms:  7 (2PB; 5SB) $52-60
Full Breakfast
Credit Cards:  A, B
Notes:  2, 5, 7, 9, 10, 11, 12

Wilmar Manor Bed and Breakfast

Homestead Lodging

## SMOKETOWN

## Homestead Lodging

184 E. Brook Rd., 17576
(717) 393-6927

Welcome to Homestead Lodging in the heart of the Pennsylvania Dutch Amish farmlands. Listen to the clippity-clop of horse and buggies go by or stroll down the lane to the scenic farmlands around us. Within walking distance of restaurants and minutes from farmers' markets; quilt, antique, and craft shops; museums; and auctions. Tours available. Family-operated B&B with clean, country rooms, each with private bath, cable color TV with remote/radio, refrigerator, air-conditioning, and heat. Microwave available.

Hosts: Robert and Lori Kepiro
Rooms: 4 (PB) $34-56
Continental Breakfast
Credit Cards: A, B
Notes: 2 (deposit only), 5, 7, 8, 9, 10, 11

## Old Road Guest Home

2501 Old Phila Pike, 17576
(717) 393-8182

Old Road Guest Home is nestled in the

NOTES:  Credit cards accepted:  A  Master Card;  B  Visa;  C  American Express;  D  Discover;
E  Diners Club;  F  Other;  2  Personal checks accepted;  3  Lunch available;  4  Dinner available;

rolling farmlands in the heart of Pennsylvania Dutch Country. Comfortable air conditioned rooms with TV. Ground floor rooms available. Spacious shaded lawn to enjoy picnics. Easy parking. Private and shared baths. Near fine restaurants. Alcoholic beverages and indoor smoking prohibited.

Hostess: Marian Buckwalter
Rooms: 6 (3PB; 3SB) $28-35
No Breakfast
Credit Cards: none
Notes: 2, 5, 7, 9, 10

## Smoketown Lodging and Carriage House Bed and Breakfast

190 E. Brook Rd., 17576
(717) 397-6944

Nestled on three beautiful acres of an original Amish homestead. Our guests call it their "home away from home." Enjoy a walk down the lane to our Amish neighbors or by the stream to feed the ducks. Relax on our two patios or in our non-smoking lounge, or enjoy a game of tennis on our new court. Restaurants including a family-style restaurant, within walking distance; buggy rides; farmers and flea markets, and outlets just a short distance. All rooms have full bath, AC, CA/TV, clock radio, and refrigerator.

Hosts: Don and Phyllis Ringuette
Rooms: 17 (PB) $34-56
Continental Breakfast
Credit Cards: A, B
Notes: 2, 5, 7, 8, 9 (on premises), 10, 12

# SOMERSET

## H.B.'s Cottage

231 W. Church St., 15501
(814) 443-1204

H.B.'s Cottage, an exclusive and elegant B&B located within the Borough of Somerset, is a stone and frame 1920s cottage with an oversize fireplace in the living room. It is furnished in the traditional manner with accent pieces from the innkeepers' overseas travels—a retired Naval Officer and his wife—and collectible Teddy Bears from the hostess' extensive collection. The guest rooms are warmly and romantically decorated and have a porch attached. Downhill and cross-country skiing, mountain biking, and tennis are specialties of the hosts. Located close to Seven Springs Mountain Resort, Falling Water Hidden Valley Resort, biking and hiking trails, and white water sports. Advance reservations are suggested.

Hosts: Hank and Phyllis Vogt
Rooms: 2 (PB) $65
Full Breakfast
Credit Cards: A, B
Notes: 2, 6 (limited), 8, 9, 10, 11

# SPRUCE CREEK

## The Dell's B&B at Cedar Hill Farm

HC-01, Box 26, Route 45 E., 16683
(814) 632-8319

This early 1800s farmhouse is located in Huntingdon County on an active livestock farm. Individual and family activities are available at Old Bedford

---

5 Open all year; 6 Pets welcome; 7 Children welcome; 8 Tennis nearby; 9 Swimming nearby; 10 Golf nearby; 11 Skiing nearby; 12 May be booked through travel agent.

Village, Horse Shoe Curve, Bland's Park, Raystown Lake, Lincoln and Indian Caverns, and Penn State University. Member of the Pennsylvania Farm Vacation Association. Fishing and hunting available on private and state game lands during stated seasons; proper licenses required.

Hostess: Sharon M. Dell
Rooms: 4 (SB) $35-50
Full Breakfast
Credit Cards: A, B
Notes: 2, 5, 7, 11

## STAHLSTOWN

### Thorn's Cottage Bed and Breakfast

RD 1, Box 254, 15687
(412) 593-6429

Located in the natural, cultural, and historic Ligonier Valley area of Pennsylvania's scenic Laurel Mountains, PA turnpike eight miles away, fifty miles east of Pittsburgh, the secluded three-room cottage offers guests homey, woodland privacy. In addition, the hosts offer one bedroom (shared bath) in their cozy, arts and crafts bungalow. Porches and herb garden complement the European, country-inspired ambiance. Breakfast includes homebaked muffins and scones to complement country, gourmet-style dishes.

Hosts: Larry and Beth Thorn
Rooms: 1 + 1 cottage (1PB; 1SB) $40-55
Full Breakfast
Credit Cards: none
Notes: 2, 5, 7, 9, 10, 11

## STARRUCCA

### Nethercott Inn

P.O. Box 26, 18462
(717) 727-2211; FAX (717) 727-3811

This lovely, 1893 Victorian home is nestled in a small village in the Endless Mountains and furnished in a pleasing mixture of country and antiques. All rooms have queen-size beds and private baths. A full breakfast is included. Located three and one half hours from New York City and Philadelphia, and eight hours from Toronto, Canada.

Hosts: Charlotte and John Keyser
Rooms: 5 (PB) $75 (midweek discounts available)
Full Breakfast
Credit Cards: A, B, C, D
Notes: 2, 5, 7, 10, 11, 12 (10%)

## STRASBURG

### The Decoy Bed and Breakfast

958 Gisenberger Rd., 17579
(717) 687-8585 (voice and FAX);
(800) 726-2287

This former Amish home is set in farmland with spectacular views and an informal atmosphere. Craft shops and attractions are nearby, and bicycle tours can be arranged. Two cats in residence.

Hosts: Debby and Hap Joy
Rooms: 5 (PB) $53.00-74.20
Full Breakfast
Credit Cards: none
Notes: 2, 5, 7, 8, 10, 12

---

NOTES: Credit cards accepted: A Master Card; B Visa; C American Express; D Discover; E Diners Club; F Other; 2 Personal checks accepted; 3 Lunch available; 4 Dinner available;

## SWIFTWATER

### *Holiday Glen Resort*

P.O. Box 96, Bush Rd., 18370
(717) 839-7015

Does the hectic pace of civilization
make you long for tranquillity? Come
to the Holiday Glen, a quiet little country resort tucked away in the scenic
Paradise Valley of the Poconos. On our
17 acres, wooded trails lead you into a
quiet forest and a world of peace, or fish
in our pond and stream. Cottages have
queen beds, air-conditioning, minifridges, TVs, and fireplaces. A country breakfast is served compliments of
your Scottish host, Sarah.

Hostess: Sarah Caulfield
Cabins: 9 (PB) $75-90
Full Breakfast
Credit Cards: A, B
Notes: 5, 7, 8, 9, 10, 11

## THOMPSON

### *Farmhouse Bed and Breakfast*

Campsite Rd., RR 2, Box 57, 18465
(717) 727-3061

An 1864 farmstead that raises sheep and
other farm animals. Enjoy the quiet of
our country home. Secluded getaway
decorated in period pieces and paintings
with antique woodstove and glass enclosed sunporch and parlor. Full, country breakfast included. Delectable pasta
dishes prepared by your Italian hostess
upon advance request. Also private loft
for groups.

Hosts: Marian and Harold Hartnett
Rooms: 5 (PB) $25-65
Full Breakfast
Credit Cards: none
Notes: 2, 4, 5, 7, 11

Jefferson Inn

### *Jefferson Inn*

RR 2, Box 36, Main St., Route 171, 18465
(717) 727-2625; (800) JEFF INN

Built in 1871, the Inn offers reasonably
priced accommodations and a full-
service restaurant. Situated in the rolling hills of northeast Pennsylvania,
there are thousands of acres available
nearby for fishing, boating, and some
of the best deer and turkey hunting
around. Other seasonal activities include skiing, snowmobiling, horseback
riding, and golf. Good, Gospel-preach-
ing churches are nearby.

Hosts: Douglas and Margaret Stark
Rooms: 6 (3PB; 3SB) $30-50
Full or Continental Breakfast
Credit Cards: A, B
Notes: 2, 3, 4, 5, 6, 7, 8, 9, 10, 11, 12

---

5  Open all year;  6  Pets welcome;  7  Children welcome;  8  Tennis nearby;  9  Swimming nearby;
10  Golf nearby;  11  Skiing nearby;  12  May be booked through travel agent.

## THORTON

### Pace One Restaurant and Country Inn

P.O. Box 108, 19373
(610) 459-3702; FAX (610) 558-0852

Pace One is a beautifully renovated 1740s stone barn. We have six overnight rooms, all with private baths and queen-size beds. Pace One is known for its restaurant. The seventy five seat restaurant and bar is very relaxed and rustic. The menu is country imaginative and has an offering of fresh seafood, steaks, fowl, and lamb. All desserts are homemade. Private rooms are also available for meetings and dining. Reservations for the Inn's rooms are taken Monday through Friday 9 AM to 5 PM by the sales office.

Proprietor: Ted Pace
Rooms: 6 (PB)
Continental Plus Breakfast
Credit Cards: A, B, C, E
Notes: 2, 3, 4, 5, 7, 8, 10, 12

## VALLEY FORGE

### Association of Bed and Breakfasts in Philadelphia, Valley Forge, and Brandywine

P.O. Box 562, 19481
(610) 783-7838; (800) 344-0123;
FAX (610) 783-7783

There is a B&B for you!—whether business, vacation, getaways, or relocating. Also serving **Bucks** and **Lancaster** **Counties**. Over 500 rooms available in historic city/country inn, town houses, unhosted estate cottages, and apartments. Request a free brochure, family plan, jacuzzi, fireplace, pool, or descriptive directory ($3). Special services include gift certificates, dinner reservations, wedding/special occasions/photography at unique B&Bs, personal attention, and gracious hospitality. No fee for reservations. Featured in *Philadelphia Magazine*. Rates range from $35 to $135. Major credit cards accepted. Carolyn J. Williams, coordinator.

### The Great Valley House of Valley Forge

110 Swedesford Rd., Rd. 3, **Malvern** 19355
(610) 644-6759; FAX (610) 644-7019

"Did George Washington sleep here?" is the most often asked question at this 300-year-old stone farmhouse dating back to 1690. The house retains original fireplaces, random-width wood floors, and hand-forged nails. Each of the guest rooms are hand-stenciled, decorated with antiques, and accented with handmade quilts. The surrounding four acres contain an old smokehouse, a cold storage keep, and ancient trees, as well as a modern diversion: a large swimming pool.

Hostess: Pattye Benson
Rooms: 3 (2PB; 2 SB) $75-85
Full Breakfast
Credit Cards: none
Notes: 2, 5, 7, 8, 9, 11, 12

---

NOTES: Credit cards accepted: A Master Card; B Visa; C American Express; D Discover; E Diners Club; F Other; 2 Personal checks accepted; 3 Lunch available; 4 Dinner available;

# WELLSBORO

## *Kaltenbach's Bed and Breakfast*

RD #6 Box 106A, Stony Fork Rd., 16901
(717) 724-4954; (800) 722-4954

This sprawling, country home with room for 32 guests offers visitors comfortable lodging, home-style breakfasts, and warm hospitality. Set on a 72-acre farm, Kaltenbach's provides ample opportunity for walks through meadows, pastures, and forests; picnicing; and watching the sheep, pigs, rabbits, and wildlife. All-you-can-eat country breakfasts are served. Honeymoon suites have tubs for two. Hunting and golf packages are available. Pennsylvania Grand Canyon. Kaltenbach's was awarded a three-Crown rating from the American Bed and Breakfast Association for its accommodations and hospitality.

Host: Lee Kaltenbach
Rooms: 10 (8PB; 2SB) $60-125
Full Breakfast
Credit Cards: A, B
Notes: 2, 3, 4, 5, 7, 8, 9, 10, 11

## *Wood's Rustic Inn*

Little Marsh Village, RR 2, Box 98A,
**Middlebury Center** 16935
(717) 376-3331

Relaxed, friendly atmosphere with beautiful flowers on a well groomed three-acre lawn. Clean, modern rooms with cable TV. Full, country, cooked breakfast served in an elegant manner on our lovely patio outside—weather permitting. . .large furnished porches for your enjoyment and fresh air. Golfing just ten minutes away. Near four lakes—all with swimming, camping, boating, and fishing. Great for bicycling, walking, sitting along the creeks and ponds, and enjoying our Belgian horses and wildlife on 600 acres of land that is great for hunting.

Hosts: Waldo and Olive Wood
Rooms: 6 (PB) $44 and up
Full Breakfast
Credit Cards: none
Notes: 2 (and travelers'), 7, 8, 9, 10

Ponda-Rowland Bed and Breakfast Inn

# WILKES-BARRE

## *Ponda-Rowland Bed and Breakfast Inn*

RR 1, Box 349, **Dallas** 18612
(717) 639-3245; (800) 854-3286;
FAX (717) 639-5531

The farmhouse, circa 1850, features a large stone fireplace, beamed ceilings, fireplaces in rooms, and museum-quality, country antiques. On this large, scenic farm in the Endless Mountain region of Pennsylvania, guests can see

---

5 Open all year; 6 Pets welcome; 7 Children welcome; 8 Tennis nearby; 9 Swimming nearby; 10 Golf nearby; 11 Skiing nearby; 12 May be booked through travel agent.

and touch pigs, goats, sheep, cows, rabbits, and horses. They also can enjoy 34 acres of private wildlife refuge, including six ponds, walking and skiing trails, canoeing, swimming, and ice skating. Nearby are horseback riding, air tours, state parks, trout fishing, hunting, restaurants, county fairs, and downhill skiing.

Hosts: Jeanette and Cliff Rowland
Rooms: 5 (PB) $55-85
Full Breakfast
Credit Cards: A, B, C, D
Notes: 2, 5, 7, 10, 11, 12

## WILLOW STREET

### The Inn at Hayward Heath

2048 Silver Lane, 17584
(717) 464-0994

The Inn at Hayward Heath is located in the heart of Amish Country in beautiful Lancaster County, Pennsylvania. This country farmhouse, built in 1890, has been restored to replicate Colonial living. It features a walk-in fireplace, spacious air-conditioned bedrooms with private and shared baths, a jacuzzi, a large living room for guests and close proximity to historic areas and tourist attractions. A sumptuous breakfast is served in the formal dining room each morning.

Hosts: Joan and David Smith
Rooms: 3 (2PB; 1SB) $80-100
Full Breakfast
Credit Cards: none
Notes: 2, 5, 8, 10

## YORK

### Friendship House

728 E. Philadelphia St., 17403
(717) 843-8299

"A touch of country in the city" describes this turn-of-the-century bed and breakfast home. Relax in the privacy of the side yard and patio. Then retire to one of three comfortable guestrooms with private baths. Country breakfast served most mornings. Off-street parking, locked garage available. Only minutes to York's historic area, fairgrounds, outlet shops, and fine restaurants.

Hostesses: Becky Detwiler and Karen Maust
Rooms: 3 (PB) $50-60
Full Breakfast
Credit Cards: none
Notes: 2, 5, 7, 8, 9, 10, 11

Friendship House

Historic Benvenue Manor Bed and Breakfast

## ZELIENOPLE

## *Historic Benvenue Manor Bed and Breakfast*

160 Manor Drive, 16063
(412) 452-1710

"Benvenue" original name of our 1816 stone manor home means a "Good Welcome." Enjoy a spectacular view, relax by the open fire, feast on a gourmet breakfast, four Victorian bedrooms, two private baths, guest livingroom, gracious hospitality. Children welcome, 35 minutes downtown Pittsburgh.

Hostess: Margo L. Hogan
Rooms: 4 (2PB; 2SB) $55-70
Full Breakfast
Credit Cards: none
Notes: 2, 3, 4, 5, 7, 8, 9, 10

## *The Inn on Grandview*

310 E. Grandview Ave., 16063
(412) 452-0469

Nestled in historic Zelienople, The Inn on Grandview was built in the early 19th century. Originally known as the Zimmerman Hotel, it has been completely renovated to its original charm and splendor. The comfortable and beautiful bedrooms are located on the second floor with private baths, television, and air-conditioning. Within a half hour you can reach Pittsburgh to the south or Amish farms to the north. Your hosts will be happy to direct you to the many antique and craft/gift shops that grace to country side.

Hosts: Rich and Juanita Eppinger
Rooms: 4 (PB) $75-95
Full Breakfast
Credit Cards: A, B, D
Notes: 2, 5, 8, 9, 10, 11, 12

The Inn on Grandview

---

5 Open all year; 6 Pets welcome; 7 Children welcome; 8 Tennis nearby; 9 Swimming nearby; 10 Golf nearby; 11 Skiing nearby; 12 May be booked through travel agent.

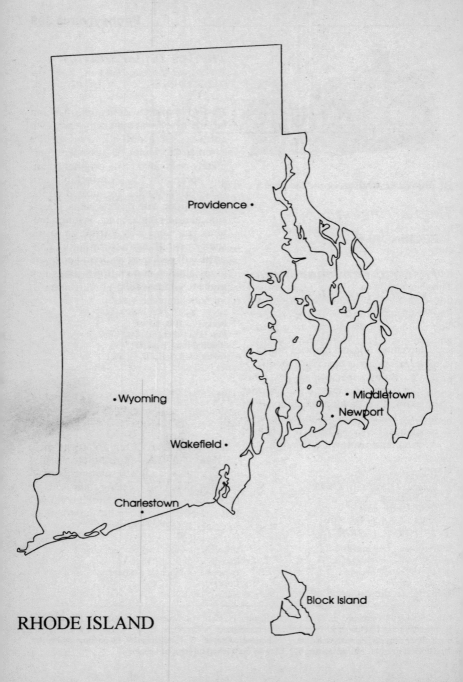

Providence •

• Wyoming

• Middletown

• Newport

Wakefield •

Charlestown •

Block Island

RHODE ISLAND

# Rhode Island

## BLOCK ISLAND

### The Barrington Inn

P.O. Box 397, (Corner of Beach and Ocean Ave.), 02807
(401) 466-5510; FAX (401) 466-5170

Known for its warmth and hospitality, The Barrington Inn is an 1886 farmhouse situated on a knoll overlooking the New Harbor area of Block Island. There are six individually decorated guest rooms with private baths, and two housekeeping apartments. A light breakfast is served each morning by the hosts. Amenities include two guests' sitting rooms (one with TV), guests' refrigerator, ceiling fans, comfortable beds, front porch, back deck, and afternoon beverages. No smoking.

Hosts: Joan and Howard Ballard
Rooms: 6 (PB) $45-145
Continental Plus Breakfast
Credit Cards: A, B
Notes: 2, 7 (over 12), 8, 9

### The Rose Farm Inn

Roslyn Road - Box E, 02807
(401) 466-2034 or (401) 466-2021;
FAX (401) 466-2053

Experience the romance of the Victo-rian era. Treat yourself to a romantic room beautifully furnished with antiques and king- or queen-size bed. Enjoy the peaceful tranquillity of the farm from shaded decks cooled by gentle breezes. Gaze at the ocean from your window or share a whirlpool bath for two. Awaken to a light buffet breakfast served in our charming porch dining room with an ocean view.

Hostess: Judith B. Rose
Rooms: 19 (17PB;2SB) $90-175
Continental Plus Breakfast
Credit Card: A, B, C, D
Notes: 2, 7 (over 11), 8, 9

### The Sheffield House

Box C-Z High Street, 02807
(401) 466-2494; FAX (401) 466-5067

Lovely Victorian set amid gardens in the historic district—five minute walk to ferry dock, shops, restaurants, and beaches. Porch with rocking chairs adds to the tranquil ambiance. Buffet breakfast and afternoon tea in the day room. Special off season prices.

Hosts: Steve and Claire McQueeny
Rooms: 7 (5PB; 2SB) $50-150
Expansive Continental Breakfast
Credit Cards: A, B, C, E
Notes: 2, 5, 8, 9, 12

---

NOTES: Credit cards accepted: A Master Card; B Visa; C American Express; D Discover; E Diners Club; F Other; 2 Personal checks accepted; 3 Lunch available; 4 Dinner available; 5 Open all year; 6 Pets welcome; 7 Children welcome; 8 Tennis nearby; 9 Swimming nearby; 10 Golf nearby; 11 Skiing nearby; 12 May be booked through travel agent.

Hotel Manisses

## CHARLESTOWN

### Hotel Manisses

1 Spring Street, 02807
(401) 466-2421; FAX (401) 466-2858

Restored Victorian hotel with authentic turn-of-the-century furnishings and today's comforts. All rooms with private bath and telephone; some have jacuzzis. Fine dining in our dining room overlooking the fountains and gardens. After-dinner drinks and flaming coffees served in upstairs parlor.

Hosts: Justin and Joan Abrams with Steve and Rita Draper
Rooms: 17 (PB) $100-350
Full Breakfast
Credit Cards: A, B, C
Notes: 2, 4, 5, 7 (over 10), 8, 9, 10, 12

## MIDDLETOWN

### Finnegan's Inn at Shadow Lawn

120 Miantonomi Ave., 02842
(401) 849-1298; (800) 828-0000;
FAX (401) 849-1306

Finnegan's Inn is one of Newport

County's finest B&B inns, set on two acres of beautifully landscaped lawns and gardens. This 1850's Victorian mansion, with its crystal chandeliers and stained-glassed windows, has eight large bedrooms each with private bath, TV, refrigerator, and air-conditioning. Five rooms also have attached kitchens. Come and enjoy a bottle of complimentary wine.

Hosts: Randy and Selma Fabricant
Rooms: 8 (PB)
Full Breakfast
Credit Cards: A, B
Notes: 5, 7 (over 12), 8, 9, 10, 12

### Lindsey's Guest House

6 James Street, 02842
(401) 846-9386

Walk to beaches and restaurants. Five minutes to Newport's famous mansions, Ocean Drive, Cliff Walk, boat and bus tours, and bird sanctuary. Quiet residential neighborhood with off-street parking. Large yard and deck with hostess available for information about events and discounts. Split-level, owner-occupied home with expanded continental breakfast. One room is wheel chair accessible for 28-inch wheelchair.

Hostess: Anne Lindsey
Rooms: 4 (wPB;2SB) $45-85
Full Breakfast
Credit Cards: A, B
Notes: 2, 5, 7, 8, 9, 10, 12

---

NOTES: Credit cards accepted: A Master Card; B Visa; C American Express; D Discover; E Diners Club; F Other; 2 Personal checks accepted; 3 Lunch available; 4 Dinner available;

## NEWPORT

### Brinley Victorian Inn

23 Brinley Street, 02840
(401) 849-7649; (800) 999-8523

Romantic year round, the Inn becomes
a Victorian Christmas dream come true.
Comfortable antiques and fresh flowers fill every room. Easy walking to
most attractions with off-road parking
on site. Friendly, unpretentious, service
AAA rated.

Hosts: John and Jennifer Sweetman (owners)
Rooms: 17 (13 PB, 4 SB) $55-149
Credit Cards: A, B
Notes: 2, 5, 7 (over 8), 8, 9, 10, 12

The Burbank Rose

### The Burbank Rose

111 Memorial Blvd. West, 02840
(401) 849-9457

Named for American horticulturist
Luther Burbank, this 1850's federal
style home is located in Newport's historic downtown. Harbor with world
class restaurants and shopping is just
steps from our door. Less than one-half
mile to mansions and beach. Clean,
comfortable rooms with queen-size
beds, air-conditioning, cable TV, and
telephone in guest sitting room.

Hosts: John and Bonnie McNeely
Rooms: 3 (PB) $49-129
Full Breakfast
Credit Cards: C
Notes: 2, 5, 8, 9, 10, 12

### Cliffside Inn

2 Seaview Avenue, 02840
(401) 847-1811; (800) 845-1811;
FAX (401) 848-5850

Nestled upon a quiet neighborhood
street just steps away from the historic
Cliff Walk, the Cliffside Inn displays
the grandure of a Victorian manor with
the warmth and comfort of a home. A
full breakfast, consisting of homemade
muffins, granola, fresh fruit, and a hot
entree, such as eggs benidect or
whipped cream topped French toast, is
served each morning in the spacious
parlor. In the evening between 5-7PM
appetizers are also served. There are
thirteen guest rooms, each uniquely
decorated in period Victorian antiques
blended with luxurious Laura Ashley
linens and drapes. Each room contains
a telephone and private bath, some with
working fireplaces and jacuzzis or
steambaths. Smoking is permitted on
the large front verandah, furnished with
wicker furniture and covered with floral cushions. All rooms are air-conditioned.

Hosts: Stephen Nicolas
Rooms: 13 (PB) $145-325
Full Hot Gourmet Breakfast
Credit Cards: A, B, C, D
Notes: 2, 5, 7 (14 and over), 8, 9, 10, 12

---

5 Open all year; 6 Pets welcome; 7 Children welcome; 8 Tennis nearby; 9 Swimming nearby;
10 Golf nearby; 11 Skiing nearby; 12 May be booked through travel agent.

La Forge Cottage

## *La Forge Cottage*

96 Pelham Street, 02840
(401) 847-4400 (voice and FAX)

A Victorian B&B in the heart of Newport's Historic Hill area. Close to beaches or downtown, and all rooms have private baths, TV, refrigerator, telephone, air-conditioning, and full breakfast room service. French, German, Spanish, and English are spoken. Minimum stay on weekends is two nights and on holidays, three nights.

Hosts: Louis and Margot Droual
Rooms: 6 + 4 suites (PB) $56.00-173.60
(includes tax)
Full or Continental Breakfast
Credit Cards: A, B, C, D
Notes: 2, 5, 7, 8, 9, 10, 12

## PROVIDENCE

## *Old Court Bed and Breakfast*

144 Bed and Breakfast, 02903
(401) 751-2002; FAX (401) 272-6566

The Old Court is filled with antique furniture, chandeliers, and memorabilia from the nineteenth century, with each room designed to reflect period tastes. All rooms have private baths, and the antique, Victorian beds are comfortable and spacious. Just a three-minute walk from the center of downtown Providence, near Brown University and Rhode Island School of Design.

Hostess: Christine Nation
Rooms: 10 + 1 suite (PB) $85-250
Full Breakfast
Credit Cards: A, B, D
Notes: 2, 5, 8, 9, 12

## *State House Inn*

43 Jewett Street, 02908
(401) 351-6111; FAX (401) 351-4261

A country inn usually means peace and quiet, friendly hosts, comfort and simplicity, with beautiful furnishings. The State House Inn has all of these qualifications, but just happens to be located in the city of Providence. Our inn has fireplaces, hardwood floors, Shaker or Colonial furnishings, canopy beds, and modern conveniences such as FAX, TV, and phone. Located near downtown and local colleges and universities.

Hosts: Frank and Monica Hopton
Rooms: 10 (PB) $59-99
Full Breakfast
Credit Cards: A, B, C
Notes: 2 (with CC for ID), 5, 7, 8, 12

## WAKEFIELD

## *Larchwood Inn*

521 Main Street, 02879
(401) 783-5454; (800) 275-5450;
FAX (401) 783-1800

Watching over the main street of the quaint New England town for over 160 years, this grand old house, surrounded by lawns and shaded by stately trees, dispenses hospitality and good food and spirits from early morning to late at night. Historic Newport, picturesque Mystic Seaport, salty Block Island, and Foxwoods Casino are a short ride away.

Hosts: Francis and Diann Browning
Rooms: 19 (12PB; 7SB) $40-100
Full Breakfast
Credit Cards: A, B, C, D, E
Notes: 2, 3, 4, 5, 6, 7, 8, 9, 10, 11, 12

## The Villa Bed and Breakfast

190 Shore Road, 02891
(401) 596-1054; (800) 722-9240;
FAX (401) 596-6268

Leave the pressures behind! Treat yourself to an award-winning private hide-a-way. Romantic jacuzzi suites, fireplace suites, and outdoor hot tub and pool. Excellent restaurants nearby. All rooms have color cable TV, refrigerators, and private baths. Breakfast is served in our dining area, in your private room, or poolside, in season. Approved by Mobile, *** AB&BA, selected by Fodor's.

Host: Jerry Maiorano
Rooms: 7 (PB) $75-195
Breakfast Buffet
Credit Cards: A, B, C
Notes: 2, 5, 6, 8, 9, 10, 12

## Woody Hill Bed and Breakfast

149 South Woody Hill Road, 02891
(401) 322-0452

This Colonial reproduction is set on a hilltop overlooking 20 acres of informal gardens, woods, and fields. Antiques, wide-board floors, handmade quilts, and fireplaces create an early American atmosphere. A full breakfast and use of secluded 40-foot, in-ground pool are included. Close to Newport, Block Island, Mystic, and Casino.

Hostess: Dr. Ellen L. Madison
Rooms: 4 (3PB; 2 SB) $60-105
Full Breakfast
Credit Cards: none
Notes: 2, 5, 7, 8, 9, 10, 12

## WYOMING

## The Cookie Jar Bed and Breakfast

64 Kingstown Road (Exit 3A off I-95), 02898
(401) 539-2680; (800) 767-4262

The heart of our home, the living room, was built in 1732 as a blacksmith's shop. Later, the forge was removed and a large granite fireplace was built by an American Indian stonemason. The original wood ceiling, hand-hewn beams, and granite walls remain today. The property was called the Perry Plantation, and, yes, they had two slaves who lived above the blacksmith's shop. All bedrooms have color TV and are air-conditioned. We offer friendly, home-style living in a comfortable, country setting. We also have two rooms with sitting rooms. On Route 138 just off I-95.

Hosts: Dick and Madelein Sohl
Rooms: 3 (PB) $75
Full Breakfast
Credit Cards: none
Notes: 2, 5, 7, 8, 9, 10, 12

5 Open all year; 6 Pets welcome; 7 Children welcome; 8 Tennis nearby; 9 Swimming nearby; 10 Golf nearby; 11 Skiing nearby; 12 May be booked through travel agent.

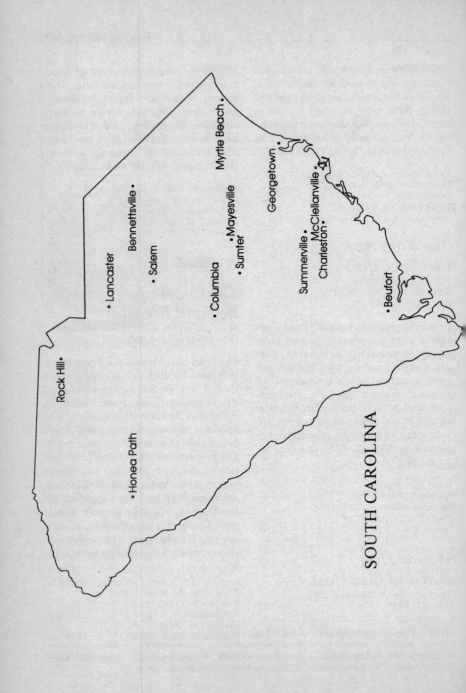

Rock Hill •

Honea Path •

Lancaster •

Bennettsville •

Salem •

Columbia •

Mayesville •
Sumter •

Myrtle Beach •

Georgetown •

Summerville •
McClellanville •
Charleston •

Beufort •

SOUTH CAROLINA

# South Carolina

## BEAUFORT

### TwoSuns Inn
### Bed and Breakfast

1705 Bay Street, 29902
(803) 522-1122; (800) 532-4244;
FAX (803) 522-1122

Enjoy the charm of a small, resident host B&B in a remarkably beautiful Nationally Landmarked Historic District about midway between Charleston and Savannah—complete with a panoramic bayview verandah, individually appointed king or queen guestrooms, an informal afternoon "Tea and Toddy Hour," and sumptuous breakfasts. The setting is idyllic, the atmosphere is casually elegant—a restored 1917 grand home with modern baths and amenities accented with collectibles and antiques. Carrol and Ron are gracious.

Hosts: Carrol and Ron Kay
Rooms: 5 (PB) $99-129
Full Breakfast
Credit Cards: A, B, C
Notes: 2, 5, 8, 9, 10, 12

TwoSuns Inn Bed and Breakfast

## BENNETTSVILLE

### The Breeden Inn
### and Carriage House

404 East Main Street, 29512
(803) 479-3665; FAX (803) 479-1040

Built in 1886, this romantic Southern mansion is situated on two acres in Bennettsville's historic district. Beautiful decor and comfortable surroundings will capture your interest and inspire your imagination. A haven for antique lovers. Listed on the National Register of Historic Places, the Inn is

---

NOTES: Credit cards accepted: A Master Card; B Visa; C American Express; D Discover; E Diners Club; F Other; 2 Personal checks accepted; 3 Lunch available; 4 Dinner available; 5 Open all year; 6 Pets welcome; 7 Children welcome; 8 Tennis nearby; 9 Swimming nearby; 10 Golf nearby; 11 Skiing nearby; 12 May be booked through travel agent.

located 25 minutes from I-95—a great halfway point between Florida and New York. Our porches and grounds...truly a Southern tradition can be enjoyed at both guest houses. Swings, rockers, wicker, cast iron, adirondacks, and even ceiling fans await to play a part in helping you unwind. Curl up with a book under the old magnolia tree...sun by the pool—there's a comfy spot for everyone. Come...we have some peace, quiet, and comfort for you. No smoking. Owned and operated by a Christian family.

Hosts: Wesley and Bonnie Park
Rooms: 7 (PB) $65
Full Breakfast
Credit Cards: A, B, D
Notes: 2, 5, 7, 9, 10, 12

## CHARLESTON

## 133 Broad Street Bed and Breakfast

133 Broad Street, 29401
(803) 577-5965

Classic Charleston townhome (circa 1870) located in the heart of the historic district. The house is completely furnished with period antiques. Three suites feature spacious rooms with ceiling fans, color cable TV, central air, telephones, private baths, and kitchens. Walking distance to countless boutiques, antique shops, museums, and excellent restaurants. Bikes are available to guests. Tennis courts are two blocks away and beautiful beaches a mere 20-minute drive. Let us share with

you America's most beautiful city!

Hosts: Doll and Jim Ward
Rooms: 3 suites (PB) $120-150
Food provided for guests to prepare
Credit Cards: none
Notes: 2, 5, 8, 9, 10

## 1837 Bed and Breakfast

126 Wentworth Street, 29401
(803) 723-7166

Enjoy accommodations in a wealthy cotton planter's home and brick carriage house centrally located in Charleston's historic district. Canopied, poster, rice beds. Walk to boat tours, the old market, antique shops, restaurants, and main attractions. Near the Omni and College of Charleston. Full, gourmet breakfast is served in the formal dining room and includes sausage pie, Eggs Benedict, ham omelets, and home-baked breads. The 1837 Tea Room serves afternoon tea to our guests and the public. Off-street parking.

Hosts: Sherri and Richard Dunn
Rooms: 8 (PB) $74-119
Special Winter Rates December - February
Full Breakfast
Credit Cards: A, B, C
Notes: 2, 5, 8, 9, 10

## Ashley Inn Bed and Breakfast

201 Ashley Avenue, 29403
(803) 723-1848; FAX (803) 768-1230

Stay in a stately, historic, circa 1835 home. So warm and hospitable, the Ashley Inn offers seven intimate bed-

NOTES: Credit cards accepted: A Master Card; B Visa; C American Express; D Discover; E Diners Club; F Other; 2 Personal checks accepted; 3 Lunch available; 4 Dinner available;

rooms featuring canopy beds, private baths, fireplace, and air-conditioning. Delicious breakfasts are served on a grand columned piazza overlooking a beautiful Charleston garden or in the formal dining room. Relax with tea and cookies after touring nearby historic sites or enjoying the complimentary touring bicycles. Simple elegance in a warm, friendly home noted for true Southern hospitality.

Hosts: Sally and Bud Allen
Rooms: 7 (PB) $69-160
Full Breakfast
Credit Cards: A, B, C, D
Notes: 2, 5, 7 (over 12), 8, 9, 10, 12

## The Belvedere Bed and Breakfast

40 Rutledge Avenue, 29401
(803) 722-0973

A late 1800s Colonial mansion in the downtown historic district on Colonial Lake has an 1800 Georgian interior with mantels and woodwork. Three large bedrooms have antiques, Oriental rugs, and family collections. Easy access to everything in the area.

Hosts: David Spell (innkeeper) and Rick Zender (manager)
Rooms: 3 (PB) $110-125
Continental Plus Breakfast
Credit Cards: none
Closed December 1-February 15
Notes: 2, 7 (over 8), 8, 9, 10

## Cannonboro Inn

184 Ashley Avenue, 29403
(803) 723-8572; FAX (803) 768-1230

This 1853 historic home offers six beau-

tifully decorated bedrooms with antique four poster and canopied beds. A place to be pampered, where you sleep in until the aroma of sizzling sausage and home baked biscuits lure you to a full breakfast on the columned piazza overlooking a low country garden and fountain. After breakfast, tour nearby historic sites on complimentary bicycles and return to more pampering with afternoon sherry, tea, and sumptuous home baked goods. Our private baths, off-street parking, color TV, and air-conditioning along with that very special Southern hospitality, says this is what Charleston is all about!

Hosts: Sally and Bud Allen
Rooms: 6 (PB) $69-150
Full Breakfast
Credit Cards: A, B, C, D
Notes: 2, 5, 7 (over 12), 8, 9, 10, 12

## Country Victorian Bed and Breakfast

105 Tradd Street, 29401-2422
(803) 577-0682

Come relive the charm of the past. Relax in a rocker on the piazza of this historic home and watch the carriages go by. Walk to antique shops, churches, restaurants, art galleries, museums, and all historic points of interest. The house, built in 1820, is located in the historic district south of Broad. Rooms have private entrances and contain antique iron and brass beds, old quilts, antique oak and wicker furniture, and braided rugs over heart-of-pine floors. Home-

5 Open all year; 6 Pets welcome; 7 Children welcome; 8 Tennis nearby; 9 Swimming nearby; 10 Golf nearby; 11 Skiing nearby; 12 May be booked through travel agent.

made cookies will be waiting. Many extras!

Hostess: Diane Deardurff Weed
Rooms: 2 (PB) $65-90
Expanded Continental Breakfast
Credit Cards: none
Notes: 2, 5, 7 (over 10), 8, 9, 10

## King George IV Inn

32 George Street, 29401
(803) 723-9339; FAX (803) 727-0065

A 200-year old, circa 1790, Charleston historic house located in the heart of historic district. The Inn is Federal style with three levels of Charleston side porches. All rooms have 10'-12' ceilings with decorative plaster moldings, wide-planked hardwood floors, old furnishings, and antiques. Private baths, parking, AC, TVs. One minute walk to historic King Street; five-minute walk to historic market. A step back in time!

Hosts: Debbie, Mike, and BJ
Rooms: 10 (8PB; 2SB) $65-130
Continental Plus Breakfast
Credit Cards: A, B
Notes: 2, 5, 6 (by arrangement), 7, 8, 9, 10, 12

The Kitchen House

## The Kitchen House Circa 1732

126 Tradd Street, 29401
(803) 577-6362

Nestled in the heart of the historic district, The Kitchen House is a totally restored 18th Century dwelling. Southern hospitality, absolute privacy, fireplaces, and antiques. Private patio, Colonial herb garden, fish pond, and fountain. Full breakfast, plus concierge service. This pre-Revolutionary home was featured in *Colonial Homes Magazine*, the *New York Times*, and *Best Places to Stay in the South*.

Hostess: Lois Evans
Rooms: 3 (PB) $95-195
Full Breakfast
Credit Cards: A, B
Notes: 2, 5, 7, 8, 9, 10, 12

## Rutledge Victorian Inn

114 Rutledge Ave., 29401
(803) 722-7551; FAX (803) 727-0065

Welcome to the past! This century old Victorian house in Charleston's downtown Historic District is an elegant Italianate style architecture with a lovely 100-foot wraparound porch, formal lobby, and dining room. The authentic bedrooms have fireplaces, hardwood floors, 12-foot ceilings with decorative moldings, 10-foot doors and windows, and antiques. Modern amenities include TVs, air-conditioning, ice machine, refrigerators, and private or shared baths. Walk to all historic attractions. Conti-

---

NOTES: Credit cards accepted: A Master Card; B Visa; C American Express; D Discover; E Diners Club; F Other; 2 Personal checks accepted; 3 Lunch available; 4 Dinner available;

nental plus breakfast, refreshments, parking.

Hosts: Lynn, Mike, and BJ
Rooms: 11 (8PB; 3SB) $65-130
Continental Plus Breakfast
Credit Cards: A, B
Notes: 2, 5, 6 (some), 7, 8, 9, 10, 12

## COLUMBIA

### Richland Street Bed and Breakfast

1425 Richland Street, 29201
(803) 779-7001

Richland Street Bed and Breakfast is a Victorian home located in the heart of Columbia's Historic District in walking distance of tour homes, restaurants, and downtown shopping. Inside your are greeted with a large gathering area, seven oversize guest rooms with private baths, and loads of hospitality. Each room has its own personality, decorated with period antiques. The Bridal Suite with whirlpool tub is especially inviting. You will enjoy the front porches with gazebo and rockers. Special attention given to each guest includes a deluxe continental breakfast served in classic Victorian style. Rated Four-Diamond American Auto Association.

Hosts: Naomi S. Perryman
Rooms: 7 (PB) $79-99; suite $120
Deluxe Breakfast
Credit Cards: A, B, C
Notes: 2 (in advance), 5, 10

## GEORGETOWN

### The Shaw House

613 Cypress Court, 29440
(803) 546-9663

A spacious, two-story, Colonial home in a natural setting with a beautiful view overlooking miles of marshland perfect for bird watchers. Within walking distance to downtown and great restaurants on the waterfront. Rooms are large with many antiques and private baths. Breakfast is served at our guests' convenience. Also included are nighttime chocolates on each pillow, turn backs, and some loving extras. Guests always leave with a little gift like prayers, recipes, and/or jellies. AAA, Mobile, and ABBA approved.

Hosts: Mary and Joe Shaw
Rooms: 3 (PB) $50-60
Full Breakfast
Credit Cards: none
Notes: 2, 5, 7, 8, 9, 10

"ShipWrights" Bed and Breakfast

### "ShipWrights" Bed and Breakfast

609 Cypress Court, 29440
(803) 527-4475

Three thousand-plus square feet of

---

beautiful, quiet, clean home is yours to use when you stay. It's nautically attired and tastefully laced with family heirlooms. Guests say they feel like they just stayed at their bestfriend's home. The bedrooms and baths are beautiful and very comfortable. You'll never get "Grandma Eicker's Pancakes" anywhere else (the inn is famous for them). There's a great story behind the pancakes! The view from the large porch is breathtaking, perfect for bird-watching. Five minutes from Ocean Beach. AAA approved.

Hosts: Leatrice M. Wright
Rooms: 2 (PB) $55-60
Full Breakfast
Credit Cards: none
Notes: 2, 5, 7, 8, 9, 10

## Winyah Bay Bed and Breakfast

403 Helena Street, 29440
(803) 546-9051; (800) 681-6176

Winyah Bay is a private efficiency suite. A deck overlooks the bay, so does the charming sitting area/breakfast room. Shell Room and Wimbeldom Room both have private baths, phone, cable TV, and VCR. You have access to the Bay by the longest private dock in the state. Also offers sunbathing on a small private island.

Hostess: Peggy Wheeler
Rooms: 2 (PB) $50-65
Continental Plus Breakfast
Credit Cards: A, B
Notes: 5, 8, 9, 10, 11, 12

"Sugarfoot Castle"

## HONEA PATH

## "Sugarfoot Castle"

211 S. Main St., 29654
(803) 369-6565

Enormous trees umbrella this 19th Century, brick, Victorian home. Fresh flowers grace the 14-inch thick walled rooms furnished with family heirlooms. Enjoy the living room's interesting collections or the library's comfy chairs, TV, VCR, books, fireplace, desk, and game table. Upon arising, guests find coffee and juice outside their doors, followed by breakfast of hot breads, cereal, fresh fruit, and beverages served by candlelight in the dining room. Rock away the world's cares on a screened porch overlooking peaceful grounds. AAA approved.

Hosts: Gail and Cecil Evans
Rooms: 3 (PB) $48-51
Heavy Continental Breakfast
Credit Cards: A, B
Notes: 2, 5, 8, 9, 10

---

NOTES: Credit cards accepted: A Master Card; B Visa; C American Express; D Discover; E Diners Club; F Other; 2 Personal checks accepted; 3 Lunch available; 4 Dinner available;

## LANCASTER

## *Wade-Beckham House*

3385 Great-Falls Hwy., 29720
(803) 285-1105

A circa 1832 plantation house listed on the National Register of Historic Places. Rural setting offering the Rose Room, the Summer House Room, and the Wade Hampton Room. Antique and craft stores on premises. Peaceful homey environment.

Hosts: Bill and Jan Duke
Rooms: 3 (SB) $60
Full Breakfast
Credit Cards: none
Notes: 2, 8, 10

Shakedown Plantation Bed and Breakfast

## MAYESVILLE

## *Shakedown Plantation Bed and Breakfast*

Route 1, Box 300, 29104
(803) 453-5004; (800) 453-5004

Large country home on flat farm land. Big porches with swings and rocking chairs. Remote walk-in area. Quiet and very private. The B&B is operated by run of the mill people, plain and simple, but *enjoyable*. Guests keep coming back.

Hosts: Billy and Lynde Dabbs
Rooms: 4 (2SB; 2PB) $55
Full Breakfast
Credit Cards: none
Notes: 2, 4 (advanced request), 5, 7, 10

## MCCLELLANVILLE

## *Laurel Hill Plantation*

8913 N. Hwy. 17, PO Box 190, 29458
(803) 887-3708

A nature lover's delight! Laurel Hill faces the Atlantic Ocean. Wraparound porches provide spectacular views of creeks and marshes. The reconstructed house is furnished with antiques that reflect the Low Country lifestyle. A perfect blend of yesterday's nostalgia and today's comfort in a setting of unparalleled coastal vistas. Located on Highway 17, 30 miles north of Charleston, 25 miles south of Georgetown, and 60 miles south of Myrtle Beach.

Hosts: Jackie and Lee Morrison
Rooms: 4 (PB) $75-85
Full Breakfast
Credit Cards: A, B
Notes: 2, 5, 7 (restricted), 9, 10, 12

## MYRTLE BEACH

## *Serendipity Inn*

407 - 71st Ave. N., 29572
(803) 449-5268; (800) 762-3229

An award-winning, mission-style inn is just 300 yards from the ocean beach and

---

5 Open all year; 6 Pets welcome; 7 Children welcome; 8 Tennis nearby; 9 Swimming nearby;
10 Golf nearby; 11 Skiing nearby; 12 May be booked through travel agent.

has a heated pool and jacuzzi. All rooms have air-conditioning, color TV, private baths, and refrigerators. Secluded patio, ping-pong, and shuffleboard. Over 70 golf courses nearby, as well as fishing, tennis, restaurants, theaters, and shopping. Ninety miles to historic Charleston Near all country music theaters.

Hosts: Terry and Sheila Johnson
Rooms: 14 (PB) $52-92
Hearty Continental Breakfast
Credit Cards: A, B, C, D
Notes: 7, 8, 9, 10, 12

## ROCK HILL

### East Main Guest House

600 E. Main St., 29730
(803) 366-1161

After extensive renovations, the upstairs contains three professionally decorated guest rooms with private baths, TV, and sitting room. The honeymoon suite features a canopy bed, fireplace, and whirlpool bath. A gourmet continental breakfast is served in the gracious dining room and, weather permitting, under the patio garden percola. We are located 20 minutes from downtown Charlotte, NC.

Hosts: Jerry and Melba Peterson
Rooms: 3 (PB) $59-79
Expanded Continental Breakfast
Credit Cards: A, B, C
Notes: 2, 5, 8, 9, 10, 11, 12

## SALEM

### Sunrise Farm Bed and Breakfast

P.O. Box 164, 325 Sunrise Dr., 29676
(803) 944-0121

This gracious 1890 Victorian farmhouse is set in the scenic foothills of the Blue Ridge Mountains. Surrounded by a 74-acre cattle farm and located near waterfalls, nature trails, and mountain lakes. Well decorated rooms in the main house and two charming cottages with kitchens.

Hosts: James and Jean Webb
Rooms: 3 + 2 cottages (PB) $65-95
Continental Plus Breakfast
Credit Cards: A, B
Notes: 2, 5, 7 (over 6), 12

"Linwood Bed and Breakfast"

## SUMMERVILLE

### "Linwood Bed and Breakfast"

200 South Palmetto St., 29483
(803) 871-2620

Once the home of a 19th Century plantation owner, gracious hospitality

---

abounds at "LINWOOD," a beautifully restored Victorian home with high ceilings, chandeliers, period antiques, and wide porches. Nestled on two acres of lush gardens, "LINWOOD" is in the center of the charming village of Summerville near shops and restaurants. Tramons plantations, golf courses, beaches, and historic Charleston are nearby. Recreation or retreat—we are here to serve you.

Hosts: Peter and Linda Shelbourne
Rooms: 4 (3PB; 1SB) $75-90
Continental Breakfast and afternoon English tea is served.
Credit Cards: B
Notes: 2, 5, 7, 8, 9, 10, 12

## SUMTER

### The Bed and Breakfast of Sumter

6 Park Avenue, 29150
(803) 773-2903; FAX (803) 775-6943

Charming, 1896 home facing a lush park in the historic district. Large front porch with swing and rocking chairs. Gracious guest rooms with antiques, fireplaces, and all private baths. Formal Victorian parlor and TV sitting area. FAX machine is also available. Gourmet breakfast includes fruit, entree, and homebaked breads. Antiques, Swan Lake, and 15 golf courses closeby.

Hosts: Jess and Suzanne Begley
Rooms: 5 (PB) $65-70
Full Breakfast
Credit Cards: A, B
Notes: 2, 5, 8, 10, 12

Six Park Avenue, Sumter SC
CIRCA 1896

The Bed and Breakfast of Sumter

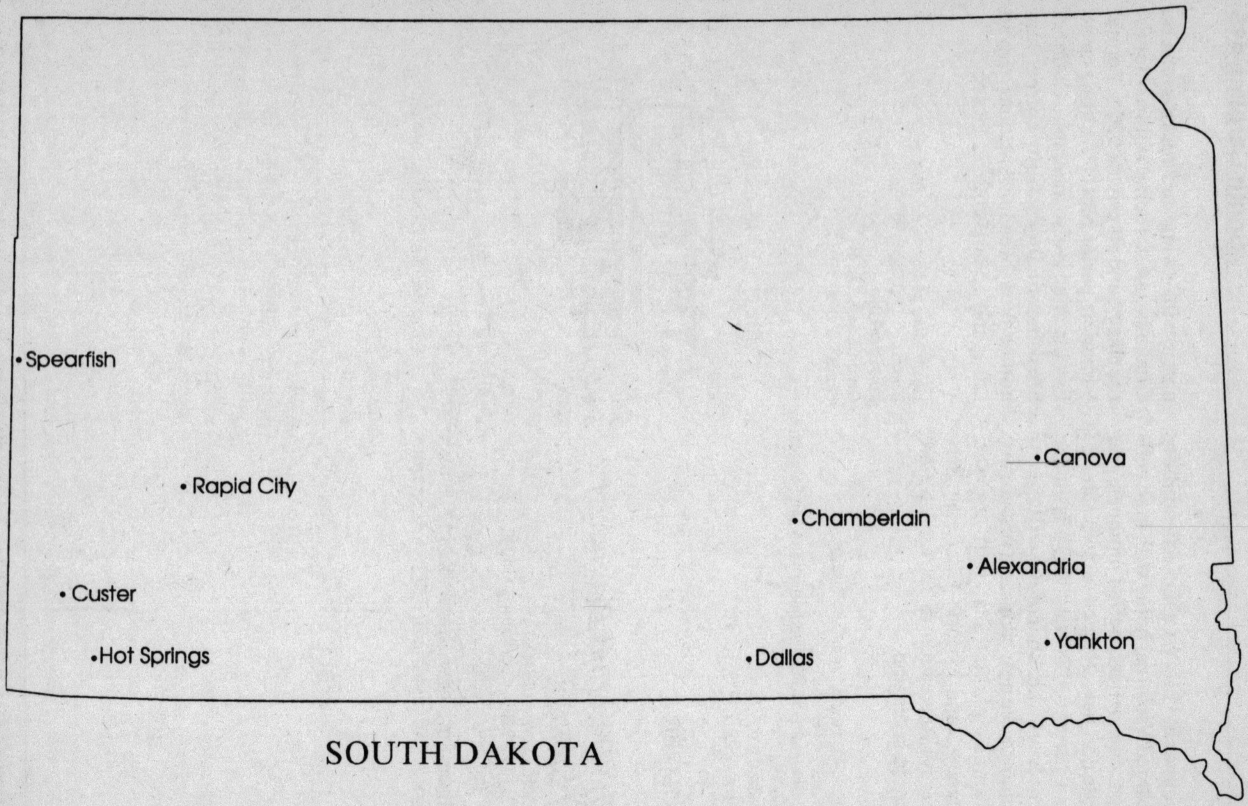

SOUTH DAKOTA

- Spearfish
- Rapid City
- Custer
- Hot Springs
- Canova
- Chamberlain
- Alexandria
- Yankton
- Dallas

# South Dakota

## ALEXANDRIA

### *B's Bed and Breakfast*

RR 2, Box 123, 57311
(605) 239-4671

We have a comfortable home with a covered deck that overlooks a lake just four miles off I-90 or 15 miles east of Mitchell which has the world's only Corn Palace. St. Mary of Mercy Church in Alexandria, four miles from us, has a Mid-America Fatima Family Shrine. The third weekend in each June a spiritual congress is conducted with national and international speakers and special liturgical services. Registration or information obtained through Fatima Family Apostolate, P.O. Box 55, Redfield, SD 57469. The gas grill is available to guests, as are paddleboats.

Hosts: Leonard and Marie Bettmeng
Rooms: 2 (SB) $30
Full or Continental Breakfast
Credit Cards: none
Notes: 2, 3, 5, 6 (if chained), 7, 9, and winter sledding

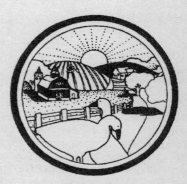

Skoglund Farm

## CANOVA

### *Skoglund Farm*

Route 1 Box 45, 57321
(605) 247-3445

Skoglund Farm brings back memories of Grandpa and Grandma's home. It is furnished with antiques and collectibles. A full, home-cooked evening meal and breakfast are served. You can sightsee in the surrounding area, visit Little

NOTES: Credit cards accepted: A Master Card; B Visa; C American Express; D Discover; E Diners Club; F Other; 2 Personal checks accepted; 3 Lunch available; 4 Dinner available; 5 Open all year; 6 Pets welcome; 7 Children welcome; 8 Tennis nearby; 9 Swimming nearby; 10 Golf nearby; 11 Skiing nearby; 12 May be booked through travel agent.

House on the Prairie Village, hike, or just relax. Several country churches are located nearby.

Hosts: Alden and Delores Skoglund
Rooms: 5 (SB) $30 each adult; $20 each teen; $15 each child; children 5 and under free.
Full Breakfast
Credit Cards: none
Notes: 2, 3, 4 (included), 5, 6, 7, 8, 9, 10, 12

## CHAMBERLAIN

### Riverview Ridge

HC 69, Box 82A, 57325
(605) 734-6084

Contemporary home built on a bluff overlooking a scenic bend in the Missouri River. King and queen beds, full breakfast, and secluded country peace and quiet. Three and one half miles north of downtown Chamberlain on Hwy 50. Enjoy outdoor recreation; visit museums, Indian reservations, and casinos; or just relax and make our home your home.

Hosts: Frank and Alta Cable
Rooms: 3 (1PB; 2SB) $50-65
Full Breakfast
Credit Cards: A, B (5% service charge)
Notes: 2, 5, 7, 9, 10

## CUSTER

### Custer Mansion Bed and Breakfast

35 Centennial Drive, 57730
(605) 673-3333

Historic 1891, Victorian Gothic home, listed on National Register of Historic Places, features a blend of Victorian elegance and country charm with Western hospitality. Clean, quiet accommodations (one room has a jacuzzi tub) and delicious home-cooked breakfasts. Central to all Black Hills attractions such as Mt. Rushmore, Crazy Horse Memorial, Custer State Park, and many more. Minimum stay of two nights, holidays and peak season. Reduced rates off season. Recommended by *Bon Appetit*, AAA, and Mobil Travel Guide.

Hosts: Mill and Carole Seaman
Rooms: 6 (4PB; 2SB) $50-90
Full Breakfast
Credit Cards: none
Notes: 2, 5, 7, 8, 9, 10, 11

Custer Mansion Bed and Breakfast

### The Rose Garden Bed and Breakfast

Route 1, Box 108A, 57730
(605) 673-2714

The Rose Garden is one mile south of Custer, the mother city of the Black Hills. Our suites are furnished with quaint, nostalgic atmosphere including clawfoot tubs, mirrored canopy beds, hot tub, and fresh fruit. Full, home-cooked, candlelight breakfasts are served in our gracious dining room. Short drives to Mt. Rushmore, Crazy Horse, Custer State Park, and Wind Cave National Park. Beautiful scenery, including rock formations, beckons you! Custer Chamber, BHBL&L Assn., BBISD, and AAA Approved.

Hosts: Ted and Charlene Hartman
Rooms: 6 (PB) $69-125
Full Breakfast
Credit Cards: A, B
Notes: 2, 5, 8, 9, 10, 12

## DALLAS

### Bolton Ranch

Route 2, Box 80, 57529
(605) 835-8960

The Bolton Ranch includes 7,000 acres in South Central South Dakota. Guests stay in a modern ranch home with a private bath. We offer an all-you-can-eat breakfast, lunches, and country suppers flavored with cowboy conversation. Ask about our cabin on the Keyapaha River if you are interested in total seclusion. There is plenty to do; fishing, hiking, and horseback riding. Lots of wildlife, sunsets and quiet. Listen to the coyotes howl.

Hosts: Brad and Kay Bolton
Rooms: 2 (SB) $50
Full Breakfast
Credit Cards: none
Notes: 2, 3, 4, 5, 6, 7

The "B and J" Bed and Breakfast

## HOT SPRINGS

### The "B and J" Bed and Breakfast

HCR 52, Box 101-B, 57747
(605) 745-4243

Nestled in the Southern Black Hills, this charming, historic 1880 log cabin, decorated in local antiques, provides guests with a unique pioneer setting. Enjoy the peaceful mountain scenery while listening to the bubble of the famous Fall River that never freezes. Early morning, in the surrounding meadows, deer and wild turkey may be seen. True Western hospitality and a good home-cooked breakfast are always available in Jeananne's kitchen. The "B and J" is located one mile south of Hot Springs on US 385/18. In Hot Springs, swim at the historic Evans Plunge where the water is always 87 degrees; visit the Mammoth Site, the World's Largest Find of Columbian Mammoth Bones; fish nearby in cold Brook Lake; and golf at one of the Midwest's most challenging and beautiful courses. Just minutes to Angostura Lake Recreation area, Wind Cave National Park, and Custer

State Park where buffalo, antelope, elk, and prairie dogs roam freely.

Hosts: Bill and Jeananne Wintz
Rooms: one 450 sq. ft. cabin (PB) $95-125
Full Breakfast
Credit Cards: none
Notes: 2, 7, 8, 9, 10, 11

## RAPID CITY

### Abend Haus Cottage and Audrie's Cranbury Corner B&B

23029 Thunderhead Falls Road, 57702
(605) 342-7788

The ultimate in charm and Old World hospitality, our country home and five-acre estate is surrounded by thousands of acres of national forest in a secluded, Black Hills setting. Each quiet, comfortable suite and cottage has private entrance, hot tub, patio, cable TV, and refrigerator. Free trout fishing, hiking, and biking available on property.

Hosts: Hank and Audry Kuhnhauser
Rooms: 6 (PB) $85
Full Breakfast
Credit Cards: none
Notes: 2, 5, 8, 9, 10, 11

Abend Haus Cottage

Historic Hotel Alex Johnson

### Historic Hotel Alex Johnson

523 Sixth Street, 57701
(605) 342-1210 (voice and FAX);
(800) 888-ALEX

Visit the Hotel Alex Johnson and stay at a historic landmark. 141 newly restored guest rooms. Old World charm combined with award-winning hospitality, this legend offers a piece of Old West history in the heart of downtown Rapid City. Listed on the National Registry of Historic Places.

Rooms: 141(PB) $58-88
Full Breakfast in Restaurant Setting
Credit Cards: A, B, C, D, E, F
Notes: 2, 3, 4, 5, 7, 8, 10, 12

### St. Charles Bed and Breakfast

613 St. Charles Street, 57701
(605) 394-0343

St. Charles B&B provides warm hospitality and invites you to relax in a comfortable atmosphere. Each room has

NOTES: Credit cards accepted: A Master Card; B Visa; C American Express; D Discover; E Diners Club; F Other; 2 Personal checks accepted; 3 Lunch available; 4 Dinner available;

been decorated to make you feel cared for. A homemade breakfast is served each morning and is different each day. Dinner is available by reservation. St. Charles B&B is located a short distance from Mount Rushmore, Custer State Park, the Badlands, Needles Highway, and the beautiful Black Hills.

Hosts: Wally and Pat Steele
Rooms: 2 (SB) $35-51
Full Breakfast
Credit Cards: none
Notes: 2, 4, 5, 7, 8, 9, 10, 11

## SPEARFISH

## *Tamarack Inn*
706 University, 57783
(605) 642-8660; (800) 380-8089

Stay in the relaxing atmosphere of this 1942 contemporary home, situated in a quiet neighborhood overlooking Spearfish. Designed and built by Miss Hesseltine, a single female math professor at Black Hills State Teacher's College in the '40s. Several inviting features include a large brick fireplace in the living room, rustic TV room, unique pine lathed ceilings in the upstairs bedrooms, antiques, and artwork. Effie, the hostess, is interested in sketching, quilting, crocheting, sewing, antique refinishing, etc. The Tamarack Inn is located within walking distance of the Passion Play, Black Hills State University, hiking and biking trails, historical sites, the city park, D.C. Booth Fish Hatchery, Matthews Opera House, and downtown Spearfish. Spearfish is a

short drive to historical Deadwood, gambling, and the Strugis Rally.

Hostess: Effie Johnson
Rooms: 4 (SB) $55-65
Full Breakfast
Credit Cards: A, B
Notes: 2, 8, 9, 10, 12

## YANKTON

## *Mulberry Inn*
512 Mulberry Street, 57078
(605) 665-7116

The beautiful Mulberry Inn offers the ultimate in comfort and charm in a traditional setting. Built in 1873, the Inn features parquet floors, six guest rooms furnished with antiques, two parlors with marble fireplaces, and a large porch. Minutes from the Lewis and Clark Lake and within walking distance of the Missouri River, fine restaurants, and downtown. The Inn is listed on the National Register of Historic Places.

Hostess: Millie Cameron
Rooms: 6 (2PB; 4SB) $35-51 May-September; $32-45 October-April
Continental (Full breakfast extra charge)
Credit Cards: A, B, C
Notes: 2, 5, 7, 8, 9, 10

Mulberry Inn

---

5 Open all year; 6 Pets welcome; 7 Children welcome; 8 Tennis nearby; 9 Swimming nearby; 10 Golf nearby; 11 Skiing nearby; 12 May be booked through travel agent.

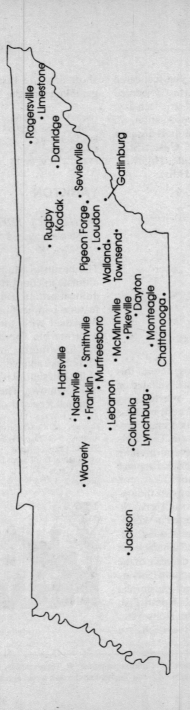

TENNESSEE

Ragersville •
Limestone •
Danridge •
Gatlinburg •
Sevierville •
Rugby • Kodak •
Pigeon Forge •
Loudon •
Walland •
Townsend •
Hartsville •
Smithville •
Nashville • Franklin •
Murfreesboro •
McMinnville •
Pikeville •
Dayton •
Monteagle •
Chattanooga •
Lebanon •
Waverly •
Columbia •
Lynchburg •
Jackson •

# Tennessee

**ALSO SEE RESERVATION SERVICES UNDER GEORGIA AND MISSISSIPPI**

## Natchez Trace Bed and Breakfast Reservation Service

P.O. Box 193, **Hampshire**, TN 38461
(615) 285-2777; (800) 377-2770

This reservation service is unusual in that all the homes listed are close to the Natchez Trace, the delightful National Parkway running from Nashville, Tennessee, to Natchez, Mississippi. Kay can help you plan your trip along the Trace, with homestays in interesting and historic homes along the way. Locations of homes include Ashland City, FairView, Leipers Fork, Coumbia, Hohenwald, Culleoka, Nashville, Franklin, and Hampshire, **Tennessee;** Florence, and Cherokee, **Alabama**; and Port Gibson, Corinth, French Camp, Kosciusko, Vicksburg, Loeman, Church Hill, and Natchez, **Mississippi.** Rates $60-125.

Adams Hilborne

## CHATTANOOGA

## Adams Hilborne

801 Vine Street, 37403
(615) 265-5000; FAX (615) 265-5555

Cornerstone to Chattanooga's Fort Wood Historic District. Rare Victorian Romanesque design with original coffered ceilings, handcarved oak stairway, beveled glass windows, and ceramic tile embellishments. Old World charm and hospitality in a tree-shaded setting rich with Civil War history and turn-of-the-century architecture. Small European-style hotel accommodations in 15 tastefully restored, exquisitely decorated guest rooms. Private baths, fireplaces, and complimentary breakfast for guests.

---

NOTES: Credit cards accepted: A Master Card; B Visa; C American Express; D Discover; E Diners Club; F Other; 2 Personal checks accepted; 3 Lunch available; 4 Dinner available; 5 Open all year; 6 Pets welcome; 7 Children welcome; 8 Tennis nearby; 9 Swimming nearby; 10 Golf nearby; 11 Skiing nearby; 12 May be booked through travel agent.

Ballroom, meeting and reception areas, private dining, and catering available to the public by arrangement. Minutes from Chattanooga museums, fine shops and restaurants, the aquarium, UTC arena, and other cultural events and attractions. Private off-street parking.

Hosts: Wendy and Dave Adams
Rooms: 15 (PB) $100-295
Continental Breakfast
Credit Cards: A, B, C
Notes: none

## Alford House Bed and Breakfast

5515 Alford Hill Drive, 37419
(615) 821-7625

This half-century, 15 room house welcomes you! Family owned and operated, in a peaceful Christian atmosphere, the B&B is ten minutes to Tennessee Aquarium, Rock City, and all other attractions. In our Gathering Room there's a piano, and on wintery nights a cozy fire awaits you. Enjoy early morning coffee and breakfast in the dining room or, weather permitting, on the upper deck. Surrounded by tall oaks and bordering the Chicamauga National Park. A large collection of antique glass baskets are displayed for your pleasure, and many antiques throughout our home. You will be blessed with restful sleep on our beauty rest bedding. Ask about our discounts.

Hosts: Rhoda (Troyer) Alford
Rooms: 4 (2PB; 2SB) $65-95
Lite Breakfast
Credit Cards: none
Notes: 8, 9, 10, 11, 12

Locust Hill Inn

## COLUMBIA

## Locust Hill Inn

1185 Mooresville Pike, 38401
(615) 388-8531; (800) 577-8264

Beautifully restored, 1840 ante-bellum home, decorated with family antiques. Pamper yourself with morning coffee in your room and evening refreshments at the fireside. Spacious rooms with private baths and comfortable sitting areas. Delicious gourmet breakfasts feature country ham, featherlight biscuits, and homemade jams enjoyed in the dining room or sunroom. Enjoy the fireplaces and relax in the library, flower gardens, or on the three porches. Romantic weekend packages are available; and gourmet dinners also available. French and German spoken.

Hosts: Bill and Beverly Beard
Rooms: 3 (PB) $80-120
Full Breakfast
Credit Cards: A, B
Notes: 2, 3, 4, 5, 10, 12

NOTES: Credit cards accepted: A Master Card; B Visa; C American Express; D Discover; E Diners Club; F Other; 2 Personal checks accepted; 3 Lunch available; 4 Dinner available;

# DANDRIDGE

## Sugar Fork Bed and Breakfast

743 Garrett Road, 37725
(615) 397-7327; (800) 487-6534

Guests will appreciate the tranquil setting of Sugar Fork, a short distance to the Great Smoky Mountains. Situated on Douglas Lake, the B&B has private access and floating dock. Enjoy warm-weather water sports and fishing year-round. Fireplace in common room, quest kitchenette, wraparound deck, swings, and park bench by the lake. A hearty breakfast is served family-style in the dining room or, weather permitting, on the deck. No smoking in guestrooms.

Hosts: Mary and Sam Price
Rooms: 3 (2PB; 2SB) $55 (SB) $65 (PB) + tax
Full Breakfast
Credit Cards: A, B
Notes: 2, 5, 7, 8, 9, 10, 11

# DAYTON

## Rose House

123 Idaho Street, 37321
(615) 775-3311; FAX (615) 775-6644

Built in 1892, our charming Victorian cottage brings an enjoyable touch of the past to the modern visitor. High ceilings, doors with transoms, solid wood floors, and period antiques refresh the eye. Dainty roses, descriptive of each guest room, bloom in the pleasant yard and can be seen from the front porch, as well as the white picket fence and delightful arbor over the mountain stone walkway. Truly a colorful, relaxing, and enjoyable lodging experience.

Hosts: Bud and Ginny Schatz
Rooms: 3 (2PB; 1SB) $65-75
Full Breakfast
Credit Cards: A, B, C, D, E
Notes: 2, 5, 8, 9

Rose House

# FRANKLIN

## Lyric Springs Country Inn

7306 S. Harpeth Rd., 37064
(615) 329-3385; (800) 621-7824;
FAX (615) 329-3381

Elegant, antique-filled, creek-side inn featured in *Better Homes and Gardens*, *Country Inns*, *USA Today*, *Fodor's*, and *Women's Wear Daily*. A haven for romance and retreat. Gourmet food. Picnics. Spa services: message, manicure, pedicure, facial. Billiards, fishing, hiking, swimming, biking, horseback riding, board games, and puzzles. Music. Waterfalls. Separate cabin available. Restricted smoking.

Hostess: Patsy Bruce
Rooms: 4 (PB) $110-115
Full Breakfast
Credit Cards: A, B, C
Notes: 2, 4 (by reservation), 5, 9, 10, 12

---

5 Open all year; 6 Pets welcome; 7 Children welcome; 8 Tennis nearby; 9 Swimming nearby; 10 Golf nearby; 11 Skiing nearby; 12 May be booked through travel agent.

## GATLINBURG

### Butcher House in the Mountains

1520 Garrett Lane, 37738
(615) 436-9457

Nestled 2,800 feet above the main entrance to the Smokies, Butcher House in the Mountains offers mountain seclusion as well as convenience. The Swisslike cedar and stone chalet enjoys one of the most beautiful views in the state. Antiques are tastefully placed throughout the house and a guest kitchen is available for coffee and lavish dessert. European gourmet brunch served. AAA rated three-Diamond; ABBA rated excellent.

Hosts: Hugh and Gloria Butcher
Rooms: 5 (PB) $79-109
Full European Gourmet Breakfast
Credit Cards: A, B, C
Notes: 2, 5, 8, 9, 10, 11, 12

### Eight Gables Inn

219 North Mountain Trail, 37738
(615) 430-3344; (800) 279-5716

For the perfect bed and breakfast getaway, Eight Gables is the answer. Reserve your accommodations from among ten spacious guest rooms which appeal to even the most discriminating taste. At the foot of the great Smokey Mountains National Park, Eight Gables Inn's location is easily accessible to all area attractions. The Inn offers bedrooms with private baths and luxurious living space and has an additional covered porch area. AAA approved-Four Diamond. Family owned and operated

by Don and Kim Casons.

Hosts: Don and Kim Cason
Rooms: 10 (PB) $95-115
Full Breakfast
Credit Cards: A, B, C, D
Notes: 2, 3 and 4 (available on request), 5, 6, 7, 8, 10, 11, 12

Olde English Tudor Inn

### Olde English Tudor Inn

135 West Holly Ridge Rd., 37738
(615) 436-7760; (800) 541-3798

The Olde English Tudor Inn Bed and Breakfast is set on a hillside overlooking the beautiful mountain resort of Gatlinburg. It is ideally located within a few minutes walk to downtown and a few minutes drive to The Great Smoky Mountain National Park. The Inn has seven spacious guest rooms with their own modern bath and cable TV (HBO). Each guest is made to feel at home in the large community room, furnished with TV/VCR and freestanding woodburning stove. Call toll free for a brochure.

Hosts: Larry and Kathy Schuh
Rooms: 7 (PB) $69-99
Full Breakfast
Credit Cards: A, B
Notes: 2, 5, 7, 8, 9, 10, 11, 12

---

NOTES: Credit cards accepted: A Master Card; B Visa; C American Express; D Discover; E Diners Club; F Other; 2 Personal checks accepted; 3 Lunch available; 4 Dinner available;

## HARTSVILLE

### Miss Alice's Bed and Breakfast

8325 Hwy. 141 South, 37074
(615) 374-3015 or (615) 444-4401

Relax, enjoy Tennessee's Southern hospitality in a restored early 1900's farmhouse. Walk through the woods, read, play horseshoes, sit on the deck, lie in the hammock, have lemonade in the wellhouse, or draw up a bucket of cool sulfur water for a treat. Wake up with a cup of gourmet coffee and afterwards enjoy a farmer's breakfast. Area attractions include Stones River Battlefield, The Hermitage, Opryland, Cragfont, Vice President Gore's hometown, Cumberland University, and many antique shops.

Hostess: Volene B. Barnes
Rooms: 2 (1PB; 1SB) $65
Full Breakfast
Credit Cards: none
Notes: 2, 5, 9, 10

Highland Place Bed and Breakfast

## JACKSON

### Highland Place Bed and Breakfast

519 N. Highland Ave., 38301
(901) 427-1472

A stately home of distinct charm, offering comfortable accommodations and Southern hospitality. Highland Place B&B is West Tennessee's 1995 Designers Showplace. Each room, hall, staircase, and even hidden away nooks has have been designed and decorated by the outstanding designers of West TN. Experience the pleasure of sharing the surroundings of one of the state's finest homes. Circa 1911, the inn was totally renovated in early 1995 and reopened in April of 1995.

Hosts: Glenn and Janice Wall
Rooms: 3 (2PB; 1SB) $65-85
Full Breakfast
Credit Cards: A, B
Notes: 2, 5, 10, 12

## KODAK

### Grandma's House Bed and Breakfast

734 Pollard Road, P.O. Box 445, 37764
(615) 933-3512; (800) 676-3512;
FAX (615) 933-0748

Colonial-style home on three acres at the base of the Great Smoky Mountains. Only two miles off I-40 at the 407 exit. Owners live on premises and are both native East Tennesseans. Country decor with handmade quilts and crafts. Farm-style, "loosen your belt" break-

5 Open all year; 6 Pets welcome; 7 Children welcome; 8 Tennis nearby; 9 Swimming nearby;
10 Golf nearby; 11 Skiing nearby; 12 May be booked through travel agent.

fast begins when guests gather around the big oak table and Hilda says the blessing. Death by Design Murder Mystery weekends held during the winter months. Call for a brochure.

Hosts: Charlie and Hilda Hickman
Rooms: 3 (PB) $65-75
Full Breakfast
Credit Cards: A, B
Notes: 2, 5, 10, 11, 12

Grandma's House Bed and Breakfast

## LEBANON

## Chanticleer Country Bed and Breakfast

8148C Trousdale Ferry Pike, 37090
(615) 449-4051

Nashville area B&B located on 48 secluded acres with walking trails and majestic views of middle Tennessee hills. Rooms with whirlpool baths and fireplaces. Grand piano for guest playing in great room. Golf, tennis, and swimming available. Two miles from Interstate 40 and 30 minutes from Nashville International Airpot and Opryland.

Hosts: Norma and Martin Amacher
Rooms: 3 (PB) $85
Full Breakfast
Credit Cards: A
Notes: 2, 3 and 4 (by reservation), 5, 8, 9, 10, 12

Snapp Inn

## LIMESTONE

## Snapp Inn B&B

1990 Davy Crockett Park Rd., 37681
(423) 257-2482

Gracious c. 1815 Federal style home, furnished with antiques. Come to the country for a relaxing weekend getaway. Enjoy the peaceful mountain view or play a game of pool. Located close to Davy Crockett Birthplace State Park. A 15-minute drive to historic Jonesborough or Greenville.

Hosts: Dan and Ruth Dorgan
Rooms: 2 (PB) $50
Full Breakfast
Credit Cards: none
Notes: 2, 5, 6, 7 (one only), 8, 9, 10, 12

## LOUDON

## Mason Place B&B

600 Commerce Street, 37774
(615) 458-3921

Nestled in a quaint Civil War town along the Tennessee River is a lovely, impeccably restored, 1865 plantation home that offers quality lodging and an opportunity to truly wander back to

---

yester-year without sacrificing the conveniences of today. A grand entrance hall, ten working fireplaces, Grecian swimming pool, gazebo and wisteria-covered arbor are but a few of the amenities available for your enjoyment. Listed on the National Registry of Historic Places, the Mason Place is situated on three acres of lawns and gardens where Civil War bullets and artifacts are still being found. Five delightful antique filled rooms, each complete with a cozy gas-log fireplace, authentic feather bed, and en-suite bathroom. Bountiful breakfast included.

Hosts: Bob and Donna Siewert
Rooms: 5 (PB) $96-120
Full Candlelight Breakfast
Credit Cards: A, B
Notes: 2, 3 (picnic baskets), 5, 8, 9 (on grounds), 10, 11, 12

Mason Place Bed and Breakfast

## LYNCHBURG

### Lynchburg Bed and Breakfast

Mechanic St., P.O. Box 34, 37352
(615) 759-7158

A 19th century home located within walking distance to the Jack Daniels

Distillery, the oldest registered distillery in the USA. One of the oldest homes in Moore County, also the home of the first Moore County Sheriff. Begin your day with our special continental breakfast, served at your convenience, then relax with a view from our shady front porch.

Hostess: Virginia Tipps
Rooms: 3 (PB) $50-60
Continental Breakfast
Credit Cards: A, B
Notes: 5, 7, 8, 9

Falcon Manor Bed and Breakfast

## MCMINNVILLE

### Falcon Manor Bed and Breakfast

2645 Faulkner Springs Road, 37110
(615) 668-4444

Relive the peaceful romance of the 1890's in one of the South's finest Victorian mansions. Rock on "gingerbread" verandas, shaded by giant trees. Indulge in the luxury of museum-quality antiques. Enjoy stories about the 10,000 square-foot mansion's history and the innkeepers' adventures restoring it. Ideal base for Tennessee vacation: halfway between Nashville and Chattanooga with easy access from I-24 and

5 Open all year; 6 Pets welcome; 7 Children welcome; 8 Tennis nearby; 9 Swimming nearby; 10 Golf nearby; 11 Skiing nearby; 12 May be booked through travel agent.

I-40. McMinnville is the world's "nurs-
ery capital." Fall Creek Falls Park and
Cumberland Caverns nearby.

Hosts: George and Charlien McGlothin
Rooms: 5 (1PB; 4SB) $75-85 + tax (8%)
Full Breakfast
Credit Cards: A, B
Notes: 2, 5, 7 (over 11), 8, 9, 10, 12

Adams Edgeworth Inn

## MONTEAGLE

## *Adams Edgeworth Inn*

Monteagle Assembly, 37356
(615) 924-4000; FAX (615) 924-3236

Circa 1896, Adams Edgeworth Inn cel-
ebrates 100 years of fine lodging and
still is the region's leader in elegance
and quality. Recently refurbished in English Manor decor, the Inn is a showcase for fine antiques, important original paintings and sculptures, and a
prize-winning rose garden. Stroll
through the 96-acre Victorian village
which surrounds the Inn, or drive six
miles to the Gothic campus of Sewanee,
University of the South. Cultural activities are year round. 150 miles of hiking
trails, scenic vistas, and waterfalls.
Tennis, swimming, golf, and riding
nearby. Five-course, fine dining by
candlelight every night. "One of the
best inns I've ever visited anywhere..."
(Sara Pitzer, recommended by "Country Inns" in *Country Inns Magazine).*

Hosts: Wendy and Dave Adams
Rooms: 14 (PB) $65-150
Continental Breakfast
Credit Cards: A, B, C, D
Notes: 2, 4, 5, 7, 8, 9, 10, 12

## MURFREESBORO

## *Clardy's Guest House*

435 E. Main Street, 37130
(615) 893-6030

This large Victorian home was built in
1898 and is located in Murfreesboro's
historic district. You will marvel at the
ornate woodwork, beautiful fireplaces,
and magnificent stained glass overlooking the staircase. The house is filled
with antiques, as are local shops and
malls. The hosts will help you with dining, shopping, and touring plans.

Hosts: Robert and Barbara Deaton
Rooms: 3 (2PB; 1SB) $35-50
Continental Breakfast
Credit Cards: none
Notes: 2, 5, 8, 9, 10

Clardy's Guest House

NOTES: Credit cards accepted: A Master Card; B Visa; C American Express; D Discover;
E Diners Club; F Other; 2 Personal checks accepted; 3 Lunch available; 4 Dinner available;

**NATCHEZTRACE—SEE PAGE 422 OR NATCHEZTRACE, MISSISSIPPI**

## NASHVILLE

### Bed and Breakfast—About Tennessee

P.O. Box 110227, 37222
(615) 331-5244; (800) 428-2421;
FAX (615) 833-7701

Bed and Breakfast—About Tennessee

From the Great Smoky Mountains to the Mississippi, here is a diversity of attractions that includes fabulous scenery, Tennessee's Grand Ole Opry and Opryland, universities, Civil War sites, horse farms, and much more. With Bed and Breakfast in Tennessee, you make your visit a special occasion. Bed and Breakfast provides an intimate alternative to hotels and motels. You will stay in a private home or inn with a host who will share firsthand knowledge of the area with you. This home-style atmosphere includes the offer of a freshly prepared continental breakfast each morning. Send your guest reservation in today so that we may place you in accommodations which are best suited to your needs. Confirmation and directions will be sent to you immediately.

Owner: Fredda Odom
Rooms: 100 (90PB; 10SB) $55-150
Continental Plus Breakfast
Credit Cards: A, B, C, D, E
Notes: 2, 5, 7 (at some); 8 and 9 (at some), 12

## PIGEON FORGE

### Day Dreams Country Inn

2720 Colonial Drive, 37863
(423) 428-0370; (800) 377-1469

Delight in the true country charm of this antique-filled, secluded two-story log home with its six uniquely decorated guestrooms. Enjoy an evening by our cozy fireplace, relax on the front porch to the soothing sound of Mill Creek, or take a stroll around our three wooded acres. Treat your tastebuds to our bountiful country breakfast each morning. Within walking distance of parkway. Perfect for family reunions and retreats. From Parkway, take 321 S., go one block, turn left on Florence Drive, go three blocks, and turn right on Colonial Drive.

Hosts: Bob and Joyce Guerrera
Rooms: 6 (PB) $79-99
Full Breakfast
Credit Cards: A, B
Notes: 2, 3, 4, 5, 7, 8, 9, 10, 11, 12

---

5 Open all year; 6 Pets welcome; 7 Children welcome; 8 Tennis nearby; 9 Swimming nearby; 10 Golf nearby; 11 Skiing nearby; 12 May be booked through travel agent.

## Hilton's Bluff B&B Inn

2654 Valley Heights Drive, 37863
(423) 428-9765; (800) 441-4188

Truly elegant country living. Secluded hilltop setting only ½ mile from heart of Pigeon Forge. Minutes from outlet shopping, Dollywood, and Smoky Mountain National Park. The honeymoon, executive, and deluxe rooms, all have private baths; five with two-person jacuzzis, king beds, and waterbeds. Tastefully decorated in romantic mingling of the old and new. Private balconies, covered decks with rockers and checkerboard tables. Den with mountain-stone fireplace; game room/conference room. Southern gourmet breakfast. Group rates for corporate seminars and church groups.

Hosts: Jack and Norma Hilton
Rooms: 10 (PB) $79-129
Full Breakfast
Credit Cards: A, B, C
Notes: 5, 8, 9, 10, 11, 12

## Little Greenbrier Lodge

3685 Lyon Springs Rd., 37862
(615) 429-2500; (800) 277-8100;
FAX (615) 429-4093

Little Greenbrier Lodge Bed and Breakfast is uniquely located on the side of a mountain at the back entrance to the Great Smoky Mountains National Park. The lodge is 150 yards from a hiking trailhead that can connect you to most of the hiking trails in the park. Each of the eleven tastefully decorated Victorian rooms have full access to relaxing decks overlooking tranquil Wears Valley. You're guaranteed to remember the aroma of the hot pecan rolls as you pre-

pare to head for the dining room each morning where a spectacular breakfast awaits!!

Hosts: Barbara and David Matthews
Rooms: 11 (7PB; 4SB) $65-95
Full Breakfast
Credit Cards: A, B, D
Notes: 5, 10, 12

## PIKEVILLE

## Fall Creek Falls B&B Inn

Route 3, Box 298B, 37367
(423) 881-5494; FAX (423) 881-5040

Elegant mountain inn featured in August '94, *Tennessee* magazine. Eight air-conditioned guest rooms all with private baths. Some heart-shaped whirlpools, and fireplace. Victorian or country decor. One mile from Fall Creek Falls State Resort Park. Beautiful mountains, waterfalls, golfing, boating, fishing, tennis, and hiking. AAA rated, no smoking, full breakfast. Romantic, scenic, and quiet.

Hosts: Doug and Rita Pruett
Rooms: 8 (PB) $75-130
Full Breakfast
Credit Cards: A, B, C
Notes: 2, 3, 4, 5, 8, 9, 10, 12

## ROGERSVILLE

## Hale Springs Inn

Town Square, 37857
(615) 272-5171

Tennessee's oldest operational inn built in 1824 and recently restored to its former glory. Air-conditioned and cen-

---

NOTES: Credit cards accepted: A Master Card; B Visa; C American Express; D Discover; E Diners Club; F Other; 2 Personal checks accepted; 3 Lunch available; 4 Dinner available;

tral heat. Most rooms have workable fireplaces. Private, modern bathrooms, antique furniture, and poster beds. Dine fireside in candlelit dining room. Presidents Andrew Jackson, James Polk, and Andrew Johnson stayed here. Easy one-hour drive to historic sites and mountain resorts.

Hosts: Bill Testerman and Sue Livesay
Rooms: 9 (PB) $35-60
Continental Breakfast
Credit Cards: A, B
Notes: 4, 5, 8, 10, 11, 12

## RUGBY

### Newbury House Bed and Breakfast
P.O. Box 8, 37733
(615) 628-2441

Restored 1880 Newbury House boasts bedrooms with Victorian antiques, guest parlor, front veranda, and complimentary tea and coffee. Pioneer and Percy cottages sleep from one to eight; kitchen facilities. Historic Rugby is listed on the National Register of Historic Places. Daily guided tours include School House Visitor Centre, Thomas Hughes Library 1882, Kingstone Lisle (the founder's home, 1884), and the Christ Church Episcopal (1887) with original hanging lamps and 1849 rosewood organ still played for Sunday services.

Hosts: Mrs. Pearl Lee Nester
Rooms: 5 + 2 cottages (3PB; 2SB) $60-70
Full Breakfast
Credit Cards: A, B
Notes: 2, 3, 4, 5, 7 (at cottages), 9, 10, 12 (no commision)

## SEVIERVILLE

NOTE: AREA CODE WILL BE CHANGING TO 423.

### Blue Mountain Mist Country Inn and Cottages
1811 Pullen Road, 37862
(615) 428-2335; (800) 497-2335;
FAX (615) 453-1720

Experience the silent beauty of mountain scenery while rocking on the big wraparound porch of this Victorian-style farmhouse. Common rooms filled with antiques lead to twelve individually decorated guest rooms. Enjoy many special touches such as old-fashioned clawfoot tubs, high antique headboards, quilts, and jacuzzi. Nestled in the woods behind the Inn are five country cottages designed for romantic getaways. The Great Smoky Mountains National Park and Gatlinbug are only twenty minutes away.

Hosts: Norman and Sarah Ball
Rooms: 12 + 5 cottages (PB) $79-125
Full Breakfast
Credit Cards: A, B
Notes: 2, 5, 7, 8, 9, 10, 11, 12

Blue Mountain Mist Country Inn and Cottages

5 Open all year; 6 Pets welcome; 7 Children welcome; 8 Tennis nearby; 9 Swimming nearby; 10 Golf nearby; 11 Skiing nearby; 12 May be booked through travel agent.

Calico Inn

## Calico Inn

757 Ranch Way, 37862
(423) 428-3833; (800) 235-1054

The Calico Inn is an authentic Log Inn
with touches of elegance. It is decorated with antiques, collectibles and
country charm. It has a spectacular
Mountain view and is situated on a hill
top with 25 acres surrounding it. Each
guest room has its own private bath.
You will be served a full delicious
breakfast daily. Only minutes away
from the Smoky Mountain National
Park, Dollywood, Gatlinburg, hiking,
fishing, golfing, and all other attractions. Yet completely secluded.

Hosts: Lill and Jim Katzbeck
Rooms: 3 (PB) $85-95
Full Breakfast
Credit Cards: A, B
Notes: 2, 5, 7, 8, 9, 10, 11, 12

Huckleberry Inn

## Huckleberry Inn

1754 Sandstone Way, 37876
(615) 428-2475

Relax and enjoy yourself as we welcome you into this hand-crafted, authentic, two-story log home. Four guest
rooms all have private baths and whirlpool tubs. Three fireplaces add warmth
to this cozy, unique home. We offer hiking trails, beautiful mountain views,
homemade desserts, and morning coffee at your door. A rustic getaway, but
very convenient to local attractions.
Group rates.

Hosts: Rich and Barb Thomas
Rooms: 4 (PB) $79-89 + tax
Full Country Breakfast
Credit Cards: A, B
Notes: 2, 4, 5, 7, 10, 11, 12

## Persephone's Retreat

2279 Hodges Ferry Rd., 37876
(615) 428-3904; FAX (615) 453-7089

A peaceful rural estate nestled in a grove
of huge shade trees. Convenient to
Gatlinburg, Pigeon Forge, or Knoxville,
but ideal for rest and relaxation from
busy tourist activities. An elegant two-
story home offers three extremely comfortable bedrooms with private baths
and large porches overlooking pastures
and a beautiful river valley. Enjoy two-
hole golf course, spacious grounds, yard
games, farm animals, miniature horses,
and hiking. Children welcome; restricted smoking.

Hosts: Bob Gonia and Victoria Nicholson
Rooms: 3 (PB) $75-95
Continental or Full Breakfast
Credit Cards: A, B
Notes: 2, 5, 7

NOTES: Credit cards accepted: A Master Card; B Visa; C American Express; D Discover;
E Diners Club; F Other; 2 Personal checks accepted; 3 Lunch available; 4 Dinner available;

Place of the Blue Smoke

## Place of the Blue Smoke

3760 Cove Mountain Rd., 37862
(615) 453-6355; (800) 453-4216

Secluded Mountain B&B has breath-taking views. The Inn is on 115 acres and has a beautiful waterfall reflection area, hiking trails, large porches, and decks. Gourmet breakfast, hot tea, and apple cider in rooms. Minutes from Dollywood and Gatlinburg. Borders Smoky Mountains National Park.

Hosts: Charlie and Nonnie Knight
Rooms: 4 (PB) $95-105
Full Gourmet Breakfast
Credit Cards: A, B
Notes: 2, 5, 7 (12 and over)

## Von-Bryan Inn

2402 Hatcher Mountain Road, 37862
(615) 453-9832; (800) 633-1459;
FAX (615) 428-8634

A mountaintop log inn with an unsurpassed panoramic view of the Great Smoky Mountains. Greet the sunrise with singing birds and the aroma of breakfast. Swim, hike, rock, rest, read, and relax the day away, then watch the sunset just before the whippoorwills begin their nightly calls. Swimming

pool, hot tub, steam shower, whirlpool tubs, library, complimentary dessert, refreshments, and breakfast. Three-bedroom, log chalet is great for families.

Hosts: The Vaughn Family (D.J, JoAnn, David, and Patrick)
Rooms: 6 + 3 bedroom chalet (PB) $80-125
Full Breakfast
Credit Cards: A, B, C, D
Notes: 2, 5, 7, 9 (on-site), 10, 11, 12 (10% com.)

## SMITHVILLE

## Evins Mill Retreat

P.O. Box 606, 37166
(615) 597-2088; FAX (615) 597-2090

Situated on the Highland Rim by Center Hill Lake, Evins Mill offers a variety of activities amongst spectacular scenery, including 90 foot Carmac Falls, hiking trails along wooded bluffs, swimming holes, a fishing pond with bass and bluegill, and much more—both on-site and nearby. It also boasts historic and award winning facilities, including the main lodge and a working grist mill built in 1939, as well as three new guest cottages. Complimenting the

5 Open all year;  6 Pets welcome;  7 Children welcome;  8 Tennis nearby;  9 Swimming nearby;
10 Golf nearby;  11 Skiing nearby;  12 May be booked through travel agent.

property and facilities are sumptuous meals served in our own Millstone Restaurant.

Host: William S. Cochran, Jr.
Rooms: 14 (PB) $105-130
Hybrid Breakfast
Credit Cards: A, B
Notes: 2, 3 and 4 (depends), 5, 7, 8, 9, 10, 11 (water), 12

## TOWNSEND

### Richmont Inn
220 Winterberry Lane, 37882
(615) 448-6751

Situated on "the peaceful side of the Smokies," this Appalachian barn is beautifully furnished with eighteenth-century English antiques and French paintings. Breathtaking mountain views, graciously appointed rooms with sitting areas, woodburning fireplaces, spa tubs for two, and balconies. French and Swiss cuisine are served at breakfast with flavored coffees and gourmet desserts by candlelight in the evenings. Featured in *Country Inn* B&B magazine as one of their "Top Inns of 1994" and received *Gourmet Magazine's* grand prize award for one of its desserts. The Smoky Mountains, art/craft shops, outlet shopping, and historic Cades Cove are all nearby.

Hosts: Susan and Jim Hind
Rooms: 10 (PB) $90-140
Full Breakfast
Credit Cards: none
Notes: 2, 5, 9, 10, 12

## WALLAND

### Misty Morning Bed and Breakfast
5515 Old Walland Hwy., 37886
(423) 681-6373

A three-story log home situated on eight beautiful acres nestled in the foothills of the Smoky mountains. The B&B offers a sense of family and Southern hospitality with full amenities. A restful mountain getaway convenient to Pigeon Forge, Knoxville, Gatlinburg, Cade's Cove, and Knoxville Airport.

Hosts: Darnell and Herman Davis
Rooms: 2 (PB) $69-79
Full Breakfast
Credit Cards: A, B, D
Notes: 9 (on-site), 10, 11

## WAVERLY

### Nolan House Inn
385 Hwy. 13 N., 37185
(615) 296-9063; (615) 296-2511

A Victorian home built in 1870, the B&B has five rooms, four with private baths. The large recreation room accommodates teas, showers, dinners, etc. There are a dogtrot, cisterns, cellars, and a stone fountain. The Inn is seven miles from Loretta Lynn's Dude Ranch.

Hostess: LaVerne Turner
Rooms: 5 (4PB; 1SB) $35
Continental Breakfast
Credit Cards: none
Notes: 2, 7, 8, 9, 10

NOTES: Credit cards accepted: A Master Card; B Visa; C American Express; D Discover; E Diners Club; F Other; 2 Personal checks accepted; 3 Lunch available; 4 Dinner available;

# Texas

## Reservation Service
## Bed and Breakfast
## Texas Style, Inc.

4224 W. Red Bird Lane, **Dallas** 75237
(214) 298-8586; (800) 899-4538;
FAX (214) 298-7118

Bed and Breakfast Texas Style, Inc. is a reservation service established in 1982. We offer you a wide variety of accommodations in private homes, cottages, and small inns. We carefully inspect and approve lodgings to insure comfort and convenience. If you prefer more privacy, you may choose a log cabin on a ranch, cottage on a farm, or a guest house in the woods. Many of our B&B's are historical mansions with Victorian decor. Let us know your desire, we will try to find just the right place for your special needs. For more information, call or write us. Approx. 340 room.; $ 59-150. Major credit cards welcomed. Coordinator, Ruth Wilson.

## BULVERDE

## Das Holz Haus

1450 Bulverde Road, 78163
(210) 438-2463; FAX (210) 438-3888

Real log home located on seven acres with beautiful oak trees in the hills of western Comal County. Area attractions and historical places are 15, 30, or 45 minutes away, including Natural Bridge Caverns, Sea World, and Fiesta Texas. Enjoy the sounds of country living. Relax in the large living room with 12-foot ceiling and antiques from Opa and Oma's grandparents.

Owner: The Master
Hosts: Lloyd (opa) and Elva Nell (oma) Lenz
Rooms: 2 (SB) $70
Full Breakfast
Credit Cards: none
Notes: 2, 5, 7, 8

## Homestead Bed and Breakfast

1324 Bulverde Road, 78163
(210) 980-2571

A private cottage facility located in the heart of a 300-acre working ranch where cattle, deer, jack rabbits, turkey, and foxes still roam. 30 minutes from historic Boerne, New Braunfels, and downtown San Antonio Riverwalk and other major attractions like Sea World and Fiesta Texas. Homestead sits on the original homestead founded by the Krause-Bremer families. It houses many of their original antique furnishings. The interior features a beaded board ceiling in the kitchen and dining room, two bed-

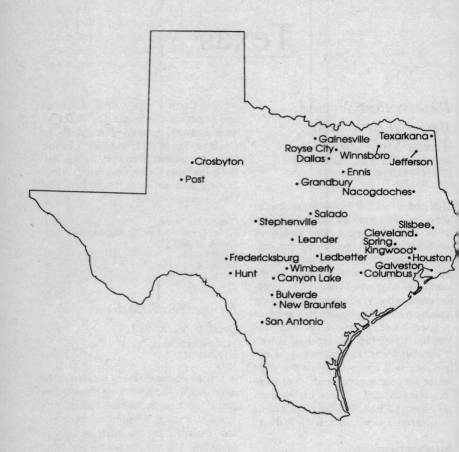

TEXAS

rooms, living room, and bath. Breakfast fixings are in the fridge; fresh breads baked each morning.

Hosts: James and MaryJane Jahnsen
Rooms: 2 in private cottage (PB) $75
Continental Breakfast fixings in refrigerator
Credit Cards: none
Notes: 2, 5, 7, 8, 9, 10

## CANYON LAKE

## *Aunt Nora's Bed and Breakfast*

120 Naked Indian Trail, 78132
(210) 905-3989

In the Texas hill country, minutes from New Braunfels, Guadeloupe River at Canyon Lake, is a country house with a touch of Victorian, nestled on a hillside. Breathe fresh country air from the front porch swing, and enjoy patio hot tub and hand built queen beds. Tastefully decorated cottages all in a delightful hill country setting.

Hosts: Alton and Iralee Haley
Rooms: 3 (PB) $85-150
Full Breakfast
Credit Cards: none
Notes: 2, 5, 8, 9, 10

## CLEVELAND

## *Chain-O-Lakes*

One Country Lane, 77327
(713) 592-2150

Chain-O-Lakes Resort, nature's heart of the Big Thicket. Spend cozy winters by a crackling fireplace in your own log cabin. Enjoy the colorful palette of springtime flowers and have a splashing good time swimming in pure artesian water. Breakfast is expertly prepared by Hilltop Herb Farm and a seasonal horse drawn carriage can take you to the restaurant.

Hosts: Jimmy and Beverly Smith (owners);
Audrey Waldrop (manager)
Rooms: 48 (PB) $120-150
Full Breakfast
Credit Cards: A, B, C, D, E
Notes: 2, 3 and 4 (in season), 5, 7, 9, 10

Raumonda Bed and Breakfast

## COLUMBUS

## *Raumonda B&B*

1100 Bowie St., P.O. Box 112, 78934
(409) 732-2190

In this Victorian home, built in 1887, you will be greeted with warmth and hospitality reminiscent of the Old South. Three fireplaces with white marble mantles, original, grained, painted woodwork, and Victorian bronze hardware make this one of the most outstanding houses in Texas. We

---

NOTES: Credit cards accepted: A Master Card; B Visa; C American Express; D Discover; E Diners Club; F Other; 2 Personal checks accepted; 3 Lunch available; 4 Dinner available; 5 Open all year; 6 Pets welcome; 7 Children welcome; 8 Tennis nearby; 9 Swimming nearby; 10 Golf nearby; 11 Skiing nearby; 12 May be booked through travel agent.

also manage the Gant Guest House.

Host: R.F. "Buddy" Rau
Rooms: 3 (PB) $80
Enhanced Continental Breakfast
Credit Cards: none
Notes: 2, 5, 8, 9, 10, 12

## The Victorian Bed and Breakfast

1336 Milam St., P.O. Box 325, 78934
(409) 732-2125; FAX (409) 732-5212

This beautiful two-story, newly re-stored, Victorian home dates from 1883. It features gingerbread, porches, 14-foot ceilings, and wainscoting. It was included on the 1993 tour of homes. Tree-lined streets of town sit on site of an old Indian village. General Sam Houston camped here. Today Columbus boasts a large number of historic markers and an 1886 opera house with productions. Tennis, golf, canoeing, bicycling area, antique shows, auctions, and more. Complimentary, guided tour. Houston is one hour away; a short drive to Festival Hill and Winedale.

Hostess: Carolyn Youens Hastedt
Rooms: 3 (1PB; 2SB) $65-80 + tax
Continental Breakfast
Credit Cards: none
Notes: 2, 5, 8, 9, 10

## CROSBYTON

## Smith House

306 West Aspen, 79322
(806) 675-2178; FAX (806) 675-2619

The Inn was built in 1921 by J. Frank Smith, a cowboy from the nearby Two Buckle Ranch. The original oak furniture and iron beds highlight the early West Texas charm. The Inn has a large dining room, a separate meeting room, and a parlor for entertaining. Guests can enjoy a rocking chair on the large front porch. Available for groups, retreats, or dinners.

Hosts: Terry and Sandy Cash
Rooms: 12 (8PB; 4SB) $50-85
Full Breakfast
Credit Cards: A, B
Notes: 2, 5, 7, 8, 9, 12

## DALLAS—SEE PAGE 437

## ENNIS

## Raphael House

500 W. Ennis Ave., 75119
(214) 875-1555; FAX (214) 875-0308

This elegant, 1906 Neoclassic Revival mansion is on the National Register and for the last four years was voted one of the top B&B's in the USA. The 19-room mansion is a showcase of quality antiques, rich wall coverings, and luxurious fabrics. Amenities include large baths with antique clawfoot tubs, down comforters and pillows, imported toiletries, afternoon refreshments and turn down service. Swedish massage, honeymoon packages, and corporate deals available. Very romantic!

Hosts: Brian and Danna Cody Wolf
Rooms: 6 (PB) $60-100
Full Breakfast; Continental Plus midweek
Credit Cards: A, B, C, D, E, F
Notes: 2, 5, 8, 9, 10

---

NOTES: Credit cards accepted: A Master Card; B Visa; C American Express; D Discover; E Diners Club; F Other; 2 Personal checks accepted; 3 Lunch available; 4 Dinner available;

## FREDERICKSBURG

### Gastehaus Schmidt Reservation Service

231 West Main Street, 78624
(210) 997-5612; FAX (210) 997-8282

*Put Yourself In our Place!* Plan a stay in one of our Traditional B&B's or guest houses. Our Reservation Service offers a pleasing variety of "out of the ordinary" overnight experiences. Whether you want to escape to the country, stay close to town, relive history, or rekindle romance, each home is special and the varieties are endless. You will discover that "our" place is truly "your" place. 100 homes to choose from. Open daily. Catalogs available.

Owner: Donna Mittel
Rooms: 100 (PB) $65-165
Full and/or Continental Breakfast
Credit Cards: A, B, D
Notes: 2, 5, 6, 7, 8, 9, 10, 12

### Magnolia House

101 E. Hackberry, 78624
(210) 997-0306

Circa 1923; restored 1991. Enjoy Southern hospitality in a grand and gracious manner. Outside, lovely magnolias and a bubbling fish pond and waterfall set a soothing mood. Inside, a beautiful living room and a formal dining room provide areas for guests to mingle. Four romantic rooms and two suites have been thoughtfully planned. A Southern-style breakfast completes a memorable experience.

Hosts: Joyce and Patrick Kennard
Rooms: 4 + 2 suites (4PB; 2SB) $80-110
Full Breakfast
Credit Cards: A, B
Notes: 2, 5, 8, 9, 10

### Schmidt Barn Bed and Breakfast

Route 2, Box 112A3, 78624
(210) 997-3234—Ask for Schmidt Barn

The Schmidt Barn is located one and one-half miles outside historic Fredericksbug. This 1860's limestone structure has been turned into a charming guesthouse with loft bedroom, living room, bath, and kitchen. The hosts live next door. German-style breakfast is left in the guest house for you. The house has been featured in *Country Living* and *Travel and Leisure* and is decorated with antiques.

Hosts: Dr. Charles and Loretta Schmidt
Guest House: 1 (PB) $77-107
Continental Plus Breakfast
Credit Cards: A, B, D
Notes: 2, 5, 6, 7, 8, 9, 10, 12

Schmidt Barn Bed and Breakfast

---

5 Open all year; 6 Pets welcome; 7 Children welcome; 8 Tennis nearby; 9 Swimming nearby; 10 Golf nearby; 11 Skiing nearby; 12 May be booked through travel agent.

## *Way of the Wolf*

HC 12 Box 92H, 78624
(210) 997-0711

This B&B/retreat, on 61 acres in the hill country, offers swimming pool, space for picnics and hikes, wildlife, and scenic views. The four bedrooms and common living area with fireplace are furnished with antiques. This destination B&B is peaceful and secluded while only 15 minutes from shopping, golf, and churches in either Kerrville or Fredericksburg. Assistance in preparing for personal or group retreats is available.

Hosts: Ron and Karen Poidevin
Rooms: 4 (2PB; 2SB) $75-100
Full Breakfast
Credit Cards: none
Notes: 2, 5, 9, 10, 12

## GAINESVILLE

## *Alexander Bed and Breakfast Acres (ABBA)*

Route 7, Box 788, 76240
(903) 564-7440; (800) 887-8794

Charming three-story Queen Anne home and guest cottage nestled peacefully in the woods and meadows of 65 acres just south of Whitesboro, Texas in the Lake Texoma area. Main house offers parlor and dining room plus third floor sitting area with TV, and wraparound porch for relaxing; five guest bedrooms with private baths and full breakfast. The two-story cottage has three bedrooms which share one bath,

there are full kitchen facilities for preparing own breakfast, and it is perfect for families with children.

Hosts: Jim and Pamela Alexander
Rooms: Main house-5 + cottage-3 (5PB; 3SB) $59-125
Full Breakfast for main house
Credit Cards: none
Notes: 2, 5, 7 (at cottage), 9, 10, 11

## GALVESTON

## *Coppersmith Inn Bed and Breakfast*

1914 Avenue M, 77550
(409) 763-7004

Queen Anne style mansion built in 1887 and designed by a famous architect. The Inn boasts gingerbread trim, double verandah, turret tower, spectacular winding staircase of teak, walnut and curly pine highlighted by stained glass and ornate newel post, large windows with original glass, exquisite heirloom antiques, Victorian decorations with romantic themes and interesting faux painting techniques used during restoration, fireplaces, clawfoot porcelain tub, antique tin tub used in Kenny Rogers movie with five water spouts, lovely landscaped gardens, large wooden deck and brick sidewalks, and a generous country breakfast.

Hostess: Lisa Hering
Rooms: 4 (1PB; 3SB) $90-135
Full and/or Continental Breakfast
Credit Cards: A, B, C, D
Notes: 2, 5, 7 (over 5), 9, 12

---

NOTES: Credit cards accepted: A Master Card; B Visa; C American Express; D Discover; E Diners Club; F Other; 2 Personal checks accepted; 3 Lunch available; 4 Dinner available;

## Madame Dyer's Bed and Breakfast

1720 Postoffice Street, 77550
(409) 765-5692

From the moment you enter this carefully restored, turn-of-the-century home, you will be entranced by period details such as wraparound porches, high airy ceilings, wooden floors, and lace curtains. Each room is furnished with delightful antiques that bring back memories of days gone by. Come and enjoy a night or weekend in this 1889 home located in a quiet, historical, residential neighborhood offering its guests a feeling of elegance from the past and still the luxury, comfort, and pleasures of today.

Hostess: Linda Wells
Rooms: 3 (PB) $95-125
Full Breakfast
Credit Cards: A, B
Notes: 2, 5, 9, 10, 12

Madame Dyer's Bed and Breakfast

## GRANDBURY

## Dabney House Bed and Breakfast

106 South Jones, 76048
(817) 579-1260; FAX (817) 579-0426

Craftsman-style one-story home built in 1907 by a local banker and furnished with antiques, hardwood floors, and original woodwork. Long-term business rates available per request; romance dinner by reservation only. We offer custom, special occasion baskets in room upon arrival, by advance order only. Book whole house for family occasions, staff retreats, or Bible retreats at discount rates. Hot tub is now available for all registered guests.

Hosts: John and Gwen Hurley
Rooms: 4 (PB) $60-105
Full Breakfast
Credit Cards: A, B, C
Notes: 2, 5, 8, 9, 10, 12

## HOUSTON

## Sara's Bed and Breakfast Inn

941 Heights Boulevard, 77008
(713) 868-1130; (800) 593-1130;
FAX (713) 868-1160

This Queen Anne Victorian with its turret and widow's walk is located in Houston Heights, a neighborhood of historic homes, many of which are on the National Historic Register. Each bedroom is uniquely furnished, having either single, double, queen, or king

---

5 Open all year; 6 Pets welcome; 7 Children welcome; 8 Tennis nearby; 9 Swimming nearby; 10 Golf nearby; 11 Skiing nearby; 12 May be booked through travel agent.

beds. The Balcony Suite consists of two bedrooms, two baths, kitchen/living area, and balcony. Breakfast is served in the beautiful garden room in the Inn. The sights and sounds of downtown Houston are five miles away.

Hosts: Donna and Tillman Arledge
Rooms: 14 (12PB; 2SB) $55-95
Continental Plus Breakfast
Credit Cards: A, B, C, D, E, F
Notes: 2, 5, 7, 8, 9, 10, 12

Sara's Bed and Breakfast Inn

## HUNT

## River Bend Bed and Breakfast

Route 1, Box 114, 78024
(210) 238-4681; (800) 472-3933;
FAX (210) 238-3180

"A peaceful and relaxing retreat," nestled in the Hill Country along the beautiful Guadalupe River. Wake to the smell of freshly brewed coffee, feast on a gourmet breakfast buffet, and relax in a quaint, Victorian room filled with an-

tique furnishings, wrought iron beds, lace curtains, and clawfooted tubs. Outside the river offers summer refreshment or winter tranquillity. Hike, fish, tube, and canoe. River Bend is only a short drive to antique shops, art galleries, museums, and many wonderful restaurants.

Hostess: Becky Key (manager)
Owners: Conrad and Terri Pyle
Rooms: 15 (PB) $85-145
Full Breakfast
Credit Cards: A, B, C, D
Notes: 2, 5, 7, 8, 9, 10, 12

## JEFFERSON

## McKay House Bed and Breakfast Inn

306 East Delta, 75657
(903) 665-7322; (214) 348-1929

Jefferson is a town where one can relax, rather than get tired. The McKay House, an 1851 Greek Revival cottage, features a pillared front porch and many fireplaces and offers genuine hospitality in a Christian atmosphere. Heart-of-pine floors, 14-foot ceilings, and documented wallpapers complement antique furnishings. Guests enjoy a full "gentleman's" breakfast. Victorian nightshirts and gowns await pampered guests in each bed chamber.

Hosts: Alma Anne and Joseph Parker
Rooms: 4 + 3 suites (PB) $75-145 (corporate rates available)
Full Sit-down Breakfast
Credit Cards: A, B
Notes: 2, 5, 10, 12

---

NOTES: Credit cards accepted: A Master Card; B Visa; C American Express; D Discover; E Diners Club; F Other; 2 Personal checks accepted; 3 Lunch available; 4 Dinner available;

## Pride House

409 Broadway, 75657
(903) 665-2675; (800) 894-3526

Breathtaking, East Texas landmark, Victorian mansion in a historic, former steamboat, port. Myth America lives in this town of 2,200, on the banks of the Cypress, along brick streets, behind picket fences, and in antique houses. Pride House has luscious interiors, luxurious amenities, and legendary breakfasts! We have ten rooms with private baths, big beds, spacious rooms, and just about everything anybody's asked for over the past fourteen years!

Hostesses: Carol and Lois
Rooms: 10 (PB) $65-100
Full Breakfast
Credit Cards: A, B, D
Notes: 2, 5, 7, 10, 12

Longhill Home

## KINGWOOD

## Longhill Home

1919 Lakeville Dr., 77339
(713) 358-3360

Located six miles east of Fredericksburg on a hill overlooking the Perdenales Valley. Full kitchen stocked with coffee, tea, hot chocolate, and juices. King-size bed upstairs; trundle bed downstairs (house sleeps four). Bath has tub/shower. House is of country decor and located on 30 acres. You are free to roam the area and share it with the cattle that graze here. Central heat/air plus ceiling fans. No firearms or smoking.

Hosts: Danny and Mary Beth Richarson (out-of-town)
Rooms: whole house sleeps 4 (1PB) $80
Breakfast not provided
Credit Cards: A, B, D
Notes: 2, 5, 7, 12

## LEANDER

## Trails End Bed and Breakfast

12223 Trails End Rd. #7, 78641
(512) 267-2901; (800) 850-2901

Trail's End Bed and Breakfast has an elegant main house with two guest rooms upstairs. The private guest house is in a wooded country setting on six acres within easy driving distance from Lake Travis, Austin, and other quaint Hill Country towns. The many romantic porches, decks, patios, and garden areas with gazebo provide lots of inviting outdoor spaces. The two fireplaces and lots of seating areas in both houses provide a romantic and cozy togetherness inside. You may also shop in the B&B store in the main house. We provide business people a comfortable lodging alternative—a great place to have that getaway and work or play. We

---

5 Open all year; 6 Pets welcome; 7 Children welcome; 8 Tennis nearby; 9 Swimming nearby; 10 Golf nearby; 11 Skiing nearby; 12 May be booked through travel agent.

look forward to serving you and hope you'll try our B&B. We know you will not be disappointed. Amenities include pool, gazebo, and bicycles.

Hosts: JoAnn and Tom Patty
Rooms: 4 (2PB; 2SB) $65-95
Full Breakfast
Credit Cards: A, B, C
Notes: 2, 4, 5, 7, 9, 12 (10%)

# LEDBETTER

## *Ledbetter Bed and Breakfast*

P.O. Box 212, 78946
(409) 249-3066; (800) 240-3066;
FAX (409) 249-3330

Ledbetter B&B, established in 1988, is a collection of multigeneration, family, 1800-1900's homes within walking distance of the remaining 1870s downtown businesses. Full country breakfast buffet can serve up to 70 guests daily. Hayrides, walks, horse and buggy rides, games, Christmas lights, chuck wagon or romantic dinners, indoor heated swimming pool, VCR, TV, and phone on advance request. Each unit accommodates approximately four people. Only non-alcoholic beverages are allowed outside private quarters. Only outdoor smoking is allowed.

Hosts: Chris and Jay Jervis
Rooms: 16-22 depending on grouping (17PB; 8SB) $70-150
Full Country Buffet Breakfast
Credit Cards: A, B (no deposit refunded)
Notes: 2, 3, 4, 5, 7, 8, 9, 10, 12

# NACOGDOCHES

## *Pine Creek Lodge Bed and Breakfast Country Inn*

Route 3 Box 1238, 75964
(409) 560-6282

On a beautiful tree covered hill overlooking a springfed creek sits Pine Creek Lodge. Built on a 140-acre property with lots of lawns, rose gardens, and a multitude of flowers, deep in the East Texas woods yet only ten miles from historic Nacogdoches. Our rustic lodge features king-size beds in tastefully decorated rooms with phone, TV/VCR, lots of decks, swimming pool, spa, fishing, biking, and much more. We have become the destination for many city dwellers.

Hosts: The Pitts Family
Rooms: 7 (PB) $45-65
Full Breakfast
Credit Cards: A, B, C
Notes: 2, 3, 4, 5, 7, 9, 10

# NEW BRAUNFELS

## *The Rose Garden*

195 S. Academy, 78130
(210) 629-DAWN (3296)

Come to our Rose Garden with designer bedrooms, fluffy towels, scented soaps, and potpourri-filled rooms. Our half-century old home is only one block from downtown. Enjoy a movie, browse our antique shops, or stroll along the Comal

---

NOTES: Credit cards accepted: A Master Card; B Visa; C American Express; D Discover; E Diners Club; F Other; 2 Personal checks accepted; 3 Lunch available; 4 Dinner available;

Springs—all within walking distance. We offer two guest rooms. The Royal Rose Room has a four poster rice, queen bed with a crystal chandelier and country French decor. The Country Rose Room has a Victorian-style, iron-and-brass queen bed with pine walls also done in country French. A full gourmet breakfast is served in the formal dining room.

Hostess: Dawn Mann
Rooms: 2 (PB) $65-95
Full Breakfast
Credit Cards: none
Notes: 2, 5, 8, 9, 10, 12

## POST

## *Hotel Garza Bed and Breakfast*

302 E. Main Street, 79356
(806) 495-3962

This restored 1915 hotel projects friendliness and history of this "Main Street City" where cereal magnate C.W. Post settled in 1907 to create his "Utopia." Guests can enjoy live theatre, colorful shops, museums, and the monthly event of Old Mill Trade Days. The guest rooms boast original furniture. From the comfy library you can look down on a quaint lobby and the dining area where a hearty breakfast is served. Suites are available.

Hosts: Janice and Jim Plummer
Rooms: 14 (10PB; 4SB) $35-95
Full Breakfast (Sat.-Sun.)
Continental (Mon.-Fri.)
Credit Cards: A, B
Notes: 2, 3, 4, 5, 7, 8, 9, 10

Country Lane Bed and Breakfast

## ROYSE CITY

## *Country Lane Bed and Breakfast*

Route 2, Box 94B, 75189
(214) 636-2600; FAX (214) 635-2300

Just 28 miles east of Dallas, this country getaway has a private pond which is a favorite stopover of egrets and herons. Four guest rooms with private baths are themed to movie characters—Mae West, Roy Rogers, Natalie Wood, and Film Noir Mysteries. Hundreds of vintage and new movies are among the collectibles for your enjoyment.

Hosts: James and Annie Cornelius
Rooms: 4 (PB) $50-85
Full Breakfast
Credit Cards: A, B, C
Notes: 2, 4, 5, 7, 10, 11 (water), 12 (10%)

## SALADO

## *The Rose Mansion*

P.O. Box 500, (in Victorian Oaks on Royal St.), 76571
(817) 947-8200; (800) 948-1004;
FAX (817) 947-1003

Nestled among towering oaks, the tra-

---

5 Open all year; 6 Pets welcome; 7 Children welcome; 8 Tennis nearby; 9 Swimming nearby; 10 Golf nearby; 11 Skiing nearby; 12 May be booked through travel agent.

ditional Greek Revival style mansion and complimentary cottage and 1850's log cabins offer a return to yesterday, with class. Four acres of beautiful grounds, memorabilia, antiques, shaded seating, swings, and games are complemented by a gourmet breakfast, queen beds, private baths, fireplace, and central heat and air. Elegant in a cozy atmosphere.

Hostess: Lynette Pellerin
Rooms: 10 (PB) $90-120
Full Breakfast (by excellent chef)
Credit Cards: A, B, C, D
Notes: 2, 3 and 4 (by request), 5, 7 (well behaved), 9, 10, 12

The Rose Mansion

## SAN ANTONIO

## Beauregard House Bed and Breakfast

215 Beauregard, 78204
(210) 222-1198; (800) 841-9377

Charming two-story Victorian home (1910) is in the historic King William neighborhood. The home has hardwood floors throughout and rooms are filled with furnishings appropriate to the era. Central air and heat. Each room is designed for your comfort and has a private bath. One room offers a fireplace. One block from convenient downtown trolley connecting you to the Alamo, Alamodome, Convention Center Arena, Market Square, and more. Also only one block from the famous River Walk. Spacious off-street, lighted parking. No smoking indoors.

Hostess: Ann Trabal (owner)
Rooms: 3-4 (PB) $85-105; single $79
Full Breakfast
Credit Cards: A, B
Notes: 2, 5, 7 (depends on circumstances), 10, 12

## Beckmann Inn and Carriage House

222 E. Guenther Street, 78204
(210) 229-1449; (800) 945-1449

A wonderful Victorian house (1886) located in the King William historic district, across the street from the start of the Riverwalk. Beautifully landscaped, it will take you on a leisurely stroll to the Alamo, downtown shops, and restaurants. You can also take the trolley which stops at the corner and within minutes you're there in style. The beautiful wraparound porch welcomes you to the main house and warm, gracious, Victorian hospitality. The large guest rooms feature antique, ornately carved, Victorian, queen-size beds; private baths; and ceiling fans. Gourmet breakfast, with breakfast dessert, is served in the dining room with china, crystal, and silver.

Hosts: Betty Jo and Don Schwartz
Rooms: 5 (PB) $80-130
Full Breakfast
Credit Cards: A, B, C, D, E
Notes: 2, 5, 7 (over 12), 10, 12

Beckmann Inn and Carriage House

## The Belle of Monte Vista

505 Belknap Place, 78212
(713) 732-4006 (voice and FAX)

J. Riely Gordon designed this 1890
Queen Anne Victorian home located
conveniently in this famous Monte
Vista historic district, one mile from
downtown San Antonio. The house has
eight fireplaces, stained glass windows,
hand-carved oak interior, and Victorian
furnishings. Near zoo, churches, Riverwalk, El Mercado, arts, and universities. Transportation to and from airport,
bus, and train station upon request.
Easy access from all major highways.

Hosts: Dave and JoAnn Bell
Rooms: 7 (1PB; 6SB) $40-75
Full Breakfast
Credit Cards: A, B, C
Notes: 2, 5, 7, 8, 10

## Brackenridge Blansett Bed and Breakfast Inn

230 Madison Street, 78204
(210) 271-3442 (voice and FAX);
(800) 221-1412

A Greek Revival home (1903) set in the
King William historic district with four
two-story white Corinthian columns
and first and second floor verdas. The
original pine floor, double-hung windows, and high ceilings are enhanced
by antique furnishings, many of them
family heirlooms. All guest rooms have
private baths and entrances, phones, and
mini-refrigerators. A bridal suite decorated in all white is available. Breakfast is served in the guest dining room
on the second floor. Located only six
blocks from downtown, two blocks
from the Riverwalk, and one block from
the ten cent trolley and the San Antonio Mission Trail. Convenient walking to four delightful restaurants.

Hosts: Bennie and Sue Blansett
Rooms: 5 (PB) $80-115
Full Breakfast
Credit Cards: A, B, C, D
Notes: 2, 5, 12

## The Victorian Lady Inn

421 Howard Street, 78212
( 210) 224-2524 (voice and FAX);
(800) 879-7116

Rediscover the genteel ambiance of 100
years ago in this 1898 historic mansion.
Guestrooms are some of the largest in

---

5 Open all year; 6 Pets welcome; 7 Children welcome; 8 Tennis nearby; 9 Swimming nearby;
10 Golf nearby; 11 Skiing nearby; 12 May be booked through travel agent.

San Antonio and feature period antiques. Your pampered retreat includes a private bath, fireplace, verandah, TV, and phone. Fabulous full breakfasts served daily in the grand dining room. Bicycles and book exchange on premises. Just blocks away are the Riverwalk, Alamo, and Convention Center. Swimming, golf, horseback riding, and antiquing are all very closeby. AAA rate three diamonds.

Hosts: Joe and Kate Bowski
Rooms: 7 (PB) $89-149
Full Breakfast
Credit Cards: A, B, C, D
Notes: 2, 5, 8, 9, 10, 12

## SILSBEE

## Sherwood Train Depot Bed and Breakfast

134 Sherwood Trail, P.O. Bxo 2281, 77656
(409) 385-0188

A beautiful wooded setting of a two-story cypress home in the midst of beech and oak trees. Within the home is a unique design of knottie cypress wood. Fireplaced living room which at the ceiling begins a "G" scale "LGB" train system that runs on a cypress ceiling-hung rail system that is 130 feet long and runs throughout the downstairs and even spiraling to the upstairs. You have to see this unusual track layout to believe it. Both suites feature king bed, private bath, cable TV/VCR, phone, and

one suite even has a two-person hot tub. Guests can also enjoy exercise equipment, walking trails, bird watching, and much more.

Host: Jerry Allen
Rooms: 2 (PB) $60-75
Continental and Full Breakfast
Credit Cards: none
Notes: 2, 3, 4, 5, 7, 9, 10

## SPRING

## McLachlan Farm Bed and Breakfast

P.O. Box 538, 77383
(713) 350-2400; (800) 382-3988

The McLachlan family homestead, built in 1911, was restored and enlarged in 1989 by the great-granddaughter, and her husband, of the original McLachlan family who settled the land in 1862. Set back among 35 acres of towering sycamore and pecan trees, neatly mowed grounds, and winding forest trails. It is a quiet oasis that returns guests to a time when life was simpler. Visitors may swing on the porches, walk in the woods, or visit Old Town Spring (one mile south) where there are more than 100 shops to enjoy.

Hosts: Jim and Joycelyn Clairmonte
Rooms: 4 (2PB; 2SB) $75-85
Full Country Breakfast
Credit Cards: A, B, C, D
Notes: 2, 5, 10, 12

# STEPHENVILLE

## *The Oxford House*
900 Harbin Drive, 76401
(817) 968-8171; FAX (817) 965-7555

The Oxford House is a completely restored, two-story Victorian home constructed in 1898. It's spacious porches
surround the magnificent structure
which houses antique furnishings, including a pump organ, a sleigh bed, and
a fainting couch. Four bedrooms with
privacy bathes, a reading room, and a
beautiful garden gazebo—ust the right
setting for the perfect wedding or reception—are all part of this wonderful
escape. Enjoy a home cooked country
breakfast and a candlelight dinner, and
relax and enjoy a memorably romantic
weekend at The Oxford House.

Hosts: Bill and Paula Oxford
Rooms: 4 (PB) $60-75
Full Breakfast
Credit Cards: A, B
Notes: 2, 4 (by reservation), 5, 7, 9, 10, 12

The Oxford House

# TEXARKANA

## *Mansion on Main Bed and Breakfast Inn*
802 Main Street, 75501
(903) 792-1835

"Twice as Nice," the motto of
Texarkana, USA (Texas and Arkansas),
is standard practice at Mansion on Main.
The 1895 Neoclassic Colonial mansion,
surrounded by 14 tall columns, was recently restored by the owners of McKay
House, the popular bed and breakfast
in nearby Jerrson. Six bed chambers
vary from the Governor's Suite to the
Butler's Garret. Guests enjoy Southern
hospitality, period furnishings, fireplaces, and a gentleman's breakfast.
Thirty miles away is the town of Hope,
birthplace of President Clinton.

Host: Javeta Hawthorne
Rooms: 4 + 2 suites (PB) $60-99 (corporate
rates available)
Full Sit-Down Breakfast
Credit Cards: A, B, C
Notes: 2, 5, 10, 12

# WIMBERLY

## *Southwind Bed and Breakfast*
2701 FM 3237, 78676
(512) 847-5277; (800) 508-5277

Southwind, a prayerful place, sets on
25 secluded acres of hills and trees.
Two long porches are provided with
rocking chairs to enjoy the fresh air,

5  Open all year;  6  Pets welcome;  7  Children welcome;  8  Tennis nearby;  9  Swimming nearby;
10  Golf nearby;  11  Skiing nearby;  12  May be booked through travel agent.

wildlife, and sunsets. Star gazing is especially grand from the hot tub. A guest living room with fireplace and kitchen and dining room privileges complement the three spacious, private guest rooms. A full, tasty breakfast with coffee or tea served on the porch is a wonderful way to start the day at Southwind.

Hostess: Carrie Watson
Rooms: 3 (PB) $70-80
Full Breakfast
Credit Cards: A, B, D
Notes: 2, 5, 8, 9, 10, 12

## WINNSBORO

### *Thee Hubbell House*

307 West Elm, 75494
(903) 342-5629; (800) 227-0639;
FAX (903) 342-6627

We spell "Thee" that way on purpose! This is not only the Old English spelling but represents our religious heritage as well. We have twelve rooms all with private baths, two acres of landscaped grounds, and four historical homes all restored and furnished in antiques. Spa House by reservation and romantic candlelight dinners also by reservation. Seven golf courses, ten lakes, and over one hundred antique/craft shops in the area. Antique shop on premises also.

Hosts: Dan and Laurel Hubbell
Rooms: 12 (PB) $75-175
Full Breakfast (Continental available)
Credit Cards: A, B, C, D, E, F (Carte Blanche)
Notes: 2, 4, 5, 7 (cottage only), 8, 9, 10, 12

Thee Hubbell House

---

NOTES: Credit cards accepted: A Master Card; B Visa; C American Express; D Discover; E Diners Club; F Other; 2 Personal checks accepted; 3 Lunch available; 4 Dinner available;

# Utah

## BLANDING

### Grayson Country Inn
### Bed and Breakfast

118 East 300 South (86-6), 84511
(801) 678-2388

Grayson Country Inn was first built in
1908 as the home of the William W.
Nix family. Located one block east of
Main Street at 300 South, the Inn offers country hospitality while adding the
modern conveniences of a private bath
and television in each of the seven guest
rooms. The cozy dining and living
rooms are favorite gathering spots for
browsing, reading, and enjoying a country breakfast while you stay for a night,
a week's vacation, or a special family
event. A great retreat for couples,
singles, and family! We specialize in
home atmosphere and home cooking.
We welcome children and family pets
can stay (if requested).

Hosts: Dennis and Lurlene Gutke
Rooms: 8 (PB) $42 (Nov.-March)—$52
(April-Oct.)
Full Breakfast
Credit Cards: A, B, C
Notes: 5, 6 ,7

## MOUNTAIN GREEN

### Hubbard House
### Bed and Breakfast

5648 W. Old Highway Rd., 84050
(801) 876-2005; (800) 815-2220;
FAX (801) 876-2020

Hubbard House, built in the 1920's, has
the warmth and charm of days gone by
with hardwood floors and stained glass
windows. It has an awesome view of
God's majestic mountains. Three ski
resorts within the area, also fishing,
boating, golfing, hiking, and hunting.
Piano in dining room. Come and enjoy
homemade goodies, laughter, and good

---

5 Open all year; 6 Pets welcome; 7 Children welcome; 8 Tennis nearby; 9 Swimming nearby;
10 Golf nearby; 11 Skiing nearby; 12 May be booked through travel agent.

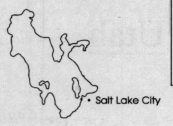

UTAH

• Salt Lake City

• Sandy

• Blanding

• St. George

old hospitality at Hubbard House. One mile east from Exit 92 off I-84.

Hosts: Donald and Gloria Hubbard
Rooms: 3 (1PB; 2SB) $55-75
Full Country Breakfast
Credit Cards: A, B
Notes: 5, 7, 8, 9, 10, 11

## ST. GEORGE

### *Aunt Annie's Inn*

139 North 100 West, 84770
(801) 673-5504; (800) 257-5504

Built in 1891 for an early cattleman, the home has been carefully renovated, restored, and decorated with a variety of fine American antiques. Located in the heart of the historic district, the Inn is within walking distance of Brigham Young's winter home, Pioneer Museum, many convenient stores, fine restaurants, gift shops, and much more. A recent guest said, "Your hospitality was the best. . .you made us feel like friends, as well as guests."

Hosts: Bob and Claudia Tribe
Rooms: 4 (PB) $45-60
Full Breakfast
Credit Cards: A, B, C, D
Notes: 2, 5, 7, 8, 9, 10, 11, 12

Aunt Annie's Inn

### *Green Gate Village*

76 W. Tabernacle St., 84770
(801) 628-6999; (800) 350-6999;
FAX (801) 628-6989

Behind the green gates, nine beautifully restored homes proved modern comfort in pioneer elegance. Our guests love the nostalgic charm of the Bentley House with elegant Victorian decor and the quaint Tolley House, where eleven children were born and raised. The Grainery sleeps three in rooms where early settlers loaded supplies for their trek to California. The Orson Pratt Home, built by another early Mormon leader, is on the National Register of Historic Places. Green Hedge, with one of the village's two bridal suites, was originally built in another part of town but was moved to Green Gate Village in 1991. Family reunions or other large groups (up to 22) may share the comfort and charm of the Greenehouse, built in 1872. The Greenehouse has all the modern conveniences of a full kitchen, swimming pool, and tennis court. Greene Gate Village also caters to corporate retreats.

Hosts: John and Barbara Greene
Rooms: 17 (PB) $50-110
Full Breakfast
Credit Cards: A, B, C, D
Notes: 2, 4, 5, 7, 8, 9, 10, 11, 12

### *Seven Wives Inn*

217 North 100 West, 84770
(801) 628-3737; (800) 600-3737

The Inn consists of two adjacent pioneer adobe homes with massive handgrained moldings framing win-

NOTES: Credit cards accepted: A Master Card; B Visa; C American Express; D Discover; E Diners Club; F Other; 2 Personal checks accepted; 3 Lunch available; 4 Dinner available; 5 Open all year; 6 Pets welcome; 7 Children welcome; 8 Tennis nearby; 9 Swimming nearby; 10 Golf nearby; 11 Skiing nearby; 12 May be booked through travel agent.

dows and doors. Bedrooms are furnished with period antiques and handmade quilts. Some rooms have fireplaces; two have a whirlpool tub. Swimming pool on premises.

Hosts: Donna and Jay Curtis; Alison and Jon Bowcutt
Rooms: 12 (PB) $55-85; suites $125
Full Breakfast
Credit Cards: A, B, C, D, E
Notes: 2, 5, 7, 8, 9, 10, 12

Armstrong Mansion Bed and Breakfast

## SALT LAKE CITY

## *Armstrong Mansion Bed and Breakfast*

667 East 100 South, 84010
(801) 531-1333; (800) 708-1333;
FAX (801) 531-0282

The Armstrong Mansion was built in 1893 in fulfillment of a wedding-day promise by Frank Armstrong, then Mayor of Salt Lake City. This Queen Anne Style mansion, alive with the oak staircase in the entry, will take your breath away. The beautiful stenciling in the rooms and the carpeting in the parlor and dining room are reproductions of the original, thanks to photographs which have been made available by the Armstrong descendants. Besides the ornate woodwork and the beautiful stained glass windows, there are fourteen splendidly restored rooms. You are within walking distance of downtown businesses, shopping, entertainment, and historical/cultural attractions. Only a 30-45 minute drive will take you from the Mansion to ten world class ski resorts with the "greatest snow on earth," snowmobiling, and water sports.

Rooms: 14 (PB) $75-184
Full Gourmet Breakfast
Credit Cards: A, B, C, D
Notes: 2, 5, 10, 11, 12

## SANDY

## *Mountain Hollow Bed and Breakfast Inn*

10209 S. Dimple Dell Road, 84092
(801) 942-3428

Nestled at the base of little Cottonwood Canyon, just minutes from world class skiing and 18 miles from downtown Salt Lake City. Wooded country estate with streams, waterfall, and outdoor hot tub. Beautiful cathedral ceilings in lounge, gameroom video library, and breakfast buffet.

Hosts: Doug and Kathy Larson
Rooms: 11 (2PB; 9SB) $58-150
Continental Plus Breakfast
Credit Cards: A, B, C
Notes: 2, 5, 7 (over 5), 8, 9, 10, 11, 12

NOTES: Credit cards accepted: A Master Card; B Visa; C American Express; D Discover; E Diners Club; F Other; 2 Personal checks accepted; 3 Lunch available; 4 Dinner available;

# Vermont

## American Country Collection of B&B

4 Greenwood Ln., **Delmar**, NY 12054
(518) 439-7001 (information and reservations);
FAX (518) 439-4301

This reservation service provides reservations for eastern **New York**, western **Massachusetts**, all of **Vermont**, and **St. Thomas/St. John, U.S.V.I.** Just one call does it all. Relax and unwind at any of our 120 immaculate, personally inspected bed and breakfasts and country inns. Many include fireplace, jacuzzi, and/or Modified American Plan. We cater to the budget-minded, yet also offer luxurious accommodations in older Colonial homes and inns. Urban, suburban, and rural locations available. $35-180. Carol Metos, coordinator.

Thomas Mott Homestead Bed and Breakfast

## ALBURG

## Thomas Mott Homestead Bed and Breakfast

Rt. 2, Box 149-B, (Blue Rock Road on Lake Champlain) 05440
(802) 796-3736 (voice and FAX);
(800) 348-0843

Formerly an importer and distributor of fine wines, your host also enjoys gourmet cooking. His completely restored farmhouse has a guest living room with TV and fireplace overlooking the lake, game room with bumper pool and darts, and quilt decor. Full view of Mt. Mansfield and Jay Peak. One hour to Montreal/Burlington; one and one-half hours to Lake Placid and Stowe. Lake activities in winter and summer. Amenities include Ben and Jerry's ice cream, lawn games, and horseshoes. Prodigy accessible; boat dock. Gift Certificates also available.

Host: Patrick J. Schallert, Sr., M.S., B.A.
Rooms: 5 (PB) $59-76
Full Breakfast
Credit Cards: A, B, D
Notes: 2, 3, 4 (gourmet dinner w/advance notice), 5, 7 (over 6), 8, 9, 10, 11, 12

---

5 Open all year; 6 Pets welcome; 7 Children welcome; 8 Tennis nearby; 9 Swimming nearby; 10 Golf nearby; 11 Skiing nearby; 12 May be booked through travel agent.

## ARLINGTON

### The Arlington Inn
Historic Rt. 7A, P.O. Box 369, 05250
(802) 375-6532; (800) 443-9442

A stately Greek Revival mansion set on lush, landscaped lawns. Elegantly appointed rooms filled with antiques and amenities. All rooms have private baths and air-conditioning and include breakfast. Located between Bennington and Manchester. Antique shops, boutiques, museums, skiing, hiking, biking, canoeing, fly fishing, golf, and many other outdoor activities are nearby. Tennis on our private court. Outstanding cuisine is served by romantic candlelight in our fireplaced, award-winning dining room with superb service. A non-smoking inn. AAA—3 diamonds. Mobile—3 stars.

Hosts: Mark and Deborah Gagnon
Rooms: 13 (PB) $70-185
Full Breakfast
Credit Cards: A, B, C, D, E
Notes: 2 (deposits only), 4, 5, 7, 8 (on-site), 9, 10, 11, 12

### Hill Farm Inn
R.R. 2, Box 2015, 05250
(802) 375-2269; (800) 882-2545;
FAX (802) 375-9918

Hill Farm is one of Vermont's original farmsteads granted from King George III in 1775. It has been an inn since 1905 and still retains the character of an old farm vacation inn on 60 beautiful acres between the Taconic and Green Mountains with a mile frontage on the Battenkill River. We offer hearty home cooking, charming rooms, hiking, biking, canoeing, and relaxing with spectacular views.

Hosts: George and Joanne Hardy
rooms: 13 (8PB; 5SB) $70-120
Full Hot Country Breakfast
Credit Cards: A, B, C, D
Notes: 2, 4, 5, 6 (limited), 7, 8, 9, 10, 11, 12

### Shenandoah Farm
Battenkill Road, 05250
(802) 375-6372

Experience New England in this lovingly restored 1820 Colonial overlooking the Battenkill River. Wonderful "Americana" year-round. Full "farm-fresh" breakfast is served daily and is included.

Hosts: Woody Masterson
Rooms: 5 (1PB; 4SB) $60-75
Full Breakfast
Credit Cards: A, B
Notes: 2, 5, 8, 10, 11, 12

## BELLOW FALLS

### Blue Haven Christian Bed and Breakfast
227 Westminster Road, 05101
(802-463-9008; (800) 228-9008;
FAX (802) 463-1454

Explore Vermont's beauty from our 1830 restored schoolhouse. Experience canopy beds, hand-painted touches, and a big country kitchen where hearth-

NOTES: Credit cards accepted: A Master Card; B Visa; C American Express; D Discover; E Diners Club; F Other; 2 Personal checks accepted; 3 Lunch available; 4 Dinner available; 5 Open all year; 6 Pets welcome; 7 Children welcome; 8 Tennis nearby; 9 Swimming nearby; 10 Golf nearby; 11 Skiing nearby; 12 May be booked through travel agent.

Green Trails Inn

baked Vermont breakfasts are served. Have tea time treats at the antique glass laden sideboard, or in the ruddy pine common room. Expect a peaceful and pleasant time here. Christian fellowship available. Open to one and all in God's love. Please come!

Hostess: Helene A. Champgne
Rooms: 6 (4PB; 2SB) $45-75
Full Breakfast (weekends); Continental Breakfast (weekdays)
Credit Cards: A, B, C
Notes: 2, 5, 7, 8, 9, 10, 11, 12

## BROOKFIELD

## Green Trails Inn
By the Floating Bridge, 05036
(802) 276-3412; (800) 243-3412

*Green Trails Inn...* Relax and be pampered...enjoy comfortable elegance and true Vermont hospitality on our seventeen-acre country estate in the heart of historic Brookfield. Outdoor lover's paradise—biking, hiking, fishing, swimming, canoeing, ice skating,

and cross-country skiing (over 30km) from our front door. Scrumptious meals, spacious lounging areas, and comfy beds to fall into at night. Fabulous antique clock collection!

Hosts: Sue and Mark Erwin
Rooms: 14 (8PB; 6SB) $70-110
Full Breakfast
Credit Cards: A, B
Notes: 2, 4, 5, 9, 10, 11, 12

## CHESTER

## Greenleaf Inn
Depot Street, P.O. Box 188, 05143
(802) 875-3171

Beautiful 1860's Victorian just off the Village Green. Five spacious, quiet guest rooms tastefully decorated with antiques, queen-sized beds, and country quilts. All with private baths. Full Vermont breakfast in our sunny dining room always included with your stay. Enjoy afternoon refreshments served by the fire or baby grand piano. Walk to churches, giftshops, antiques, and restaurants. Swimming, boating, golf, hiking, biking, cross-country, downhill skiing, and snowmobiling all nearby. Gift certificates available for that special someone.

Hosts: Jerry and Robin Szawerda
Rooms: 5 (PB) $70-95
Full Breakfast
Credit Cards: A, B, C, D
Notes: 2, 5, 8, 9, 10, 11

## Henry Farm Inn

P.O. Box 646, 05143
(802) 875-2674; (800) 723-8213

The Henry Farm Inn supplies the beauty of Vermont with old-time simplicity. Nestled on 50 acres of rolling hills and meadows, assuring peace and quiet. Spacious rooms, private baths, country sitting areas, and a sunny dining room all guarantee a feeling of home. Come and visit for a day or more!

Hosts: The Bowmans
Rooms: 7 (PB) $50-90
Full Breakfast
Credit Cards: A, B, C
Notes: 2, 5, 7, 8, 9, 10, 11, 12

## The Hugging Bear Inn and Shoppe

Main Street, 05143
(802) 875-2412; (800) 325-0519;
FAX (802) 875-3823

Teddy bears peek out the windows and are tucked in all the corners of this beautiful Victorian house built in 1850. If you love teddy bears, you'll love the Hugging Bear. There are six guest rooms with private shower baths and a teddy bear in every bed. Full breakfast

and afternoon snack are served.

Hosts: Georgette, Diane, and Paul Thomas
Rooms: 6 (PB) $55-90
Full Breakfast
Credit Cards: A, B, C, D
Notes: 2, 5, 7, 8, 9, 10, 11

## The Old Town Farm Inn

RR 4 Box 383B, State Route 10, 05143
(802) 875-2346

Built in 1861, the Inn is a handsome 20-room New England Colonial farmhouse. The original farm had 150 acres and was the "Chester Town Farm" that periods answer to public assistance. Every town had a town farm. People needing assistance could live here and work on the farm. Located in the hamlet of Gassetts, a part of Chester, the Inn has been painstakingly restored with eleven comfortable guest rooms partially furnished with period antiques. Also featuring quilts and stenciling.

Hosts: Fred and Jan Baldwin
Rooms: 11 (4PB; 7SB) $58-72
Full Breakfast
Credit Cards: A, B, E
Notes: 2, 5, 7 (6 and over), 8, 9, 10, 11

## CUTTINGSVILLE

## Buckmaster Inn

Lincoln Hill Road, 05738
(802) 492-3485

The Buckmaster Inn (1801) was an early stagecoach stop in Shrewsbury. Standing on a knoll overlooking a picturesque barn scene and rolling hills, the Inn is situated in the Green Mountains. A center hall, grand staircase, and wide-

---

5 Open all year; 6 Pets welcome; 7 Children welcome; 8 Tennis nearby; 9 Swimming nearby; 10 Golf nearby; 11 Skiing nearby; 12 May be booked through travel agent.

pine floors grace the home which is decorated with family antiques and crewel handiwork done by your hostess. Extremely large, airy rooms; wood-burning stove; four fireplaces; and two large porches.

Hosts: Sam and Grace Husselman
Rooms: 4 (2PB; 2SB) $55-65 + tax
Full Breakfast
Credit Cards: none
Notes: 5, 7, 8, 9, 10, 11

## Maple Crest Farm

R.R. Box 120 Lincoln Hill, 05738
(802) 492-3367

This 27-room, 1808 farmhouse has been preserved for five generations and is located in the heart of the Green Mountains in Shrewsbury. It has been a bed and breakfast for 23 years. Ten miles north of Ludlow and ten miles south of Rutland, an area that offers much to visitors. Pico, Killington, and Okemo are nearby for downhill skiing. Cross-country skiing and hiking are offered on the premises.

Hosts: William and Donna Smith
Rooms: 4 (SB) $25-35 per person
Full Breakfast
Credit Cards: none
Notes: 2, 7, 8, 9, 10, 11, 12

## DANBY

## The Quail's Nest

P.O. Box 221, Main Street, 05739
(802) 293-5099; (802) 293-6300

Nestled in a quiet mountain village, our inn offers guests friendly conversation around the fireplace, rooms filled with cozy quilts and antiques, and a hearty, home-cooked breakfast in the morning. Hiking, skiing, swimming, and outlet shopping are all very close by as well as our local craft and antique shops. Our guests are all treated as part of the family, which is what makes a real difference.

Hosts: Gregory and Nancy Diaz
Rooms: 6 (4PB; 2SB) $60-85
Full Breakfast
Credit Cards: A, B
Notes: 2, 5, 7, 8, 9, 10, 11

## Silas Griffith Inn

R.R. 1, Box 66F, 05739
(800) 545-1509

Built by Vermont's first millionaire, this Victorian inn was built in 1891 in the heart of the Green Mountains, with a spectacular mountain view. It features 17 delightful, antique-furnished rooms and a fireplace in the living and dining room. Hiking, skiing, and antiquing nearby. Come and enjoy our elegant meals and New England hospitality.

Hosts: Paul and Lois Dansereau
Rooms: 17 (11PB; 6SB) $70-88
Full Breakfast
Credit Cards: A, B
Notes: 2, 4, 5, 7, 9, 10, 11, 12

## DERBY LINE

## Derby Village Inn

46 Main Street, 05830
(802) 873-3604

Enjoy this charming, old, Victorian mansion situated in the quiet village of Derby Line, within walking distance of

---

NOTES: Credit cards accepted: A Master Card; B Visa; C American Express; D Discover; E Diners Club; F Other; 2 Personal checks accepted; 3 Lunch available; 4 Dinner available;

the Canadian border and the world's only international library and opera house. The nearby countryside offers year-round recreation: downhill and cross-country skiing, water sports, cycling, fishing, hiking, golf, snowmobiling, sleigh rides, antiquing, and most of all peace and tranquillity. We are a non-smoking facility.

Hosts: Tom and Phyllis Moreau
Rooms: 5 (PB) $55-65
Full Breakfast
Credit Cards: A, B, D
Notes: 2, 5, 7, 8, 9, 10, 11

## DUCK CREEK VILLAGE

## Meadeau View Lodge

P.O. Box 1331, Movie Ranch Road, 84762
(801) 682-2495; (800) 332-0568

A unique mountain inn located within beautiful Dixie National Forest. Our common area boasts a large circular fireplace where we serve homemade goodies during our evening "social hour." Rooms of knotty pine have a warm country feel. Within minutes of Bryce Canyon and Zion National Parks and Cedar Breaks National Monument. Paradise for fishermen, mountain bikers, hikers, snowmobilers, and skiers! Let us spoil you with gourmet, delicious, homey, comfort, and warm hospitality.

Hosts: Craig and Kimberly Simmerman
Rooms: 9 (PB) $50-60
Full Country Breakfast
Credit Cards: A, B
Notes: 3, 4, 5, 6, 7, 12

## EAST DOVER

## Cooper Hill Inn

P.O. Box 146, 05341
(802) 348-6333; (800) 783-3229

Set high on a hill in Southern Vermont's Green Mountains Cooper Hill Inn commands a view to the east proclaimed by the *Boston Globe* as "one of the most spectacular mountain panoramas in all New England." A small portion of the Inn was a farmhouse built in 1797. The Inn has ten rooms, all with private bath. The atmosphere is always homey and informal. Country breakfast included in rate. Families welcome.

Hosts: Pat and Marilyn Hunt
Rooms: 10 (PB) $68-110
Full Breakfast
Credit Cards: A, B, D
Notes: 2, 4, 5, 7, 8, 9, 10, 11, 12

Maplewood Inn

## FAIR HAVEN

## Maplewood Inn

Route 22A South, 05743
(802) 265-8039; (800) 253-7729;
FAX (802) 265-8210

Exquisite 1843 Greek Revival on the Vermont Register of Historic Places and a romantic, antique-filled haven! Keep-

---

5 Open all year; 6 Pets welcome; 7 Children welcome; 8 Tennis nearby; 9 Swimming nearby; 10 Golf nearby; 11 Skiing nearby; 12 May be booked through travel agent.

ing room with fireplace, gathering room with books and games, parlor with complimentary cordials. Elegant rooms and suites are air-conditioned, have fireplaces, color cable TVs, radios, and in-room phone available. Near everything! Bikes and canoe on sight. Lakes region. Pet boarding arranged. A true four-season experience! Recommended by Guidebook, Mobil—3 stars, and AAA—3 diamonds.

Hosts: Doug and Cindy Baird
Rooms: 5 (PB) $70-105
Continental Plus Breakfast
Credit Cards: A, B, C, D, E, F
Notes: 2, 5, 7 (over 5), 8, 9, 10, 11, 12

## FAIRLEE

### Silver Maple Lodge and Cottages

R.R. 1, Box 8, 05045
(802) 333-4326; (800) 666-1946

A historic bed and breakfast country inn is located in a four-season recreational area. Enjoy canoeing, fishing, golf, tennis, and skiing within a few miles of the lodge. Visit nearby flea markets and country auctions. Choose a newly renovated room in our antique farmhouse or a handsome, pine-paneled cottage room. Three cottages with working fireplaces. Many fine restaurants are nearby. Darmouth College is 17 miles away. Also offered are hot air balloon packages, inn-to-inn bicycling, canoeing, and walking tours. Brochures available.

Hosts: Scott and Sharon Wright
Rooms: 16 (14PB; 2SB) $50-74
Continental Breakfast
Credit Cards: A, B, C, D
Notes: 2, 5, 7, 8, 9, 10, 11, 12

Silver Maple Lodge and Cottages

## KILLINGTON

### The Peak Chalet

P.O. Bxo 551, South View Path, 05751
(802) 422-4278

The Peak Chalet is a four room B&B located within the beautiful Green Mountains. The exterior is authentically European alpine. The interior is furnished with a fine country inn flavor and reflects high quality with attention to detail. We offer panoramic mountain views with a cozy stone fireplace to unwind by. All rooms have queen-size beds and private baths. Centrally located within Killington Ski Resort, this is a truly relaxing experience.

Hosts: Gregory and Diane Becker
Rooms: 4 (PB) $50-110
Continental Breakfast
Credit Cards: A, B, C, E
Notes; 5, 7 (over 12), 8, 9, 10, 11, 12

### Vermont Inn

HC 34, Box 37J, Route 4, 05751
(802) 775-0708; (800) 541-7795;
FAX (802) 773-2440

Please join us in our small c. 1840 country inn on five acres in the Green Mountains. We offer the charm of a family run inn with award-winning New En-

---

NOTES: Credit cards accepted: A Master Card; B Visa; C American Express; D Discover; E Diners Club; F Other; 2 Personal checks accepted; 3 Lunch available; 4 Dinner available;

gland cuisine. We are in an area that provides year-round activity for all ages. Fireplace rooms available. 3-Diamonds from AAA.

Hosts: Greg and Megan Smith
Rooms: 19 (15PB; 4SB) $50-160 (Full Breakfast) $90-200 (Full Breakfast and Dinner)
Credit Cards: A, B, C
Notes: 2, 4, 5 (except May), 7 (over 6), 8, 9

## LONDONBERRY

### Blue Gentian Lodge (Koinonia of Vermont)

R.R. 1 Box 29, 05148
(802) 824-5908 (voice and FAX)

A special place to stay, nestled at the foot of Magic Mountain—all rooms have private baths, cable color TV, and include a full breakfast in the dining room. Seasonal activities on the grounds, a swimming pool, and walking trails. Recreation Room offers ping pong, bumper pool, board games, and library. There is golf, tennis, fishing, outlet shopping, antiquing, horseback riding, and skiing (downhill and cross-country) nearby.

Hosts: Paul and Dorothy Alberti
Rooms: 13 (PB) $50-80
Full Breakfast
Credit Cards: none
Notes: 2, 5, 7, 8, 9, 10, 11

Rabbit Hill Inn

## LOWER WATERFORD

### Rabbit Hill Inn

Box 55, Route 18, 05848
(802) 748-5168; (800) 76-BUNNY;
FAX (802) 748-8342

Full of whimsical and charming surprises, this Federal-period inn, established in 1795, has been lavished with love and attention. Many guest rooms have fireplaces and canopied beds. Chamber music, candlelit gourmet dining, and turn-down service make this an enchanting and romantic hideaway in a tiny, restore village overlooking the mountains. Award-winning, nationally acclaimed inn. Our service is inspired by Philippians 2:7.

Hosts: John and Maureen Magee
Rooms: 18 (PB) $105-209; $55-159 single
Full Breakfast
Credit Cards: A, B, C
Closed first two weeks of Nov. and all of April
Notes: 2, 3 (picnic), 4, 8, 9 (on-site), 10, 11 (on-site), 12

## MANCHESTER VILLAGE

### The Battenkill Inn

P.O. Box 948, 05254
(802) 362-4213; (800) 441-1628

Enjoy afternoon croquet on sweeping lawns with mountain views, or savor evening hors d'oeuvres by a marble mantled fire. The Battenkill Inn offers warm hospitality in the dramatic elegance of an 1840 Italianate Victorian setting. Convenient to skiing, hiking, biking, fishing, canoeing, outlet shopping, and some of the finest dining in New England. Sumptuous breakfasts included. Some fireplaced rooms, all with private baths and air-conditioning.

Hosts: Ramsay and Mary Jo Gourd
Rooms: 10 (PB) $75-160
Very Full Breakfast
Credit Cards: A, B, C
Notes: 3 (boxed), 5, 7 (well attended), 9, 10, 11, 12

## MIDDLEBURY

### The Middlebury Inn

14 Courthouse Square, 05753
(802) 388-4961; (800) 842-4666

This 1827, historic, 75-room landmark overlooks the village green in a picturesque New England college town. Discover Middlebury, Vermont—the splendor of its historic district—Vermont State Craft Center, Middlebury College, boutique shopping, and four season recreation. Elegantly restored rooms, private bath, telephone, color TV, and air-conditioning (in season). The Inn offers breakfast, lunch, dinner, seasonal porch dining, afternoon tea, and Sunday brunch. Recommended by AAA and a member of Historic Hotels of America.

Hosts: Jane and Frank Emanuel, Innkeepers
Rooms: 75 (PB) $86-200 per room, per night (double occupancy)
Full and Continental Breakfast (not included in rate but can be added)
Credit Cards: A, B, C, E
Notes: 3, 4, 5, 6 (limited), 7, 8, 9, 10, 11, 12

## MORETOWN

### Camel's Hump View

Box 720, 05660
(802) 496-3614

Camel's Hump View is a unique old-style country inn dating back to 1831, with the Mad River to the east and Camel's Hump Mountain to the west. Warm up by the glowing fire in the winter, or enjoy cattle grazing in the fields during the summer. The inn can accommodate 16 guests and serves hearty country meals from the gardens. Skiing, golf, fishing, horseback riding, and hiking are all available. No smoking.

Hosts: Jerry and Wilma Maynard
Rooms: 8 (1PB; 7SB) $50-60
Full Breakfast
Credit Cards: F
Notes: 2, 4, 5, 7, 8, 9, 10, 11

## PITTSFIELD

### Swiss Farm Lodge

P.O. Box 630, Route 100, 05762
(802) 746-8341; (800) 245-5126

Working Hereford beef farm. Enjoy the casual, family-type atmosphere in our living room with fireplace and TV or in the game room. Home-cooked meals and baking served family style. Our own maple syrup, jams, and jellies. Walk-in cooler available for guests' use. Cross-country trails on site. B&B available all year. M.A.P provided November to April only. Mountain bike trails close by. Owned and operated by the same family for 50 years. Lower rates for children in same room as parents.

Hosts: Mark and Sandy Begin
Rooms: 17 (14PB; 3SB) $40-60
Full Breakfast
Credit Cards: A, B, D
Notes: 2, 4, 5, 7, 8, 9, 10, 11, 12

---

NOTES: Credit cards accepted: A Master Card; B Visa; C American Express; D Discover; E Diners Club; F Other; 2 Personal checks accepted; 3 Lunch available; 4 Dinner available;

# ROCHESTER

## Liberty Hill Farm

R.R. 1 Box 158, Liberty Hill Rd., 05767
(802) 767-3926

Come enjoy exploring our award-winning dairy farm in the Green Mountains.
Families are welcome to share in the
barn chores. Excellent home-cooked
meals are served family style in our
1825 farmhouse. Hiking, fishing, swimming, skiing, horseback riding, and golf
available. Refresh and restore your spirit
and become a member of our *"family"*.

Hosts:  Bob and Beth Kennett
Rooms:  7 (SB) $100-120
Full Breakfast and Dinner
Credit Cards:  none
Notes:  2, 4, 5, 7, 8, 9, 10, 11, 12

# RUTLAND

## The Inn at Rutland

70 N. Main Street, 05701
(802) 773-0575; (800) 808-0575;
FAX (802) 775-3506

Beautifully restored 1890's Victorian
mansion with ten large, comfortable
rooms all with private baths, remote
color cable TV, and phones. Some
rooms have A/C. Gourmet breakfast
included. Large front porch with beautiful views of mountains and valleys.
Close to all central Vermont attractions.
Common rooms with fireplaces, TV/
VCR, and games. Carriage house for ski
and bike storage. Ten minutes to Pico
and Killington ski areas. Call our toll-

free number.

Hosts:  Bob and Tanya Liberman
Rooms:  10 (PB) $69-179
Full Breakfast
Credit Cards:  A, B, D, E
Notes:  2, 5, 7 (over 8), 8, 9, 10, 11, 12

# STOWE

## Brass Lantern Inn

717 Maple Street, 05672
(802) 253-2229; (800) 729-2980;
FAX (802) 253-7425

Award winning traditional bed and
breakfast inn, in the heart of Stowe,
overlooking Mt. Mansfield, Vermont's
most prominent mountain. The features
period antiques, hand made quilts local
artisian wares and A/C. Most rooms
have view, some have fireplaces and
some have whirlpools. A hint of romance abounds in each room, an intimate Inn for romatics. Special packages include; honeymoon/anniversary,
romance, skiing, golf, historic, and
more. Non-smoking.

Host:  Andy Aldrich
Rooms:  9 (PB) $75-175
Full Breakfast
Credit Cards:  A, B, C
Notes:  2, 5, 8, 9, 10, 11, 12

## The Siebeness Inn

3681 Mountain Rd., 05672
(802) 253-8942; (800) 426-9001;
FAX (802) 253-9232

A warm welcome awaits you at our
charming country inn nestled in the
foothills of Mt. Mansfield. Romantic

---

5  Open all year;  6  Pets welcome;  7  Children welcome;  8  Tennis nearby;  9  Swimming nearby;
10  Golf nearby;  11  Skiing nearby;  12  May be booked through travel agent.

rooms have country antiques, private baths, and air-conditioning. Awake to the aroma of freshly baked muffins, which accompany your hearty New England breakfast. Relax in our outdoor hot tub in winter or our pool with mountain views in summer. Fireplace in lounge. Bike, walk, or cross-country ski from the Inn on a recreation path. Honeymoon, golf, and ski packages.

Hosts: Sue and Nils Andersen
Rooms: 11 (PB) $65-125
Full Breakfast
Credit Cards: A, B, C, D
Notes: 2, 4 (winter), 5, 7, 8, 9, 10, 11, 12

Ski Inn

## Ski Inn

Route 108, 05672
(802) 253-4050

In appearance the Ski Inn is a traditionally old New England inn, but comfortably modern. Built and operated by the Heyer family, original owners. Rooms are large and colorful with both a double

and single bed. Located back from the traveled road, it is a quiet place to relax and enjoy. In winter, a skier's delight, the Inn is close to Mt. Mansfield's downhill trails, with miles of cross-country trails at our back door.

Hostess: Mrs. Larry Heyer
Rooms: 10 (5PB; 5SB) $40-55
Continental Breakfast
Credit Cards: C
Notes: 2, 4 (winter), 5, 6 (advance notice), 7, 8, 9, 10, 11

## Timberhölm Inn

452 Cottage Club Rd., 05672
(802) 253-7603; (800) 753-7603;
FAX (802) 253-8559

This delightful country inn in a quiet, secluded, wooded setting has a wonderful view of the Worchester Mountains. We serve afternoon tea and refreshments in the summer and après ski soup in the winter. We have ten individually decorated rooms with quilts and antiques. Two are two-bedroom suites ideal for families. There is a very large common room with an oversized fieldstone fireplace. Large outdoor deck and hot tub. Game room, shuffleboard, cable TV/VCR, refrigerator, and microwave. No smoking.

Hosts: Pete and Louise Hunter
Rooms: 10 (PB) $70-130
Full Country Breakfast
Credit Cards: A, B, D
Notes: 2, 5, 7, 8, 9, 10, 11, 12

---

NOTES: Credit cards accepted: A Master Card; B Visa; C American Express; D Discover; E Diners Club; F Other; 2 Personal checks accepted; 3 Lunch available; 4 Dinner available;

# VERGENNES

## Strong House Inn

82 West Main Street, 05491
(802) 877-3337

Experience elegant lodging in a grand 1834 Federal home listed on the National Register of Historic Places. Located in the heart of the Champlain Valley, the area provides superb cycling, hiking, antique shopping, and nearby Shelburne Museum. The fully air-conditioned inn situated on six acres with walking trails and gardens, offers seven rooms, two suites, three working fireplaces, and a full country breakfast.

Hosts: Mary and Hugh Bargiel
Rooms: 7 (5PB; 2SB) $65-140
Full Breakfast
Credit Cards: A, B, C
Notes: 2, 4, 5, 9, 10, 11, 12

# WAITSFIELD

## 1824 House Inn

Route 100, Box 159, 05673
(802) 496-7555; (800) 426-6398;
FAX (802) 496-7558

Enjoy relaxed elegance in one of seven beautiful guest rooms at this quintessential farmhouse on 52 acres. The Inn features antiques, original art, fireplaces, and classical music. Breakfast by the fire includes such whimsical gourmet delights as soufflés, crepes, blueberry buttermilk pancakes, and freshly squeezed orange juice. Cross-country skiing and private river swim-

ming hole are nearby. Featured in *Glamour* and *Vermont Life*. National Historic Registered. AAA three-diamond and Mobile three-star rated.

Hosts: Susan and Lawrence McKay
Rooms: 7 (PB) $90-135
Full Breakfast
Credit Cards: A, B, C, D
Notes: 2, 5, 8, 9, 10, 11, 12

## Inn at Mad River Barn

Route 17, 05673
(802) 496-3310; (800) 631-0466

Premier country lodge with 15 rooms, private baths, gardens, and outdoor pool in the heart of the Green Mountain Forest. Superb downhill and cross-country skiing. Fireplace; pub. Three miles from Route 100.

Hostess: Becky Pratt
Rooms: 15 (PB) $50-95
Full Breakfast
Credit Cards: A, B, C
Notes: 2, 5, 7, 9, 10, 11, 12

## Mountain View Inn

RFD Box 69, 05673
(802) 496-2426

The Mountain View Inn is an old farmhouse, circa 1826, that was made into a lodge in 1948 to accommodate skiers at nearby Mad River Glen. Today it is a country inn with seven rooms. Meals are served family style around the antique harvest table where good fellowship prevails. Sip mulled cider around a crackling fire in our living room when

---

5 Open all year; 6 Pets welcome; 7 Children welcome; 8 Tennis nearby; 9 Swimming nearby; 10 Golf nearby; 11 Skiing nearby; 12 May be booked through travel agent.

the weather turns chilly.

Hosts: Fred and Susan Spencer
Rooms: 7 (PB) $35-65 per person
Full Breakfast
Credit Cards: none
Notes: 2, 4, 5, 7, 8, 9, 10, 11, 12

## Tucker Hill Lodge

Rd. 1, Box 147 Waitsfield, 05673
(802) 496-3983; (800) 543-7841;
FAX (802) 496-3203

Escape to the beautiful Sugarbush/Mad
River Valley, Vermont. Situated on 14
acres of wooded land, Tucker Hill
Lodge has 22 cozy guest rooms (including two suites), a charming cafe and
rustic bar. Restaurant specialties include
scallops Veneziana, stone oven pizza,
and wood grilled chicken. Pool, tennis,
hiking, and cycling on site. Ten minutes to fishing, golf, and horseback
riding. Two miles from downhill and
cross-country skiing. One mile from
village shops. Group rates available.

Hosts: Susan and Gorgio Noaro
Rooms: 22 (16PB; 6SB) $60-115
Full Country Breakfast includes cold buffet and
hot entree from menu.
Credit Cards: A, B, C
Notes: 2, 4, 5, 7, 8 and 9 (on-site), 10, 11, 12

Tucker Hill Lodge

Beaver Pond Farm Inn

## WARREN

## Beaver Pond Farm Inn

Golf Course Rd., R.D. Box 306, 05674
(802) 583-2861; FAX (802) 583-2860

Beaver Pond Farm Inn, a small gracious
country inn near the Sugarbush ski area,
is located 100 yards from the first tee
of the Sugarbush Golf Course, transformed into 25 kilometers of cross-
country ski trails in the winter. *Bed and
Breakfast in New England* calls it "The
best of the best." Rooms have down
comforters and beautiful views. Hearty
breakfasts are served, and snacks are enjoyed by the fireplace. Continental dinners are offered three times a week during the winter. Hiking, biking, soaring,
and fishing nearby. Bob will take guests
out for fly fishing instruction. Ski and
golf packages are available.

Hosts: Bob and Betty Hansen
Rooms: 6 (4PB; 2SB) $72-96
Full Breakfast
Credit Cards: A, B, C
Notes: 2, 4 (3 times a week), 7 (over 6), 8, 9,
10, 11, 12

---

NOTES: Credit cards accepted: A Master Card; B Visa; C American Express; D Discover;
E Diners Club; F Other; 2 Personal checks accepted; 3 Lunch available; 4 Dinner available;

## WATERBURY

### *Grünberg Haus Bed and Breakfast and Cabins*
R.R. 2, Box 1595 CB, Route 100 South, 05676
(802) 244-7726; (800) 800-7760

Handbuilt Austrian inn offering romantic guestrooms (each with balcony, antiques, comforters, and quilts), secluded cabins (each with fireplace and mountain-view deck) and a carriage house suite (with skywindow, kitchen, sitting area, and two balconies). Central location is close to Stowe, Burlington, Sugarbush, and Montpelier. All accommodations include full, musical breakfast. Enjoy our jacuzzi, sauna, BYOB pub, fireplaces, tennis court, and groomed cross-country ski trails. Help Mark feed the chickens.

Hosts: Chris Sellers and Mark Frohman
Rooms: 15 (10PB; 5SB) $55-140
Full Musical Breakfast
Credit Cards: A, B, C, D
Notes: 2, 5, 7, 8, 9, 10, 11, 12

Grünberg Haus

Inn at Blush Hill

### *Inn at Blush Hill*
R.R. 1 Box 1266, 05676
(802) 244-7529; (800) 736-7522;
FAX (802) 244-7314

This Cape Cod bed and breakfast, circa 1790, sits on five acres with spectacular mountain views. The Inn has a large common room, library, antiques, and four fireplaces, one in a guest room. Enjoy a breakfast of Vermont products at a ten-foot farmland's table in front of a bay window overlooking the Worcester Mountains. Afternoon refreshments are served. We are adjacent to Ben and Jerry's ice cream factory, and the skiing at Stowe and Sugarbush is only minutes away.

Hosts: Gary and Pamela Gosselin
Rooms: 5 (PB) $75-130 seasonal
Full Breakfast
Credit Cards: A, B, C, D
Notes: 2, 5, 7 (over 6), 8, 9, 10, 11, 12

## WESTON

### *The Colonial House*
287 Route 100, 05161
(802) 824-6286; (800) 639-5033;
FAX (802) 824-3934

Family oriented with old-fashioned hos-

---

5 Open all year; 6 Pets welcome; 7 Children welcome; 8 Tennis nearby; 9 Swimming nearby; 10 Golf nearby; 11 Skiing nearby; 12 May be booked through travel agent.

pitality, a comfortable inn and motel. "Vermont's Favorite Breakfast" with dinners to match. Conveniently located on Route 100 outside Weston, with summer theater, shops, and museums, and seven minutes from Weston Priory. Three downhill ski areas and 400 km of cross-country within 20 minutes. The place to stay while visiting southern Vermont. 2-Star Mobil Travel Guide; 2 Diamond AAA.

Hosts: John and Betty Nunnikhoven
Rooms: 15 (9PB; 6SB) $50-84
Full Breakfast
Credit Cards: A, B, D
Notes: 2, 4, 5, 7, 8, 9, 10, 11

The Wilder Homestead Inn

## The Wilder Homestead Inn

25 Lawrence Hill Road, 05161
(802) 824-8172

Built in 1827 with Rumford fireplaces and original Moses Eaton stenciling, the Inn has been carefully restored by us and has quiet surroundings and antique furnishings. Walk to village shops, museums, and summer theater. Nearby are Weston Priory, fine restaurants, and skiing. Weston is a village that takes you back in time. Craft Shoppe on premises.

No smoking.

Hosts: Peg and Roy Varner
Rooms: 7 (5PB; 2SB) $65-100
Full Breakfast
Credit Cards: A, B (deposit only)
Notes: 2, 7 (over 6), 8, 9, 10, 11

## WILLISTON

## Partridge Hill B&B

P.O. Box 52, 102 Partridge Hill, 05495
(802) 878-4741

On top of a hill with a great view of the Vermont Green Mountains to the east, Partridge Hill is ideal for a summer visit with Shelburne museum nearby. The colors surrounding the grounds are ablaze in the fall. We have three rooms for different combinations of guests, but we only take two different families at a time. No smoking.

Hosts: Roger and Sally Bryant
Rooms: 3 (SB) $65-75
Full Breakfast
Credit Cards: none
Notes: 2, 5, 7

## WILMINGTON

## Misty Mountain Lodge

326 Stowe Hill Rd., Box 114, 05363
(802) 464-3961

A cozy, 1803 Farmhouse Inn for over 30 years. Four recently renovated rooms with private baths, one with whirlpool tub. Other rooms have shared baths. Rural setting, beautiful views, living room fireplace, and bountiful meals. Native Vermonter host owns, operates, and entertains with banjo and guitar. Summer walking trails. MAP, B&B, and dinner by reservation.

Hosts: Lensey (Buzz) and Elizabeth Cole
Rooms: 6 (4PB; 2SB) $55-105
Full Breakfast
Credit Cards: A, B, D
Notes: 2, 4, 5, 7, 8, 9, 10, 11, 12

## Shearer Hill Farm B&B

P.O. Box 1453, 05363
(802) 464-3253; (800) 437-3104

Pristine farm setting on country road, large rooms (king, queen, twin), private baths, and delicious Vermont breakfast. Cross-country trails on property. Near downhill skiing, shopping, swimming, fishing, and horseback riding. Only 210 miles from New York, 120 miles from Boston, 90 miles from Hartland, and 70 miles from Albany.

Hosts: Bill and Patti Pusey
Rooms: 6 (PB) $80
Full Vermont Breakfast
Credit Cards: A, B, C, D
Notes: 2 (preferred), 5, 8, 9, 10, 12

## WOODSTOCK

## Canterbury House B&B

43 Pleasant Street, 05091
(802) 457-3077; (800) 390-3077

115 year-old Victorian town house is just a stroll to the village green and fine dining. The Inn is beautifully decorated with era antiques and is for the discriminating traveler. The Inn has won awards from *Yankee* magazine and the American B&B Association, and it is recommended as the best value in town by *Glamour* magazine. Each room is decorated to a different theme.

Hosts: Celeste and Fred Holden
Rooms: 8 (PB) $85-140
Full Gourmet Breakfast
Credit Cards: A, B, C
Notes: 2, 5, 7 (over 7), 8, 9, 10, 11, 12

## Deer Brook Inn

HCR 68, Box 443 Route 4 W., 05091
(802) 672-3713

Handmade quilts, original pine floors and an immaculately maintained country decor are just a few of the charming features of this 1820 farmhouse. Four spacious guestrooms with private baths and queen- or king-sized beds. Enjoy a crackling fire in the winter or a view of the Ottauquechee River from the porch in the summer. A bountiful breakfast provides the perfect start for your day. AAA three diamonds. ABBA approved.

Hosts: Brian and Rosemary McGinty
Rooms: 4 (PB) $70-95
Full Breakfast
Credit Cards: A, B
Notes: 2, 5, 7, 8, 9, 10, 11, 12 (no commission)

---

5 Open all year; 6 Pets welcome; 7 Children welcome; 8 Tennis nearby; 9 Swimming nearby; 10 Golf nearby; 11 Skiing nearby; 12 May be booked through travel agent.

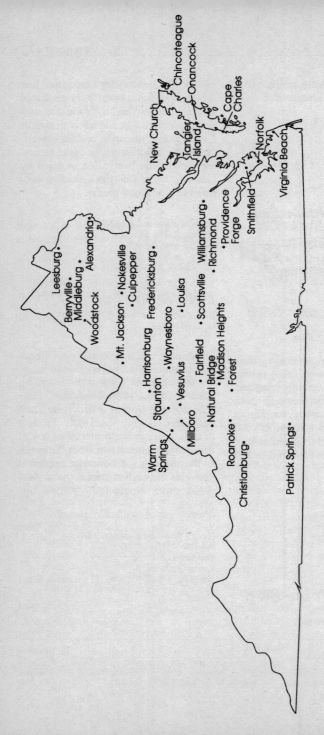

Chincoteague
Onancock
New Church
Tangier Island
Cape Charles
Norfolk
Virginia Beach
Williamsburg
Providence Forge
Richmond
Smithfield
Leesburg
Berryville
Middleburg
Alexandria
Woodstock
Nokesville
Culpepper
Mt. Jackson
Fredericksburg
Harrisonburg
Waynesboro
Louisa
Scottsville
Staunton
Vesuvius
Fairfield
Madison Heights
Millboro
Natural Bridge
Forest
Warm Springs
Roanoke
Christiansburg
Patrick Springs

VIRGINIA

# Virginia

**ALSO SEE RESERVATION SERVICES UNDER DELAWARE AND D.C.**

## ALEXANDRIA

### Morrison House

116 South Alfred Street, 22314
(703) 838-8000; FAX (703) 684-6283

Built in the style of an 18th-century manor house, award-winning Morrison House offers 45 elegantly appointed guest rooms, each different from the others, including three suites. All guest rooms are enhanced by fine Federal-period reproductions, including mahogany four-poster beds, brass chandeliers, decorative fireplaces, and Italian marble baths. 24-hour butler, concierge, and room services; indoor valet parking, specialized laundry and valet services including shoeshine; newspaper delivery to each room, nightly turndown with chocolates; and health club privileges. Afternoon tea served daily from 3-5PM in the parlor. Centrally located in Old Town Alexandria, Morrison House is a stroll from historic landmarks, quaint boutiques, and international dining. Downtown Washington, DC, is less than ten minutes away, National Airport is only three miles, and the metro is an easy ten-minute walk.

Hosts: Mr. And Mrs. Robert E. Morrison
Rooms: 45 (PB) $205-295
Complimentary Coffee and Tea in the Parlor.
Credit Cards: A, B, C, E, F (Carte Blanche)
Notes: 2, 3, 4, 5, 7, 8, 9, 10, 12

## BERRYVILLE

### Blue Ridge B&B Reservation Service

Rocks and Rills Farm, Rt. 2, Box 3895,
**Berryville** 22611
(703) 955-1246 (voice and FAX);
(800) 296-1246

Beautiful antique-filled Colonial Williamsburg reproduction nestled in the foothills of the Blue Ridge Mountains, near the Shenandoah River on eleven acres of fragrant Christmas trees. Perfect getaway; ideal for weekend bikers and hikers. Only 90 minutes from Washington, DC. Also a reservation service for numerous host homes.

Hostess: Rita Z. Duncan
Rooms: Numerous (most all PB) $50-150
Full Breakfast
Credit Cards: A, B
Notes: 2, 3 and 4 (some, w/reservations), 5, 6, 7, 8, 9, 10, 11, 12

---

NOTES: Credit cards accepted: A Master Card; B Visa; C American Express; D Discover; E Diners Club; F Other; 2 Personal checks accepted; 3 Lunch available; 4 Dinner available; 5 Open all year; 6 Pets welcome; 7 Children welcome; 8 Tennis nearby; 9 Swimming nearby; 10 Golf nearby; 11 Skiing nearby; 12 May be booked through travel agent.

## CAPE CHARLES

## *Sea Gate*

9 Tatewell Ave., 23310
(804) 331-2206

Located in the quiet and sleepy town of
Cape Charles, just steps from Chesapeake Bay, on Virginia's undiscovered
eastern shore. My home is your home!
Day begins with a full breakfast followed by leisure or hiking, birding,
bathing, and exploring our historic area.
Tea prepares you for the most glorious
sunsets on the east coast. Sea Gate is
the perfect place to rest, relax and re-
charge away from the crush of modern
America.

Host: Chris Bannon
Rooms: 4 (2PB; 2 shared shower) $70-80
(winter 2 nights $100)
Full Breakfast
Credit Cards: none
Notes: 2, 5, 7 (over 7), 8, 9, 10, 12

## CHINCOTEAGUE

## *The Watson House Bed and Breakfast*

4240 Main Street, 23336
(804) 336-1564; (800) 336-6787

The Watson House has been tastefully
restored with Victorian charm. Nestled
in the heart of Chincoteague, the House
is within walking distance of shops and
restaurants. Each guest room includes
antiques, private bath, and air-conditioning. A full, hearty breakfast and afternoon tea are served in the dining
room or on the verandah. Enjoy free use
of bicycles to tour the Chincoteague
National Wildlife Refuge and Beach.
AAA—3 diamonds.

Hosts: Tom and Jacque Derrickson and David
and Joanne Snead
Rooms: 6 (PB) $65-115
Full Breakfast plus Afternoon Tea
Credit Cards: A, B
Notes: 2, 7 (over 9), 8, 9, 10

## CHRISTIANSBURG

## *EVERGREEN—The Bell-Capozzi House*

201 E. Main Street, 24073
(703) 382-7372

Victorian Mansion (circa 1890's) on
routes I-81, 11, 460, bike Route 76, Wilderness Road, and in the historic district. Amenities include central air-conditioning, fireplaces, swimming pool,
art gallery, wisteria covered arbor, gazebo, and rockers on wraparound
porches. A non-smoking inn.

Hosts: Rocco and Barbara Bell-Capozzi
Rooms: 5 (PB) $75-105
Full, Southern-Style Breakfast
Credit Cards: A, B, C
Notes: 2, 5, 8, 9, 10, 12

EVERGREEN—The Bell-Capozzi House

## CULPEPER

### Fountain Hall

609 S. East Street, 22701
(703) 825-8200; (800) 29-VISIT;
FAX (703) 825-7716

Fountain Hall is a charming 1859 Colonial Revival bed and breakfast. All of our rooms are tastefully restored and most are furnished with antiques. Three guest rooms have private porches overlooking the grounds. Fireplaces can be found in the common rooms along with books, local literature, board games, music, and TV/VCR. Fountain Hall is within walking distance to Historic Downtown Culpeper and Amtrak. Charlottesville and Dulles airports are nearby.

Hosts: Steve, Kathi, and Leah-Marie Walker
Rooms: 5 (PB) $75-150
Expanded Continental Breakfast
Credit Cards: A, B, C, D, E
Notes: 2, 5, 7, 8, 9, 10, 12

## FAIRFIELD

### Angels Rest Farm

Route 2, Box 104, 24435
(540) 377-6449

Angels Rest Farm is located in the beautiful Shenandoah valley just eight miles north of Lexington, VA. Lexington is home to the Virginia Military Institute and Washington and Lee University as well as a number of historic landmarks and museums. Our home, located on a country road, is nestled in a quiet valley surrounded by green pastures with grazing cattle and horses nearby. The pond provides good fishing and a reflected view of the woods as you enjoy the view from either of the porches. A swimming pool is available in summer and hot tub is available year round.

Hosts: John and Carol Nothwang
Rooms: 2 (PB) $55-65
Continental Breakfast
Credit Cards: none
Notes: 2, 5, 9, 11

Angels Rest Farm

## FOREST

### The Summer Kitchen at West Manor

Route 4, Box 538, 24551
(804) 525-0923

Come enjoy a romantic English country cottage located on a beautiful working dairy farm. This private restored summer kitchen, circa 1840, sleeps four with fireplace, loft, sunroom, and jacuzzi. Enjoy a full country breakfast while overlooking 600 acres of rolling cropland, pastures, cattle, and mountains. Afternoon tea and strolls through the gardens complete each day. Come escape to our country haven. Area interests include Thomas Jefferson's Poplar Forest, antique shops, and the Blue Ridge Mountains.

Hosts: Sharon and Greg Lester
Cottage: 1; sleeps four (PB) $115
Full Breakfast
Credit Cards: none
Notes: 2, 5, 7, 10

## FREDERICKSBURG

### Fredericksburg Colonial Inn

1707 Princess Anne Street, 22401
(703) 371-5666

A restored country inn in the historic district has 32 antique-appointed lodging rooms-private baths, phones, TV, refrigerator, and Civil War motif. Continental breakfast, suites, and family rooms available. Wonderful restaurants within walking distance. Beautiful churches nearby! Over 200 antique dealers, 20 major tourist attractions, and battlefields—A Great Getaway! Less than one hour from Washington, D.C. and Richmond, VA. Open year round! AARP welcomed; special group rates upon request! Call for more information.

Hosts: Mr. Jim Crisp and Mrs. Patsy Nunnally
Rooms: 32 (PB) $45-65
Continental Breakfast
Credit Cards: A, B, C
Notes: 2, 5, 7, 10

### La Vista Plantation

4420 Guinea Station Road, 22408
(540) 898-8444; (800) 529-2823;
FAX (540) 898-1041

This Classical revival-style manor house, circa 1838, is situated on ten quiet, country acres and is surrounded by farm fields and mature trees. Stocked pond, six fireplaces, antiques, rich Civil War past, radio, phone, TV, and bicycles. Fresh eggs and homemade jams are served for breakfast; air conditioned; close to historic attractions. Choose from formal room or complete apartment.

Hosts: Edward and Michele Schiesser
Rooms: 1 + 1 large apartment (PB) $95
Full Breakfast
Credit Cards: A, B
Notes: 2, 5, 7, 9, 10, 12

## HARRISONBURG

### Kingsway Bed and Breakfast

3581 Singers Glen Road, 22801
(703) 867-9696

Enjoy the warm hospitality of your hosts who make your comfort their priority. This private home is in a quiet rural area with a view of the mountains in the beautiful Shenandoah Valley. Hosts' carpentry and homemaking skills, many house plants and outdoor flowers, a large lawn, and the in ground pool help to make your stay restful and refreshing. Just four and one-half miles from downtown; nearby is Skyline

---

NOTES: Credit cards accepted: A Master Card; B Visa; C American Express; D Discover; E Diners Club; F Other; 2 Personal checks accepted; 3 Lunch available; 4 Dinner available;

Drive, caverns, historic sites, antique shops, and flea markets.

Hosts: Chester and Verna Leaman
Rooms: 2 (PB) $50-55
Expanded Continental Breakfast
Credit Cards: none
Notes: 2, 5, 7, 9, 10, 12

## LEESBURG

### Leesburg Colonial Inn

19 South King Street, 22075
(703) 777-5000; (800) 392-1332

The Leesburg Colonial Inn has well appointed rooms, all in the 18th Century decor, but with all the modern amenities (cable TV, phone, and private bath) a true gourmet breakfast is served as part of the package while staying at the Inn. Some of our rooms have fireplace as well as whirlpool; all rooms have grand period pieces such as rustic farm dresser, fine Persian and Oriental rugs, and queen-size poster bed. The Inn is conveniently located in the center of Historic Leesburg, among many antique shops, where you can find the charm of early Virginia. Our chef can delight the most discriminate palate with his award-winning cuisine. We have conference rooms available; we can cater for two as well as hundred persons. We are surrounded by Virginia's hunt country, yet only 30 minutes from Washington, DC, and 15 minutes from Dulles International Airport.

Host: Mr. Fabian E. Saeidi
Rooms: 10 (PB) $68-150 honeymoon suite
Full Gourmet Breakfast
Credit Cards: A, B, C, D, E, F
Notes: 2, 3, 4, 5, 6, 7, 8, 9, 10, 12

### The Norris House Inn

108 Loudoin Street SW, 22075
(703) 777-1806; (800) 644-1806;
FAX (703) 771-8051

Elegant accommodations in the heart of Leesburg's historic district. Six guest rooms, all furnished with antiques, and three wood-burning fireplaces. Full country breakfast served by candlelight. Convenient in-town location with several fine restaurants within easy walking distance. Just an hour's drive from Washington, DC in Virginia's Hunt Country, rich in Colonial and Civil War history, antiquing, and quaint villages. Perfect for romantic getaways, small meetings, and weddings. Open daily by reservation. Stone House Tea Room located on the Inn's right.

Hosts: Pam and Don McMurray
Rooms: 6 (SB) $85-145
Full Breakfast
Credit Cards: A, B, C, D, E
Notes: 2, 5, 7 (over 12), 8, 10, 12

## LOUISA

### Whistle Stop

P.O. Box 1609, 318 W. Main St., 23093
(703) 967-2911; FAX (703) 967-2232

Enjoy the nostalgia of yesterday in a Queen Anne Victorian home, nestled in a small town in historical central Virginia. The original part of the house was built in 1870, with a large addition added in 1909. In 1989 the present restoration was started which now provides five guest rooms. Large halls, fireplaces,

---

5 Open all year; 6 Pets welcome; 7 Children welcome; 8 Tennis nearby; 9 Swimming nearby; 10 Golf nearby; 11 Skiing nearby; 12 May be booked through travel agent.

a library, and a parlor provide ample room for visiting, reading, or board games. The large wraparound porch with swings offer visiting, reading, or viewing an occasional train. Enjoy a walk or bike ride through the small town visiting the Museum, antique shops, or other small shops. Lake Anna, just 15 minutes away, offers boating, fishing, and swimming.

Hosts: Marvin and Dorry Lou Wharton
Rooms: 6 (3PB; 3SB) $65-75
Full Breakfast
Credit Cards: none
Notes: 2, 5, 6 and 7 (by special arrangement), 8, 9, 10

Whistle Stop

## MADISON HEIGHTS

## *Winridge B&B*

Route 1, Box 362, Winridge Drive, 24572
(804) 384-7220

Come, enjoy the warm family atmosphere in our grand country home. Stroll through the gardens where birds, butterflies, and flowers abound. Shade trees with swings and hammock. Relax on the large, inviting porches. Scenic mountain views. Hot, hearty breakfasts are served in the family dining room. Greenhouse features perennials, unusual annuals, and container gardening. Close to Blue Ridge Parkway, Lynchburg, Appomattox, and Poplar Forest.

Hosts: LoisAnn and Ed Pfister and Family
Rooms: 3 (1PB; 2SB) $65-79
Full Breakfast
Credit Cards: none
Notes: 2, 5, 7, 8, 9, 11, 12

Winridge Bed and Breakfast

## MIDDLEBURG

## *Middleburg Inn and Guest Suites*

105 W. Washington, P.O. Box 984, 22117
(703) 687-3115; (800) 432-6125

In the heart of Hunt Country, the Inn has elegantly furnished suites for short or long term stays. Our one- and two-bedroom suites are beautifully appointed with antiques and accessories in the 18th Century style. Centrally air-conditioned, the suites feature canopy beds, private baths, color TVs, direct dial phones, fresh cut flowers, and cot-

---

NOTES: Credit cards accepted: A Master Card; B Visa; C American Express; D Discover; E Diners Club; F Other; 2 Personal checks accepted; 3 Lunch available; 4 Dinner available;

ton bath robes. The spacious living room in our largest suite has a wood-burning, stone fireplace.

Hostess: Marilyn Moya
Rooms: 5 suites (PB) $130-195
Continental Breakfast at Red Fox (1 block up)
Credit Cards: A, B
Notes: 2, 7

## MILLBORO

## *Fort Lewis Lodge*

HCR 3, Box 21A, 24460
(540) 925-2314; FAX (540) 925-2352

Warm and welcoming, the Lodge's large gathering room and 13 guestrooms, decorated with wildlife art and hand-crafted furniture, feel cozy and downright comfortable. The newly renovated silo with three bedrooms "in the round" and two historic, hand-hewn log cabins are ideal for a romantic getaway. Room rates include dinner and breakfast. Countless outdoor activities are offered including four miles of exceptional trout and smallmouth bass fishing, swimming, and tubing in the unspoiled "Cowpasture River;" and miles of mountain hiking trails and

backroad bicycling. AAA

Hosts: John and Caryl Cowden
Rooms: 13 (PB) $130-180 (MAP)
Modified American Plan includes full dinner and breakfast
Credit Cards: A, B
Notes: 2, 4, 7, 9, 10

## MT. JACKSON

## *Widow Kip's Country Inn*

355 Orchard Drive, 22842
(540) 477-2400; (800) 477-2400

A stately 1830 Colonial on seven rural acres in the Shenandoah Valley overlooking the mountains. Friendly rooms filled with family photographs, bric-a-brac, and antiques. Each bedroom has a working fireplace and canopy, sleigh, or Lincoln bed. Two cozy cottages are also available. Pool on the premises. Nearby battlefields and caverns to explore, canoeing, hiking, or downhill skiing. Bicycles, picnics, and grill available.

Hostess: Betty Luse
Rooms: 5 + 2 courtyard cottages (PB) $65-85
Full Breakfast
Credit Cards: A, B
Notes: 2, 5, 6 and 7 (in cottages), 8, 9, 10, 11, 12

## NATURAL BRIDGE

## *Burger's Country Inn*

Route 2, Box 564, 24578
(703) 291-2464

This historic inn is furnished in antiques

---

5 Open all year; 6 Pets welcome; 7 Children welcome; 8 Tennis nearby; 9 Swimming nearby; 10 Golf nearby; 11 Skiing nearby; 12 May be booked through travel agent.

and country collectibles. The rambling farmhouse with wraparound porch and large columns is on ten wooded acres. Four guest rooms and three baths are available. Enjoy croquet in summer and relax by the fire in winter. Special continental breakfast is included. Visit the Natural Bridge and historic Lexington. Beautiful Blue Ridge Parkway nearby. Call or write for brochure/reservations.

Hosts: John and Diane Burger
Rooms: 4 (2PB; 2SB) $50-55
Expanded Continental Breakfast
Credit Cards: none
Notes: 2, 5, 6, 7, 9, 10

## NEW CHURCH

### Garden and Sean Inn and Restaurant

P.O. Box 275, 23415
(804) 824-0672; (800) 824-0672

Casual elegance and warm hospitality await you at this European-style country inn with its romantic, candlelight, fine dining restaurant. Near Chincoteague wildlife refuge and Assateague Island's beautiful beach. Large, luxurious guest rooms, beautifully designed; spacious private baths, some with whirlpools; Victorian detail and stained glass; Oriental rugs; antiques; bay windows; and patios and gardens. Mobile three-star, AAA three diamond, and American B&B Association three-crown ratings. Open April 1- November 26.

Hosts: Tom and Sara Baker
Rooms: 5 (PB) $75-155
Expanded Continental Breakfast
Credit Cards: A, B, C, D
Notes: 2, 3, 4, 6, 7, 8, 9, 10, 12

## NOKESVILLE

### Shiloh Bed and Breakfast

13520 Carriage Ford Rd., 22123
(703) 594-2664

Shiloh B&B is a Georgian home built in 1987 on 153 acres overlooking a five-acre bass lake with a gazebo. Amid acres of evergreen forests with many trails for walking and a black walnut grove with three hammocks, our guests find all they could ask for in desired solitude. Located one hour from Washington, DC, and Manassas and close to Civil War battlefields, tennis, farmers' markets, golf courses, and well known bike trips are available within easy commute. Two beautifully decorated suites with private entrances, baths, and kitchenettes with patio hot tub exceed guest expectations in every way.

Hosts: Alan and Carolee Fischer
Rooms: 2 (PB) $95-130
Full Breakfast
Credit Cards: A, B
Notes: 2, 5, 7 (over 12), 8, 9, 10

## NORFOLK

### Old Dominion Inn

4111 Hampton Boulevard, 23508
(804) 440-5100; (800) 653-9030;
FAX (804) 423-5238

Our new, sixty-room inn takes its name from the commonwealth of Virginia, "The Old Dominion." Located in the heart of Norfolk's west side, just one block south of the Old Dominion University Campus and only a short drive,

---

NOTES: Credit cards accepted: A Master Card; B Visa; C American Express; D Discover; E Diners Club; F Other; 2 Personal checks accepted; 3 Lunch available; 4 Dinner available;

up or down Hampton Boulevard, from many of the area's busiest facilities. Each Old Dominion Inn room gives you a remote-controled, color TV with cable service, ceiling fan, and individually controlled heat and air-conditioning. The James W. Sherrill family invites you to share in the warm hospitality of the Old Dominion Inn. As a family owned business, it is our desire that you will feel right at home when you stay with us. We treat our guests like part of "our family." Be our guest for a complimentary, light breakfast each morning of your stay.

Hosts: The Sherrill Family
Rooms: 60 (PB) $61-128
Expanded Continental Breakfast
Credit Cards: A, B, C, D, E
Notes: 2, 5, 7, 12

All guest rooms have queen beds, private baths, and air-conditioning. Guests can visit Kerr Place (1799 museum), cruise to Tangier Island from Onancock Wharf, and walk to restaurants. Bicycles, tennis, and golf are available. Chincoteague/Assateaque Island beach close by. A calm Eastern Shore getaway from D.C., Maryland, Virginia, Delaware, and New Jersey on the Chesapeake Bay, five miles from the Atlantic.

Hosts: David and Karen Tweedie
Rooms: 5 (PB) $85-95
Full Breakfast
Credit Cards: A, B
Notes: 2, 8, 9, 10, 12

The Spinning Wheel Bed and Breakfast

Old Dominion Inn

## ONANCOCK

### *The Spinning Wheel Bed and Breakfast*

31 North Street, 23417
(804) 787-7311

This 1890's Folk Victorian home in the historic waterfront town of Onancock, on Virginia's Eastern Shore, has antiques and spinning wheels throughout.

## PATRICK SPRINGS

### *Maple Springs Inn Bed and Breakfast*

Route 1 Box 327-B, 24133
(540) 629-2954

Maple Springs is located near the Blue Ridge Parkway and within a 20-mile radius of the Smith Mt. Lake, Phillpot Lake, and Fairystone State Park. The

5 Open all year; 6 Pets welcome; 7 Children welcome; 8 Tennis nearby; 9 Swimming nearby; 10 Golf nearby; 11 Skiing nearby; 12 May be booked through travel agent.

main lodge is our home, a three story log dwelling with a large dining room and living room with sky lights. Also, we have a honeymoon cottage with air-conditioning that is private and nicely furnished with antiques of the years gone by. You can walk the trails through the 27 acres to the small creeks nearby. Breakfast is a super continental plus! Also we have an afternoon snack with homemade pie or cake plus a refreshing drink at no additional charge.

Hosts: Lloyd and Virginia Barker
Rooms: 4 (2PB; 2SB) $50-60
Continental Plus Breakfast
Credit Cards: F
Notes: 2, 4 (advance notice), 5, 7 (over 12), 9 and 10 (20 miles), 11 (water)

## PROVIDENCE FORGE

### Jasmine Plantation B&B

4500 N. Courthouse Road, 23140
(804) 966-9836; (800) NEW-KENT

Restored 1750s farmhouse convenient to Williamsburg, Richmond, and the James River Plantations. Genuine hospitality, a historical setting, and rooms decorated in various period antiques await the visitor. Settled prior to 1683, guests are invited to walk the 47 acres and use their imagination as to what events have occurred here during its 300-year history. Located only 2.4 miles from I-64, the inn offers both convenience and seclusion. Fine dining located nearby.

Hosts: Joyce and Howard Vogt
Rooms: 6 (4PB; 2SB) $70-95
Full Breakfast
Credit Cards: A, B
Notes: 2, 5, 7 (over 12), 10, 12

## RICHMOND

### The William Catlin House

2304 E. Broad Street, 23223
(804) 780-3746

Richmond's first and oldest bed and breakfast features antique, canopy poster beds and working fireplaces. A delicious, full breakfast is served in the elegant dining room. Built in 1845, this richly appointed home is in the Church Hill historic district and was featured in *Colonial Homes* and *Southern Living* magazines. Directly across from St. John's Church, where Patrick Henry gave his famous "Liberty or Death" speech. Just two minutes from I-95 and Route 64.

Hosts: Robert and Josie Martin
Rooms: 5 (3PB; 2SB) $95 includes all taxes
Full Breakfast
Credit Cards: A, B, D
Notes: 2, 5, 7 (over 12), 10, 12

## ROANOKE—SMITH MOUNTAIN LAKE

### The Manor at Taylor's Store Bed and Breakfast Country Inn

Route 1, Box 533, **Smith Mountain Lake** 24184
(703) 721-3951; (800) 248-6267;
FAX (703) 721-5243

This historic 120-acre estate with an elegant manor house provides roman-

NOTES: Credit cards accepted: A Master Card; B Visa; C American Express; D Discover; E Diners Club; F Other; 2 Personal checks accepted; 3 Lunch available; 4 Dinner available;

tic accommodations in guest suites with fireplaces, antiques, canopied beds, and private porches; use of hot tub, billiards, exercise room, and guest kitchen; and many other amenities. A separate, three-bedroom, two-bath cottage is ideal for a family. Enjoy six private, springfed ponds for swimming, canoeing, fishing, and hiking. Full heart-healthy, gourmet breakfast is served in the dining room with panoramic views of the countryside.

Hosts: Lee and Mary Lynn Tucker
Rooms: 6 (4PB; 2SB) $85-150
Full Breakfast
Credit Cards: A, B
Notes: 2, 3, 5, 7, 8, 9, 10, 11, 12

Deerfield Bed and Breakfast

## SCOTTSVILLE

## *Deerfield Bed and Breakfast*

Route 3, Box 573, 24590
(804) 286-6306

Country sophisticated, classic B&B overlooks the James River Valley. Southern hospitality on 200-plus acres that are very private. Practice the lost art of "porch sitting," explore the fields and meadows, or visit the historic river town of Scottsville, renowned for its Federal architecture.Nearby are Moniecello, Ash Lawn, UVA, and Walton's Mountain Museum. At Deerfield, breakfast is an event and features homemade delicacies. Guests rarely need any lunch after our full breakfast.

Hosts: John and Callie Bowers
Rooms: 2 (PB) $95-125
Full Breakfast
Credit Cards: A, B, C
Notes: 2, 11

## SMITHFIELD

## *Isle of Wight Inn*

1607 S. Church St., 23430
(804) 357-3176

Luxurious Colonial B&B inn located in a delightful historic, river port town. Several suites with fireplaces and jacuzzis. Antique shop featuring tall case clocks and period furniture. More than 60 old homes in town dating from 1750. Just 30 minutes and a short ferry ride to Williamsburg and Jamestown; less than an hour from James River plantations, Norfolk, Hampton, and Virginia Beach.

Hosts: The Harts and the Earls
Rooms: 12 (PB) $52-119
Full Breakfast
Credit Cards: A, B, C, D
Notes: 2, 5, 7, 8, 9, 10, 12

5 Open all year; 6 Pets welcome; 7 Children welcome; 8 Tennis nearby; 9 Swimming nearby; 10 Golf nearby; 11 Skiing nearby; 12 May be booked through travel agent.

## STAUNTON

### Ashton Country House

1205 Middlebrook Rd., 24401
(540) 885-7819; (800) 296-7819

Ashton is a delightful blend of town and country. This 1860 Greek Revival home is located on 24 acres, yet one mile from the center of Staunton. There are five air-conditioned, comfortable, and attractive bedrooms, each with a private bath. Guests start each day with a hearty country breakfast. Afternoon tea is served in the grand living room or on any porch. Ashton Country House is the perfect place to soothe the spirit, share a weekend with friends, celebrate a special anniversary, or escape to the serenity of the countryside.

Hosts: Dorie and Vince Distefano
Rooms: 5 (PB) $85-105
Full Breakfast
Credit Cards: A, B, C, D
Notes: 2, 5, 7 (over 10), 8, 9, 10, 11, 12

Frederick House

### Frederick House

28 N. New Street, 24401
(800) 334-5575

An historic town house hotel in the European tradition, Frederick House is located downtown in the oldest city in the Shenandoah Valley. It is convenient to shops and restaurants, adjacent to Mary Baldwin College, and two blocks from Woodrow Wilson's birthplace. All rooms include TV, phone, air-conditioning, private bath, and private entrance.

Hosts: Joe and Evy Harman
Rooms: 14 (PB) $65-105
Full Breakfast
Credit Cards: A, B, C, D, E
Notes: 2, 3, 4, 5, 7, 8, 9, 10, 11, 12

### Thornrose House at Gypsy Hill

531 Thornrose Ave., 24401
(540) 885-7026

Outside, this turn-of-the century Georgian residence has a wraparound verandah, Greek colonnades, and lovely gardens. Inside, a fireplace and grand piano create a formal but comfortable atmosphere. Five attractive bedrooms with private baths are on the second floor. Your hosts offer afternoon tea, refreshments, and conversation. Adjacent to a 300-acre park that is great for walking, with tennis, golf, and ponds. Other nearby attractions include the Blue Ridge National Park, natural chimneys, Skyline Drive, Woodrow Wilson's birthplace, and the Museum of American Frontier Culture.

Hosts: Otis and Suzanne Huston
Rooms: 5 (PB) $55-75
Full Breakfast
Credit Cards: none
Notes: 2, 5, 7 (over 6), 8, 9, 10

NOTES: Credit cards accepted: A Master Card; B Visa; C American Express; D Discover; E Diners Club; F Other; 2 Personal checks accepted; 3 Lunch available; 4 Dinner available;

Sunset Inn

## TANGIER ISLAND

### *Sunset Inn*

Box 156, 16650 W. Ridge Rd., 23440
(804) 891-2535

Enjoy accommodations one-half block
from the beach with a view of the bay.
Deck, air-conditioning, bike riding, and
nice restaurants.

Hosts: Grace and Jim Brown
Rooms: 9 (8PB; 1SB) $50-60
Continental Breakfast
Credit Cards: none
Notes: 2, 5, 7, 9

Noah's Ark Rests

## VESUVIUS

### *Noah's Ark Rests*

P.O. Box 351, 24483
(800) 998-NOAH (6624)

An old Victorian setting between I-81
and Blue Ridge Parkway near Lexington, Virginia and Natural Bridge sur-
veyed by George Washington and
owned by Thomas Jefferson. Robert E.
Lee brought the railroad to our valley
which is very rich in Civil War history.
Noah's Ark video showing and Christian books are available. Donations accepted, $50-$60 suggested for each
room up to three people.

Rooms: 3 (1PB; 2SB) $50-60 donation
Full Breakfast
Credit Cards: none
Notes: 5, 6, 7, 12

## VIRGINIA BEACH

### *Barclay Cottage Bed and Breakfast*

400 16th Street, 23451
(804) 422-1956

Casual sophistication in a warm historic, inn-like atmosphere. Designed in
turn-of-the-century style, the Barclay
Cottage is two blocks from the beach
in the heart of the Virginia Beach recreational area. The inn is completely
restored with antique furniture to bring
together the feeling of yesterday with
the comfort of today. Formerly the
home of Lillian S. Barclay, the inn has

been a guest home for many years. We have kept the historic ambiance of the old inn while modernizing it significantly to meet today's needs. We look forward to welcoming you to the Barclay Cottage where the theme is "We go where our dream leads us."

Hosts: Peter and Claire
Rooms: 6 (3PB; 3SB) $65-80
Full Breakfast
Credit Cards: A, B, C
Notes: 8, 9, 10, 12

## WARM SPRINGS

### Three Hills Inn
P.O. Box 9, 24484
(540) 839-5381; FAX (540) 839-5199

A premier B&B inn in the heart of Bath County, Virginia. Enjoy a casually elegant retreat in a beautifully restored historic manor. Spectacular mountain views, acres of woods and trails—serenity at its best! Elegant suites available, some with kitchens and fireplaces. Four miles from the historic Homestead Resort. Your hosts have missionary backgrounds and speak fluent Spanish. From a romantic getaway to an executive retreat (meeting/conference facility), the Inn is the perfect choice for the discriminating traveler.

Hosts: Doug and Charlene Fike with Dan and Joy Adams
Rooms: 18 (PB) $47-145
Full Gourmet Breakfast (Afternoon tea weekends)
Credit Cards: A, B, D
Notes: 2, 5, 6, 7, 8, 9, 10, 11, 12

## WASHINGTON D.C. AREA

### Caledonia Farm—1812
47 Dearing Road, **Flint Hill** 22627
(703) 675-3693; (800) BNB-1812

Enjoy ultimate hospitality, comfort, scenery, and recreation adjacent to Virginia's Shenandoah National Park. This romantic getaway to history and nature includes outstanding full breakfasts, fireplaces, air-conditioning, hayrides, bicycles, lawn games, VCR, and piano. World's finest dining, caves, Skyline Drive, battlefields, stables, antiquing, hiking, and climbing are all nearby. Washington, D.C., is 68 miles away; Washington, Virginia, just four miles. A Virginia historic landmark, the farm is listed on the National Register of Historic Places. AAA three-diamond rated.

Host: Phil Irwin
Rooms: 2 + 1 suite (1PB; 2SB) $80-140
Full Breakfast
Credit Cards: A, B, D
Notes: 2, 5, 7 (over 12), 8, 9, 10, 11, 12

Caledonia Farm

## WAYNESBORO

### This Iris Inn

191 Chinquapin Drive, 22980
(540) 943-1991

The charm and grace of Southern living in a totally modern facility, nestled in a wooded tract on the western slope of the Blue Ridge, overlooking the historic Shenandoah Valley—that's what awaits you at the Iris Inn in Waynesboro. It's ideal for a weekend retreat, a refreshing change for the business traveler, and a tranquil spot for the tourist to spend a night or a week. Guest rooms are spacious, comfortably furnished, and delightfully decorated in nature and wildlife motifs. Each room has private bath and individual temperature control.

Hosts: Wayne and Iris Karl
Rooms: 7 (PB) $80-100
Full Breakfast
Credit Cards: A, B
Notes: 2, 5, 8, 9, 10

## WILLIAMSBURG

### Applewood Colonial Bed and Breakfast

605 Richmond Road, 23185
(800) 899-2753

The owner's unique apple collection is evidenced throughout this restored colonial home. Four elegant guest rooms (one suite with fireplace) are conveniently located four short blocks from Colonial Williamsburg and very close to the College of William and Mary campus. Antiques complement the romantic atmosphere. The dining room has a beautiful built-in corner cupboard and a crystal chandelier above the pedestal table where homemade breakfast is served. Afternoon tea. No smoking.

Host: Fred Strout
Rooms: 4 (PB) $75-120
Full Breakfast
Credit Cards: A, B
Notes: 2, 5, 7, 8, 10, 12

### The Cedars

616 Jamestown Rd., 23185
(804) 229-3591; (800) 296-3591

Enter this three-story brick Georgian home and the tone will be set for your visit to the 18th Century. An eight-minute walk to historic Williamsburg, across from the College of William and Mary, this elegant inn offers traditional, gracious hospitality and comfort. Candlelit breakfasts are scrumptious and bountiful. Each guest chamber reflects the romance and charm of the Colonial era. Canopy and four-poster beds abound. Each cottage suite has a fireplace. Offstreet parking. Williamsburg's oldest and largest B&B.

Hosts: Carol, Jim, and Brona Malecha
Rooms: 8 + cottages (PB) $95-160
Full Breakfast
Credit Cards: A, B
Notes: 2, 5, 7, 10, 12

---

5 Open all year; 6 Pets welcome; 7 Children welcome; 8 Tennis nearby; 9 Swimming nearby; 10 Golf nearby; 11 Skiing nearby; 12 May be booked through travel agent.

Colonial Capital Bed and Breakfast

## Colonial Capital Bed and Breakfast

501 Richmond Road, 23185
(804) 229-0233; (800) 776-0570;
FAX (804) 253-7667

Our Colonial Revival home in the Architectural Preservation District is only three blocks from the historic area. Enjoy our antiques, Oriental rugs, cozy canopied beds, and ensuite baths. Indulge in a full, cooked breakfast before the days activities. Relax afterwards on the porch, patio, or deck sharing tea and wine with friends, new and old. Inroom phone, FAX and IBM PS/1 available. Smoking outdoors only. Free bikes. Gift certificates. Inspected and approved by AAA and BBAV.

Hosts: Barbara and Phil Craig
Rooms: 5 (including one two-room suite) (PB)
$76-125
Full Cooked Breakfast
Credit Cards: A, B, C, D
Notes: 2, 5, 7 (over 6), 8, 9, 10, 12

## Fox and Grape Bed and Breakfast

701 Monumental Ave., 23185
(804) 229-6914; (800) 292-3699

Genteel accommodations located just five blocks north of Virginia's restored Colonial capital. Furnishings in this lovely two-story Colonial with a large wraparound porch include antiques, counted cross stitch, duck decoys, and a cup plate collection. Four guest rooms with private baths.

Hosts: Pat and Bob Orendorff
Rooms: 4 (PB) $78-84
Continental Plus Breakfast
Credit Cards: A, B, D
Notes: 2, 5, 7, 8, 9, 10, 12

Fox and Grape Bed and Breakfast

## Hites Bed and Breakfast

704 Monumental Ave., 23185
(804) 229-4814

An attractive Cape Cod B&B just a seven-minute walk to Colonial Williamsburg. Large rooms cleverly furnished with antiques and collectibles.

---

NOTES: Credit cards accepted: A Master Card; B Visa; C American Express; D Discover; E Diners Club; F Other; 2 Personal checks accepted; 3 Lunch available; 4 Dinner available;

Each room has TV, phone, radio, coffeemaker, robes, and private baths. You will especially like the suite with its large sitting room and old-fashioned bathroom with clawfoot tub. In the parlor for your enjoyment is an antique pump organ and hand-crank Victrola. You can swing in the back yard and enjoy the squirrels, birds, and goldfish pond.

Hosts: Faye and James Hite
Rooms: 2 (PB) 80-90 (suite)
Full Breakfast
Credit Cards: none
Notes: 2, 5, 7, 8, 9, 10

## Hughes' Guest Home

106 Newport Ave., 23185
(804) 229-3493

The Hughes' Guest Home has been in operation since 1947, located directly opposite the Williamsburg Lodge on Newport Avenue. It is a lovely two minute stroll to Colonial Williamsburg's restored district, golfing facilities, and numerous dining facilities including the Colonial taverns. The College of William and Mary, Merchant's Square, and several CW museums are also within easy walking distances. We welcome you to our home during your stay in Williamsburg. The house is decorated lavishly with family antiques and our gardens may be appreciated from the screened porch or patio. Do come and enjoy our Southern hospitality.

Hostess: Genevieve O. Hughes
Rooms: 3 + 1 two-room suite (PB) $60
Full Breakfast
Credit Cards: none
Notes: 2, 5, 7, 8, 10

## Newport House
## Bed and Breakfast

710 South Henry Street, 23185
(804) 229-1775

A reproduction of an important 1756 home, Newport House has museum-standard period furnishings, including canopy beds. A five-minute walk to the historic area. Full breakfast with Colonial recipes; Colonial dancing in the ballroom every Tuesday evening (beginners welcome). The host is a historian/author(including a book on Christ) and former museum director. The hostess is a gardener, beekeeper, 18-century seamstress, and former nurse. A pet rabit entertains at breakfast. No smoking.

Hosts: John and Cathy Millar
Rooms: 2 (PB) $110-135
Full Breakfast
Credit Cards: none
Notes: 2, 5, 7, 10, 12

## Piney Grove
## at Southall's Plantation

P.O. Box 1359, 23187
(804) 829-2480 (voice and FAX)

Only AAA-approved historic B&B in the Williamsburg area. Located just west of Williamsburg, among the James River Plantations. Elegant accommodations and gracious hospitality await you at this secluded country retreat which is a Virginia historic landmark and is listed on the National Register of Historic Places. Spacious guest rooms are furnished with antiques and include pri-

5 Open all year; 6 Pets welcome; 7 Children welcome; 8 Tennis nearby; 9 Swimming nearby; 10 Golf nearby; 11 Skiing nearby; 12 May be booked through travel agent.

vate baths, refrigerators, and coffee-makers. Guests enjoy served plantation breakfasts, turn-down service, and wood-burning fires. The Gordineer Family welcomes you to relive the Golden Age of the James River Plantations.

Hosts: The Gordineer Family
Rooms: 4 (PB) $125-140
Full Plantation Breakfast
Credit Cards: none
Notes: 2, 3 and 4 (nearby), 5, 7, 9 (on premises), 10, 12

## Primrose Cottage

706 Richmond Road, 23185
(804) 229-6421; (800) 522-1901;
FAX (804) 259-0717

Primrose Cottage is a nature-lover's delight. In the spring, the front walkway is lined with primroses. In cooler months, the front yard is abloom with banks of pansies. There are two bedrooms upstairs, each with a large, walk-in closet and private bathroom. Desks, chairs, and reading lamps add to the comfort of home. In the morning, the aroma of home cooking usually rouses even the sleepiest traveler. Within walking distance of Williamsburg Historic Area, fine restaurants, and local churches. Complimentary bikes. Off-street parking. Smoke-free atmosphere.

Hostess: Inge Curtis
Rooms: 3 (PB) $85-95
Full Breakfast
Credit Cards: A, B
Notes: 2, 10

## Spiggle Guest Home

720 College Terrace, 23185
(804) 253-0202

Spend the night with these gracious hosts in their cozy 6,000-square-foot brick home on their beautiful quiet residential street next to the campus of The College of William and Mary and away from the city noise. You'll see all of Williamsburg from this convenient location—just a 10- to 15-minute walk to the restored area of Williamsburg and a ten minute drive to shopping centers, Busch Gardens, and the Pottery Factory. Guest's rooms are comfortably furnished, some with family antiques, and all include wall-to-wall carpeting, central air, inroom refrigerators, coffee and tea maker, phone jacks, TV, and private baths. A great location for seeing all the nearby sights of Jamestown and Yorktown.

Hosts: Phil and Dot Spiggle
Rooms: 4 (3PB; 2SB) $35-50
No Breakfast
Credit Cards: none
Notes: 2, 5

## Williamsburg Sampler Bed and Breakfast

922 Jamestown Road, 23185
(804) 253-0398; (800) 722-1168;
FAX (804) 220-0245

This 18th Century, plantation-style, brick colonial was awarded the 1995 Inn Of The Year and is a AAA three Dia-

---

mond home within walking distance to the historic area. Richly furnished bedrooms and suites with king- or queen-size bed, TV, private baths, fireplaces, and Roof Top Garden. A collection of antiques, pewter, and samplers are displayed throughout the house. A "Skip Lunch" breakfast is served. Internationally recognized as a favorite spot for a romantic honeymoon or anniversary.

Hosts: Helen and Ike Sisane
Rooms: 4 + 2 suites (PB) $90-130
Full Breakfast
Credit Cards: A, B
Notes: 2, 5, 8, 9, 10, 12

ceilings. It was initially used as a parsonage, serving a church three blocks away for about 70 years. Located in the historic Shenendoah Valley, it is close to Skyline Drive and the mountains. Many Civil War sites are within short driving distance. Nearby activities include antiquing, hiking, and horseback riding.

Hosts: Price and Margaret McDonald
Rooms: 3 (PB) $50-70
Full Breakfast
Credit Cards: A, B, C
Notes: 2, 7 (over 6), 9, 10, 11

Williamsburg Sampler Bed and Breakfast

Azalea House Bed and Breakfast

## WOODSTOCK

## *Azalea House*
## *Bed and Breakfast*
551 S. Main Street, 22664
(703) 459-3500

A large Victorian house built in 1892 featuring family antiques and stenciled

---

5 Open all year; 6 Pets welcome; 7 Children welcome; 8 Tennis nearby; 9 Swimming nearby; 10 Golf nearby; 11 Skiing nearby; 12 May be booked through travel agent.

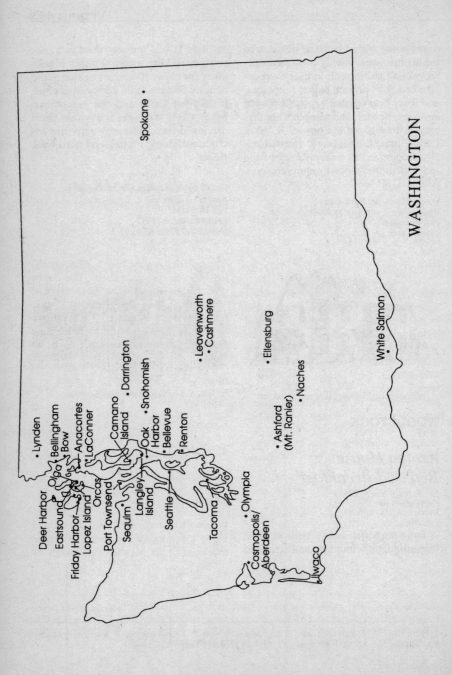

# Washington

## ANACORTES

### Albatross Bed and Breakfast

5708 Kingsway W., 98221
(360) 293-0677; (800) 622-8864

Our 1927 Cape Cod-style home offers king and queen beds and private baths in all guest rooms. The quiet, relaxing living room, patio, and deck areas view waterfront, islands, and mountains. You can walk to Washington Park, Skyline marina, fine dining, and inspirational beaches. We also offer sightseeing cruises aboard a 46-sailboat and have two-speed cross bikes available. We are close to the State Ferry Boat terminal for access to the San Juan Islands and Victoria B.C. We are also close to over 25 churches.

Hosts: Ken and Barbie
Rooms: 4 (PB) $75-90
Full Breakfast
Credit Cards: A, B, C
Notes: 2, 5, 7, 8, 9, 10, 12

### Hasty Pudding House Bed and Breakfast

1312 8th Street, 98221
(360) 293-5773; (800) 368-5588;
FAX (360) 299-9208

You will enjoy your visit to this romantic, 1913 craftsman house. The decor is Victorian and attention has been paid to restoring the original charm of this inviting, friendly place to stay. You have four beautiful rooms to choose from with comfortable beds for a good rest.

Hosts: Mikel and Melinda
Rooms: 4 (2PB; 2SB) $65-105
Full Breakfast
Credit Cards: A, B, C, D
Notes: 2, 5, 7, 8, 9, 10, 11, 12

### Sunset Beach Bed and Breakfast

100 Sunset Beach, 98221
(800) 359-3448

On exciting Rosario Straits. Relax and enjoy the view of seven major islands from our decks, stroll on the beach, or

---

NOTES: Credit cards accepted: A Master Card; B Visa; C American Express; D Discover; E Diners Club; F Other; 2 Personal checks accepted; 3 Lunch available; 4 Dinner available; 5 Open all year; 6 Pets welcome; 7 Children welcome; 8 Tennis nearby; 9 Swimming nearby; 10 Golf nearby; 11 Skiing nearby; 12 May be booked through travel agent.

walk in the beautiful Washington Park, adjacent to our private gardens. Also enjoy boating, hiking, and fishing. Private entry, bathrooms, and TV. Full breakfast. Five minutes to San Juan Ferries, fine restaurants, and marina and a convenience store nearby. Sunsets are outstanding! No smoking.

Hosts: Joann and Hal Harker
Rooms: 3 (1PB; 2SB) $59-79
Full Breakfast
Credit Cards: A, B
Notes: 2, 5, 7 (over 6), 9, 10, 11, 12

## ANDERSON ISLAND

## *The Inn at Burg's Landing*
8808 Villa Beach Road, 98303
(206) 884-9185

Catch the ferry from Steilacoom to stay at this contemporary log homestead built in 1987. It offers spectacular views of Mt. Rainier, Puget Sound, and the Cascade Mountains and is located south of Tacoma off I-5. Choose from three guest rooms, including the master bedroom with queen-size "log" bed with skylight above and private whirlpool bath. The Inn has a private beach. Collect seashells and agates, swim on two freshwater lakes nearby, and/or enjoy a game of tennis or golf. Tour the island by bicycle or on foot and watch for sailboats and deer. Hot tub. Full breakfast. Families welcome. No smoking.

Hosts: Ken and Annie Burg
Rooms: 3 (2PB; 1SB) $65-90
Full Breakfast
Credit Cards: A, B
Notes: 2, 5, 7, 8, 9, 10, 11

## ASHFORD (MT. RAINIER)

## *Jasmer's Bed and Breakfast/Cabins*
30005 SR 706 East, 98304
(360) 569-2682 (voice and FAX)

Jasmer's—A place to celebrate intimacy, historic surroundings, and nature, all at the same time. Mt. Rainier beckons you! To accommodate we offer rooms with private entrances, parking, baths, TV/VCR, queen beds, dimmer lights, and showers for two. The two rooms share an outside hot tub and half gazebo for the starry nights. Big Creek Cabin is off premises on the creek, with its own hot tub, kitchen, wood-stove, TV/VCR, queen beds, and restful solitude. Other cabins available are A-frames, chalets, and cottages, each private and completely furnished.

Hosts: Luke and Tanna Osterhaus
Rooms: 2 + 4 cabins (PB) $45-125
Continental Breakfast
Credit Cards: A, B
Notes: 2, 5, 7 (over10), 11, 12

Jasmer's Bed and Breakfast/Cabins

---

## The Lodge near Mt. Rainier

P.O. Box 86, 98304
(360) 569-2312

Four cabins and three lodges, each have modern bathrooms, kitchens, and a fireplace, but no phones. Restaurant and bar within walking distance. Relax in the tranquillity of wildlife and evergreens at the foot of Mt. Rainier. Located on 16 acres, there is a multitude of activities year around. Group accommodations are ideal for retreats, family reunions, church groups, etc. Children welcome, sorry no pets because of the wild animals. The Lodge is located 1/4 mile west of the Nisqually entrance to Mt. Rainier National Park on SR 706.

Rooms: 4 family units + 3 group lodges;
$49-79
No Breakfast
Credit Cards: A, B, D
Notes: 5, 7, 9, 11, 12

## Mt. Meadows Inn Bed and Breakfast

28912 S.R. 706 East, 98304
(360) 569-2788

Built in 1910 as a mill superintendent's house, Mountain Meadows Inn Bed and Breakfast has made a graceful transition to quiet country elegance. An era of Northwest logging passed by and was seen in vivid detail from the vantage point of spring board and misery whip. Old growth stumps scattered around the house and pond still wear spring board notches as witness to a time when trees, men, and the stories of both were tall.

The innkeeper says guests tell him its the best B&B they have ever stayed in. Model railroad museum. Evening campfires and smores.

Host: Chad Darrah
Rooms: 5 (PB) $55-95
Full Breakfast
Credit Cards: A, B
Notes: 2, 5, 7 (over 10), 8, 9, 10, 11, 12

## BELLEVUE

## Petersen Bed and Breakfast

10228 S.E. 8th, 98004
(206) 454-9334

We offer two rooms five minutes from Bellevue Square with wonderful shopping and one-half block from the bus line to Seattle. Rooms have down comforters, and we have a hot tub on the deck. Children are welcome. No smoking.

Hosts: Eunice and Carl Petersen
Rooms: 2 (SB) $50-65
Full Breakfast
Credit Cards: none
Notes: 2, 5, 7

## BELLINGHAM

## Circle F Bed and Breakfast

2399 Mt. Baker Highway, 98226
(360) 671-9825; FAX (360) 734-3816

Circle F Bed and Breakfast is a home away from home for all of our guests.

---

5 Open all year; 6 Pets welcome; 7 Children welcome; 8 Tennis nearby; 9 Swimming nearby;
10 Golf nearby; 11 Skiing nearby; 12 May be booked through travel agent.

The Victorian-style ranch house was built in 1892 and is located on 330 acres of pasture and woodlands. We are a working farm, and you can enjoy hiking trails and visits with the farm animals. A hearty breakfast is served by a friendly farm family who enjoys the company of all visitors.

Hosts: Guy J. Foster
Rooms: 4 (1PB; 3SB) $45-60
Full Breakfast
Credit Cards: none
Notes: 2, 5, 7

## BOW

### Benson Farmstead Bed and Breakfast
1009 Avon-Allen Road, 98232
(206) 757-0578

Located just minutes from the Skagit Valley, tulip fields, the historical town of LaConner, and ferries to the San Juan Islands, the Benson Farmstead is a beautiful restored farmhouse. The Bensons are a friendly couple who serve homemade desserts in the evening and a wonderful breakfast. They have filled their home with charming antiques, old quilts, and curios from their Scandinavian heritage. The extensive yard features an English Garden and a large playground.

Hosts: Jerry and Sharon Benson
Rooms: 4 (2PB; 2SB) $65-75
Full Breakfast
Credit Cards: A, B
Notes: 2, 5 (weekends only Sept.-March), 7, 8, 9, 10, 11

## CAMANO ISLAND

### Willcox House Bed and Breakfast
1462 E. Larkspur Lane, 98292
(360) 629-4746

This island retreat, a short drive from Seattle, is designed for relaxing! Enjoy the panoramic view of the Cascade Mountains. Named for early 1900s illustrator, Jesse Willcox Smith and decorated with her works. It's a step back in time to a less stressful pace. Leisurely, country breakfast of Willcox House blended coffee, assorted omelets, Swedish pancakes, muffins, and fresh fruits in season, with sunlight streaming into a cozy breakfast room.

Hostess: Sharon Boulanger
Rooms: 4 (PB) $75
Full Breakfast
Credit Cards: A, B, D
Notes: 2, 5, 8, 9, 10, 11

Cashmere Country Inn

## CASHMERE

### Cashmere Country Inn
5801 Pioneer Drive, 98815
(509) 782-4212; (800) 291-9144

This delightful 1907 farmhouse with

---

NOTES: Credit cards accepted: A Master Card; B Visa; C American Express; D Discover; E Diners Club; F Other; 2 Personal checks accepted; 3 Lunch available; 4 Dinner available;

Hemlock Hills Bed and Breakfast

five bedrooms welcomes guests with charm and hospitality. Every effort has been made to make each stay memorable. Among many outstanding features, is the food, skillfully prepared and beautifully presented. There is a pool and hot tub and a large fireplace in the living room. Looking for that extra-special inn that defines a B&B? You'll be pleased to discover Cashmere Country Inn.

Hosts: Patti and Dale Swanson
Rooms: 5 (PB) $75-80
Full Breakfast
Credit Cards: A, B, C
Notes: 2, 4, 5, 8, 9 (on-site), 10, 11, 12

## COSMOPOLIS / ABERDEEN

## Cooney Mansion

1705 Fifth Street, Box 54, 98537
(360) 533-0602

This 1908 National Historic Register home, situated in wooded seclusion, was built by Neil Cooney, owner of one of the largest sawmills of the time. It captures the adventure of the Northwest. Share the lumber baron's history and many of his original "craftsman" style antiques. Enjoy 18 holes of golf (in

backyard) or a leisurely walk around Mill Creek Park. Relax in the sauna and jacuzzi, curl up with one of the many books from the library, or watch TV in the ballroom or living room.

Hosts: Judi and Jim Lohr
Rooms: 8 (5PB; 3SB) $60-120
Full "Lumber Baron's" Breakfast
Credit Cards: A, B, C, D, E
Notes: 5, 8, 10

## DARRINGTON

## Hemlock Hills Bed and Breakfast

612 Still Aguamish, 98241
(360) 436-1274; (800) 520-1584

Hemlock Hills Bed and Breakfast is our home. It is a place to share warmth, comfort, and friendship. Our home is located in Darrington with views of the surrounding mountains. This is a place where you can enjoy country living. Inviting rooms filled with antiques, country furnishings, and quilts. Relax in the parlor or spend time in the game room. We offer two double occupancies with shared bath and serve a full country breakfast. Close to hiking, bi-

---

5 Open all year; 6 Pets welcome; 7 Children welcome; 8 Tennis nearby; 9 Swimming nearby; 10 Golf nearby; 11 Skiing nearby; 12 May be booked through travel agent.

cycling, and fishing.

Hosts: Dale and Elaine Hamlin
Rooms: 2 (SB) $50 + tax
Full Breakfast
Credit Cards: none
Notes: 2, 3 and 4 (walking distance), 5, 7, 8, 10 (20 miles), 11 (cross-country), 12

## Sauk River Farm Bed and Breakfast

32629 S.R. 530 NE, 98241
(360) 436-1794

The wild scenic Sauk River runs through this farm nestled in a valley of the North Cascades. All-season recreational opportunities await you. Wildlife abounds year-round. The Native American Loft Room is a collector's delight; The Victoria Room offers pastoral privacy. Hallmarks of the farm are its views of rugged mountains, intimate atmosphere, comfortable accommodations, and solitude for those seeking relaxation. Step back in time and sample Darrington hospitality with its Bluegrass music and crafters. No smoking.

Hosts: Leo and Sharon Mehler
Rooms: 2 (SB) $40-60
Full Breakfast
Credit Cards: none
Notes: 2, 5, 11

## ELLENSBURG

## Murphy's Country Bed and Breakfast

2830 Thorp Highway South, 98926
(509) 925-7986

Two large guest rooms in a lovely 1915

country home with a sweeping view of the valley. Full breakfast. Close to fly fishing and golfing.

Hostess: Doris Callahan-Murphy
Rooms: 2 (SB) $60
Full Breakfast
Credit Cards: A, B, C
Notes: 2, 5, 10

## FRIDAY HARBOR

## Tucker House Bed and Breakfast with Cottages

260 B Street, 98250
(360) 378-2783; (800) 965-0123;
FAX (360) 378-6437

A Victorian home(c.1898) with two upstairs bedrooms, queen beds, and shared bath. Three separate cottages with queen beds, private bath, woodstoves, kitchenettes, TV, outside hot tub, and off-street parking. A full, gourmet breakfast with homemade cinnamon bread. Property abounds in flowers and stately trees and is surrounded by a white picket fence. Two blocks from the ferry landing, and two blocks to the heart of picturesque Friday Harbor. Gift certificates available.

Hosts: Skip and Annette Metzger
Rooms: 2 (SB; upstairs in main Victorian)
3 cottages (PB) $85-135
Full Breakfast
Credit Cards: A, B, C, D
Notes: 2, 5, 6 (under 40 lbs.; $15-25 night each), 7, 8, 9, 10, 12

NOTES: Credit cards accepted: A Master Card; B Visa; C American Express; D Discover; E Diners Club; F Other; 2 Personal checks accepted; 3 Lunch available; 4 Dinner available;

# ILWACO

## *Chick-A-Dee Inn at Ilwaco*

120 Williams Street NE, 98624
(360) 642-8686; FAX (360) 642-8642

The Inn at Ilwaco had its beginning 65 years ago as the Ilwaco Presbyterian Church. This classically composed building stands proudly on a wooded knoll overlooking the fishing port of Ilwaco. It is a country inn with nine cozy guest rooms tucked into the eves and dormers and furnished with a mix of antiques and handmade furnishings. There are 28 miles of sandy beach with two rocky headlands containing lighthouses at the Ilwaco end of the peninsula and Leadbetter park bird sanctuary at the north end. The Ilwaco Heritage Museum, International Kite Museum, Astoria Maritime Museum, Fort Canby and Fort Columbia's gun emplacements and museum, art galleries, book stores, antique, and collectable shops are all nearby.

Hosts: Chick and Delaine "Dee Dee" Hinkle
Rooms: 10 (9PB; 1SB) $60-150 M.A.P.
Full Breakfast and Dinner (Sun.-Weds.) included
Credit Cards: A, B
Notes: 2, 3, 4, 5, 8, 9, 10, 11

Chick-A-Dee Inn at Ilwaco

Katy's Inn

# LACONNER

## *Katy's Inn*

503 S. Third, P.O. Box 869, 98257
(360) 466-3366; (800) 914-7767

Charming 1876 Victorian two blocks up hill from quaint LaConner that has 100 unique shops, galleries, and antique stores. Four wonderful guest rooms (two with private baths). French doors open onto a wraparound porch. View of Swinomish Channel. Warm hospitality. Evening goodies. Full breakfast. Hot tub. Accommodations are great for small retreats!

Hosts: Bruce and Kathie Hubbard
Rooms: 4 (2PB; 2SB) $69-89
Full Breakfast
Credit Cards: A, B, C, D
Notes: 2, 5, 10, 12

# LANGLEY—WHIDBEY ISLAND

## *Log Castle*

3273 E. Saratoga Rd., 98260
(360) 221-5483

A log house on a private, secluded beach features turret bedrooms, wood-

---

5 Open all year; 6 Pets welcome; 7 Children welcome; 8 Tennis nearby; 9 Swimming nearby; 10 Golf nearby; 11 Skiing nearby; 12 May be booked through travel agent.

burning stoves, porch swings, and panoramic views of the beach and mountains. Rustic elegance—with private baths. Relax before a large stone fireplace or listen to the call of gulls as you watch for bald eagles and sea lions.

Hosts: Congressman Jack and Norma Metcalf
Rooms: 4 (PB) $90-115
Full Breakfast
Credit Cards: A, B, D
Notes: 2, 8

## LEAVENWORTH

### All Seasons River Inn

8751 Icicle Rd., 98826
(509) 548-1425; (800) 254-0555

Riverfront guest rooms, magnificent Cascade views, and warm hospitality are but a few reasons why All Seasons River Inn was selected as one of the "50 most romantic getaways in the Pacific Northwest," and it is also why a stay here will call you back again and again. Built as a bed and breakfast, all guest rooms are very spacious with antique decor, river-view deck, and private bath, some with jacuzzi tub and/or fireplace. Full gourmet breakfast; adults only. No smoking on premises.

Hosts: Kathy and Jeff Falconer
Rooms: 6 (PB) $85-125
Full Breakfast
Credit Cards: A, B
Notes: 2, 5, 8, 9, 10, 11, 12 (with exceptions)

### Run of the River

P.O. Box 285, 98826
(509) 548-7171; FAX (509) 548-7547

Imagine the quintessential Northwest log bed and breakfast inn. Spacious rooms feature private baths, hand-hewn log beds, and fluffy down comforters. Or, celebrate in a suite with your own heartwarming wood-stove, jetted jacuzzi surrounded by river rock, and a bird's eye loft to laze about with a favorite book. From your room's log porch swing, drink in the Icicle River, surrounding bird refuge, and the Cascade peaks, appropriately named the Enchantments. To explore the Icicle Valley, get off the beaten path with hiking, biking, and driving guides written just for you by the innkeepers, avid bikers and hikers. Take a spin on complimentary mountain bikes. A hearty breakfast sets the day in motion.

Hosts: Monty and Karen Turner
Rooms: 6 (PB) $90-140
Full Breakfast
Credit Cards: A, B, C, D
Notes: 2, 5, 8, 9, 10, 11, 12

## LOPEZ ISLAND

### Aleck Bay Inn

Route 1, Box 1920, 98261
(360) 468-3535; FAX (360) 468-3533

The Inn has seven acres bounded by the beaches and offshore islands situated at the south end of Lopez Island. Enjoy a sun deck with hot tub overlooking the strait of San Juan De Fuca. Full breakfast is served in the solarium beside the bay. All rooms have private bath and queen bed, decorated by Victorian canopies, floral linens, etc. Two with jacuzzi tub. You may enjoy the TV/VCR, table tennis, billiards, piano, violin, and all

---

NOTES: Credit cards accepted: A Master Card; B Visa; C American Express; D Discover; E Diners Club; F Other; 2 Personal checks accepted; 3 Lunch available; 4 Dinner available;

kinds of games. Bike rental is available.

Hosts: May and David Mendez
Rooms: 4 (PB) $79-139
Full Breakfast
Credit Cards: A, B, C
Notes: 2, 5, 9, 10, 12

## MacKaye Harbor Inn
Route 1, Box 1940, 98261
(360) 468-2253; FAX (360) 468-9555

The ideal beachfront getaway. Lopez's only bed and breakfast on a low-bank, sandy beach. Kayak and mountain bike rentals and/or instructions. This 1927 Victorian home has been painstakingly restored. Guests are pampered in comfortable elegance. Eagles, deer, seals, and otters frequent this Cape Cod of the Northwest. Commendations from *Sunset, Pacific Northwest* magazine, the *Los Angeles Times*, and *Northwest Best Places.*

Hosts: Brooks and Sharon Broberg
Rooms: 5 (3PB; 2SB) $69-139
Full Breakfast
Credit Cards: A, B
Notes: 2, 5, 8, 10, 12

## LYNDEN

## Century House Bed and Breakfast
401 South B.C. Ave., 98264
(360) 354-2439; (800) 820-3617;
FAX (360) 354-6910

Located on 35 acres at the edge of town, Century House is a 108 year-old Victorian home. You'll find this completely restored home is a quiet retreat with spacious gardens and lawns for your enjoyment. The quaint Dutch village of Lynden is within an easy walk and boasts the best museums in the area and gift shops galore...but sorry, the town is closed on Sundays. Take day trips to the Cascade Mountains and Mount Baker, the sea, Seattle, Vancouver, or Victoria, British Columbia.

Hosts: Jan and Ken Stremler
Rooms: 4 (2PB; 2SB) $60-85
Full Breakfast
Credit Cards: A, B
Notes: 2, 5, 7, 8, 9, 10, 11

Century House Bed and Breakfast

## NACHES

## Apple Country Bed and Breakfast
4561 Old Naches Hwy., 98937
(509) 965-0344; FAX (509) 965-1591

This remodeled, 1911 farmhouse is located in the heart of the Naches Valley on a working ranch. Apple Country B&B is the ideal stop for any traveler who is seeking a countryside bed and breakfast. Enjoy a continental breakfast while taking in the sweeping view of the valley from your large bedroom, tastefully decorated with new and antique furniture. Apple Country B&B is just a short drive from many activities offered by its surrounding valleys: fine dining, golfing, antiquing, skiing, fishing, hiking, hunting, and wine country tours. *"Truly, A Four Season Country"*.

Hosts: Shirley and Mark Robert
Rooms: 3 (1PB; 2SB) $70-75
Continental Breakfast
Credit Cards: none
Notes: 2, 5, 7, 8, 9, 10, 11

## OAK HARBOR

## North Island Bed and Breakfast

1589 N. West Beach Rd., 98277
(360) 675-7080

North Island Bed and Breakfast is located on 175 feet of private beachfront. Each guest room has a private bath, king-size bed, individual heating, fireplace, and beautiful furnishings. From you deck or patio you'll enjoy a view of the Olympic Mountains and San Juan Islands. A separate entrance and ample parking are provided. All of Whidby Island's wonderful attractions are close by.

Hosts: Jim and MaryVern Loomis
Rooms: 2 (PB) $80-90
Continental Breakfast
Credit Cards: A, B, C, D
Notes: 2, 5, 10

## OLYMPIA

## Harbinger Inn

1136 East Bay Drive, 98506
(360) 754-0389

Built in 1910, the house is of finely detailed grey, ashler block construction with white pillars and wide balconies—all completely restored. Distinctive features of the grounds have also been kept, like the mysterious street-to-basement tunnel and the hillside waterfall fed by an artesian well. Throughout the Inn, turn-of-the-century furniture has been used in keeping with the original wall stencils and oak pocket doors of the first floor. Guests will find a warm, informal atmosphere at the Harbinger. In addition to its spectacular view of the nearby Capitol, the location makes not only boating, bicycling, and jogging readily available but also downtown shopping and fine dining.

Hosts: Terrell and Marisa Williams
Rooms: 4 (3PB; 1SB) $55-100
Continental Breakfast
Credit Cards: A, B, C
Notes: 2, 5, 6, 7 (over 12), 9, 10, 12

## ORCAS ISLAND—DEER HARBOR

## Palmer's Chart House

P.O. Box 51, 98243
(360) 376-4231

The first B&B on Orcas Island (since 1975) with a magnificent water view.

---

NOTES: Credit cards accepted: A Master Card; B Visa; C American Express; D Discover; E Diners Club; F Other; 2 Personal checks accepted; 3 Lunch available; 4 Dinner available;

The 33-foot, private yacht *Amante* is available for a minimal fee with skipper Don. Low-key, private, personal attention makes this B&B unique and attractive. Well traveled hosts speak Spanish.

Hosts: Don and Majean Palmer
Rooms: 2 (PB) $60 + tax
Full Breakfast
Credit Cards: none
Notes: 2, 5, 7 (over 12), 8, 10, 11, 12

## ORCAS ISLAND— EASTSOUND

### *Turtleback Farm Inn*

Route 1, Box 650, 98245
(360) 376-4914

Turtleback Farm Inn, built in the late 1800s, is noted for its detail, perfect restoration, elegantly comfortable and spotless rooms, and award-winning breakfasts. The Inn, centrally located in the Crow Valley and six miles from the ferry landing, overlooks 80 acres of forest and farmland in the shadow of Turtleback Mountain. Orcas Island, considered by most to be the loveliest of the San Juan Islands that dot Puget Sound, is a haven for anyone who enjoys spectacular scenery, varied outdoor activities, unique shopping, and superb food.

Hosts: William and Susan C. Fletcher
Rooms: 7 (PB) $80-160
Full Breakfast
Credit Cards: A, B
Notes: 2, 5, 8, 9, 10, 12

Turtleback Farm Inn

## ORCAS ISLAND—OLGA

### *Buck Bay Farm*

Star Route Box 45, 98279
(360) 376-2908

Buck Bay Farm is located on beautiful Orcas in the San Juan Islands of Washington State. Orcas is an idyllic vacation destination with lots of outdoor fun: hiking, bicycling, boating or kayaking, whale watching, golf, fishing, and much more. The B&B is a farmhouse recently rebuilt by the owner. A warm welcome and hearty, home-style breakfast await you.

Hosts: Rick and Janet Bronkey
Rooms: 4 (PB) $85-110
Full Breakfast
Credit Cards: A, B
Notes: 2, 5, 7 (by arrangement), 10

## PORT TOWNSEND

### *Ann Starrett Mansion Victorian B&B Inn*

744 Clay Street, 98368
(360) 385-3205; (800) 321-0644;
FAX (360) 385-2976

Situated on the bluff overlooking moun-

---

5 Open all year; 6 Pets welcome; 7 Children welcome; 8 Tennis nearby; 9 Swimming nearby; 10 Golf nearby; 11 Skiing nearby; 12 May be booked through travel agent.

tains and Puget Sound sits the lovingly restored Starrett Mansion. The Mansion is internationally renowned for its classic Victorian architecture, frescoed ceilings, and the free hung, three tiered spiral staircase, which leads to one of the most unusual domed ceilings in North America. A breathtaking vision of rose, teal green, and cream, the variety of exterior trim on the mansion is almost as extraordinary as the solar dome. You can relax amid a dozen beautiful rooms furnished with antiques, painstakingly collected from many different sources to recreate the Victorian period of 100 years ago.

Hosts: Bob and Edel Sokol
Rooms: 11 (PB) $70-225
Full Breakfast
Credit Cards: A, B, C, D
Notes: 2, 5, 8, 9, 10, 11, 12

## The English Inn
718 F Street, 98368
(360) 385-5302 (voice and FAX);
(800) 254-5302;

The English Inn was built in 1885 in the Italianate style. It is one of the more gracious Victorian mansions in Port Townsend. It has five large, sunny bedrooms, three of which have views of the Olympic Mountains. Beautiful scenery, hiking, antiquing, and only two hours from Seattle. A lovely garden, hot tub, and lots of comfort, but best of all, fresh scones for breakfast!

Hostess: Nancy Borino
Rooms: 5 (PB) $65-95
Full Breakfast
Credit Cards: A, B, C, D, E
Notes: 2, 5, 8, 10, 12

## Water Street Hotel
635 Water Street, 98368
(800) 735-9810

Built in 1889 and completely renovated in 1990 the Water Street Hotel is in a secluded waterfront community. The Hotel combines the Old World charm of historic downtown Port Townsend with a panoramic view of Puget Sound and the majestic Olympic Mountains. Yet, it's within walking distance of downtown shops, restaurants, and the Keystone Ferry.

Hostesses: Dawn Pfeiffer and Mary Hewitt
Rooms: 16 (11PB; 5SB) winter $45-100, summer $50-125
Credit Cards: A, B, C
Notes: 2 (with proper I.D.), 5, 6 (with a fee), 7, 8, 10, 12

## RENTON

## Holly Hedge House
908 Grant Avenue South, 98055
(206) 226-2555

Experience the ultimate in pampering and privacy in this meticulously restored 1900 scenic hilltop retreat. This unique lodging facility reserves the entire house for one couple at a time to indulge in the beauty and affordable luxury. Landscaped grounds; wood deck with hot tub; swimming pool; stocked gourmet kitchen; whirlpool bath tub; CD, video, and reading libraries; fireplace; glassed-in-verandah. Ten minutes from Sea Tac International Air-

---

NOTES: Credit cards accepted: A Master Card; B Visa; C American Express; D Discover; E Diners Club; F Other; 2 Personal checks accepted; 3 Lunch available; 4 Dinner available;

port; twenty minutes from Seattle; five minutes from Lake Washington. A vacation, honeymoon, or corporate travel getaway that will long be remembered! Ask about the "Spirit Package."

Hosts: Lynn and Marian Thrasher
Rooms: 1 (PB) $110
Full Breakfast
Credit Cards: A, B
Notes: 2, 5, 8, 9, 10, 11

Chambered Nautilus Bed and Breakfast Inn

## SEATTLE

## *Chambered Nautilus Bed and Breakfast Inn*

5005 - 22nd Ave. N.E., 98105
(206) 522-2536; FAX (206) 522-0404

A gracious 1915 Georgian Colonial that is nestled on a hill and furnished with a mixture of American and English antiques and fine reproductions. A touch of Mozart, Persian rugs, a grand piano, two fireplaces, four lovely porches, and national award-winning breakfasts help assure your special comfort. Excellent access to Seattle's theaters, restaurants, public transportation, shopping, bike and jogging trails, churches, Husky Stadium, and the University of Washing-

ton campus.

Hosts: Bill and Bunny Hagemeyer
Rooms: 6 (4PB; 2SB) $79.50-109.50
Full Breakfast
Credit Cards: A, B, C, E
Notes: 2, 5, 8, 9, 10, 11, 12

## *Shafer-Baillie Mansion Guest House*

907 14th Ave. E., 98112
(206) 322-4654 (voice and FAX);
(800) 922-4654

Antiques of yesteryear; a quiet and enjoyable atmosphere; formal living room and fireplace with comfortable seating for our guests; full library with TV and VCR; formal dining room seats 50; billiard room with copper fireplace; spacious grounds and garden for summer parties and weddings; port cochere and gazebos on north and south lawns with tables and seating; great food in your price range; casual buffet or gourmet sumptuous fare. With your event in mind, we will help you plan your occasion, whether it's a breakfast, luncheon, or meeting all day with both. There are telephones in every room.

Host: Erv Olssen (owner/proprietor)
Rooms: 13 (10PB; 3SB) $79-115
Continental Breakfast
Credit Cards: C, D
Notes: 2, 5, 6 (on request), 8, 9, 10, 11, 12

Shafer-Baillie Mansion Guest House

5 Open all year; 6 Pets welcome; 7 Children welcome; 8 Tennis nearby; 9 Swimming nearby; 10 Golf nearby; 11 Skiing nearby; 12 May be booked through travel agent.

## Tug Boat Challenger Bunk and Breakfast

1001 Fairview Ave. N., 98109
(206) 340-1201; FAX (206) 621-9208

Restored, 1944 tugboat in downtown.
Carpeted, fireplace, eight cabins (five
w/private baths and double beds). Also
two yachts with two cabins on each.
Featured in *Travel and Leisure*, *Cosmo-
politan*, and numerous major papers.

Hosts: Jerry and Buff Brown
Rooms: 12 (9PB; 3SB) $75-165
Full Breakfast
Credit Cards: A, B, C, D, E
Notes: 2, 5, 7, 9, 12

## SEQUIM

### Greywolf Inn

395 Keeler Road, 98382
(360) 683-5889; FAX (360) 683-1487

Nestled in a crescent of towering evergreens, this Northwest country estate
overlooking the Dungeness Valley is
the ideal starting point for year-round,
light adventure on the Olympic
peninsula...hiking, fishing, biking, boating, bird-watching, sightseeing, and
golf. Enjoy Greywolf's sunny decks,
Japanese-style hot tub, and meandering
five-acre woodswalk, or curl up by the
fire with a good book. Then, retire to
one of the Inn's cozy, comfortable
theme rooms. It is the perfect ending
to an exciting day.

Hosts: Peggy and Bill Melang
Rooms: 6 (PB) $68-115
Full Breakfast
Credit Cards: A, B, C
Notes: 2, 3, 5, 7 (over 12), 8, 9, 10, 11, 12

Greywolf Inn

## Margie's Inn on the Bay

120 Forrest Road, 98382
(360) 683-7011; (800) 730-7011

Sequim's only waterfront bed and
breakfast. A contemporary ranch-style
home with 180 feet on the water. Five
well-appointed bedrooms with private
baths. A large sitting room with VCR
and movies. Two Persian cats and a
talking parrot. Close to the marina, fishing, Dungeness National Wildlife Refuge and Spit, Olympic Game Farm, hiking, biking, Hurricane Ridge, gift shops,
and much more. Great restaurants in
the area. AAA inspected.

Hosts: Margie and Don Vorhies
Rooms: 5 (PB) $69-125
Full Breakfast
Credit Cards: A, B, D
Notes: 2, 7 (over 12), 8, 9, 10, 11, 12

Margie's Inn on the Bay

---

NOTES: Credit cards accepted: A Master Card; B Visa; C American Express; D Discover;
E Diners Club; F Other; 2 Personal checks accepted; 3 Lunch available; 4 Dinner available;

## SNOHOMISH

### Eddy's Bed and Breakfast

425 9th Street, 98290
(360) 568-7081

1884 Queen Anne style Victorian home with white picket fence, landscaped gardens, and in-ground heated pool. King and queen canopied beds in guestrooms with private baths and furnished with antiques, hand-made quilts, and resident Teddy Bears. Gourmet Breakfast. Six blocks from 400 antique dealers. Located 30 miles N.E. of Seattle on Highway 2 East.

Hosts: Ted and Marlene Bosworth
Rooms: 3 (1PB; 2SB) $65-85
Full Breakfast
Credit Cards: A, B
Notes: 2, 5, 7, 8, 9 (on-site), 10, 11, 12

Eddy's Bed and Breakfast

## SPOKANE

### Oslo's Bed and Breakfast

1821 E. 39th Avenue, 99203
(509) 838-3175

An attractive South Hill home on a quiet street. Comfortable bedrooms with private baths, and living room available where you may relax and read or visit in a Norwegian atmosphere. Central air-conditioning. A large terrace overlooking the garden may be enjoyed with a full breakfast served at 9:00 A.M., Scandinavian cuisine if desired. Earlier breakfast may be arranged if planned in advance. A small park is located ½ block away. It has tennis courts, exercise stops, and paths for walking. The network of skywalks downtown may be worth investigating, also the Cheney Cowles Museum and the Bing Crosby Library at Gonzaga University.

Host: Aslaug Stevenson
Rooms: 2 (PB) $55-65
Full Breakfast
Credit Cards: F
Notes: 2, 5, 6, 8, 10, 11, 12

## TACOMA

### Commencement Bay Bed and Breakfast

3312 N. Union Ave., 98407
(206) 752-8175;
E MAIL: GREATVIEWS@aol.com;
FAX (206) 759-4025

An elegantly decorated traditional colonial home overlooking scenic north end Tacoma. Guests can enjoy breathtaking bay and mountain views. Rooms are quite large and different with queen-size beds, private baths, closet or dresser space, as well as bedside reading lights. Relax in our bayview fireside reading area, a secluded outdoor hot tub in a lovely garden, or in the casual game

room with a large screen TV, microwave, and refrigerator. Massages and
boat charters can also be arranged. We
offer our guests cable TV, VCR, or telephones. We are close to several nice
waterfront parks, jogging, hiking trails,
restaurants, quaint and antique shops,
and easy freeway access.

Hosts: Bill and Sharon Kaufmann
Rooms: 3 (PB) $75-105
Full Breakfast
Credit Cards: A, B, C, D
Notes: 2, 5, 7 (12 and up), 8, 9, 10, 11, 12

Llama Ranch Bed and Breakfast

## WHITE SALMON

## *Llama Ranch Bed and Breakfast*
1980 Highway 141, 98672
(509) 395-2786; (800) 800-LAMA

Hospitality plus, unforgettable delight.
Jerry and Rebeka share their love of llamas on free llama walks through the
woods with each guest walking a
"llovable" llama. There are stunning
views of both Mt. Adams and Mt. Hood.
The ranch is located between the Mt.
Adams wilderness area and the Columbia Gorge national scenic area with
many varied activities close by. Picturesque views and photographic
memories abound along with the serenity, dignity, and beauty of llamas.

Hosts: Jerry and Rebeka Stone
Rooms: 7 (2PB; 5SB) $55-75
Full Breakfast
Credit Cards: A, B, D
Notes: 2, 5, 6, 7, 10, 11, 12

---

NOTES: Credit cards accepted: A Master Card; B Visa; C American Express; D Discover;
E Diners Club; F Other; 2 Personal checks accepted; 3 Lunch available; 4 Dinner available;

# West Virginia

## BERKELEY SPRINGS

### The Country Inn and Renassance Spa

207 S. Washington Street, 25411
(304) 258-2210; (800) 822-6630;
FAX (304) 258-3986

Retaining the best of the past...less than 100 miles from Balto. Enjoy the warmth and service of a unique and charming country inn. 70 distinctive rooms, creative cuisine, and light specialties. Relax in our full service spa, art gallery, and serene gardens. Many irresistible packages available. Call for reservations.

Hosts: Mr. and Mrs. Jack Barker (innkeepers)
Rooms: 70 (57PB; 13SB) $35-80
Full Breakfast
Credit Cards: A, B, C, D, E
Notes: 2, 3, 4, 5, 7, 8, 9, 10, 11, 12

Historic Charleston Bed and Breakfast

## CHARLESTON

### Historic Charleston B&B

114 Elizabeth Street, 25311
(304) 345-8156;
(800) CALLWVA (ask for Historic Charleston)

Built in 1905 this American Foursquare home was opened in 1991 as the FIRST bed and breakfast in Charleston. Located in the historic district of the city, one block from the Capitol, Cultural Center and Governor's Mansion. A great place for evening walks along the Kanawha River with a view of Charleston University and many beautiful homes. Many other attractions in the city and nearby to take part in. Three antique-filled, non-smoking guest rooms with private baths and a sitting area await your arrival. A full breakfast is included; stuffed French toast, blueberry pancakes, and Belgian waffles are just a few of the many delicious entrees served. We offer affordable elegance that will entice a return visit. While visiting in Charleston, we welcome you in our bed and breakfast.

Hosts: Jean and Bob Lambert
Rooms: 3 (PB) $65-75
Full Breakfast
Credit Cards: A, B, C
Notes: 2, 8, 9, 10

5 Open all year; 6 Pets welcome; 7 Children welcome; 8 Tennis nearby; 9 Swimming nearby; 10 Golf nearby; 11 Skiing nearby; 12 May be booked through travel agent.

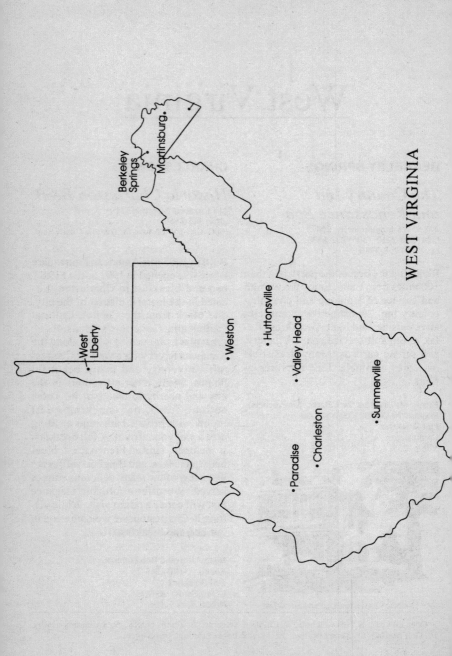

WEST VIRGINIA

West
Liberty

Berkeley
Springs

Martinsburg

Weston

Huttonsville

Valley Head

Paradise

Charleston

Summerville

Washington House Inn

## COLONIAL CHARLES TOWN

# *Washington House Inn*

216 South George St., 25414
(304) 725-7923; (800) 297-6957;
FAX (304) 726-5150

In charming Colonial Charles Town, nestled in the Blue Ridge Mountains where the Shenandoah and Potomac Rivers meet, the Washington House Inn is a wonderful example of late Victorian architecture. Built at the turn of the century, by descendants of President Washington's brothers, the Inn is graced with antique furnishings, carved oak mantles, seven fireplaces, and spacious guest rooms. Just 60 miles from Washington D.C.

Hosts: Mel and Nina Vogel
Rooms: 6 (PB) $70-125
Full Breakfast
Credit Cards: none
Notes: 2, 5, 7 (over 10), 8, 9, 10, 12

## HUTTONSVILLE

# *Hutton House*
# *Bed and Breakfast*

P.O. Box 88, Route 250 and 219, 26273
(304) 335-6701

Meticulously restored and decorated, this Queen Anne Victorian on the National Register of Historic Places is conveniently located near Elkins, Cass Railroad, and Snowshoe Ski Resort. It has a wraparound porch and deck for relaxing and enjoying the view, TV, game room, lawn for games, and a friendly kitchen. Breakfast and afternoon refreshments are served at your leisure; other meals are available with prior reservation or good luck! Come see us!

Hosts: Loretta Murray and Dean Ahren
Rooms: 6 (PB) $60-70
Full Breakfast
Credit Cards: A, B
Notes: 2, 5, 7, 8, 10, 11, 12

## MARTINSBURG

# *Boydville, The Inn*
# *at Martinsburg*

601 S. Queen Street, 25401
(304) 263-1448

A stone manor house, set well back from Queen Street. To reach the front door you turn up a drive through ten acres

---

NOTES: Credit cards accepted: A Master Card; B Visa; C American Express; D Discover; E Diners Club; F Other; 2 Personal checks accepted; 3 Lunch available; 4 Dinner available; 5 Open all year; 6 Pets welcome; 7 Children welcome; 8 Tennis nearby; 9 Swimming nearby; 10 Golf nearby; 11 Skiing nearby; 12 May be booked through travel agent.

with over-arching maples on both sides of the road. This is an experience in itself, because it feels as if you are being led away from a busy world into an earlier and more peaceful time. Handsomely appointed and furnished with English and American antiques, the Inn dates back to 1812. Guests enjoy leisurely walks on the grounds, in the brick-walled courtyard, and the surrounding gardens. Boydville is ideal for a business retreat or a romantic getaway. On the National Register of Historic Places.

Hosts: LaRue Frye, Bob Boege, Carolyn Snyder, and Pete Bailey
Rooms: 6 (4PB; 2SB) $90-110
Expanded Continental Breakfast
Credit Cards: A, B
Notes: 2, 5 (except Aug.), 7 (over 12), 8, 10, 11, 12

## SUMMERVILLE

## *Historic Brock House Bed and Breakfast Inn*

1400 Webster Road, 26651
(302) 872-4887

Tucked away among towering maples and oaks, Historic Brock House Bed and Breakfast Inn has hosted travelers for over 100 years. On lazy summer afternoons, guests can enjoy the rockers and wicker furniture on the wide, wraparound porch. On cooler days a cozy fireside is available for quiet moments, a cup of tea, card playing, or visiting with new friends. Guests can choose

from a full or light breakfast with a variety of homebaked items. Antique shops, Civil War battlefields, canoeing, water skiing, horseback trails, kayaking, rock climbing, and white water rafting abound in this area.

Hosts: Margie and Jim Martin
Rooms: 6 (4PB; 2SB) $65-75
Full Breakfast
Credit Cards: A, B
Notes: 2, 4, 10, 12

Historic Brock House Bed and Breakfast Inn

## VALLEY CHAPEL (WESTON)

## *Ingeberg Acres Bed and Breakfast*

P.O. Box 199, 26446
(304) 269-2834

An unique experience can be yours at this scenic 450-acre horse and cattle farm. Ingeberg Acres is located in the heart of West Virginia seven miles from Weston, overlooking its own private valley. Hiking, swimming, hunting, and fishing or just relaxing can be the orders of the day. Observe or participate in numerous farm activities.

Hosts: Inge and John Mann
Rooms: 3 (SB) $59
Full Breakfast
Credit Cards: none
Notes: 2, 5, 7, 9, 10

## VALLEY HEAD

### *Nakiska Chalet Bed and Breakfast*

HC 73, Box 24, 26294
(304) 339-6309

Nakiska Chalet Bed and Breakfast

Comfortable, casual wood, stone, and glass chalet on a genuine West Virginia country road. We're located near downhill and cross-country skiing, golf, hiking and biking trails, trout fishing, Cass Scenic Railroad, Greenbrier River Trail, Cranberry Glades, fall "leaf-looking," and great festivals and fairs. Less active? Nakiska Chalet is a good place to hide out with your favorite book or project. Accommodations include three guest rooms, a full hearty breakfast, and a smoke-free environment in a pastoral setting.

Hosts: Joyce and Doug Cooper
Rooms: 3 (1PB; 2SB) $60-70
Full Breakfast
Credit Cards: A, B, D
Notes: 2, 5, 10, 11

## WEST LIBERTY

### *The Atkinson Guest House*

124 Chatham Drive, 26074
(304) 336-7577

Located just minutes from Oglebay Park in the college town of West Liberty, this three-story home has two spacious guest bedrooms and breakfast served in the dining room, used at one time by the owner's grandmother. The house is decorated in the style of the Victorian era with much of the original furniture of the day.

Hostess: Karen Cappone
Rooms: 2 (SB) $40-55
Continental Breakfast
Credit Cards: A, B
Notes: 7, 8, 9, 10, 11

---

5 Open all year; 6 Pets welcome; 7 Children welcome; 8 Tennis nearby; 9 Swimming nearby; 10 Golf nearby; 11 Skiing nearby; 12 May be booked through travel agent.

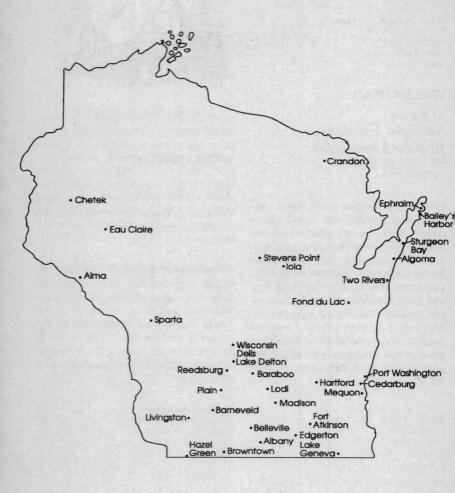

WISCONSIN

# Wisconsin

## ALBANY

### Albany Guest House

405 S. Mill Street, 53502
(608) 862-3636

A two-acre park-like setting, with flower gardens galore and a brick walk, is where you'll find the restored 1908 three story block home. With blooming plants everywhere you'll find king- and queen-sized beds, and a wood-burning fireplace in the master bedroom. Be amazed with the complete, antique, four piece, solid birdseye maple bedroom set, a family heirloom. After a full, wholesome breakfast, recover on the porch swing or rocker or stroll the grounds before exploring, biking, tubing, or canoeing the river.

Hosts: Bob and Sally Braem
Rooms: 4 (PB) $55-68
Full Breakfast
Credit Cards: none
Notes: 2, 5, 7 (disciplined), 10, 11

### Oak Hill Manor

401 E. Main Street, 53502
(608) 862-1400

A 1908 brick manor house on the Sugar River Bicycle Trail. Spacious, sunny, corner rooms are air-conditioned and all have queen-size beds. Choose a room with a fireplace, a porch, or a canopy bed. Stroll the acre of gardens or sit by the fire in the guest parlor. Gourmet fireside breakfast served daily. Hike, bike, canoe, golf, and cross-country ski. Bicycles available at no charge. No smoking.

Hosts: Lee and Mary DeWolf
Rooms: 4 (PB) $55-60
Full Breakfast
Credit Cards: A, B
Notes: 2, 5, 8, 10, 11

Oak Hill Manor

---

NOTES: Credit cards accepted: A Master Card; B Visa; C American Express; D Discover; E Diners Club; F Other; 2 Personal checks accepted; 3 Lunch available; 4 Dinner available; 5 Open all year; 6 Pets welcome; 7 Children welcome; 8 Tennis nearby; 9 Swimming nearby; 10 Golf nearby; 11 Skiing nearby; 12 May be booked through travel agent.

## Sugar River Inn
## Bed and Breakfast

304 S. Mill Street, 53502
(608) 862-1248

Our turn-of-the century inn, with many original features, has the charm of yesteryear and Christian fellowship. We are located in a quiet village in southern Wisconsin along the Sugar River. We have spacious lawn, canoeing, and fishing in the back yard. We are minutes away from the bike trail. Comfortable, light, airy rooms await you with queen-size beds, fine linens, afternoon refreshments, and wake up coffee. We are near New Glarus, House on the Rock, Little Norway, and the state capital in Madison. Only two hours from Chicago.

Hosts: Jack and Ruth Lindberg
Rooms: 4 (1PB; 3SB) $45-60
Full Breakfast
Credit Cards: A, B
Notes: 2, 5, 7 (by arrangement), 9, 10

## ALGOMA

## Amberwood Inn

N7136 Hwy. 42, 54201
(414) 487-3471

Luxury Lake Michigan beachfront accommodations. Located on two and one-half private acres with 300 feet of beach. Each suite is large, romantic, and very private. Private baths, whirlpool tubs, hot tub, sauna, and private decks open to the water. Awaken to a sunrise over water; sleep to the sound of the waves. Ten minutes to Door County.

Rooms: 5 (PB) $65-85
Full Breakfast
Credit Cards: A, B
Notes: 2, 7, 9, 10

Laue House Inn

## ALMA

## Laue House Inn

1111 S. Main St., 54610
(608) 685-4923

*Comfortable, cozy, and affordable.* In walking distance to all the stores and shops in the city. Watch the train and barges go by from the front porch or hike in the hills behind the house. The Laue House is a fine example of Italianate architecture design by the famous architecture Charles Maybury. The house was placed on the National Register of Historic Places in 1979 by Jan and Jerry who saved and restored this old and charming structure. Player piano in the lounge to sing along with. Refrigerator for refreshments and coffee bar for chatting with friends by the

NOTES: Credit cards accepted: A Master Card; B Visa; C American Express; D Discover; E Diners Club; F Other; 2 Personal checks accepted; 3 Lunch available; 4 Dinner available;

fireplace. Hope to see you sometime!

Hosts: Jan and Jerry
Rooms: 6 (SB) $25-35
Continental Breakfast
Credit Cards: none
Notes: 2, 6, 7, 8, 9, 10, 11

## BAILEY'S HARBOR

### *Loving's Guest Home*

7445 Highway 57, 54202
(414) 839-2049

Located in beautiful Door County, Wisconsin, on Kangaroo Lake (½ mile from Lake Michigan). Comfortable family home surrounded by gardens on a large lot that invite relaxing. Quiet setting, yet close to all Door Peninsula activities. Adults only. No smoking in house

Hosts: George and Margaret Loving
Rooms: 3—each with 1 double bed) (SB) $45
Full Continental Breakfast
Credit Cards: none
Notes: 2, 5, 8, 9, 10, 11

## BARABOO

### *Pinehaven Bed and Breakfast*

E13083 Highway 33, 53913
(608) 356-3489

Our home is located in a scenic valley with a small, private lake and Baraboo Bluffs in the background. The guest rooms are distinctly different with wicker furniture and antiques, queen and twin beds. Take a walk in this peaceful country setting. Area activities include Devil's Lake State Park, Circus World Museum, Wisconsin Dells, and ski resorts. Ask about our private guest cottage. No pets and no smoking. Gift certificates available.

Hosts: Lyle and Marge Getschman
Rooms: 4 (PB) $65-75
Full Breakfast
Credit Cards: A, B
Notes: 2, 5, 7 (over 5), 9, 10, 11

### *The Victorian Rose Bed and Breakfast*

423 Third Ave., 53913
(608) 356-7828

Nostalgic retreat. A place for all seasons. Spend tranquil moments with memories to treasure. Nestled in the heart of historical Baraboo. Centrally located to all area attractions. Enjoy the splendor of the Victorian era by resting on the wraparound front porch or relaxing in two formal parlors with beautiful cherub fireplace and TV/VCR. Romantic guestrooms, candlelight breakfast, and Christian hospitality.

Hosts: Robert and Carolyn Stearns
Rooms: 3 (PB) $65-80
Full Breakfast
Credit Cards: D
Notes: 2, 5, 8, 9, 10, 11, 12

The Victorian Rose Bed and Breakfast

5 Open all year; 6 Pets welcome; 7 Children welcome; 8 Tennis nearby; 9 Swimming nearby; 10 Golf nearby; 11 Skiing nearby; 12 May be booked through travel agent.

## BARNEVELD

### The Garden Bed and Breakfast

112 Arneson Road, 53507
(608) 924-2108

Your stay at The Garden B&B will be like going "home to the country." Nestled in the midst of rolling farmland and quaint small towns, you'll enjoy the leisurely escape from the bustle of the city. Choose from theme rooms like the Teddy Bear Room, the Garden Room, or the Blue Room; each has special features and touches. Also, you'll find immaculately clean, comfortable beds with handmade quilts. Fresh cut flowers and chocolate mints await your arrival and, in true tradition of coming "home to the country," feast on a delicious and bountiful breakfast every morning, served in an elegant setting.

Hosts: Richard and Lois Wilson
Rooms: 3 (2½PB; 1SB) $55-65
Full Breakfast
Credit Cards: none
Notes: 2, 5 (except holidays), 9, 10, 11

## BELLEVILLE

### Abendruh Bed and Breakfast Swisstyle

7019 Gehin Drive, 53508
(608) 424-3808

Experience B&B Swisstyle. This highly acclaimed, Wisconsin B&B offers true Swiss charm and hospitality. The serenity of this peaceful retreat is one of many treasures that keeps guests coming back. Spacious guestrooms adorned with beautiful family heirlooms. Sitting room with high cathedral ceiling and cozy fireplace. An Abendruh breakfast is a perfect way to start a new day or end a peaceful stay.

Hostess: Mathilde Jaggi
Rooms: 2 (PB) $60-65 + tax
Full Breakfast
Credit Cards: A, B
Notes: 2, 5, 8, 9, 10, 11, 12

## BROWNTOWN

### Honeywind Farm

W. 8247 County P, 53522
(608) 325-5215

Honeywind Farm is a B&B blended into a beautiful southwest Wisconsin dairy farm. We emphasize family farm vacations. On our 300 acres is a fishing stream, 20 acres of woods, natural wetlands, plus corn and hay fields, all contributing to an abundance of wildlife and numerous ways to enjoy your time. Our children will welcome yours. Depending on the season, you may have opportunity to help with various farm activities and/or take home a sampling of farm products.

Hosts: Ryan and Claudia Wilson and Family
Rooms: 2 (PB) $65-85
Full Breakfast
Credit Cards: none
Notes: 2, 5, 7

---

NOTES: Credit cards accepted: A Master Card; B Visa; C American Express; D Discover; E Diners Club; F Other; 2 Personal checks accepted; 3 Lunch available; 4 Dinner available;

Stagecoach Inn

# CEDARBURG

## Stagecoach Inn

W61 N520 Washington, 53012
(414) 375-0208; FAX (414) 375-6170

The Stagecoach Inn is a historic, re-stored, 1853 stone building of Greek Revival style and an 1847, restored, frame house annex. The Inn's twelve cozy and comfortable rooms feature stenciled walls, central air-conditioning, and private baths. Situated in the heart of historic Cedarburg within walking distance to shops and restaurants, the Inn also features an on-premises pub with a 100-year-old bar and a chocolate shop.

Hosts: Liz and Brook Brown
Rooms: 12 (PB) $70-105
Continental Plus Breakfast
Credit Cards: A, B, C, D, E
Notes: 2, 5, 7 (over 12), 8, 9, 10, 11, 12

## The Washington House Inn

W62 N573 Washington Avenue, 53012
(414) 375-3550; (800) 554-4717;
FAX (414) 375-9422

Built in 1884 and listed on the National Register of Historic Places, the Inn's 34 guest rooms feature antiques, down comforters, whirlpool baths, fireplaces, and cable TV. Located in the heart of the Cedarburg historic district, within walking distance of area antique shops, fine dining, and historic Cedar Creek settlement.

Hostess: Wendy Porterfield
Rooms: 34 (PB) $59-179
Embellished Continental Breakfast
Credit Cards: A, B, C, D, E
Notes: 2, 5, 7, 8, 9, 10, 11

# CHETEK

## Trails End Bed and Breakfast

641 Ten Mile Lake Dr., 54728
(715) 924-2641

Peace and tranquillity await you in this modern, spacious, log lodge, situated on our private island. The 4,000-square-foot, three-level, log home boasts antiques of every sort, with stories behind most every unique feature of the home from an 1887 jail door to a 300 pound, seven-foot wagon wheel and a huge stone fireplace. Each guest's bedroom—the Romantic, Indian, and Western Rooms—are decorated with antiques of yesteryear.

Hosts: Richard and Bonnie Flood
Rooms: 3 (1PB; 2SB) $80-95
Full Breakfast
Credit Cards: A, B, C, D
Notes: 2, 5, 10, 11

---

5 Open all year; 6 Pets welcome; 7 Children welcome; 8 Tennis nearby; 9 Swimming nearby; 10 Golf nearby; 11 Skiing nearby; 12 May be booked through travel agent.

## CRANDON

### Courthouse Square Bed and Breakfast

210 E. Polk, 54520
(715) 478-2549

Guests frequently comment about the peace and tranquillity of the setting. Enjoy birds and squirrels at the many benches placed throughout the flower and herb gardens or stroll down the hill to the lake through the forget-me-nots and view the wildlife. *The Rhinelander Daily News* wrote, "Traditional hospitality is emphasized at Courthouse Square B&B, and it's evident from the moment you enter this delightful home where tranquillity and peace abounds. You will no doubt smell something delicious baking in Bess's kitchen as gourmet cooking is one of her specialties."

Hosts: Les and Bess Aho
Rooms: 3 (1PB; 2SB) $50-60
Full Gourmet Candlelit Breakfast
Credit Cards: C
Notes: 2, 5, 7 (ask about 12+), 8, 9, 10, 11

## EAU CLAIRE

### The Atrium Bed and Breakfast

5572 Prill Rd., 54701
(715) 833-9045

Named for its most unique feature, the heart of this contemporary home is a 20' x 20' garden room where a palmtree and bougainvillea vines stretch toward the glassed ceiling. The home is nestled on 15 wooded acres on Otter Creek that beckons the explorer. Nearby you'll fine bicycling, canoeing, antiquing, and an Amish community. The Atrium offers the best of both worlds; relaxed seclusion, only minutes from numerous restaurants, shopping, and the University of Wisconsin-Eau Claire.

Hosts: Celia and Dick Stoltz
Rooms: 3 (1PB; 2SB) $60-75
Full Breakfast weekends; Continental Breakfast weekdays
Credit Cards: A, B
Notes: 2, 5, 7 (12 and over), 8, 9, 10, 11 (cross-country)

Otter Creek Inn

### Otter Creek Inn

2536 Hwy. 12, 54701
(715) 832-2945

Pamper yourself with breakfast in bed amid the antiques of yesteryear in this spacious 6,000 square-foot, three-story inn. Discover amenities of today tucked amidst the country Victorian decor as every guest room contains a double whirlpool, private bath, phone, AC, and cable TV. Explore the creek or snuggle up inside near the fire to watch the wildlife saunter by. All this country charm is located less than one mile from nu-

---

NOTES: Credit cards accepted: A Master Card; B Visa; C American Express; D Discover; E Diners Club; F Other; 2 Personal checks accepted; 3 Lunch available; 4 Dinner available;

merous restaurants and shops.

Hosts: Randy and Shelley Hansen
Rooms: 5 (PB) $75-139
Expanded Continental Breakfast
Credit Cards: A, B, C, D, E
Notes: 2, 5, 8, 9, 10, 11

## EDGERTON

### The Olde Parsonage Bed and Breakfast

120 Swift Street, 53534
(608) 884-6490

Retreat to this well preserved parsonage of 1906 graced with herring bone floors, leaded glass windows, and original oak woodwork. Relax in the parlor with cozy conversation or play euchre in the reading room before retiring to your own room. Located two miles off I-90 in Edgerton, the boyhood home of Sterling North. Visit antique and specialty shops or Tobacco City Museum. Enjoy golf, tennis, or water sports at Lake Koshkonong, three miles east of Edgerton.

Hostess: Connie Frank
Rooms: 4 (SB) $45-75
Hearty Continental Breakfast
Credit Cards: none
Notes: 2, 5, 8, 9, 10

## EPHRAIM

### Hillside Hotel of Ephraim

9980 Hwy. 42, P.O. Box 17, 54211
(414) 854-2417; (800) 423-7023;
FAX (414) 854-4604

Authentic, restored country, Victorian inn featuring full, specialty breakfasts and afternoon teas, feather beds, original antiques, gorgeous harbor view, 100-foot verandah overlooking the beach, individually decorated guest rooms, clawfoot tubs with showers, and brass fixtures. We have twelve years experience and *love* what we do!!

Hosts: David and Karen McNeil
Rooms: 11 (SB) $84-115
Cottages: 2 (PB) $140-180
Full Breakfast and Afternoon Tea
Credit Cards: A, B, D
Notes: 2, 5, 7, 8, 9, 10, 11

## FOND DU LAC

### White Picket Fence Bed and Breakfast

213 E. First Street, 54935
(414) 922-0870

The White Picket Fence is Fond du Lac's first B&B. This stately historical house was built by Judge Duffy at the turn-of-the-century. The spacious Italianate-style home exhibits the charm of yesteryear, furnished with antiques, and the amenities of today, including cable and air-conditioning. A full breakfast, catering to special dietary needs and your schedule, is available. Relax on the deck with orange juice or coffee. We are located mid-way between Milwaukee and Green Bay and in the heart of Fond du Lac. Gift certificates are available.

Hostess: Betty Ernest
Rooms: 2 (SB) $68-78
Full Breakfast
Credit Cards: A, B
Notes: 2, 5, 7 (inquire), 8, 9, 10, 11

---

5 Open all year; 6 Pets welcome; 7 Children welcome; 8 Tennis nearby; 9 Swimming nearby; 10 Golf nearby; 11 Skiing nearby; 12 May be booked through travel agent.

## FORT ATKINSON

### The Lamp Post Inn

408 S. Main Street, 53538
(414) 563-6561

We welcome you to the charm of our 115-year-old Victorian home filled with beautiful antiques. Five gramophones for your listening pleasure. For the modern, one of our baths features a large jacuzzi. We are located seven blocks from the famous Fireside Playhouse. You come a stranger, but leave here a friend. No smoking.

Hosts: Debbie and Mike Rusch
Rooms: 3 (2PB; 1SB) $60-95
Full Breakfast
Credit Cards: none
Notes: 2, 5, 7, 8, 9, 10, 11

## HARTFORD

### Jordan House Bed and Breakfast

81 S. Main Street, 53027
(414) 673-5643

Warm and comfortable Victorian home furnished with period antiques. Forty miles from Milwaukee. Near majestic Holy Hill Shrine, Horizon Wildlife Refuge, and Pike Lake State Park. Walk to the state's largest antique auto museum, antique malls, and downtown shops. Call or write for brochure.

Hosts: Kathy Buchanan and Art Jones
Rooms: 4 (1PB; 3SB) $55-65
Full Breakfast
Credit Cards: A, B
Notes: 2, 5, 7, 8, 9, 10, 11

## HAZEL GREEN

### Wisconsin House Stage Coach Inn

2105 E. Main, 53811
(608) 854-2233

Built as a stage coach inn in 1846, the Inn now offers six rooms and two suites for your comfort. Join us for an evening's rest. Dine and be refreshed in the parlor where General Grant spent many evenings with his friend Jefferson Crawford. Most conveniently located for all the attractions of the Tri-State Area. Galena, Illinois, is ten minutes away; Dubuque, Iowa, 15 miles away; and Platteville is 20 miles away.

Hosts: Ken and Pat Disch
Rooms: 8 (6PB; 2SB) $55-110
Full Breakfast
Credit Cards: A, B, D
Notes: 4, 5, 7, 12

## IOLA

### Taylor House Bed and Breakfast

210 E. Iola St., P.O. Box 101, 54945
(715) 445-2204

Turn-of-the-century Victorian home. Four antique-furnished rooms, one with fireplace. Parlor with fireplace. Queen-size beds. No smoking. Air-conditioned. Paved country roads are ideal for biking. Twenty minutes from the Waupaca Chain O'Lakes area. We offer a glimpse of the lifestyle of the 1800s with all the conveniences of the modern age. Call or write for a free brochure.

Hosts: Crystal and Richard Anderson
Rooms: 4 (2PB; 2SB) $46-55
Full Breakfast
Credit Cards: none
Notes: 2, 5, 7, 9, 10, 11

## LAKE DELTON

### The Swallow's Nest Bed and Breakfast

141 Sarrington, P.O. Box 418, 53940
(608) 254-6900

The unique decor is English in taste with period collectibles. New home with cathedral windows and ceiling. Offers seclusion among the trees and bird's-eye view of the lake. Relax in the library or by the fireplace. Fine restaurants nearby. Close to Wisconsin Dells, Devils Head, two state parks, and Circus World Museum. Full breakfast, four rooms, and four private baths. No pets and no smoking. Gift certificates available.

Hosts: Rod and Mary Ann Stemo
Rooms: 4 (PB) $60-70
Full Breakfast
Credit Cards: A, B
Notes: 2, 5, 9, 10, 11

## LAKE GENEVA

### Eleven Gables Inn on the Lake

493 Wrigley Drive, 53147
(414) 248-8393

Nestled in evergreen amid giant oaks in the Edgewater Historical District, this quaint lakeside Carpenter's Gothic Inn offers privacy and a prime location. Romantic bedrooms, bridal chamber, and unique "country cottages" all have fireplaces, down comforters, baths, TV's, wet-bars, or cocktail refrigerators. Some have lattice courtyards, balconies, and private entrances. A private pier provides exclusive water activities. Bike rentals are available. This charming "Newport of the Midwest" community provides fine dining, boutiques, and entertainment year round.

Host: A. Fasel Milliette
Rooms: 12 (PB) Please call for seasonal and package rates
Full or Continental Breakfast
Credit Cards: A, B, C, E
Notes: 5, 7, 8, 9, 10, 11

## LIVINGSTON

### Oak Hill Farm

9850 Highway 80, 53554
(608) 943-6006

A comfortable country home with a warm hospitable atmosphere that is enhanced with fireplaces, porches, and facilities for picnics, bird-watching, and hiking. In the area you will find state parks, museums, and lakes.

Hosts: Elizabeth Johnson and Victor Johnson
Suites: 4 (1PB; 3SB) $42
Continental Breakfast
Credit Cards: none
Notes: 2, 6, 7, 8, 9, 10, 11, 12

---

5 Open all year; 6 Pets welcome; 7 Children welcome; 8 Tennis nearby; 9 Swimming nearby; 10 Golf nearby; 11 Skiing nearby; 12 May be booked through travel agent.

Victorian Treasure Bed and Breakfast Inn

## LODI

### Victorian Treasure Bed and Breakfast Inn

115 Prairie Street, 53555
(608) 592-5199 (voice and FAX);
(800) 859-5199

The Victorian Treasure is a balance between timeless ambiance, thoughtful amenities, and gracious hospitality. Six unique guest rooms in two historic Queen Anne Victorians with architectural details and classic Victorian flair. Guests of the 1897 Bissell Mansion experience a more traditional B&B stay with a formal front parlor, sitting room with fireplace, and wraparound verandah. Afternoon refreshments are provided, as well as a full breakfast in the formal dining room. Guests of the 1893 Palmer House escape to luxurious suites with canopied bed, sitting area, fireplace, wet bar, microwave, refrigerator, stereo with CD, and whirlpool bath. Gourmet coffee and a full breakfast is delivered to the suites. The owners, also the innkeepers, are fussy about the details and genuinely interested in exceed-

ing guest's expectations!

Hosts: Todd and Kimberly Seidl
Rooms: 4 (PB) $65-110
Full Breakfast
Credit Cards: A, B
Notes: 2, 5, 8, 9, 10, 11, 12

## MADISON

### Annie's B&B

2117 Sheridan Drive, 53704
(608) 244-2224; FAX (608) 242-9611

When you want the world to go away, come to Annie's, the quiet inn on Warner Park with the beautiful view. Luxury accommodations at reasonable rates. Close to the lake and park, it is also convenient to downtown and the University of Wisconsin campus. There are unusual amenities in this charming setting, including a romantic gazebo surrounded by butterfly gardens, a shaded terrace, and pond. Two beautiful two-bedroom suites. Double jacuzzi. Full air-conditioning. Winter cross-country skiing, too!

Hosts: Anne and Larry Stuart
Suites: 2 (two-room suites) (PB) $75-115
Full Breakfast
Credit Cards: A, B, C
Notes: 2, 5, 7 (over 12), 8, 9, 10, 11

Annie's Bed and Breakfast

---

NOTES: Credit cards accepted: A Master Card; B Visa; C American Express; D Discover; E Diners Club; F Other; 2 Personal checks accepted; 3 Lunch available; 4 Dinner available;

Mansion Hill Inn

## Mansion Hill Inn

424 N. Pinckney Street, 53703
(608) 255-3999; (800) 798-9070;
FAX (608) 255-2217

Eleven luxurious rooms, each with a sumptuous bath. Whirlpool tubs with stereo headphones, hand-carved marble fireplaces, minibars, and elegant Victorian furnishings help make this restored mansion into Madison's ONLY Four Diamond Inn. Private wine cellar, VCR's, and access to private dining and athletic clubs available upon request. Turndown service and evening refreshments in our parlor. Ideal for honeymoons. Listed on the National Register of Historic Places.

Hostess: Janna Wojtal
Rooms: 11 (PB) $100-270
Continental, Silver Service Breakfast
Credit Cards: A, B, C
Notes: 2, 5, 9, 12

## MEQUON

### Port Zedler Motel

10036 North Port Washington Rd., 53092
(414) 241-5850 (voice and FAX)

AAA Approved. Air-conditioned. Convenient to downtown, casino, and excellent restaurants. Twelve minutes north of downtown Milwaukee. Touchtone, in-room phones. Full private bath/shower. Winter plug-ins. In-room refrigerator and microwave oven on request. Rates include color cable TV(HBO/Showtime). Free, ample parking and ice. No charge for children under 12. Senior/AARP/AAA discounts. German is spoken. I-43 northbound one-half mile northwest of exit 83 (Hwy. W. North). I-43 southbound exit 82A, one block east and one and one-half mile north on Port Washington Road (Hwy. W. North).

Hostess: Sheila
Rooms: 16 (PB) $34-95-59.95
Continental Breakfast
Credit Cards: A, B, C, D
Notes: 5, 6, 7, 8, 9, 10, 11, 12

## PLAIN

### Bettinger House Bed and Breakfast

Highway 23, P.O. Box 243, 53577
(608) 546-2951 (voice and FAX)

Hostess's grandparents' 1904 Victorian farmhouse; Grandma was a midwife and delivered 300 babies in this house. Choose from five spacious bedrooms that blend the old with the new, each named after note-worthy persons of Plain. Central air-conditioning. Start your day with one of the old-fashioned, full-course breakfasts we are famous for. Near "House on the Rock," Frank Lloyd Wright's original Taliesin, American Players Theatre, White

5 Open all year; 6 Pets welcome; 7 Children welcome; 8 Tennis nearby; 9 Swimming nearby; 10 Golf nearby; 11 Skiing nearby; 12 May be booked through travel agent.

Mound Park, and much more.

Hosts: Jim and Marie Neider
Rooms: 5 (2PB; 3SB) $50-65
Full Breakfast
Credit Cards: A, B
Notes: 2, 5, 7 (inquire first), 8, 9, 10, 11, 12

The Inn at Old Twelve Hundred

## PORT WASHINGTON

### The Inn at Old Twelve Hundred

806 W. Grand Ave., 53074
(414) 268-1200; FAX (414) 284-6885

Beautifully restored and decorated
Queen Anne. Original master duite features fireplace, private porch, and king-
size bed. Two rooms offer oversize
whirlpools, fireplaces, and sitting room
or private porch. Spacious yard, gazebo, croquet, and tandem bicycles
available. Port Washington is a quaint
village on Lake Michigan. Minutes to
Cedarburg, Harrison Beach, State Park,
and Kohler. Air-conditioned. Restricted smoking. Ask about the new

"Coach House".

Hostesses: Stephanie and Ellie Bresette
Rooms: 5 (PB) $75-145
Continental Breakfast
Credit Cards: A, B, C
Notes: 2, 5

## REEDSBURG

### Parkview B&B

211 N. Park Street, 53959
(608) 524-4333

Our 1895 Queen Anne Victorian home
overlooks City Park in the historic district. Many of the original features of
the home remain, such as hardware,
hardwood floors, intricate woodwork,
leaded and etched windows, plus a suit-
ors window. Wake-up coffee is followed by a full, homemade breakfast.
Central air and ceiling fans add to
guests' comfort. Located one block
from downtown. Close to Wisconsin
Dells, Baraboo, and Spring Green.
Three blocks from 400 Bike Trail.

Hosts: Tom and Donna Hofmann
Rooms: 4 (2PB; 2SB) $55-70
Full Breakfast
Credit Cards: A, B, C
Notes: 2, 5, 7 (inquire), 8, 10, 11, 12

Parkview Bed and Breakfast

NOTES: Credit cards accepted: A Master Card; B Visa; C American Express; D Discover;
E Diners Club; F Other; 2 Personal checks accepted; 3 Lunch available; 4 Dinner available;

## SPARTA

### The Franklin Victorian Bed and Breakfast

220 E. Franklin Street, 54656
(608) 269-3894; (800) 845-8767

This turn-of-the-century home welcomes you to bygone elegance with small-town quiet and comfort. The four spacious bedrooms provide a perfect setting for ultimate relaxation. Full home-cooked breakfast is served before starting you day of hiking, biking, skiing, canoeing, antiquing, or exploring this beautiful area.

Hosts: Lloyd and Jane Larson
Rooms: 4 (2PB; 2SB) $65-92
Full Breakfast
Credit Cards: A, B
Notes: 2, 5, 7 (over 10), 8, 9, 10, 11

## STEVENS POINT

### Dreams of Yesteryear Bed and Breakfast

1100 Brawley Street, 54481
(715) 341-4525; FAX (715) 344-3047

Featured in *Victorian Homes Magazine* and listed on the National Register of Historic Places. Your hosts are from Stevens Point and enjoy talking about the restoration of their turn-of-the-century home which has been in the same family for three generations. All rooms are furnished in antiques. Guests enjoy use of parlors, porches, and gardens. Two blocks from the historic downtown, antique and specialty shops, picturesque Green Circle Trails, the uni-

versity, and more. Dreams of Yesteryear is truly "a Victorian dream come true."

Hosts: Bonnie and Bill Maher
Rooms: 6 (4PB; 2SB) $55-95
Full Breakfast
Credit Cards: A, B, C, D
Notes: 2, 5, 7 (over 12), 8, 9, 10, 11, 12

### Victorian Swan on Water

1716 Water Street, 54481
(715) 345-0595

A happy memory never wears out. Create those happy memories with this historic 1889 home. Unique woodwork and antiques with air-conditioned comfort as its main ingredient. A secret room, a Roman bath, restful gardens, whirlpool, and refreshments by the fireplace—a respite for your soul. Complete those memories with a delicious full breakfast and a river walk.

Hostess: Joan Ouellette
Rooms: 4 (PB) $55-120
Full Breakfast
Credit Cards: A, B, C, D
Notes: 2, 5, 10, 11, 12

## STURGEON BAY

### Hearthside Bed and Breakfast

2136 Taube Road, 54235
(414) 746-2136

This remodeled 1800s farmhouse has a pleasant blend of contemporary and antique furnishings. Lake Michigan can be seen in the distance. The old barn still stands nearby. Within easy driv-

---

5 Open all year; 6 Pets welcome; 7 Children welcome; 8 Tennis nearby; 9 Swimming nearby;
10 Golf nearby; 11 Skiing nearby; 12 May be booked through travel agent.

ing distance are fantastic state parks, beaches for swimming in summer, or areas for skiing in the winter. Lighthouses, U.S. Coast Guard Station, lake cruises, airport, ship building, and weekend festivals. The rooms are charming; three with queen beds. The upper east wing room has three twin beds. Guests may use TVs, VCRs, living and sun rooms, plus group meeting rooms.

Hosts: Don and Lu Kleussendorf
Rooms: 4 (PB) $35-65
Full Home-cooked Breakfast
Credit Cards: A, B
Notes: 2, 5, 7, 8, 9, 10, 11

Hearthside Bed and Breakfast

## TWO RIVERS

### Red Forest Bed and Breakfast

1421 25th Street, 54241
(414) 793-1794

We invite you to step back in time to 1907 and enjoy our gracious three-story shingle style home. Highlighted with stained glass windows, heirloom antiques, and cozy fireplace. Four beautifully appointed guest rooms await your arrival. Stroll along our sugar sand beaches or through downtown antiquing. The Red Forest is located on Wisconsin's East Coast, minutes from Manitowoc, Wisconsin's port city of Lake Michigan Carferry. Also located midway from Chicago and the Door County Pennisula.

Hosts: Alan and Kay Rodewald
Rooms: 4 (2PB; 2SB) $60-75
Full Breakfast
Credit Cards: A, B, C
Notes: 2, 5, 7 (older), 8, 9 (beach), 10, 11, 12 (12% comm.)

Red Forest Bed and Breakfast

## WISCONSIN DELLS

### Historic Bennett House

825 Oak Street, 53965
(608) 254-2500

The 1863 home of an honored pioneer photographer is listed on the National Register of Historic Places. We'll pamper you with elegant lace, crystal, antiques, romantic bedrooms, and luscious fireside breakfast. The private suite has a parlor, Eastlake bedroom, and showerbath. The English Room has a walnut and lace canopy bed. And the Garden Room has a brass bed. Walk to

NOTES: Credit cards accepted: A Master Card; B Visa; C American Express; D Discover; E Diners Club; F Other; 2 Personal checks accepted; 3 Lunch available; 4 Dinner available;

river tours, antiques, and crafts. Minutes to hiking, biking, canoeing, four golf courses, five ski areas, five state parks, greyhound racing, bird-watching, and Indian culture. Bennett, Rockwell, circus, and railroad museums are also nearby. Gift certificates are available.

Hosts: Gail and Rich Obermeyer
Rooms: 3 (1PB; 2SB) $70-90
Full Breakfast
Credit Cards: none
Notes: 2, 5, 8, 9, 10, 11, 12

Historic Bennett House

## Terrace Hill
## Bed and Breakfast
922 River Road, 53965
(608) 253-9363

Serendipity, the unexpected. A quiet niche with private parking in rear and a peaceful, small city park right out the back door, yet only one block from downtown Dell and on the Wisconsin River. Enjoy summer tourism or winter fun. We are on the snowmobile trail with facilities for trailer parking and a quaint restaurant in the mansion next door. Arrangements and special rates for retreats, seminars, and family gathering. Additional lodging nearby.

Hosts: The Novak Family
Rooms: 5 (PB) $65-140 (suite)
Full Breakfast
Credit Cards: none
Notes: 2, 5, 7, 9, 10, 11

WYOMING

# Wyoming

## BIG HORN

### Spahn's Bighorn Mountain Bed and Breakfast
P.O. Box 579, 82833
(307) 674-8150

Towering log home and secluded guest cabins on the mountainside in whispering pines. Borders one million acres of public forest with deer and moose. Gracious mountain breakfast served on the deck with binoculars to enjoy the 100-mile view. Owner is former Yellowstone ranger. Ten minutes from I-90 near Sheridan.

Hosts: Ron and Bobbie Spahn
Rooms: 4 (PB) $65-100
Full Breakfast
Credit Cards: A, B
Notes: 2, 3, 4, 7

## BUFFALO

### Historic Mansion House Inn
313 North Main, 82834
(307) 684-2218

Turn-of-the-century Victorian Home located on historic Main Street and Highway 16, scenic route from the Black Hills of South Dakota to Yellowstone National Park. All rooms are comfortably decorated, each with private bath, TV, and air-conditioning. Continental Breakfast provided. Open year-round.

Hosts: Phil and Diane Mehlhaff
Rooms: 18 (PB) call for rates
Continental Breakfast
Credit Cards: A, B, D
Notes: 5, 7, 8, 9, 10, 11, 12

## CHEYENNE

### The Storyteller, Pueblo Bed and Breakfast
5201 Ogden Road, 82009
(307) 634-7036

Native American art from over 30 tribes: pottery, beadwork, baskets, and rugs. Contemporary home of country and primitive antiques. Down home hospitality on a quiet street. Convenient to shopping and major restaurants. Breakfast with all the amenities. Fireplaces and family rooms for your enjoyment.

---

NOTES: Credit cards accepted: A Master Card; B Visa; C American Express; D Discover; E Diners Club; F Other; 2 Personal checks accepted; 3 Lunch available; 4 Dinner available; 5 Open all year; 6 Pets welcome; 7 Children welcome; 8 Tennis nearby; 9 Swimming nearby; 10 Golf nearby; 11 Skiing nearby; 12 May be booked through travel agent.

Reservations recommended. Special rates during the last ten days of every July.

Hosts: Howard and Peggy Hutchings
Rooms: 3 (1PB; 12SB) $40-55
Full Breakfast
Credit Cards: none
Notes: 2, 5, 7 (by arrangement), 8, 9, 10, 11, 12

## CODY

### The Lockhart Bed and Breakfast Inn

109 W. Yellowstone Ave., 82414
(307) 587-6074; (800) 377-7255;
FAX (307) 587-8644

Historic home of famous Cody authoress, Caroline Lockhart. Circa 1890, refurbished in 1985 and again in 1994 offering antiques, parlor, dining area, wood-burning stove, piano, games, direct dial phones, and cable TV. Complimentary coffee, teas, brandy, spiced cider, and hot cocoa. Two acres overlooking Sitoshone River; three mountains. Mobile rated.

Hostess: Cindy Baldwin
Rooms: 7 (PB) $55-82
Full Breakfast
Credit Cards: A, B, D, E
Notes: 2, 3, 5, 7, 8, 9, 10, 11, 12

The Lockhart Bed and Breakfast Inn

## ENCAMPMENT

### Grand and Sierra Bed and Breakfast Lodge

P.O. Box 312, 1016 Lomax Street, 82325
(307) 327-5200

The Grand and Sierra Lodge has five bedrooms and four bathrooms. The two bedrooms upstairs have queen-size beds and private baths. The three downstairs share two bathrooms, one contains a shower. The family game room is filled with North American trophies along with a stone fireplace. There's a patio off the dining room. The spa sits on a lower patio. The lodge was constructed by the owner who cut the logs and skidded them out by horseback.

Manager: Mary Paxton
Owner: Glen Knotwell
Rooms: 5 (2PB; 3SB) $48-65
Full Breakfast
Credit Cards: A, B
Notes: 2, 5, 7, 8, 9 (20 miles), 11 (cross-country)

### Rustic Mountain Lodge

Star Route, Box 49, 82325
(307) 327-5539 (voice and FAX)

A peaceful mountain view, located on a working ranch with wholesome country atmosphere and lots of Western hospitality. Enjoy daily fishing on a private pond, big game trophy hunts, cookouts, holistic health and fitness, pack trips, photo safaries, youth programs, cattle drives, trail rides, hiking, rock hunting, numerous ranch activities, mountain

---

NOTES: Credit cards accepted: A Master Card; B Visa; C American Express; D Discover; E Diners Club; F Other; 2 Personal checks accepted; 3 Lunch available; 4 Dinner available;

biking and four wheeling trails, and survival workshops. Individuals, families, and groups welcome! A terrific atmosphere for workshops. Lodge and cabin rentals available. Reservations only. Private fishing cabins available May through September. Write for a complete brochure!

Hosts: Mayvon and Ron Platt
Rooms: 3 (SB) $55
Full Breakfast
Credit Cards: none
Notes: 2, 3, 4, 5, 6, 7, 8, 9, 10, 11

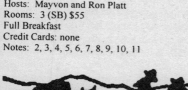

Rustic Mountain Lodge

## JACKSON

## *H.C. Richards Bed and Breakfast*

P.O. Box 2606, 83001
(307) 733-6704; FAX (307) 733-0930

One and one-half blocks from the center of town. Homer and Eliza Richards' granddaughter, Jackie will be your hostess. Amenities included in every room: private baths, goosedown comforters, tea service, telephones, and cable TV.

Gourmet breakfasts. Take your afternoon tea in the sitting room in front of a glowing fire. Many of the beautiful antiques were Homer and Eliza's and you feel the warmth of their presence and the love that they shared just relaxing amidst their treasured belongings.

Hostess: Jackie Williams
Rooms: 3 (PB) $81.00 - 97.20
Full Breakfast
Credit Cards: A, B
Notes: 2, 5, 6, 7 (over 9), 8, 9, 10, 11, 12

## WILSON

## *Teton View Bed and Breakfast*

2136 Coyote Loop, P.O. Box 652, 83014
(307) 733-7954

Rooms have mountain views. The lounge/eating area, where homemade pastries, fresh fruit, and coffee are served, connects to a private upper deck with fantastic mountain and ski resort views. Private, guest entrance. Convenient to Yellowstone and Grand Teton National Parks. Approximately four miles from the ski area.

Hosts: John and Joanna Engelhart
Rooms: 3 (1PB; 2SB) $60-90
Full Breakfast
Credit Cards: A, B
Close April and November
Notes: 2, 4, 7, 8, 9, 10, 11, 12

---

5 Open all year; 6 Pets welcome; 7 Children welcome; 8 Tennis nearby; 9 Swimming nearby; 10 Golf nearby; 11 Skiing nearby; 12 May be booked through travel agent.

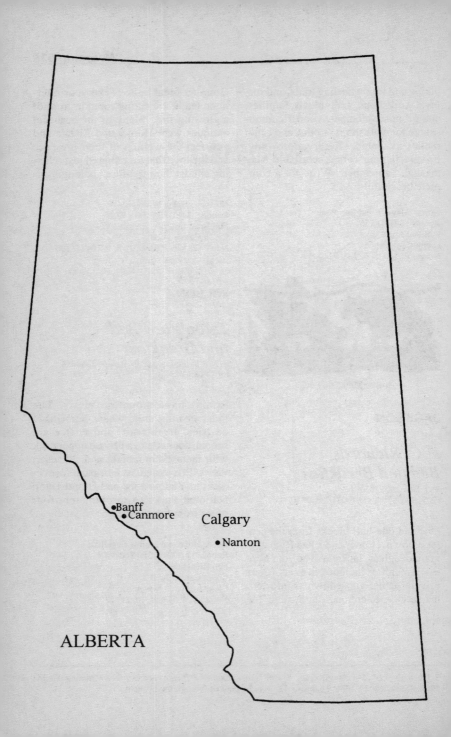

# Alberta

Cougar Creek Inn Bed and Breakfast

## BANFF

## Pension Tannenhof
121 Cave Ave., T0L 0C0
(403) 762-4636; FAX (403) 762-5660

Quietly located on the foot of Sulphur Mountain, fifteen minutes walking to downtown on the Eave and Basin (birthplace of Banff and Banff North Park). Featuring a large living room with wood-burning fireplace, CCTV, lovely breakfast room, and a homey, yet elegant, atmosphere. Recreational facili-

ties within short walking distance.

Hosts: Herbert and Fannye Riedinger
Rooms: 14 (3PB; 11SB) $70-130 (Canada $)
Full Breakfast
Credit Cards: A, B
Notes: 2, 5, 7, 8, 9, 10, 11

## CANMORE

## Cougar Creek Inn Bed and Breakfast
P.O. Box 1162, T0L 0M0
(403) 678-4751

Quiet, rustic, cedar chalet with mountain views in every direction. Grounds border on Cougar Creek and are surrounded by rugged mountain scenery which invites all types of outdoor activity. Hostess has strong love for the mountains and can assist with plans for local hiking, skiing, canoeing, mountain biking, backpacking, etc., as well as scenic drives. The Bed and Breakfast has a private entrance with sitting area, fireplace, games, TV, sauna, and numerous reading materials for guests' use. Breakfasts are hearty and whole-

---

NOTES: Credit cards accepted: A Master Card; B Visa; C American Express; D Discover; E Diners Club; F Other; 2 Personal checks accepted; 3 Lunch available; 4 Dinner available; 5 Open all year; 6 Pets welcome; 7 Children welcome; 8 Tennis nearby; 9 Swimming nearby; 10 Golf nearby; 11 Skiing nearby; 12 May be booked through travel agent.

some with many home-baked items.

Hostess: Mrs. Patricia Doucette
Rooms: 4 (2PB; 2SB) $55-60 (Canada $)
Full Breakfast
Credit Cards: none
Notes: 2, 3, 5, 7, 8, 9, 10, 11

## MEETING CREEK

### *Log and Hearth Bed and Breakfast*

Box 150, T0B 2Z0
(403) 877-2403; FAX (403) 877-2695

Seclusion and privacy are a contrast to the easy accessibility of this uniquely decorated, classically modern vacation chalet. Return to yesteryear in one of our four distinctive theme rooms, each with their own private bathroom. All this packaged together in a rustic log cabin complete with open fireplace, cozy tea nooks, and dormer library. Part of the scenic beauty of this place is a lake with trout fishing. Nature hikes add to the local interest. We invite you to experience the wonder of friendly and fascinating community.

Hosts: Denver and Janet Klassen
Rooms: 4 (PB) $55 (Canadian $)
Full Breakfast
Credit Cards: B
Notes: 2, 3, 4, 5, 7, 9, 10, 11, 12 (Tower Travel; Camrose, AB)

Log and Hearth Bed and Breakfast

## NANTON

### *Timber Ridge Homestead*

Box 94, T0L 1R0
(403) 646-5683; Winter: (403) 646-2480

Timber Ridge Homestead is a rustic establishment in beautiful foothills ranching country about 70 miles SW of Calgary. We have good, quiet horses to help you see the abundant wildflowers, wildlife, and wonderful views of the Rockies. Good plain cooking if you want it. To get here, go to Nanton, 50 miles south of Calgary, drive West on Highway 533 for four miles, turn south, and follow winding road into hills for twelve miles and the gate is on the right.

Hostess: Bridget Jones
Rooms: 3 (SB) $50
Full Breakfast
Credit Cards: none
Notes: 2, 3, 4, 7

---

NOTES: Credit cards accepted: A Master Card; B Visa; C American Express; D Discover E Diners Club; F Other; 2 Personal checks accepted; 3 Lunch available; 4 Dinner available

# British Columbia

## ABBOTSFORD

### Everett House B&B

1990 Everett Road, V2S 7S3
(604) 859-2944

We invite you to join us in our Victorian styled home in Abbotsford. Easily accessible to the freeway and overlooking the Fraser Valley, our home is the perfect retreat removed from the hustle of the city. It is also that "someplace special" for you while you conduct your business in the Fraser Valley. A stay at our home will provide you with a refreshing break from ordinary life.

Hosts: David and Cindy Sahlstrom
Rooms: 3 (PB) $60-90
Full Breakfast (early departure; Continental)
Credit Cards: A, B
Notes: 5, 7, 8, 9 (public pools), 10, 11, 12

## CAMPBELL RIVER

### Arbour's Guest House

375 S. Murphy St., V9W 1Y8
(604) 287-9873; FAX (604) 287-2353

Arbour's Guest House Bed and Breakfast, reservations suggested, offers seasonal, complimentary glass of wine on arrival. Antique decor, with spectacular view of the mountains, ocean, and fishing grounds, from large treed property. TV room, bicycle rentals available, golf courses close by. Boat rental arrangements made and experienced fishing guides available for salt water salmon fishing. No smoking and no pets, please. Adult oriented.

Hosts: Ted and Sharon Arbour
Rooms: 2 (1PB; 1SB) $70-95
Continental Breakfast
Credit Cards: A, B
Open April through October
Notes: 8, 9, 10, 12

### Campbell River Lodge and Fishing Resort

1760 Island Highway, V9W 2E7
(604) 287-7446; FAX (604) 287-4063

The Campbell River Lodge and Fishing Resort is a small lodge nestled on the banks of the "famous" Campbell River. The Lodge itself was built from logs in 1948, in the style of the Hudson Bay trading posts. Magnificent wood carvings adorn many of the beams, walls, and railings inside the lodge. Our surrounding grounds host an extraordinary collection of chainsaw carvings. We boast great fishing, great food and great fun! One of our experienced

---

5 Open all year; 6 Pets welcome; 7 Children welcome; 8 Tennis nearby; 9 Swimming nearby;
10 Golf nearby; 11 Skiing nearby; 12 May be booked through travel agent.

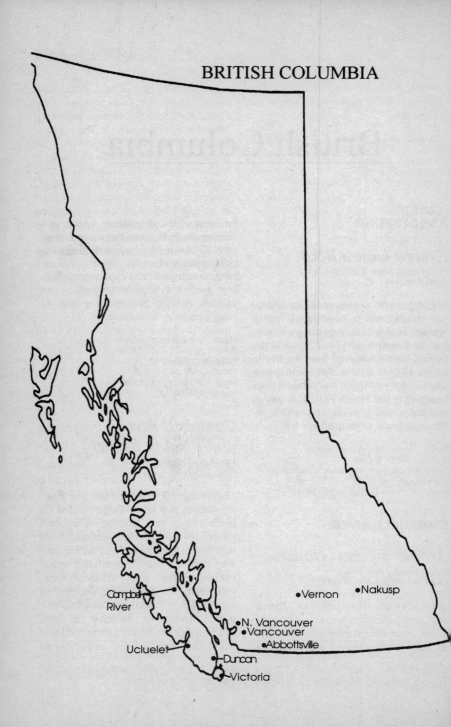

BRITISH COLUMBIA

Campbell
River

Ucluelet

N. Vancouver
Vancouver
Abbottsville

Duncan

Victoria

Vernon    Nakusp

guides will take you salt water sport-fishing. We'll cook your catch in our restaurant.

Manager: Brian Clarkson
Rooms: 28 (PB) $49-93
Continental Breakfast
Credit Cards: A, B
Notes: 3, 4, 5, 6, 7, 8, 9, 10, 11, 12

## DUNCAN

### *Fairburn Farm Country Manor*

3310 Jackson Rd., RR 7, V9L 4W4
(604) 746-4637 (voice and FAX)

Secluded 130 area farm 30 miles north of Victoria. Victorian manor house. Organic fruit and vegetables, ground wheat for flour, and churned golden butter from brown Swiss cows. Bedrooms with queen or twin beds and private bathrooms. Library, sitting room, and terrace. Trails, mountain stream, fields, virgin timber, reforestation, working sheep dogs, antique sawmill, and barns. Approved by Fodor Canada's *Great Country Inns and Sanctuaries*.

Hosts: Darrel and Anthea Archer
Rooms: 6 (PB) $80-110 (US equivalent)
Full Breakfast
Credit Cards: A
Notes: 2, 7, 8, 9, 10, 12

## FORT STEELE

### *Wild Horse Farm B&B*

Box 7, V0B 1N0
(604) 426-6000

Step back into a time of leisure and luxury at Wild Horse Farm, a secluded, historic, park-like, 80-acre estate in the Canadian Rocky Mountains adjoining Fort Steele Historic Town. The log covered home was built by the New York Astors in the early 1900s with spacious high ceilinged rooms, five fieldstone fireplaces, and antique furnishings. Screened verandas invite you to relax in a setting which reflects generations of tradition and comfort. Awaken to hot tea or coffee brought to your room. Enjoy a leisurely gourmet breakfast later in the dining room.

Hosts: Bob and Orma Termuende
Rooms: 3 (PB) $58-93
Full Breakfast
Credit Cards: B
Notes: 2, 5, 7 (by arrangement), 8, 9, 10, 11, 12

## NAKUSP

### *Country Hills Bed and Breakfast*

RR 1, 510 C17, V0G 1R0
(604) 265-3004; FAX (604) 265-3244

Country Hills is located in the exquisite setting of Arrow Lakes Vacation Country in central British Columbia. It's back borders a nine-hole golf course and driving range and is within an hour drive of three other nine hole golf courses. Nearby trails offer walking in summer and cross-country skiing in winter. Nakusp Hot Springs is only a 20-minute drive away through gorgeous mountain scenery. Fishing, swimming, water skiing, and marina are all available on Upper Arrow Lake in Nakusp.

---

NOTES: Credit cards accepted: A Master Card; B Visa; C American Express; D Discover; E Diners Club; F Other; 2 Personal checks accepted; 3 Lunch available; 4 Dinner available; 5 Open all year; 6 Pets welcome; 7 Children welcome; 8 Tennis nearby; 9 Swimming nearby; 10 Golf nearby; 11 Skiing nearby; 12 May be booked through travel agent.

A full country breakfast is served daily.

Hostesses: Anne Lang and Audrey Shandro
Rooms: 3 (SB)
Full Breakfast
Credit Cards: none
Notes: 5, 6, 7, 8, 9, 10, 11, 12

## Secret Inn Nakusp

P.O. Box 1114, 204 Third Ave. NW, V0G1R0
(604) 265-4748

A home away from home. Victorian elegance with verandah and gliding swing in an enchanting garden setting in the heart of the village of Nakusp. Nakusp offers bike riding, boating, bird watching, and picnics on the beach. Visit the museum and then promenade along the waterfront to the Japanese garden. The Nakusp area has many good streams and lakes for fishing. End your day with a relaxing soak in the soothing waters of Nakusp Hot Springs. Then return for a restful and comfortable sleep in the quiet surroundings of Secret Inn Nakusp.

Hosts: Jan and Pat Dion
Rooms: 2 (PB) $50-60
Full Breakfast
Credit Cards: none
Notes: 2, 3, 4, 5, 6, 7, 8, 9, 10, 11

Secret Inn Nakusp

## NORTH DELTA (VANCOUVER AREA)

## "Sunshine Hills Bed and Breakfast"

11200 Bond Blvd., V4E 1M7
(604) 596-6496; FAX (604) 596-2560

Private entrance. Two cozy bedrooms with TV, shared bathroom, and a beautiful garden. Close to US Border, airport, and ferries (20 minutes). Kitchenette. We are originally Dutch, very European. Breakfast includes fresh fruit, orange juice, and much more. Your host knows the city very well and can be of help to all the guests.

Hosts: Putzi and Wim Honing
Rooms: 2 (SB) $50 (Canada $)
Full Breakfast
Credit Cards: none
Notes: 7, 8, 10

## NORTH VANCOUVER

## Lynn Canyon Bed and Breakfast

1910 Peters Rd., V7J 1Y9
(604) 987-2569

Luxury accommodations; gourmet breakfast; adult-oriented. The grounds of this large West Coast-style home, border on a 600-acre wilderness park just fifteen minutes from downtown Vancouver. Minimum two night stay.

Hostess: Giselle Paaliwe
Rooms: 3 (1PB; 2SB) $55-65 (US $)
Full Breakfast
Credit Cards: A, B
Notes: 5, 6, 8, 9, 10, 11, 12

---

NOTES: Credit cards accepted: A Master Card; B Visa; C American Express; D Discover; E Diners Club; F Other; 2 Personal checks accepted; 3 Lunch available; 4 Dinner available;

## *Sue's Victorian Guest House—Circa 1904*

152 E. Third Street, V7L 1E6
(604) 985-1523; (800) 776-1811

Located centrally for many tourist attractions, this lovely, restored, 1904, non-smoking home, just four blocks from the harbor, seabus terminal, and Quay market; and even closer are restaurants, ships and public transportation. We have Victorian soaker baths (no showers), and each room is individually keyed, has a fan, TV, video, and phone (for short local calls). Minimum stay of three nights. Cats in residence; shoes off at door. Longer stays encouraged. Parking behind 152 and 158 East Third Street.

Hostess: Sue Chalmers
Rooms: 3 (1PB; 2SB) $60 (Canada $)
Self-serve kitchen privileges (4 PM - 10AM)
Credit Cards: B (for deposit only)
Notes: 5

Sue's Victorian Guest House

Burley's

## UCLUELET

## *Burley's*

Box 550, 1078 Helen Rd, V0R 3A0
(604) 726-4444

A waterfront home on a small "drive to" island at the harbor mouth. Watch the ducks and birds play, heron and kingfisher work, and eagles soar. In the Harbor, trollers, draggers, and seiners attract the gulls. Loggers work in the distant hills. There is a view from every window, a large living room, fireplace, books, and recreation room with pool table.

Hosts: Ron Burley and Micheline Burley
Rooms: 6 (SB) $45-65
Continental Breakfast
Credit Cards: A, B
Notes: 8, 9, 10

---

5 Open all year; 6 Pets welcome; 7 Children welcome; 8 Tennis nearby; 9 Swimming nearby; 10 Golf nearby; 11 Skiing nearby; 12 May be booked through travel agent.

## VANCOUVER

### AB&C Bed and Breakfast Agency

4390 Frances St., **Burnaby**, V5C 2R3
(604) 298-8815; (604) 488-1941 (US only);
FAX (604) 298-5917

A professional reservation agency offering modest to luxurious accommodations. Single, twin, queen, and king beds, private and shared baths. Vancouver, Victoria, and throughout BC. 18 years in tourism.

Manager: Norma McCurrach
Homes: 60; $75-160
Full Breakfast
Credit Cards: A, B
Notes: 5, 8, 9, 10, 11, 12

## VERNON

### City Lights Bed and Breakfast

5800 Ranch Road, V1B 3J9
(604) 542-5086 (voice and FAX)

New home on ten acres with panoramic view of the Okanagan Valley and the city. Enjoy our friendly, relaxed atmosphere in our country setting. We serve a healthy European-style breakfast. Each room has its own private bath. Separate entrance. Laundry facilities available. Please, no smoking or pets. Adult oriented. German speaking; *wir sprechen deutsch.*

Hosts: Frank and Lotte Meissner
Rooms: 3 (PB) $65-85
Full European-style Breakfast
Credit Cards: B
Notes: 2, 3, 4, 5, 9, 10, 11, 12

## VICTORIA

### AAccommodations West Reservation Service

660 Jones Terrace, V8Z 2L7
(604) 479-1986; FAX (604) 479-9999

No reservation fee. Over seventy choice locations inspected and approved. Ocean view, farm tranquillity, cozy cottage, city convenience, and historic heritage! Assistance with itineraries includes **Victoria**, **Vancouver Island**, and some adjacent islands. For competent, caring service, call Doreen. 9AM - 9PM Monday through Saturday and 2PM - 9PM on Sundays.

Manager: Doreen Wensley
Credit Cards: A, B, C
Notes: 2, 5, 6, 7, 8, 9, 10, 11, 12

### All Seasons Bed and Breakfast Agency Inc.

P.O. Box 5511 Station B, V8R 6S4
(604) 655-7173

All the best B&B of **Victoria**, **Vancouver Island**, and the **Gulf Is-**

---

NOTES: Credit cards accepted: A Master Card; B Visa; C American Express; D Discover; E Diners Club; F Other; 2 Personal checks accepted; 3 Lunch available; 4 Dinner available;

lands. Specializing in waterfront and garden homes and inns. There's an accommodation style for everyone. When you want to get away from it all, trips are much more enjoyable with a bit of advance planning. You know where you'll be welcome at night, so you can travel for the mere fun of it. Listing approximately 40 B&B's. Visa, Master-Card, and personal checks accepted. Kate Catterill, coordinator.

## Battery Street Guest House

670 Battery St., V8V 1E5
(604) 385-4632

Newly renovated guest house built in 1898 with four bright comfortable rooms, two with bathrooms. Centrally located within walking distance to downtown, Beacon Hill Park, and Victoria's scenic Marine Drive, only one block away. A full, hearty breakfast served by a Dutch hostess. No smoking.

Hostess: Pamela Verduyn
Rooms: 4 (2PB; 2SB) $65-85 (US $)
Full Breakfast
Credit Cards: B
Notes: 2, 5

## Borthwick Country Manor Bed and Breakfast

9750 Ardmore Drive, **Sidney** V8L 5H5
(604) 656-9498; FAX (604) 656-9498

An English Tudor manor house is set on an acre of gorgeous landscaped gardens in the quite countryside area of Patricia Bay on Vancouver Island. Relax in the outdoor hot tub or walk to the nearby beach. Enjoy a delicious gourmet breakfast on the patio. Large bedrooms, king- and queen-size beds. Minutes from Butchart Gardens, Victoria, airport, BC and Washington State Ferries, golf, fishing, boating, and beaches.

Hostess: Susan Siems
Rooms: 4 (PB) $89-130 (Canadian $)
Full Breakfast
Credit Cards: A, B, C, E
Notes: 5, 10, 12

## Camelot Bed and Breakfast

Box 5038 Sta. 'B', V8R 6N3
(604) 592-8589 (voice and FAX)

Treat yourself to a bed and breakfast experience at Camelot. Enjoy a refreshing taste of Old World charm and old fashioned hospitality at this turn-of-the-century McClure mansion nestled on an acre of ancient Oaks, giant firs, and country gardens. Located only seven minutes from downtown Victoria and four blocks to quaint Oak Bay Village. Three spacious rooms are decorated in period furnishings and collectibles. One room features a wood-burning fireplace. Start the day with tea and coffee service and the morning paper delivered to your room. Breakfasts, prepared by a professional gourmet cook, is served in the chandeliered dining room near a cheerful fire. Outdoor hot tub. Fax/

5 Open all year; 6 Pets welcome; 7 Children welcome; 8 Tennis nearby; 9 Swimming nearby; 10 Golf nearby; 11 Skiing nearby; 12 May be booked through travel agent.

telephone/message service. Laundry service. Limousine pick-up by arrangement.

Hostesses: Rozanne Shuey and Sonja Maans
Rooms: 3 (2PB; 1SB) $95-145
Full Breakfast
Credit Cards: none
Notes: 2, 5, 8, 9, 10, 12

Camelot Bed and Breakfast

## *Dashwood Seaside Manor*

1 Cook St., V8V 3W6
(604) 385-5517

Enjoy the comfort and privacy of your own elegant suite in one of Victoria's traditional Tudor mansions. Gaze out your window at the ocean and America's Olympic Mountains. If you're an early riser, you may see seals, killer whales, or sea otters frolicking offshore. Watch an eagle cruise by. Help yourself to breakfast from your private, well-stocked kitchen. You're minutes away from the attractions of town. Stroll there through beautiful Beacon Hill Park.

Hosts: Derek Dashwood, family, and staff
Rooms: 14 (PB) $65-240
Self-catered Full Breakfast
Credit Cards: A, B, C
Notes: 2, 5, 6 (small), 7, 8, 10, 12

## *Graham's Cedar House Bed and Breakfast*

1825 Lands End Road, **Sidney** V8L 5J2
(604) 655-3699; (800) 655-3699;
FAX (604) 655-1422

Modern air-conditioned Chalet style home nestled in a secluded six-acre country estate next to ocean, where tall Douglas firs sprinkle sunlight over lush fern beds. Spacious, graciously appointed, four-room suite with king bed and private, romantic, jacuzzi room (jacuzzi for two). Bedroom, living room, and private patio deck all overlook natural strolling gardens that feature statuary, fountains, and benches. Explore our forest or walk to the beach, marinas, or British style "pub." Breakfast served at your convenience. Close to Victoria, Butchart Gardens, and USA/Canadian ferries.

Hosts: Dennis and Kay Graham
Rooms: 1 luxury suite (PB) $95-159 (Canada $)
Full Breakfast
Credit Cards: A, B
Notes: 5, 7, (over 10), 8, 9, 10, 12

## *Gregory's Guest House*

5373 Patricia Bay Hwy., V8Y 1S9
(604) 658-8404; FAX (604) 658-4604

Early 1900's farmstead overlooking Elk Lake features farm animals, gardens, and country setting, only ten minutes from downtown. Bountiful, complimentary breakfast served in the cozy parlor with fireplace and antique furnishings. Convenient to ferries, airport, and

NOTES: Credit cards accepted: A Master Card; B Visa; C American Express; D Discover; E Diners Club; F Other; 2 Personal checks accepted; 3 Lunch available; 4 Dinner available;

Burchart Gardens.

Hosts: Elizabeth and Paul Gregory
Rooms: 4 (2PB; 2SB) $65-75
Full Breakfast
Credit Cards: A
Notes: 2, 7, 8, 9, 10 , 12

## Lavigne's Gourmet Bed and Breakfast

999 Easter Rd., V8X 2Z9
(604) 480-0999

Lovely 1940 home located in a charming residential area surrounded by historic Garry Oaks. Guests will enjoy the beautifully decorated guest rooms, coved ceilings, the Samuel McClure stone fireplace, and the private garden. A gourmet breakfast is often served on the sunny deck with hillside views. Fresh fruit and home baking precede such specialties as smoked salmon soufflé. Within walking distance to Swan Lake Nature Sanctuary and Playfair Park.

Hosts: Len and Lynne Lavigne
Rooms: 2 (1PB; 2SB) $55-80 (Canada $)
Full Breakfast
Credit Cards: none
Notes: 2, 5, 7 (over 10), 8, 9, 10, 12

Lavigne's Gourmet Bed and Breakfast

## Maplewood Bed and Breakfast

3430 Maplewood Rd., V8P3N3
(604) 383-2781

The Maplewood Bed and Breakfast accommodations include a private suite with your own courtyard, king size bed, refrigerator, TV, three piece bath, sauna, and fireplace. Only a five-minute walk to many main Victoria attractions, such as the beautiful Butchars Gardens, the Craig Darroch Castle, Government House, and the Emperors Hotel where you can enjoy a cup of high tea. Golfing is also nearby (five minutes). The B&B is located ten minutes from the ocean. After a peaceful night sleep, enjoy a hearty, fulfilling breakfast in the morning when you rise. No smoking is allowed in the home. Ask Adelle about her homemade scones.

Hostess: Adelle Caird
Rooms: 2 (1 suite PB; 1rm SB) $55-85 (US $)
Full, Hearty, Country Breakfast
Credit Cards: none
Notes: 2, 5, 7 (13 or older), 8, 9, 10

## Oak Bay Guest House

1052 Newport Avenue, V8S 5E3
(604) 598-3812; FAX (604) 598-0369

Built from designs by famous architect Samuel McLure. This classic 1912 inn, established since 1922, has your comfort at heart. Set in beautiful gardens in the prime, peaceful location of Oak Bay, only one block from the water and minutes from downtown. Eleven rooms with private bathrooms and antiques;

5 Open all year; 6 Pets welcome; 7 Children welcome; 8 Tennis nearby; 9 Swimming nearby;
10 Golf nearby; 11 Skiing nearby; 12 May be booked through travel agent.

sitting room with Inglenook fireplace; sunroom with library and TV. Home-cooked breakfast. Golf, shopping, and the city bus at door.

Hosts: Karl and Jackie Morris
Rooms: 11 (PB) $79-165 (Canadian $)
Full Breakfast
Credit Cards: A, B
Notes: 5, 8, 9, 10, 12

Prior House Bed and Breakfast Inn

## *Peggy's Cove Bed and Breakfast*

279 Coal Point Lane, **Sidney**, V8L 5P1
(604) 656-5656; FAX (604) 655-3118

**Spoil yourself!** Come join me in my beautiful home bordered by spectacular ocean views on all sides. Imagine a gourmet breakfast on the sundeck, watching sea lions at play, eagles soaring, and if you are lucky, a family of killer whales may appear. Enjoy fishing at your doorstep, a stroll on the beach, and, in the evening, canoe into the sunset then spend a romantic moment in the **"hot tub under the stars."** Victoria's world famous Butchart Gardens, BC and Anacortes Ferries are only minutes away. Many consider Peggy's Cove a honeymoon paradise.

Hostess: Peggy Waibel
Rooms: 2 (1PB; 2SB) $100 + (US $)
Full Gourmet Breakfast
Credit Cards: none
Notes: 2, 5, 5, 7, 8, 9, 10, 12

## *Prior House Bed and Breakfast Inn*

620 St. Charles Street, V8S 3N7
(604) 592-8847; FAX (604) 592-8223

Formerly a private residence of the English Crown's representative, this grand B&B inn has all the amenities of the finest European inn. Featuring rooms with fireplaces, marble jacuzzi tubs, ocean and mountain views, sumptuous breakfasts, and afternoon tea. Special private suites available for families. Rated as *"Outstanding"* by *Northwest Best Places* and AAA—three diamond.

Hostess: Candis C. Cooperrider
Rooms: 7 (PB) $180-200 (US $)
Full Breakfast
Credit Cards: A, B
Notes: 5, 7 (9 and over), 8, 10

---

NOTES: Credit cards accepted: A Master Card; B Visa; C American Express; D Discover; E Diners Club; F Other; 2 Personal checks accepted; 3 Lunch available; 4 Dinner available;

## The Sea Rose

1250 Dallas Road, V8V 1C4
(604) 381-7932; FAX (604) 480-1298

A wonderful 1927 character house on the oceanfront just a few blocks south of Beacon Hill Park and a 20-minute walk to downtown Victoria. All accommodations are full suites with kitchenettes, private baths, and private entrances. Healthy breakfast served. No smoking. Watch the killer whales from our oceanfront sunroom.

Hosts: Gail and Herm Hamhuis
Rooms: 4 (PB) $89-109 (US $)
Guest's Choice of Full or Continental Breakfast
Credit Cards: A, B
Notes: 7, 10, 12

The Sea Rose

## Top O' Triangle Mountain

3442 Karger Terrace, V9C 3K5
(604) 478-7853; FAX (604) 478-2245

Our home, built of solid cedar construction, boasts a spectacular view of Victoria, the Juan de Fuca Strait, and the Olympia Mountains in Washington.

We are a relaxed household with few rules, lots of hospitality, and clean, comfortable rooms. A hearty breakfast is different each morning.

Hosts: Henry and Patricia Hansen
Rooms: 3 (PB) $65-85 (Canadian $)
Full Home-cooked Breakfast
Credit Cards: A, B
Notes: 5, 7, 8, 9, 10, 12

Top O'Triangle Mountain

## Welling Bed and Breakfast

66 Wellington Avenue, V8V 4H5
(604) 383-5976 (voice and FAX)

You're in for a treat of the finest Victorian hospitality in this 1912, fully restored, Edwardian B&B. Inge is an interior designer and each room is specially designed with private baths, queen or king bed, walk-in closet, duvets, lace, and some fireplaces. A guest living room offers books and relaxation. Only a half block from ocean and bus. A 20-minute walk will take you

---

5 Open all year; 6 Pets welcome; 7 Children welcome; 8 Tennis nearby; 9 Swimming nearby; 10 Golf nearby; 11 Skiing nearby; 12 May be booked through travel agent.

to downtown through the park. Only minutes from shops, restaurants, and sites. A full, delicious breakfast is served in the dining room.

Hosts: Inge Ranzinger
Rooms: 3 (3PB) $70-95 (Canada $) or $50-70 (US)
Full Breakfast
Credit Cards: A
Notes: 2, 5, 7 (over 12), 8, 9, 10, 12

## WEST VANCOUVER

### Beachside Bed and Breakfast

4208 Evergreen Avenue, V7V 1H1
(604) 922-7773; (800) 563-3311;
FAX (604) 926-8073

Guests are welcomed to this beautiful waterfront home with a basket of fruit and fresh flowers. Situated on a quiet cul-de-sac in an exclusive area of the city, the house, with Spanish architecture accented by antique stained glass windows, affords a panoramic view of Vancouver's busy harbor. There are private baths, a patio leading to the beach, and a large jacuzzi at the seashore, where you can watch seals swim by daily. Near sailing, fishing, hiking, golf, downhill skiing, and antique shopping.

Hosts: Gordon and Joan Gibbs
Rooms: 3 (PB) $110-180
Full Breakfast
Credit Cards: A, B
Notes: 2, 5, 8, 10, 11, 12, 13

## WHISTLER

### Golden Dreams Bed and Breakfast

6412 Easy Street, V0N 1B6
(604) 932-2667; (800) 668-7055;
FAX (604) 932-7055

Uniquely decorated Victorian, Oriental, and Aztec theme rooms feature sherry decanter and cozy duvets. Relax in the luxurious, private jacuzzi and awake to a nutritious vegetarian breakfast including homemade jams and fresh herbs served in the country kitchen. A short walk to the valley trail to village activities and restaurants.

Hosts: Ann and Terry Spence
Rooms: 3 (1PB; 2SB) $75-105 (Canada $)
Full Breakfast
Credit Cards: A, B
Notes: 2, 5, 7, 8, 9, 10, 11

---

NOTES: Credit cards accepted: A Master Card; B Visa; C American Express; D Discover; E Diners Club; F Other; 2 Personal checks accepted; 3 Lunch available; 4 Dinner available;

# New Brunswick

Applelot Bed and Breakfast

## FREDERICTON

### Applelot Bed and Breakfast

R.R. 4 (located on Hwy. 105), E3B 4X5
(506) 444-8083

Attractive farmhouse overlooking the St. John River. Three bedrooms with a view in a restful country atmosphere. Full homemade breakfast served on the spacious sunporch. Orchards and woodlands with walking trails, "a bird-watcher's delight." Board games, TV, VCR, books, and piano inside; picnic table, gas BBQ, and lawn swing outside. Area attractions include several

golf courses, Mactaquac Park, Kings Landing Historical Village, museums in Fredericton, the Beaverbrook Art Gallery, and the Provincial Archives.

Hostess: Elsie Myshrall
Rooms: 3 (1PB;2SB) $55
Full Breakfast
Credit Cards: none
Open May 1 through Oct. 31
Notes: 2, 9, 10, 12

Carriage House Inn

### Carriage House Inn

230 University Ave., E3B 4H7
(506) 452-9924; (800) 267-6068;
FAX (506) 458-0799

The Carriage House may be Fredericton's Heritage Inn, but is offers modern conveniences: off-street parking, wake-up calls, a library, and FAX

---

5 Open all year; 6 Pets welcome; 7 Children welcome; 8 Tennis nearby; 9 Swimming nearby; 10 Golf nearby; 11 Skiing nearby; 12 May be booked through travel agent.

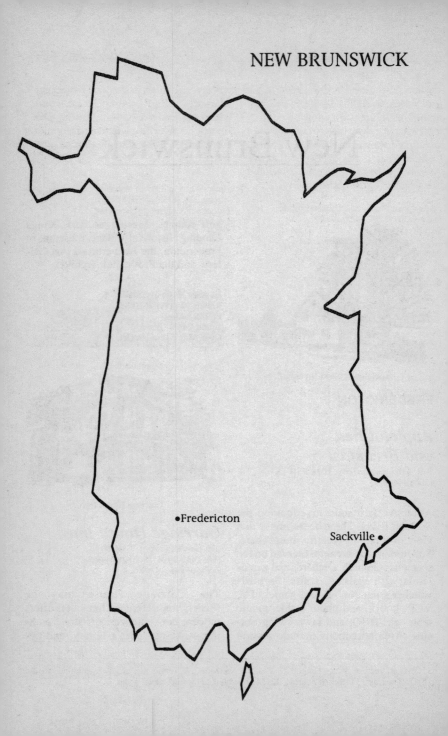

NEW BRUNSWICK

•Fredericton

Sackville •

service. The location is perfect, just a few paces from Fredericton's Green along the St. John River at the edge of the historic preservation area. Within strolling distance are the Christ Church Cathedral, art galleries, the Legislative Assembly Building, restaurants, and craft shops. Three-star property.

Hosts: Joan, Frank, and Nathan Gorham
Rooms: 10 (5 PB; 5SB) $60-75
Full Breakfast
Credit Cards: A, B, D, F (Enroute)
Notes: 2, 5, 7, 8, 9, 10, 11, 12

## SACKVILLE

## *Marshlands Inn*

59 Bridge Street, P.O. Box 1440, E0A 3C0
(506) 536-0170; (800) 561-1266;
FAX (506) 536-0721

One of Canada's oldest and best known country inns...located in a small univer-

sity town, adjacent to famous Tantramar Marshes, in the geographic centre of Marritive Canada Famous for its fine dining, wonderful gardens and antique furnishings. Come relax, replenish, and retire.

Hosts: Peter and Diane Weedon
Rooms: 20 (17PB; 3SB) $65-95
Full and/or Continental Breakfast
Credit Cards: A, B, C, E
Notes: 3, 4, 5, 7, 9, 10, 11, 12

Marshlands Inn

---

NOTES: Credit cards accepted: A Master Card; B Visa; C American Express; D Discover; E Diners Club; F Other; 2 Personal checks accepted; 3 Lunch available; 4 Dinner available; 5 Open all year; 6 Pets welcome; 7 Children welcome; 8 Tennis nearby; 9 Swimming nearby; 10 Golf nearby; 11 Skiing nearby; 12 May be booked through travel agent.

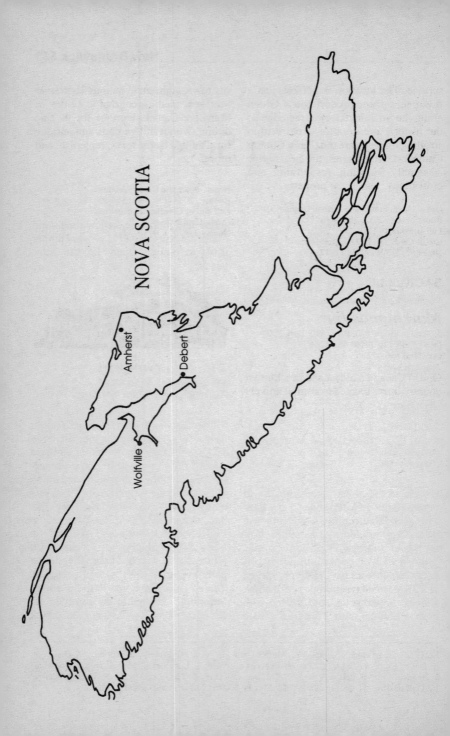

NOVA SCOTIA

Amherst

Debert

Wolfville

# Nova Scotia

Amherst Shore Country Inn

sauce, and meringue torte with almond butter are representative of what dinner is like each night. Open May 1 to October 13.

Hostess: Donna Laceby
Rooms: 8 (PB) $79-129
Full Breakfast (additional fee)
Credit Cards: A, B
Notes: 4 (by reservation), 9, 10, 12

## AMHERST

## Amherst Shore Country Inn

R.R. #2 Route 366 at Lorneville, B4H 3X9
(902) 661-4800 (voice and FAX);
(800) 661-ASCI

Escape to the quiet, natural beauty of Nova Scotia's Northumberland Strait. This renovated century-old farmhouse offers comfortable rooms, suites, cottages, and country-style, gourmet meals. Enjoy a walk on our 600-foot long private beach before having dinner served at 7:30 PM (with reservation) each night. Curried potato soup, sole stuffed with crab, chicken with brandied cream

## Victoria Gardens

196 Victoria St. East, B4H 1Y9
(902) 667-2278; FAX (902) 667-6161

Situated on the famous Sunrise Trail in downtown Amherst is an elegant, circa 1903, Victorian home on a tree-lined street in the midst of heritage properties. Each room is tastefully decorated and has antique furniture. For the guests enjoyment, we also have fireplaces, piano, organ, TV/VCR, and barbecue. Full breakfast; the house specialty is Nova Scotia blueberry pancakes with Nova Scotia maple syrup. Pleased to cater to special diets with prior notice. Tea and sweets served in the evening. Smoking is limited to the out of doors. Rated 3½ stars by the Tourism Indus-

---

NOTES: Credit cards accepted: A Master Card; B Visa; C American Express; D Discover; E Diners Club; F Other; 2 Personal checks accepted; 3 Lunch available; 4 Dinner available; 5 Open all year; 6 Pets welcome; 7 Children welcome; 8 Tennis nearby; 9 Swimming nearby; 10 Golf nearby; 11 Skiing nearby; 12 May be booked through travel agent.

try of Nova Scotia Canada Select.

Hosts: Carl and Bea Brander
Rooms: 3 (1PB; 2SB) $50-60
Full Breakfast
Credit Cards: A, B
Notes: 8, 9, 10, 11, 12

## DEBERT

### Shady Maple B&B
R.R. 1, Masstown, B0M 1G0
(902) 662-3565

Welcome to our fully operating farm;
Exit 12 off Highway 104. Travel 1½
miles into Masstown or, Exit 14A off
Hwy. 102, six miles to Masstown. Walk
through fields and wooded trails, view
the milking, pet the animals, or have a
swim in our outdoor, heated pool and
an outdoor year-round spa. In the
evening, come and sit by the fireplace
in our country home. Close proximity
to the Tidal Bore, Truro, Ski
Wentworth, and only 45 minutes from
Halifax Airport. We offer homemade
jams, jellies, and maple syrup. Farm
fresh eggs and an in-house gift shop.
Cribs and cots available. Honeymoon
package available. Open all year.

Hosts: James and Ellen Eisses
Rooms: 3 (1 suite PB; 2SB) $40-75
Full Breakfast and Evening Snack
Credit Cards: B
Notes: 5, 6, 7, 9, 10, 11, 12

## WOLFVILLE

### Blomidon Inn
P.O. Box 839, 127 Main St., B0P 1X0
(902) 542-2291; (800) 565-2291;
FAX (902) 542-7461

Escape to Nova Scotia's Annapolis
Valley and visit our beautifully restored,
19th Century, sea-captain's mansion for
a relaxed lunch or dinner. We offer
Christmas parties, corporate gatherings,
and other memorable times, or perhaps
a getaway in one of our 26 guest rooms
all with ensuite baths and many with
four-poster beds. Either way, you'll find
yourself transported back to the style
and relaxation of the Victorian era,
without sacrificing the modern amenities. Come, be our guests.

Hosts: Jim and Donna Laceby
Rooms: 29 (PB) $79-129 (Canadian $)
Continental Buffet Breakfast
Credit Cards: A, B
Notes: 3, 4, 5 (except Christmas), 7 (limited),
8, 10, 11, 12

Blomidon Inn

---

NOTES: Credit cards accepted: A Master Card; B Visa; C American Express; D Discover;
E Diners Club; F Other; 2 Personal checks accepted; 3 Lunch available; 4 Dinner available;

# Ontario

Cozy Corner Bed and Breakfast

## BARRIE

### *Cozy Corner*
### *Bed and Breakfast*

2 Morton Crescent, L4N 7T3
(705) 739-0157

Escape to peace and tranquillity in this comfortable home, nestled amidst sparkling lakes and forests. 36 miles north of Toronto. Charita, a former school teacher, spent four years as governess to Julio Iglesias's children. Her English born husband completed three years of culinary training in Germany before moving to the Savoy Hotel, London. Sample Harry's expertise at breakfast and other meals. Sandy beaches and golf on our doorstep. Air-conditioned.

Jacuzzi. Brochure available.

Hosts: Charita and Harry Kirby
Suite: 1 (4 piece bath and jacuzzi)
Rooms: 2 (1SB) $55-85
Full Breakfast
Credit Cards: B
Notes: 2, 4, 5, 8, 9, 10, 11, 12

## BRAESIDE

### *Glenroy Farm*
### *Bed and Breakfast*

R.R 1, Braeside, K0A 1G0
(613) 432-6248

Beautiful, quiet farm setting just one hour's drive from Ottawa. Situated in historic McNab Township of Renfrew County in the heart of the Ottawa Valley, halfway between the towns of Renfrew and Arnprior. We live in an 1884 stone house that has been well maintained by the three generations of McGregors who built the home and lived in it. We have a farming operation growing strawberries and corn and raising beef cattle. Located within driving distance of the Ottawa river raft rides, Storyland, Logos land,

---

5 Open all year; 6 Pets welcome; 7 Children welcome; 8 Tennis nearby; 9 Swimming nearby; 10 Golf nearby; 11 Skiing nearby; 12 May be booked through travel agent.

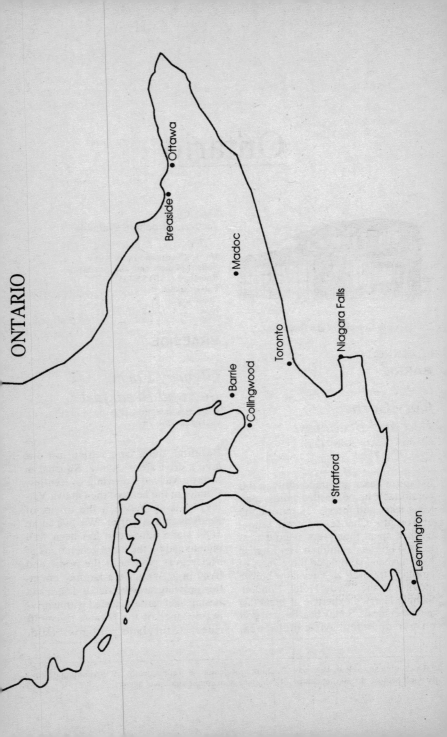

Bonnechere Caves, and many other attractions.

Hosts: Steve and Noreen McGregor
Rooms: 5 (1PB; 4SB) $45-50
Full Breakfast
Credit Cards: none
Notes: 4, 5, 7

Home Suite Home Bed and Breakfast

## LEAMINGTON

## *Home Suite Home*
## *Bed and Breakfast*
115 Erie Street South, N8H 3B5
(519) 326-7169

*Near Point Pelee National Park* and
enroute from Detroit to Niagara Falls,
Home Suite Home features two honeymoon suites, two additional rooms, and
a large in-ground pool. Large, traditional home decorated Victorian Country. Four and one-half baths, plush carpet, and fine linen. In house, central air
and a hearty, full, country breakfast.
Area attractions include dinner theaters,
cycling and canoeing, tropical gardens,
and trips to Pelee Island. Log-burning
fireplace for cool winter evenings. No

smoking. No pets. Agatha is coordinator for Point Pelee Bed and Breakfast Association.

Hosts: Harry and Agatha Tiessen
Rooms: 4 (2PB; 2SB) $58-68
Full Breakfast
Credit Cards: none
Notes: 5, 9, 10

## MADOC

## *Camelot Country Inn*
R.R. 5, K0K 2K0
(613) 473-0441

Relax in the quiet, country setting of our
1853 brick and stone home. It is surrounded by plantings of red and white
pine on 25 acres of land in the heart of
Hastings County. Original woodwork
and oak floors have been lovingly preserved. There are three guest rooms
available with two doubles and one
twin. The full breakfast may be chosen
by guests from the country breakfast or
one of two gourmet breakfasts.

Hostess: Marian Foster
Rooms: 3 (SB) $45
Full Breakfast
Credit Cards: none
Notes: 5, 7, 8, 10

## NIAGARA FALLS

## *Bed of Roses*
## *Bed and Breakfast*
4877 River Road, L2E 3G5
(905) 356-0529 (voice and FAX)

Christian hosts welcome you. We have

---

NOTES: Credit cards accepted: A Master Card; B Visa; C American Express; D Discover;
E Diners Club; F Other; 2 Personal checks accepted; 3 Lunch available; 4 Dinner available;
5 Open all year; 6 Pets welcome; 7 Children welcome; 8 Tennis nearby; 9 Swimming nearby;
10 Golf nearby; 11 Skiing nearby; 12 May be booked through travel agent.

two efficiency units with bedroom, living room with pull out sofa bed, furnished kitchenette, dining area, bath and a private entrance. A full breakfast is served "room service style." We are located on the famous River Road near Niagara Falls, bridges to U.S.A, bike and hiking trails, golf course, and all major attractions. Free pick up from bus and train station. Come and enjoy your stay in Niagara Falls, Ontario.

Hosts: Norma Lambertson
Rooms: 2 Efficiency Apts. (PB) $75-95
Full Breakfast
Credit Cards: B
Notes: 5, 7, 10

Gretna Green Bed and Breakfast

## Gretna Green Bed and Breakfast

5077 River Road, L2E 3G7
(905) 357-2081

A warm welcome awaits you in this Scots-Canadian home overlooking the Niagara River Gorge. All rooms are air-conditioned and have their own TV. Included in the rate is a full breakfast with homemade scones and muffins. We also pick up at the train or bus stations. Many people have called this a "home away from home."

Hosts: Stan and Marg Gardiner
Rooms: 4 (PB) $45-65
Full Breakfast
Credit Cards: none
Notes: 5, 7, 8, 10

## NOTTAWA (NEAR COLLINGWOOD)

## Pretty River Valley "Country" Inn

RR #1, L0M 1P0
(705) 445-7598 (voice and FAX)

Cozy, quiet, country inn in the scenic Blue Mountains overlooking Pretty River Valley Wilderness Park. Distinctive pine furnished studios and suites with **fireplaces and in-room whirlpools for two.** Spa and air-conditioning. Close to Collingwood, beaches, golfing, fishing, hiking (Bruce Trail), bicycle paths, antique shops, and restaurants. Complimentary tea served upon arrival. No smoking.

Hosts: Steve and Diane Szelestowski
Rooms: 8 (6 studios + 2 suites) (PB) $69-110 (Canada $)
Full Breakfast
Credit Cards: A, B
Notes: 5, 7 (well-behaved), 8, 9, 10, 11, 12

Pretty River Valley "Country" Inn

NOTES: Credit cards accepted: A Master Card; B Visa; C American Express; D Discover; E Diners Club; F Other; 2 Personal checks accepted; 3 Lunch available; 4 Dinner available;

## OTTAWA

## Auberg McGEE'S Inn

185 Daly Ave., K1N 6E8
(613) 237-6089; (800) 2 MCGEES;
FAX (613) 237-6021

A 14-room, smoke-free, historic Victorian inn celebrating ten-plus years of award-winning hospitality! Centrally located downtown on a quiet avenue within walking distance of excellent restaurants, museums, Parliament, canal, and University of Ottawa. Rooms with cable TV, phone, and jacuzzi ensuites. Kitchenette facilities for longer stays. Recommended by AAA. Full breakfast served in Art Deco dining room. All denominations welcome.

Hostesses: Anne Schutte and Mary Unger
Rooms: 14 (10PB; 4SB) $58-150 (Canada $)
Full Breakfast
Credit Cards: A, B
Notes: 5, 7, 8, 9, 10, 11

## Australis Guest House

35 Marlborough Avenue, K1N 8E6
(613) 235-8461

We are the oldest, established, and still operating bed and breakfast in the Ottawa area. Located on a quiet, tree-lined street one block from the Redeau River with ducks and swans, and Strathcona Park. We are a 20-minute walk from the Parliament buildings. This period house boasts leaded-glass windows, fireplaces, oak floors, and unique eight-foot high stained-glass windows overlooking the hall. Hearty, home-cooked breakfasts with home-baked breads and pastries. Past winner of the Ottawa Hospitality Award, recommended by *Newsweek* and featured in the *Ottawa Sun* newspaper for our Australian bread.

Hosts: Carol and Brain Waters
Rooms: 3 (1PB; 2SB) $58-72 (Canadian $)
Full Breakfast
Credit Cards: none
Notes: 5, 7, 8

## STRATFORD

## Burnside Guest Home

139 William Street, N5A 4X9
(519) 271-7076 (voice and FAX)

Burnside is a turn-of-the century home on the north shore of Lake Victoria, the site of the first Stratford logging mill. The home features many family heirlooms and antiques and is central air-conditioned. Our rooms have been redecorated with light and cheery colors. Relax in the gardens overlooking the Avon River on hand-crafted furniture amid the rose, herb, herbaceous, and annual flower gardens. Within walking distance of Shakespearean theaters. Stratford is the home of a world renowned Shakespearean festival from early-May to mid-November. Also enjoy farmers' market, Mennonite country, art and craft shops, outstanding architecture, and the outdoor Art in the Park.

Host: Lester J. Wilker
Rooms: 4 (SB) $50-70
Full Breakfast
Credit Cards: A
Notes: 2, 5, 7, 8, 9, 10, 11

---

5 Open all year; 6 Pets welcome; 7 Children welcome; 8 Tennis nearby; 9 Swimming nearby; 10 Golf nearby; 11 Skiing nearby; 12 May be booked through travel agent.

## TORONTO

### The Palmerston Inn Bed and Breakfast

322 Palmerston Blvd., M6G 2N6
(416) 920-7842 or (416) 964-2566;
FAX (416) 960-9529

Elegant old mansion, circa 1906, located in downtown close to all attractions. Eight guest rooms furnished with antiques, wash basin, telephone, and ceiling fans. Some rooms have air-conditioning. Full breakfast, guest kitchen, outdoor deck, free parking, and maid service. No Smoking.

Hostess: Judy Carr
Rooms: 8 (SB) $65-95 (Canada $)
Full Breakfast
Credit Cards: A, B
Notes: 5, 7, 8, 9, 10, 12

### Toronto Bed and Breakfast, Inc.

Box 269, 253 College St., M5T 1R5
(416) 588-8800 or (416) 690-1407;
FAX (416) 690-5089

Let us simplify your travel plans throughout **Metro Toronto, Ottowa, Kingston, and Niagara Falls!** Now in its 17th year, Toronto's oldest and original bed and breakfast registry is serving the entire area. Our reservation service of quality, inspected B&B homes provides a high level of safety, comfort, cleanliness, and hospitality. Advance reservations recommended; free brochure on request. Traveler's checks, MasterCard, Visa, and American Express.

# Prince Edward Island

## MURRAY RIVER

### Bayberry Cliff Inn
R.R. 4, Little Sands, C0A 1W0
(902) 962-3395

Located on the edge of a 40-foot cliff
are two uniquely decorated post-and-
beam barns, antiques, and marine art.
Seven rooms have double beds, three
with extra sleeping lofts. One room has
two single beds. Two rooms, including
the honeymoon suite, have private bath.
Seals, occasional whale sightings, restaurants, swimming, inner-tubing, and
crafts shops are all nearby.

Hosts: Don and Nancy Perkins
Rooms: 8 (2PB; 6SB) $60-95
Full Breakfast
Credit Cards: A, B
Notes: 2, 9, 10, 12

## O'LEARY

### Smallman's Bed and Breakfast
Knutsford, R.R. 1, C0B 1V0
(902) 859-3469 or (902) 859-2664 (please call
AM or after 6PM)

We have a split-level house with a garage on the west end and brick gate
posts. We have a horse racetrack behind
the house where some guests like to go
for a walk. There are churches, stores,
craft shops, tennis, golf, and museums.
Lovely beaches for relaxing, walking,
and watching the sun on the waters. We
live in a quiet, country area on Route
142 off Hwy. 2 or Hwy. 14. Come into
O'Leary and go four miles west. Travelers checks accepted. Three-star rating.

Hostess: Eileen Smallman
Rooms: 4 (SB) $25-40
Full or Continental Breakfast
Credit Cards: none
Notes: 3, 4, 5, 6 (on leash), 7, 8, 9, 10, 11, 12

---

NOTES: Credit cards accepted: A Master Card; B Visa; C American Express; D Discover;
E Diners Club; F Other; 2 Personal checks accepted; 3 Lunch available; 4 Dinner available;
5 Open all year; 6 Pets welcome; 7 Children welcome; 8 Tennis nearby; 9 Swimming nearby;
10 Golf nearby; 11 Skiing nearby; 12 May be booked through travel agent

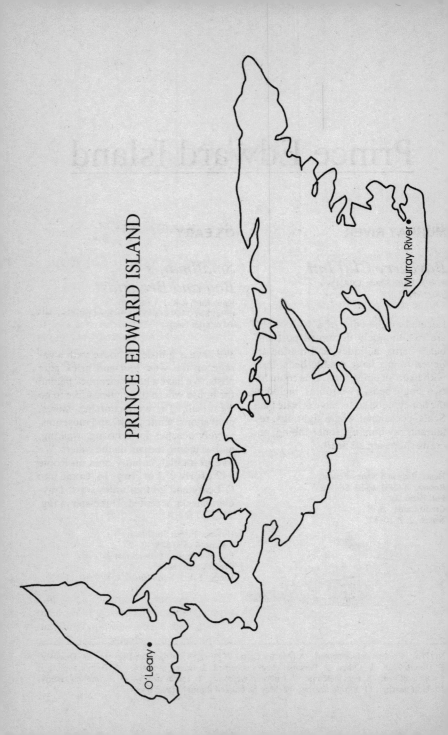

PRINCE EDWARD ISLAND

Murray River •

O'Leary •

# Quebec

## BIC

### Aux Cormorans
P.O. Box 627, G0L 1B0
(418) 736-8113

On the shore of the St. Lawrence, in Bic Bay, our century-old house awaits you in its calm, serene setting and old-fashioned decor and ambiance. Idyllically situated, my flower garden leads directly to the sea. From the encircling porch, observe a continuous spectacle of sea birds following the eternal movement of tides. The nearby 18-hole golf course as well as the Bic Conservation Park, compliment the wild, natural coastline making your stay memorable.

Hostess:  Judy Parceaud
Rooms:  5 (SB) $50-65
Full Breakfast
Credit Cards:  B
Notes:  5, 7, 8, 10

Aux Cormorans

## DESCHAMBAULT

### Auberg Chemin Ou Roy
106-rue St. Laurent, G0A 1S0
(418) 286-6958

Between Montreal and Quebec, the town of Deschambault invites you to discover its historic past by staying at our Victorian inn. Our antiques will make you feel serenity and romance near our fireplace. Our guests can also relax with the murmuring waterfall and the St. Lawrence breezes. We hope to see your smile soon.

Hosts:  Francine Bouthat and Gilles LaBerge
Rooms:  8 (4PB; 4SB) $59-74
Full Breakfast
Credit Cards:  B
Notes:  4, 5, 7, 8, 9, 10, 12

## MONTREAL

### Armor Inn
151 Sherbrooke Est., H2X 1C7
(514) 285-0140; FAX (514) 284-1126

The Armor Inn is a small hotel with a typical European character. In the heart of Montreal, it offers a warm family atmosphere and is ideally situated close to Métro, Saint Denis, and Prince Arthur

---

5  Open all year;  6  Pets welcome;  7  Children welcome;  8  Tennis nearby;  9  Swimming nearby;
10  Golf nearby;  11  Skiing nearby;  12  May be booked through travel agent.

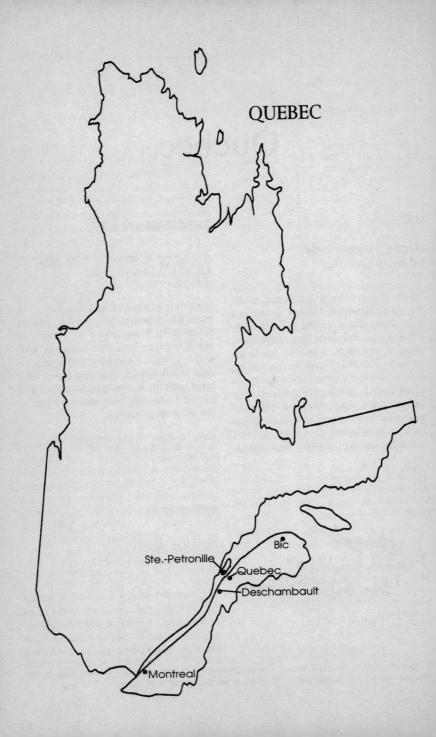

QUEBEC

Bic

Ste.-Petronille

Quebec

Deschambault

Montreal

Streets. It is a 15-minute walk to Old Montréal, the Palais of Congress, and numerous underground shopping centers.

Hosts: Annick Morvan
Rooms: 15 (7 PB; 8 SB) $38-55
Continental Breakfast
Credit Cards: A, B
Notes: 5, 7, 12

## Auberge de la Fountaine

1301 Rachel St. E., H2J 2K1
(514) 597-0166; (800) 597-0597;
FAX (514) 597-0496

The Auberge de la Fountaine is a nice stone house, newly renovated, where the 21 rooms, in a warm and modern decor, are of unique style in Montréal. Comfortable, friendly atmosphere and attentive, personal service are greatly appreciated by our corporate and leisure travelers. Each room is tastefully decorated. The suites with whirlpool baths, as well as the luxurious rooms, have brick walls and exclusive fabrics. It will settle you in an elegant and quiet environment. Duvet and decorative pillows will ensure you a cozy comfort. Breakfast is a given at the Auberg. A delicious variety of breakfast foods are set out each morning and you have access to the kitchen for snacks. There are no parking fees. We want our guests to feel comfortable and be entirely satisfied with their stay.

Hostesses: Céline Boudreau and Jean Lamothe
Rooms: 21 (PB) $99-175 (Canada $)
Generous Continental Buffet Breakfast
Credit Cards: A, B, C, E, F
Notes: 5, 7, 8, 9, 12

## Hotel Casa Bella Inc.

264 Sherbrooke West, H2X 1X9
(514) 849-2777; FAX (514) 849-3650

The same owner has operated this charming hotel for 21 years. The 100-year-old European-style house has been renovated and is located downtown, near "La Place Des Arts," U.S. Consulate, Metro, and bus, and within walking distance of Old Montreal, Prince Arthur Street, and shopping center. Rooms are comfortable for a low price. Parking is available.

Hosts: Louise Rannou
Rooms: 20 (14PB; 6SB) $45-80
Continental Breakfast
Credit Cards: A, B
Notes: 5, 7

## Le Jardin d' Antoine

2024-rue St. Denis, H2X 3K7
(514) 843-4506; (800) 361-4506;
FAX (514) 281-1491

Located in the heart of French Montréal in the midst of the Latin Quarter, an area known for its boutiques, restaurants, and terraces. All rooms are fully renovated and have private bathrooms, some have a double whirlpool. Fifteen-minute drive from Dorval Airport. One block from a main subway station; fifteen-minute walk to Old Montréal.

Hosts: Antoine and Francine Giardina
Rooms: 20 (PB) $59-130
Full Breakfast
Credit Cards: A, B, C, E
Notes: 5, 12

---

NOTES: Credit cards accepted: A Master Card; B Visa; C American Express; D Discover; E Diners Club; F Other; 2 Personal checks accepted; 3 Lunch available; 4 Dinner available; 5 Open all year; 6 Pets welcome; 7 Children welcome; 8 Tennis nearby; 9 Swimming nearby; 10 Golf nearby; 11 Skiing nearby; 12 May be booked through travel agent.

## *Manoir Sherbrooke*

157 Sherbrooke Est., H2X 1C7
(514) 845-0915; (800) 203-5485;
FAX (516) 284-1126

The Manoir Sherbrooke is a small hotel with European character and offering a family atmosphere. It is convenient to Métro, Saint Denis, and Prince Arthur streets. It is within walking distance of Old Montréal, the Palais of Congress, and numerous shopping centers.

Hosts: Annick Le Gall
Rooms: 22 (14 PB; 8 SB) $42-70
Continental Breakfast
Credit Cards: A, B
Notes: 5, 7, 12

Bay View Farm

## NEW CARLISLE WEST

## *Bay View Farm*

337 Main Hwy., Route 132, Box 21, G0C 1Z0
(418) 752-2725 or (418) 752-6718

On the coastline of Quebec's picturesque Gaspé Peninsula, guests are welcomed into our comfortable home located on Route 132 Main Highway. Enjoy fresh sea air from our wraparound veranda, walk or swim at the beach. Visit natural and historic sites. Country breakfast; fresh farm, garden and orchard produce; home baking; and genuine Gaspesian hospitality. Light dinners by reservation. Craft, quilting, and folk music workshops. August Folk Festival. Also, a small cottage for $350 per week. English and French spoken.

Hostess: Helen Sawyer
Rooms: 5 (SB) $35
Full Breakfast
Credit Cards: none
Notes: 3, 4, 5, 7, 8, 9, 10, 11

## QUEBEC

## *Au Petit Hôtel des Ursulines Enr. (Au Petit Hotel)*

3, Ruelle des Ursulines, G1R 3Y6
(418) 694-0965; FAX (418) 692-4320

True to its name, the Au Petit Hôtel provides the ideal mix between the intimacy of a family operated bed and breakfast and a full service hotel. Located near the St. Louis gate in the small Ursulines street within the old city of Quebec, the Au Petit Hotel opens it doors to you, offering the kind of lodging which effectively combines a quiet surrounding within the warm and hospitable atmosphere of the Old City.

Hosts: The Tims Family
Rooms: 16 (PB) $55-85 (Canada $)
Continental Breakfast
Credit Cards: A, B, C
Notes: 2 (for deposit only), 5, 7, 11, 12

NOTES: Credit cards accepted: A Master Card; B Visa; C American Express; D Discover; E Diners Club; F Other; 2 Personal checks accepted; 3 Lunch available; 4 Dinner available;

## Hayden's Wexford House

450-rue Champlain, G1K 4J3
(418) 524-0525; FAX (418) 648-8995

Ancestral home built in the beginning of the 18th Century, at the heart of our heritage, located in the Old Quebec, and very near the main points of interest. In the summer, relax in the flower garden and in the winter, by the fireside. Enjoy breakfast in a warm decor and relaxed atmosphere. Also, featuring three furnished apartments.

Hostess: Michelle Paquet Rivière
Rooms: 3 (SB) $65-85
Full Breakfast
Credit Cards: B
Notes: 5, 7, 9, 10, 11

## Manoir des Remparts

3½-rue des Remparts, G1R 3R4
(418) 692-2056; FAX (418) 692-1125

Located minutes from the train/bus terminal and the famed Chateau Frontenac, with some rooms overlooking the majestic St. Lawrence River, the Manoir des Remparts boasts having one of the most coveted locations available in the old city of Quebec. Newly renovated, it is able to offer its guests a vast choice of rooms, ranging from a budget room with shared washrooms to an all inclusive room with private terrace.

Hostess: Sitheary Ngor
Rooms: 36 (22PB; 14SB) $35-75
Continental Breakfast
Credit Cards: A, B, C
Notes: 5, 7, 11, 12

## Tim House (La Maison Tim)

84-rue St. Louis, G1R 3Z5
(418) 694-0776 or (418) 694-0104;
FAX (418) 692-4320

Built in 1900 on what is now one of Quebec City's main streets, Tim House offers its guests the luxury and charm of its Victorian architecture, complemented by the convenience of its very central location. Breakfast is served daily between 8 and 10 AM in the beautiful dining room located on the second floor. Free parking available.

Host: Supheauy Tim
Rooms: 3 (1PB; 2SB) $44-75 (Canada $) includes tax
Continental Breakfast
Credit Cards: A, B, C
Notes: 2 (deposit only), 5, 7, 11, 12

## ST. PÉTRONILLE

## Auberge La Goéliche

22 Chemin Du Quai, G0A 4C0
(418) 828-2248; FAX (418) 828-2745

Overhanging the St. Lawrence River, this castle-like inn offers a breathtaking view of Quebec City, a 15-minute drive away. It is also close to famous Mt. St. Anne Ski Center. Its 24 rooms are warmly decorated in Victorian style. Outdoor swimming pool.

Host: Andrée Marchand
Rooms: 24 (PB) $52
Full Breakfast
Credit Cards: A, B, C, F
Notes: 3, 4, 5, 7, 8, 9, 10, 11, 12

Open all year; 6 Pets welcome; 7 Children welcome; 8 Tennis nearby; 9 Swimming nearby; 10 Golf nearby; 11 Skiing nearby; 12 May be booked through travel agent.

# SASKATCHEWAN

- Paradise Hill

- Gull Lake

# Saskatchewan

## GULL LAKE

### Magee's Farm
Box 428, S0N 1A0
(306) 672-3970 (voice and FAX)

Let us show you some real Western hospitality on our working family farm. Enjoy home cooking made with our own produce. We share our farmyard with our grandchildren and we have some small animals. Our interests include photography and nature. Access to Hutterite Colony. Hunters welcome.

Hosts: Beatrice and Tom Magee
Rooms: 2 (PB) $40 (Canada $)
Full Breakfast
Credit Cards: none
Notes: 2, 3, 4, 5, 6, 7, 8, 9, 10

## PARADISE HILL

### Country Cottage Bed and Breakfast
Box 126, S0M 2G0
(306) 344-2137

Accommodations in a 16x32 foot guest house with kitchen facilities (hot plate) and separate bathroom. Quiet, relaxing, rural setting on our cattle and mixed farm. Log home, antique machinery, birds, flowers, berries, lots of trees and bush, and miles of scenic hiking. Beautiful northern lakes, swimming, historic sites, skiing, tennis, and shopping nearby. Continental breakfast upon request with homegrown organic produce. Motor homes, campers, tenters, and HUNTERS especially welcome. Good white-tail deer hunting (in season)! Families with children welcome and pets on leash.

Hosts: Robert and Marla Rauser
Rooms: 1 (PB) $35
Continental Breakfast
Credit Cards: none
Notes: 5, 6 (on leash), 7, 8, 9, 11

---

NOTES: Credit cards accepted: A Master Card; B Visa; C American Express; D Discover; E Diners Club; F Other; 2 Personal checks accepted; 3 Lunch available; 4 Dinner available; 5 Open all year; 6 Pets welcome; 7 Children welcome; 8 Tennis nearby; 9 Swimming nearby; 10 Golf nearby; 11 Skiing nearby; 12 May be booked through travel agent.

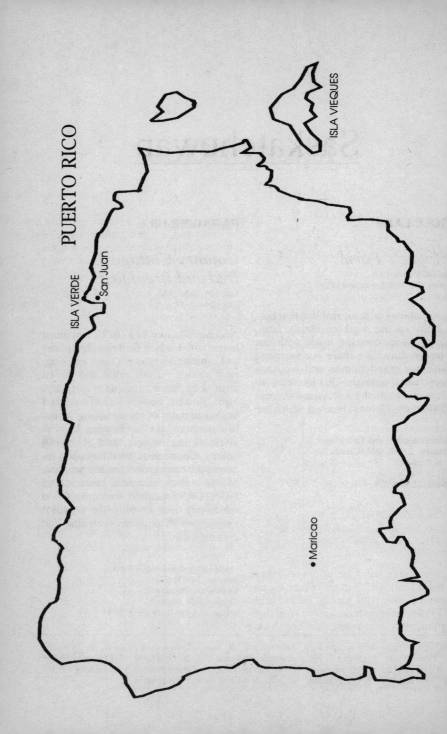

PUERTO RICO

ISLA VERDE

San Juan

Maricao

ISLA VIEQUES

# Puerto Rico

## MARICAO

### Parador La Hacienda Juanita

P.O. Box 777, Rd. 105, KM 23-5, 00606
(809) 838-2550; FAX (809) 2551

C. 1830. This hacienda-style building once served as the main lodge for a coffee plantation. Twenty-four acres, 1,600 feet above sea level in the cool tropical mountains of the Puerto Rican rain forest. Bird watchers' paradise.

Hosts: Luis J. Rivera Lugo
Rooms: 21 (PB) $65
Continental Breakfast
Credit Cards: A, B, C
Notes: 2, 3, 4, 5, 7, 8, 9, 12

## SAN JUAN

### El Canario Inn

1317 Ashford Ave. Condado, 00907
(809) 722-3861; (800) 533-2649;
FAX (809) 722-0391

San Juan's most historic and unique B&B inn. All 25 guest rooms are air-conditioned with private baths, cable TV, and telephone, and come with complimentary continental breakfast. Our tropical patios and sundeck provide a friendly and informal atmosphere. Centrally located near beach, casinos, restaurants, boutiques, and public transportation.

Hosts: Jude and Keith Olson
Rooms: 25 (PB) $65 -95
Continental Breakfast
Credit Cards: A, B, C, D, E
Notes: 5, 7, 8, 9, 12

### Tres Palmas Guesthouse

2212 Park Boulevard, 00913
(809) 727-4617; FAX (809) 727-5434

Remodeled in 1990, all rooms include air-conditioners, ceiling fans, CATV with remote control, AM/FM clock radio, small decorative refrigerator, and continental breakfast. Oceanfront, beautiful sandy beach; daily maid service; newspapers; magazines; games; oceanview sun deck; fresh beach towels; and chairs. Tourist information available. Centrally located ten minutes from the airport and Old San Juan.

Hostess: Yvette Velez
Rooms: 9 + 3 apartments (11PB; 1SB)
$50-90; $45-60 off season
Continental Breakfast
Credit Cards: A, B, C
Notes: 3, 4, 5, 7, 9

---

NOTES: Credit cards accepted: A Master Card; B Visa; C American Express; D Discover; E Diners Club; F Other; 2 Personal checks accepted; 3 Lunch available; 4 Dinner available; 5 Open all year; 6 Pets welcome; 7 Children welcome; 8 Tennis nearby; 9 Swimming nearby; 10 Golf nearby; 11 Skiing nearby; 12 May be booked through travel agent.

# Virgin Islands

## American Country Collection of Bed and Breakfasts

4 Greenwood Ln., **Delmar**, NY 12054
(518) 439-7001 (information and reservations);
FAX (518) 439-4301

This reservation service provides reservations for eastern **New York**, western **Massachusetts**, all of **Vermont**, and **St. Thomas/St. John, U.S.V.I.** Just one call does it all. Relax and unwind at any of our 120 immaculate, personally inspected bed and breakfasts and country inns. Many include fireplace, jacuzzi, and/or Modified American Plan. We cater to the budget-minded, yet also offer luxurious accommodations in older Colonial homes and inns. Urban, suburban, and rural locations available. $35-180. Carol Matos, coordinator.

## ST. THOMAS

### Villa Elaine

44 Water Island, 00802
(809) 774-0290

Lovely oceanfront apartment: fully furnished, kitchen, living room, dining room, two bedrooms, two baths, and veranda. Swim and snorkel from our own private beach. Spend an hour hiking around a 500-acre water island. Beautiful, peaceful, and secure retreat. Ten-minute ferry ride to St. Thomas. Minimum stay of three days.

Hostess: Elaine Grissom
Rooms: 2-bedroom apartment (PB) $125-165
Continental Breakfast
Credit Cards: none

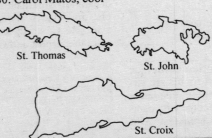

St. Thomas

St. John

St. Croix

---

NOTES: Credit cards accepted: A Master Card; B Visa; C American Express; D Discover; E Diners Club; F Other; 2 Personal checks accepted; 3 Lunch available; 4 Dinner available; 5 Open all year; 6 Pets welcome; 7 Children welcome; 8 Tennis nearby; 9 Swimming nearby; 10 Golf nearby; 11 Skiing nearby; 12 May be booked through travel agent.

## The Christian Bed and Breakfast Directory

P.O. Box 719
Uhrichsville, OH 44683

# INN EVALUATION FORM

Please copy and complete this form for each stay and mail to the address above. Since 1990 we have maintained files that include thousands of evaluations from inngoers. We value your comments. These help us to keep abreast of the hundreds of new inns that open each year and to follow the changes in established inns.

Name of inn: _____

City and State: _____

Date of stay: _____

Length of stay: _____

**Please use the following rating scales for the next items.**
**A: Outstanding. B: Good. C: Average. D: Fair. F: Poor.**

Attitude of innkeepers: _____     Attitude of helpers: _____

Food Service: _____     Handling of Reservations: _____

Cleanliness: _____     Privacy: _____

Beds: _____     Bathrooms: _____

Parking: _____     Worth of price: _____

Comments on the above: _____

_____

_____

_____

_____

What did you especially like? _____

_____

_____

_____

Suggestions for improvements: _____

_____

_____

_____

1996-97

# ...an Bed & Breakfast Directory
## Listing Reservation Form

***You will receive a complimentary copy of the Directory upon publication.***

PLEASE TYPE OR PRINT CLEARLY, answering all questions. Return with your check, money order, or credit card information for the **$25.00 fee** to *The Christian Bed & Breakfast Directory,* P.O. Box 719, 1810 Barbour Drive, Uhrichsville, OH 44683 or to FAX (614) 922-5948. **All materials must be in by August 12, 1995, to be included in the 1997-1998 edition.**

NAME OF INN _____

ADDRESS _____

CITY_____ STATE_____ ZIP_____

TELEPHONE _____ FAX _____

___Enclosed is my check or money order for $25.00 United States Dollars.
___Charge $25.00 to my credit card:  Visa___MC___American Express___Discover

Credit Card Number_____ Exp. Date _____

Signature _____

**PLEASE ATTACH A DESCRIPTION OF YOUR BED AND BREAKFAST OF 50 TO 70 WORDS.**

Host(s)/Hostess _____
Number of guest rooms _____
Number with private baths_____ Number with shared baths _____
Rate range for two people sharing one room (lowest to highest) _____
Full or continental breakfast? _____

**Circle those that apply:**

1. Credit Cards
   A. MasterCard
   B. Visa
   C. American Express
   D. Discover Card
   E. Diners Club
   F. Other
2. Personal checks accepted
3. Lunch available
4. Dinner available
5. Open all year
6. Pets welcome
7. Children welcome
8. Tennis nearby
9. Swimming nearby
10. Golf nearby
11. Skiing nearby
12. May be booked by a travel agent